Toward a Science of Consciousnes

MW01153329

Toward a Science of Consciousness III
The Third Tucson Discussions and Debates

edited by Stuart R. Hameroff, Alfred W. Kaszniak, and David J. Chalmers

A Bradford Book
The MIT Press
Cambridge, Massachusetts
London, England

This book was set in Times New Roman by Asco Typesetters, Hong Kong

Printed and bound in the United States of America.

Library of Congress Cataloging-in-Publication Data

Toward a science of consciousness III : the third Tucson discussions and debates / edited by Stuart R. Hameroff, Alfred W. Kaszniak, David J. Chalmers.
    p. m. — (Complex adaptive systems)
"A Bradford book."
Conference proceedings.
Includes bibliographical references and index.
ISBN 0-262-58181-7 (alk. paper)
    1. Consciousness—Congresses. I. Hameroff, Stuart R. II. Kaszniak, Alfred W., 1949–   .
III. Chalmers, David John, 1966–   . IV. Title: Toward a science of consciousness three.   V. Title: Third Tucson discussions and debates.
BF311.T67   1999
153—dc21   99-36574
                                                                         CIP

A Tree Tickles Its Branches
Carol Ebbecke

We are the laughing rats.
Our private approaches to reflection still require
a second perspective.

We can clearly see through our psychoscope
the hot spot of vision and awareness
our perception of the vision at hand

versus science itself—
a cat versus a kitten, a model versus a reality.
A scan will tell us, second hand,

that no amount of mythmaking will maintain
a memory of private subjectivity in the mind's past.

Moony blue rays on the mountainscape lasso
the self in the name of qualia,
the synchronicity of the coyote's rapture

a shaman caught in the feather of physicality.
Awareness invariably entails awareness

of something, the mechanics of variables,
fuzzy virtual memory eludes the paradigm.
Rescind the sensory, dreams are the stories

we tell upon waking—experience
plus explanation ...

Fire of the breathless continuum begs the answer:
can I know you through one eye?

and opens a non-human border to the mind,
captures language before we can focus the space,
or consider the time.

Contents

Acknowledgments

The editors would like to express their appreciation to all of the hard-working people who put in time and effort every day in order to keep the Tucson conferences and related activities running smoothly. Carol Ebbecke, our editorial assistant and poetry slam mistress, has now guided two Tucson volumes to press. Without her organizational skills, communication, and aesthetic taste these books would not be possible. The Fetzer Institute continues to provide generous support for our endeavors. Our forthcoming Center for Consciousness Studies, which would not be in its current guise without Fetzer's input, is part and parcel of all of our present and future Tucson conferences. The *Journal of Consciousness Studies* and *Trends in Cognitive Science* have generously permitted us to reprint material from their pages. The Program Committee, including Christof Koch, Marilyn Schlitz, Al Scott, Petra Stoerig, Keith Sutherland, Michael Winkelman, and Jim Laukes, scattered all around the world, came together by e-mail and in Tucson to assemble the multi-disciplinary line-up for the conference. Artist Dave Cantrell re-created some of the trickier figures, and Al Scott gave us his blessing and turned his editorship over to Dave Chalmers beginning with this book. Finally, Jim Laukes kept the starch in our sails and always made certain that we could deliver on what we promised though his attention to every imaginable detail.

We must also thank our families and colleagues in our home departments of Anesthesiology, Psychology, Neurology, Psychiatry, and Philosophy, and the University of Arizona for providing an academic environment amenable to our intellectual pursuits.

Finally, we are grateful to Bradford Books and the MIT Press for their continued support. In particular we thank Betty Stanton for her stewardship, vision and courage in continuing in her late husband's role.

Contributors

Dick Bierman
University of Amsterdam
Roetersstraat 15
1018 WB Amsterdam, The Netherlands

Jeffrey Burgdorf
Dept. of Psychology
Bowling Green State University
Bowling Green, OH 43403

A. G. Cairns-Smith
Department of Chemistry
Glasgow University
Glasgow G12 8QQ
Scotland, UK

William H. Calvin
Department of Psychiatry and
Behavioral Sciences
University of Washington
Seattle WA 98195-1800

David J. Chalmers
Department of Philosophy
The University of Arizona
Tucson, AZ 85721

Christian de Quincey
Institute of Noetic Sciences and the John
F. Kennedy University
IONS, 475 Gate Five Road, Suite 300
Sausalito, CA 94965

Frank H. Durgin
Department of Psychology
Swarthmore College
500 College Avenue
Swarthmore, PA 19081

Carol Ebbecke
Department of English
The University of Arizona
Tucson, AZ 85721

Vittorio Gallese
Institute of Human Physiology
University of Parma
via Gramsci, 14-I43100 Parma, Italy

Alex Gamma
Psychiatric University Hospital Zürich
Research Department
Box 68
CH-8029 Zürich, Switzerland

Elizabeth L. Glisky
Department of Psychology
The University of Arizona
Tucson, AZ 85721

Melvyn A. Goodale
The University of Western Ontario
Department of Psychology
Social Science Centre
London, Ontario N6A 5C2, Canada

Richard L. Gregory
University of Bristol
Department of Experimental Psychology
8 Woodland Road
Bristol BS8 1TN, UK

Scott Hagan
Computational Modeling Lab
Dept. of Information Science, N.A.R.C.
3-1-1 Kannondai, Tsukuba, Ibaraki,
305 Japan

Stuart R. Hameroff
Department of Anesthesiology
Arizona Health Sciences Center
Tucson, AZ 85724

C. Larry Hardin
Department of Philosophy
Syracuse University
Syracuse, NY 13244

Charles A. Heywood
Department of Psychology
Science Laboratories
South Road, Durham, DH1 3LE, UK

Masayuki Hirafuji
Computational Modeling Lab
Dept. of Information Science, N.A.R.C.
3-1-1 Kannondai, Tsukuba, Ibaraki,
305 Japan

Nicholas Humphrey
Department of Psychology
New School for Social Research
65 Fifth Avenue
New York, NY 10003

Harry T. Hunt
Department of Psychology
Brock University
St. Catherines, Ontario
L2S 3A1 Canada

Piet Hut
Institute for Advanced Study
Olden Lane
Princeton, NJ 08540

Alfred W. Kaszniak
Departments of Psychology and
Psychiatry
The University of Arizona
Tucson, AZ 85721

Robert W. Kentridge
Department of Psychology
Science Laboratories
South Road, Durham, DH1 3LE, UK

Stanley A. Klein
Vision Science
University of California, Berkeley
Berkeley, CA 94720-2020

Charles D. Laughlin
Department of Sociology and
Anthropology
Carleton University
Ottawa, Ontario, CANADA K1S 5B6
and
International Consciousness Research
Laboratories (ICRL)

Joseph Levine
North Carolina State University
Department of Philosophy and Religion
Raleigh, NC, 27695

Lianggang Lou
Department of Psychology
The University of Hong Kong
Pokfulam Road
Hong Kong

Shimon Malin
Department of Physics and Astronomy
Colgate University
13 Oak Drive
Hamilton, NY 13346

A. David Milner
School of Psychology
University of St Andrews
Fife KY16 9JU
Scotland, UK

Steven Mithen
Department of Archaeology
University of Reading
Whiteknights
PO Box 218
Reading RG6 6AA, UK

Martine Nida-Rümelin
Institut fur Philosophie, Logik und
Wissenschaftstheorie
Ludwigstrasse 31
80539 Munich, Germany

Stephen E. Palmer
Department of Psychology
University of California at Berkeley
Berkeley, CA 94720

Jaak Panksepp
Dept. of Psychology
Bowling Green State University
Bowling Green, OH 43403

Dean Radin
Interval Research Corporation
1801 Page Mill Road, Building C
Palo Alto, CA 94304

Steven Z. Rapcsak
Department of Psychology
The University of Arizona
Tucson, AZ 85721

Sheryl L. Reminger
Department of Psychology
The University of Arizona
Tucson, AZ 85721

Antti Revonsuo
Department of Philosophy
Center for Cognitive Neuroscience
University of Turku
FIN-20014 Turku, Finland

Gregg H. Rosenberg
Artificial Intelligence Center
The University of Georgia
Athens, GA 30602

Yves Rossetti
Espace et Action
INSERM 94
16, avenue doyen Lepine
case 13
F-69676 BRON CEDEX FRANCE

Jeffrey M. Schwartz, M.D.
UCLA Department of Psychiatry
760 Westwood Plaza
Room 67-468
Los Angeles, CA 90024-1759

Jonathan Shear
Dept. of Philosophy
Virginia Commonwealth University
Richmond, VA 23284

Galen Strawson
Department of Philosophy
Oxford University
10 Merton Street
Oxford OX1 4JJ, UK

Robert Van Gulick
Dept. of Philosophy
541 Hall of Languages
Syracuse University
Syracuse, NY 13244-1170

Franz X. Vollenweider
Psychiatric University Hospital Zurich
Research Department
Box 68
CH-8029 Zurich, Switzerland

Margreet F. I. Vollenweider-
Scherpenhuyzen
University Hospital of Zurich
Department of Anesthesiology
Rämistrasse 100
CH-8092 Zurich, Switzerland

B. Alan Wallace
Department of Religious Studies
University of California Santa Barbara
Santa Barbara, CA 93106

Douglas F. Watt
Director of Neuropsychology
Quincy Hospital
Quincy, MA 02169

Lawrence Weiskrantz
Department of Psychology
Science Laboratories
South Road, Durham, DH1 3LE, UK

Fred Alan Wolf
Have Brains / Will Travel
435 15th Avenue, #3
San Francisco, CA 94118-2828

Kunio Yasue
Research Institute for Informatics and
Science
Notre Dame Seishin University
2-16-9 Ifuku-cho, Okayama 700-8516,
Japan

Arthur Zajonc
Department of Physics
Amherst College
Amherst, MA 01002

Preface

What is consciousness? How and why do we have conscious experience, an inner life textured and comprised of the feelings and sensations that philosophers call "qualia"? As a new millennium beckons, these questions have emerged from a long darkness that dominated psychology for much of the last century. This international and interdisciplinary introspection has stemmed in part from a number of high-profile books in the area, in part from a development of new experimental techniques for addressing the problem, and in part simply from a sense that now is the time for the science of the mind to address its central and most difficult problem.

The most burning issue is that of whether conscious experience—feelings, qualia, our "inner life"—can be accommodated within present-day science. Many see conscious experience as just another physical process in the brain. Others see conscious experience as outside science, or believe that science must expand to include experience. These philosophical battle lines were originally drawn between Socrates, who believed that the "cerebrum created consciousness," and Democritus, who argued that mental processes were fundamental constituents of reality.

Riding and facilitating the late twentieth century wave of interest in the nature of conscious experience, three interdisciplinary and international Tucson conferences (Toward a Science of Consciousness) have been held in 1994, 1996, and 1998 (the fourth is scheduled for April 10–15, 2000). The conferences have been integrative, attempting to assimilate and synthesize a variety of approaches toward understanding the conscious mind. Five major areas are delineated: philosophy, neuroscience, cognitive science, math/physics/biology, and experiental/cultural approaches. The idea from the beginning has been to bring proponents and researchers in each of these areas under one tent, to avoid tunnel vision in this tricky and potentially overwhelming mystery.

The first Tucson conference in 1994 was relatively small and tentative. Could an interdisciplinary consciousness conference work? Would proponents of the varied approaches be able to communicate, or would the gathering degenerate into a modern Tower of Babel? "Tucson I" succeeded beyond expectations, and a second, expanded Tucson II was held in 1996, moving from the University of Arizona campus to the larger facilities at the Tucson Convention Center and Music Hall. Many of the central figures in the newly forming field of consciousness studies were invited and participated, and the issues were fiercely debated amid 1000 attendees, producing numerous print and electronic reports. Following Tucson II, more focused conferences on consciousness sprang up across the globe. Consciousness had become part of the consciousness of the scientific world.

Following the giddiness of Tucson II, questions arose about the future of the field. The history of psychology is replete with flashes-in-the-pan, new movements and ideas that did not sustain. Could a stable, self-sustaining science of consciousness get off the ground? Could modern neuroscience, cognitive science, physics, and other fields raise enough new ideas to maintain the interest of a scientific community with a short attention span and an impatience for results?

With these considerations in mind, organizers of the Tucson III conference made some decisions. First, in response to numerous requests, work in the areas of cultural anthropology and aesthetics were incorporated. Second, all abstracts submitted for presentation were reviewed to a higher standard than for Tucson II. Third, the Tucson III conference focused centrally on data—experimental results relevant to consciousness. The result was a conference that was not as fiery as Tucson II, but which showcased the solid scientific progress in the study of consciousness on numerous fronts. More talks were evolutionary than revolutionary, which we take to be a sign that this young field is taking some steps toward maturity. There has been considerable progress, especially in the study of neural correlates of consciousness (especially visual consciousness), and of the contrast between conscious and unconscious processes. Of course there is still much room for bold ideas and for passionate debate, and we expect no shortage of those things at future meetings.

The Tucson III conference opened on April 17, 1998, with an announcement that the Fetzer Institute had awarded $1.4 million to the University of Arizona to establish a Center for Consciousness Studies. The Center is intended to continue and expand efforts begun with the conferences and related projects, online courses, visiting scholars and research awards (ten $20,000 grants per year for studies in various fields aimed directly at the problem of consciousness).

On a lighter note, the conference concluded with the first ever Consciousness Poetry Slam, organized and masterfully compered by poet Carol Ebbecke. This included the first public performance of the "Zombie Blues," an evolving commentary on central issues in the field by a ragtag bunch of consciousness scholars.

This book is the third in a series accompanying the Tucson conferences, and is a collection of chapters from among papers presented at the conference. They were invited based on authors' recognized expertise, quality of the work, and their place in a balanced representation of material filling out the spectrum of approaches to consciousness. The chapters are divided into thematic sections, each preceded by some integrative summary remarks.

I THE EXPLANATORY GAP—INTRODUCTION

David J. Chalmers

It is natural to hope that an explanation of consciousness might be a physical explanation. Physical explanations have had extraordinary success elsewhere in science. In biology, chemistry, geology, physiology, and even in aspects of psychology, we have found that physical analyses can account for all sorts of phenomena in a reasonably complete and satisfying way. Given this track record, one might well expect that a physical explanation of consciousness is on its way. And indeed, investigation of the neurophysiological basis of consciousness has already yielded many insights into the phenomenon.

But some have argued that any purely physical explanation of consciousness will be incomplete. Neurophysiology will very likely yield a systematic correlation between states of the brain and states of consciousness, but will this correlation be a complete explanation? It has often been suggested that no physical account tells us why there should be states of subjective experience—the direct experience of colors, pains, emotions, and other phenomenological aspects of our mental lives. Given any physical account, one can ask why *that* process should yield consciousness; and many have suggested that a physical theory alone cannot answer this question.

One can argue, for example, that it is a least internally consistent to suppose that there could be a being physically identical to one of us, but who is not conscious at all. This is an odd possibility, and there is little reason to believe it corresponds to anything in the actual world, but it is arguably at least *logically* possible, in that the notion is not contradictory. If so, this suggests that physical theory is logically compatible with both the presence and the absence of consciousness. And this in turn suggests that no purely physical theory can explain why consciousness exists in the first place. Levine (1983) has put the point by saying that there is an *explanatory gap* between physical processes and conscious experience.

Theorists of consciousness are divided both on whether there is an explanatory gap, and on what follows. Some deny that there is any gap, or suggest that it has already been closed. It is probably fair to say, however, that most think that there is at least a *prima facie* explanatory gap. From here, some go on to argue that consciousness is not a wholly physical phenomenon, while others resist this conclusion.

The four contributors to this section all accept that there is at least a *prima facie* explanatory gap, but they differ in where they go from there. In different ways, each of them is looking for a way to accommodate consciousness within a physical view of the world, while still taking the first-person phenomena as real. This leads down numerous interesting pathways.

Joseph Levine, who introduced the term *explanatory gap*, thinks that the gap may be uncloseable, but that consciousness may be physical all the same. That is, there is an epistemological gap, but no ontological gap. In this chapter, he analyzes the roots of the gap. In particular, he investigates how it can be that given that water and consciousness are both physical processes, one can be explainable while the other is not.

Robert Van Gulick holds that there is a *prima facie* explanatory gap, but that it may eventually be closed. To close the explanatory gap, we need to revise our concepts, in a way that we cannot yet anticipate. With such a revision, it may no longer seem internally consistent to suppose that any physical process could take place without consciousness. He uses this idea to address some arguments by Chalmers (1996) for the conclusion that consciousness is nonphysical.

Galen Strawson, whose 1994 book discusses the problems of experience in depth, holds that experiential phenomena are physical. But this does not mean we need to deflate experience to something less than it is; rather, we have to expand our concept of the physical. He argues that there is more to the physical world than physical theory specifies. Once we understand the physical as it is in itself, rather than as described by physical theory, we will see that it has room for experience in its underlying intrinsic nature. He calls the resulting position "realistic monism."

Gregg Rosenberg pursues a related idea, arguing that we have to "re-enchant" our conception of the physical world for reasons that are independent of consciousness, and that once we do so, we will see how consciousness can fit in. By making an analogy with Conway's game of Life, he argues that our theory of the physical world is incomplete: it specifies abstract patterns and bare differences, but no underlying nature. He argues that causation has two aspects: an external aspect characterized by physical theory, and an internal aspect about which physical theory is silent. He argues that consciousness may be tied to the internal aspect of physical causation, giving it a deep and fundamental place in the natural order.

Many more papers on these issues can be found in Block, Flanagan, and Güzeldere (1997) and Shear (1997).

References

Block, N., Flanagan, O., and Güzeldere, G. (eds.) 1997. *The Nature of Consciousness: Philosophical Debates.* MIT Press.

Chalmers, D. J. 1996. *The Conscious Mind: In Search of a Fundamental Theory.* Oxford University Press.

Levine, J. 1983. Materialism and qualia: The explanatory gap. *Pacific Philosophical Quarterly* 64:354–61.

Shear, J. (ed.) 1997. *Explaining Consciousness: The Hard Problem.* MIT Press.

Strawson, G. 1994. *Mental Reality.* MIT Press.

1 Conceivability, Identity, and the Explanatory Gap

Joseph Levine

Materialism in the philosophy of mind is the thesis that the ultimate nature of the mind is physical; there is no sharp discontinuity in nature between the mental and the nonmental. Antimaterialists assert that, on the contrary, mental phenomena are different in kind from physical phenomena. Among the weapons in the arsenal of antimaterialists, one of the most potent has been the conceivability argument. When I conceive of the mental, it seems utterly unlike the physical. Antimaterialists insist that from this intuitive difference we can infer a genuine metaphysical difference. Materialists retort that the nature of reality, including the ultimate natures of its constituents, is a matter for discovery; an objective fact that cannot be discerned *a priori*.

The antimaterialist conceivability argument traces back (at least) to Descartes's famous demonstration of the distinction between mind and body.[1] Descartes argued that since he can coherently conceive of a situation in which his mind exists but his body does not, there must in reality be a genuine, metaphysical distinction between the two. Of course one can justifiably take issue with Descartes's claim that he really can coherently conceive of himself as a disembodied mind. But the most common materialist response, as mentioned above, is to challenge his inference from what's conceivable to what's possible. Why think that what's possible, a metaphysical, mind-independent fact, should necessarily coincide with what's conceivable, an epistemic, mind-dependent fact?

While I think this materialist response is right in the end,[2] it does not suffice to put the mind-body problem to rest. Even if conceivability considerations do not establish that the mind is in fact distinct from the body, or that mental properties are metaphysically irreducible to physical properties, still they do demonstrate that we lack an explanation of the mental in terms of the physical. The idea is this. It seems conceivable that there could be a creature physically like us (or functionally like us) and yet for which there is nothing it is like to be this creature; or, for whom sensory states are very different from what they are like for us. If we really understood what it is about our physical, or functional structure that is responsible for our sensory states being like what they're like (or being like anything at all), then it would no longer be conceivable that such a creature could exist. Thus what the conceivability argument demonstrates is the existence of an explanatory gap between the mental and the physical.[3]

In this chapter I want to consider an objection to the explanatory gap argument. According to the objection, there is no explanatory gap because the phenomenon that is allegedly lacking an explanation is not really a proper candidate for explanation. In order to present the objection, I will first need to present the original explanatory gap argument in a little detail. After presenting the objection, I'll argue that it doesn't succeed in removing the problem. Finally, I'll briefly explore the implications of my reply to the objection for the metaphysical question concerning the actual identity of mental properties with physical (or functional) properties.

1   Water vs. Qualia

One way to appreciate the explanatory gap is to contrast the case of explaining the existence of various sensory qualia (e.g., the way pain feels, or the way red things look) in terms of underlying physical (or computational) processes with the case of explaining other macro phenomena in terms of underlying microphysical processes. So, for instance, let's compare how we explain the boiling point of water at sea level with how we might explain the reddish character of certain visual sensations. Consider then, the following two explanation sketches:

ESI: Boiling Point of Water

(1) H_2O molecules exert vapor pressure P at kinetic energy E

(2) At sea level exerting vapor pressure P causes molecules to rapidly escape into air

(3) Rapidly escaping into air is boiling

(4) 212° F. is kinetic energy E

(5) Water is H_2O

(6) Water boils at 212° F. at sea level

ESII: Presence of Reddish Qualia

(7) S occupies brain state B

(8) Occupying brain state B is to experience a reddish quale (state R)

(9) S is experiencing a reddish quale

Notice that I have presented both explanation sketches as arguments, where the explanans (i.e., the statements that do the explaining) function as premises from which the explanandum (i.e., the statement describing what is to be explained) is deductively derived. This is no doubt a tendentious characterization of scientific explanation, but I don't believe that the crucial issues at stake here really depend on any of the tendentious features.[4] Also, I call these "explanation sketches" because they clearly do not contain all the relevant information.

At first blush, there is nothing significant to distinguish the two explanation sketches. (Of course there's more detail in the first one, but that's an artifact of the example.) In both cases we have deductively valid arguments. Also, in both cases there is crucial use of a "bridge" premise ((5) in ESI and (8) in ESII); that is, a premise that identifies the phenomenon to be explained with some phenomenon describable in the relevant micro-vocabulary. So what is it about ESII that leaves us with the feeling that an explanatory gap remains, but not with ESI? The answer lies in the nature of the bridge premises.

There are actually two accounts I want to offer of the difference between the two bridge premises used in the explanation sketches above. The first is one that I will eventually reject, but it has initial plausibility, adherents among contemporary philosophers,[5] and it sets us up for the objection I want to consider. The second one constitutes my reply to the objection.

On the first account, what distinguishes (5) from (8) is that (5) is itself derivable from a combination of statements that are either analytic (i.e., can be known *a priori*, purely on the basis of competency with the relevant concepts) or descriptions of underlying microphysical phenomena. No such derivation of (8) is possible. Thus the difference between the two cases is this. In the case of water, the crucial bridge premise is itself susceptible of explanation, whereas this is not the case with qualia.

Let me elaborate. On this account, statement (5) can be derived in something like the following manner:

(i) Water is the stuff that manifests the "watery" properties

(ii) H_2O manifests the "watery" properties

(5) Water is H_2O

By the "watery properties" I mean whatever superficial properties they are by which we normally identify water (e.g., liquidity at room temperature, being located in lakes and oceans, falling from the sky, etc.). There are two crucial features of premise (i) that are responsible for this derivation constituting an adequate explanation of (5): it is analytic, and "watery" is ultimately characterizable in "topic-neutral" terms.

To say that it is analytic, for these purposes, is just to say that one knows it's true purely by knowing what the relevant terms mean; or purely by having the relevant concepts. So it's supposed to be entailed by what we mean by "water" that it manifests the watery properties. A "topic-neutral" expression, for these purposes, is one that does not contain any nonlogical vocabulary that is not already included in the vocabulary of the theory that's doing the explaining. Thus terms like "liquid," "lake," etc., that might reasonably be expected to appear in any full-fledged characterization of "watery," must themselves be definable in topic-neutral terms (or, more likely, in terms that are themselves definable in topic-neutral terms). The point is that the chain of analytic definitions must bottom out in topic-neutral vocabulary.

Both of these features—being analytic and (ultimately) topic-neutral—are crucial to the explanatory adequacy of the derivation of (5), and, thereby, to the explanatory adequacy of ESI, which depends essentially on (5). Premise (i) serves as a bridge premise for the explanation of (5), and we clearly won't have made any progress in removing an explanatory gap if it stands as much in need of explanation as (5) itself. If, however, it is knowable *a priori*, because it expresses an analytic truth, then there really isn't any question of explaining it after all. It's true by definition. We couldn't claim analytic status for (5) itself, but so long as it rests on an analytic truth, together with statements describing various micro-phenomena, it is fully explicable.

That "watery" is (ultimately) topic-neutral is required for a similar reason. For suppose it weren't; that is, suppose one of the constituent terms in the expansion of "watery" were not definable in topic-neutral terms. If so, then when we turn to premise (ii) we can ask what explains it, and the answer can't be given in terms exclusively of micro-physical processes since (ii) contains at least one unreduced term. So we'll need another bridge premise, and we can then ask what explains it. Thus both requirements—that (i) be analytic and that "watery" be definable in topic-neutral terms—are necessary to the explanatory adequacy of ESI.

Now, suppose we tried to construct an explanatory derivation of (8), along the lines of the one we constructed for (5). It would probably look something like this:

(iii) Qualitative state R is the state that plays causal role C

(iv) Brain state B plays causal role C
_____

(8) Brain state B is qualitative state R

The problem is that (iii) isn't analytic. While it may be true that experiences with a certain reddish qualitative character tend to play a certain causal, or functional role, it doesn't seem to be a conceptual truth that they do. What justifies this claim? Here is where the conceivability argument comes in. It just seems conceivable that one could have a conscious experience of a certain sort without its playing the typical causal role for that state. Perhaps this isn't genuinely, metaphysically possible. Still, the fact that it's coherently conceivable (a premise that the materialist we're interested in grants) shows at least that the claim that this experience plays this causal role isn't analytic; and that's all the explanatory gap argument needs. So (8), unlike (5), still stands in need of explanation. This is why ESI doesn't leave a gap, whereas ESII does.

2   The Objection

The objection I wish to consider involves a two-pronged attack on the argument. First, the objector takes issue with the claim that statements like (i) above are analytic, or that they can be rendered in topic-neutral terms. Second, the objector responds to the obvious question that arises as a result of the first prong of the attack: namely, if (i) is neither analytic nor topic-neutral, then why is there no explanatory gap in ESI, given its reliance on the bridge premise (5)? The answer is to challenge the assumption on which the question is based, that (5) itself requires an explanation.

The denial of analytic status to (i) is part of a general challenge to the analytic-synthetic distinction, which dates back to Quine (1953). For one thing, no one has ever produced a convincing example of a conceptual analysis, aside from marginal cases like "bachelor" or mathematical concepts. After all, what would really go into the expansion of "watery"? Is it really analytic that water falls from the sky, or is liquid at room temperature? Of course, one can always say that we just haven't found the right analysis, or that it is best understood as a cluster concept with no one necessary condition but a weighted sum of necessary conditions. At this point the burden shifts to the advocate of analyticity to show why we should believe there is such a thing as the right analysis to be found.

There are a lot of moves and counter-moves to make at this point, and I can't delve into them here.[6] But surely one reason for thinking there has to be an analysis for terms like "water" is that without one we would be at a loss to explain identities like (5). This brings us to the second prong of the attack, removing one of the principal reasons for believing in the necessity of analysis. The argument here is that identities, unlike correlations, do not require explanation. That something is itself is precisely the sort of situation that we accept as a brute fact. What else could it be? What really would count as explaining an object's identity with itself?

Of course it does seem as if we often ask for explanations of identities. Doesn't it make sense to ask why, or how it is, that water is H_2O? But whenever such a question makes sense, it is possible to reinterpret it in one of two ways: either as a justificatory question, or as a question about the coinstantiation of distinct properties. So, with respect to asking for an explanation of (5), we might be asking not why water is H_2O, but rather why we should think that water is H_2O. This is a way of seeking evidence for its truth, not an explanation of its truth.

On the other hand, we might be asking something like this: How is it that this substance made out of H_2O molecules appears continuously divisible? Here we are asking for an explanation, but what we want explained is how two distinct properties—in this case, being composed of H_2O molecules and appearing continuously divisible—could be instantiated in the same substance. This is a quite proper object of explanation, but notice that it involves a connection between two distinct properties. What, goes the argument, you never have is, strictly, why is this the same as that? To this question, if it were ever asked, the only possible answer is, "because it is, that's why."

If the foregoing is right, and I think it is, then the reason we don't find a gap in ESI has nothing to do with the availability of an analysis of "water," and so nothing to do with our ability to explain the bridge identity (5). There is no gap because bridge identities don't generally require explanations. But if there is no gap in ESI because (5) doesn't require an explanation, why should there be a gap in ESII either? Isn't (8) on a par with (5)? If (5) requires no explanation, then neither should (8). Thus, there is no explanatory gap between the mental (conscious experience) and the physical.

3   The Reply

The objection presented in the last section was based on the idea that identity claims do not themselves require explanation. Therefore, we can use identity claims as premises in explanatory arguments without thereby introducing new demands for explanation. This view works out nicely for ESI, involving water. The objector argues that we should view ESII, involving qualitative character, the same way. But the problem is that they clearly aren't the same. Something must be wrong with the idea about identity claims on which the objection is based.

Where the objector points to the explanatory adequacy of ESI as a model for ESII, I would emphasize the fact that we don't need to be convinced of the adequacy of ESI, which shows how different it is from ESII. I will introduce the term "gappy identity" to express this difference. An identity claim is "gappy" if it admits of an intelligible request for explanation, and "nongappy" otherwise. It seems to me that (5) is nongappy, whereas (8) is gappy. I will elaborate.

With respect to (5), imagine that all the micro-physical facts relevant to the behavior of water are known, but someone still asks, why is (5) true? As discussed above, such a request for explanation might really be a request for justification, in which case the explanatory potential of accepting (5)—that we can explain such facts as water's boiling and freezing points—would suffice as an answer. Alternatively, the questioner might be wondering how water could simultaneously instantiate certain (distinct) properties. This too could be answered. But suppose that the questioner refuses both of these attempts at reinterpreting the question. She just insists that she wants to know how water could be H_2O. It seems to me at that point that we could only respond with an incredulous look. After all, what could she really be asking? It just is H_2O; that's all there is to it.

On the other hand, when it comes to psycho-physical identity claims like (8), the situation is quite different. Let's again imagine that we have all the relevant neuro-physiological and functional facts. If someone were to press the question, but how is it (or, why should it be) that brain state B is a reddish experience, the question is quite intelligible. Of course some would insist that the identity must be true, since accepting it would explain a lot of phenomena (such as how reddish experiences cause us to call things "red"). But even someone convinced by causal considerations to accept the identity would still understand what someone was asking when requesting an explanation. We don't just stare blankly wondering what they could possibly have in mind. On the contrary, the sense of puzzlement is all too familiar.

If this distinction between gappy and nongappy identities holds up, then I think we can reply to the objection of the previous section. Granted, the difference between (5) and (8) is not that (5) is derivable from analytic and micro-physical premises whereas (8) is not. There is no analysis of our concept of water underlying our acceptance of its identity with H_2O. We accept it because of its explanatory power. (5) itself doesn't require an explanation. However, (5) is different in this respect from (8). (5) is a nongappy identity, a fact that is manifest by our not finding a request to explain it intelligible (that is, once we remove the possible reinterpretations of the request). (8) is a gappy identity, manifest by the fact that a request to explain it seems to be quite intelligible. So, given the intelligibility of a request to explain it, our inability to explain leaves an explanatory gap. Thus, the difference between the two explanation sketches is just this. The one that leaves an explanatory gap is the one that relies essentially on a gappy identity!

4   Metaphysical Implications

At the start of the chapter I distinguished between the explanatory gap argument we've been discussing and the traditional antimaterialist conceivability argument. The latter attempts to establish a metaphysical thesis, to the effect that mental properties are irreducible to physical properties (in whatever sense of reduction is required by materialism). The former attempts to establish a more modest, epistemological thesis, to the effect that mental properties cannot be explained in terms of physical properties, though they nonetheless might be metaphysically reducible to physical properties. However, given the defense of the explanatory gap argument presented in the last section, it's not hard to see how the metaphysical antimaterialist can turn it to her own purposes.

In section 2 it was argued that identity claims *per se* never require explanation. Whenever it seems as if someone is intelligibly asking for an explanation of an identity claim, it turns out that their request can be reinterpreted in one of two ways: either as a request for justification, or as an explanation for the coinstantiation of distinct properties. The latter is not really a question about why an identity is true, but why (or how) distinct properties are manifested by the same thing. Now, given the argument of section 3, we can say that this argument only applies to nongappy identities, not to gappy ones. For in the case of gappy identities it does seem as if one can intelligibly ask for an explanation of the identity claim *per se*.

But, the metaphysical antimaterialist is likely to press, why think the reinterpretation model just proposed for nongappy identities isn't fully general? In fact, given the independent plausibility of the position that when it comes to a pure identity claim there is nothing really to explain, the idea that there are identities for which this rule doesn't hold seems extremely doubtful. Rather, what makes more sense is to account for gappy identities in terms of the standard form of reinterpretation. If an identity is gappy, it's because we really have in mind two distinct properties that are alleged to be instantiated in the same thing, and that's what our request for an explanation targets. But if that is our account of the gappy psychophysical identity claim (8), then there must be two distinct properties for the coinstantiation of which we are requesting an explanation. But this is just to say that being a quale of type R, or some related mental property by which we are acquainted with a quale of type R, is not reducible to a neurophysiological property after all. Thus we now have derived a metaphysical conclusion from an epistemic premise concerning what is or is not intelligibly an object of explanation.

The original basis for rejecting the metaphysical antimaterialist argument was that the inference from what we can conceive to what's genuinely possible didn't seem warranted. The general idea is that the ultimate metaphysical nature of reality—including the nature of the mind itself—is independent of our cognitive access to it. So, the question now is how this materialist move concerning the limits of our cognitive access can be applied to the specific argument about the proper interpretation of gappy identities.

I don't think there's an easy answer here. The existence of gappy identities like (8) is a puzzle that itself requires explanation, and it's not easy to see how to do that within a materialist framework.[7] However, I don't think the puzzlement arising from gappy identities justifies dualism either. Let me end by briefly presenting a way of understanding how there could be gappy identities even though materialism is true.

The apparently troublesome fact is that pure identity claims don't require explanation. But to understand this fact properly, we need to appreciate that explanation is not purely an epistemological matter; it has a metaphysical side as well. When I say that phenomenon A explains phenomenon B, one thing I mean is that A's obtaining is responsible for B's obtaining. This is a metaphysical notion. I also mean that I can understand why B obtains, B's obtaining becomes intelligible to me, once I know that A obtains (together with B's connection to A). This is an epistemological notion.

Now, when it's said that a pure identity requires no explanation, this too has both a metaphysical and an epistemological side. On the metaphysical side, what this means is that there is no sense in which there is a responsible source for the identity, other than the identity itself. Identities are brute facts; what else could they be? On the epistemological side, what this means is that once we have removed any questions about the coinstantiation of distinct properties (or about justification), we recognize that we are dealing with a brute fact and therefore requests for further explanation come to seem otiose.

The materialist who recognizes the phenomenon of gappy psycho-physical identities must say this. Metaphysically speaking, there is nothing to explain. That is, we are dealing with a brute fact and there is no further source (beyond the fact itself) responsible for its obtaining. The fact that we still find a request for an explanation intelligible in this case shows that we still conceive of the relata in the identity claim as distinct properties, or, perhaps, the one thing as manifesting distinct properties. We can't seem to see the mental property as the same thing as its physical correlate. But though our inability to see this is indeed puzzling, it doesn't show, it can't show, that in fact they aren't the same thing. For what is the case cannot be guaranteed by how we conceive of it.

In the end, we are right back where we started. The explanatory gap argument doesn't demonstrate a gap in nature, but a gap in our understanding of nature. Of course a plausible explanation for there being a gap in our understanding of nature is that there is a genuine gap in nature. But so long as we have countervailing reasons for doubting the latter, we have to look elsewhere for an explanation of the former.

Notes

1. The most widely known source for this argument is Descartes's *Meditations on First Philosophy*, Sixth Meditation. See Rosenthal (1991), p. 26.

2. However, I don't think it's nearly as straightforward as many materialists believe. See Jackson (1993) and Chalmers (1996) for counterarguments, and Levine (1998) for extended discussion of the debate surrounding the metaphysical implications of the conceivability argument.

3. Nagel (1974), in a seminal article, emphasized how we don't have a clue how physical processes can give rise to conscious experience, "what it's like" to be us. The term "explanatory gap" was introduced in Levine (1983), and the argument further elaborated in Levine (1993b).

4. For the *locus classicus* on treating explanations as deductions, see Hempel (1965). For a wide range of views on the nature of explanation, see Kitcher and Salmon (1989).

5. Among them, Jackson (1993) and Chalmers (1996).

6. I discuss this issue at length in Levine (1998). Also see Fodor and Lepore (1992), Levine (1993a), and Rey (1993).

7. Again, for more in-depth discussion see Levine (1998). Also, for a different and quite illuminating approach to the problem, see Loar (1997).

References

Chalmers, D. 1996. *The Conscious Mind*. Oxford: Oxford University Press.

Fodor, J. and Lepore, E. 1992. *Holism: A Shopper's Guide*. Blackwell: Oxford.

Hempel, C. G. 1965. *Aspects of Scientific Explanation*. New York: The Free Press.

Jackson, F. 1993. Armchair Metaphysics, in *Philosophy in Mind*, O'Leary-Hawthorne and Michael, eds., Dordrecht: Kluwer.

Kitcher, P., and Salmon, W. C., eds. 1989. *Scientific Explanation*, Minneapolis, MN: University of Minnesota Press.

Levine, J. 1983. Materialism and Qualia: The Explanatory Gap, *Pacific Philosophical Quarterly* 64.

Levine, J. 1993a. Intentional Chemistry, in Fodor, J. and Lepore, E., eds., *Holism: A Consumer Update*, special issue of *Grazer Philosophische Studien*, vol. 46.

Levine, J. 1993b. On Leaving Out What It's Like, in Davies, M. and Humphreys, G., eds., *Consciousness: Psychological and Philosophical Essays*, Oxford: Blackwell.

Levine, J. 1998. Conceivability and the Metaphysics of Mind, *Noûs* 32.

Loar, B. 1997. Phenomenal States, in Block, N., Flanagan, O., and Güzeldere, G. eds., *The Nature of Consciousness*. Cambridge: MIT Press.

Nagel, T. 1974. What Is It Like to Be a Bat? *The Philosophical Review*, vol. 82.

Quine, W. V. 1953. Two Dogmas of Empiricism, in *From a Logical Point of View*, Harvard University Press: Cambridge, Mass.

Rey, G. 1993. The Unavailability of What We Mean I: A Reply to Quine, in Fodor, J. and Lepore, E., eds., *Holism: A Consumer Update*, special issue of *Grazer Philosophische Studien*, vol. 46, 61–10.

Rosenthal, D., ed. 1991 *The Nature of Mind*. Oxford: Oxford University Press.

2 Conceiving beyond Our Means: The Limits of Thought Experiments

Robert Van Gulick

How must consciousness supervene on the physical to validate the materialist view that all mental properties, including conscious phenomenal ones, derive from underlying physical structure? It would seem at the least that no two beings with the same underlying physical causal structure and organization could differ in any mental property (leaving aside all the qualifications and nuances that would have to be built in to accommodate the "wide" or contextual dimension of mental states and their contents.)[1]

However neo-dualists, like David Chalmers,[2] argue that more is needed since causal supervenience could meet that condition yet not suffice for materialism. It's compatible with property dualism as long as there are nomic connections linking physical and mental properties. According to the property dualist, mental properties are distinct from physical properties in the same way that electromagnetic and gravitational forces are distinct. Just as we can have lawlike links between fundamental physical properties, so too the neo-dualist claims we can have lawlike relations among fundamental physical and mental properties. Given the existence of such natural laws, it may be *nomically impossible* to have a mental difference without a physical difference. If so, systems globally alike in all physical respects must as a matter of nomic necessity be alike in all mental respects

The neo-dualist contends that materialism is nonetheless false since mental properties do not *logically supervene* on physical properties but only *nomically supervene* on them. There are logically possible worlds, he alleges, that are just like ours in all physical respects but differ mentally (especially with regard to conscious mental states). It is these logical possibilities that establish the distinctness of mental properties; if mental properties were merely a special type of physical property then it would be logically impossible for them to vary while holding all physical properties constant, but since they can vary (or so the neo-dualist claims) they can not be physical properties of any kind. At most they are a distinct class of nonphysical properties that are tied to physical properties by nomically necessary but not logically necessary links.

I agree that mere nomic supervenience would not by itself secure materialism. Thus the key issue becomes the sort(s) of supervenience that can be shown to hold or not to hold between the mental and the physical. Is there a form of supervenience that the dualist can show *not to hold* that will establish his/her position? Or alternatively is there a form of supervenience that the materialist can show *does hold* that demonstrates his/her view? And how can one determine which dependencies and possibilities there are?

The burden of proof will vary with the specific claim is at issue. To prove the truth of materialism, one would need to show that any imagined world that purports to separate the mental from the physical in fact embodies a contradiction and violates the law of identity. One and the same thing can not at the same time both be and not be; if phenomenal consciousness is just a complex physical property, then its existence can not be distinct or independent from the totality of the physical facts. The materialist's aim may be, however, more modest: simply to challenge various alleged possibilities with which the dualist claims to refute materialism. His burden in that case is far less; he need show only that the dualist lacks an adequate basis for regarding the alleged possibilities as genuinely free from contradiction. The mere fact that none is obvious will not suffice, and so the focus shifts to how well the dualist can defend his purported possibility.

Dualists since Descartes[3] have used tried to use conceivability arguments to show the nonmateriality of mind. Descartes claimed that he could clearly and distinctly imagine his conscious mind continuing to exist in the total absence of his physical body. He thus concluded that the two could not be one and same. In recent years imagined zombie cases have been called upon to play a similar argumentative role. Chalmers[4] for example asks us to imagine a world W2 satisfying the following conditions:

1. There are beings who are molecule-for-molecule duplicates of conscious humans in the actual world,

2. Our molecule-for-molecule doppelgangers in W2 are not conscious, and

3. The physical laws in W2 are the same as those that hold in the actual world.

On the basis of this claim about what he can *conceive* Chalmers concludes that such molecule-for-molecule zombies are *logically possible*.

The standard reply distinguishes between two senses of "conceivability," a weak or subjective sense and a strong or objective sense. Arguments such as the zombie one rely on two premises or claims: first a claim that the existence of one sort of property without the other is indeed conceivable, and second the linking proposition that what is conceivable is logically possible. For example,

P1 I can conceive of a without b (e.g., zombie world)

P2 Whatever is conceivable is logically possible or more specifically

P2* If I can conceive of a without b then it is logically possible for a to exist without b.

C3 Therefore it is logically possible for a to exist without b.

P4 If it is logically possible for a to exist without b, then a is distinct from b (not identical with b)

C5 a is distinct from b (not identical with b)

Such an argument must either equivocate on its use of the word "conceivable" or fail to support at least one of its first two premises. To make (P1) plausible, one needs to read it in the weak subjective sense, as meaning merely that imagining a without b, (or any other mental difference without a physical difference), *does not seem to* involve a contradiction, that is, merely that we can tell ourselves what seems to be a coherent story. But while this makes P1 plausible, it undercuts the second step (P2), which links conceivability to logical possibility. That an imagined state of affairs does not *seem* to involve a contradiction does not entail that it in fact involves none. If we opt for the stronger or objective notion of conceivability, which requires that there not be any contradiction (as opposed to merely seeming such,) the link to logical possibility goes through directly. But then the earlier claim that one can conceive of a without b (or the mental without the physical) collapses into question-begging. Thus if we read "conceivable" strongly we lose P1, if we read weakly we lose P2, and if we equivocate the inference to C3 is invalid. Thus the argument is unsound.

This line of criticism is often illustrated with familiar scientific examples such as those of water and H_2O or heat and molecular kinetic energy. The fact that a chemically ignorant person might conceive (in the weak or subjective sense) of water existing without H_2O shows nothing about their nonidentity, and because water *is* H_2O—as established a posteriori—it is not logically possible for the one to exist without the other.

Chalmers is fully aware of these objections but believes his own arguments escape such criticism.[5] First it is worth noting that he uses "logical possibility" with a sense that would rehabilitate the move to C3 while leaving the argument unsound overall. As he uses it, "logical possibility" means little more than conceivability, what he calls "a priori possibility" and which concerns only what we can infer from the concepts involved by a priori means. If "logical possibility" is read in that way, P2 becomes more or less a tautology even on the weak reading of "conceivable," and the move to C3 is automatic. The original problem, however recurs at the next step. If the "logical possibility" of separation means merely its "a priori conceivability" then, as the scientific cases show, it does not entail distinctness, and the general argument fails.

Chalmers acknowledges this and, unlike some of his predecessors, does not rely on any general linking principle such as P4. Moreover he acknowledges that a priori conceivability (what he calls logical possibility) does not in itself entails what he calls "metaphysical possibility," the strong relation needed to license the move from *possibility* of separation to nonidentity.[6]

In analyzing the familiar scientific examples, he carefully distinguishes between what he calls primary and secondary intensions associated with terms. The primary intension of the word "water" involves having various watery characteristics (color, liquidity, taste, smell, etc.). However, through its use in context by our linguistic group to refer to the stuff around here that has those characteristics, it acquires the secondary intension [H_2O]. Thus when someone in our linguistic community claims to be imagining a situation with water but without H_2O, he/she is misdescribing his/her state; when he/she uses "water" it means H_2O (secondary intension). Such a person is in fact imagining a situation in which some substance satisfies the primary intension associated with "water" without being water.

However, according to Chalmers the analogy breaks down in the consciousness/material properties case. The disanalogy is this: anything that satisfied the primary intension associated with "consciousness" would *be* a case of consciousness. Thus if one can conceive of that concept (primary intension) being satisfied in a world that lacks the materialist's proposed physical properties, then consciousness must be distinct from them. More importantly, if one can conceive of the primary intension associated with "consciousness" *not* being satisfied in a world that contains all the relevant physical properties, then consciousness cannot be identical with them nor logically supervenient on them.

To be precise, what Chalmers claims is just a bit weaker: namely that as a matter of a priori/logical possibility the phenomenal aspect associated with the primary intension can exist independently of any supposed physical basis and thus must be distinct from it.[7] But since that aspect involves the existence of phenomenal awareness, whether or not we identify it outright with consciousness matters little. What counts is the supposed logical possibility that phenomenal what-it's-like-to-be-ness can exist or not exist independently of the physical facts.

However, even if successful, this reply would merely weaken the analogy with certain examples (e.g., water/H_2O) that are standardly used to illustrate the problems with modal conceivability arguments; it would not in itself resolve those issues. Though some analogies are broken, other remain that may suffice to undermine the zombie thought experiment. And more importantly there are residual questions about the adequacy of the concepts that Chalmers and the neodualists use in their thought experiments. Are those concepts well enough developed and anchored to support the argumentative use to which they are put? I think not.

Consider the analogies kept and broken. There are allegedly two sorts of worlds. First those in which the primary intension of "consciousness," the phenomenal aspect, is satisfied despite the absence of the materialist's purported physical referent. These are worlds like those in which there is watery XYZ without any H_2O. This is where the disanalogy intrudes; although we can imagine something watery that is not water, we can't imagine something that involves phenomenal awareness without imagining what amounts to consciousness in the philosophically important sense. The primary intension of "water," refers to relatively superficial properties that demonstratively link us to its referent in context. But the primary intension of "consciousness" incorporates so much that its imagined satisfaction in the absence of its materialist counterpart shows the two to be distinct.

But this wouldn't suffice to refute materialism; it shows that consciousness can be realized by multiple substrates, but that's a materialist platitude. To get a dualist result, one needs to claim that one can imagine consciousness occurring in the absence of any physical substrate at all—a true Cartesian disembodied mind. Materialists typically object to such claims as begging the question. If being in a state of phenomenal awareness is in fact being in special sort of dynamically organized physical state, then when one imagines a world with phenomenal awareness, one imagines some physical substrate whether one recognizes that one is doing so or not. If "being-a-something-that-it's-like-to-be" is a matter of being a certain sort of physical system that interacts with itself in a special way, then when one imagines the former, one imagines the latter whether one conceives of it *as such* or not. The materialist may be wrong, but to *show* him so one needs assumptions that don't prejudge the issue.

Imagined worlds of the second sort are even more problematic; these are the zombie worlds in which our exact physical duplicates completely lack consciousness. The materialist will reply that this is just as contradictory as imagining a world in which there is a substance that is physically and behaviorally just like the water in Lake Erie for some extended stretch of time, but that is not liquid. Obviously when one imagines the Lake Erie doppelganger, one in effect imagines its liquidity. Though it is not so obvious, the materialist claims we do the same when we imagine our physical duplicates; whether we realize it or not, in doing so we imagine conscious beings just as we imagine liquid lakes. Is he right? That remains an open question, but to assume he's wrong again seems to beg the question.

The neodualist will deny the parallel. With Lake Erie, we can reductively explain just why and how the underlying physical substrate satisfies all the functional conditions to count as liquid, but we can't do the same for consciousness. Indeed we can not at this time come close to doing so, but that need reflect only the poverty of our current theories and concepts. It shows we have a current explanatory gap, but no metaphysical implications follow. The fault may lie not in the world but in our concepts of it.

We come thus to the second and more general question about the dualist's thought experiments. Are the concepts that he uses adequate to the task to which he puts them? Is our concept of phenomenal consciousness or our concept of its possible physical basis well enough developed to allow us to draw metaphysical conclusions about their relation? As noted above, I think they are not.

Consider first another nonmental example. Imagine a mid-nineteenth-century vitalist who argues as follows:

1. I can conceive of creatures that are just like actual creatures (say actual cats) in all physical respects but that have no ability to reproduce.

2. Therefore the ability to reproduce does not logically supervene on a creature's physical structure.

With the benefit of late twentieth century science we know the vitalist's conclusion is dead wrong; the ability to reproduce *does* logically supervene on physical structure. More interestingly we can see diagnostically where the vitalist went wrong; he had neither an adequate concept of reproduction nor an adequate concept of the total physical structure of a living organism, and he also lacked an adequate theory of how the two might fit together. He had no idea of the way in which reproduction involves the replication and transfer of genetic information, and he had not the slightest grasp of what we now know to be the biochemical basis of that process, of how genetic information can be coded by sequences of DNA and RNA. What was conceivable from the vitalist's perspective shows little if anything about what is logically (or metaphysically) possible in matters reproductive and physical. The vitalist might have conjoined *his concept* of the total physical structure of a cat with the negation of *his concept of* the ability to reproduce without generating any a priori contradictions, but given the radical incompleteness of his concepts vis-à-vis the natures of the two phenomena to which he applied them, nothing really follows regarding what relations of logical (or metaphysical) possibility might hold between those phenomena themselves.

Are the concepts used by Chalmers and the neodualist more adequate than the vitalist's? First we must ask, "what specific concepts do they use?" On the mental side they use a concept of experience derived from our first person awareness of our own conscious mental states and processes. The nature of these concepts derives from their representational and regulatory role in the monitoring and control of our conscious mental life. They surely meet conditions of adequacy relative to that role. But in what other respects might they be adequate or inadequate? For the neodualist's purposes his concept of conscious experience, call it CCE, must be adequate to limn the boundaries of consciousness; whatever satisfies CCE in any world must be an instance of consciousness and whatever fails to fall under CCE must equally fail to be an instance of consciousness. The neodualist treats his concept CCE as the universal (Protagorean) standard of consciousness, but that assumption seems less than plausible or at least problematic. Why should that concept of experience derived from its role in regulating our specific form of consciousness provide a characterization of consciousness sufficiently general to determine the logically possible boundaries of consciousness. Please note I am not saying that the neodualist assumes that all logically possible conscious experience must involve the same specific phenomenal properties associated with human consciousness; he most surely and rightly does not say that. But what he does implicitly assume, though more modest, is still upon reflection implausible, namely that the concepts of consciousness that we command on the basis of their application within our own self-awareness can provide us with a general means of delimiting the logically possible boundaries of consciousness.

Moreover, there is a further dimension of adequacy in which the neodualist's concept of consciousness is even less plausibly up to the task, one that is directly relevant to his thought experiment. The question is whether or not the neodualist's concept of consciousness is adequate for assessing whether or not and how it might be instantiated by a material substrate. Recall the vitalist's concept of reproduction, which failed to include the idea of information transfer. Given the incompleteness of the vitalist's concept it is not surprising that he could not see how reproduction might be a fully material process. The situation, I believe is comparable with respect to the neodualist's concept of consciousness. Here too our current understanding of consciousness *qua consciousness* is far too incomplete to be able to say with any confidence how it might or might not be physically realized.

This conceptual inadequacy on the mental side is compounded by the fact that the concepts that the neodualist invokes on the physical side of his conceivability experiment are terribly nonspecific and even less adequate to the task at hand. Indeed the physical concepts that are used are little more than dummy concepts, such as "beings like actual conscious humans in all physical respects." No real detailed concepts that might characterize the physical substrate of consciousness are given. It's akin to the vitalist's blanket claim about the possibility of physically identical creatures without the ability to reproduce. The vitalist really knew nothing in any specific way about what the physical substrate of inheritance might be; he knew nothing of biochemistry, nothing of nucleic acids, or their structure or operation within the cell.

The vitalist had no remotely adequate or detailed concept of the physical basis of reproduction. He lacked an adequate conception of what reproduction required. And thus he couldn't understand how to fit together the two inadequately conceptualized pieces of his puzzle. Ditto for the neodualist.

Chalmers explicitly denies that there is any valid analogy between his conceivability argument and vitalist arguments for antimaterialism, though he does not consider any parallels drawn in the way I have done just above, that is, he does not consider an analogy based on parallel conceptual inadequacy. Nonetheless we should consider his basis for denying that there is a valid analogy. He argues that all the phenomena that the vitalist saw as beyond physical explanation were functional in nature; according to Chalmers what the vitalist couldn't see was how any physical structures or processes could perform the requisite function. To refute the vitalist we needed only to show how they could in fact do so.

Chalmers, however, denies that the same might happen with respect to consciousness and the physical because on his reckoning—and this is a key claim—consciousness is *not* a fundamentally functional process. He admits consciousness and conscious mental states perform various functional roles, but he denies that an account of such roles can explain what consciousness *is*, that is, he denies we can *analyze* or *explicate* the nature of consciousness in functional terms. To support his claim, he considers various functional roles that have been associated with or proposed for consciousness—such as information processing roles or behavior regulating roles—and argues that in each case we can conceive or imagine that role being filled in the complete absence of phenomenal consciousness; that is, he offers a variety of absent qualia arguments each directed at one or another functional role that has been or might be proposed for consciousness. But here again we need to ask about the adequacy of the concepts that Chalmers uses to reach his general antifunctionalist conclusion. I agree that consciousness does not logically supervene on the specific functional phenomena that he considers, but that reflects negatively only on the specific inadequate functionalist proposals he considers not on the prospects for functionally explicating consciousness per se.

The functionalist has his own modest embarrassments. In the absence of a detailed functionalist account of consciousness, he is left in a position like that of a mid-nineteenth-century materialist trying to reply to his vitalist critic. He has a wide explanatory gap to bridge and needs to write a hefty IOU. But carrying the burden of a large promissory note is not the same as having been refuted. And that as yet the functionalist has not been, nor has the materialist—zombie thought experiments not with standing.

Notes

1. On the contextual nature of the mental see for example, Burge (1979).
2. Chalmers (1996).

3. As in Descartes (1972) originally published in 1642.

4. Chalmers (1996) p. 94.

5. Chalmers (1996), chapter 3.

6. Chalmers (1996), chapter 4.

7. I am here indebted to personal communication from David Chalmers by email, May 1998.

References

Burge, T. 1979. Individualism and the mental in *Midwest Studies in Philosophy*. Vol. 4, Peter French, Thomas Uehling, and Howard Wettstein, eds. Minneapolis: University of Minnesota Press, 73–121.

Chalmers, D. 1996. *The Conscious Mind*. New York: Oxford University Press.

Descartes, R. 1972. *Meditations on First Philosophy*. In *The Philosophical Works of Descartes* translated by Elizabeth Haldane and G. R. T Ross. Cambridge: Cambridge University Press, (Original publication of *The Meditations* was in 1642.)

3 Realistic Materialist Monism

Galen Strawson

1

Materialists hold that every thing and event in the universe is physical in every respect. They hold that "physical phenomenon" is coextensive with "real phenomenon," or at least with "real, concrete phenomenon," and for the purposes of this chapter I am going to assume that they are right.[1]

Monists hold that there is, fundamentally, only one kind of stuff in reality—in a sense that I will discuss further in §6.

Realistic monists—realistic anybodys—grant that experiential phenomena are real, where by "experiential phenomena" and "experience" I mean the phenomena of consciousness considered just and only in respect of the qualitative character that they have for those who have them as they have them.

Realistic materialist monists, then, grant that experiential phenomena are real, and are wholly physical, strictly on a par with the phenomena of extension and mass as characterized by physics. For if they do not, they are not realistic materialists. This is the part of the reason why genuine, reflective endorsement of materialism is a very considerable achievement. I think, in fact, that it requires concerted meditative effort. If one hasn't felt a kind of vertigo of astonishment, when facing the thought that consciousness is a wholly physical phenomenon in every respect, then one hasn't begun to be a thoughtful materialist. One hasn't got to the starting line.

Materialism has been characterized in other ways. David Lewis has defined it as "metaphysics built to endorse the truth and descriptive completeness of physics more or less as we know it" (1986: x). This cannot be faulted as a terminological decision, but it seems unwise to burden materialism—the view that everything in the universe is *physical*—with a commitment to the descriptive completeness of *physics* more or less as we know it. There may be physical phenomena that physics (and any non-revolutionary extension of it) cannot describe, and of which it has no inkling. Physics is one thing, the physical is another. "Physical" is the ultimate natural-kind term, and no sensible person thinks that physics has nailed all the essential properties of the physical. Current physics is profoundly beautiful and useful, but it is in a state of chronic internal tension (consider the old quarrel between general relativity theory and quantum mechanics). It may be added, with Russell and others, that although physics appears to tell us a great deal about certain of the general structural or mathematical characteristics of the physical, it fails to give us any real insight into the nature of whatever it is that has these characteristics—apart from making it plain that it is utterly bizarre relative to our ordinary conception of it.

It is unclear exactly what this last remark amounts to (is it being suggested that physics is failing to do something it could do?). But it already amounts to something very important when it comes to what is known as the "mind-body problem." For many take this to be the problem of how mental phenomena can be physical phenomena *given what we already know about the nature of the physical*. And this is the great mistake of our time. The truth is that we have no good reason to think that we know *anything* about the physical that gives us *any* reason to find *any* problem in the idea that mental or experiential phenomena are physical phenomena.

Arnauld made the essential point in 1641, and he was not the first. So did Locke in 1690, Hume in 1739, Priestley in 1777, Kant in 1781. Russell put the point in a strong form in 1927, when he argued that "the physical world is only known as regards certain abstract features of its space-time structure—features that, because of their abstractness, do not suffice to show whether the physical world is, or is not, different in intrinsic character from the world of mind" (1948: 240). "Physics is mathematical," he said,

not because we know so much about the physical world, but because we know so little: it is only its mathematical properties that we can discover. For the rest, our knowledge is negative.... We know nothing about the intrinsic quality of physical events except when these are mental events that we directly experience ... as regards the world in general, both physical and mental, everything that we know of its intrinsic character is derived from the mental side.[2]

2

Realistic materialism, then, first divides the world into experiential and non-experiential phenomena (it cannot deny the existence of experiential phenomena, and it *assumes* that physical reality does not consist entirely of experiential phenomena). It then requires one to drain one's conception of the non-experiential of any element that, in a puzzling world, makes it seem especially puzzling that the experiential is physical.

Some philosophers think this is the wrong way round. They think we have to drain our conception of the experiential of any element that produces special puzzlement, leaving our existing conception of the non-experiential in place. But no substantial draining can be done on the experiential side, for in having experience in the way we do, we are directly acquainted with certain features of the fundamental or ultimate nature of reality, as Russell and many others have remarked—whether or not we can put what we know into words in any theoretically tractable way.

Some deny this. "Look," they say, "in having experience we only have access to an appearance of how things are, and are not acquainted, in the mere having of the experience, with how anything is in itself."

The reply is immediate. Here, how things appear or seem is how they really are: the reality that is in question just is the appearing or seeming. In the case of any experience E there may be something X of which it is true to say that in having E we only have access to an appearance of X, and not to how X is in itself. But serious materialists must hold that E itself, the event of being-appeared-to, with all the qualitative character that it has, is itself part of physical reality. They cannot say that it too is just an appearance, and not part of how things are, on pain of infinite regress. They must grant that it is itself a reality, and a reality with which we must be allowed to have some sort of direct acquaintance.

3

The puzzlement remains—the deep puzzlement one still feels, as a beginner in materialism, when one considers experiential properties and non-experiential properties and grants that they are equally part of physical reality. The puzzlement is legitimate in a way: it is legitimate insofar as we have no positive understanding of how the two sorts of properties connect up. But it is completely illegitimate if it contains any trace of the thought "How *can* consciousness be physical, given what we know about what matter is like?" If one thinks this then one is, in Russell's words, "guilty, unconsciously and in spite of explicit disavowals, of a confusion in one's imaginative picture of matter" (1927a: 382). One thinks one knows more about the nature of matter—of the non-experiential—than one does. This is the fundamental error.

Consider the old, natural intuition that there is a "deep repugnance" between the nature of experience or consciousness and the nature of space. It is powerful but unsupported. The truth is that we have no good reason to think that we know enough about the nature of space—or rather, about the nature of matter-in-space-considered-in-its-nonmental-being—to be able to assert that there is any such repugnance. Colin McGinn develops the the idea that there is a deep repugnance between consciousness and space with great force, until he finds himself driven to the suggestion that consciousness may be a manifestation of the nonspatial nature of pre Big Bang reality. Later, and more moderately, he says that consciousness "tests the adequacy of our spatial understanding. It marks the place of deep lack of knowledge about space" (1995: 223–224; 230).

This is right: the concept of space, like the concept of the physical, is a natural-kind concept, and there are very good reasons for thinking that there is more to space than we know or can understand. Even when I put aside the (already weighty) points that physical space is non-Euclidean, and is itself something that is literally expanding, and the nonlocality results, I can't fully understand how space and time can be interdependent in the way that they demonstrably are. We are also told on very good authority that gravity is really just a matter of the curvature of space; and that string theory is an immensely promising theory of matter that entails that there are at least ten spatial dimensions.

4

So we suffer from confusion in our imaginative picture of matter. Can anything be done? I think it can. Physics can help us by diluting or undermining features of our natural conception of the physical that make nonmental phenomena appear utterly different from mental phenomena. The basic point is simple and can be elaborated as follows.

At first, perhaps, one takes it that matter is simply solid stuff, uniform, non-particulate—the ultimate Scandinavian cheese. Then one learns that it is composed of distinct atoms—solid particles that cohere more or less closely together to make up objects, but that have empty space (to put it simplistically but intelligibly) between them. Then one learns that these atoms are themselves made up of tiny, separate particles, and full of empty space themselves. One learns that matter is not at all what one thought.

One may accept this while holding on to the idea that matter is at root solid and dense. For so far this picture retains the idea that there are particles of matter: minuscule grainy bits of ultimate stuff that are in themselves truly solid, continuum-dense. And one may say that only these, strictly speaking, are matter: matter as such. But it is more than two hundred years since Joseph Priestley (alluding to Boscovich) observed that there is no positive observational or theoretical reason to suppose that the fundamental constituents of matter have any truly solid central part, and the picture of grainy, inert bits of matter has suffered many further blows in modern (post-1925) quantum mechanics and in quantum field theory. It was in any case already undermined by the discovery that matter is a form of energy.

To put it dramatically: Physics thinks of matter considered in its non-experiential being is a thing of forces, energy, fields, and it can also seem rather natural to conceive of experience or consciousness as a form or manifestation of energy, as a kind of force, and even, perhaps, as a kind of field. The two things may still seem deeply heterogeneous, but we really have no good reason to believe this. We just don't know enough about the nature of matter considered in its nonmental being. In fact—and it had to come back to this—we don't really know enough to say that there is any nonmental being. All the appearances of a nonmental world may just be the way that physical phenomena—in themselves entirely mental phenomena—appear; the appearance being another mental phenomenon.

Whether this is so or not, lumpish, inert matter has given way to fields of energy, essentially active diaphanous process-stuff that—intuitively—seems far less unlike the process of consciousness. When McGinn, Greenfield, and Nagel talk of "soggy grey matter" a "sludgy mass," and the "squishy brain," they vividly express the "imaginative . . . confusion" in the ordinary idea of matter.[3] But we can avoid some of the confusion without much difficulty. There is a clear sense in which the best description of the nature of the nonmental *even in common-sense terms* comes from physics. For what, expressed in common-sense terms, does physics find in the volume of spacetime occupied by a brain? Not a sludgy mass, but a—to us—astonishingly insubstantial play of energy, an ethereally radiant form.

It finds, in other words, a physical object that, thus far examined, is like any other. Examined further, this particular physical object—the living brain—turns out to have a vast further set of remarkable properties: all the sweeping sheets and scudding fountains of electrochemical activity that physics and neurophysiology apprehend as a further level of extraordinarily complex intensities of movement and organization.

All this being so, does one really have good reason to think that the phenomenon of consciousness or experience is not a physical thing, strictly on a par with the phenomena of mass and extension as apprehended by physics? I think not.

5

This point is negative. It destroys one common source of intuitive puzzlement, but it doesn't offer any sort of positive account of the relation between the play of energy non-experientially conceived and the play of energy experientially apprehended, and some will find it no help. They may even object that it is a positive mistake to think that it is helpful, on the grounds that there is in the end no more difficulty in the thought that the existence of matter naively and grossly conceived involves the existence of consciousness than there is in the thought that matter scientifically and quantum-mechanically conceived does so.

We can grant them their objection for their own consumption (they are likely to be fairly sophisticated philosophers). Others—including philosophers—may find the negative point useful, and it may be worth relating it briefly to three currently popular issues: eliminativism, the "hard problem," and "zombies."

Eliminativism

Consider any philosopher who has ever been tempted, even momentarily, by the "eliminativist" suggestion that one has to question the reality of the Experiential in some way in order to be a thoroughgoing materialist. It is an extraordinary suggestion (it is considerably more bizarre than Xenocrates' suggestion that the soul is a self-moving number), and what is most striking about it in the present context is that it constitutes the most perfect demonstration in the history of philosophy of the grip of the very thing that it seeks to reject: dualist thinking. The eliminativists make the same initial mistake as Descartes—the mistake of assuming that they understand more about the nature of the physical than they do—but their subjugation to dualist thinking is much deeper than Descartes: they are so certain that the physical excludes the Experiential that they are prepared to deny the reality of the Experiential in some (admittedly unclear) way—that is, to make the most ridiculous claim ever made in philosophy—in order to retain the physical.

The "Hard Problem"

It is seriously misleading to talk too freely about "the hard part of the mind-body problem," as if the "mind-body" problem were clearly posed.[4] It is not, as Chomsky has observed. In fact it is not sufficiently well-defined for us to be able to say that it is hard; for although we have a clear positive fix on the notion of experiential reality, we have no clear positive fix on the notion of non-experiential reality. Certainly we have no reason to think that it is a harder problem than the problem posed for our understanding by the peculiarities of quantum physics.

Zombies

It is, finally, a mistake to think that we can know that "zombies" could exist—where zombies are understood to be creatures that have no experiential properties although they are *perfect physical duplicates* (PPDs) of currently experiencing human beings like you and me.[5]

The argument that PPD-zombies could exist proceeds from two premises—[1] it is conceivable that PPD-zombies exist, [2] if something is conceivable, then it is possible. It is plainly valid, and (unlike many) I have no insuperable problem with [2]. The problem is that we can't know [1] to be true, and have no reason to think it is. To be a materialist is, precisely, to hold that it is false, and while materialism cannot be known to be true, it cannot be refuted a priori—as it could be if [1] were established. "Physical," recall, is a natural-kind term, and since we know that there is much that we do not know about the nature of the physical, we we cannot possibly claim to know that a experienceless PPD of a currently experiencing human being is conceivable, and could possibly (or "in some possible world") exist.[6] Note that anyone who holds that it is as a matter of *physical* fact impossible for a PPD of an actual, living normally experiencing human being to be experienceless must hold that PPD-zombies are *metaphysically* impossible. Physical impossibility entails metaphysical impossibility in this case, because the question is precisely what is possible given the actual nature of the physical.

6

In §1 I pointed out that the word "physical," as used by genuine materialists, is coextensive with "real and concrete"—so that to say something is a physical phenomenon is simply to say that it is a real (spatiotemporal) phenomenon. But then why use "physical"? Why not simply use "real"? And why bother with "real," when talking about concrete things that are assumed to exist? It is clearly redundant. All one needs, to mark the distinctions that are centrally at issue in discussion of the unfortunately named "mind-body problem," are "mental" and "nonmental," "experiential" and "non-experiential." One can simply declare oneself to be a *experiential-and-non-experiential* monist: one who registers the indubitable reality of experiential phenomena and takes it that there are also non-experiential phenomena. I nominate this position for the title "realistic materialist monism."

"But if one can do without "physical," then the word "materialist," used so diligently in this chapter, is just as superfluous; and it is deeply compromised by its history."

I think, nevertheless, that the word "materialist," as an adjective formed from the natural-kind term "matter," can be harmlessly and even illuminatingly retained. What is matter? It is whatever we are actually talking about when we talk about concrete reality, and realistic materialist monists who take it that experiential phenomena are wholly material in nature can assert with certainty that there is such a thing as matter, for they can know with certainty that there is such a thing as concrete reality (i.e. experiential phenomena). What they will want to add to this is an acknowledgement that nothing can count as matter unless it has some sort of non-experiential being—together with the working presumption (modulated by awareness of the extent of our ignorance) that current physics's best account of the structure of reality is genuinely reality-mirroring in certain ways. If in fact current physics gets nothing right, then one might say that their claim to be materialists effectively lapses; but so does everyone else's.

As a realistic materialist monist, then, I presume that physics's best account of the structure of reality is genuinely reality-mirroring in substantive ways, and that the term "materialist" is in good order. It has travelled far from some of its past uses, but there is no good reason to think that its meaning is especially tied to its past use, still less to one particular part of its past use,[7] and there is a sense in which its past use makes it particularly well worth retaining: it makes the claim that the present position is materialist vivid by prompting resistance that turns out to be groundless when the position is properly understood.

What about "monist"? There is serious unclarity in this notion, for monists hold that there is, in spite of all the variety in the world, a fundamental sense in which there is only one basic kind of stuff or being. But questions about how many kinds of stuff or being there are are answerable only relative to a particular point of view or interest; and what point of view is so privileged that it allows one to say that it is an absolute metaphysical fact that there is only one kind stuff or being in reality? Materialists call themselves monists because they think that all things are of one kind—the physical kind. But many of them also hold that there is more than one kind of fundamental particle, and this claim, taken literally, entails that there isn't after all any one basic kind of being out of which everything is constituted. For it is the claim that these particles are themselves, in their diversity, the ultimate constituents of reality; in which case there is kind-plurality or stuff-plurality right at the bottom of things.

"But these particles are nevertheless all *physical*, and in that sense of one kind."

But to say that they can be classed together as single-substanced in this way is question-begging until it is backed by a positive theoretical account of why it is correct to say that they are all ultimately (constituted) of one kind (of substance). To claim that their causal interaction sufficiently proves their same-substancehood is to beg the question in another way, on the terms of the classical debate, for classical substance-dualists simply deny that causal interaction entails same-substancehood. The claim that they are all spatiotemporally located also begs the question. For how does this prove same substancehood?

It may be replied that all the particles are just different forms of the same stuff—energy. And it may be added that the so-called fundamental particles—quarks and leptons—are not strictly speaking fundamental, and are in fact all constituted of just one kind of thing: superstrings. And these approaches deserve investigation—to be conducted with an appropriately respectful attitude to panpsychism. But one can overleap them by simply rejecting the terms of the classical debate: one can take causal interaction to be a sufficient condition of same-substancehood.

I think that this is what one should do, if one is going to retain any version of the terminology of substance. Dualists who postulate two distinct substances while holding that they interact causally not only face the old problem of how to give an honest account of this interaction. They also face the (far more difficult) problem of justifying the claim that there are two substances. As far as I can see, *the only justification that has ever been attempted* has consisted in an appeal to the intuition that the mental, or the experiential, is utterly different in nature from matter. But this intuition lacks any remotely respectable theoretical support, if the argument of this chapter is even roughly right; and this has been clear for hundreds of years (cf., e.g., Locke 1690: IV.iii.6). The truth is that dualism has *nothing* in its favour—to think that it has does is simply to reveal that one thinks one knows more than one does—and it has Occam's razor (that blunt sharp instrument) against it. It may be that substance dualism—or pluralism—is in fact the best view to take about our universe for reasons of which we know nothing. So be it: the objection to dualism just given remains decisive when dualism is considered specifically as a theoretical response to the "mind-body problem."

"But why persist with "monist"? You might as well call yourself a "neutral pluralist," for all the difference it makes, and "monist" carries bad baggage. Why not simply call yourself a "noncommittal naturalist," or, with Chomsky, a "methodological naturalist"? Or a '"?-ist"?'[8]

These are very good questions. For the moment, though, the physics idea (the ancient idea) that everything is made of the same ultimate stuff—that the deep diversity of the universe is a matter of different arrangements of the same fundamental *ens* or *entia*—seems to me as compelling as it is remarkable, and I choose to register my attraction to it with the word '*monism*'.[9]

Notes

1. I use "phenomenon" as a completely general word for any sort of existent, abstracting from its meaning of *appearance*, and without any implication as to ontological category (the trouble with "entity" is that it now has a strongly substantival connotation). I add "concrete" to "real" because some say numbers are real things, but agree that they are abstract, not concrete, entities.

2. Russell 1927b/1992b: 125; 1956: 153; 1927a/1992a: 402. Lockwood (1989: ch. 10) has a useful historical note on versions of the idea that precede Russell's. Cp. Chomsky 1995: 1–10, Crane and Mellor 1990.

3. McGinn 1991: 1, 100, Greenfield BBC 21 June 1997, Nagel 1998: 338.

4. Strawson 1994: 93. Cf. McGinn 1989: 349, Chalmers 1995: 200, and many others through the ages.

5. I don't know where these zombies come from. Ten years or so ago, philosophical zombies were far more plausible creatures: they were defined to be *outwardly* and *behaviorally* indistinguishable from human beings, while having unknown (possibly nonbiological) insides, and were of considerable interest to functionalists and behaviorists.

6. To be a perfect physical duplicate, one would of course have to be governed by the same physical laws.

7. There is no good reason to think that it is especially tied to the seventeenth-century conception of matter as something passive and inert, and the conception of matter as essentially energy-involving, or at least as something to which motion is intrinsic, is already present in the work of Democritus and Epicurus.

8. Sebastian Gardner once suggested that I might call myself a "'?-ist" (cf. Strawson 1994: 105).

9. This is a trailer for Strawson (forthcoming). I am very grateful to Noam Chomsky, Michael Lockwood, and Undo Uus for the leads they have given me, and would also like to thank Harvey Brown, Jeremy Butterfield, Tim Crane, Mark Greenberg, Isaac Levi, Barry Loewer, Philip Pettit, Mark Sainsbury, Simon Saunders, Stephen Schiffer, Peter Unger, and audiences at the University of Birmingham, CUNY Graduate Center, and Columbia University.

References

Chalmers, D. (1995) "Facing up to the Problem of Consciousness." *Journal of Consciousness Studies*, 2, 200–219.

Chomsky, N. (1995) "Language and Nature." *Mind* 104, 1–60.

Crane, T. and Mellor, D. H. (1990) "There Is No Question of Physicalism." *Mind* 99, 185.

Dennett, D. (1991) *Consciousness Explained*. Boston: Little, Brown.

Hume, D. (1739/1978) *A Treatise of Human Nature*, ed. L. A. Selby-Bigge and P. H. Nidditch. Oxford: Oxford University Press.

Kant, I. (1781/1933) *Critique of Pure Reason*, trans. N. Kemp Smith. London: Macmillan.

Levine, J. (1983) "Materialism and qualia: the explanatory gap." *Pacific Philosophical Quarterly* 64, 354–361.

Lewis, David (1983) "Introduction." In D. Lewis, *Philosophical Papers*, vol. 2. Oxford: Oxford University Press.

Locke, J. (1690/1975) *An Essay Concerning Human Understanding*, edited by P. Nidditch. Oxford: Clarendon Press.

Lockwood, M. (1989) *Mind, Brain, and the Quantum*. Oxford: Blackwell.

McGinn, C. (1991) *The Problem of Consciousness*. Oxford: Blackwell.

McGinn, C. (1995) "Consciousness and Space." *Journal of Consciousness Studies* 2, 221–230.

Nagel, T. (1998) "Conceiving the Impossible and the Mind-Body Problem." *Philosophy* 73, 337–352.

Priestley, J. (1777/1965) *Priestley's Writings on Philosophy, Science and Politics*, ed. J. A Passmore. New York: Collier.

Russell, B. (1927a/1992a) *The Analysis of Matter*. London: Routledge.

Russell, B. (1927b/1992b) *An Outline of Philosophy*. London: Routledge.

Russell, B. (1948/1992c) *Human Knowledge: Its Scope and Limits*. London: Routledge.

Russell, B. (1956/1995) "Mind and Matter." In *Portraits from Memory*. Nottingham: Spokesman.

Strawson, G. (1994) *Mental Reality*. Cambridge, Mass.: MIT Press.

Strawson, G. (forthcoming) "Realistic monism." In *Chomsky and His Critics*, ed. L. Antony and N. Hornstein. Oxford: Blackwell.

4 On the Intrinsic Nature of the Physical

Gregg H. Rosenberg

"Even if there is only one possible unified theory, it is just a set of rules and equations. What is it that breathes fire into the equations and makes a universe for them to describe?"
—Stephen Hawking, *A Brief History of Time*

I Introduction

In its original context Hawking was writing about the significance of physics for questions about God's existence and responsibility for creation. I am co-opting the sentiment for another purpose, though. As stated Hawking could equally be directing the question at concerns about the seemingly abstract information physics conveys about the world, and the full body of facts contained in the substance of the world. Would even a complete and adequate physics tell us all the general facts about the stuff the world is made of? In this chapter I am going to argue that the answer is "no." I am also going to argue that the missing facts are like the kinds of facts we can use to cross the explanatory gap. I am going to argue, in short, that we have reasons to re-enchant matter that are independent of the mind-body problem.

In a recent anthology on consciousness (1997) Güven Güzeldere wrote,

a principle reason underlying the confusion and seeming mystery surrounding the concept and phenomenon of consciousness lies in the presence of two influential, equally attractive, pre-theoretic characterizations.... They can be summarized in the following mottos: "Consciousness is as consciousness does" and "Consciousness is as consciousness *seems.*"

Güzeldere calls these the "two faces" of consciousness. Face one of consciousness concerns the causal role that being conscious enables a cognitive element to play in our mental economy. Face two of consciousness concerns the way conscious elements feel or appear to the experiencer. These two faces correspond to the functional and experiential aspects of the problem, respectively.

By using this distinction we can produce a useful and quick diagnosis of why the explanatory gap exists. Science describes the way the external world seems to us largely by explaining why things *do what they do*. At intermediate levels we involve structural descriptions in the project, but these are typically only important because of their role in helping us to fulfill the primary goal of understanding the behavior of things. Most centrally, at the bottom level the basic physical things have one "face": when one explains what things at this level *do*, one has explained all the facts about how they *seem*. The "one face" of physical things concerns how they behave with respect to other physical things.

The gap arises because the experiential face of consciousness involves facts that seem to go beyond just facts about what it does. In Güzeldere's phrase, unlike physical things, consciousness has "two faces." Facts about the phenomenal qualities, and the experiencing of these qualities, exist as further targets of explanation. So even after our physical theories explain what consciousness does, there are further questions about its nature that we need to ask and answer. These are the "hard problem" questions about its other "face."

II The Landscape of Responses

Even though some flatly deny the existence of the explanatory gap, its existence is widely perceived and acknowledged by members of the consciousness studies community. Three strategies to address it have been well-explored without yielding a stable consensus. The first strategy involves trying to produce arguments that, despite first appearances, no gap exists. The troublesome experiential face is more or less an illusion, and no facts other than facts about what consciousness does (Dennett 1988, Wilkes 1988, Rey 1995) exist. The second strategy is to argue that, even though there *is* an explanatory gap, that does not mean we need to draw any conclusions about our theories leaving out any facts (Levine 1993). The gap is *merely* one of explanation, and so it only draws our attention to a peculiarity in our situation with respect to the facts. Nothing else important follows from it. A closely related third strategy is to argue that a gap merely *seems* to exist because of some cognitive limitation on our part (McGinn 1989)—we are too stupid (or have the wrong type of intelligence) to appreciate the explanatory connection. A proper understanding of the physical and phenomenal facts would, in reality, show us that one explains the other.

I do not believe any of these three strategies are acceptable. The first simply flatly conflicts with the evidence. Its proponents need to produce much stronger arguments than they have produced to make it a serious contender, and I am pessimistic that such arguments exist. Each of the other two strategies suffers from another serious fault: they are exercises in excuse making. The explanatory gap is an instance of explanatory failure. When confronted with explanatory failure, standard practice in science is to re-evaluate the theory for inaccuracy or incompleteness. These moves attempt to blame the psychology or perspective of the theory makers rather than the ontology of the theory, and are completely anomalous. They stand in the way of the real possibility that we can find a better theory.

In this chapter I will pursue a fourth strategy by tackling the problem more directly. I will show fault in the theories, rather than the theory-makers. My methodology, then, is more traditional than the methodology of the other strategies. The conclusion I reach, however, may seem more radical. I am going to argue that physical things are "two faced" also. More facts than just the facts about what they do are true of them, and these further facts may fill the gap. If this conclusion is correct then the form of the theories traditionally employed in the sciences needs to be supplemented before we can cross the explanatory gap.

Someone pursuing this strategy needs to meet three challenges, which I will try to do. The first challenge is to avoid being *ad hoc*. To make the strategy work, the motivation for introducing these extra facts should be independent of the mind-body problem. Otherwise the theory is likely to seem—and probably be—indulgent, and will compete poorly in the marketplace of ideas.

The second challenge is to avoid the dualist dilemma. Whatever facts one introduces must be tied to the physical facts in a way that does not make them causally irrelevant, or spookily interactive.

The third challenge is to be relevant to the explanatory gap. The theory must give reasons why these further facts about the physical, whose existence one has independent reason to believe in, may fill the explanatory gap between the physical and phenomenal facts.

III   The Physics of *Life*

In pursuit of this strategy, I am now going to examine the character of the physical facts. By "the physical facts" I mean, stipulatively, the facts as they are conveyed by physics (or an ideal science relevantly like physics, in a sense of "relevantly" that will become clear). This stipulation immediately produces an expository problem for me, because real physics is complicated and still evolving. Also, people tend to bring distracting suppositions to discussions of it. To get around these problems I am going to work in a simplified context—a simplified physics—that still raises the crucial issues in a clear and direct way. After discussing the issues in this simplified context, I will bring the discussion back to real physics and, ultimately, to the problem of experience.

The toy physics that I am going to consider describes the class of cellular automata called *Life* worlds. A *Life* world consists of a two dimensional grid of cells that we visualize as squares with eight neighbors: one neighbor touching each side, and one neighbor touching each corner. Figure 4.1 shows a cell and its neighbors. At any given time, each cell may have exactly one of two properties: the "on" property or the "off" property. For the sake of argument, I am going to stipulate that a cell's

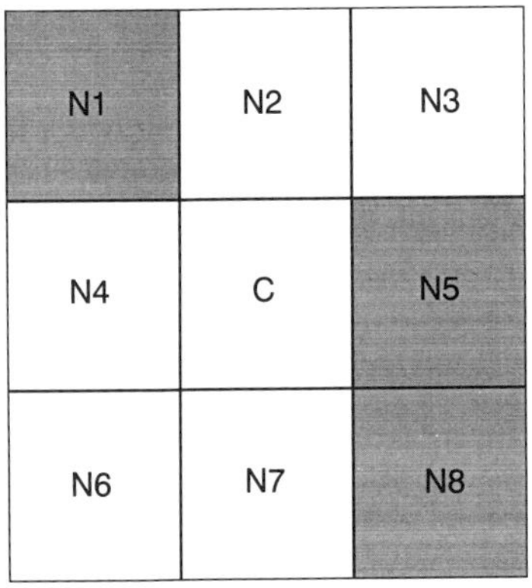

N1	N2	N3
N4	C	N5
N6	N7	N8

Figure 4.1

being "off" consists in its having some positive property rather than merely the absence of the "on" property. *Life*'s physics consists of three simple rules:

1) If a cell has exactly two "on" neighbors it maintains its property, "on" or "off," in the next time step.

2) If a cell has exactly three on neighbors it will be "on" in the next time step.

3) Otherwise the cell will be "off" in the next time step.

This very simple physics can produce very complex phenomena. The automaton gets the name "*Life*" from the fact that it can produce patterns of "on" and "off" properties that are nontrivial self-replicators in the same mathematical sense that DNA are. One can also build a Universal Turing machine inside a *Life* world. Let us assume, for the sake of argument, that we have a dimensional viewer that gives us access to another reality, one that is a *Life* world with a *Life* world's physics. Since a *Life* world can support the existence of complexly functioning objects let us also assume that this world supports the existence of objects that function analogously to cognitive systems in our world. That is, their behavior is complex and purposeful seeming, and it is driven by what seems to be an information processing cognitive engine responding to perceptions of its environment. These objects consist of patterns evolving atop the grid, subsisting in huge arrays of cells blinking on and off through time.

Would such *Life* objects be phenomenally conscious? Most people agree that an explanatory gap seems to exist here also, as a skeptic would have a consistent position (the gap is argued for in Rosenberg 1997). *If* consciousness were to exist in such a world, its existence would seem like a *brute* fact relative to the specification of its physics, and relative to the existence of the kinds of properties its physics can transparently support. The presence of consciousness would seem to us like the result of some kind of law of nature, or a "metaphysical" law, or a "metaphysical" identity of some kind. This is just like the situation with respect to the explanatory gap in our world.

Why does the gap exist in the *Life* world? One very deep reason for the existence of the gap here is that we presume that *Life's* physics *completely* characterizes the basic properties in a **pure** *Life*. That means these basic properties are completely characterized by:

1) A bare difference of type between them;

2) The roles they occupy in the physical laws.

Focusing on the first condition, what is a bare difference? The phrase is meant to express an intuitive point that can be loosely stated this way. *Life's* physics leaves us in the dark about what the "on" and "off" differences are themselves. We just know the facts that they are different and enter into certain dynamic relations. Moreover, if we are viewing a **pure** *Life* world then we can assume that there just *are* no other facts about those properties. The difference is "bare" because it does not rest on any further facts about the properties.

This distinguishes the *Life* world's bare difference from other cases of difference. In other cases of difference, the facts about difference are implied by other facts. One naturally says that these differences rest on, or arise from, these further facts. For instance, benzene molecules and sodium chloride molecules are different molecules, but all their differences are implied by further, more fundamental facts about their structure and content. As another example, the fact that red and green are different colors seems to rest on further facts about their hues, intrinsic and observable facts about the appearances of those hues.

In more philosophically technical terms, a "bare" difference is a difference relation that is ontologically primary instead of being implied by other facts. When a "bare" difference obtains, the natures of the relata are constituted by their participation in the relation but not vice versa. In this way the relation of difference is the ontological ground, and the existence of the things related is derivative on it. This is in contrast to the usual kind of difference relation in which the relata are the ontological ground, and the relation is derivative on intrinsic facts about them.

The skeptic about the existence of consciousness in a **pure** *Life* world doubts that a mosaic of bare difference could support the existence of consciousness. A pure *Life* world would be constituted by a mosaic of bare difference, and the absence of consciousness seems consistent with the presence of any mosaic of bare difference. Consciousness, the skeptic claims, is not pure pattern. The skeptic even has an argument for this position:

1) Difference relations between phenomenal qualities are observable.

2) These difference relations are observably contentful relations: it is not a formal relation of bare difference. For example the difference between red and green holds because of facts intrinsic to redness and greenness.

3) These phenomenal contents themselves are observably not structures of bare differences.

For the skeptic these are not just "intuitions." They are observable facts about a class of everyday phenomena. As observations go, they can in principle be overturned, but that will take an extremely strong argument. At this point, how will the argument with the skeptic go? I can report from experience that there will be stubbornness and fist pounding on both sides. The skeptic's opponents will make appeals to something called *metaphysical* necessity that neither of them really understands, or to a fact of primitive identity that is unlike any identity discovered elsewhere. Someone will make an appeal to the skeptic's epistemic frailty, charging that the skeptic cannot reliably make the consistency judgments needed.

Among all this sound and fury something is being overlooked. The debate with the skeptic suggests a question. *Could* there be a **pure** *Life* world? That is, could a world exist in which no fundamental facts were true except those completely characterized by the *Life* physics? If not, then even a completely adequate physics for a *Life* world would fail to deliver all the facts about that world. Some further facts would need to be present to complement the physics and complete the world.

I think several reasons exist for believing that a pure *Life* world could not exist. First, the basic "on" and "off" properties of *Life* are characterized by their dispositional relations to one another, and the dispositional network is circular. The kind of circularity present is a special kind of logical regress. If one wishes to know what the "on" property is, one is told that it is the property that is *not* the "off" property, but is dispositionally related to it in a special way. That is acceptable as long as we know what the "off" property is. What is it? According to the physics, it is the property that is *not* the "on" property, but is dispositionally related to it in a certain way. This would be adequate if we knew what the "on" property is, but that is where we started.

The description is completed by positing that the relation of difference is one of bare difference, an ontological ground that constitutes the properties. This is difficult, though, because a difference relation between properties is—in all other instances—grounded in further facts. We have no precedent for understanding what a bare difference between properties is. The precedents we do have tell us that properties characterized by circularly defined categories and higher-order relations belong to abstract *schemas*. That raises the question of how nature instantiates these schemas, and the properties internal to them. Are they self-sufficient?

In all other instances, the elements of a schema require *carriers*. What is a carrier? A carrier is something that exists within an instance of a schema even though it has a nature outrunning the categories of that schema. To be a carrier this nature must be capable, in the proper context, of playing the part of a schema element by helping to instantiate the structure of relations required by the schema. When this happens we often say that the carrier is *implementing* some element of the scheme.

To qualify as carriers items must have intrinsic relations to other carriers—relations of difference or dynamics—that mirror the stipulated relations in the schema. These "intrinsic" relations are just relations that hold between their schema independent natures. For instance, we can implement a game of *Life* on a checkerboard by using red and black checkers; or in a computer using voltages. The red and black checkers can be carriers because of a prior relation of difference between their hues. This prior relation of difference can stand in for the stipulated relation of difference between the "on" and the "off" properties. Finally, by affecting the humans in their surroundings in ways that cause them to manipulate the board in accord with the physics, the checkers acquire the dispositional properties needed, albeit in a roundabout way. Similarly, the voltages in a computer have natures outrunning the categories of *Life*, but which, in the proper context, exhibit relations to one another that mirror the stipulated relations of the schema.

A carrier that has a nature outrunning one schema—a nature external to that schema—may still be internal to another schema. The relationship between molecules and genes follows this pattern. In describing genes, genetics describes a schema for transmitting information. Its elements are carried by organic molecules like DNA. But molecules themselves belong to another schema, that of molecular chemistry, which is described by the rules of the periodic table. The schema of the periodic table is itself carried by the schema of atomic chemistry, and, ultimately, quantum physics.

Nested layers of pattern and being could also exist in the *Life* world, creating a similar ladder of embedded schema within schema. What happens when we get to the bottom (i.e., *Life* physics?) We do not want to regress indefinitely, but we still have a schema. We still need carriers for the basic properties. To avoid a regress these carriers will have natures that are partially *external* to the fundamental system of categories in the fundamental schema, while not being *internal* to any other schema. To meet these conditions these fundamental carriers will need to be intrinsic properties, understood as properties that cannot be fully characterized through the relations they enter into with other properties. For any physical story about them—stories about the difference structures they instantiate and the lawful relations they enter into—there will be further facts to know. These further facts will be intrinsic facts that *carry* the fundamental nomic dispositions, and that *carry* the fundamental facts of difference in type and quantity.

If this view is right, there could *not* be a "pure" *Life* world. The notion of a "bare" difference, in the end, does not make sense. Any *Life* world would *at least* have to contain further facts about the intrinsic natures of the carriers. These facts would not be reducible to the facts about the relations specified in its physics. These points raise the question, "Is our physics in any better shape than *Life's* physics?"

An examination of our physics does not yield reasons to believe that it is. We have fundamental properties like "mass," "spin," and "charge." We characterize these almost exactly like we characterize the "on" and "off" properties. There is one difference in that our physics contains added indexical facts. These facts allow us to pick out the various roles by using our community as a kind of central pivot point from which we can begin plotting the system of relations. Such indexical facts anchor how the schema should be mapped onto the elements of our world, but they do not touch the fundamental problem. That problem concerns the natures of the things that we are mapping to.

From these points it seems to follow that there is at least one category of fact left out by our physical explanations: facts about the carriers. Furthermore, these facts will be facts about intrinsic natures that have internal relations of difference, scalar variation along selected dimensions, and that carry lawful dispositions with respect to one another. The main point of this chapter should now be apparent: this description fits the phenomenal qualities perfectly. The two "problems," that of finding a place for the phenomenal qualities and conceiving of what the carriers must be like, fit together like lock and key.

The view also meets the three challenges laid out at the beginning of the investigation. First, it is not ad hoc. Both the carrier problem and the hypothesis about their natures were introduced independently of the mind-body problem, and of any strong theoretical suppositions about the nature of the phenomenal properties. Second, it avoids both epiphenomenalism and interactionism. In a sense, the phenomenal properties show up as the deep nature of the physical. They are the stuff that is doing the work. Physics is only a partial description of the work that is getting done. Finally, making the supposition that phenomenal properties are the carriers in this world holds promise as a way of crossing the explanatory gap. For we would no longer be trying to derive the existence of the contentful character of experience from an abstract description. Instead we would be trying to understand how such an abstract description, a description of structural and quantitative variation, and of nomic compatibility, could derive from a contentful base. This seems like an easier task, especially since we already know that phenomenal contents do have internal difference relations, scalar variations within families of qualities, and intrinsic compatibility and incompatibility relations. Points like this have been made several times before (e.g., Whitehead 1929, Russell 1927, Maxwell 1978, and Lockwood 1989) but the idea's potential seems to have been lost in all the commotion about zombies, "metaphysical" necessity, epistemic limitations, and the like.

IV   The Two Faces of Causation

As intriguing as the argument for the two faces of the physical is, the problem of crossing the explanatory gap lies deeper still. The argument so far only provides a reason for believing in some intrinsic facts about the physical that are not characterized by physical science. To successfully cross the explanatory gap we need to answer at least two further questions. The first question concerns why these intrinsic properties should be experiential in character. A gap seems to exist between mere intrinsicness and experiential intrinsicness, as the experiential character seems to be an added aspect. A skeptic might ask, "Couldn't there be intrinsic properties that are not experiential?" This gap may not seem as large as the physical/phenomenal gap, but it is real. The second question concerns how one climbs the ladder of nature to account for animal consciousness. While the arguments for the second face of the physical provide reasons for postulating an intrinsic aspect to the elements of the fundamental schema, these elements are just the basic quarks or strings that might lie at the base of physics. There is still a huge gap between that level, and the level where we need an explanation of the intrinsic content that one would identify with animal consciousness.

In this section I am going to gesture toward a place in theory space where we can address these further questions, and I am going to do this by outlining a proposal that I develop in detail in Rosenberg (1997). The key proposal begins with two points. First, the fundamental schema will be the schema that describes the world's causal structure. Second, the schema of physics describes only an aspect of this more fundamental schema. Fundamental physics describes the regularities in the ways that the basic effective properties instantiate, but there is more to causation than this. The schema of the world's causal structure has two faces itself, and these faces correspond to the effective *and* receptive aspects of causation. In general, physics does not contain a theory about the nature of the causal connection, nor of the structure of the causal nexus once such natures are included. Huw Price (1997) argues for the this conclusion about physics, and then draws an irrealist conclusion about the existence of causal connections. Rosenberg (1997) argues for the conclusion about physics also, but then motivates and develops a realist theory of causal connection. If this latter reaction is correct, then even a completed physics would be an incomplete description of the world's fundamental facts.

Under the realist alternative the causal nexus has two aspects, its effective and its receptive faces. These two faces are logically inseparable, as one cannot have receptiveness without effectiveness, and vice versa. The natural relation between these two faces will constitute a causal nexus. Since a realist wishes to find a theory of this nexus, a theory of the causal nexus must be a theory of the detailed relation between these two faces.

First, finding the most general theory of the causal nexus requires overcoming one tempting view. This is the view that conceives of the receptive and the effective properties of individuals as each being monadic properties of those individuals. In place of this common sense picture, one must substitute a picture of receptivity as a *connection* between the effective sides of distinct individuals. Figure 4.2 illustrates these two

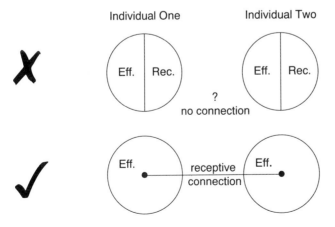

Figure 4.2

alternatives. When one models receptivity as a connection, the receptive connection does the work of the causal connection, and causation emerges by detailing the conditions under which this connection might bind two or more effective states.

Modeling receptivity in the way described above yields several important explanatory benefits. Among these are,

1) It enables the theory to sidestep questions about adding further conditions for deciding when an individual is receptive to another individual (e.g., spatiotemporal contiguity) over and above sharing a receptive connection. This allows it to take a simpler form by making fewer assumptions at the outset, and ultimately makes it more compatible with modern physics.

2) It yields a simple inductive definition of natural individuation that enables the theory to elegantly model levels of nature, where those levels each contain irreducible individuals with irreducible aspects. The definition is as follows: an individual is a natural individual IFF **Base case**: It is an instance of a basic effective property. **Inductive case**: It is a set of natural individuals that share a common receptive connection.

3) It yields a topology to the causal mesh that increases the explanatory power of the theory by allowing for a reduction of the facts about spacetime to facts about causal connection and causal significance.

4) It yields a structure for the causal nexus that ties into the hypothesis that consciousness is a carrier for causal content, and does so at a deep and detailed level.

When developed the theory yields an intriguing way to view the world, one that endows it with an intricate *vertical* structure that is more than merely pattern atop pattern. This way of viewing the world is depicted in figure 4.3.

To understand what this view involves one must fully appreciate the role of receptivity in the creation of natural individuals at different levels. A natural individual's receptivity is an element of its being that binds lower level individuals within it, making those individuals effective states relevant to one another in a direct way. As such, receptivity is an irreducible global property of a natural individual. The term "irreducible" here is being used in its strongest sense: a higher-level individual's receptivity is not the sum, either linearly or nonlinearly, of the receptiveness of its lower-level constituents. It is a novel element in the world, unique to the individual that it helps constitute.

The role receptivity plays is that of a *possibility filter*. By opening a group of individuals to the constraints presented by one another's effective properties, it maps a set of prior possibilities for the joint states of its constituents onto one of that set's proper subsets. That is what allows it to play the role of a causal connection, as its presence

Nature is partitioned into individuals at many levels. Each level's individuals are constituted by the existence of a receptive connection binding individuals from a lower level into a common receptive field.

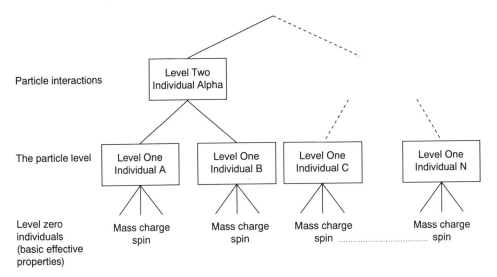

Figure 4.3

imposes a condition on the joint instantiation of states that sunders their independence from one another. The theory, then, is highly nontrivial. The addition of receptivity to a model of the causal nexus not only represents a substantial metaphysical hypothesis, but, in principle, one should be able to draw substantial empirical hypotheses from it also. As an irreducible global property it echoes of the sort of thing that draws people to quantum mechanical theories involving global *coherence*; as a possibility filter it echoes the sort of thing that attracts people to theories of quantum *decoherence*. In the end it is a sort of hybrid notion whose full implications need to be explored.

Because of the irreducible nature of each receptivity, the theory needs something to carry each instance of it, and also the effective constraints active within that individual. Here we see a duality to causation: it divides into the existence of effective constraints, and the binding of those constraints within a shared receptivity. Furthermore, these two aspects are logically connected to one another in a kind of compositional circularity. For an instance of receptivity to exist, it must bind effective constraints; and for the effective constraints to exist, they must be bound within an instance of receptivity. Although they are distinct kinds, they are logically interdependent.

Consciousness, we have already noted, also divides into a kind of duality. At the beginning of this section, I noted the intrinsic properties that are its contents, and the experiencing of those properties. This division in consciousness seems conditioned by a mutual dependence similar to the mutual dependence of the effective and receptive aspects of the causal nexus. The qualities of experience must be bound within an experiencing subject (for them, to be is to be experienced); and for a subject of experience to exist, it must experience phenomenal qualities. Perhaps this is an instance of a kind of *de re* logical relationship between distinct essences, as their independence is (arguably) inconceivable. This point holds promise in solving one of the problems the carrier view is confronted with. Namely, it may help us to understand why the intrinsic properties of the world are experiential properties. The answer may be that the intrinsic content is carrying effective constraints, and the experiencing of that content is the result of a shared receptivity.

Further, we have a natural ladder of nature in our picture already, and climbing it does not require combining qualities from lower levels into a mix that somehow yields the qualities at the higher levels. It merely requires mapping each lower-level effective property appropriately to an irreducible carrier at the next level. What qualifies a carrier in a particular instance is an appropriate match with the constraint it must carry from the lower-level individuals. This constraint should be mathematically describable using a set number of degrees of freedom along which the constraint may vary, and laws describing the ways that other states are effected by its variance. To carry it, the phenomenal quality would need to instantiate the dimensional structure of this characterization, and belong to a family of qualities whose internal compatibility and incompatibility relations mirror the laws.

To understand how the ascent is achieved, one can use an analogy to vector addition. Such addition directs you to a new vector in the space in a rulelike way, but it does not mix the old vectors as if they were building blocks of the new. To understand how to get from level to level in the view I have proposed, imagine a vast quality space that partitions into families. These qualities are potential carriers for effective constraints. The effective states of lower-level individuals present these effective constraints to other individuals when they become bound within a common receptivity. This constraint may have degrees of freedom corresponding to the structure of the individual that presents it. Think of the lower-level individual as being constituted by a set of vectors, and the constraint it presents is like doing a sum over those vectors. It yields a new vector that takes us to a new place in quality space. Thus what we are searching for are *projection* operators that jump us through quality space, moving us from one family of qualities to another. We are not faced with the problem of finding combinatorial operators that create new qualities from alien ones.

Table 4.1
How phenomenal properties map to the carrier role

Phenomenal properties	Causal content
1. The possibility of being experienced is essential to phenomenal qualities.	1. The possibility of being receptively bound is essential to effective properties.
2. Being an experiencing subject implies the experiencing of phenomenal qualities.	2. Being a receptive individual implies receiving the constraint of effective properties.
3. Phenomenal qualities are only potential unless actually being experienced.	3. Effective properties are only potential unless actually receptively bound.
4. An experiencer is only potential unless it is experiencing phenomenal quality.	4. A receptive connection is only potential unless it is binding effective properties.
5. Relations of inclusion, exclusion, compatibility and incompatibility exist between phenomenal properties.	5. Relations of inclusion, exclusion, compatibility and incompatibility exist between effective properties.
6. Scalar relations and relations of intrinsic difference exist between phenomenal properties.	6. Scalar relations and relations of stipulative difference exist between effective properties.
7. Despite mutually participating in one another's nature, phenomenal properties and the experiencing of them mark distinct essences.	7. Despite mutually participating in one another's nature, effective properties and the receptive binding of them mark distinct essences.

In short, the intrinsic qualities at lower-levels are stepping stones to the qualities at the higher-levels, not constituents of those qualities. If this is correct, we can solve both of the original problems this section started with. The instrinsic nature of the world is experiential because experience is needed to carry the receptivity of the causal nexus. Nature does not create the qualities of animal consciousness by throwing together alien qualities at lower-levels. They are reached by taking an orderly walk through quality space as nature drafts different carriers into duty in service of individuals at different levels.

These suggestions are intriguing enough to make one wonder if consciousness can map to the carrier role. Table 4.1 lists a partial answer to this question (in fact, the mapping can get much more detailed).

In conclusion, this view of the two faces of causation yields two fundamental hypotheses that hold promise that we may yet bridge the explanatory gap. These hypotheses are:

The Carrier Hypotheses   Phenomenal qualities carry the effective constraints in the world; the experiencing of those qualities by a subject carries the receptivity of an individual to those constraints.

The Consciousness Hypotheses   Human consciousness is carrying the causal content of a high-level, cognitively structured, natural individual. Human awareness is experiential acquaintance with the intrinsic content that carries nature's effective side.

References

Dennett, D. C. 1988. Quining Qualia. In *Consciousness in Contemporary Science*, A. Marcel and E. Bisiach, eds., Clarenden Press, Oxford: 42–77.

Güzeldere, G. 1997. The Many Faces of Consciousness: A Field Guide. in *The Nature of Consciousness: Philosophical Debates*. Block, Ned; Flanagan, Owen; Güzeldere, Güven, eds. The MIT Press, Cambridge, Mass.: 1–68.

Levine, J. 1993. On Leaving Out What It's Like in *Consciousness*, Davies and Humphreys, ed. Blackwell Publishers, Cambridge, Mass.: 121–136.

Lockwood, M. 1989. *Mind, Brain, and Quanta*. Basil Blackwell, Cambridge, Mass.

Maxwell, G. 1979. Rigid designators and mind-brain identity. in *Minnesota Studies in Philosophy of Science*, 9.

McGinn, C. 1989. Can We Solve The Mind–Body Problem? *Mind* 98:349–66.

Rey, G. 1995. Towards a Projectivist Account of Conscious Experience. in *Conscious Experience*, Thomas Metzinger, ed. Imprint Academic, Schöningh: 123–144.

Rosenberg, G. H. 1997. *A Place for Consciousness: Probing the deep structure of the natural world*. Dissertation, Indiana University.

Russell, B. 1927. *The Analysis of Matter*. Kegan Paul, London.

Whitehead, A. N. 1929. *Process and Reality corrected edition*. Griffin, Donald Ray; Sherburne, Donald W. eds. The Free Press, New York, 1978.

Wilkes, K. 1988. yishi, duh, um, and consciousness *Consciousness in Contemporary Science*, A. Marcel and E. Bisiach, eds., Clarenden Press, Oxford: 16–41.

II COLOR—INTRODUCTION

David J. Chalmers

Color experience is a microcosm of consciousness. Many of the deepest philosophical questions about consciousness can be vividly illustrated in the case of color. Why do experiences of red and blue have the particular subjective qualities (or qualia) that they do? Jackson (1982) has argued that a neuroscientist with black-and-white vision might know all the physical facts about color processing in the brain and in the world, but would still not know what it is like to have a red experience. If so, it seems that there might be a deep explanatory gap between knowledge of physical facts and knowledge of qualia.

Another traditional philosophical problem about color is the problem of the inverted spectrum. At some point in our lives, many of us have entertained the hypothesis that when others look at red objects, they have the sort of experience that we have when we look at blue objects. It might be argued that this would be undetectable, since we will call our different experiences by the same names ("red" or "blue"), associate them to the same objects, and so on. But even so, and even if one thinks it unlikely that such cases actually exist, the mere logical possibility of such cases raises questions about whether we can explain facts about color experience in terms of facts about processing.

In this section, three theorists of color apply empirical results from the science of color to these ancient philosophical problems. Much is known about color processing now that was not known a few decades ago, and some of these results are highly relevant to the philosophical debate. In this way we see how science and philosophy can interact productively, with benefits for both sides.

Stephen Palmer discusses ways in which the idea of a behaviorally undetectable inversion of color experience may or may not make sense. The most obvious ways to understand an inverted spectrum turn out to be deeply problematic, since they will violate certain asymmetries in the space of colors. But certain inversions involving the red-green dimension may hold promise, though this is affected in turn by questions about basic color terms in human culture. Palmer goes on to draw a general moral for the science of consciousness, proposing an "isomorphism constraint" relating processing to experience. Processing facts can characterize the abstract structure of the space of color qualia, but they may not be able to tell us about the underlying qualia themselves.

C. L. Hardin is more skeptical about the idea of a spectrum inversion. He argues that once we truly understand all the facts about the structure of color space, the idea of an inversion will not make sense even as a logical possibility: color structure tells us all there is to know about color qualia. He discusses a number of deep asymmetries in color space, drawn from work in both anthropology and psychophysics, which he argues rule out any possible inversion. Hardin suggests that this sort of result has the promise of closing the explanatory gap between physical processes and color experiences.

Martine Nida-Rümelin discusses the intriguing possibility that there may be some *actual* cases of spectrum inversion. It turns out that there is a theoretical possibility that some subjects (about 1 in 700 males) have two forms of colorblindness simultaneously, which would switch the responses of the cones in the retina, plausibly resulting in a systematic transposition in their color space. Nida-Rümelin discusses philosophical consequences of this "pseudonormal vision," and goes on to address the arguments given by Hardin. She argues that even if complete qualia inversions are impossible, this leaves the explanatory gap between physical processes and color qualia intact.

Further philosophical and scientific papers on color can be found in the two-volume anthology edited by Byrne and Hilbert (1997).

References

Byrne, A., and Hilbert, D. R. 1997. *Readings on Color.* (Volume 1: *The Philosophy of Color.* Volume 2: *The Science of Color*). MIT Press.

Jackson, F. 1982. Epiphenomenal qualia. *Philosophical Quarterly* 32:127–136.

5 Of Color and Consciousness

Stephen E. Palmer

The issues I discuss in this chapter concern whether your conscious experiences of color are the same as mine when we both look at the same environmental objects under the same physical conditions, and how we could possibly know. Together, I will refer to them as the "color question."

The reader may wonder why color should be the focus of this discussion about conscious experiences. Different people have different reasons for focusing on color. My own reasons are twofold. First, we know an enormous amount about color perception, and this background of scientific knowledge makes it a good domain in which to ask such questions. Second, there is a well known and persuasive argument due to John Locke (1690/1987) in the philosophical literature—called the "inverted spectrum argument"—that claims to show that we simply cannot know whether your color experiences are the same as mine. It goes like this.

Locke argued that there isn't any way you could know whether my experiences of colors are the same as yours or whether they are "inverted." The most straightforward interpretation of this inversion would be simply reversing the order of colors experienced in viewing a rainbow. If this were the case, you would experience the rainbow with red at the top and violet at the bottom, but I would experience it with violet at the top and red at the bottom. We would both call the top color "red" and the bottom color "violet," of course, because that is what we have all been taught by our parents, teachers, and society at large. Everyone calls blood, ripe tomatoes, and Macintosh apples "red," so we all associate our internal color experiences on viewing these objects—whatever they might be—with this verbal label. But my internal experiences of color might be inverted in just the way Locke suggested without its having any effect on how I behave in naming colors. Indeed, Locke's argument is that spectral inversion of color experiences might conceivably exist without there being any external manifestation of the difference. It seems there just isn't any way to tell, because I can't "get inside your head," and "have your experiences"—nor you mine.

But in this chapter, I will claim that there *are* ways of rejecting this particular argument without getting inside each other's heads and having each other's experiences. Good, solid behavioral evidence from vision science allows us to reject conclusively this literal interpretation of Locke's argument. Once we see why, we will ask whether there is *any* transformation of your color experience that I might have without it being detectable in my behavior relative to yours.

Symmetries of Color Space

One important thing we can measure behaviorally about color experiences is their relative similarities. Everybody with normal color vision would agree, for example, that red is more similar to orange than it is to green. These relative similarities can be obtained for a large sample of triples of colors. It turns out that the results of measuring these three-way similarities can be summarized quite neatly in a geometric model of color experiences known as a color space. Each point in a color space corresponds to a color experience, and proximities between points correspond to similarities between colors. This means that nearby points in color space correspond to similar color experiences, and distant points in color space correspond to different color experiences.

Perhaps the simplest and best known color space is Newton's color circle, which is represented in figure 5.1. The saturated colors of the rainbow are arrayed around most of the perimeter of the circle, approximately as indicated by the color names around the outside. A few wavelengths of monochromatic light are also indicated in this diagram at the appropriate places. This color circle is not the most complete or accurate representation of human color experiences, but it is a good starting point for understanding how behavioral data can constrain the answer to the color question.

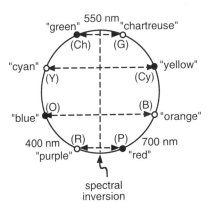

Figure 5.1
Newton's color circle and spectral inversion. Colors are arranged along the perimeter of a color circle, as indicated by the names on the outside of the circle. Black dots correspond to unique colors (red, green, blue, and yellow), which look subjectively pure. The dashed diameter indicates the axis of reflection corresponding to literal spectral inversion, and the dashed arrows indicate corresponding experiences under this transformation. Letters in parentheses inside the circle indicate the color experiences a spectrally inverted individual would have to the same physical stimuli a normal individual would experience as the colors indicated on the outside of the circle.

One of the interesting things about this geometrical representation of color similarities is that it allows a simple and transparent way to determine whether Locke's hypothetical spectral inversion could be detected by behavioral measurements of color similarities. Within the color circle, inverting the spectrum is just a reflection about the diameter passing through 550 nm. (the dashed line in figure 5.1), which lies at the middle of the visible spectrum from 400 to 700 nm. This reflection sets up the correspondence between your color experiences (as indicated by the quoted labels on the outside of the circle in lowercase letters) and my color experiences (as indicated by the parenthesize abbreviations on the inside of the circle in capital letters). When you experience red, I experience purple; when you experience yellow, I experience blue-green (cyan); and so forth.

Would these differences be detectible through measures of color similarity relations? You would say that red is more similar to orange than to green (because the point for red on the outside of the circle is closer to the outside point for orange than it is to the outside point for green). But I would say the same thing, even though, for me, it would correspond to experiencing purple as more similar to blue than to yellow-green (as reflected by proximities of the same points, but with respect to the experiences indicated on the inside of the circle). And in fact, all the color similarity judgments you and I make would be outwardly the same, even though our experiences would be inwardly different.

The reason such differences could not be detected by similarity measures is that the color circle is symmetric with respect to reflection about this axis. We can therefore conclude that so-called spectral inversion of color experiences could not be detected by measurements of color similarity. Furthermore, we can see that this particular inversion is only one of many ways that my color experiences might differ from yours without the difference being detected by measuring color similarities. Any reflection about a line passing through the center of the color circle would do as well, and so would any rotation about the center. In all these cases, our color experiences would indeed differ, but all our statements about the relative similarities of color samples would be the same. This is precisely the kind of result Locke expected when he proposed his inverted spectrum argument, for it seems we cannot tell whether there are differences in experiences or not.

But there is a great deal more that we can measure behaviorally about color experiences than just their similarities. Among the most important additional factors are relations of color composition. Most colors look like they are composed of other more primitive colors. Orange looks like it contains both red and yellow. Purple looks like it contains both red and blue. But there is a particular shade of red that is pure in the sense that it contains no traces of yellow or blue or any other color—it looks "just plain red." People with so-called normal color vision agree about this fact. Nobody claims that red actually looks like the composition of orange and purple, even though it lies between these two colors in color space. Color scientists call these experientially pure colors "unique hues," and there are four of them: unique red, unique yellow, unique green, and unique blue.

The existence of these four unique colors provides another behavioral tool for detecting color transformations. Consider rainbow reversal again, this time from the perspective of unique hues. You will indicate unique colors at particular shades of red, blue, green, and yellow, whereas I will indicate them at orange, purple, cyan, and chartreuse. The reason is simply that the experience of mine that is the same as your experience of unique red, results from my looking at color samples that we all call "purple." So for me, there is some shade of purple that appears chromatically pure in a way that no shade of red does, whereas for you, there is some shade of red that is pure in a way that no shade of purple is. This behavioral difference can thus be used to unmask a rainbow-reversed individual, if such a person existed.

This example shows that unique colors and other relations of color composition further constrain the set of color transformations that can escape detection. We can now rule out literal spectral inversion in the sense of simply reversing the rainbow. Even so, there are still several color transformations that will pass all behavioral tests of color similarity and color composition with respect to the color circle shown in figure 5.1. They are the four central reflections about the axes passing through opposite unique colors (i.e., the red-green axis and the blue-yellow axis) and the angular bisectors of these axes, plus the three central rotations of 90°, 180°, and 270°. All have the crucial property that they map unique colors into unique colors, even though at least some of them are different.

By now, it should be apparent where this argument leads. Color transformations that can escape behavioral detection correspond to symmetries in an empirically constrained color space. The important issue for answering the general version of Locke's color question, then, boils down to whether there are any symmetries in human color space. If there are, then my color experiences might differ from yours by the corresponding symmetry transformation.

Until now we have pretended that the color circle, as augmented by the distinguished set of unique hues, is sufficient to represent what is known about human color experience. But there is a great deal more known about color that is relevant to answering the color question. Most importantly, human color space is actually three dimensional rather than two dimensional. The three dimensions are hue, saturation, and lightness, and together they form the lopsided spindle structure diagrammed in figure 5.2A. The important fact about the 3-D color spindle for present purposes is that it breaks many of the symmetries in the color circle.

One of the most salient features of this 3-D color space is that highly saturated yellows are quite a bit lighter than highly saturated blues. This asymmetry makes some further color transformations detectable by purely behavioral means. Transformations in which your experience of yellow is supposed to be the same as my experience of blue (or vice versa) will be detectable because you will say that yellow is lighter than blue, whereas I will say that blue is lighter than yellow (because, remember, yellow looks to me like blue does to you). This difference can certainly be detected behaviorally—*unless* the lightness dimension of my color experience is also reversed, so that what looks black to you looks white to me, and what looks white to you looks black to me.

The upshot of such considerations is that if human color space has approximately the structure shown in figure 5.2A, there are just three possible color transformations that might escape detection in experiments that assess color similarity and composition relations. They correspond to the three approximate symmetries of human color space shown in figures 5.2B, 5.2C, and 5.2D. Relative to the so-called "normal" space in figure 5.2A, one transformation (figure 5.2B) reverses just the red-green dimension. The second (figure 5.2C) reverses two dimensions: blue-for-yellow and black-for-white. The third (figure 5.2D) is the composition of the other two, which calls for a complete reversal, red-for-green, blue-for-yellow and black-for-white.

Although all three are logically possible, by far the most plausible is reflecting just the red-green dimension. Indeed, a persuasive argument can be made that such red-green reversed perceivers actually exist in the population of so-called "normal trichromats" (see Nida-Rümelin, this volume). The argument goes like this. Normal trichromats have three different pigments in their three cone types. Some people, called *protanopes*, are red-green color blind because they have a gene that causes their long-wavelength (L) cones to have the same pigment as their medium-wavelength (M) cones. Other people, called *deuteranopes*, have a different form of red-green color blindness because they have a different gene that causes their M-cones to have the same pigment as their L-cones. In both cases, people with these genetic defects lose the ability to experience the red-green dimension of color space because the visual system codes it by taking the difference between the outputs of the M- and L-cones. Now suppose that someone had the genes for *both* forms of red-green color blindness simultaneously. Their L-cones would have the M-pigment, and their M-cones would have the L-pigment. Such people, would therefore not be red-green color blind at all, but simply red-green reversed trichromats. They should exist. Assuming they do, they

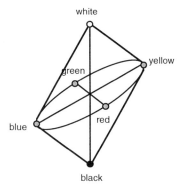

A. "NORMAL" COLOR SPACE

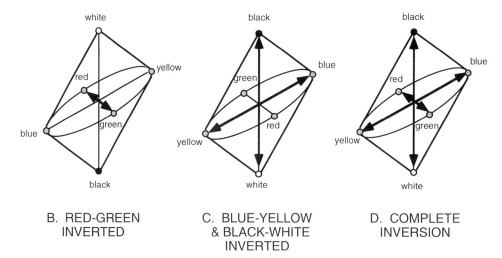

B. RED-GREEN INVERTED	C. BLUE-YELLOW & BLACK-WHITE INVERTED	D. COMPLETE INVERSION

Figure 5.2
Three-dimensional color space and its symmetries. (A) Colors are represented as points in the three-dimensional space of a normal trichromat according to the dimensions of hue, saturation, and lightness. The positions of the six unique colors (or Hering primaries) within this space are shown as circles. This color space has three approximate symmetries: reversal of the red-green dimension only (B), reversal of the blue-yellow and black-white dimensions (C), and reversal of all three dimensions (D).

are proof that this color transformation is either undetectable or very difficult to detect by purely behavioral means, because nobody has ever managed to identify one!

There is a great deal more that can be said about the behavioral detectability of color transformations (see Hardin, this volume). One key issue is the possible relevance of the basic color categories discovered by Berlin and Kay (1969) in cross-linguistic analysis of color naming. Briefly, the argument goes like this. There is a subset of 16 color names, called *basic color terms* (BCTs): single, frequently used, general-purpose words that refer primarily to colors. Together, they appear to form a universal system for linguistic description of colors. In English, there are 11 BCTs: RED, GREEN, BLUE, YELLOW, BLACK, WHITE, GRAY, ORANGE, PURPLE, PINK, and BROWN. The BCTs that do not exist in English can be glossed as LIGHT-BLUE, WARM (reds, oranges, and yellows), COOL (greens, blues, and violets), LIGHT-WARM (whites plus warm colors), and DARK-COOL (blacks plus cool colors). The fact that they appear to be linguistic universals suggests that they have some basis in human color experience and/or human physiology.

The important fact for present purposes is that some BCTs are symmetrically distributed in color space whereas others are not. In particular, RED, GREEN, BLUE, YELLOW, BLACK, WHITE, and GRAY are symmetric with respect to the three candidate color transformations shown in figures 5.2B, 5.2C, and 5.2D. The distribution of the other BCTs breaks all three of these symmetries, however. Therefore, if all of the BCTs arise from underlying asymmetries in the experiential structure of human color space, then any color transformation could be detected by behavioral means.

To illustrate, consider how I could, in theory, be unmasked as a "red-green inver-tomat" by my behavior concerning BCTs. Due to the reversal of the red-green axis of my color space, I would experience orange as yellow-green and purple as blue-green (and vice versa). This would not make any difference to my judgments of color similarity or color composition, but it should cause me to find it strange that there are BCTs for orange and purple rather than for blue-green and yellow-green. If systematic and reliable data on this matter could be obtained, it would reveal the fact of my red-green reversal.

It is not clear to me that I can easily make such fine distinctions, at least in direct introspective judgments. I am hard-pressed to say with certainty that orange and purple are "better" or "more natural" as basic color categories than cyan (blue-green) or chartreuse (yellow-green) would be if I had grown up in a culture that had these alternative BCTs. Perhaps they would, but it seems equally likely that I would not find the alternative strange at all.

Regardless of how the issue of BCTs is ultimately settled, the key question in evaluating the color question behaviorally is the existence of symmetries in human color space. That much seems clear. The question I want to turn to now is why this might be so. What is it about symmetries that makes them so crucial in answering the color question?

The Isomorphism Constraint

Symmetries have two important structural properties. First, they are what mathematicians call *automorphisms*: they map a given domain onto itself. This is important for Locke's original argument because one of its ground rules is that both you and I have the same set of color experiences; they are just differently hooked up to external stimuli. However, I do not think automorphism is actually important for the more general issue of color consciousness. The reason is that my experience in response to stimulation by different wavelengths of light might be nothing at all like yours. You and I could live in entirely different areas of experiential space, so to speak, and I don't believe it would matter with respect to what could be inferred about our color experiences from behavioral measures. I could even be a "color zombie" with no experiences of color at all, and no one would be able to tell, provided I behaved in the same ways toward them as you do.

The second property of symmetries is that they are what mathematicians call *isomorphisms*: they map a source domain onto a target domain in such a way that relational structure is preserved. In the case of symmetries, the source and target domains are the same (i.e., both automorphism and isomorphism hold), but this is not the case for isomorphisms in general. For example, color experiences can be represented by spatial models such as the ones shown in figure 5.2 because the objects of the source domain (color experiences) can be mapped into those of the target domain (points in 3-D space) so that experiential relations between colors (lighter than, more similar to, redder than, etc.) are preserved by corresponding spatial relations between points in color space (higher than, farther away from, closer to the position of focal-red than, etc.).

I want to argue that it is isomorphism—"having the same structure"—that is crucial for behavioral equivalence of conscious experiences. As long as two people have the same structure of relations among their color experiences, whatever those experiences might be in and of themselves, they will always give the same behavioral responses and therefore be behaviorally indistinguishable.

It is universally acknowledged that there is a behaviorally defined brick wall—the *subjectivity barrier*—that limits which aspects of experience can be shared with others and which aspects cannot be, no matter how hard we might try. The importance of the isomorphism constraint is that it provides a clear dividing line for the subjectivity barrier. The part we can share is the abstract relational structure of our experiences; the part we cannot share is the nature of the experiences themselves. In the case of color experience, this means that we share facts such as that red is more like orange than it is like green, that gray is intermediate between black and white, that purple looks like it contains both red and blue, and that there is a shade of red that is compositionally pure. We can share them because they are about the relational structure of experiences. We may implicitly (or even explicitly) believe that we also share the experiences themselves, but Locke and Wittgenstein have disabused many of us of saying so, at least in public.

What I am calling the isomorphism constraint is simply the conjecture that behavior is sufficient to specify experience to the level of isomorphism and not beyond. It proposes that the nature of individual color experiences cannot be uniquely fixed by behavioral means, but their structural interrelations can be. In case anyone feels disappointed in this, I hasten to point out that structural relations are absolutely crucial to the fabric of mental life. Without them, redness would be as much like greenness as it is like orangeness—or squareness, or middle-C, or the taste of pumpkin pie. Without them, perceptual qualities would just be so many equally different experiences, and this certainly is not so. But, by the same token, structural relations do not reflect everything one would like to know about experiences. Logically speaking, the isomorphism constraint implies that *any* set of underlying experiences will do for color, provided they relate to each other in the required way. The same argument can be extended to other perceptual and conceptual domains, although both the underlying experiential components and their relational structure will necessarily differ.

Behavioral scientists aren't alone in working within the constraint of isomorphism, for it also exists in mathematics. A mathematical domain is formalized by specifying a set of primitive elements (such as the points, lines, and planes of Euclidean geometry) plus a set of axioms that specify the relations among them (such as the fact that two points uniquely determine a line, and three noncollinear points determine a plane). But the elements to which the axioms and theorems refer cannot be fixed in any way except by the nature of the relations among them; they refer equally to any entities that satisfy the set of axioms. That is why mathematicians sometimes discover an alternative interpretation of the primitive elements—called a dual system—in which all the same axioms and theorems hold. The brilliant French mathematician Poincaré (1952) put the situation very clearly. "Mathematicians do not study objects," he said, "but the relations between objects. To them it is a matter of indifference if

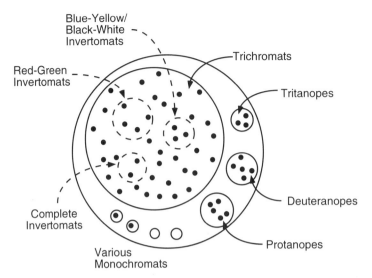

Figure 5.3
Equivalence classes of color perceivers. The Venn diagrams with solid lines indicate the behaviorally
defined equivalence classes of color perceivers who have isomorphic color experiences, but not necessarily
equivalent color experiences. Dashed circles indicate the possible existence of three classes of trichromats
with color experiences that differ from those of normal trichromats at a subisomorphic level, corresponding
to the three symmetries of color space indicated in figures 5.2B, 5.2C, and 5.2D.

these objects are replaced by others, provided that the relations do not change." The
same can be said about behavioral scientists with respect to consciousness: we do not
study experiences, but the relations among experiences.

The Appeal to Biology

As I have formulated it, the isomorphism constraint defines the limits of what can
be known via behavior. Figure 5.3 shows how far this can take us in the domain of
color. Behavioral measures define the standard equivalence classes of color perception: so-called normal trichromats, three varieties of dichromats, and four types of
monochromats. There are some further classes of so-called "color weakness" among
trichromats, but this classification will do for now.

With respect to behavior these are indeed "equivalence classes," but with respect to
statements about color experience, it would be more accurate to call them "difference
classes." Pairs of individuals in different difference classes certainly have different
color experiences, and within each difference class the isomorphism constraint cer-

tainly holds. But beyond that, we cannot say. There may be many varieties of color experience within the set of normal trichromats, many others within the set of protanopes, and so forth. We just cannot tell on the basis of behavior alone.

This raises the important question of whether we can go beyond the level of isomorphism by applying biological methods, either alone or in concert with behavioral ones. It is tempting to believe that if consciousness is fundamentally a biological phenomenon, the answer must be, "Of course we can!" I am less optimistic, but do not see the situation as completely hopeless, at least in principle, for reasons I will now explain.

It seems at first blush that one should be able to study subisomorphic differences in color experiences between two individuals by identifying relevant neurobiological differences between them and correlating them with differences in color experience. But this will not work. The problem is not in finding biological differences. We will presumably be able to work out the hardware differences at whatever level current technology allows. The problem is that, try as we might, we cannot identify any subisomorphic differences between our experiences to correlate with the biological differences. The reason is simply that the subjectivity barrier is still very much in place. Whenever we try to asses how two people's experiences might differ, we can get no further than the isomorphism constraint.

Even so, quite a different line of thought suggests that, at some level, biology must provide important constraints on the answer to the Color Question. It seems highly plausible, for example, that two clones, who have identical nervous systems, should have the same color experiences in response to the same stimulation. This is, in effect, a corollary of Kim's (1978) principle of supervenience: If the underlying biology is the same, the experiences will be the same. Most cognitive scientists and neuroscientists tend to believe something like this, although it is logically possible that the nature of experience depends on sub biological facts about quarks, quantum gravitational fields, or some other physical feature by which clones can be differentiated. Nevertheless, I will proceed on the assumption that clones have the same color experiences.

Assuming this clone-assumption to be well-founded, is there any way this presumed subisomorphic level of conscious experience can be tapped? The only effective route I can see is to avoid the subjectivity barrier by using within-subject designs. The idea is to use a biological intervention on an individual and ask for his or her report about any changes in color experience from before to after the intervention. Suppose, for instance, there were a drug called invertacillin that exchanged the light-sensitive pigments in the M- and L-cones. Assuming that the drug acted reasonably quickly and that it didn't also mysteriously alter people's long-term memories for object colors or the associations between internal experiences and verbal labels, subjects would indeed notice, and could reliably report, changes in their color experiences due to taking the drug. They might report that blood now looks green and that grass now looks red. These are extreme examples, and subtler changes in experience would, one hopes, also be detectable. But the crucial point is that the same subisomorphic color transformations that are quite impossible to detect *between* individuals seem, in principle, quite easy to detect *within* individuals. Notice that we, as experimenters, have still not penetrated anyone's subjectivity barrier, for we don't actually know how blood or grass appeared to the subject either before or after the change. We only know that it changed by reversing the red-green dimension of color experience, whatever that dimension might be like for that observer.

For the sake of argument, let us further suppose that we can figure out what the biological effects of the drug are and that it affects everyone's color experiences in the same way: namely, by reversing the red-green dimension of color space. Armed with this information, we can then divide the set of behaviorally defined trichromats into those who naturally have the biological structure associated with the result of the invertacillin intervention (the dashed circle labelled "Red-Green Invertomats" in figure 5.3) versus those who do not. Notice that this biologically defined class does not imply equivalent color experiences for individuals within it. With respect to color experiences, they still constitute a difference class, just like the behaviorally defined difference classes we mentioned earlier. People in different difference classes have different color experiences, but people in the same class may or may not have the same color experiences. We could not know that until we had exhausted the set of all the relevant biological factors and all their possible interactions, which is a pretty large set.

But suppose, for the sake of argument, that we could determine the complete catalog of the biological factors that are relevant to color experience in this way. Then we could, in principle, define true equivalence classes of people who have the same color experiences as people whose color systems all have the same values on the set of relevant biological features (e.g., association between photosensitive pigments and cone types). Notice that such statements would always be *inferences* about whether two people have the same experiences based on indirect evidence, much like our earlier inference that two clones would have the same experiences based on knowledge that their biology is the same. We have plausible scientific reasons to believe that they would, but no way of testing it directly because of the subjectivity barrier. The clones themselves can neither confirm nor deny the conjecture, of course, because the subjectivity barrier exists for them as much as for everyone else.

If we were able to carry out this research program—and that is a very big assumption—it seems that we would, in principle, be able to infer what colors look like to other people. People who are in the same biological equivalence class as yourself would experience colors in the world as you do, within some reasonable margin of error. And people who are in a different equivalence class would have color experiences that differ from yours. In some cases the nature of those differences can be specified; in others, not. If I am a red-green invertomat, for example, and you are a "normal trichromat" and if the corresponding physiological difference were the only one in our chromatic neurobiology, then our experiences would differ specifically by the red-green inversion transformation reported by subjects who took the invertacillin drug.

You could then know what my color experiences of the world by taking invertacillin yourself or undergoing whatever biological intervention it was that supported the establishment of the differences between our subisomorphic biological classes in the first place. But the possibility that these color-transformed experiences enable you to know what the world looks like to me is necessarily based on inferences. You cannot have my experiences in any direct fashion because of the subjectivity barrier. The inference is based on at least two important assumptions. One is what we called the clone assumption: that any differences in experience must necessarily rest on standard biological differences. The other is that all the relevant biological differences have been exhaustively cataloged. If either is false, then the conclusion that you know what it is like to have my color experience by taking invertacillin may also be false. Given the dubious nature of at least one of these assumptions, the chances of being able to bring this project off in reality are vanishingly small. Even so, the very possibility is intriguing.

Acknowledgment

This chapter was facilitated by grant 1-R01-MH46141 from the National Institute of Mental Health to the author. It is based in part on an article currently in press in *The Behavioral and Brain Sciences*.

References

Berlin, B., and Kay, P. 1969. *Basic color terms: Their universality and evolution*. Berkeley: University of California Press.

Kim, J. 1978. Supervenience and nomological incommensurables. *American Philosophical Quarterly*, 15:149–156.

Locke, J. 1690/1987. *An essay concerning human understanding*. Oxford: Clarendon Press.

Poincare, H. 1952. *Science and hypothesis*. New York: Dover.

6 Color Quality and Color Structure

C. L. Hardin

Spectral inversion arguments have been used for many purposes. I shall here focus on a version of the argument purporting to show that even an explanatory relationship between qualitative experiences and brain processes—let alone an identity of one with the other—is unintelligible. For instance, Joseph Levine (1983) argues that although mental processes and physical process might in fact be identical, we can never have scientific grounds for supposing them to be so:

Let's call the physical story for seeing red 'R' and the physical story for seeing green 'G'. . . . When we consider the qualitative character of our visual experiences when looking at ripe McIntosh apples, as opposed to looking at ripe cucumbers, the difference is not explained by appeal to G and R. For R doesn't really explain why I have the one kind of qualitative experience—the kind I have when looking at McIntosh apples—and not the other. As evidence for this, note that it seems just as easy to imagine G as to imagine R underlying the qualitative experience that is in fact associated with R. The reverse, of course, also seems quite imaginable.

Levine argues that, in the absence of an intelligible connection between seeing red and the 'R' story and seeing green and the 'G' story, we can never be entitled to take seeing red to be identical with having neural processes R. The very possibility that somebody could have had the same physical constitution and display the very same behavior that she does now and yet have seen as red what she now sees as green (and, generally, for the same set of stimuli, experiencing all colors as interchanged with their actual-world complements) is sufficient to show that no physical story can ever capture what it is to experience a color.

I do not think that the prospect for a reduction of color experiencing to neural functioning is so bleak. There is enough factual evidence to suggest that the possibility of an undetectable spectral inversion may be an illusion based upon our ignorance, and that if the facts were to be filled in further, the possibility of an undetectable spectral inversion would come to seem as fanciful as the possibility of a human being having Superman's x-ray vision.

In the previous chapter, Stephen Palmer has shown that many mappings of color space onto itself are "symmetry breakers," because they map unitary (unique) colors onto binary colors, and vice-versa. Any "spectral inversion" that would carry a binary color like orange into a unitary color like blue would be readily detectable. But why could there not be a transformation in which elementary colors go into elementary colors? As Palmer pointed out, nothing in the simple opponent-process scheme forbids such an interchange, and this would give us an inversion that preserves symmetry. In the quest to find further symmetry breakers, we must therefore look to other aspects of color phenomenology. Perhaps these will suggest deeper reasons, based in the qualitative features of the colors themselves, for thinking that the colors of human experience are intrinsically not invertable. I believe that these deeper reasons will emerge when we consider some characteristics of color categories.

Categories are equivalence classes of items that need not be identical. When we call a particular surface "blue," we do not mean to say that it is identical in color to every other surface that is blue. Things that you take to be blue—your neighbor's car, your boss's dress, the sky, the sea—typically differ from each other in tint, shade, or hue. There are light blues, navy blues, electric blues, powder blues. Yet all of them resemble each other more than any of them resembles something that you see as yellow, or as red. It is important to understand that the resemblance that connects two instances of the same color category is not necessarily a function of the perceptual distance between them. It is not hard to find three color samples A, B, and C, which are such that B is separated from A on the one side and from C on the other by the same number of just-noticeable differences, and yet A and B are seen to belong to the same color category whereas C is seen to belong to a different color category. A spectrum looks banded, even though each of its constituent regions blends smoothly into its neighbors.

Is color categorization exclusively a cultural phenomenon, or does it have a biological component? Let's address this question by considering some data about human infants and other primates. Four-month infants know precious little English, and they cannot describe what they see. Nevertheless, by watching their eye fixations one can tell whether they see two stimuli as similar or different. Infants will lose interest in a stimulus that looks similar to its predecessor, but continue looking at a stimulus that they regard as different from what went before. By exposing infants to sequences of colored lights whose dominant wavelengths are 20 nm apart, and recording their eye movements, Bornstein and his collaborators were able to map out their spectral color categories (Bornstein, Kessen, and Weiskopf 1976). These proved to line up rather well with the spectral categories of adults that are mapped with color-naming procedures (for the latter, see Sternheim and Boynton 1966). In a similar fashion, a macaque was trained to respond differentially to spectral lights that human beings would see as good representatives of their categories, and then presented with randomized sequences of lights that did not match the training lights. These lights were categorized by the macaque in pretty much the same way as adult human English speakers would classify them (Sandell, Gross, and Bornstein 1979).

So there must be innate mechanisms not only for detecting resemblances amongst colors, but for categorizing them as well. We should not of course suppose that color categories are consciously or explicitly born in mind by monkeys or infants, but rather that their brains are so wired as to incline them to respond to certain classificatory demands in a characteristic fashion. This was strikingly demonstrated in a series of chimpanzee categorization experiments by Matsuzawa (1985).

In order to see what motivated Matsuzawa, we need to take a brief look at Berlin and Kay's famous work on basic color terms (Berlin and Kay 1969). Basic color terms are distinguished from nonbasic terms by their salience and their generality. Applying criteria based on these characteristics, Berlin and Kay were able to show that, with one possible exception, no language currently has more than eleven basic color terms, that each of the terms has a small set of best, or focal examples, that the focal examples from different languages cluster tightly in perceptual color space, and that, in consequence, basic color terms are readily translatable from one language to another. In English, the basic color terms are, as one might expect, the names for the Hering primaries, "red," "yellow," "green," "blue," "black," and "white," as well as "brown," "gray," "orange," "purple," and "pink." The stimuli in the Berlin and Kay work were a selection of Munsell color chips, a collection of color samples carefully scaled and reproduced to exacting standards. The selection consisted of maximally saturated chips taken from the outer shell of the Munsell color space. Using alternative color order systems, other investigators, notably Boynton and Olson (1987) in the United States and Sivik and Taft (1994) in Sweden, have carefully studied the ranges of these terms with very good overall agreement, exploring the interior of the color solid as well as its outer skin. Among other findings, they showed that some colors, such as blue and green, are seen over wide regions of the space, whereas other colors, such as red, orange, and yellow, are of much more restricted extent. We will look at the implications of this shortly.

In the Matsuzawa experiment that was mentioned above, the chimp, whose name was Ai, was trained on a set of eleven focal samples, learning to press the key that contained a contrived character for the appropriate basic color term. She was then presented with 215 of the Berlin and Kay chips that she had not seen. They were shown to her one at a time and in random order, and she was asked to name them. Following the sessions with the training chips, she did not receive reinforcement for her choices. The experimenter assigned a label to a chip when the chimpanzee gave it that label on at least 75 percent of the trials. The results were compared to those generated in a human color-naming experiment, again using the 75 percent consistency criterion. The outcomes were closely similar. The chimp had generalized from focal chips in essentially the same fashion as the human being.

This is a striking result, but what is its application to our problem? Think of it this way. Ai was presumably not doing what she was doing because of cultural bias, the grammar of color concepts, or any other such fancy hoo-ha. She was guided by what she saw, by what looked like what, by, if you will, the intrinsic qualities of her sensory experience. The array of Munsell chips is scaled so that the samples are a constant number of just-noticeable-hue-differences apart, and a constant number of just-noticeable-lightness-differences apart. At one level of resemblance ordering, everything is smooth and orderly. But at the level of categorization, this is not at all the case, as we have already seen. (I might note parenthetically that other measures of perceptual distance are used in other color-order systems, but the results of categorization are essentially independent of this fact. The principles of scaling in the Swedish Natural Color System yield a solid of entirely regular shape, but the categorized areas are as irregular in shape and strikingly diverse in extent in the Natural Color System as they are in the Munsell solid.) If red occupies a small volume in the solid, and green a large one, what does this betoken but a substantial difference in phenomenal structure between red and green? Moreover, this difference is surely intrinsic to the qualities themselves. What else could serve as the basis for categorization? After all, the whole procedure only involves assessing the qualitative similarities and differences between one color and another.

Here is another categorical asymmetry. Brown is a blackened orange or yellow. An orange fruit has in fact the same chromaticity as a chocolate bar. This assertion is commonly met with disbelief, for brown looks to have a very different quality from yellow and orange. This is why people are surprised when they see a demonstration in which a projected orange spot is first dimmed, looking orange to the very edge of invisibility. The same spot is then blackened by surrounding it with an annulus of bright white light. When the blackening occurs, the orange spot is transformed into a rich brown. It is as if the original quality has been lost, and replaced by another.

This appearance of strong qualitative differences is not a general characteristic of blackened colors, most of which resemble their parent hues. Blackened blues, such as navy blue, continue to look blue, and blackened greens—olive greens—continue to look green. Only oranges and yellows seem to lose the parental connection when blackened. Then what would happen in the hypothetical case of spectral inversion in which hues are carried into their complements? The inverse of orange is turquoise, the inverse of yellow, blue. Therefore the inverse of the browns would be blackened turquoises and navy blues. If you are like most people, you will find brown and yellow to be far more different from each other than light blue is from navy blue. In many languages, as in English, the difference between yellow and brown is marked by the use of two distinct basic color terms, but in no language whatever is the light blue-dark blue difference marked with distinct basic color terms, while the yellow-brown difference is left unmarked. In fact, with the possible exception of Russian, no language even has separate basic terms for light blue and dark blue.

It is thus fair to conclude that something has got lost in the inversion, and that if a human being were to be born with such an inversion, it would not go undetected. More to the point, since the blackness in a blackened yellow is the same as the blackness in a blackened blue, or, for that matter, red, or green, there must be some characteristic of yellow that is not present in blue or in any of the other Hering primaries. This probably has to do with the fact that yellow, unlike any other chromatic primary, is most pronounced only at high lightness levels.

But why is this? The most helpful, indeed, I think, the only helpful explanation of this phenomenon would be in terms of a neural mechanism. Recent neurophysiological evidence indicates that color-sensitive color cells in the cerebral cortex statistically "prefer" their yellows light and their reds dark (Yoshioka et al. 1996). This is of course only the first step in a long journey that will, if we are lucky, bring us to suitably rich mechanisms to account for the properties of yellow. Finding such mechanisms would be the way to understand other phenomenal features of yellow, such as why it is that yellowish greens look as though they ought to be classified as greens, even though we judge the yellow content to be well above 50 per cent. The very fact that the internal relations between yellow and its neighbors do not have the same form as the internal relationships between blue and its neighbors suggests that although yellow may be elementary with respect to phenomenal color mixture, it is not elementary simpliciter, any more than a proposition that is commonly used as an axiom for certain purposes is an axiom simpliciter.

The only way to understand why yellow, or any other color, has its particular phenomenal structure is to devise a good functional model, consistent with what we know about the underlying neurophysiology. Such models have already helped us to understand the unitary-binary and opponent structures of phenomenal color space (Hardin 1988). More recently, there has been progress in understanding how the intrinsic similarities and differences revealed in color naming might be grounded in the workings of our visual systems. Guest and Van Laar (1997), using the CIE Uniform Color Space realized on video displays, have investigated the size and distribution of the regions of basic color naming and connected them to features of Hunt's quantitative opponent color model. Hunt's complex model was derived from considerations of color appearance that are quite independent of color naming. Once again, quality is expressed in structure, structure is anchored in functional configuration, and functional configuration is presumably rooted in patterns of neural activity.

As a final example, let us consider the well-known distinction between "warm" and "cool" colors. Although this cross-culturally robust division is commonly believed to arise in consequence of environmental associations, it has always seemed to some people, including me, that it reflects intrinsic phenomenal similarities and differences. Recently, Katra and Wooten asked ten subjects to rate eight color samples as "warm" or "cool" on a ten-point scale, with ten as "very warm." As one might have expected, the mean results gave the lowest rating (3.5) to the unitary blue sample, and the highest rating (6.75) to the orange sample. There was a high level of agreement among subjects. Katra and Wooten compared the group data with summed averaged opponent-response cancellation data, which can be interpreted as giving the level of activation of opponent channels. To quote Katra and Wooten's conclusion:

The remarkable correspondence between the obtained ratings of warmth and coolness and the activation levels in the opponent channels ... suggests that the attribution of thermal properties to colors may be linked to the low-level physiological processes involved in color perception. Higher ratings of warmth corresponded with levels of activation of the opponent channels in one direction, while cooler ratings corresponded with activation in the opposite direction. This suggests that a link to the activation level of the opponent channels, rather than the psychological quality of hue, drives the association of temperature with color, and that the association is more than simply a cognitive process.

They thus trace the connection between the warm-cool of temperature and the warm-cool of color to the corresponding activation levels of their respective neural systems rather than to stereotypical environmental associations such as red with fire and blue with water. This does not by itself warrant the conclusion that the respective intrinsic characters of the warm colors and the cool colors are a function of opponent activation levels, but it is consonant with that stronger claim. Furthermore, if one reflects on just how Katra and Wooten's subjects could gain information about the state of activation of their visual opponent cells, it becomes clear that it could only be by experiencing the colors of which these cells are the neural substrate. In other words, the color qualities themselves are the natural expression of neural activation, and we implicitly read them as such.

Now let us sum up these considerations. Color space has an irregular structure. The structure of color space is arrived at entirely by comparing the colors with each other, so the irregularity of structure is intrinsic to the domain of colors. Experiments with nonhuman primates strongly suggest that this irregular, intrinsic structure is of biological rather than cultural origin. The peculiarities of chromatic structure invite explanation in terms of biological mechanisms, and in some cases it is possible to produce such explanations, at least in outline. The details of the chromatic structural irregularities prohibit putative undetectable interchanges of color experiences: small rotations of the hue circuit carry unitary into binary hues; interchanges of warm and cool colors carry negative opponent-channel activations into positive ones, and vice-versa; interchange of yellows with blues exchanges dark blues and cyans with browns; interchange of reds with greens maps a small categorical region into a large one, and a large region into a small one.

What has here been given is an empirical argument, and as such has predictive consequences. In particular, it should be possible to test it with the pseudonormal observers (if such there be) that Martine Nida-Rümelin describes in the next chapter.

A pseudonormal would see green at spectral loci at which normal observers see red, and red at loci where normal observers see green. If the present argument is correct, the region of a standard color space that a pseudonormal observer labels "red" should be large, and the region that such an observer labels "green" should be small. Since pseudonormality could presumably be determined by genetic tests, one would only have to see whether there is a correlation between the genetic marker and differences in the size, shape, and location of color-naming regions.

Some proponents of the possibility of an inverted spectrum (e.g., Shoemaker 1984) have conceded that human color space may not as a matter of fact be invertable. They have, however, urged that this does not show that no creature could possibly have inverted sensory qualities, and some of them (e.g., Levine 1991) have go on to argue that the mere possibility of inverted sensory qualities is sufficient to make any functionalist account of the qualities of experience suspect.

In one respect, they are right. Empirical arguments cannot (nontrivially) yield necessary truths. We philosophers rather tenaciously cling to this truism, perhaps because we sense that the independence of our discipline depends upon it. But we must beware of letting it bear too much weight. That we can in some fashion imagine that water is not H_2O, or that heat is a fluid, or that there exists a perfectly rigid body, does not license us to suppose that any of these things is possible in any scientifically interesting sense. At our present state of knowledge, to regard any of them as genuinely possible is to exchange hard-won intelligibility for a murky mess of imagery. Given as background what we now know about fluids and heat, it becomes much harder for us even to imagine that heat is a fluid. Granted, there is still no knockdown argument that there is no possible world in which the heat of a gas is a fluid, but we are not thereby tempted to suspect that the heat of a gas might not after all be identical with molecular kinetic energy. When it comes to scientific identities, logical possibility is trumped by overwhelming implausibility.

The case at hand is similar. Much of the appeal of the inverted spectrum as an antifunctionalist or antimaterialist weapon has lain in its intuitiveness: what looks to me to be THIS color (inwardly ostending red) could have looked to me to be THAT color (inwardly ostending green) without anyone being the wiser. This simple intuition has doubtless been aided and abetted by the wide currency of oversimplified models of color space, such as the color sphere and hue circle, in which the structure of color qualities is presented as smoothly symmetrical. But once we do the phenomenology of THIS and THAT, becoming aware of their intrinsic structure, and elaborating the functional structure that underlies them, the initial plausibility of interchange begins to fade, just as the plausibility of heat's being a fluid begins to fade once one understands how the ideas of the kinetic theory engage the empirical facts about heat. And when this paradigmatic example of qualitative interchange

loses its grip on our imaginations, the idea of there being abstractly specified qualitative states being interchangeable in abstractly specified creatures with abstractly
specified physical workings ought to lose its grip on our intuitions.

Merely schematic specification of the subject matter plagues both sides of the disputes about functionalism. One the one hand a defender of functionalism (Lewis
1980) gives us Martians with plumbing instead of neurons, and on the other, a critic
of functionalism (Block 1980) presents us with the spectacle of the whole nation of
China acting as a Turing machine. Amusing though these fantasies may be, they are
as desperately lacking in the details of what is to be explained as they are lacking in
constraints on the putative explanatory mechanisms. It is as if we were asked to judge
the possibility of a physical account of living organisms based only on a thorough
knowledge of Lucretius's *On the Nature of Things*. To judge rightly the adequacy of
functionalism or materialism to capture the qualitative character of experience, we
must carefully describe both sides of the equation. To do so, we need good ideas, the
right distinctions, and lots of careful empirical work. That work must take place on
several levels, regimenting the phenomenology, developing functional models that are
capable of imaging that phenomenology, and investigating how those models might
be realized by the available neural resources (cf. Clark 1993). The patient application
of these methods can, in principle, capture any expressible fact about sensory qualities, and bring that fact within the ambit of scientific explanation. Will there be a
plurality of plausible functional models adequate to the total phenomenology, or will
there be but one? Will the preferred future explanations of sensory qualities take the
form only of correlations among the behavioral, phenomenal, and neural domains,
or will they involve a proper reduction of phenomenology to neural mechanisms? We
are simply too ignorant of the relevant facts to answer these questions now, and we
ought not to pretend that clever conceptual analysis can offset this epistemic defi-
ciency. We must go much further in solving the "easy" problems of consciousness
before we can clearly understand just what the "hard" problem consists in, or
whether there really is a "hard" problem at all. And anyway, aren't the "easy"
problems hard enough?

Longer versions of this chapter have appeared under the title "Reinventing the
Spectrum" in the following two books:

Mindscapes: Philosophy, Science, and the Mind. Edited by Martin Carrier and Peter
K. Machamer. UVK/University of Pittsburgh Press, 1997.

Readings on Color: The Philosophy of Color. Edited by Alex Byrne and David R.
Hilbert. MIT Press, 1997.

References

Berlin, B. and Kay, P. 1969. *Basic Color Terms*. Berkeley and Los Angeles: University of California Press.

Block, N. 1980. Troubles with Functionalism, in N. Block (ed.), *Readings in Philosophy of Psychology*, vol. 1. Cambridge, Mass.: Harvard University Press.

Bornstein, M. H., Kessen, W. and Weiskopf, S. 1976. Color Vision and Hue Categorization in Young Human Infants, in *Journal of Experimental Psychology* 2:115–19.

Boynton, R. M. and Olson, C. X. 1987. Locating Basic Colors in the OSA Space, in *Color Research and Application* 12, no. 2:94–105.

Clark, A. 1993. *Sensory Qualities*. Oxford: The Clarendon Press.

Guest, S. and Van Laar, D. 1997. All Colours Are not Created Equal: The Psychology of Categorical Colour Naming, in L. Sivik (ed.), *Colour Report F50: Colour and Psychology*. Stockholm: Scandinavian Colour Institute.

Hardin, C. L. 1988. *Color for Philosophers: Unweaving the Rainbow*. Indianapolis and Cambridge, Mass.: Hackett Publishing Company.

Hardin, C. L. 1997. Reinverting the Spectrum, in A. Byrne and D. R. Hilbert (eds.), *Readings on Color*, vol. 1. Cambridge, Mass.: MIT Press.

Hardin, C. L. and Maffi, L. (eds.) 1997. *Color Categories in Thought and Language*. Cambridge and New York: Cambridge University Press.

Katra, B. and Wooten, B. H. nd. Perceived Lightness/Darkness and Warmth/Coolness in Chromatic Experience, unpublished ms. 38 pp.

Levine, J. 1983. Materialism and Qualia: The Explanatory Gap, *Pacific Philosophical Quarterly* 64:354–361.

Levine, J. 1991. Cool Red: A Reply to Hardin, *Philosophical Psychology* 4(1):27–40.

Lewis, D. 1980. "Mad Pain and Martian Pain." In N. Block (ed.), *Readings in Philosophy of Psychology*, vol. 1. Cambridge, Mass.: Harvard University Press.

Matsuzawa, T. 1985. Colour Naming and Classification in a Chimpanzee (Pan Troglodytes), in *Journal of Human Evolution* 14:283–91.

Quinn, P. C., Rosano, J. L. and Wooten, B. R. 1988. Evidence that Brown is not an Elemental Color, in *Perception and Psychophysics* 37(3):198–202.

Sandell, J. H., Gross, C. G. and Bornstein, M. H. 1979. Color Categories in Macaques, in *Journal of Comparative and Physiological Psychology* 93:626–35.

Shoemaker, S. 1984. The Inverted Spectrum, in *Identity, Cause, and Mind: Philosophical Essays*. Cambridge: Cambridge University Press.

Sivik, L. and Taft, C. 1994. Color Naming: A Mapping in the NCS of Common Color Terms, in *Scandinavian Journal of Psychology* 35:144–64.

Sternheim, C. E. and Boynton, R. M. 1966. Uniqueness of Perceived Hues Investigated with a Continuous Judgmental Technique, in *Journal of Experimental Psychology* 72:770–86.

Yoshioka, T., Dow, B. M. and R. G. Vautin 1996. Neural Mechanisms of Color Categorization in Areas V1, V2, and V4 of Macaque Monkey Cortex. *Behavioral Brain Research* 76:51–80.

7 Pseudonormal Vision and Color Qualia[1]

Martine Nida-Rümelin

1 Pseudonormal Vision and Functionalism

Is it possible that a person who behaves just like you and me in normal life situations and applies color words to objects just as we do and makes the same color discriminations, see green where we see red and red where we see green? Or, to put the same question from another perspective: Is it possible that you are yourself red-green inverted with respect to all or most other people and that you thus are and have always been radically wrong about what other people see when looking at a sunset or the moving leaves of a tree?

Philosophers normally discuss the possibility of Qualia Inversion by considering thought experiments. But there is, in fact, scientific evidence for the existence of such cases. Theories about the physiological basis of color vision deficiencies together with theories about the genetics of color vision deficiencies lead to the prediction that some people are "pseudonormal."[2] Pseudonormal people "would be expected to have normal color vision except that the sensations of red and green would be reversed—something that would be difficult, if not impossible, to prove."[3] This inversion would affect the perception of any color that contains a red or green component. A greenish blue river would appear violet to a pseudonormal person. Remember, however, that this description will give you a correct idea of what pseudonormal people experience only if you are not yourself one of them. But there is a chance that you are. According to a model of the genetics of color vision deficiencies that was first presented by Piantanida in 1974 pseudonormality occurs in 14 of 10 000 males.[4] It is instructive to see how the prediction of pseudonormal vision follows from the combination of several empirically supported assumptions.

There are three types of photoreceptors on the retina that play a central role in human color vision and that are called B-cones, G- and R-cones. Although this is in many ways misleading, one should keep in mind that these labels derive from "blue" (in the case of B-cones), "green" (in the case of G-Cones) and "red" (in the case of R-Cones). These three cone types contain in normal people three chemically different photopigments. The photopigment contained in a receptor determines its characteristic sensitivity to light of different wavelengths. This assumption is central to the following discussion. It implies that a G-cone will react to a specific light stimulus exactly like a normal R-cone if it is filled with the photopigment normally contained in R-cones and vice versa. The amount of redness, greenness, yellowness and blueness in a perceived color depends on the average stimulation of the cones of the three types on the relevant area of the retina. The perceived color contains some amount of redness iff the relevant higher areas of the brain get the information that R-cone activity prevails G-cone activity and it contains a component of green iff G-cone activity prevails R-cone activity. In an analogous manner, a comparison between the activity of B-cones and the activity of R- and G-cones together determines whether the perceived color contains a component of blue or of yellow.

Let's see what happens if for some mistake of nature a given person has her R- and her G-cones filled with the same photopigment. The average stimulation of R- and G-cones will always be the same independently of the wavelengths composition of the light stimulus and so nothing will appear greenish or reddish to the person at issue. The mistake can occur in two ways: G and R-cones could both be filled with the R-cone-photopigment or could both be filled with the G-cone-photopigment. These two conditions actually correspond to the two main forms of red-green-blindness. According to Piantanida's model mentioned before, both genes, the one that causes production of the G-cone photopigment in R-cones and the one that causes production of the R-cone photopigment in G-cones, may be active in one single individual. In this case two mistakes are much better than one: The wrong filling in both cone types simply leads to an exchange of the photopigments in the two cone types. As a result, the discriminative capacities of the person at issue will not be impaired and his or her visual life will not be impoverished. But, whenever a pseudonormal person looks at a red tomato, her brain will get the information that G-cone-acticity prevails, so the red tomato will appear green to him or her. In general one can predict: What appears red to a normal person to a certain degree, will appear green to a pseudonormal person to roughly the same degree and vice versa. In this sense pseudonormal people are red-green-inverted. Contrary to this result, several *philosophical* theories imply that pseudonormal people, if they existed, would not be red-green-inverted. This is, as I will argue, reason to reject the philosophical theory at issue.

Any philosophical theory about mind should meet the following *prima facie constraint*: No hypothesis accepted or seriously considered in color vision science should be regarded according to a philosophical theory to be either incoherent or unstatable or false. A view that denies that red objects appear green to pseudonormals obviously violates this principle. The constraint just formulated is, however, only *prima facie*. Surely it may follow from a convincing philosophical theory that the terminology of some specific science is somehow confused and should be revised. However, the philosopher whose theory does not meet the above formulated constraint has the burden of proof on his side. In particular, he should be able to argue that the empirical theory at issue can be reformulated in a way compatible with the philosopher's theory without change of its empirical content and without contradicting its most central assumptions. But, as we will see in a moment, this is not possible with respect to color vision sicence for a philosopher who denies that pseudonormal people are red-green-inverted.

The prediction of red-green-inversion for pseudonormal people is a direct consequence of a general and highly plausible assumption about the dependence of phenomenal experience on physiological properties that may be put as a supervenience thesis:

(ST)   There can be no difference between two persons with respect to their phenomenal experience unless there is also a difference in their relevant physiological properties.

Two remarks about the intended class of "relevant" physiological properties refered to in (ST) are necessary. (1) This class only includes physiological properties of the brain and not of the retina. The reason is this: If there were a difference between two individuals with respect to their retina that would not cause a physiological difference in their brain, then it would be mysterious if the corresponding phenomenal experiences were all the same different. Mysterious cases of this kind are excluded by (ST) if the relevant class of physiological properties is restricted to properties of the brain. (2) Also, it would be quite mysterious if the mere fact that a person learns to associate specific linguistic expressions with his or her phenomenal experience would suffice to change its qualitative character. Therefore, physiological properties that underly causal connections of this irrelevant kind to the language center of the brain, are also excluded from the intended class of physiological properties either. With these explanation of relevance in mind it is clear that there is no difference in the relevant physiological properties between a normal person who is looking at a red tomato and a pseudonormal person who is looking at a green tomato and vice versa. So, who denies that pseudonormal people are red-green inverted thereby denies (ST).[5]

This result can be used for an argument against functionalism. According to functionalism to have a sensation of red is to be in a state that is caused by a certain kind of stimuli, leads to specific other internal states (e.g., the belief that there is something red), and causes—together with other internal states characteristic outputs (e.g., the utterance "this is red"). This rough characterization of functionalism is precise enough to clarify why pseudonormal vision represents a problem for most functionalist theories of mind.[6] According to functionalism there is a characteristic type of inputs I_G that causes sensations of green (and to be caused by inputs of this type is an *essential* property of sensations of green) and there is a specific type of outputs O_G that is typically caused by sensations of green (and to be a partial cause of output of this type is again an *essential* property of sensations of green). Now, most versions of functionalism are either committed to the claim that

(A)   The inputs received by a pseudonormal person when looking at a red tomato are not of the type I_G

or to the claim that

(B)   The outputs partially caused by the internal state of pseudonormal people when looking at red tomatoes are not of type O_G

or to both of these claims. In each case, the functionalist must deny that red tomatoes appear green to pseudonormal people. But, as we have seen, this shows that his theory is in conflict with a central and highly plausible assumption of color vision science.

2   The Unexplainability of Color Qualia

Two questions in the debate about the so-called explantory gap thesis should not be conflated:

Q1:   Is it possible to understand why certain physical properties of physical systems lead to the occurrence of consciousness at all?

Q2:   Is it possible to understand why certain physical processes in the brain of sentient beings lead to experiences of a given qualitative type?

I will only discuss the second question here.If we call the physical process that actually underlies sensations of green "G" and the physical process that actually underlies sensations of red "R," then a negative answer to the second question may be put as follows:

(T1)   Explanatory Gap Thesis
Even if we knew everything there is to know about the physical[7] properties of R and G, we still would not *understand* why R is correlated with sensations of red and why G is correlated with sensations of green.

Most proponents of the explanatory gap thesis defend their claim by an intuition captured by T2[8]:

(T2)   Qualia Inversion Hypothesis
Even if we knew everything there is to know about the physical properties of R and G, we could still coherently conceive of circumstances where experiences of red are correlated with G and experiences of green are correlated with R.

It is quite generally accepted in the ongoing debate that T1 and T2 stand or fall together. In what follows I will challenge this common assumption. In my view, there is some reason to doubt the Qualia Inversion Hypothesis and still there is good reason to believe in the Explanatory Gap Thesis.[9]

In several papers and talks Hardin has argued simultaneously against T1 and T2.[10] I will describe what seems to me to be the abstract common structure behind these arguments and I will call any argument of this common structure "the Hardin-Argument." There are mainly two reasons why I think it is worthwhile to look at Hardin's work from this abstract viewpoint: One thereby is led to see quite clearly why (T1) does not depend on the truth of (T2) and one is led to more general insights about what kind of explanations of conscious experience can at best be expected from the empirical sciences.

The Hardin-Argument starts from the following two basic assumptions:

(P1)   The color qualities we are acquainted with have a necessary phenomenal structure.

(P2)   Any conceivable empirical correlation between hue sensations and brain processes is structure preserving.

The following observation by Hardin clarifies the idea behind (P1): If a creature sees neither reddishness nor yellowishness in a perceived color, then this *constitutes*, as Hardin says, its failing to see orange.[11] The same point may be put in another way: Being composed of red and yellow is not just an actual but rather a necessary property of orange. Note that P1 can be used in an argument against (T2) only if "necessity" is interpreted in a specific way. In the sense of necessity required for the purposes at issue, the following implication holds: If a given property is a necessary property of a color, then we cannot coherently conceive of circumstances where this color does not have the property at issue. Who wishes to argue against the thesis that qualia inversion cases are coherently conceivable must refer to properties of colors that these colors have not just under the actually given circumstances but under all coherently conceivable circumstances as well. This is why the Hardin argument needs the philosophical premise that certain structural properties of colors are necessary and cannot be based on the corresponding empirical claims about their actual structure alone.

The idea behind (P2) can be seen by means of an example: There should be some functional property P such that the amount of redness in the color perceived by a person increases with the degree to which the correlated brain process exemplifies the property P. A similar statement should be true for every phenomenal property of colors. An exact formulation of the idea behind (P2) requires using the mathematical notion of an isomorphic mapping. But the idea will be clear enough without going into these technical details.[12] One might object to the premiss (P2) that we can in some sense coherently think of psychophysical correlations that do not preserve structure. After all, it is even coherently conceivable in some sense of conceivability that a being has color sensations without having a brain at all. However, I doubt that the sense of conceivability involved here is helpful for somenone who wishes to defend the Explanatory Gap Thesis (T1) on the basis of the Qualia Inversion Hypothesis (T2). I will therefore conceed (P2).

It is quite clear how an argument against (T2) has to proceed, once (P1) and (P2) are accepted. One must show, using concrete knowledge about both, the phenomenal and partly necessary structure of our color sensations on the one hand and knowledge about the functional structure of the underlying physiological processes on the other, that there is only one way to correlate color sensations and brain processes to each other in a structure preserving way, namely the one actually chosen by nature. Hardin has presented material that makes it appear very plausible that this part of the argument can be stated successfully.[13] So, if we decide to accept the two fundamental premisses stated before, we have to admit that the Qualia Inversion Hypothesis (T2) is false. However, this does not help to close the explanatory gap. To see this it is helpful to state the result we have reached in a slightly different way. I will use the following abbreviations: "S_p" stands for the necessary phenomenal structure of our color experiences and "S_f" for the actual functional structure of the physiological processes that underly our color experiences. The material presented by Hardin supports the following claim:

(R1)   If a creature has visual sensations with the phenomenal structure S_p and a visual system with the functional structure S_f, then there is just one structure-preserving way to correlate hue sensations with neural processes.

If we concede (a) that psychophysical correlations that do not preserve structure are unconceivable (see premiss P2) and (b) that we cannot coherently conceive of a creature that has sensations of red, green, yellow and blue without having color experiences that realize the phenomenal structure S_p (compare premiss P1), then (R1) leads to the stronger result (R2):

(R2)   If we already know of a creature that it has sensations of red, green, yellow and blue, and that its visual system realizes the functional structure S_f, then the actual psychophysical correlations between hue sensations and brain processes are the only correlations we can still coherently conceive of.

(R2) clearly contradicts the Qualia Inversion Hypothesis (T2), but, it does not undermine (T1). To close the explanatory gap, we need a quite different result. We wish to see why the functional structure of our brain processes necessarily leads to sensations of red, green, and so on. So what we need is an argument for something like the following result:

(R*)   We cannot coherently conceive of a creature whose visual system realizes S_f and yet does not have sensations of red, green, yellow and blue.

(R2) starts from the assumption that we already know that the creature at issue has *our* basic color sensations (red, green, yellow and blue). Therefore it obviously cannot establish (R*). But, maybe the philosophical opponent is really a bit closer to his philosophical aim than might appear after what has been said so far. It is quite plausible that an argument very much *like* the Hardin-Argument can show that functional structure determines phenomenal structure in the following sense:

(R3)   It is not coherently conceivable that a sentient being has a visual system that realizes the functional structure S_f and yet does not have color experiences that realize the phenomenal structure S_p

With an argument for (R3) we would have established the explainability of phenomenal structure on the basis of functional structure, but still this is not enough. An explanation of why our color experiences have a specific phenomenal structure is not yet an explanation of why we have sensations of the concrete qualities red, green, yellow and blue. *So we are still left with an explanatory gap between phenomenal structure and concrete phenomenal qualities.* One might try to close this remaining gap by proposing the following further premise:

(P3)   A creature who has visual experiences that realize the phenomenal structure S_p necessarily has experiences of red, green, blue, and yellow.

Maybe (P3) is acceptable if "necessity" is read as natural or nomological necessity. I doubt this, but we do not need to decide this issue. (P3) does not help to close the explanatory gap if necessity is read in this sense. Maybe it is a law of nature that sensations of red, green, yellow and blue necessarily occur whenever there is the phenomenal structure S_p. But, if we had to accept this regularity as a brute fact about how the world really is, we still would be left with the original puzzle: Why do we have sensations of red (this concrete quality)? Who wishes to attack the explanatory gap thesis in this way must claim that (P3) is still true when necessity is read as conceptual necessity. On this reading however, (P3) is quite obviously false. There is, as Hardin has pointed out convincingly, I think, a conceptual link that leads from concrete phenomenal qualities to phenomenal structure, but there is no conceptual link that turns an explanation of phenomenal structure into an explanation of the occurrence of concrete phenomenal qualities. This observation has its parallel in the epistemological fact that knowledge about phenomenal structure does not imply knowledge about concrete phenomenal qualities. An example may illustrate this epistemological fact. Let us assume that we find somewhere in the universe a sentient being who distinguishes surfaces of objects according to the wavelengths composition of the light reflected by these objects. In some way we find out that the alien creature has not just two channels that inform the brain about the result of comparing average acticities of different receptor types, but three such channels. If we knew that the creature has visual sensations at all, we would then have reason to assume that it is acquainted not with four but with six basic colors and that the colors it perceives have one more hue dimension: Our colors are phenomenally composed of at most two hue components, the colors experienced by these creatures are composed of up to three components (the painters of this alien society would have incredibly more possibilities of artistic expression). On the basis of the functional structure of the visual system of these creatures we might gain rich knowledge about the phenomenal structure of their experiences, but this does not help us to find out which are the six basic colors they experience.[14]

We are thus led to the following diagnosis: The explanatory gap, as far as the explanation of specific phenomenal sensations are concerned, basically rests on the partial epistemological independence between phenomenal structure on the one hand and concrete phenomenal qualities on the other. So maybe the proponent of the explanatory gap thesis, instead of insisting on the Qualia Inversion Hypothesis should rather concentrate on this specific independence claim and its philosophical consequences.

3   Concluding Remark

What kinds of explanation of phenomenal experience may we at best expect from the empirical sciences? (1) We can of course expect what one might call single case explanations for the occurrence of a phenomenal experience of a specific kind in a given situation. For example, why do you see a rose as red? Answer: The rose produces a physiological state that is, in humans generally, correlated with sensations of red. A single case explanation of this kind presupposes psychophysical laws. (2) We can expect explanations of phenomenal structure. Why is it impossible to see a surface as greenish and reddish in the same place? Answer: the underlying physiological processes have causal properties that make it impossible for them to occur simultanously. Explanations of phenomenal structure of this kind again presuppose psychophysical laws. (3) We may expect even explanations of psychophysical laws in the following sense: Any alternative psychophysical correlation would not be structure preserving. As we have seen, explaining psychophysical laws in this manner, presupposes the fact that we have sensations of the specific qualities red, green, yellow and blue, and does not explain this fact. (4) Under the assumption that *by law of nature* the phenomenal structure S_p of visual experiences can only be found in individuals whose basic hue qualities are those known to *us* (red, green, yellow, and blue), we even may get an explanation of why we have sensations of this specific phenomenal character. This explanation, however, presupposes and does not explain why a specific phenomenal structure is nomologically associated with these concrete phenomenal qualities.—The possibility to explain phenomenal structure in the senses just sketched may be more of an explanation than some philosophers might have expected. But still it does not close the explanatory gap and we are left with our original puzzle about the occurrence of concrete phenomenal qualities.

One common feature of the four kinds of explanation just mentioned should be kept in mind: They all presuppose and do not explain the fact that the creature at issue is a sentient being, that is has a subjective perspective, that there is consciousness at all. This aspect of the explanatory gap debate certainly concerns the more fundamental and still more puzzling mystery about consciousness.

Notes

1. When invited to the Tucson III conference, I was asked to talk about pseudonormal vision *and* about Hardin's arguments against the explanatory gap thesis. This is why the chapter consists of two relatively independent parts.

2. See T. P. Piantanida, "A replacement model of X-linked recessive colour vision defects." *Annals of Human Genetics* 37 (1974): 393–404 and Robert M. Boynton "Human Color Vision," New York, Holt Rinehart and Winston, 1979, pp. 351–358.

3. Boynton in "Human Color Vision" op. cit., pp. 356.

4. I don't know the estimation for females.

5. A more detailed discussion would, of course, have to include (a) a precise account of (ST) and the involved concept of relevance, (b) more evidence for the claim that (ST) is actually accepted in color vision science and (c) independent philosophical reasons for the acceptance of (ST).

6. Some versions of functionalism have a reply to the argument that follows but have other problems with the case of pseudonormal vision (see my paper [1996], in particular section 4).

7. Note that "physical" is used here in the very broad sense common in the relevant debate: Chemical, physiological, and functional properties are included.

8. Compare, e.g., Joseph Levine [1983].

9. The case of pseudonormal vision is, of course, irrelevant to the present question. The qualia inversion hypothesis states the conceivability of cases where two individuals differ in their phenomenal experience while there is no relevant physical difference between the two. But there *are* relevant physical differences between normals and pseudonormals when looking at red objects.

10. See Hardin [1987], [1996], and his contribution to this volume.

11. Compare Hardin [1996], p. 101 and his contribution to this volume.

12. For a more detailed examination of (P2) compare my paper [1998].

13. Compare his contribution to this volume and his [1996] paper.

14. The observation that knowledge about physical properties (including functional properties) does not guarantee knowledge about qualitative states has been discussed in detail (see, e.g., Jackson's famous paper [1982] and the discussion that followed). The point here is slightly different: Even knowledge about *phenomenal* structure (not to confuse with *functional* structure!) does not include knowledge about concrete qualia.

References

Boynton, R. M. 1979. *Human Color Vision, New York*, Holt Rinehart & Winston: 351–358.

Jackson, F. 1982. Epiphenomenal Qualia, *Philosophical Quarterly* 32:127–136.

Hardin, Clyde L., 1996. Reinverting the Spectrum, in Carrier and Machamer: *Mindscapes: Philosophy, Science, and the Mind*, Pittsburgh, Konstanz: University of Pittsburgh Press, Universitätsverlag Konstanz, 99–112.

Hardin, C. L., 1987. Qualia and Materialism: Closing the Explanatory Gap, *Philosophy and Phenomenological Research* 48:281–298.

Levine, J., 1983. Materialism and Qualia: The Explanatory Gap, *Pacific Philosophical Quarterly* 64:354–361.

Nida-Rümelin, M. 1996. Pseudonormal Vision. An Actual Case of Qualia Inversion?, *Philosophical Studies* 82:145–157.

Nida-Rümelin, M. 1998. Vertauschte Sinnesqualitäten und die Frage der Erklärbarkeit von Bewußtsein, in Frank Esken and Dieter Heckmann (eds.), *Bewußtsein und Repräsentation*, Paderborn, Ferdinand Schöningh: 299–324.

Piantanida, T. P., 1974. A replacement model of X-linked recessive color vision defects, *Annals of Human Genetics*, 37:393–404.

III NEURAL CORRELATES—INTRODUCTION

The search for neural correlates of consciousness (NCC) occupies the laboratory efforts of an increasing number of scientists, and has gained the interest of many philosophers. While some investigators have focused their attention on one particular domain of sensory qualia, such as visual experience (e.g., Crick and Koch 1995), others (e.g., Bogen 1998, Newman 1997) have sought for commonalities across domains in attempts to develop general theories of NCC. The three chapters within this section continue the search for the NC of visual awareness, as well as extend the exploration of NCC into the realms of altered states of consciousness and psychiatric disorder.

In the first chapter of this section, Antti Revonsuo examines the close interaction between theoretical and empirical issues that is required for development of a theoretically driven cognitive neuroscience of consciousness. He begins his examination by conceptualizing consciousness as the phenomenal level of organization in the brain, and argues that the science of consciousness needs to develop a phenomenal level of description that captures this level of organization. He goes on to describe how metaphors and model systems can be used to capture essential features of phenomena, and presents an argument for taking the concept of Virtual Reality as a metaphor for consciousness. In this metaphor, Revonsuo posits the phenomenal level of organization as being conceivable as the brain's "natural virtual reality system," and uses this metaphor to define the framework for an empirically based phenomenology. As an example of implications of such an approach, the chapter closes with a description of recent empirical research conducted by Revonsuo and his colleagues in which cortical magnetic responses to visual object awareness were found to support the hypotheses of Crick and Koch (1995).

In the second chapter, Vollenweider reviews his search for the NC of hallucinogen-induced altered states of consciousness. Vollenweider and his colleagues have investigated the effects of various psychoactive drugs on cerebral metabolism (employing positron emission tomography; PET) and psychometric ratings. Different psychometrically related aspects of altered states (i.e., experiences of oceanic boundlessness, visionary restructuralization and hallucinatory experience, and fear of ego-dissolution) were found to be related to distinctly different patterns of cerebral metabolic changes, implicating different cerebral systems.

In the third and final chapter of this section, Jeffrey Schwartz describes his PET imaging studies of cerebral metabolic changes after psychological treatment of obsessive-compulsive disorder (OCD). Following a discussion of how OCD provides a potentially important source of information about mind-brain relations, the chapter gives a brief overview of what is know about brain mechanisms in OCD, particularly implicating the basal ganglia, orbital frontal cortex, and the anterior cingulate gyrus. Schwartz then describes a cognitive-behavioral treatment for OCD in which an attempt is made to help the patient appreciate that intrusive OCD thoughts and urges are "false brain messages" that can safely be ignored. He draws analogies between the treatment goal of patients' developing the ability to observe their own internal sensations "with the calm clarity of an external witness," and the mindful awareness of traditional Buddhist practice. Schwartz then summarizes the results of his PET studies, in which systematic changes in cerebral glucose metabolism were found to accompany clinical improvement following the cognitive-behavioral treatment. These changes included bilateral decreases in caudate nucleus metabolism and a decrease in the correlations between metabolic activity in the orbital cortex, caudate nucleus, cingulate gyrus, and thalamus. These data are interpreted by Schwartz as providing evidence associating "new consciously chosen response patterns with statistically significant changes of energy use in the very brain circuitry" that underlie the painful intrusive thoughts and urges of OCD. Schwartz closes the chapter with a proposal for considering the term "mental force" as aptly describing the process by which OCD patients are able to effect the cerebral metabolic changes observed.

As each of the three chapters in this section illustrate, current technologies of human neuroscience are providing exciting new opportunities for examining relationships between brain and consciousness. As also well-illustrated by these chapters, the yield of such technologies in revealing the NCC continues to be heavily dependent upon how well the phenomenology of conscious experience can be assessed or reliably manipulated within the experimental paradigms employed.

References

Bogen, J. E. 1998. Locating the subjectivity pump: The thalamic intralaminar nuclei. In S. R. Hameroff, A. W. Kaszniak, and A. C. Scott, eds., *Toward a Science of Consciousness II: The Second Tucson Discussions and Debates*. Cambridge, Mass.: MIT Press, pp. 237–246.

Crick, F., and C. Koch. 1995. Are we aware of neural activity in primary visual cortex? *Nature* 375:121–123.

Newman, J. 1997. Putting the puzzle together: Towards a general theory of the neural correlates of consciousness. *Journal of Consciousness Studies* 4:47–66.

8 Toward a Cognitive Neuroscience of Consciousness

Antti Revonsuo

Consciousness as a Biological Phenomenon

An essential element of any scientific understanding of consciousness is a systematic, natural-science approach to consciousness, which links consciousness studies with cognitive neuroscience and more generally with the biological sciences. Let us call such a branch of science "Cognitive Neuroscience of Consciousness" (CNC).

Although a substantial part of current empirical work on consciousness, especially on the neural correlates of consciousness, is carried out within a natural science framework, there seems to be no unifying *theoretical* view of consciousness guiding such work. This is a serious weakness for the scientific approach to consciousness, for unless consciousness studies can be theoretically firmly linked with mainstream biological and cognitive science, there is little hope that it will become the widely respected, progressive multidisciplinary field of inquiry that it strives to be.

Developing a theoretical basis for CNC requires close interaction between theoretical and empirical issues. What we first and foremost need is a philosophy of consciousness that could be taken seriously even by empirical neuroscientists. However, if one looks at what several respectable philosophers currently say about the nature of consciousness, one finds a lot of rather peculiar views that could hardly be taken seriously by the craftsmen of a natural-science approach to consciousness. Some, like Dennett (1991), suggest that subjective phenomenal consciousness doesn't *really* exist at all, others, like Chalmers (1996), propose that perhaps consciousness is *everywhere*—even electrons, stones, thermostats and other very simple systems might possess some sort of consciousness. Dretske (1995) and Tye (1995) deny that phenomenal consciousness could be explained by studying the brain—in their view, phenomenology is not inside the brain.

Instead of taking any of those highly exotic philosophical views of consciousness as a starting point, I propose that an empirically based CNC should start with the following simple, clear, and not highly implausible assumption concerning the nature and place of consciousness: "Consciousness (phenomenal experience) is a real, natural, biological phenomenon that literally resides in the brain." That sounds like a reasonable working hypothesis for CNC. Although there are some philosophers who would probably agree with this kind of a view (Searle 1992, Flanagan 1992), it seems that the majority of recent philosophy on consciousness is inconsistent with these assumptions. Indeed, one is inclined to agree with Bruce Mangan's (1998) observation that most philosophy today works *against* viewing consciousness as a biological system.

My intention here is not to analyze in detail all the various views that deny that consciousness is a biological phenomenon in the brain; suffice it to say that they all have deep philosophical problems of their own, in addition to the fact that they could never serve as the theoretical basis of an empirically based CNC. Instead of wasting ammunition for nothing—philosophers rarely give up their views anyway—I believe it is far more fruitful to try to see how we could actually start developing a theoretical basis for empirical CNC. What is needed for CNC to progress is an active interaction between the theoretical and the empirical points of view when trying to understand consciousness as a biological phenomenon, instead of endless arguments with the defenders of all kinds of far-fetched antibiological views.

Consciousness as a Level of Organization

How should we depict consciousness as a biological phenomenon? The general framework used in understanding complex biological systems conceives of them as composed of several different *levels of organization*. Phenomena at different levels of organization in nature (e.g., molecules, cells, organs) are usually quite dissimilar to each other, have distinct causal powers, and require different sorts of approaches to be studied empirically. For example, a single cell is quite dissimilar from the molecules that it is composed of and from the tissues and organs that it may be a part of. Levels of organization are seen as really existing out there in nature. Our biological theories attempt to capture these levels by postulating abstract models and conceptual systems that describe the levels and explain the relations between the different levels. Our theories thus have levels of description and explanation thought to correspond to the levels of organization actually existing in nature.

If this general framework is taken seriously in consciousness research, then CNC should *reconceptualize* consciousness as *the phenomenal level of organization in the brain*. This sort of characterization makes it perfectly clear that we are dealing with a real biological phenomenon; an integral feature of the brain as a biological system. This view leaves no room for arguments that try to separate consciousness from the brain by insisting that we can imagine a complete neurobiological description of the brain that does not tell us anything about consciousness. A complete description of the brain as a biological system *necessarily includes* a description of the phenomenal level of organization in the brain. If we fail to understand subjective phenomenal consciousness we will have failed to exhaustively understand the brain as a biological system.

Explaining consciousness involves finding answers to the following questions: What is the phenomenal level of organization like? Where can it be found? How could it be revealed to the methods of empirical science? How is it brought about by the underlying lower levels of organization? The first question is the one we have to start with, for it is the basic question concerning the systematic *description* of the phenomenon we are interested in. Any empirically based scientific discipline must start with systematic description, and it is the indispensable foundation of all explanatory research in biology as well (Mayr 1996).

Here we encounter one of the principal problems in current research on consciousness: it seems to operate at two levels of description only: first, the level of the cognitive (information-processing) mechanisms and second, the level of the neural mechanisms or neural correlates of those cognitive mechanisms. The most important level of description in consciousness research, namely that of phenomenal organization, surprisingly enough has no central role in current theorizing. Without a systematic description of the phenomenal level, however, it does not make much sense to chart the cognitive or neural mechanisms of consciousness, for it remains quite unclear what all those detailed mechanisms are supposed to be mechanisms *of*. The point is that a science of consciousness must first treat the phenomenal level of organization as a proper level of description. The lower levels of explanatory mechanisms can be invoked only after we have a clear conception of the phenomenon that these mechanisms are supposed to explain.

It is not too difficult to see why this lack of phenomenological description prevails in consciousness research: there is no well-established empirically based framework to turn to. In the history of psychology, introspectionism once failed, and many still feel that an empirically based scientific phenomenology is outright impossible. Phenomenology as practiced in philosophical circles seems to be too obscure and conceptually isolated from current cognitive neuroscience to be of any real value for the empirically minded scientist. Furthermore, some philosophers are not too optimistic about the prospects of an "objective phenomenology" (Nagel 1974). Thus, it is no wonder that in consciousness research conceptual frameworks are primarily taken from the empirically respectable and well-established branches of cognitive science and neuroscience. The problem, however, is that the science of consciousness is not simply a trivial further branch of those fields: standard mainstream cognitive science and neuroscience largely ignore consciousness; they will not provide us with adequate levels of description to handle phenomenal experience.

I suggest that the science of consciousness needs to develop *a phenomenal level of description* that systematically captures the phenomenal level of organization in the brain. This level of description cannot be imported from any other existing branch of science—it must be contributed by the science of consciousness itself.

Metaphors and Model Systems

How should we go about developing a better understanding of the phenomenal level? I propose that we compare this task with previous attempts to describe and understand other complex biological phenomena. At a stage when no well-developed theory of a given phenomenon is available, the researchers tend to describe it in terms of a suitable metaphor. For example at the time when biologists had little idea what the internal structure and chemical composition of genes was, they nevertheless were able to construct very useful models of genes by treating them as distinct units that are arranged linearly just like "beads on a string." This was a simple, powerful metaphor that guided the thinking in classical genetics for a long time. To take another example, cell cleavage patterns were represented in what were called *soap-bubble models*, and this analogy even allowed researchers to suggest theoretical explanations about cells based on knowledge about soap bubbles (Maienschein 1991). Thus, a good metaphor captures some of the essential features of the phenomenon in a form that is easily comprehensible and visualizable.

Metaphors have been used in current consciousness research, but I am afraid that most of them have not been constructed so as to capture the phenomenal level of organization specifically. The lack of phenomenology is reflected in the Theater Metaphor of consciousness (Baars 1997), which may be a fitting metaphor of the cognitive *mechanisms* of consciousness, but does not seem to catch the level of phenomenology at all that well. To be conscious does not typically feel like sitting in a dark theater and looking at characters or events appearing on a faraway stage. Rather, my moment-to-moment consciousness feels like being immersed into the center of a multimodal world that is present for me all at once, though I may pay focal attention only to a certain feature of it. The phenomenal level includes the externalized sensory events, my own body-image, and those events that I feel going on inside my body or my mind (emotions, inner speech). Therefore, we need a different kind of metaphor and a different conceptual framework in order to capture the level of phenomenal representation, or consciousness *itself* (but not necessarily its neurocognitive mechanisms).

A model system is a system in which the phenomenon of interest manifests itself in a particularly clear form. In the ideal case the phenomenon is clearly isolated from others with which it might otherwise be confused, and it is accessible to easy observation or manipulation by the researchers. The model system may otherwise not be prominent in any way; just consider the significance of the lowly fruit fly *Drosophila melanogaster* for the development of genetics.

I believe that the dreaming brain is an excellent source of both a model system and a metaphor of the phenomenal level of organization. We know from empirical dream research that *the phenomenal level of organization is fully realized in the dreaming brain*. The visual appearance of dreams is practically identical with that of the waking world (Rechschaffen and Buchignani 1992). When we dream, we typically have the experience of being in the center of a spatially extended world of objects and people, with all kinds of events going on around us. We have a body-image much like the one we experience during waking, and we apparently can control its actions and sense our own movement through dreamed space. We know that during REM-sleep, with which vivid dreaming typically is associated, the brain suppresses the processing of sensory information, but at the same time it activates itself internally. The motor output mechanisms are inhibited and voluntary muscles are virtually paralyzed, although motor commands are actively produced in the brain.

The dreaming brain shows us that sensory input and motor output are not *necessary* for producing a fully realized phenomenal level of organization. The dreaming brain creates the phenomenal level in an isolated form and in that sense provides us with insights into the processes that are *sufficient* for producing the phenomenal level. At the same time the dreaming brain is an excellent reminder of the subjectivity of conscious states: there is no way we can directly "see" another person's dream world. However, we have a large body of empirical data on the phenomenological contents of dreaming, thanks to the development of systematic collection of dream reports and quantitative methods in dream content analysis (Domhoff 1996). Quantitative dream content analysis may be the sole example of a field in which systematic empirically based descriptive phenomenology is practiced today.

So the dreaming brain is a good model system for consciousness research because it isolates the phenomenal level from other systems that it might be confused with, it underscores the subjectivity of the phenomenon, invites questions as to the possibilities of directly observing or imaging the phenomenal level, and it has resulted in empirical research with a systematic methodology and body of quantitative data based on phenomenological description.

The dreaming brain furthermore provides us with a proper metaphor of the phenomenal level itself. When the phenomenal level is fully realized, as it is in the dreaming brain, it is characterized by the *sense of presence in* or *immersion into* a multimodal experiential reality. These terms were originally launched to describe experiences created with the help of a virtual reality (VR) system. But of course these terms do not describe the computers or the programs in a VR system, but the subjective *experience* that such systems at their best can create. In developing such vocabulary I think the VR-community has done a valuable service to consciousness research, because what they have come up with are terms that capture the realization of subjective phenomenal organization from the first person's point of view.

The Virtual Reality Metaphor of Consciousness

I have proposed (Revonsuo 1995, 1997) that we should take the concept of Virtual Reality as a metaphor for consciousness. To briefly summarize the ideas behind the VR-metaphor, when the brain realizes the phenomenal level it is actually creating the experience that *I am directly present in a world outside my brain* although the experience itself is brought about by neural systems buried *inside* the brain. The brain is essentially creating an "Out-of-the-Brain-Experience": the sense of presence in and the full immersion into a seemingly real world outside the brain. This is immediately obvious when we consider dreaming: there we are, in the middle of a strange dream world, but it never occurs to us to conceptualize it in any other terms than as a *world* or a *place* where we find ourselves in. Almost all dream reports begin by specifying the place in which the subject has found himself in the dream. We never come to think about the dream world as showing us how our own brain looks from the inside, although we know quite certainly that that's where all the fun is really taking place.

The phenomenal level of organization realizes what I call "Virtual Presence." Dreaming involves it in two different senses: first, there is the illusion that the experiential events do not take place inside my brain, but somewhere in an externalized perceptual world. Second, dreaming involves the further illusion that I am not present in the environment where my physical body actually is located and sleeping. In this sense dreaming creates a completely imaginary presence, just like the technological variety of virtual reality does. Waking perception, however, only involves the first kind of illusion and thus creates a sort of *telepresence* for the brain: the sense of direct presence in the world currently surrounding the body and modulating sensory input. The brain and the phenomenal level together with it, actually constituting this experience, reside deep inside the skull, never actually directly in touch with external objects.

The phenomenal level of organization can thus be seen as the brain's *natural virtual reality system*, a level of organization the purpose of which it is to construct a real-time simulation of the organism and its place in the world. This simulation is modulated by sensory information during waking perception, but during dreaming it is realized off-line, by recombining materials from experiences stored in long-term memory. In everyday thinking we rarely realize that what we directly experience is merely a clever *simulation* or *model* of the world, provided by the brain, not the world itself. In order to be an *effective* simulation, we are supposed to take it as the real thing, and that is exactly what we do even during dreaming.

Why does the brain bother to create a detailed model of the world for us (or rather for itself)? Obviously in order to guide the organism through paths that enhance its chances of survival and succesful reproduction in the real world. An excellent example of the importance of the phenomenal level in the guidance of behavior is a sleep disorder called *REM Sleep Behavior Disorder (RBD)*. Patients with RBD do not become paralyzed during REM sleep as they ought to: the mechanisms of motor inhibition fail. Consequently, the patients act out the behavior that they dream about. If they are chased in the dream, they jump out of their beds and start to run for their lives. If they are attacked in the dream, they defend themselves and may kick around or throw punches at invisible enemies.

A subject with RBD is phenomenologically immersed into a dream world, but behaviorally interacting with the real physical environment, often with unfortunate consequences. Obviously, one cannot get very far in the real world if one has an entirely erroneous model of the world in consciousness. Thus, these patients often suffer all kinds of physical injuries during their attempted dream enactments and may even get seriously injured. For example, a 73-year-old man with RBD, when dreaming, attempted to catch a running man. His wife reported that he jumped off the end of the bed and awoke on the floor, badly injured (Dyken et al. 1995). If an epidemic of RBD suddenly were to spread, all of us would behave in bizarre ways every night, guided by whatever the nocturnal contents of the phenomenal level of organization would happen to be.

The brain constructs the phenomenal level of organization because that level is needed in mediating voluntary behavior. The content of the phenomenal level is ultimately the world as it is *for* the conscious organism: the world that the individual attempts to *interact with* and to which it attempts to *adapt to* through voluntary behavior. This crucial role in mediating voluntary, adaptive behavior, although functioning all the time in waking perception, becomes dramatically revealed when a full-scale hallucinatory world, such as we have during dreaming, guides our behavior.

An important implication of the Virtual Reality Metaphor is that this metaphor defines a framework for an empirically based phenomenology. The scope of a science of phenomenology could be depicted as *the systematical description of the normal structure and the pathological breakdown of the phenomenal level of organization in the brain*. We need to develop conceptual frameworks to systematically describe the different ways in which the structure of the phenomenal level can be distorted or break down in consequence of brain injury or in altered states of consciousness. The binding problem can be seen as the question of how the organization at the phenomenal level can become integrated or disintegrated as a result of normal or abnormal functioning of underlying integrative neurocognitive mechanisms. Similarly, the bizarreness of dream images could be conceptualized as specific distortions of the contents at the phenomenal level.

I believe that the critical question for the future of consciousness research is: Can we describe consciousness systematically even on its own terms? If not, the prospects for being able to understand its relations to other levels of organization look dim at best. Without a description of the phenomenal level of organization, cognitive neuroscience explanations of consciousness seem futile. The Virtual Reality Metaphor is my suggestion as to where we could start looking for such a description.

Empirical Approaches in the Science of Consciousness

Discovering the neural correlates of conscious states is certainly one of the most important tasks for an empirical science of consciousness. When engaged in such work we should, however, be quite well aware of what it is that we are actually measuring, and whether it has anything to do with the phenomenal level of organization at all.

Many highly interesting studies have been published lately, for example, on the neural correlates of binocular rivalry and on the neural representation of perceptual unity as high-frequency synchronization of neural activity. When it comes to the science of consciousness one annoying point is that most of this data is from animal subjects, mostly cats and monkeys. The unfortunate fact is that we are able to have any real access only to human phenomenology, and therefore the science of consciousness should mostly (but not solely) be based on results from human studies. In the rest of the present chapter, I review our studies on the neural correlates of human visual awareness.

We tested two hypotheses that were originally presented by Crick and Koch (1990, 1995). First, in which visual cortical areas are the neural correlates of visual awareness located? Crick and Koch (1995) argue that primates are not directly aware of neural activation in V1, but that they may be aware of activity in other visual cortical areas. We measured cortical magnetic responses (122-channel MEG) to visual awareness of objects in an object detection task (Vanni, Revonsuo, Saarinen, and Hari 1996).

In the task, the subjects (N = 8) were shown pictures of coherent and meaningful objects as well as disorganized and meaningless nonobjects (one picture at a time), using brief stimulus durations (30, 46 and 106 milliseconds) and masked stimuli. The subject's task was to detect the objects and to report (by lifting a finger) when he saw a coherent and meaningful object. If nothing at all or nothing coherent and meaningful was perceived, the subject lifted another finger. Less than 50% of the objects were detected at the shortest stimulus duration (30 ms), but performance was very close to 100% of correct detections at the longest stimulus duration (106 ms).

Source modeling of the evoked neuromagnetic signals was used in order to reveal the location of active brain areas. Although several different areas were more strongly activated by objects than nonobjects, the activation of only one area (the right lateral occipital cortex, possibly human V4) became stronger with increasing stimulus duration and directly correlated with the proportion of correct object detections (i.e., with visual awareness of the objects). Visual objects are represented and processed at multiple levels in the brain, but not all these representations are directly reflected in visual awareness. The right lateral occipital cortex seems to be specifically involved in the emergence of visual awareness of coherent objects. This is in accordance with the Crick and Koch hypothesis that the direct neural correlates of visual awareness are located in the extrastriatal visual areas, not in V1.

Second, the hypothesis that high-frequency neural oscillations around 40-Hz are associated with the binding of visual percepts into coherent wholes (Crick and Koch 1990) was tested by measuring EEG in a task in which the subjects perceived the same stimulus (a random dot stereogram) in one condition as an incoherent collection of random dots and in another as a coherent three-dimensional Gestalt (Revonsuo, Wilenius-Emet, Kuusela and Lehto 1997). Continuous viewing of the same stimulus in the incoherent vs. coherent condition was not associated with significant differences in 40-Hz synchronization. Thus, although there is *a radical phenomenological difference* between these two stable views of the stimulus, *no corresponding difference at the neurophysiological level* in 40-Hz power was detected. Next, we tested the hypothesis that the *construction* of the coherent Gestalt in visual awareness is perhaps accompanied by transient 40-Hz synchronization. The subjects free-fused the random-dot stereogram and pushed a button as soon as they saw the three-dimensional Gestalt clearly. In a control condition, they fused a stimulus from which no unified percept emerged. Event-related 40-Hz synchronization was observed 500–300 milliseconds before visual awareness of the coherent percept was reported, at right posterior and occipital electrode sites. 40-Hz activity thus seems to participate in the construction of the unified percept, perhaps by rapidly binding spatially distributed neural populations together. Consequently, the hypotheses presented by Crick and Koch on the neural basis of visual awareness were supported by our studies with human subjects.

Conclusions

The further development of an empirically based science of consciousness will, I believe, depend on whether we are able to take consciousness seriously as a biological phenomenon in the brain, and start creating the appropriate theoretical and empirical basis for such a science. If this attempt fails, or worse yet, if we fail to give it a serious try, we might see consciousness studies slowly fading from mainstream cognitive neuroscience, in spite of it being precisely the branch of empirical science supposed to explain how the brain generates the mind and consciousness. As I have attempted to show in the present chapter, the cognitive neuroscience of consciousness surely deserves to be given a serious try right now, instead of our resorting to increasingly bizarre philosophical speculations on the nature of consciousness.

Acknowledgment

The writing of this chapter was supported by the Academy of Finland (project 36106).

References

Baars, B. J. 1997. *In the Theater of Consciousness: The Workspace of the Mind.* New York: Oxford University Press.

Chalmers, D. J. 1996. *The Conscious Mind.* Oxford: Oxford University Press.

Crick, F. and Koch, C. 1990. *Towards a neurobiological theory of consciousness.* Seminars in the Neurosciences 2:273–304.

Crick, F. and Koch, C. 1995. Are we aware of neural activity in primary visual cortex? *Nature* 375:121–123.

Dennett, D. C. 1991. *Consciousness Explained,* Boston: Little, Brown.

Domhoff, G. W. 1996. *Finding Meaning in Dreams.* New York: Plenum.

Dretske, F. 1995. *Naturalizing the Mind.* Cambridge, MA.: MIT Press.

Dyken, M. E., Lin-Dyken, D. C., Seaba, P. and Yamada, T. 1995. Violent sleep-related behavior leading to subdural hemorrhage. *Archives of Neurology* 52:318–321.

Flanagan, O. 1992. *Consciousness Reconsidered,* Cambridge, Mass.: MIT Press.

Mangan, B. 1998. Consciousness, biological systems, and the fallacy of functional exclusion. *Consciousness Research Abstracts,* Toward a Science of Consciousness, Tucson III, p. 52.

Maienschein, J. 1991. From presentation to representation in E. B. Wilson's The Cell. *Biology and Philosophy* 6:227–254.

Mayr, E. 1996. *This is Biology.* Cambridge, Mass.: Belknap / Harvard University Press.

Rechtschaffen, A. and Buchignani, C. 1992. The visual appearance of dreams. In: *The Neuropsychology of Sleep and Dreaming,* ed. J. S. Antrobus and M. Bertini, 143–155. Hillsdale, N.J.: Lawrence Erlbaum.

Revonsuo, A. 1995. Consciousness, dreams, and virtual realities. *Philosophical Psychology* 8:35–58.

Revonsuo, A. 1997. How to take consciousness seriously in cognitive neuroscience. *Consciousness and Cognition* 30:185–206.

Revonsuo, A., Wilenius-Emet, M., Kuusela, J. and Lehto, M. 1997. The neural generation of a unified illusion in human vision. *NeuroReport* 8 18:3867–3870.

Searle, J. R. 1992. *The Rediscovery of the Mind*, Cambridge, Mass.: MIT Press.

Tye, M. 1995. *Ten Problems of Consciousness. A Representational Theory of the Phenomenal Mind.* Cambridge, Mass.: MIT Press.

Vanni, S., Revonsuo, A., Saarinen, J. and Hari, R. 1996. Visual awareness of objects correlates with activity of right occipital cortex. *NeuroReport* 8:183–186.

9 Neural Correlates of Hallucinogen-induced Altered States of Consciousness

F. X. Vollenweider, A. Gamma, and M. F. I. Vollenweider-Scherpenhuyzen

The study of hallucinogens ("psychedelics") and related substances offers a promising avenue to investigate biological correlates of altered states of consciousness (ASC) (Vollenweider 1998a). In combination with functional brain imaging techniques and pharmacological methodologies, these compounds are remarkable molecular probes into the biochemistry and functional organization of the brain in nonordinary states. The study of hallucinogens in humans is important firstly because they profoundly affect a number of brain functions that characterize the human mind, including cognition, volition, emotion, ego and self-awareness, which cannot be reliably studied in behavioral animal models. Secondly, they are important because they elicit a clinical syndrome resembling in several aspects the first manifestation of schizophrenic disorders (Gouzoulis-Mayfrank et al. 1998). The various forms of ego alterations are especially prominent features of psychedelic and naturally occurring psychoses. These alterations may range from a slight loosening of ego boundaries to a dissolving of ego into an ecstatic oneness with the cosmos. The dissolution of the self as a center of reference, however, can also evoke anxiety and feelings of fragmentation, confusion and disorganization resembling the core features of schizophrenic ego disorders. Hence, studies of the neuronal mechanisms of hallucinogen action should provide not only novel insights into the pathophysiology of psychiatric disorders and their treatment, but, in a broader sense, into the biology of consciousness as a whole, for example, into the biology of ego structuring processes.

In the present contribution, we wish to summarize some of our recent results and advances in hallucinogen research, which are the result of human studies conducted in our group. We have developed different strategies to explore the pharmacological effects of hallucinogens on brain functions. The basic approaches are to investigate hallucinogen-induced metabolic changes with fluorodeoxyglucose (FDG) and to characterize functional interactions of neurotransmitter systems by assessing hallucinogen-induced displacement of specific radiolabeled receptor ligands using positron emission tomography (PET) (Vollenweider 1998a). A human model of sensory gating deficits, the cortico-striato-thalamo-cortical (CSTC) loop model, will be introduced to provide a perspective how current knowledge about hallucinogen drug action could be visualized within a synthetic framework to explain its subjective effects in humans. Hypotheses derived from this model were tested in several FDG-PET studies, and correlational analyses between hallucinogen-induced brain activity changes and phenomenological dimensions of ASC were computed to elucidate the neuronal correlates of ASC.

Measurement of Psychological Dimensions of ASC

In the context of the present theme—relating psychological and biological effects of hallucinogens—the assessment and characterization of altered states of consciousness (ASC) is of fundamental importance. Among several rating scales, the APZ questionnaire has become the standard in Europe for measuring specific states of consciousness and has been used on a routine basis by our group. The APZ questionnaire was developed based on a large prospective study with 393 subjects tested with cannabinoids, dimethyltryptamine, psilocybin, mescaline, harmaline, nitrous oxide, hypnosis, autogenic training, and meditation techniques (Dittrich 1998). It measures three primary and one secondary etiology-independent dimensions of ASC. The first dimension designated "oceanic boundlessness" (OSE) measures derealization phenomena and ego-dissolution, which are associated with a pleasurable emotional state ranging from heightened mood to sublime happiness and exaltation. Ego-dissolution can start with a mere loosening of ego-boundaries but may end up in a feeling of merging with the cosmos, where the experience of time has changed or completely vanished. If fully developed, this state might be comparable to a mystical experience. The second dimension "Anxious ego-dissolution" (AIA) measures thought disorder, ego-disintegration, loss of autonomy and self-control variously associated with arousal, anxiety, and paranoid feelings. The third subscale "visionary restructuralization" (VUS) refers to auditory and visual illusions, hallucinations, synesthetic phenomena, as well as altered experience of meaning and ideas of reference. The intercultural consistency of the APZ dimensions OSE, AIA and VUS has been rigorously tested in a subsequent study, the International Study on Altered States of Consciousness (ISASC), and the dimensions have been shown to be altered consistently in a manner that is independent of the particular treatment, disorder, or condition that led to the ASC (Dittrich 1998).

So far, the APZ questionnaire has been used by our group to characterize the psychological effects of hallucinogens (psilocybin) (Vollenweider et al. 1997c), dissociative anesthetics (ketamine) (Vollenweider et al. 1997a, Vollenweider et al. 1997b), stimulants (amphetamine) (Vollenweider et al. 1998b), and entactogens (MDMA) (Vollenweider et al. 1998c) (figure 9.1).

Another psychometric scale that has proved useful for assessing specific dimensions of ego disorders is the "Ego Pathology Inventory" (EPI) developed by Scharfetter (Scharfetter 1981). The EPI has been divided empirically into five dimensions describing ego pathology and related behavior: ego identity, ego demarcation, ego consistency, ego activity and ego vitality. The "ego identity" scale includes items of doubts, changes or loss of one's identity in respect to "gestalt," physiognomy, gender,

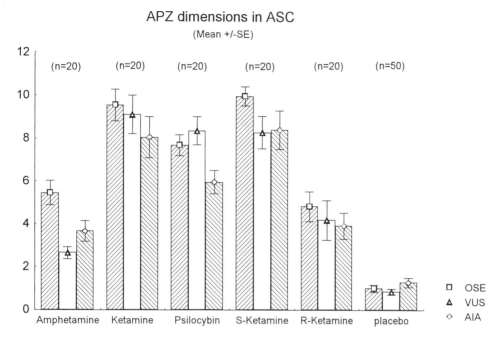

Figure 9.1
Mean values of APZ scores under hallucinogenic and stimulant drugs compared to placebo. The euphoric-submanic state induced by amphetamine is clearly different from the hallucinogenic state induced by psilocybin and ketamine. See text for abbreviations.

genealogical origin and biography. The "ego demarcation" scale refers to one's uncertainty or lack of differentiation between ego and non-ego spheres concerning thought process, affective state and body experience. The "ego consistency" scale comprises dissolution, splitting and destruction in experiencing a coherent self, body, thought process, chain of feelings and a structured external world. The "ego activity" scale refers to the deficit in one's ability, potency or power for self-determined action, thinking, feeling and perceiving. The "ego vitality" scale includes the experience or fear of one's death, of the fading away of liveliness, of the demise of mankind or the universe.

As seen in figure 9.2, acute first-break schizophrenics differ from psilocybin and ketamine subjects most markedly in the extent of their impairment of ego activity and ego vitality. Notwithstanding, the similar range of values for the ego identity, ego demarcation and ego consisteny score indicates the similarity between hallucinogen-induced and endogenous psychotic states.

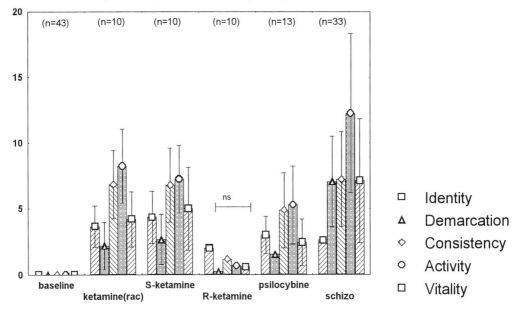

Figure 9.2
Mean EPI scores obtained from human subjects in drug-induced ASC and drug-free state compared to first episode schizophrenics. See text for explanations.

The CSTC Model of Sensory Information Processing and ASC

Based on the available neuroanatomical evidence and pharmacological findings of psychedelic drug action, we propose a cortico-subcortical model of psychosensory information processing that can be used as a starting point to analyze and integrate the effects of different chemical types of hallucinogens at a system level. The model advances that psychedelic states can be conceptualized as complex disturbances arising from more elementary deficits of sensory information processing in cortico-striato-thalamo-cortical (CSTC) feedback loops. The model is not entirely new, it incorporates the idea that psychotic symptoms might relate to a dopaminergic and/or dopaminergic-glutamatergic neurotransmitter dysbalance in mesolimbic and/or mesolimbic-corticostriatal pathways (Carlsson and Carlsson 1990), but it extends this hypothesis, insofar that the serotonergic and GABAergic neurotransmission are also brought into the scheme (Vollenweider 1992, Vollenweider 1994).

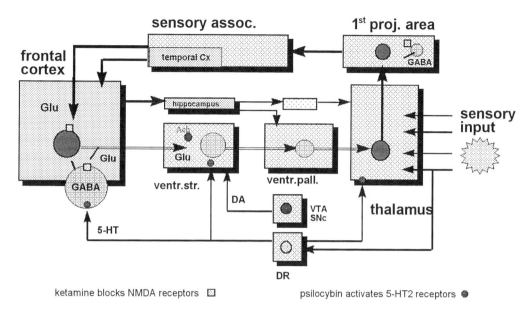

Figure 9.3
The CSTC loop model of sensory information processing. See text for explanations.

In short, five CSTC loops have been identified and each loop, functioning in parallel, is thought to mediate a different set of functions; the motor, the oculomotor, the prefrontal, the association and the limbic loop. The limbic loop is involved in memory, learning and self-nonself discrimination by linking of cortical categorized exteroceptive perception and internal stimuli of the value system. The limbic loop originates in the medial and lateral temporal lobe and hippocampal formation and projects to the ventral striatum. Projections from this region then converge on the ventral pallidum and feed back via the thalamus to the anterior cingulate and the orbitofrontal cortex (figure 9.3).

The CSTC model posits that the thalamus acts as a filter or gating mechanism for the extero- and interoceptive information flow to the cerebral cortex and that deficits in thalamic gating may lead to a sensory overload of the cortex, which in turn may cause the sensory flooding, cognitive fragmentation and ego-dissolution seen in drug-induced ASC and endogenous psychotic states. The filter capability of the thalamus is thought to be under the control of cortico-striato-thalamic (CST) feedback loops. Specifically, it is hypothesized that the striatum and pallidum exert an inhibitory influence on the thalamus. Inhibition of the thalamus should result in a decrease of sensory input to the cortex and in a reduction of arousal, protecting the cerebral cortex from sensory overload and breakdown of its integrative capacity. The striatal activity is modulated by a number of subsidiary circuits and neurotransmitter systems, respectively. The mesostriatal and mesolimbic projections provide an inhibitory dopaminergic input to the striatum. Under physiological conditions, the inhibitory influence of the dopaminergic systems on the striatum is, however, thought to be counterbalanced by the glutamatergic excitatory input from cortico-striatal pathways. This assumption implies that an increase in dopaminergic tone (e.g., by amphetamine) as well as a decrease in glutamatergic neurotransmission (e.g., by ketamine) should lead to a reduction of the inhibitory influence of the striatum on the thalamus and result in a opening of the thalamic "filter" and, subsequently, in a sensory overload of the cerebral cortex and psychotic symptom formation. Finally, the reticular formation, which is activated by input from all sensory modalities, gives rise to serotonergic projections to the components of the CST loops. Excessive activation of the postsynaptic elements of the serotonergic projection sites (e.g., by psilocybin) should also result in a reduction of thalamic gating and, consequently, in a sensory overload of frontal cortex and psychosis.

First Results Testing the CSTC Model

Although the CSTC model is an oversimplification, it provides a set of testable hypotheses. According to the CSTC model we have hypothesized that both the reduction of glutamatergic transmission by the NMDA antagonist ketamine and stimulation of the serotonergic system by the mixed 5-HT$_{2/1}$ agonist psilocybin should lead to a sensory overload and metabolic activation of the frontal cortex (hyperfrontality). This hypothesis has been tested in healthy volunteers using positron emission tomography (PET) and the radioligand [18F]fluorodeoxyglucose (FDG). In fact, it was possible to confirm the central hypothesis of a frontocortical activation in psychedelic states. Both ketamine and psilocybin led to a marked metabolic activation of the frontal cortex, including the anterior cingulate, and a number of overlapping metabolic changes in other brain regions (Vollenweider et al. 1997b, Vollenweider et al. 1997c).

The observed hyperfrontality is interesting in several ways. First, the marked stimulation of the frontal cortex, the anterior cingulate, the temporomedial cortex and the thalamus seen in psilocybin and ketamine subjects accords with the thalamic filter theory suggesting that a disruption of the cortico-striato-thalamic (CST-) loop should lead to a sensory overload of the frontal cortex and its limbic relay stations. Second, hallucinogen-induced hyperfrontality is of particular interest because it appears to parallel similar findings in acutely ill schizophrenic and nonschizophrenic psychotic patients (Ebmeier et al. 1995, Sabri et al. 1997). Third, the hyperfrontality after ketamine and psilocybin also supports the idea that the psychedelics used in these studies may mediate their effects through a common final pathway or neurotransmitter system, downstream to their primary locus of action (see Vollenweider 1998a for a review).

Patterns of Cortical Activity in ASC

A multivariate analysis of metabolic and psychological data and a relatively large sample size (e.g., 50–100 subjects) are imperative if the common neuroanatomical substrates of ASC are to be identified accurately. Therefore, a number of additional placebo-controlled FDG-PET experiments with S-ketamine, R-ketamine and amphetamine were performed in normal subjects (Vollenweider et al. 1997a, Vollenweider et al. 1998b). To identify the interactive organization of the brain in resting state and ASC, normalized metabolic PET data from placebo and corresponding drug conditions were subjected to a factor analysis, and factor scores for each individual subjects were computed (n = 106). Surprisingly, this computation revealed that the cortical-subcortical organization (based on a five-factor solution) during ASC was very similar to that seen under placebo, indicating that the functional integrity of interrelated brain regions (factors), which might be interpreted as functional "units" or "modules," is not disrupted in ASC (see figure 9.4). According to their content, the factors were labeled "fronto-parietal cortex," "temporal cortex," "occipital cortex," "striatum" (which included the caudate nucleus and putamen) and "thalamus." Subsequent comparison of the factor scores of drug and placebo condition revealed that subjects had significantly higher scores on the "frontal-parietal" and "striatal" network and lower scores on the "occipital cortex" during hallucinatory states than in resting states. This finding indicates that the neuronal activity within these modules and the more global relationship between these modules differs markedly between ASC and normal waking state.

Multiple regression analysis of psychological scores (APZ scores) and factor scores (normalized metabolic activity) revealed, firstly, that the dimension OSE (oceanic boundlessness) relates to changes in metabolic activity in the frontal-parietal cortex, occipital cortex and striatum. Secondly, VUS (visionary restructuralization including hallucinatory phenomena) is associated with activity changes in the same network as the OSE dimension, but additionally relates to temporal activity. Thirdly, AIA (anxious ego-dissolution) is primarily associated with metabolic changes in the

- ◆ Factor I: frontomedial, frontolateral, cingulate ant. and post., parietal, and sensorimotor Cortex
- ◆ Factor II: occipitomedial and -lateral Cortex
- ◆ Factor III: temporomedial and lateral Cortex
- ◆ Factor IV: caudate nucleus, putamen
- ◆ Factor V: thalamus

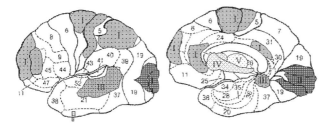

Figure 9.4
Anatomical localization of the five cortical-subcortical area factors identified by factor analysis from 14 cortical/subcortical regions of interest. Each factor represents a functional "unit" or "module" of highly intercorrelated brain regions. Descriptive names of the brain regions involved in each factor are given in the figure.

thalamus (table 9.1). The observed association between AIA and increased relative metabolic activity in the thalamus is underscored by the finding of a positive correlation between ego-identity impairment and the thalamic factor.

The present data show that the positively experienced form of ego-dissolution, OSE, can be clearly differentiated in terms of neurometabolic activity from the more fragmented and anxious ego-dissolution AIA. The OSE dimension, which relates to the pleasurable experience of dissolution of ego-boundaries, possibly culminating in transcendental or "mystical" states, and the altered perception of time and space, substantially loads on the fronto-parietal factor. Indeed, according to current views, the frontal cortex in conjunction with parietal and limbic areas, is critical for the construction and maintenance of a coherent self. In its executive faculty, the frontal cortex, including the anterior cingulate, has an active role in structuring time, directing attention to relevant extero- or interoceptive stimuli and initiating and expressing appropriate behaviors (Milner et al. 1985, Fuster 1989, Posner and Petersen 1990). The parietal cortex is important for determining the relationship of the self to extrapersonal space, based on visuospatial input from the dorsal stream (Pribram 1991). It is noteworthy that the fronto-parietal factor also includes somatosensory and motor cortical areas, which contribute essential information to the formation of

Table 9.1
The relationship between the APZ scores OSE, VUS and AIA, and the EPI score ego-identity impairment and normalized metabolic activity in the five functional brain modules (factors) identified by factor analysis. F1 (fronto-parietal factor), F2 (occipital factor), F3 (temporal factor), F4 (striatal factor), F5 (thalamic factor). Factors which significantly contribute to the computation are indicated by asterisks *p < 0.05.

OSE	$= 0.32\ F_1{}^*$	$-0.20\ F_2{}^*$	$+0.11\ F_3$	$+0.20\ F_4{}^*$	$+0.05\ F_5$
VUS	$= 0.20\ F_1{}^*$	$-0.27\ F_2{}^*$	$+0.17\ F_3{}^*$	$+0.32\ F_4{}^*$	$+0.10\ F_5$
AIA	$= 0.00\ F_1$	$+0.09\ F_2$	$+0.01\ F_3$	$+0.17\ F_4$	$+0.28\ F_5{}^*$
Identity	$= 0.04\ F_1$	$-0.04\ F_2$	$+0.05\ F_3$	$+0.10\ F_4$	$+0.20\ F_5{}^*$

body image and physical representation of the self. As an interrelated network, the areas of the fronto-parietal factor are sometimes called "Central Neural Authority" (Hernegger 1995) to express the idea that they constitute a functional system crucially involved in ego-structuring processes and the formation of a coherent self defined in time and space. Based on these theoretical concepts, it appears well plausible that overstimulation of the Central Neural Authority may lead to profound alterations of self-experience and space/time perception, as reflected by the increased OSE scores in hallucinogen-induced ASC.

Anxious ego-dissolution (AIA) and ego-identity impairment appear to depend mainly on thalamic activity. This finding is in line with the view that dysfunction of the thalamic filter could lead to sensory overload, cognitive fragmentation and psychosis, as it is postulated by the CSTC model. Interestingly, increased thalamic activity with new exacerbation of psychotic symptoms was also observed in neuroleptic-stabilized patients after ketamine administration.

Outlook

Hallucinogen research offers the exciting possibility to explore how our experience of self and ego relates to the complex interplay of neural networks in the brain, and, more generally, to narrow the gap between the mental and the physical. Due to the similarity of hallucinogen-induced states and endogenous psychoses, it can also enhance our understanding of the pathophysiology of neuropsychiatric disorders. The CSTC model presented here provides a useful starting point from which to approach the functional organization of the brain in drug-induced or naturally occurring ASC.

It should be noted, however, that the present correlations, which are based on aggregated observations over time (APZ ratings, metabolism) and space (brain regions), though probably correct in the order of magnitude, might be inadequate at a finer level of resolution. New methodologies with a high time resolution such as

3D-electromagnetic tomography (Pasqual-Marqui et al. 1994) will allow us to also capture the temporal microdynamics of brain processes in ASC.

Acknowledgments

This study was supported in part by the Swiss National Science Foundation (Grants: 32-28746, 32-32418, and 32-04090). The authors wish to thank Prof. Ch. Scharfetter for providing data on schizophrenia patients and Prof. A. Dittrich, PSIN, for statistical advice.

References

Carlsson, M., and Carlsson, A. 1990. Schizophrenia: A subcortical neurotransmitter imbalance syndrome? *Schizophrenia Bull* 16:425–432.

Dittrich, A. 1998. The standardized psychometric assessment of altered states of consciousness (ASCs) in humans. *Pharmacopsychiat* 31:80–84.

Ebmeier, K. P., Lawrie, S. M., Blackwood, D. H., Johnstone, E. C., and Goodwin, G. M. (1995). Hypofrontality revisited: a high resolution single photon emission computed tomography study in schizophrenia. *J Neurol Neurosurg Psychiat* 58:452–456.

Fuster, J. M. (1989). *The prefrontal cortex*. New York: Raven Press.

Gouzoulis-Mayfrank, E., Hermle, L., Thelen, B., and Sass, H. (1998): History, rationale and potential of human experimental hallucinogen drug research in psychiatry. *Pharmacopsychiat* 31:63–68.

Hernegger R. (1995). *Wahrnehmung und Bewusstsein. Ein Diskussionsbeitrag zur Neuropsychologie*. Berlin: Spectrum Akademischer Verlag.

Milner, B., Pertrides, M., and Smith, M. L. (1985). Frontal lobes and the temporal organisation of memory. *Hum Neurobiol* 4:137–142.

Pasqual-Marqui, R. D., Michel, C. M., and Lehmann, D. (1994). Low resolution electromagnetic tomography: a new method for localizing electrical activity in the brain. *Int J Psychophysiol* 18:49–65.

Posner, M. I., Petersen, S. E. (1990). The attention system of the human brain. *Ann Rev Neurosci* 13:25–42.

Pribram, K. H. (1991). *Brain and Perception*. Hillsdale, N.J.: Lawrence Erlbaum Associates.

Sabri, O., Erkwoh, R., Schreckenberger, M., Owega, A., Sass, H., and Buell, U. (1997). Correlation of positive symptoms exclusively to hyperperfusion or hypoperfusion of cerebral cortex in never-treated schizophrenics. *Lancet* 349:1735–1739.

Scharfetter, C. (1981). Ego-pychopathology: the concept and its empirical evaluation. *Psychol Med* 11:273–280.

Vollenweider, F. X. (1992). Die Anwendung von Psychotomimetika in der Schizophrenieforschung unter besonderer Berücksichtigung der Ketamin/PCP-Modell-Psychose [The use of psychotomimetics in schizophrenia research with special emphasis on the PCP/ketamine model psychosis]. *SUCHT* 38:389–409.

Vollenweider, F. X. (1994). Evidence for a cortical-subcortical dysbalance of sensory information processing during altered states of consciousness using PET and FDG. In Pletscher A, Ladewig D (eds.), *50 Years of LSD: State of the Art and Perspectives of Hallucinogens*. London, Parthenon Publishing, pp. 67–86.

Vollenweider, F. X. (1998a). Advances and pathophysiological models of hallucinogen drug actions in humans: a preamble to schizophrenia research. *Pharmacopsychiat* 31:92–103.

Vollenweider, F. X., Antonini, A., Leenders, K. L., and Mathys, K. (1998b). Effects of high amphetamine doses on mood and cerebral glucose metabolism in normals using positron emission tomography (PET). [In Press] *Psychiatry Research: Neuroimaging* 83:149–162.

Vollenweider, F. X., Antonini, A., Leenders, K. L., Oye, I., Hell, D., and Angst, J. (1997a). Differential Psychopathology and patterns of cerebral glucose utilisation produced by (S)- and (R)-ketamine in healthy volunteers measured by FDG-PET. *Eur Neuropsychopharmacol* 7:25–38.

Vollenweider, F. X., Leenders, K. L., Scharfetter, C., Antonini, A., Maguire, P., Missimer, J., and Angst, J. (1997b). Metabolic hyperfrontality and psychopathology in the ketamine model of psychosis using positron emission tomography (PET) and [F–18]-fluorodeoxyglocose (FDG). *Eur Neuropsychopharmacol* 7:9–24.

Vollenweider, F. X., Leenders, K. L., Scharfetter, C., Maguire, P., Stadelmann, O., and Angst, J. (1997c). Positron emission tomography and fluorodeoxyglucose studies of metabolic hyperfrontality and psychopathology in the psilocybin model of psychosis. *Neuropsychopharmacology* 16:357–372.

Vollenweider, F. X., Liechti, M., Gamma, A., and Huber, T. (1998c). Psychological and cardiovascular effects and short-term sequelae of MDMA ("Ecstasy") on MDMA-naive healthy volunteers. *Neuropsychopharmacology* 19:241–251.

10 First Steps toward a Theory of Mental Force: PET Imaging of Systematic Cerebral Changes after Psychological Treatment of Obsessive-Compulsive Disorder

Jeffrey M. Schwartz

Obsessive-compulsive disorder (OCD) is a common neuropsychiatric condition, affecting approximately 2% of the general population (Jenike et al. 1998). It is characterized by bothersome intrusive thoughts and urges that frequently lead to dysfunctional repetitive behaviors such as excessive hand washing or ritualistic counting and checking. As the result of a concerted research effort over the past two decades there has emerged a growing consensus that brain circuitry contained within the orbital frontal cortex, anterior cingulate gyrus and the basal ganglia is intimately involved in the expression of the symptoms of OCD (for recent reviews see Schwartz 1997a and b, Jenike et al. 1998).

There are several aspects of OCD that make it a potentially rich source of information about the sorts of natural phenomena that occur at the mind-brain interface. First, because the neurobiology of this condition is reasonably well understood, and its symptom presentation fairly distinct and readily describable, studying OCD provides substantial information about how functional activity in the affected brain regions is experienced by humans. Second, the nature of this disease state is such that people who are affected by it are generally quite aware that the bothersome intrusive thoughts and urges with which they are suffering are inappropriate and adventitious in the literal sense i.e., the symptoms are experienced as unwanted and extraneous intrusions into consciousness, and have a quality that has classically been described in the clinical literature as "ego-dystonic" or "ego-alien" implying "foreign to one's experience of oneself as a psychological being" (Nehmiah and Uhde 1989). Because of this, sufferers from OCD can frequently give clear and graphic descriptions of how the symptoms are subjectively experienced and how those conscious experiences change with treatment. Third, there are now very effective treatments of OCD involving both pharmacological and cognitive-behavioral psychological approaches, which can be administered either in conjunction or separately. Of particular interest are the recent findings that each of these treatments independently cause similar changes in patterns of brain metabolism in patients who respond to them (Baxter et al. 1992, Schwartz et al. 1996). Thus it becomes possible to track how changes in brain metabolism in specific brain circuits relate to changes in the internal conscious experience of well-defined neuropsychiatric symptoms.

One aspect of the study of cerebral metabolism in OCD and how it changes in conjunction with drug-free psychological treatment seems particularly relevant to the those interested in the study of the mind-brain interface. This involves the use of cognitive training as a means of enabling people suffering from this condition to come to a new understanding of the relationship between their brain, their conscious experience, and their choice of behavioral responses to that experience. It is on that aspect of the study of OCD that this chapter will focus. But first, let's take a brief look at the behavioral pathophysiology of OCD.

OCD: Overview of Brain Mechanisms

The major function of the basal ganglia, a set of gray matter structures lying deep within each brain hemisphere, is the processing of circuitry in the cerebral cortex for the purpose of efficiently initiating and guiding environmentally relevant behaviors. There is a substantial clinical literature that suggests a link between obsessive-compulsive symptoms and basal ganglia neuropathology. For instance, there have been numerous reports in the clinical literature describing the onset of obsessions and compulsions after a wide variety of insults to the basal ganglia, including even moderate decreases in oxygen supply or damage secondary to exposure to neurotoxic agents. Especially interesting are the findings of Susan Swedo of the NIMH, whose group has demonstrated a relationship between OCD in children and autoimmune attack on the basal ganglia occurring as a complication of streptococcal infection.

Numerous studies of the behavioral genetics of OCD also implicate the basal ganglia. James Leckman and David Pauls of Yale University have demonstrated a significant familial association between OCD and Tourette's Disorder, a condition that manifests with multiple motor and vocal tics and very likely involves the basal ganglia in its core pathophysiology. Other work has demonstrated marked increases in a variety of motor tic disorders among family members of patients with OCD (see Piacentini 1997, Jenike et al. 1998 for review). Thus the notion that OCD is a disorder in which brain pathology is related to what are essentially "multiple mental tics" is one that has significant clinical support.

The aspect of cortical circuitry that has been particularly implicated in OCD pathophysiology involves the connections between the orbital frontal cortex (OFC) and the caudate nucleus, the part of the basal ganglia that primarily processes input from the brain's frontal lobe. In 1987 our PET brain imaging group at UCLA found that metabolic activity in these two structures was increased in subjects with OCD. This finding has now been replicated in a series of subsequent studies by several other groups, with increased activity in the OFC and a closely associated structure called the anterior cingulate gyrus being consistently seen in symptomatic OCD patients. Of particular interest are the findings of Scott Rauch and Hans Breiter of Harvard University demonstrating acute increases in the activity of these structures in patients subjected to sudden exacerbation of their OCD symptoms (see Baxter 1995 for review of all these findings). There is now a significant consensus among neurobiologists that an impairment in the modulation of OFC and cingulate activity by the caudate nucleus is a key aspect in the pathophysiology of OCD.

Studies of cellular physiology in behaving monkeys (Rolls 1995) helps clarify possible mechanisms underlying these clinical findings. The group of E. T. Rolls of Oxford University investigated neuronal firing patterns in the OFC in monkeys trained to respond to various visual cues in order to receive juice as a reward. These experiments revealed several important aspects of OFC function. First, neurons in OFC change their firing pattern in response to visual cues depending on whether these cues are associated with rewarding or aversive stimuli. Seeing something associated with either reward or punishment triggers discrete patterns of neuronal firing in OFC. Further, OFC responses are very sensitive to the expectations the organism has concerning the stimuli to which it is exposed. For instance, if a monkey comes to expect that a blue light is associated with receiving juice, but no juice is delivered after the blue light appears, bursts of neuronal firing will occur in OFC. These cellular responses, which can be understood as an "error detection" mechanism, can underlie an internal sense in an organism that "something is wrong" in the environment, and are conducive to the acquisition of adaptive behavioral changes. Cellular responses of this kind are also seen in the anterior cingulate gyrus.

Thus, a malfunction of these structures can impair an organism's capacity to recognize that stimuli that once were behaviorally meaningful no longer are. This helps explain why primates, including humans, with damage to the frontal lobe often demonstrate much slower and less effective forms of behavioral adaptation when confronting changed environmental circumstances, frequently associated with repetitive inappropriate behavioral responses.

In contrast to the kinds of perseverative behaviors that are performed as the result of a failure of OFC and anterior cingulate to generate appropriate "error detection" signals, OCD symptoms can be understood as behavioral perseverations associated with a persistent internal sense that "something is wrong," which is inappropriately generated by a pathological hyperactivity of these structures. The cognitive foundation of our approach to treating OCD at UCLA Medical Center relies on enhancing the patients' insight into the fact that their adventitious thoughts and urges are caused by "false brain messages"—and then helping them utilize that insight to change the choices they make when selecting behavioral responses to those internal experiences. When this results in significant clinical improvement due to the performance of more adaptive behavioral responses, there are associated significant alterations in their patterns of brain metabolism in the OFC anterior cingulate and caudate. Before presenting that data I will briefly overview the method of the psychological treatment.

Table 10.1
Summary of the four steps of cognitive-biobehavioral self-treatment for obsessive-compulsive disorder (OCD). (From Schwartz 1997c)

---

1. **RELABEL:**
Recognize the intrusive obsessive thoughts and urges as a RESULT of OCD.

2. **REATTRIBUTE:**
Realize that the intensity and intrusiveness of the thought or urge is CAUSED BY OCD; it is probably related to a brain biochemical imbalance.
REMEMBER: IT'S NOT ME, IT'S THE OCD

3. **REFOCUS:**
'Work Around' the OCD thoughts by focusing attention on something else for at least a few minutes, i.e., DO ANOTHER BEHAVIOR

4. **REVALUE:**
Do not take the OCD thought at 'face value'. It is not significant in itself.

Mindful Awareness and the Impartial Spectator

In behavioral approaches to the psychological treatment of OCD patients learn to perform adaptive behaviors instead of pathological ones in response to the intrusive thoughts and urges that comprise the core symptoms of OCD. To successfully complete therapy patients must tolerate and effectively re-direct their responses to the acutely uncomfortable feeling states that arise as a result of OCD pathophysiology. There is now substantial evidence that the acquisition of specific cognitive skills by patients enables them to perform behavioral therapy techniques more effectively by increasing their ability to manage the intensely uncomfortable feelings that arise during treatment (Tallis 1995).

At UCLA we have developed a four-step cognitive-behavioral training method (see table 10.1) that is organized around the working hypothesis that the intrusive thoughts and urges of OCD are caused to a significant degree by a biomedical disease state (Schwartz 1997c). Because the cognitive aspect of this method accentuates the biomedical aspects of OCD symptom etiology, we use the term cognitive-biobehavioral to describe the overall treatment strategy.

What we are trying to achieve by this training is a deepening appreciation of the intimacy of the relationship between intrusive OCD thoughts and urges and what are basically "false brain messages" that can safely be ignored. The treatment goal, of course, is to learn to respond to these "false brain messages" in a new and much more adaptive way. This is done by applying techniques of behavioral refocusing in which functional activities are systematically performed in place of habitual OCD responses. These cognitive-behavioral treatment techniques enable patients to better manage the intense anxiety caused by OCD symptoms; this enhances their ability to perform consciously chosen adaptive behaviors rather than automaton-like compulsive responses when besieged by the excruciatingly unpleasant thoughts and urges elicited by the brain biochemical abnormalities associated with OCD.

One aspect of this training method has emerged as being of particular importance. As the concept that intrusive OCD symptoms are merely "false brain messages" becomes increasingly well integrated into the patient's cognitive framework, an important transition begins to take place. The nature of how the patient consciously experiences the uncomfortable feeling of an OCD symptom begins to change in a way that allows him/her to create a distance between the experience of self and the experience of the symptom. While it is true that this change in how the symptom is perceived is in some sense an accentuation of the "ego-dystonic" or "ego-alien" aspect of it, that is only one small component of the therapeutic process. The essence of this adaptive change in perspective is that the person with OCD becomes increasingly able to experience the intrusive symptom from the point of view of a clear-minded observer, and thus comes to see the symptom as merely the result of a malfunctioning mechanical process in the brain that, while unpleasant, is not of any great personal concern.

It is the ability to observe one's own internal sensations with the calm clarity of an external witness that is the most noteworthy aspect of this experience. Within the terminology of traditional Buddhist philosophy this sort of mental action is called mindfulness or mindful awareness (Silananda 1990). Noting the sense in which it involves clear observation by, as it were, " a man within," the Scottish philosopher Adam Smith (1976) described this sort of mental experience as the perspective of "the impartial spectator." Both of these descriptions are used during treatment to help clarify for patients how to use their new insight into the biomedical nature of OCD symptoms to create a distance between the symptom and their self-concept. Thus, for example, patients learn to stop making self-statements like, "I feel like I need to wash my hands again," and instead make statements of the type, "That nasty compulsive urge is bothering me again." This process, which requires profound and painstaking effort, can significantly enhance patients' abilities to manage the fears and anxieties associated with OCD symptoms, which enables them to more consistently alter their behavioral responses in increasingly adaptive ways.

Effects of Cognitive Behavioral Treatment on Cerebral Function

Systematic changes in cerebral glucose metabolism accompany the clinical improvements achieved using this method of cognitive-biobehavioral therapy (Schwartz et al. 1996). We investigated cerebral metabolic rate changes in eighteen drug-free subjects

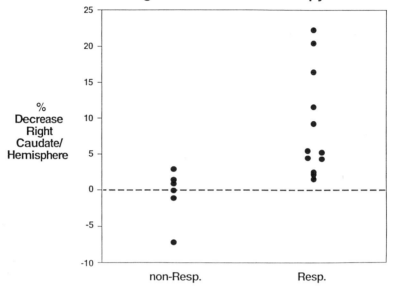

Change in Right Caudate Glucose Metabolic Rate in Non-Responders and Responders to Cognitive-Behavioral Therapy

Figure 10.1

studied with PET scans before and after ten weeks of out-patient treatment. Twelve of them demonstrated clinically significant decreases in OCD symptom severity during the treatment period, and six did not. There were two main findings in this study:

1. Bilateral decreases in caudate nucleus metabolism, divided by ipsilateral hemisphere metabolism (Cd/hem), were seen in responders to treatment compared to nonresponders. This finding was more robust on the right ($p = .003$) than on the left ($p = .02$). (See figure 10.1.)

2. There were significant correlations of metabolic activity prior to treatment between the orbital cortex and the caudate nucleus, cingulate gyrus, and thalamus on the right. After effective treatment these correlations decreased significantly. (See table 10.2.)

Assessing the Data of Inner Experience

The philosophical position known as epiphenomenalism views conscious experience as the result, but not the cause, of physical activity in the cerebrum. However, the

Table 10.2
Normalized region of interest correlations (r) before and after treatment, for behavior treatment responders (n = 12). (Modified from Schwartz et al., 1996)

	Before treatment	After treatment
left Orbit to left Caudate	.46	−.01
right Orbit to right Caudate	.74**	.28 ¶
left Orbit to left Cingulate	.11	.58*
right Orbit to right Cingulate	.87****	.22 ¶
left Orbit to left Thalamus	.34	.05
right Orbit to right Thalamus	.81***	.14 ¶
left Caudate to left Thalamus	.66*	.36
right Caudate to right Thalamus	.69*	.41

Note: significance (one-tailed) of individual pre- and post-treatment correlations—
$* p < .05$
$** p < .01$
$*** p < .001$
$**** p < .0005$
¶ = significant ($p < 0.05$) difference in pre- to post-treatment correlation.

issue of the role of interpretation in the response to brain activity, specifically the question of what meaning and/or value the human mind places on the internal experience of any particular electro-chemical event in the cerebrum, does not seem to be adequately addressed by this view. This is especially so insofar as it involves the relationship between any particular act of understanding and/or valuing of the internal experience that arises in association with a given brain signal, the type and quality of behavior that follows it, and the nature of subsequent brain signals. Because OCD is a condition in which data concerning all three of these factors can currently be acquired, it provides an excellent vehicle for investigating how changes in the valuation one places on the inner experience of an electro-chemical brain event relates to subsequent behaviors and brain events.

The Austrian economist Ludwig von Mises stated that, "Valuing is man's emotional reaction to the various states of his environment, both that of the external world and that of the physiological conditions of his own body" (Mises 1978). It is a major task of both economists and the psychotherapists (among a wide variety of other investigators) to discern coherent relationships between the way people value their experience and the kinds of choices and actions they subsequently make. Given recent technological advances in the fields of brain imaging, it is now also possible to acquire data concerning brain events occurring in conjunction with these events. Has the use of brain imaging to study the pathophysiology and psychological treatment of OCD taught us anything useful about possible relationships between these various factors?

Let us attempt the beginnings of an answer to this question by examining the therapeutic process in the case of a man with typical OCD. (The clinical aspects of this case will, to save space, be markedly abbreviated. See Schwartz 1997c for details) At the outset of treatment this man is besieged by very intrusive and persistent thoughts and urges associated with a gnawing gut-level feeling of dread that his hands are contaminated with germs. This almost invariably leads to hand washing of such severity that it causes the skin to become red, raw and chapped. Although he knows that his concerns about germ contamination are excessive to the point of being nonsensical, the gnawing anxiety associated with the obsessive thoughts of possible contamination is so intense he almost invariably succumbs to it with bouts of hand washing. A large body of research data is consistent with the statement that the intrusive gnawing fear that "something is wrong" with his hands (e.g., they are "contaminated by germs") is caused by an error-detection circuit that is "locked in gear" as the result of faulty circuitry connecting his caudate nucleus, anterior cingulate and orbital cortex. When we explain this to the man, and give him associated instructional materials, emotional support and time, he comes to readily understand it. This learning process comprises the first two steps, Relabel and Reattribute, of the Four Step Method (see table 10.1) that is used as part of the treatment process.

From a clinical perspective, what has the man learned: what is it that he now understands? The essence of his new knowledge is definitely *not* that his fear of being contaminated is a false cognition, because he already knew that to a significant degree when he appeared for treatment—in fact that's largely *why* he sought treatment. (To properly understand the clinical phenomena of OCD it is critical to remember that sufferers are still "in touch" with reality—the core problem is that their judgment gets overwhelmed by intense doubt, fear, and anxiety, which compulsions are a vain attempt to relieve. Indeed, compulsions tend to exacerbate the anxiety.) The essence of his new knowledge is that the reason his intrusive persistent thoughts and urges *don't go away* is that a biochemical imbalance in his brain results in his conscious mind being bombarded with a steady stream of "false error messages" or (as many patients prefer to call them) "false alarms." So what does that knowledge accomplish?

Well one thing it definitely does *not* accomplish is any meaningful change in the raw perception of the *actual feelings* of fear and anxiety—the gut is still churning and the gnawing sense that "your hands are dirty" is very definitely still present. That's almost certainly because the brain mechanisms underlying those inner experiences (the mechanisms upon which, to use the technical term, those experiences supervene) has not changed in any significant way. What *has* begun to change is the **value** the man now puts on those feelings and sensations. What he is beginning to do is learn how to control his *emotional reactions* to those feelings and sensations, by which I specifically mean the kinds of interpretations and meanings he attributes to them. At this point in treatment he basically *feels* the same—but he has changed in a critical way how he *understands* those feelings. With that change in understanding he has set the stage for making different choices about how to act on those feelings and sensations. Now, by consistently Refocusing his behavioral output onto healthful rather than pathological behaviors, while systematically Revaluing his inner experience of OCD symptoms on a regular basis (steps three and four in table 10.1), he can consciously establish new and much more adaptive response patterns to internal experiences that, prior to treatment, were almost always followed by nearly automatic pathological hand washing. And controlled scientific data now exist associating those new consciously chosen response patterns with statistically significant changes of energy use in the very brain circuitry that underlie his painful intrusive thoughts and urges, changes that bring with them a marked amelioration of the intensity and severity of his mental suffering.

How to Generate New Brain Circuits

From the perspective of a classically trained neurophysiologist there must exist new patterns of nervous system activity that are intimately related to the new understanding our man now has begun to attain regarding the unpleasant sensations his OCD pathology is bombarding him with—sensations that are, in all probability, causally linked to hyperactivity in brain circuitry involving the OFC, anterior cingulate and caudate nucleus. The key question from a philosophical perspective is what kind of process **generates** those new patterns of brain activity that arise in association with the man's new understanding. For an epiphenomenalist this question must be answered by statements that in essence "map out" or "specify a blueprint for" the kinds of neuronal process that lead to the new pattern of brain activity—no other type of answer is permissible given the constraints epiphenomenalism imposes with respect to the kinds of causal processes that effect changes in conscious activity. The epiphenomenalist position is that changes in the nervous system cause all changes in consciousness.

When asked to further specify what kind of process it is that relates a new moment of conscious understanding to the generation of new patterns of brain activity, the epiphenomenalist has no choice but to try to turn the question around and say that there was no new moment of understanding until the new brain patterns emerged— and when asked about what kind of process it is that causes those new brain patterns to emerge they will defer to some unknown future when the classically trained neurophysiologist will be able to answer that kind of question.

Fortunately, our man with OCD already has a good answer to that question, as he will proceed to demonstrate by exerting his will in order to endure and ultimately overcome his pain. Through a process that involves making the hard choices and performing the courageous actions that it takes to mindfully nurture and deepen his new understanding, he will begin to consciously alter his behavioral responses to his nasty OCD feelings—and in so doing he will systematically change the very brain circuitry that is causing his suffering.

There is one particularly key point, both clinically and philosophically, to comprehend about what occurs at the interface of conscious experience and brain activity during the moments of therapeutic breakthrough in the course of our man's treatment—those very special moments always involve an **ACTIVE** process. For at the moment when the man with OCD summons the mental strength to exert his will and physically actualize his new understanding by adaptively changing his behavior, he will be overcoming tremendous biological forces that are operating in order to resist that change. And the force it takes to surmount that resistance is in no sense a manifestation of any passive or random process—indeed, that force represents the essence of what the words *active* and *purposeful* really mean.

Assuming that his new understanding about the "false brain messages" underlying his intense urge to wash his hands is itself related to new patterns of brain activity (which, however they are generated, I believe is a very fair assumption), a major difficulty still confronts our man: How does he focus his attention on the "true message" those new and still frail and developing circuits are sending to his consciousness when he is simultaneously being bombarded by intense, powerful, and extremely distracting "false messages" that are very much still being "transmitted" by his hyperactive cortical-basal ganglia circuitry. Where, in other words, does he find the energy to strengthen the "good message" signal in his fragile and still developing new circuitry? And further, how does he now activate motor circuitry that will take him *away from* rather than *toward* the bathroom sink—for movement toward the sink, and the initiation of further damaging hand washing has been his habitual motor response to the urge from the "false brain message" for many years now, and so that particular motor response itself will have a very well-developed brain circuitry associated with it, with its own associated drives and urges.

The answer to this question, as every good OCD therapist knows, is that he generates the energy to activate his new health giving and life affirming circuitry through the exertion of his will, and the power of his striving—a power that can generate a real and palpable force, which I propose to term **mental force**. It is just this mental force, directed in our OCD patient's case by focusing his attention on his new "good message," that will strengthen and enhance his new brain circuitry's "message transmitting" capacity.

Now without question this newly proposed term, mental force, represents a still largely hypothetical entity at the present moment. But there does seem to be a theoretical need for a force of this kind in nature. For once one acknowledges the clinical fact that in order to change one's behavior in the midst of a barrage of intense dreadful feelings produced by pathological OCD brain circuitry, one must utilize an *active* process; and further reflects on the type of mechanism it would require for such an active process to cause the kind of systematic energy use changes those pathological circuits have undergone in the data presented in figure 10.1 and table 10.2, one may well come to the conclusion that a mental force, or something very much like it, is a necessary condition to accomplish the task. Without such a force the demonstrated changes in cerebral energy use, which are statistically significant only for those OCD subjects who demonstrate clinically meaningful improvement, would have to be generated by a passive process—but that is plainly inconsistent with a very large amount of clinical data, most especially the verbal reports of patients who have undergone treatments of this type. To precipitously reject such verbal reports as an unimportant source of data is not only scientifically and methodologically unjustified, it reflects an ad hoc perspective adopted merely to protect a profoundly counterintuitive way of thinking.

In the course of preparing this chapter I discussed its cental point—the very special, yet palpably familiar, force required to activate the newly forming healthy brain circuits that are called upon when one engages in cognitive-biobehavioral treatment—with the patients in my OCD therapy group. One group member commented by suggesting that it seemed to him that this force was the internal world equivalent of the kind of force that it takes "to make water run uphill" in the external world. This insight seems very germane, perhaps even precise, to me. For with the availability of brain imaging techniques that can quantitatively measure energy fluxes in the brains of freely acting humans, the possibility of quantitatively characterizing the mental force involved in altering those fluxes in the course of well-defined conscious processes becomes a real possibility. Much work remains to be done as we proceed on the path toward a science of consciousness.

Acknowledgments

This work was made possible by generous donations from the Charles and Lelah Hilton Family. Stimulating discussions with Dr. Henry P. Stapp, Dr. Ann Graybiel, and Dr. David Chalmers helped me formulate these ideas.

References

Baxter, L. R. 1995. Neuroimaging studies of human anxiety disorders: cutting paths of knowledge through the field of neurotic phenomena. In *Psychopharmacology: The Fourth Generation of Progress*. Ed. F. E. Bloom and D. J. Kupfer, pp. 1287–1299. New York: Raven Press.

Baxter, L. R., J. M. Schwartz, K. S Bergman, et al. 1992. Caudate glucose metabolic rate changes with both drug and behavior therapy for obsessive-compulsive disorder. *Archives of General Psychiatry* 49:681–689.

Jenike, M. A., L. Baer and W. E. Minichiello (eds.) 1998. *Obsessive-Compulsive Disorders: Practical Management* (3d ed.). St. Louis: Mosby.

Mises, L. von. 1978. *The Ultimate Foundation of Economic Science: An Essay on Method*. 2nd ed. Mission, KS: Andrews & McMeel.

Nemiah, J. C. and T. W. Uhde. 1989. Obsessive-compulsive disorder. In *Comprehensive Textbook of Psychiatry*. Ed. H. I. Kaplan and B. J. Sadock, pp. 984–1000. Baltimore: Williams & Wilkins.

Piacentini, J. and Graae, F. 1997. Childhood OCD. In *Obsessive-Compulsive Disorders: Diagnosis, Etiology, Treatment*. Ed. E. Hollander and D. J. Stein, pp. 23–46. New York: Marcel Dekker.

Rolls, E. T. 1995. A theory of emotion and consciousness, and its application to understanding the neural basis of emotion. In *The Cognitive Neurosciences*. Ed. M. S. Gazzaniga, pp. 1091–1106. Cambridge, Mass.: MIT Press.

Schwartz, J. M., P. W Stoessel, Baxter, L. R., et al. 1996. Systematic changes in cerebral glucose metabolic rate after successful behavior modification treatment of obsessive-compulsive disorder. *Archives of General Psychiatry*, 53:109–113.

Schwartz, J. M. 1997a. Cognitive-behavioral self-treatment for obsessive-compulsive disorder systematically alters cerebral metabolism: A mind-brain interaction paradigm for psychotherapists. In *Obsessive-Compulsive Disorders: Diagnosis, Etiology, Treatment*. Ed. E. Hollander and D. J. Stein, pp. 257–281. New York: Marcel Dekker.

Schwartz, J. M. 1997b. Obsessive-Compulsive Disorder. *Science and Medicine* 4, no. 2 (March/April): 14–23.

Schwartz, J. M. 1997c. *Brain Lock: Free Yourself From Obsessive-Compulsive Behavior*. New York: Harper Collins.

Schwartz, J. M. 1998. Neuroanatomical aspects of cognitive-behavioral therapy response in obsessive-compulsive disorder: An evolving perspective on brain and behavior. *British Journal of Psychiatry* 173 (suppl. 35): 38–44.

Silananda, U. 1990. *The Four Foundations of Mindfulness*. Boston: Wisdom Press.

Smith, A. 1976. *The Theory of Moral Sentiments* (sixth edn, 1790). Ed. D. D. Raphael and A. L. Macfie. Oxford: Oxford University Press.

Tallis, F. 1995. *Obsessive-Compulsive Disorder: A cognitive and neuropsychological perspective*. New York: John Wiley & Sons.

IV VISION AND CONSCIOUSNESS—INTRODUCTION

David J. Chalmers

Much of the most exciting recent scientific work on consciousness has come from the study of vision. Visual consciousness is many ways the easiest aspect of consciousness to study: it is ubiquitous, it is highly structured, it has properties that are easy to articulate, it is relatively easy to monitor, and we have a reasonably good understanding of its basis in the brain. The fields of neurophysiology, neuropsychology, and cognitive psychology have all contributed to the recent explosion of work on visual consciousness.

Within neurophysiology, there has been much work on isolating the neural correlates of visual consciousness. The structure of visual pathways is becoming well-understood, and we have reached a point where it is reasonable to ask which structures are most closely associated with consciousness. Research on monkeys and other mammals has focused on the question of whether the correlates of visual consciousness are located in primary visual cortex (V1) or later visual areas. Intriguing recent work on binocular rivalry by Logothetis and colleagues (e.g., Logothetis and Leopold 1998) suggests a special role for inferior temporal cortex (IT). And much attention has been focused on the ventral stream of processing, as discussed below.

Within neuropsychology, there have been intense studies of syndromes that involve a disruption of visual consciousness, and in particular that bring about dissociations between visual consciousness and action. The best-known of these syndromes is blindsight, in which subjects are seen to respond accurately when forced to guess about stimuli that they say they have no conscious awareness of. Syndromes such as visual agnosia and optic ataxia also suggest intriguing dissociations. Knowledge of the neural basis of these syndromes has given several important clues about the brain basis of consciousness.

Within cognitive psychology, there has been much attention to the capacities of unconscious visual perception. More broadly, there has been a good deal of psychophysical work on dissociations between information available for verbal report and that available for control of action, in various implicit processes. And there has been much recent research on the extent of visual consciousness, with a number of studies suggesting that we are not visually conscious of as much as we think we are.

Most of these directions are explored in the chapters in this section. In this way we can see how neurophysiology, neuropsychology, and cognitive psychology complement each other to yield a powerful tool in the study of conscious experience.

The chapter by David Milner and Mel Goodale gives an overview of their important work on visual pathways. It is well-known that vision in the brain involves at least two main pathways, the ventral and dorsal streams. Milner and Goodale (1995) have suggested that the ventral stream is devoted to cognitive representations of objects and events, which is largely conscious, and that the dorsal stream is devoted to the online control of action, which is largely unconscious. This fits much evidence from neuropsychology, including some dissociation syndromes that Milner and Goodale discuss. It also meshes with work from cognitive psychology on dissociations between motor action and verbal report, and provides a suggestive guide to the neural basis of visual consciousness.

The chapter by Yves Rossetti forms an interesting complement to this work, by discussing psychophysical evidence for "immaculate" motor representations that are not affected by top-down cognitive influences. Insofar as there is such evidence, the case for separate pathways for conscious identification and motor action is strengthened.

The contribution by Kentridge, Heywood, and Weiskrantz discusses the relation between awareness and attention in a subject with blindsight. Intriguingly, it turns that that the subject can direct his attention to stimuli with positive results, even when he is not conscious of the stimuli. This suggests that attention and consciousness may be less closely tied than is often thought to be the case.

At the Tucson III conference, Petra Stoerig presented some recent work on functional magnetic resonance imaging studies of blindsight, showing that there is activity in the ventral as well as the visual stream when a subject's blind field is stimulated. This unconscious ventral activation might be seen as a challenge to the Milner and Goodale hypothesis. In his introduction to the Blindsight and Vision section here (reprinted from *Trends in Cognitive Sciences*), David Milner addresses Stoerig's work as well as that of Kentridge et al., and discusses how this work relates to the Milner/Goodale hypothesis.

Vittorio Gallese discusses the extraordinary recent discovery of "mirror neurons" in area F5 of the monkey premotor cortex. These neurons fire when a monkey performs a certain action, and they also fire when the monkey perceives someone else perform that action. Gallese also discusses evidence that such mirror systems exist in humans, and speculates on possible functional roles for mirror systems in social interaction and the origin of language.

In recent years, there has been a swelling of evidence for what is sometimes called the "grand illusion" hypothesis: that we are visually conscious of much less than we think we are. One source of evidence involves eye movements: our eyes are constantly focusing on different locations, but we usually do not notice this and have the impression of a constant and detailed visual field. In his contribution, Frank H. Durgin gives evidence suggesting that subjects' eye movements can become sensitive to information of which the subject is not consciously aware. This suggests another way in much visual processing is unconscious.

Finally, Lianggang Lou discusses another intriguing relationship between attention and visual consciousness. It seems that in certain circumstances, phenomenology indicates that paying attention to a stimulus can cause it to "fade" from visual consciousness. Lou backs this up with psychophysical evidence that this fading affects attended stimuli rather than unattended stimuli. This counterintuitive phenomenon has implications for various theories of attention, consciousness, and their neural bases, some of which Lou discusses.

References

Logothetis, N. K. and Leopold, D. A. 1998. Single-neuron activity and visual perception. In (S. Hameroff, A. Kaszniak, and A. Scott, eds) *Toward a Science of Consciousness II*. MIT Press.

Milner, A. D., and Goodale, M. A. 1995. *The Visual Brain in Action*. Oxford University Press.

11 The Visual Brain in Action

A. David Milner and Melvyn A. Goodale

The Functions of Vision

Standard accounts of vision implicitly assume that the purpose of the visual system is to construct some sort of internal model of the world outside—a kind of simulacrum of the real thing, which can then serve as the perceptual foundation for all visually derived thought and action. The association of rich and distinctive conscious experiences with most of our perceptions gives credence to the idea that they must constitute a vital and necessary prerequisite for all of our visually based behavior.

But even though the perceptual representation of objects and events in the world is an important function of vision, it should not be forgotten that vision evolved in the first place, not to provide perception of the world per se, but to provide distal sensory control of the many different movements that organisms make. Many of the visual control systems for the different motor outputs evolved as relatively independent input-output modules. Thus, the different patterns of behavior exhibited by vertebrates, from catching prey to avoiding obstacles, can be shown to depend on independent pathways from the visual receptors through to the motor nuclei, each pathway processing a particular constellation of inputs and each evoking a particular combination of effector outputs.

Of course, the visually guided behavior of many animals, particularly complex animals such as humans, is not rigidly bound to a set of visuomotor modules, however subtle those mechanisms might be. Much of our behavior is quite arbitrary with respect to sensory input and is clearly mediated by some sort of internal model of the world in which we live. In other words, representational systems have evolved—systems that permit the brain to model the world, to identify objects and events, to attach meaning and significance to them, and to establish their causal relations. In humans and other primates, vision provides some of the most important inputs to these representational systems. Such systems are not linked directly to specific motor outputs but are linked instead to cognitive systems subserving memory, semantics, planning, and communication. Of course the ultimate function even of these higher-order systems has to be the production of adaptive behavior. The distinction between systems of this kind and the dedicated visuomotor modules described earlier is that the former enable us to select appropriate courses of action with respect to patterns of visual input, while the latter provide the immediate visual control required to execute those actions.

In our book *The Visual Brain in Action* (Milner and Goodale 1995), we argue that these two broad kinds of vision can be distinguished not only on functional grounds, but also by the fact that they are subserved by anatomically distinct substrates in the brain. Thus the distinction between vision for action and vision for perception helps us to understand the logic lying behind the organization of the visual pathways in the brain.

The Visual Brain

Evolution has provided primates with a complex patchwork of visual areas occupying the posterior 50% or so of the cerebral cortex (for review see Zeki 1993). But despite the complexity of the interconnections between these different areas, two broad "streams" of projections have been identified in the macaque monkey brain, each originating from the primary visual area (V1): a ventral stream projecting eventually to the inferior temporal (IT) cortex, and a dorsal stream projecting to the posterior parietal (PP) cortex (Ungerleider and Mishkin 1982). The two streams and the cortical regions to which they project are illustrated in figure 11.1. Of course, these regions also receive inputs from a number of other subcortical visual structures, such as the superior colliculus (via the thalamus). Although some caution must be

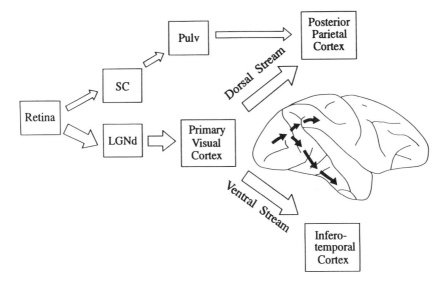

Figure 11.1
Major routes whereby retinal input reaches the dorsal and ventral streams. The diagram of the macaque brain (right hemisphere) on the right of the figure shows the approximate routes of the cortico-cortical projections from primary visual cortex to the posterior parietal and the inferotemporal cortex, respectively. LGNd: lateral geniculate nucleus, pars dorsalis; Pulv: pulvinar; SC: superior colliculus. Adapted with permission from Goodale et al. (1994b).

exercised in generalizing from monkey to human, it seems likely that the visual projections from primary visual cortex to the temporal and parietal lobes in the human brain will involve a separation into ventral and dorsal streams similar to those seen in the monkey.

In 1982, Ungerleider and Mishkin argued that the two streams of visual processing play different but complementary roles in the perception of incoming visual information. According to their original account, the ventral stream plays a critical role in the identification and recognition of objects, while the dorsal stream mediates the localization of those same objects. Some have referred to this distinction in visual processing as one between object vision and spatial vision—"what" versus "where." Apparent support for this idea came from work with monkeys. Lesions of inferior temporal cortex produced deficits in the animal's ability to discriminate between objects on the basis of their visual features but did not affect their performance on a spatially demanding "landmark" task. Conversely, lesions of the posterior parietal cortex produced deficits in performance on the landmark task but did not affect object discrimination learning. Although the evidence available at the time fitted well with Ungerleider and Mishkin's proposal, recent findings from a broad range of studies in both humans and monkeys are more consistent with a distinction not between subdomains of perception, but between perception on the one hand and the guidance of action on the other.

One source of evidence for the perception-action distinction comes from the study of the visual properties of neurons in the ventral and dorsal streams. Neurons in ventral stream areas such as IT are tuned to the features of objects, and many of them show remarkable categorical specificity; some of these category-specific cells maintain their selectivity irrespective of viewpoint, retinal image size, and even color. They are little affected by the monkey's motor behavior, but many are modulated by how often the visual stimulus has been presented and others by whether or not it has been associated with reward. Such observations are consistent with the suggestion that the ventral stream is more concerned with the enduring characteristics and significance of objects than with moment-to-moment changes in the visual array.

Neurons in the dorsal stream show quite different properties from those in the ventral stream. In fact, the visual properties of neurons in this stream were discovered only when methodological advances permitted the experimenter to record from awake monkeys performing visuomotor tasks. Different subsets of neurons in PP cortex turned out to be activated by visual stimuli as a function of the different kinds of responses the monkey makes to those stimuli. For example, some cells respond when the stimulus is the target of an arm reach; others when it is the object of a grasp response; others when it is the target of a saccadic eye movement; others when the stimulus is moving and is followed by a slow pursuit eye movement; and still others when the stimulus is stationary and the object of an ocular fixation. In addition, of course, there are many cells in the dorsal stream, as there are in the ventral stream, that can be activated passively by visual stimuli—indeed logic requires that the visuomotor neurons must receive their visual inputs from visual cells that are not themselves visuomotor. These purely visual neurons are now known to include some that are selective for the orientation of a stimulus object. One important characteristic of many PP neurons is that they respond better to a visual stimulus when the monkey is attending to it, in readiness to make a saccadic or manual response. This phenomenon is known as neuronal enhancement.

The electrophysiology can readily explain why posterior parietal lesions impair landmark task performance: quite simply, the monkey fails to orient toward the landmark. Recent behavioral studies bear out this interpretation. The electrophysiology also explains one of the most obvious effects of PP lesions, namely the monkeys' inability to reach accurately to grasp a moving or stationary food morsel, and why they fail to shape and orient their hands and fingers appropriately to pick up the morsel. The most recent development in this area has been the elegant experiments of Gallese and his colleagues (1997). They have demonstrated that micro-injections of a drug (muscimol) into a particular part of the PP cortex will cause a temporary impairment in hand shaping when the monkey reaches to grasp objects. This fits well with the recent discovery of visually responsive cells within that same part of PP cortex, as well as in anatomically linked areas of premotor cortex, which respond selectively during the grasping of particular objects (Sakata et al. 1997; Rizzolatti et al. 1988). Such evidence is consistent with the proposal that visual networks in the dorsal stream compute more than just spatial location. Indeed, in agreement with the electrophysiology, the behavioral literature is fully consistent with the idea that the dorsal stream has a primary role in mediating the visual control and guidance of a wide range of behavioral acts (Milner and Goodale 1993). Furthermore, even though the egocentric locations of visual targets are indeed computed within the PP cortex, it has now been clearly shown that this is done separately for guiding movements of the eyes and for movements of the hands, both in the monkey brain (Snyder et al. 1997) and in the human brain (Kawashima et al. 1996).

While lesions of one system (the dorsal stream) can thus disrupt visuomotor control without affecting perception, the converse is also true. The classic studies of bilateral temporal lobe lesions in monkeys showed unequivocally that visual recognition was severely affected (Klüver and Bucy 1938), but the investigators noticed that the monkeys retained a wide range of visuomotor skills. For example, they observed that the lesioned monkeys did not bump into obstacles or misjudge distances when jumping. In a more recent study, IT-lesioned monkeys that had failed to learn a pattern discrimination despite many weeks of training, nevertheless remained highly adept at catching gnats flying within the cage room. In another study, infero-temporal monkeys were found able to track and seize a rapidly and erratically moving peanut. Thus the evidence from IT lesions allows us to delineate a range of residual visual skills that do not depend on the ventral stream.

The same dissociations following brain damage have been observed in humans. The first systematic description of a patient of bilateral posterior parietal damage was published by Bálint (see Harvey 1995). Bálint's patient had three major groups of symptoms: attentional (including a narrowing of visual attention), visuomotor (what Bálint called optic ataxia), and oculomotor (fixed gaze). Optic ataxia was manifest as a difficulty in accurately reaching in space to pick up objects with the right hand. In many respects, these disorders closely resemble those seen in the PP-lesioned monkey. In both monkey and man, for example, optic ataxia appears to be visuomotor rather than purely visual or purely motor.

Accordingly, similar lesions in the superior parietal lobule and the neighboring intraparietal sulcus also cause difficulties in executing visually controlled saccadic eye movements in space. Furthermore, patients with optic ataxia not only fail to reach in the right direction but also have difficulty orienting their hand and forming their grasp appropriately with respect to target objects. For example, Perenin and Vighetto (1988) found that their optic ataxic subjects made errors in hand rotation as they tried to reach toward and into a large oriented slot. Often such patients are also unable to use visual information to form their grip as they reach toward an object. Although a normal individual opens the hand in anticipation of the target object, the maximum aperture being scaled in proportion to the size of the object, patients with lesions in the superior parietal cortex often show deficient grip scaling as they reach out to pick up an object (Jeannerod 1986). Yet despite the failure of these patients to orient their hands, to scale their grip appropriately, or to reach toward the right location, they have comparatively little difficulty in giving perceptual reports of the orientation and location of the very objects they fail to grasp.

On the other side of the equation, an impairment of ventral stream function seems to occur in humans who suffer from the condition known as visual form agnosia. The classic case of this disorder was described by Benson and Greenberg (1969). Their patient was not only unable to recognize faces or objects, he could not even reliably identify geometric shapes visually, nor distinguish reliably between a square and a rectangle with a 2:1 aspect ratio. Yet the patient was certainly not cortically blind. Recently we have described a very similar patient, D. F. (Milner et al. 1991). We have examined her spared abilities to use visual information in a series of experimental studies. We have found that her attempts to make a perceptual report of the orientation of an oriented slot show little relationship to its actual orientation, whether her reports are made verbally or by manual means. However, when she was asked to insert her hand or a hand-held card into the slot, she shows no difficulty, moving her hand or the card toward the slot in the correct orientation and inserting it quite accurately. Videorecordings have shown that her hand begins to rotate in the appropriate direction as soon as it leaves the start position. In short, although she cannot report the orientation of the slot, she can insert her hand or post a card into it with considerable skill. This dissociation is illustrated in figure 11.2.

Similar dissociations between perceptual report and visuomotor control were also observed in D. F. when she was asked to deal with the intrinsic properties of objects such as their size and shape. Thus, she showed excellent visual control of anticipatory hand posture when she was asked to reach out to pick up blocks of different sizes that she could not distinguish perceptually. Just like normal subjects, D. F. adjusted her finger-thumb separation well in advance of her hand's arrival at the object, and scaled her grip size in a perfectly normal and linear fashion in relation to the target width (Goodale et al. 1991). Yet when she was asked to use her finger and thumb to make a perceptual judgment of the object's width on a separate series of trials, D. F.'s responses were unrelated to the actual stimulus dimensions, and showed high variation from trial to trial.

D. F.'s accurate calibration of grip size during reaching to grasp contrasts markedly with the poor performance of optic ataxic patients with occipito-parietal damage. D. F. is as adept as normal subjects in many grasping tasks. In a recent study (Carey et al. 1996), for example, we have shown that when reaching to pick up rectangular shapes that varied in their orientation as well as their width, D. F. showed simultaneously both normal sensitivity to orientation and normal sensitivity to width. She is not entirely normal in dealing with complex shapes however. We found no evidence, for example, that she is able to deal with two different orientations present in a single target object, such as a cross, when reaching to grasp it. Yet, despite this difficulty with two oriented contours, we have found some evidence that the gross shape of an object can influence where D. F. places her fingers when picking it up (Goodale et al. 1994b, Carey et al. 1996).

If, then, we make the plausible assumption that the ventral stream is severely damaged and/or disconnected in D. F. (an assumption that is quite consistent with her pattern of brain damage), it is reasonable to infer that the calibration of these various residual visuomotor skills must depend on intact mechanisms within the dorsal stream. The visual inputs to this stream, which provide the necessary information for coding orientation, size, and shape, could possibly arise via V1, or via the

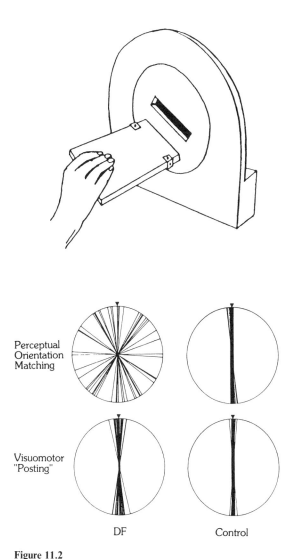

Figure 11.2
A. Apparatus that was used to test sensitivity to orientation in the patient D.F. The slot could be placed in any one of a number of orientations around the clock. Subjects were required either to rotate a hand-held card to match the orientation of the slot or to 'post' the card into the slot as shown in this figure. B. Polar plots of the orientation of the hand-held card on the perceptual matching task and the visuomotor posting task for D.F. and an age-matched control subject. The correct orientation on each trial has been rotated to vertical. Note that although D.F. was unable to match the orientation of the card to that of the slot in the perceptual matching card, she did rotate the card to the correct orientation as she attempted to insert it into the slot on the posting task. Adapted with permission from Goodale et al. (1991).

collicular-thalamic route, or via both. Both routes would appear to be available to
D. F., since MRI evidence indicates a substantial sparing of V1 in this patient, with
no suggestion of collicular or thalamic damage. Patients with lesions of V1, however,
although in some cases able to perform such visuomotor tasks at an above-chance
level ('blindsight': Perenin and Rossetti 1996, Rossetti 1998), do so far less profi-
ciently than D. F. We therefore believe that the collicular-pulvinar route alone cannot account for her preserved abilities.

Our various studies of D. F. show that she is able to govern many of her actions
using visual information of which she has no awareness. But it is clear that this is only
true of actions that are targeted directly at the visual stimulus. She cannot successfully use the same visual information to guide an identical but displaced response—a
response using the same distal musculature but at another location. Presumably the
difference is that a response displaced in this way is necessarily an arbitrary or symbolic one—not one that would fall within the natural repertoire of a hard-wired
visuomotor control system. Thus D. F. seems to be using a visual processing system
dedicated for motor control, which will normally only come into play when she
carries out natural goal-directed actions.

There are temporal as well as spatial limits on D. F.s ability to drive her motor
behavior visually. After showing her a rectangular block, Goodale et al. (1994a)
asked D. F. to delay for either 2 or 30 seconds with eyes closed, before allowing her
to reach out as if to grasp it. Even after a 30 second delay, the preparatory grip size of
normal subjects still correlated well with object width. In D. F., however, all evidence
of grip scaling during her reaches had evaporated after a delay of even 2 seconds.
This failure was not due to a general impairment in short-term memory. Instead, it
seems that a delayed reach is no longer a natural movement, and indeed this is so
even for normal subjects. A detailed kinematic analysis of the control subjects
showed that they moved their hand abnormally in the delay conditions, as if their
apparently normal grip scaling was actually generated artificially by imagining the
object and then "pantomiming" the grasp. This pantomiming strategy would not
have been open to D. F., since she could not have generated a visual image of
something that she failed to perceive in the first place. Presumably the visual processing that is available to her has a very short time constant, because it is designed to
deal with present or imminent states of the visual world, and to disregard past states
that may no longer be relevant (for example as a result of self-motion). Rossetti
(1998) has recently described a similar loss of visuomotor control in the hemianopic
field of a "blindsight" patient following a brief delay. Perhaps more surprisingly, we
have recently observed a complementary *improvement* in visuomotor performance in
a bilateral optic ataxic patient (A.T.) after a 5-second delay. Presumably in this case

the patient was able to throw off the dominance of the dorsal stream under the delay condition, allowing her to make use of her better-preserved ventral system.

Visual Awareness

According to the present interpretation, D. F.'s brain damage has uncovered a visual processing system (specifically the human dorsal stream) that can operate in relative isolation within the domains of size, shape and orientation. D. F. has no explicit awareness of the shapes and sizes that she is able to grasp by virtue of her remaining visual apparatus. We suggest that like D. F., we too carry out these functions using visual information that is not present in our awareness. Indeed, we suggest that in providing visual guidance for our actions the dorsal stream acts in large part alone and independent of any acquired "knowledge base."

One of the ways in which the visual information used by the motor system can be shown to be quite different from that which we experience perceptually is through the study of visual illusions. Gregory (1997) has argued over many years that higher-level visual illusions, including geometric illusions, deceive the perceptual system because the system makes (false) assumptions about the structure of the world based on stored knowledge. These include, for example, assumptions about perceptual stability and spatial constancy. It seems that the dorsal system, by and large, is not deceived by such spatial illusions (Bridgeman et al. 1979, 1981; Wong and Mack 1981; Goodale et al. 1986), perhaps because evolution has taught it that a little "knowledge" can be quite literally a dangerous thing. Instead, the dorsal stream directs our saccadic eye movements and our hand movements to where a target really is, which is not always where our perceptual system tells us it is. Similarly, under appropriate circumstances geometric illusions can be seen to affect visually guided reaching (Gentilucci et al. 1996) and grasping (Aglioti et al. 1995; Brenner and Smeets 1996; Haffenden and Goodale 1998) far less than they affect our perceptual judgments (see figures 11.3 and 11.4). Thus we may perceive an object as bigger than it really is, but we open our finger-thumb grip veridically when reaching for it.

We propose that the processing accomplished by the ventral stream both generates and is informed by stored abstract visual knowledge about objects and their spatial relationships. We further surmise that the particular kinds of coding that are necessary to achieve these ends coincide with those that render the representations accessible to our awareness. This would fit with the idea that coded descriptions of enduring object properties, rather than transitory egocentric views, are precisely what we need for mental manipulations such as those required for the planning of action sequences and the mental rehearsal of alternative courses of action.

a.

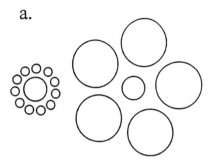

b.

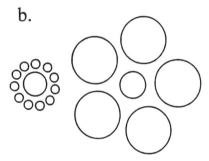

Figure 11.3
The "Ebbinghaus" illusion. Panel A shows the standard version of the illusion in which physically identical target circles appear perceptually different. Most people judge the target circle surrounded by the annulus of smaller circles to be larger than the other target circle. Panel B shows a version of the illusion in which the target circle surrounded by the annulus of larger circles has been made physically larger than the other target, compensating for the effect of the illusion. Most people now see the two target circles as equivalent in size. Adapted with permission from Aglioti et al. (1995).

But of course, the mere fact that processing occurs in this generalized way in the ventral stream could not be a sufficient condition for its reaching visual awareness. For example, there are generally many items processed in parallel at any given time, most of which will be filtered out of awareness by the operation of selective attention. We have therefore proposed that it is only those items that receive more than a certain threshold level of relative activation, for example through the sharpening effects of spatial gating processes known to be active during selective attention (e.g., Moran and Desimone 1985, Chelazzi et al. 1993), that will reach awareness. That is, we are proposing a conjoint requirement for an item to attain visual awareness: (a) a certain kind of coding (one that is object-based and abstracted from the viewer-centered and

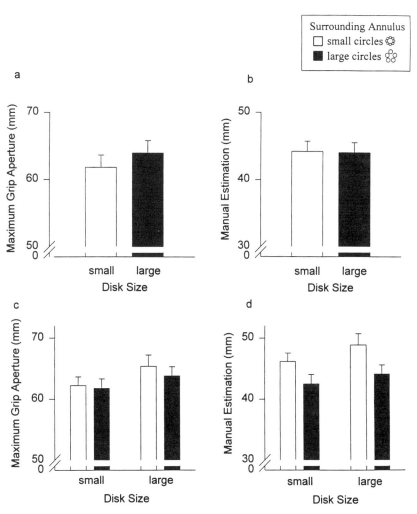

Figure 11.4
Calibration of the grasp (on left) and manual estimations (on right) for disks surrounded by the illusory annuli: (a & b) perceptually identical conditions, and (c & d) perceptually different conditions. The difference between the maximum grip aperture achieved during a grasping movement was significantly greater for large disks than the maximum grip aperture for small disks independent of whether or not the subject perceived the disks to be the same or different sizes (p < .05). Manual estimations were influenced by the illusory display. The difference between manual estimations of the large and small disks in the perceptually identical condition was not significant (p > .05). Perceptually different, but physically identical disk pairs produced significantly different manual estimations. The small disk surrounded by the small circle annulus was estimated to be larger than the small disk surrounded by the large circle annulus (p < .01). Manual estimations of the pair of large disks produced a similar result. The large disk surrounded by the small circle annulus was estimated to be larger than the large disk surrounded by the large circle annulus (p < .05). Error bars indicate the standard error of the mean averaged within each condition for all subjects. Adapted with permission from Haffenden and Goodale (1998).

egocentric particulars of the visual stimulation that gives rise to it) and (b) a certain level of activation of these coding circuits above the background level of neighbouring circuits.

We do not deny, then, that perception can proceed unconsciously under some circumstances, for example, when the stimuli are degraded by masking or short exposure, or when they are outside the current focus of selective attention. We believe that there is good empirical evidence for such "subliminal" perception of complex patterns, processing that is capable of activating semantic representations of certain kinds. Our assumption is that this form of unconscious perception arises through the partial or diffused activation of neuronal assemblies in the ventral stream, and that it does not reach awareness due to the fact that there is insufficient focussing of the activation above the noise of the surrounding assemblies. If this notion is correct, we would predict that such subconscious stimulation, although able to prime certain kinds of semantic decision tasks, would not provide usable inputs to the visuomotor system. Conversely, visual form information that can successfully guide action in a patient like D. F. should not be expected to have significant priming effects on semantic tasks—precisely because that visual processing is never available to conscious experience, even in the normal observer. In short, it may be the case that for an "undetected" visual stimulus to be able to prime decision tasks, it must at least in principle be accessible to consciousness.

The Visual Brain in Action

Although we have emphasized the separation of the dorsal and ventral streams, there are of course multiple connections between them, and indeed adaptive goal-directed behavior in humans and other primates must depend on a successful integration of their complementary contributions. Thus the execution of a goal-directed action might depend on dedicated control systems in the dorsal stream, but the selection of appropriate goal objects and the action to be performed depends on the perceptual machinery of the ventral stream. One of the important questions that remains to be answered is how the two streams interact both with each other and with other brain regions in the production of purposive behavior.

At the level of visual processing, however, the visuomotor modules in the primate parietal lobe function quite independently from the occipitotemporal mechanisms generating perception-based knowledge of the world. Only this latter, perceptual, system can provide suitable raw materials for our thought processes to act upon. In contrast, the other is designed to guide actions purely in the "here and now," and its products are consequently useless for later reference. To put it another way, it is only through knowledge gained via the ventral stream that we can exercise insight, hindsight and foresight about the visual world. The visuomotor system may be able to give us "blindsight," but in doing so can offer no direct input to our mental life (Weiskrantz 1997).

References

Aglioti, S., Goodale, M. A., and DeSouza, J. F. X. 1995. Size-contrast illusions deceive the eye but not the hand. *Curr. Biol.* 5:679–685.

Benson, D. F., and Greenberg, J. P. 1969. Visual form agnosia: a specific deficit in visual discrimination. *Arch. Neurol.*, 20:82–89.

Brenner, E., and Smeets, J. B. J. 1996. Size illusion influences how we lift but not how we grasp an object. *Exp. Brain Res.*, 111:473–476.

Bridgeman, B., Lewis, S., Heit, G., and Nagle, M. 1979. Relation between cognitive and motor-oriented systems of visual position perception. *J. Exp. Psychol.* (Hum. Percept.), 5:692–800.

Bridgeman, B., Kirch, M., and Sperling, A. 1981. Segregation of cognitive and motor aspects of visual function using induced motion. *Percept. Psychophys.*, 29:336–342.

Carey, D. P., Harvey, M., and Milner, A. D. 1996. Visuomotor sensitivity for shape and orientation in a patient with visual form agnosia. *Neuropsychologia*, 34:329–338.

Chelazzi, L., Miller, E. K., Duncan, J., and Desimone, R. 1993. A neural basis for visual search in inferior temporal cortex. *Nature* 363:345–347.

Gallese, V., Fadiga, L., Fogassi, L., Luppino, G., and Murata, A. 1997. A parietal-frontal circuit for hand grasping movements in the monkey: evidence from reversible inactivation experiments. In: *Parietal lobe contributions to orientation in 3D-space*, (ed. P. Thier and H.-O. Karnath) pp. 255–270. Springer-Verlag, Heidelberg.

Gentilucci, M., Chieffi, S. Daprati, E., Saetti, M. C., and Toni, I. 1996. Visual illusion and action. *Neuropsychologia*, 34, 369–376.

Goodale, M. A., Pélisson, D., and Prablanc, C. 1986. Large adjustments in visually guided reaching do not depend on vision of the hand or perception of target displacement. *Nature* 320:748–850.

Goodale, M. A., Milner, A. D., Jakobson, L. S., and Carey, D. P. 1991. A neurological dissociation between perceiving objects and grasping them. *Nature* 349:154–156.

Goodale, M. A., Jakobson, L. S., and Keillor, J. M. 1994a. Differences in the visual control of pantomimed and natural grasping movements. *Neuropsychologia* 32:1159–1178.

Goodale, M. A., Meenan, J. P., Bülthoff, H. H., Nicolle, D. A., Murphy, K. J., and Racicot, C. I. 1994b. Separate neural pathways for the visual analysis of object shape in perception and prehension. *Current Biol.* 4:604–610.

Gregory, R. 1997. Knowledge in perception and illusion. *Phil. Trans. R. Soc. Lond. B* 352:1121–1127.

Haffenden, A. M., and Goodale, M. A. 1998. The effect of pictorial illusion on prehension and perception. *J. Cogn. Neurosci.* 10:122–136.

Harvey, M. 1995. Translation of "Psychic paralysis of gaze, optic ataxia, and spatial disorder of attention" by Rudolph Bálint. *Cognitive Neuropsychol.* 12:261–282.

Jeannerod, M. 1986. The formation of finger grip during prehension: a cortically mediated visuomotor pattern. *Behav. Brain Res.*, 19:99–116.

Kawashima, R., Naitoh, E., Matsumura, M., Itoh, H., Ono, S., Satoh, K., Gotoh, R., Koyama, M., Inoue, K., Yoshioka, S., and Fukuda, H. 1996. Topographic representation in human intraparietal sulcus of reaching and saccade. *Neuroreport* 7:1253–1256.

Klüver, H., and Bucy, P. C. 1938. An analysis of certain effects of bilateral temporal lobectomy in the rhesus monkey, with special reference to "psychic blindness." *J. Psychol.* 5:33–54.

Milner, A. D., and Goodale, M. A. 1993. Visual pathways to perception and action. In: *Progress in Brain Research*, Vol. 95, (ed. T. P. Hicks, S. Molotchnikoff, and T. Ono) pp. 317–337. Elsevier, Amsterdam.

Milner, A. D., and Goodale, M. A. 1995. *The Visual Brain in Action*. Oxford: Oxford University Press.

Milner, A. D., Perrett, D. I., Johnston, R. S., Benson, P. J., Jordan, T. R., Heeley, D. W., Bettucci, D., Mortara, F., Mutani, R., Terazzi, E., and Davidson, D. L. W. 1991. Perception and action in visual form agnosia. *Brain* 114:405–428.

Moran, J., and Desimone, R. 1985. Selective attention gates visual processing in the extrastriate cortex. *Science* 229:782–884.

Perenin, M.-T., and Rossetti, Y. 1996. Grasping without form discrimination in a hemianopic field. *Neuroreport* 7:793–897.

Perenin, M.-T., and Vighetto, A. 1988. Optic ataxia: a specific disruption in visuomotor mechanisms. I. Different aspects of the deficit in reaching for objects. *Brain* 111:643–674.

Rizzolatti, G., Camarda, R., Fogassi, L., Gentilucci, M., Luppino, G., and Matelli, M. 1988. Functional organization of inferior area 6 in the macaque monkey. II. Area F5 and the control of distal movements. *Exp. Brain Res.* 71:491–507.

Rossetti, Y. 1998. Implicit perception in action: short-lived motor representations of space. *Consciousness and Cognition*, 7:520–558.

Sakata, H., Taira, M., Murata, A., Gallese, V., Tanaka, Y., Shikata, E., and Kusunoki, M. 1997. Parietal visual neurons coding 3-D characteristics of objects and their relation to hand action. In: *Parietal lobe contributions to orientation in 3D space*, (ed. P. Thier and H.-O. Karnath), pp. 237–254. Springer-Verlag, Heidelberg.

Snyder, L. H., Batista, A. P., and Andersen, R. A. 1997. Coding of intention in the posterior parietal cortex. *Nature* 386:167–170.

Ungerleider, L. G., and Mishkin, M. 1982. Two cortical visual systems. In D. J. Ingle, M. A. Goodale, and R. J. W. Mansfield (eds.). *Analysis of Visual Behavior* (pp. 549–586). Cambridge, Mass.: MIT Press

Weiskrantz, L. 1997. *Consciousness Lost and Found*. Oxford: Oxford University Press.

Wong, E., and Mack, A. 1981. Saccadic programming and perceived location. *Acta Psychol.* 48:123–131.

Zeki, S. 1993. *A Vision of the Brain.* Oxford: Blackwell.

12 In Search of Immaculate Perception: Evidence from Motor Representations of Space

Yves Rossetti

Contrasting with naive conceptions of perception as a pure bottom-up process, the idea has been proposed by von Helmoltz that perception results from unconscious inductive inferences (Gregory 1987). Although physiological studies of the visual system have long been focused on how visual images are constructed through hierarchically organized stages of processing, the same idea of a dialogue between bottom-up and top-down processes is now being applied to the understanding of vision (Salin and Bullier 1995, Thorpe et al. 1996). This two-way description of vision and perception in general is also widely acknowledged by psychologists (e.g., Gregory 1987, Cave and Kosslyn 1989) and philosophers (Dretske 1990, Jacob 1985), so much so that the idea that "there is no such thing as immaculate perception" has been defended (Kosslyn and Sussman 1995). The most cited experimental evidence for the implication of descending influences on perception is the case of ambiguous figures, for which perception can alternate between two possible interpretations of the visual input, even though the memorized image can be subjected to other interpretation (Peterson et al. 1994). Visual illusions are also often considered as a clear example of the interpretation (and contamination) of retinal information involved in perception (Dretske 1990, Jacob 1985, Gregory 1987, Meini 1996). In their attempt to rule out the possibility for "immaculate perception," Kosslyn and Sussman (1990) review evidence for the use of imagery in perception suggesting that a match is being created between descending expectations and ascending signals. Then they present possible anatomical substrate of descending feedback from higher visual centers, and consider possible ways to transform an internal image so as to match the peripheral retinal image. This latter issue leads them to consider the strong link between this mental transformation and sensori-motor processing. This chapter will consider these and other observations as a way to demonstrate that instances of immaculate perception can be precisely found in the field of action.

The current knowledge of visual processes does not allow to challenge the idea that most instances of perception involve downward projections from mental images. This is particularly true for high-level perception, for example when subjects are required to identify a given shape or letter. Indeed many of the examples presented in Kosslyn and Sussman's paper (1995) deal with pattern recognition. As stressed in their introduction, it is especially at the level of on-line input processing that the idea of immaculate perception can be questioned. The best examples of on-line processing of visual input are found in the field of action, because simple actions can be the locus of extremely fast processing of visual changes. Just as is the case for the "role of imagery in recognition" (Kosslyn and Sussman 1995), the role of motor representations "may be counter-intuitive because we are not aware of generating" them when we perform an action (cf. Jeannerod 1994). But examples of specific motor representations can be found from a variety of studies ranging from neuropsychology to motor psychophysics (reviews: Rossetti 1998 and Milner and Goodale in this volume).

The first example can be taken from the Prablanc, Pélisson, and Goodale study (1986), in which a better pointing accuracy was found when the target remained in view during the entire movement time than when it was removed shortly after movement initiation. This result has been considered by Kosslyn and Sussman as a demonstration that "a tight linkage exists between what one expects to see and an error-correction motor output system." The same authors (Goodale et al. 1986, Pélisson et al. 1986) also studied the effect of unexpectedly displacing the target during the eye saccade toward it, so that subjects were never aware of this target jump. Strikingly however, subjects corrected their movement and reached the second location of the target without increasing their movement time. In addition, they were not aware of their own arm trajectory change (Pélisson et al. 1986). This result clearly indicates that a discrepancy can be found between the on-line processing of the visual information used for driving the hand toward its target and the subjects expectation about the target location. In addition, the same error-correction mechanism is at work when the target jump can be consciously detected because it is not synchronized with the saccade (e.g., Castiello et al. 1991, Komilis et al. 1993). Although it would certainly be misleading to assume that all brain inferences are associated with conscious awareness (c.f. supra), it is difficult to conceive how the processing of an *unexpected* target perturbation would benefit from top-down imagery about where the target should have jumped. It may rather be argued that the speed of the motor reactions to a visual perturbation may preclude the influence of top-down projection in these mechanisms.

An even stronger demonstration of this discrepancy is obtained when the subject is required to stop his movement whenever the target jumps (Pisella et al. 1998). Under this particular condition, fast movements are found to reach the secondary location of the target, whereas they should have been interrupted (Rossetti and Pisella 1998). This result suggests not only that a motor representation of the target is used to drive the hand toward a new position despite there is no expectation of the jump (Pélisson et al. 1986), but also that this motor representation can be stronger than the expectation, so as to reach even a "prohibited" target. As a conclusion to these observations, it may be emphasized that the temporal issue is crucial here. When movements are slow enough, the discrepancy between the subject's expectation and the automatic motor corrections carried out by the hand can be resolved before the action ends, even though the motor reaction is initiated prior to awareness of the target perturbation (e.g., Castiello et al. 1991). This agreement can be achieved also because the detection of the unexpected event does not imply further modification of the ongoing corrective action. In the case of faster movements, and the unexpected jump being associated with an interruption of the automatic behavior, the subjects reached the prohibited target before to become apt to control their movement (Rossetti and Pisella 1998). In this particular case a clear dissociation can be observed between the fast motor representation automatically driving the hand toward a goal and the slower control processes.

Examples of pure spatial (re)presentations (not contaminated by higher level cognitive representation) can be observed in brain-damaged patients. Blindsight and Numbsense provide examples of the complete loss of sensory experience in the visual or in the somesthetic modality, where actions can still be performed toward undetected target objects (review in Rossetti 1998). Blindsight patients may be able to gaze or to point at unseen visual targets (e.g., Pöppel et al. 1973, Weiskrantz et al. 1974, Perenin and Jeannerod 1975), or even to significantly size their grasp or orient their hand while reaching to an object (Perenin and Rossetti 1996). Blindfolded numbsense patients are able to point to unfelt tactile stimuli applied to their arm (Paillard et al. 1987, Rossetti et al. 1995) and to point to unfelt proprioceptive targets (Rossetti et al. 1995) with above-chance performance. In the same way, patients with visual agnosia exhibit good goal-directed motor performances, whereas they may remain unable to describe any feature of the target object verbally (see Milner in this volume). These arguments are consistent with the idea that pure motor representations can be spared in patients with lesion of higher-level perceptual systems. The example of patient J. A. is presented in figure 12.1. This patient presented a complete loss of all somatosensory processing on the left half of his whole body when he was tested clinically for light touch, deep pressure, moving tactile stimulation, pain, warm and cold, vibration, segment position, passive movement, etc. When blindfolded and required to guess verbally the locus of tactile stimuli delivered to his forearm and hand, he performed at chance level. Figure 12.1 shows his significant ability to point at stimuli delivered to his right arm despite he could not otherwise indicate *where* the stimulus was applied.

A crucial argument in this debate about specific motor representations has been brought by investigations of motor responses to visual illusions (see also Milner and Goodale in this volume). For example, Gentilucci et al. (1996) required subjects to point from one end to the other end of Müller-Lyer lines, in order to investigate whether subjects would produce longer movements for the open configuration of the line (>———<, which appears longer) as compared to the closed configuration (<———>, which appears shorter). Although the perceptual effect of Müller-Lyer

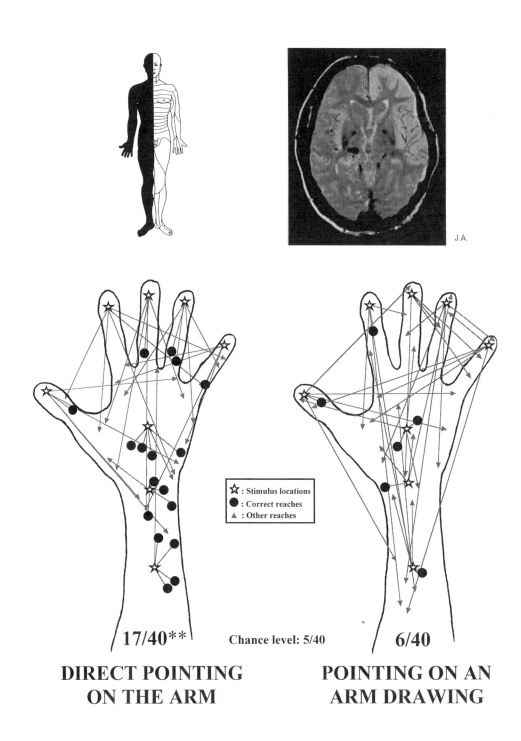

J.A.

☆ : Stimulus locations
● : Correct reaches
▲ : Other reaches

17/40**   Chance level: 5/40   6/40

DIRECT POINTING
ON THE ARM

POINTING ON AN
ARM DRAWING

illusion can be estimated about 20% of the actual length (Rossetti 1998), the motor performance was not biased by more than 2–3%. These results are consistent with previous results that demonstrated that the frame of reference used by the action system was different from that used by conscious perception (Bridgeman et al. 1997). The action system would compute the position of targets in an egocentric reference frame, whereas perception would locate objects relative to the surrounding frame or objects (see also Goodale and Milner 1992, Jeannerod and Rossetti 1993, Milner and Goodale 1995). These results also suggest that despite the very strong and reliable effect of this illusion, that has been used to argue for the extensive interpretation of visual input by cognitive processes, the motor representation of the line length was only very marginally contaminated by such interpretation (especially if one considers that a component of Müller-Lyer illusion can be explained by retinal factors, as mentioned by Gentilucci et al. 1996). Interestingly, the effect of the illusion on pointing was dramatically increased when a delay was introduced between the line presentation and the motor response (Gentilucci et al. 1996). A very similar effect of delay on pointing actions as shown previously has been described by Rossetti and Régnier (1995) for proprioceptive targets and by Bridgeman (1997, 1998) for visual targets. In these two studies the introduction of a memory delay between the target presentation and the response induced a change in the reference frame used by the action system to located the target. Analyses of the delayed pointing errors revealed that they resulted from the computation of the goal with respect to the surrounding information. These results suggest that motor representations are short-lived, and that the information processed by higher cognitive representation is being fed into the motor system when the delay exceeds its limited memory capacity, therefore contaminating the outcome of the action.

This reliable effect of delay is compatible with the idea that "... imagery is a bridge between perception and motor control" (Kosslyn and Sussman 1995: 1040) (see Rossetti and Procyk 1997). When the life time of motor representations is too short to allow them to participate in the action, the motor response has to rely on spatial

Figure 12.1
Numbsense for touch. Patient J.A. presented a complete clinical loss of somatosensory processing on the right side of the whole body following a lesion to the VL and VPL nuclei of the left thalamus. The lower left panel represent his performance when required to point to unfelt stimuli delivered to one out of 8 possible locations (stars). Arrows indicate the distance between the stimulus and the inappropriate responses, whereas black dots display trials with reaches on the stimulated area. Out of a 40 trial session, correct responses were obtained from the blindfolded patient in more than three times the chance level. When the patient was asked to point on a seen drawing of his own arm in response to the unseen stimulus delivery, his performance dropped to chance level. This dissociation demonstrates the specificity of motor representation: knowing **How** to reach to a stimulus can be dissociated from knowing **Where** the stimulus has been delivered. Redrawn from Rossetti et al. 1995.

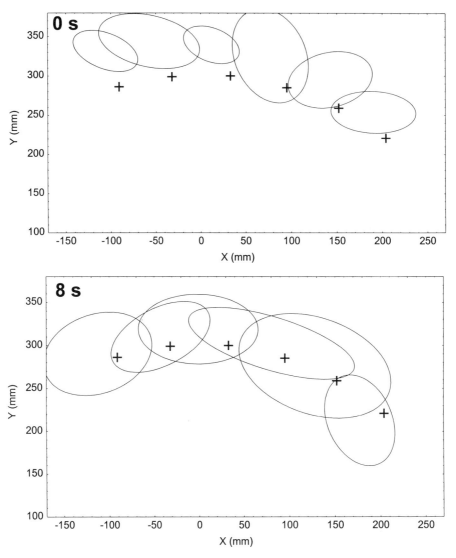

Figure 12.2
Immediate vs delayed action. Blindfolded healthy subjects were required to point to proprioceptive targets presented along an arc array of 6 locations. For each trial the target fingertip was briefly placed on one location and the subject was instructed by a computer-generated tone when to point at it with the other hand. The starting point coordinates were (0, 0). Pointing distributions obtained for each target location and each delay are presented as confidence ellipses. As expected, these confidence ellipses were larger for the 8 s delay (lower panel) than for the 0 s delay (upper panel). The most interesting observation was made on the ellipse orientation: delayed responses were influenced by the target array, such that the ellipse's major axes tended to be aligned with this arc, whereas immediate responses did not.

memory. Just as ambiguous images benefit from visual imagery, the spatial memory used to guide a delayed action can be contaminated by higher-level interpretation of the spatial relationship between the target and its surrounding. Figure 12.2 exemplifies this specific influence of imagery on a delayed action: immediate pointings are not influenced by the spatial context of the experimental session, whereas delayed pointing are strongly influenced by the integration in time of the successive target location used in the same session (Rossetti and Régnier 1995, Rossetti et al. 1996).

Is it possible to conclude that motor representations provide one example of immaculate perception? It could be argued that motor representations are not innate and benefit from early-childhood learning, such that they could not be considered as immaculate perception. One interesting aspect of this learning, however, is that what is learned by the motor system results from a direct confrontation with surrounding objects. Motor responses are necessarily constrained by the metric properties of the physical environment, whereas perception is not (see also Bridgeman 1998). If there is a perfect metric correspondence between the space representation used to drive an action and the physical space of the action goal, as supported by the data presented here, then motor (re)presentations are clearly pure from distorting brain inferences, and can be considered as an instance of immaculate perception. Their very short-lived feature may be the characteristic that prevent them from being influenced by visual imagery.

References

Bridgeman, B. 1998. Interactions between vision for perception and vision for behavior. In Y. Rossetti and A. Revonsuo (eds.), Beyond dissociation: interactions between dissociated implicit and explicit processing. In press.

Bridgeman, B., Peery, S., and Anand, S. 1997. Interaction of cognitive and sensorimotor maps of visual space. *Percept Psychophys* 59(3):456–469.

Castiello, U. 1991. Temporal dissociation of motor responses and subjective awareness. A study in normal subjects. *Brain* 114:2639–2655.

Cave, K. R., and Kosslyn, S. M. 1989. Varieties of size-specific visual selection. *J. Exp. Psychol.* [Gen] 118:148–164.

Dretske, F. 1990. Seeing, believing, and knowing; in Osherson, D. N., Kosslyn, S. M., and Hollerbach, J. M. (eds.): *An invitation to cognitive science.* MIT Press, 129–148.

Gentilucci, M., Chieffi, S., Daprati, E., and Toni, I. 1996. Visual illusion and action. *Neuropsychologia* 34:369–376.

Goodale, M. A., and Milner, A. D. 1992. Separate visual pathways for perception and action. *Trends in Neurosc.* 15:20–25.

Goodale, M. A., Pélisson, D., and Prablanc, C. 1986. Large adjustments in visually guided reaching do not depend on vision of the hand or perception of target displacement. *Nature* 320(6064):748–850.

Gregory, R. L. 1987. *The Oxford companion to the mind.* Oxford: Oxford University Press.

Jacob, P. 1985. Voit-on ce que l'on croit? *Philosophie* 7:53–82.

Jeannerod, M., and Rossetti, Y. 1993. Visuomotor coordination as a dissociable function: experimental and clinical evidence; in Kennard, C. (ed): Visual perceptual defects. London, Ballière Tindall, pp. 439–460.

Jeannerod, M. 1994. The representating brain: Neural correlates of motor intention and imagery. *Behavioral and Brain Sciences* 17(2):187–245.

Komilis, E., Pelisson, D., and Prablanc, D. 1993. Error processing in pointing at randomly feedback-induced double-step stimuli. *Journal of Motor Behavior* 25(4):299–308.

Kosslyn, S. M., and Sussman, A. L. 1995. Roles of imagery in perception: or, there is no such thing as immaculate perception; in Gazzaniga, M. S. (ed): *The cognitive neurosciences*. Cambridge, Massachussetts, MIT Press, pp. 1035–1042.

Meini, C. 1996. La frontière entre percept et concept: la théorie de Fred Dretzke à l'épreuve des illusions d'optique. In *Cognito*, (6), 27–38.

Milner, A. D., and Goodale, M. A. 1995. *The visual brain in action* (Oxford Psychology Series 27). Oxford: Oxford University Press. 248 pp.

Pélisson, D., Prablanc, C., Goodale, M. A., and Jeannerod, M. 1986. Visual control of reaching movements without vision of the limb. II. evidence of fast unconscious processes correcting the trajectory of the hand to the final position of a double-step stimulus. *Experimental Brain Research* 62:303–311.

Perenin, M-T., and Rossetti, Y. 1996. Grasping in an hemianopic field. Another instance of dissociation between perception and action. *Neuroreport* 7:793–897.

Perenin, M-T., and Jeannerod, M. 1975. Residual vision in cortically blind hemifields. *Neuropsychologia*, 13:1–8.

Peterson, M. A., Kihlstrom, J. F., Rose, P. M., and Glisky, M. L. 1992. Mental images can be ambiguous: reconstruals and reference-frame reversals. *Memory and Cognition* 20(2):107–123.

Pisella, L., Arzi, M., and Rossetti, Y. 1998. The timing of color and location processing in the motor context. *Experimental Brain Research*, in press.

Pöppel, E., Held, R., and Frost, D. 1973. Residual visual function after brain wounds involving central visual pathways in man. *Nature* 243:295–296.

Prablanc, C., Pelisson, D., and Goodale, M. A. 1986. Visual control of reaching movements without vision of the limb. I. Role of retinal feedback of target position in guiding the hand. *Exp Brain Res.* 62(2):293–302.

Rossetti, Y., Gaunet, F., and Thinus-Blanc, C. 1996. Early visual experience affects memorization and spatial representation of proprioceptive targets. *Neuroreport* 7(6):1219–1223.

Rossetti, Y., and Régnier, C. 1995. Representations in action: pointing to a target with various representations; in Bardy, B. G., Bootsma, R. J., and Guiard, Y. (eds.): *Studies in Perception and Action III*. Mahwah, N.J., Lawrence Erlbaum Associates, Inc., pp. 233–236.

Rossetti, Y., Rode, G., and Boisson, D. 1995. Implicit processing of somaesthetic information: a dissociation between where and how? *Neuroreport* 6:506–510.

Rossetti, Y. 1998. Short-lived motor representation of space in brain-damaged and healthy subjects. *Consciousness and Cognition*, in press.

Rossetti, Y., and Pisella, L. 1998. Temporal asynchrony between sensory and between motor components of a visuo-motor response: a time-grounded dissociation between implicit and explicit processing. Tucson III abstract No 217.

Rossetti, Y., and Procyk, E. 1997. What memory is for action: the gap between percepts and concepts. *Behavioral and Brain Sciences* 20(1):34–36.

Salin, P. A., and Bullier, J. 1995. Corticocortical connections in the visual system: structure and function. *Phyiol. Reviews* 75:107–154.

Thorpe, S., Fize, D., and Marlot, C. 1996. Speed of processing in the human visual system. *Nature* 381:520–522.

Weiskrantz, L., Warrington, E. R., Sanders, M. D., and Marshall, J. C. 1974. Visual capacity in the hemianopic field following a restricted occipital ablation. *Brain* 97:709–828.

13 Attending, Seeing and Knowing in Blindsight

Robert W. Kentridge, Charles A. Heywood, and Lawrence Weiskrantz

Blindsight is the term coined by Weiskrantz (see Weiskrantz et al. 1974) to describe the condition in which subjects with damage to their primary visual cortex are able to perform simple visual tasks in the area of visual space corresponding to their brain-damage while maintaining that they have no visual experience there. In other words, they retain some visual abilities in an area where they report that they are phenomenally blind. This dissociation between conscious experience and visual performance is usually revealed in forced-choice tasks involving discriminations of simple stimulus properties such as location, contrast, orientation, color and so on. However, while conducting an experiment mapping the area of one subject's residual vision (Kentridge et al. 1997), we recently chanced upon an exception. In this experiment the subject had to decide which of two tones was accompanied by a flashing spot of light. By examining how his performance varied as the spot of light was presented in different positions we could map the area over which his blindsight extended. Quite by chance, during one of the breaks in testing the subject (known as GY) remarked that he had just realised that the stimuli were sometimes being presented well above the horizontal and so now he was trying to pay attention higher up in his blind visual field. This is an extraordinary remark since one's intuition is that it is attention that gives rise to consciousness. Our subjective experience is that we are most conscious of that part of the world to which we are attending. This apparently close relationship between attention and consciousness was remarked upon from the birth of modern psychology (see, for example, James [1890], Wundt [1912]) and still influences many modern theories of consciousness. We followed the observation up in a series of experiments designed to establish exactly which aspects of attention continue to function in the blind region of GY's visual field. These experiments are reported in detail elsewhere (Kentridge et al., submitted), in the present chapter we will briefly summarize their results and then consider their implications for theories of consciousness and the central bases of visual attention.

Types of Attention

Attention has been studied, subdivided and categorized extensively (see, e.g., Pashler 1998). Two aspects of attention may influence awareness. First, the nature of the stimulus to which we are attending—are we simply attending to a specific location within the visual field or are we looking out for objects with a particular property, for example red things? Second, how was our attention initially directed—did we decide to attend voluntarily or did something unexpected or sudden catch our attention by itself? Both of these aspects of attention, the nature of its objective and the nature of its control, have featured in modern theories linking attention and consciousness.

Milner and Goodale (1996) suggested that we are conscious of stimuli that match a property to which we are attending, in other words, attention in the service of object identification gives rise to awareness. In contrast, stimuli appearing at an attended spatial location do not necessarily give rise to awareness. In other words, attention in the service of object location need not give rise to awareness. On the basis of neuro-psychological evidence Milner and Goodale identify processes leading to object identification with pathways leaving the primary visual cortex and passing ventrally toward inferotemporal cortex. In contrast, processes associated with directing actions toward objects, and hence with their spatial characteristics, with pathways leaving the visual cortex and passing dorsally toward the parietal cortex (see figure 13.1).

Posner (1994) has suggested that a dissociation between attention and awareness can also be made in terms of the nature of attentional control. The voluntary direction of attention, in which memories are invoked in order to guide attention, is

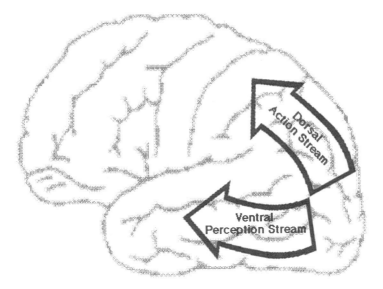

Figure 13.1
On leaving the visual cortex at the rear of the brain (on the right in this figure) visual information passes along a dorsal stream reaching the parietal cortex and a ventral stream reaching the temporal lobe. Milner and Goodale propose that the dorsal stream is involved in processing visual stimuli in the service of action whereas the ventral stream is involved in the process of identifying objects.

associated with awareness, whereas automatic direction of attention, in which a sensory stimulus captures attention for the processing of subsequent stimuli, can take place without awareness. Using brain-imaging Posner identifies the voluntary control of attention with activity in anterior cingulate and dorsolateral prefrontal cortex and automatic direction of attention with parietal cortex (see figure 13.2).

It should be clear that Milner and Goodale's and Posner's proposals are not in conflict with one another, they are, however, not entirely orthogonal. The automatic direction of attention is almost inevitably spatial whereas attention can be voluntarily directed either on the basis of location or object features. Our experiments addressed the question of whether attention could be automatically or voluntarily directed to target locations within the scotoma of a blindsight patient. It has been found that blindsight patients can exhibit different modes of awareness within their scotomata. In addition to blindsight, the presence of residual visual function with no acknowledged awareness, these patients also sometimes report awareness of events within their scotoma. This awareness is not accompanied by report of normal visual experience, rather, it is described as a sense that "something happened," that a stimulus

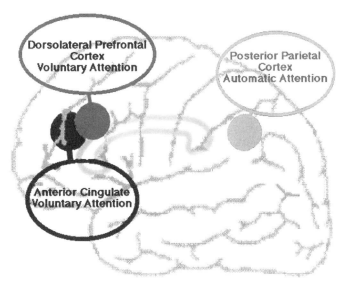

Figure 13.2
Posner identifies a number of different brain areas involved in voluntary and automatic attention. The posterior parietal cortex is implicated in the automatic direction of attention. Both the dorsolateral prefrontal cortex and the anterior cingulate are involved in the voluntary control of attention. The anterior cingulate does not lie on the surface of the brain, rather it lies on the brain's medial surface just forward of and above the corpus callosum.

gives rise to "awareness, but you don't see it," that decisions are not being based purely on guesswork. This "aware" mode of perception can be produced using moving or transient stimuli of high contrast (see, e.g., Weiskrantz et al. 1995). The ability to manipulate awareness in a blindsight patient without producing any report of visual qualia allowed us to investigate the role of awareness in both the automatic and voluntary direction of attention.

Attention without Awareness in Blindsight

We used Posner's attentional cueing paradigm (Posner 1980) to assess the effects of various cues on GY's reaction time to stimuli presented within his scotoma. GY's task was to determine whether or not a tone was accompanied by a visual target presented within his scotoma. A cue preceded each trial that usually indicated the likely location of a subsequent visual target. One some trials, however, the cue signalled an incorrect location. If the cues were being used to direct attention then we would expect to find significantly quicker reaction times on trials where the cue indicated the correct location compared to those from trials where the cue was misleading. In addition to measuring the effects of cueing on his reaction time we could also assess GY's accuracy in discriminaing the presence of targets. The possibility that reaction-time advantages produced by cueing were due to changes in strategy, trading-off accuracy for speed rather than gaining a speed advantage with no loss of accuracy by virtue of attending to the target location, could be discounted if reaction-time advantages are not accompanied by decreases in discrimination accuracy.

First we established that GY could indeed direct attention within his scotoma using cues that we presented in an undamaged area of his visual field pointing toward target locations in his blind field (the sequence of stimuli used in this experiment and those about to be desribed are shown in figure 13.3). We then went on to assess the role of awareness in voluntary and automatic direction of spatial attention. All cues were now presented within GY's scotoma, as were the targets. We manipulated GY's awareness of cues by using two different cue contrasts. In one set of experiments cues (apart from the misleading ones) and targets were presented at the same locations. These cues could automatically direct attention to the target location. In a second set of experiments we instructed GY that when a cue appeared at one location it indicated that a target was likely to appear at a second specified location. Appropriate direction of attention relied on recall of this instruction and so was necessarily voluntary—automatic engagement of attention to the location of the cue would not aid detection of the target, which was at another location in these experiments. We

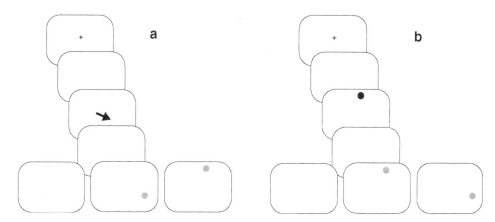

Figure 13.3
Stimulus sequences used in each trial. Panel **a** shows the sequence in the experiment using centrally presented arrow cues. The left frame at the bottom illustrates a trial where no target was presented, the middle
frame one where the target was presented in the location indicated by the cue and the right frame one
where it was presented at the other, invalid, location. The sequences used in the other experiments where
the cues were peripherally presented discs are shown in panel **b**. In this example the upper location is cued
and the left, middle and right frames again illustrate target-absent, valid and invalidly cued target trials
respectively. The displays were identical in the experiments where peripheral cues had to be interpreted in
the light of a rule relating cue and target location. The only difference being that in these experiments,
rather that the cue indicating the location at which a subsequent target is most likely to appear, it now
indicates that the target is more likely to appear at the other of the two possible locations. For these
experiments if the cue appeared at the upper location (as in panel **b**) then the left, middle and right frames
at the bottom would illustrate target-absent, invalidly and validly cued target trials respectively.

found that GY could only direct his attention voluntarily with high contrast cues that
produced reports of awareness on nearly all trials. GY's attention could, however, be
directed automatically regardless of the cue-contrast. These results are summarised in
figure 13.4.

Anatomical Bases for Blindsight

What implications do these results have for our understanding of the anatomy of
attention, awareness and qualia? GY's scotoma resulted from a road accident he
suffered aged 8. The accident produced a unilateral occipital lesion, apparently
restricted to striate cortex (area V1) as revealed by neuroimaging (Blythe et al. 1987,
Barbur et al. 1993). There are a number of possible bases for GY's residual vision
given this lesion. One suggestion (Campion et al. 1983, Fendrich et al. 1995) is that
the damage to GY's striate cortex is incomplete and his residual vision depends upon

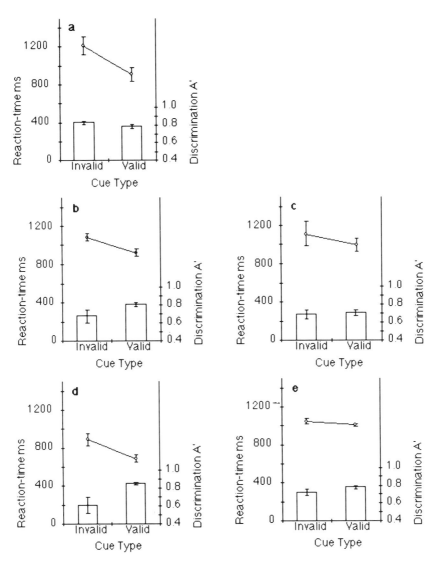

Figure 13.4
Each panel shows reaction times (o) and the discrimination measure A′ (bars) for valid and invalid cues. Analyses were conducted on a block by block basis. A′ scores for valid and invalid cues were calculated from all trials in each block. An average reaction time was calculated for each cueing condition, in each block, from all trials in which a target was correctly identified as being present, after discarding anticipatory responses (RT < 100 ms) and mis-hits of the buttons (RT > 2000 ms). The measures were entered into analyses of variance with the repeated-measures factor "Cue-validity" for experiment 1 and the additional independent-samples factor 'Cue-contrast' for the other two experiments. Panel **a** shows results for centrally presented arrow cues: RT F(1, 5) = 20.13, p < 0.01; A′ F(1, 5) = 2.57 ns. Panels **b** and **c** show results

small patches of spared cortex within the volume of the apparent lesion. There are a number of reasons to doubt this explanation. First the area of GY's residual vision did not appear patchy when mapped using procedures to eliminate possible confounding effects of eye-movements (Kentridge et al. 1997). Second, functional magnetic resonance imaging of brain activity in another blindsight patient showed that stimuli presented in his blind field did not produce any detectable activation of primary visual cortex but did result in an increase in activity in extrastirate visual areas (Stoerig et al. 1998). This evidence shows that blindsight cannot be a purely subcortical phenomenon. Blindsight may, under some circumstances, be mediated by pathways that reach extrastriate cortical areas without passing through primary visual cortex. There are two possible sources, direct projections from the lateral geniculate nucleus to areas V2 and V4 (Cowey and Stoerig 1989) and projections, possibly via the superior colliculus, to the pulvinar and on to areas MT (Standage and Benvenuto 1983) and V4 (Ungerleider and Desimone 1986).

Anatomical Bases for Attention

How could these potential sources of residual function in blindsight link up with the anatomies of voluntary and automatic attention? Should we be surprised that attention can be directed in the absence of primary visual cortex? An elegant experiment by He et al. (1996) showed that the after-effects of looking at a pattern with a particular orientation in a particular location and the ability to attend to just that location could be dissociated. The range over which the after-effect occurred was much smaller than the distance over which distactors items could be suppressed in an attentional task. The scale over which the after-effect and the focus of attention act are likely to depend on the receptive field sizes of cells in the brain areas that mediate these two processes. As the after-effect is known to be due adaptation in primary visual cortex and the scale over which the focus of attention operates is different from the scale over which the after effect operates it is unlikely that attentional selection is

Figure 13.4 (continued)
for direct indication of target location with high (panel **b**) and low (panel **c**) contrast cues. RT analysis: cue-validity $F_{(1, 13)} = 16.76$, $p > 0.001$, cue-contrast $F < 1$, interaction $F < 1$ A' analysis: cue-validity $F_{(1, 13)} = 1.90$, ns, cue-contrast $F < 1$, interaction $F_{(1, 13)} = 1.20$, ns. Panels **d** and **e** show results for indirect indication of target location with high (panel **d**) and low (panel **e**) contrast cues. RT analysis: cue-validity $F_{(1, 19)} = 19.65$, $p > 0.0001$, cue-contrast $F_{(1, 19)} = 25.99$, $p < 0.0001$, interaction $F_{(1, 19)} = 9.28$, $p < 0.0001$. The simple main effect of cue-validity is significant for high contrast cues ($F_{(1, 19)} = 22.78$, $p < 0.001$) but not low contrast ones ($F < 1$). A' analysis: cue-validity $F_{(1, 19)} = 13.08$, $p < 0.005$, cue-contrast $F < 1$, interaction $F_{(1, 19)} = 5.11$, $p < 0.05$.

occurring is primary visual cortex. This aspect of their conclusion is unsurprising since it has been known since the mid 1980s that attention modulates neuronal activity in extrastriate cortex but has little effect on striate cortex (Moran and Desimone 1985). The key conclusion of the He et al. paper, however, is that is "that the attentional filter acts in one or more higher visual cortical areas to restrict the availability of visual information to conscious awareness" (p. 335). We show that this cannot be the case. Attentional selection can take place without awareness, so selection per se, is not sufficient for awareness.

There is more to attention than selection. Consider the steps involving attention in our experimental designs using peripheral cues. Initially, as the subject's attention is not directed to either of the target locations, the appearance of a cue in the periphery must capture attention, disengaging it from its current focus. Once attention has been captured by the cue, attention must be redirected to its new focus. This redirection may be automatic or voluntary. The newly redirected focus of attention must now selectively enhance the processing of stimuli that match the focus of attention (in this case, location). The consequences of this enhanced processing may be an increased likelihood of perceiving the attended stimulus or a predisposition to act in response to it.

The posterior parietal lobe is clearly implicated in the capture of attention. Hemispatial neglect is a neuropsychological disorder usually caused by unilateral damage to the parietal lobe. Although parietal syndrome may have many components, including somatosensory and oculomotor deficits (see, e.g., Cole et al. 1962, Ishiai et al. 1979) its most studied aspect is patients inability to redirect their attention to the visual hemifield contralateral to their lesion (Posner et al. 1984). This attentional component has been specifically associated with lesions of the inferior parietal lobule (Galletti et al. 1997). Electrophysiological studies in monkeys have shown that attending to a location at which subsequent targets are likely to appear reduces the sensitivity of a majority of parietal neurons (in area 7a) to stimuli (Steinmetz et al. 1994) at the attended location. The implication is that the sensitivity of neurons in nonattended locations is enhanced in order to allow peripheral events to capture attention. Posterior parietal cortex receives many projections from the pulvinar (see, e.g., Asanuma et al. 1985) in addition to those from striate and extrastriate cortex. It is reasonable to assume that it can be activated in blindsight in the absence of striate cortex.

The automatic redirection of attention to the location at which a cue appeared may not require control by areas beyond parietal cortex. Activity in parietal areas is revealed by PET studies in tasks both voluntary and automatic attention (e.g.,

Corbetta et al. 1993). Constantinidis and Steinmetz (1996) showed that during the interval between the presentation of cue and target, when no stimulus was therefore present, activity in a subpopulation of neurons within area 7a of parietal cortex of monkeys was elevated in the region corresponding to the cue's location. The relationship between the set of neurons whose sensitivity is suppressed once attention has been captured by a stimulus and the set of neurons whose activity is enhanced is not known. These studies indicate that the automatic redirection of attention may not require control from areas beyond the parietal lobe. This is not the case when attention must be voluntarily redirected. In this case the new focus of attention is depends on interpreting cues in the light of some remembered rule or meaning. When tasks in which attention is automatically engaged are compared to those requiring voluntary control differences in PET are found in frontal areas but not parietal ones. Corbetta et al. (1993) report activation of superior frontal cortex and anterior cingulate cortex in voluntary but not in automatic tasks.

In 1985 Moran and Desimone (1985) reported that cells in cortical area V4 and in the inferior temporal cortex of monkeys responded much more strongly to stimuli when the monkeys were attending to them than when the stimuli were being ignored. The enhancement of the response of a specific subset of cells is a very good candidate for the selective mechanism of attention. Since Moran and Desimone's (1985) paper similar selective enhancements have been reported in a number of visual areas, for example, MT and MST (Treue and Maunsell 1996), V1 (striate cortex), V2, V4 (Motter 1993). There is some controversy over evidence for attention modulation of responsivity in striate cortex. Motter (1993) reports attentional modulation when using large number of distractors whereas Moran and Desimone (1985) failed to find any. Although selection may take place in V1, it probably operates more strongly in extrastriate areas, particularly V4 (Desimone and Duncan 1995). Given the fact that, among the many thalamo-cortical connections that bypass striate cortex, there are projections from both the LGN and the pulvinar to V4 we should not be surprised that attentional selection can operate in blindsight.

Awareness, Control and Qualia

The evidence outlined above is compatible with the capture, redirection and selection mechanism of attention in blindsight. Remember, however, that all of this is occurring without normal visual experience. One of the most curious features of attention in blindsight is its voluntary control in response to cues within the blind field. Although this was only effective when GY reported awareness of stimuli, he still denied normal visual experience of them. Although he was aware of stimuli he did not "see" them. As we have seen, studies of voluntary attention suggest that it involves prefrontal areas, in particular dorsolateral prefrontal cortex and anterior cingulate cortex. Willed action (Frith et al. 1991), spatial memory (Ungerleider et al. 1998) and the suppression of habitual responses to remembered instructions (Jahanshahi et al. 1998) have also all been associated with activity in dorsolateral prefrontal cortex. Dorsolateral prefrontal cortex has also been shown to be active in GY when he reports awareness of a stimulus but not when he makes successful discriminations without awareness (Sahraie et al. 1997), although superior colliculus and medial and orbital prefrontal cortices are activated in this unaware blindsight mode. It therefore appears that while the involvement of dorsolateral prefrontal cortex in the voluntary direction of attention may give rise to awareness, on its own it does not give rise to visual qualia, but rather to a feeling of knowing free from qualia, what James (1890) referred to as fringe consciousness (see Mangan 1993 for a modern review of this concept). This fringe consciousness is sufficient to allow the retrieval of a rule from memory and a resultant attentional modulation of responses to targets, but, it does not give rise to visual qualia. This awareness is sufficient for control but not experience. Although awareness of visual cues defined by luminance contrast may be mediated by activity reaching dorsolateral prefrontal cortex by a route that bypasses striate cortex, the experience of visual qualia is not complete without striate cortex.

We can draw the following conclusions.

• Attention can be directed to locations within the scotoma of a blindsight patient.

• Attention can be directed by cues within the scotoma of a blindsight patient.

• Although the automatic direction of attention need not be associated with awareness, the voluntary direction of attention requires awareness.

• There is no conflict between current understanding of the anatomy of attention and both voluntary and automatic control of attention bypassing striate cortex.

• The activation of dosrolateral prefrontal cortex in GY's aware mode revealed with functional magnetic resonance imaging by Sahraie et al. (1997) and the selective involvement of dosrolateral prefrontal cortex in voluntary but not automatic control of attention indicate that GY's "aware" mode is sufficient for the engagement of rules from memory and the control of action via attention.

• 'Aware' mode is not seeing, activation of dosrolateral prefrontal cortex may coincide with consciousness in the form of a feeling of knowing, but, without striate cortex it is does not produce visual qualia.

References

Asanuma, C., Andersen, R. A., and Cowan, W. M. 1985. The thalamic relations of the caudal inferior parietal lobule and the lateral prefrontal cortex in monkeys: divergent cortical projections from cell clusters in the medial pulvinar nucleus. *J. Comp. Neurol.* 241:357–81.

Barbur, J. L., Watson, J. D. G., Frakowiak, R. S. J., and Zeki, S. 1993. Conscious visual perception without V1. *Brain* 116:1293–1302.

Blythe, I. M., Kennard, C., and Ruddock, K. H. 1987. Residual vision in patients with retrogeniculate lesions of the visual pathways. *Brain* 110:887–894.

Cole, M., Shutta, H. S., and Warrington, W. K. 1962. Visual disorientation in homonymous halffields. *Neurology* 12:257–263.

Constantinidis, C., and Steinmetz, M. A. 1996. Neuronal activity in posterior parietal area 7a during the delay periods of a spatial memory task. *J. Neurophysiol.* 76:1352–1355.

Corbetta, M., Miezin, F. M., Shulman, G. L., and Petersen, S. E. 1993. A PET study of visuospatial attention. *J. Neurosci.* 13:1202–1226.

Cowey, A., and Stoerig, P. 1989. Projection patterns of surviving neurons in the dorsal lateral geniculate nucleus following discrete lesions of striate cortex: implications for residual vision. *Exp. Brain Res.* 75:631–638

Desimone, R., and Duncan, J. 1995. Neural mechanisms of selective visual attenton. *Ann. Rev. Neurosci.* 18:193–222.

Frith, C. D., Friston, K., Liddle, P. F., and Frackowiak, R. S. 1991. Willed action and the prefrontal cortex in man: a study with PET. *Proc. R. Soc. Lond. B. Biol. Sci.* 244:241–6.

Galletti, C., Battaglini, P. P., and Fattori, P. 1997. The posterior parietal cortex in humans and monkeys. *News in Physiol. Sci.* 12:166–171.

He, S., Cavanagh, P., and Intriligator, J. 1996. Attentional resolution and the locus of visual awareness. *Nature* 383:334–337.

Ishiai, S., Furukawa, T., and Tsukagoshi, H. 1987. Eye-fixation patterns in homonymous hemianopia and unilateral spatial neglect. *Neuropsychologia* 25:675–679.

Jahanshahi, M., Profice, P., Brown, R. G., Ridding, M. C., Dirnberger, G., and Rothwell, J. C. 1998. The effects of transcranial magnetic stimulation on suppression of habitual counting during random number generation. *Brain* 121:1533–1544.

James, W. 1890. *Principles of psychology*. London: Macmillan.

Kentridge, R. W., Heywood, C. A., and Weiskrantz, L. Attention without awareness in blindsight. submitted to *Proc. Roy. Soc. B.*

Kentridge, R. W., Heywood, C. A.. and Weiskrantz, L. 1997. Residual vision in multiple retinal locations within a scotoma: Implications for blindsight. *J. Cog. Neurosci.* 9:191–202.

Mangan, B. 1993. Taking pheomenology seriously: The "fringe" and its implications for cognitive research. *Consciousness and Cognition* 2:89–108.

Milner, A. D. and Goodale, M. A. 1996. *The visual brain in action*. Oxford: Oxford University Press.

Moran, J., and Desimone, R. 1985. Selective attention gates visual processing in the extrastriate cortex. *Science* 229:782–884.

Motter, B. C. 1993. Focal attention produces spatially selective processing in visual cortical areas V1, V2, and V4 in the presence of competing stimuli. *J. Neurophysiol.* 70:909–19

Pashler, H. E. 1998. The psychology of attention. Cambridge, Mass.: MIT Press.

Posner, M. I. 1980. Orienting of attention. *Q. J. Exp. Psychol.* 32:3–25.

Posner, M. I. 1994. Attention: the mechanisms of consciousness. *Proc. Natl. Acad. Sci. USA* 91:7398–8403.

Posner, M. I., Walker, J. A., Friedrich, F. J., and Rafal, R. D. Effects of parietal injury on covert orienting of attention. *J. Neurosci.* **4**:1863–84.

Sahraie, A., Weiskrantz, L., Barbur, J. L., Simmons, A., Williams, S. C., and Brammer, M. J. 1997. Pattern of neuronal activity associated with conscious and unconscious processing of visual signals. *Proc. Natl. Acad. Sci. USA* 94:9406–11.

Standage, G. P., and Benevento, L. A. 1983. The organization of connections between the pulvinar and visual area MT in the macaque monkey. *Brain. Res.* 262:288–94.

Steinmetz, M. A., Connor, C. E., Constantinidis, C., and McLaughlin, J. R. 1994. Covert attention suppresses neuronal responses in area 7a of the posterior parietal cortex. *J. Neurophysiol.* 72:1020–3.

Stoerig, P., Kleinschmidt, A., and Frahm, J. 1998. No visual responses in denervated V1: high-resolution functional magnetic resonance imaging of a blindsight patient. *Neuroreport* 9:21–5.

Treue, S., and Maunsell, J. H. 1996. Attentional modulation of visual motion processing in cortical areas MT and MST. *Nature* 382:539–41.

Ungerleider, L. G., Courtney, S. M., and Haxby, J. V. 1998. A neural system for human visual working memory. *Proc. Natl. Acad. Sci. USA* 95:883–90.

Ungerleider, L. G., and Desimone, R. 1986. Cortical connections of visual area MT in the macaque. *J. Comp. Neurol.* 248:190–222.

Weiskrantz, L. ; Barbur, J. L., and Sahraie, A. 1995. Parameters affecting conscious versus unconscious visual discrimination with damage to the visual cortex (V1) *Proc. Natl. Acad. Sci. USA* 92:6122–6126.

Weiskrantz, L., Warrington, E. K., Sanders, M. D., and Marshall, J. 1974. Visual capacity in the hemianopic field following a restricted occipital ablation. *Brain* 97:709–28.

Wundt, W. 1912. *Introduction to psychology* (Trans. R. Pintner). London: George Allen.

14 Insights into Blindsight

A. David Milner

One of the highlights of the third meeting of "Toward a Science of Consciousness," was the plenary session on Blindsight. The definition of the term *blindsight* remains, some 25 years after its coinage by Larry Weiskrantz, controversial. In the general view, it refers to any residual visual function, unaccompanied by visual awareness, that can be observed in patients who have suffered major (usually hemianopic) field defects following damage to the striate cortex (V1) or to the optic radiations (which connect the lateral geniculate nucleus to the cortex). Despite the controversy, the term seems destined to stick, and to survive the recent attempt by Zeki and ffytche (1998) to introduce the (arguably more respectable) Greek-derived term *agnosopsia* to refer to such phenomena of vision without awareness.

The two presentations in the plenary session at Tucson were given by Petra Stoerig (with co-authors A. Cowey and R. Goebel) and by Robert Kentridge (with co-authors C. A. Heywood and L. Weiskrantz). Stoerig first reviewed briefly the evidence for blindsight in humans and monkey subjects, and described how increasingly careful studies have been done to control for the possible artifacts that critics have identified over the years. She then went on to present new neuroimaging data that revealed an intriguing pattern of activation in the occipito-temporal regions of the cerebral cortex of three hemianopic patients when they viewed complex visual stimuli in the "blind" hemifield. The activated areas included those that have been designated V4 and LO, which may be regarded as likely homologues of areas V4 and TEO in the monkey's ventral stream. The stimuli consisted of colored drawings of natural objects, such as fruit. Importantly, there was no activation in the damaged or deafferented area V1 on the lesioned side of the brain, even when reversing checkerboard patterns (a powerful stimulus to striate cortex) were presented. In separate observations, the investigators also found activation of the motion complex (including MT/V5) ipsilateral to the lesion, in response to spiral checkerboard motion.

The reported activation of the motion complex, which forms a part of the "dorsal stream" of cortical visual areas, replicates a previous neuroimaging study of a blindsight patient (Barbur et al. 1993). It is reasonable to assume that the activation comes about via the second major visual route from the eye to the brain, which passes through the superior colliculus in the midbrain and pulvinar nucleus of the thalamus. The activation of areas within the occipito-temporal "ventral" stream however, has not been previously reported in hemianopic subjects, and is surprising in the light of animal research. This work has shown that (at least in anesthetized monkeys) neurons in the ventral stream lose their responsiveness to visual stimuli when area V1 is removed, or deactivated through cooling, although neurons in the dorsal stream (e.g., in area MT) remain active (Gross 1991, Bullier et al. 1994).

There are several possible interpretations of these new results, each of which should lead to even more interesting experiments. For example, it could be that the ventral-stream activation comes about through pathways that convey color information to the cortex through extra-striate routes. Cowey and Stoerig (e.g., 1992) have shown in several studies that "color blindsight" can occur, and indeed have argued that this phenomenon might be mediated by neurons surviving in the LGN that could carry information directly to extrastriate visual areas such as V2 and V4, by-passing the striate cortex. This route could be more fully elucidated by carrying out further neuroimaging studies with hemianopic patients in which color variations in an abstract pattern are contrasted with luminance variations only (cf. Zeki et al. 1991), or in which colored line drawings are contrasted with achromatic line drawings.

A second possibility is that the activation seen in response to the drawings reflects form processing, or at least the processing of object contours, in the absence of striate cortex (any apparent blindsight for form is probably reducible to blindsight for line orientation and perhaps other elementary attributes like line length—see Weiskrantz 1987). However work by Perenin and Rossetti (1996) suggests that, as with motion processing, such contour processing is dependent upon dorsal-stream systems rather than ventral ones in hemianopic patients. These authors reported that their hemianopic patient was able to carry out visually guided motor acts (rotating the wrist to mail a card, or opening the hand to grasp a block) in response to stimuli in the blind field, but was not able to report them verbally or manually. They interpret their data in the light of the model of Milner and Goodale (1995) in which the dorsal stream is seen as primarily dedicated for the visual control of action. Milner and Goodale suggested that where blindsight for contour was demonstrated, it might be the result of the activation of such visuomotor systems. They took a similar line in explaining blindsight for location and motion (e.g., in terms of incipient eye movement control), while accepting Cowey and Stoerig's evidence for the involvement of ventral stream areas in color blindsight.

The third and perhaps most intriguing possibility for explaining the ventral stream activation found by Stoerig and colleagues was raised by a questioner from the floor at the Plenary session. No doubt inspired by an earlier presentation by Richard Gregory, this questioner asked whether the ventral stream activation might be generated by a top-down process, in which the person tries to make sense of the absent or rudimentary information available from the "blind" field by constructing perceptual "hypotheses." This idea could be tested in a number of ways. For example, it might be predicted that even when no blindsight for contour was present in a hemianopic patient (perhaps even when blindness is caused by ocular or peripheral optic pathway damage, such that no visual information can reach the brain at all), one might still be able to record activity in the occipito-temporal region if the person is led to expect shapes in the blind field.

The other presentation, by Bob Kentridge, was equally thought-provoking. It included work that tells against the recent idea by Fendrich and colleagues (1992) that apparent blindsight might be attributable to preserved islands of intact cortex within area V1. The work of Kentridge and colleagues shows that in at least one well-studied patient (GY), there is no patchiness of blindsight across the hemianopic field as would be expected if there were such preserved cortical islands. They failed to find any such variation even when eye movements were minimized by various means and monitored by a dual-Purkinje image eye tracker (see Kentridge et al. 1997). Kentridge went on to describe more recent studies in which GY's ability to attend selectively within his hemianopic field was examined. This question touches on one of the most basic issues in modern research into consciousness—namely, what is the relationship between attention and consciousness, and can the two be dissociated?

Milner and Goodale (1995) summarized physiological evidence that the gating processes correlated with selective attention are widely distributed among the cortical areas subserving visual processing, and in particular that these processes can be seen within both the dorsal and ventral streams. More recent research has strengthened this conclusion. Milner and Goodale also proposed that the conscious experience that (generally) goes with visual perception receives its contents via the ventral stream, whereas the visuomotor control mediated by the dorsal stream proceeds without directly influencing or requiring visual awareness. They went on to make the inference that attentional processes can operate either to select for action or to select for perception, and that only in the latter case would they be closely correlated with awareness.

Kentridge reported data that are consistent with these ideas. Using variations of the Posner cueing paradigm, he and his colleagues have found highly convincing evidence that GY can direct his visuospatial attention within his hemianopic field. For example, GY showed much more rapid reaction times to targets in a location that was validly cued by a central symbolic prime, than to target locations that were invalidly cued. Thus GY seems to be well able to distribute his attention differentially within his "blind" field. Furthermore, the authors went on to show that GY was even responsive to attentional cues placed in his hemianopic field itself—in other words his attention could be directed by cues that he could not see to targets that he could not see! Admittedly, however, the use of a brighter attentional cue (for which GY more often reports some kind of indefinable sensation) did yield larger attentional effects.

Moreover, when asked to use a cue at one of two locations in his blind field to direct his attention to the *other* location, GY succeeded only when the brighter cues were used. Kentridge inferred from this that the *voluntary* use of cues to direct attention may require conscious processing of the cue, while more automatic orienting of attention may not.

Where does this new burst of blindsight research take us? I believe it marks at last a move away from the somewhat sterile debates over the reality of blindsight, into more interesting realms of investigation, in which the *fact* of blindsight allows us to ask important new questions about the neural and psychological correlates of visual awareness. If this optimism is justified, then the second 25 years of blindsight research promise to build on the first 25 years in some profoundly exciting ways.

This article was previously published in *Trends in Cognitive Science* 2, no. 7 (1998): 237–238.

References

Barbur, J. L., Watson, J. D. G., Frackowiak, R. S. J., and Zeki, S. M. 1993. Conscious visual perception without V1. *Brain* 116:1293–1302.

Bullier, J., Girard, P., and Salin, P.-A. 1994. The role of area 17 in the transfer of information to extrastriate visual cortex, in *Cerebral Cortex, Volume 10: Primary Visual Cortex in Primates* (Peters, A. and Rockland, K. S., eds.), pp. 301–330, Plenum Press.

Cowey, A., and Stoerig, P. 1992. Reflections on blindsight, in *The Neuropsychology of Consciousness* (Milner, A. D. and Rugg, M. D., eds.), pp. 11–38, Academic Press.

Fendrich, R., Wessinger, C. M., and Gazzaniga, M. S. 1992. Residual vision in a scotoma: implications for blindsight. *Science* 258:1489–1491.

Gross, C. G. 1991. Contribution of striate cortex and the superior colliculus to visual function in area MT, the superior temporal polysensory area and inferior temporal cortex. *Neuropsychologia* 29:497–515.

Kentridge, R. W., Heywood, C. A., and Weiskrantz, L. 1997. Residual vision in multiple retinal locations within a scotoma: implications for blindsight. *Journal of Cognitive Neuroscience* 9:191–202.

Milner, A. D., and Goodale, M. A. 1995. *The Visual Brain in Action*, Oxford University Press.

Perenin, M. T., and Rossetti, Y. 1996. Grasping without form discrimination in a hemianopic field. *NeuroReport* 7:793–897.

Weiskrantz, L. 1987. Residual vision in a scotoma. A follow-up study of "form" discrimination. *Brain* 110:77–92.

Zeki, S. and ffytche, D. H. 1998. The Riddoch syndrome: insights into the neurobiology of conscious vision. *Brain* 121:25–45.

Zeki, S., Watson, J. D. G., Lueck, C. J., Friston, K. J., Kennard, C.. and Frackowiak, R. S. J. 1991. A direct demonstration of functional specialization in human visual cortex. *Journal of Neuroscience* 11:641–649.

15 From Grasping to Language: Mirror Neurons and the Origin of Social Communication

Vittorio Gallese

There are many different ways to approach the study of brain functions. The data that will be reported here have been acquired by using a "naturalistic" approach. What does it mean? A naturalistic approach, when applied to neurophysiology, consists in choosing the most appropriate way of testing neurons activity, by figuring out what would be the stimuli or the behavioral situation that more closely approximate what the animal we are recording from would experience in its natural environment. The "answers" we are seeking from neuronal activity are strongly influenced by the way in which we pose our "questions." Too many experimental data are collected by routinely applying behavioral paradigms good for all purposes. Another flaw commonly encountered in part of the contemporary neurophysiological literature is the poor, if any, attention paid to investigate *where from* is recorded *what*. Altogether, these factors have induced among many scholars of this discipline a growing sense of discomfort with the single neuron recording approach.

My point, as neurophysiologist, is that the single neuron recording approach still represents a very powerful and creative tool to unravel the neural correlates of many cognitive functions. This goal can be achieved provided that we are able to broaden the theoretical background in which the experimental data are to be framed, by integrating the findings and the contributions coming from other disciplines such as psychology, cognitive ethology, and philosophy.

In the following sections I will expose results which are in line with the theoretical and methodological principles that I have only briefly sketched above. I will show how some of the visuo-motor processes occurring in the macaque monkey premotor cortex may provide new insights on issues such as action understanding and the origin of language.

The Monkey Premotor Cortex and Area F5

Let us examine a very "simple" empirical problem: what happens in a macaque monkey brain when it is about to grasp a raisin? Grasping is, apparently, a very simple action. Monkeys, as humans, perform it hundred times everyday. Grasping can be described in terms of the goal that has to be achieved: to take possession of an object. It can also be described in terms of its temporal development, decomposing it into a premovement phase, during which the physical properties of the object to be grasped like its size, its shape, its axis orientation, are analyzed, and into an executive phase, during which the monkey's hand is aimed at the object in such a way as to properly match its previously analyzed intrinsic properties. How does the monkey brain addresses these problems? And even more important, how can we investigate it? According to the "naturalistic" approach I was advocating in the introduction, the best way is to present some interesting objects like raisin, apples, etc., to the monkey, let it grasp them, and correlate the single neuron activity we are recording with the ongoing behavior.

This approach led during the last two decades to the discovery of the existence of multiple cortical representations of hand movements in the inferior parietal lobule and in the ventral premotor cortex (Hyvärinen and Poranen 1974, Mountcastle et al. 1975, Rizzolatti et al. 1981, Rizzolatti 1987, Gentilucci et al. 1988, Rizzolatti et al. 1988, Sakata et al. 1995). The anticipatory discharge with respect to movement onset of many neurons of these areas lead to hypothesize for them an important role in the planning of movements.

I will focus my attention on the premotor cortex, the cortex that lies rostral to the primary motor cortex. Converging anatomical evidence (see Matelli and Luppino 1997) supports the notion that the ventral premotor cortex (referred to also as inferior area 6) is composed of two distinct areas, designated as F4 and F5 (Matelli et al. 1985). As shown in figure 15.1, area F5 occupies the rostralmost part of inferior area

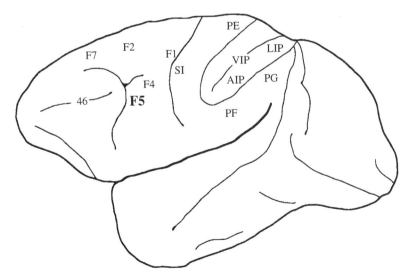

Figure 15.1
Lateral view of the macaque brain showing the cytoarchitectonic parcellation of the ventral premotor cortex according to Matelli et al., 1985. Mirror neurons were recorded in area F5, indicated in bold, which represents the rostralmost part of the ventral premotor cortex.

6, extending rostrally within the posterior bank of the inferior limb of the arcuate sulcus. Area F5 is reciprocally connected with the hand field of the primary motor cortex (Matelli et al. 1986) and has direct, although limited, projections to the upper cervical segments of the spinal chord (He et al. 1993). Intracortical microstimulation evokes in F5 hand and mouth movements at thresholds generally higher than in the primary motor cortex (Gentilucci et al. 1988, Hepp-Reymond et al. 1994). The functional properties of F5 neurons were assessed in a series of single unit recording experiments (Rizzolatti et al. 1981, Okano and Tanji 1987, Rizzolatti et al. 1988). These experiments showed that the activity of F5 neurons is correlated with specific distal motor acts and not with the execution of individual movements. What makes of a movement a motor act is the presence of a goal. Using the effective motor act as the classification criterion, the following types of neurons were described: "Grasping neurons," "Holding neurons," "Tearing neurons," and "Manipulation neurons." Let us concentrate on the first class: grasping neurons discharge when the monkey performs movements aimed to take possession of objects with the hand ("Grasping-with-the-hand neurons"), with the mouth ("Grasping-with-the-mouth neurons"), or with both ("Grasping-with-the-hand-and-the-mouth neurons"). Grasping-with-the-hand neurons form the largest class of F5 neurons. Most neurons of this class are selective for different types of grip. By observing the way in which the monkey grasped objects, three basic types of hand prehension were distinguished: *precision grip* (opposition of the pulpar surface of the index finger and thumb) normally used to grasp small objects, *finger prehension* (opposition of the thumb to the other fingers) used to grasp middle-size objects and *whole hand prehension* (flexion of all fingers around an object) used to grasp large objects. The majority of F5 grasping neurons is selective for precision grip.

The most interesting aspect of F5 neurons is that they code movement in quite abstract terms. What is coded is not simply a parameter such as force or movement direction, but rather the relationship, in motor terms, between the agent and the object of the action. F5 neurons become active only if a particular type of action (e.g., grasp, hold, etc.) is executed to achieve a particular type of goal (e.g., to take possession of a piece of food, to throw away an object, etc.). The metaphor of a "motor vocabulary" has been introduced (Rizzolatti and Gentilucci 1988) in order to conceptualize the function of these neurons. The presence in the motor system of a "vocabulary" of motor acts allows a much simpler selection of a particular action within a given context. Either when the action is self-generated or externally generated, only a few "words" need to be selected. Let us imagine that a monkey is presented with a small object, say a raisin, within its reaching distance. If the motivational value of the stimulus is powerful enough to trigger an appetitive behavior, it will evoke a command for a grasping action; then the command will address a specific finger configuration, suitable to grasp the raisin in that particular context. Within the context of a motor "vocabulary," motor action can be conceived as a simple assembly of words, instead of being described in the less economical terms of the control of individual movements.

Since most grasping actions are executed under visual guidance, it is extremely interesting to elucidate the relationship between the features of 3D visual objects and the specific words of the motor vocabulary. According to this logic, the appearance of a graspable object in the visual space will retrieve immediately the appropriate ensemble of words. This process, in neurophysiological terms, implies that the same neuron must be able not only to code motor acts, but also to respond to the visual features triggering them. About twenty percent of F5 grasping neurons, when clinically tested, indeed responded to the visual presentation of objects of different size in absence of any detectable movement (Rizzolatti et al. 1988). Very often a strict congruence was observed between the type of grip coded by a given neuron and the size of the object effective in triggering its visual response. These neurons, which match the "intrinsic" object properties with the most appropriate type of prehension, appear to be good candidates to perform the process of visuo-motor transformation. It was during the study of the visual properties of grasping neurons that mirror neurons were discovered.

The Discovery of Mirror Neurons and Their Functional Properties

Scientific discoveries very often happen by chance: the discovery of mirror neurons makes no exception.

One afternoon, when studying a neuron motorically activated by the action of grasping with the hand, one of us brought his hand toward a food-tray to grasp a raisin that had to be showed to the monkey: in that precise moment the neuron discharged vigorously. We were really surprised and, I must admit, quite skeptical about this unprecedented and unexpected visual response. Nevertheless, after many repetition of the same action, we started thinking that a new class of visuo-motor neurons perhaps had been discovered. A class of neurons responding both when a particular action is performed by the recorded monkey *and* when the same action performed by another individual is observed. After that first neuron we decided to look systematically whether more grasping neurons could be activated not by the visual presentation of graspable objects but by the observation of grasping actions. I remember those days as marked by a growing sense of excitation as it appeared that a considerable percentage of grasping neurons could be driven by action observation. We decided to call them "Mirror neurons," (Gallese et al. 1996, Rizzolatti et al. 1996a), since their visual properties match, mirror, the motor ones. Since then, many more mirror neurons have been recorded in our lab from many monkeys. This has allowed us to study them more quantitatively, and to theorize about their possible function.

Let us briefly summarize the naturalistic approach when recording mirror neurons from area F5. The awake monkey is confortably seated on a primate chair. Single neuron activity is recorded by means of a microelectrode. Once a neuron is isolated, its visual and motor properties are studied. The monkey is presented with various objects: they consist of food items (raisins, pieces of apple, sunflower seeds) and of objects of different size and shapes. Objects are presented at different locations with respect to the monkey, within and outside its reaching distance. Prehension movements are studied by presenting the same objects used for visual testing, and by letting the monkey grasp them. Everytime a neuron becomes active during prehension movements its properties are formally tested within a behavioral controlled paradigm in which arm and hand movements of the monkey are recorded, both in light and in darkness, using a computerized movement recording system and subsequently correlated with the recorded neuronal activity.

Mirror properties were studied by performing a series of actions in different spatial locations with respect to the monkey. These actions could be transitive movements (such as grasping, holding, manipulating, or tearing objects) or intransitive movements with or without emotional content (arms lifting, waving hands, threatening gestures, and so on). In order to verify whether the recorded neuron coded specifically hand-objects interactions the following actions were also performed: hand movements mimicking object-related actions in absence of the objects; prehension movements performed by using tools such as pincers or pliers; simultaneous movements of hands and objects kept spatially separated. Finally, in order to rule out the possibility that mirror neurons activation during the observation of hand-object interactions could be due to unspecific factors such as food expectancy or motor preparation for food retrieval or reward, we studied a set of neurons by using a second monkey as action performer, being the recorded monkey with its hands restrained and thus not receiving any reward.

All mirror neurons discharged during specific goal-related motor acts. Grasping, manipulating and holding objects were by far the most effective actions that triggered their motor response. Among them about fifty percent discharged during a specific type of prehension, being precision grip the most represented one. The visual stimuli most effective in triggering mirror neurons visual responses were actions in which the experimenter, or a second monkey, interacted with objects with their hand or with their mouth. Neither the sight of the object alone or of the agent alone were effective in evoking the neuronal response. Similarly, ineffective were mimicking an action without a target object, or performing the action by using tools. In over 90% of mirror neurons a clear correlation between the most effective observed action and their motor response was observed. In one third of them this correlation was strict both in terms of the general goal of the action (e.g., grasping) and in terms of the way in which it was executed (e.g., precision grip) (Gallese et al. 1996, Rizzolatti et al. 1996a). Figure 15.2 shows two examples of mirror neurons.

On the basis of their functional properties, here briefly summarized, mirror neurons appear to form a cortical system that matches observation and execution of motor actions. What could be the possible functional role of this matching system? Before addressing this important issue it is important to stress that the existence of such a system has been demonstrated also in humans.

The Mirror System in Humans

Two lines of evidence strongly suggest that an action/observation matching system similar to that discovered in monkeys does exist also in humans. The first refers to an elegant study by Fadiga et al. (1995) in which the excitability of the motor cortex of normal human subjects was tested by using Transcranic Magnetic Stimulation (TMS). The basic assumption underlying this experiment was that, if the observation of actions activates in humans, as in monkeys, the premotor cortex, this mirror effect should elicit an enhancement of the motor evoked potentials (MEPs), recorded from hand muscles, induced by the magnetic stimulation of the motor cortex, given its strong anatomical links to premotor areas. TMS was performed during four different conditions: observation of an experimenter grasping objects; observation of an experimenter drawing meaningless shapes with his arm in the air; observation of objects; detection of the dimming of a small spot of light. The results of this study showed that during grasping observation MEPs recorded from the hand muscles markedly increased with respect to the other conditions, including the attention demanding dimming detection task. Even more intriguing was the finding that the increase of excitability was present only in those muscles that were used by subjects when actively performing the observed movements. This study provided for the first time evidence that humans have a mirror system similar to that of the monkey. Every time we are looking at someone performing an action, the same motor circuits that are recruited when we ourselves perform that action are concurrently activated.

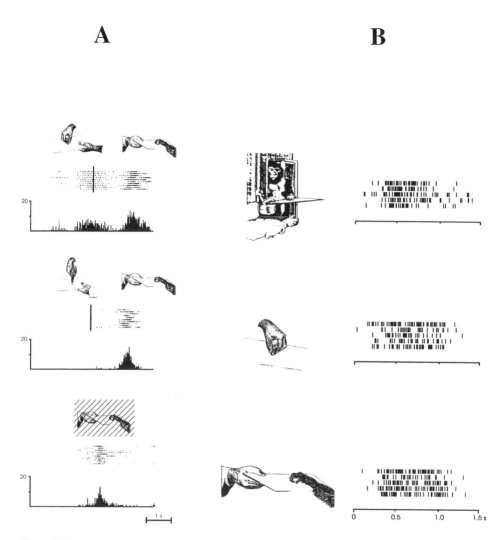

Figure 15.2

A Visual and motor responses of a mirror neuron. In the upper part of each panel the behavioral context in which the neuron was studied is shown. In the lower part of each panel a series of consecutive rasters and the relative peristimulus response histograms are shown. In the upper panel the experimenter grasps a piece of food with his hand and moves it towards the monkey who grasps it. The neuron discharges during grasping observation, it is silent when the food is moved, and discharges again when the monkey grasps it. In the middle panel the experimenter grasps the food with a tool. Subsequent series of event as in the previous panel. During grasping observation the neuron is silent. In the lower panel the monkey grasps the food in complete darkness. In the upper and middle panels rasters and histograms are aligned (vertical bar) with the moment in which the experimenter grasps the food. In the lower panel alignment is with the beginning of the grasping movement. Histograms bin width: 20 ms. Ordinates: spikes/bin. Abscissae: time. **B** Visual and motor responses of a mirror neuron. In the upper panel the recorded monkey observes another monkey grasping food. In the middle panel the recorded monkey observes the experimenter grasping food. In the lower panel the recorded monkey actively grasps food. Each panel illustrates five consecutive trials. The spontaneous activity of the neuron was virtually absent. (modified from Rizzolatti et al. 1996a).

These results posed the question of the anatomical location of the mirror system within the human brain. This issue has been addressed by two brain imaging experiments utilizing the technique of Positron Emission Tomography (PET). These two experiments (Rizzolatti et al. 1996b, Grafton et al. 1996), although different for many aspects, both shared a condition in which normal human subjects observed the experimenter grasping 3D objects. Both studies used the observation of the same objects as control condition. The results showed that grasping observation significantly activates the cortex of the left superior temporal sulcus, of the left inferior parietal lobule and of the anterior part of Broca's region. The activation during action observation of a cortical sector of the human brain traditionally linked with language raises the problem of the possible homologies between Broca's region and the premotor area F5 of the monkey, in which mirror neurons have been discovered. This point will be addressed in the section on the origin of language.

The Mirror Matching System: Possible Functional Roles

So far we have seen that both monkeys and humans possess a cortical mechanism able to match onto the same neuronal machinery action-observation and action-execution. Before trying to elucidate its functional role I will step back to review some monkey neurophysiological studies dealing with complex biological visual stimuli. This concise overview will provide a comparative perspective that may be of help in better focusing the functional relevance of the mirror system.

Neurons responding to complex biological stimuli had been previously described in the macaque brain. A series of studies showed that in the inferior temporal cortex there are neurons that discharge selectively to the presentation of faces or hands (Gross et al. 1972, Perrett et al. 1982, Gross et al. 1985). More recently it has been showed that some of these neurons respond to specific features of these stimuli (see Tanaka et al. 1991). Neurons responding to complex biological visual stimuli such as walking, climbing, approaching another individual, were reported also in the amygdala (Brothers et al. 1990). Even more relevant to the present issue is the work of Perrett and coworkers. These authors showed that in the upper bank of the superior temporal sulcus (STS) there are neurons selective to the observation of hand movements (Perrett et al. 1982 1989, 1990). These properties resemble the visual properties of F5 mirror neurons very much: both populations of neurons code the same types of actions; they both generalize their responses to the different instances of the same action; they both are not responsive to mimicked hand actions without the target object. However, the distinctive feature of F5 mirror neurons resides in the fact that they also discharge during active movements of the observer. An observed action produces the same neural pattern of activation as does the action actively made by the observer.

The presence of two brain regions with neurons endowed with similar complex visual properties, raises the question of their possible relationship. Two possibilities might be suggested. One is that F5 mirror neurons and STS neurons have different functional roles. STS neurons would code the semantic, the meaning of hand-object interactions, while F5 mirror neurons would be engaged in the pragmatic coding of the same actions. Being area F5 recipient of visual information fed mainly by the parietal lobe (see Matelli et al. 1986, 1994), this hypothesis is in line with theories positing a sharp distinction between pragmatic and semantic coding within the two main streams of visual processing (see Milner and Goodale 1995).

A second possibility, that I personally favor, is that these two "action detector" systems would represent distinct stages of the same analysis. The STS neurons would provide an initial "pictorial" description of actions that would be then fed, (likely through an intermediate step in the posterior parietal cortex), to the F5 motor vocabulary where it would acquire a meaning for the individual. This latter hypothesis stresses the importance of the motor system in providing meaning to what is "described" by the visual system, by positing a pragmatic "validation" of what is perceived. Experimental evidence so far does not allow to rule out either of the two hypotheses.

What may be the functional role of the mirror matching system? Why has evolution provided individuals with such a mechanism? Mammals are usually engaged in relationships with conspecifics. This social attitude is particularly evident among primates. Macaque monkeys live in groups characterized by several active and intense social interactions, such as grooming (see Dunbar 1993), that are usually disciplined by a well delineated hierarchical organization. It is therefore very important for each member of a given social group to be able to recognize the presence of another individual performing an action, to discriminate the observed action from others, and to "understand" the meaning of the observed action in order to appropiately react to it. Whenever an individual emits an action it is able to predict its consequences. This knowledge is likely built by associating, through learning, the goal of the action, coded in the motor centers, with its consequences as monitored by the sensory systems. The matching system represented by mirror neurons could provide the neuronal basis for such a process of "action understanding," a basic requisite for social communication.

Mirror Neurons and the Origin of Language

Language is a distinctive hallmark of the human species. By means of this extraordinarily powerful tool humans have unceasingly progressed along history: a bunch of hunters-gatherers became through millennia able to completely reshape and remodel the environment they were living in. The astonishingly successful achievements that mankind has obtained by means of science and technology would have been impossible without the ability to coordinate activities and share knowledge that only language can provide. How this unique capability emerged in the course of evolution is a far more disputed issue.

A thorough discussion of this problem, which is a key passage toward the understanding of the distinctiveness of being humans, is beyond the scope of this essay. My main concern here is to suggest that the discovery of mirror neurons may provide a new, although still sketchy, neurobiological basis to account for the emergence of language (see Rizzolatti and Arbib 1998 for a thorough discussion of these points). This assumption is founded on the following premises: a) Language skill has emerged through evolution by means of a process of preadaptation: specific behaviors and the nervous structures supporting them, originally selected for other purposes, acquire new functions that side and eventually supersede the previous one. b) A continuity can be traced between language skill and prelanguage brachio-manual behaviors, being the primate premotor cortex the common playground of this evolutionary continuity; c) The specialization for language of human Broca's region derives from an ancient mechanism, the mirror system, originally devised for action understanding.

After having delimited the theoretical background, let us examine the empirical findings upon which it can be grounded. The finding from brain imaging experiments, reported above, that in humans the observation of hand actions activates the Broca's region, an area classically considered to be mainly involved in speech control, raises queries about a possible homology between Broca's region and monkey area F5, where mirror neurons have been recorded. Once such an homology could be established, the ties between F5 and language could be more firmly asserted.

In monkey, the caudal sector of the ventral part of the frontal lobe (ventral premotor area) is constituted of two areas: area F4 caudally (FB according to Von Bonin and Bailey 1947), and area F5, rostrally (FCBm of Von Bonin and Bailey). Both areas have basically an agranular structure. Area F5 shows a rough somatotopic organization, although with a considerable overlap: hand movements are represented mostly in its rostral part (Rizzolatti 1987, Okano and Tanji 1987, Gentilucci et al. 1988, Rizzolatti et al. 1988, Hepp-Reymond et al. 1994), while face, mouth and larynx movements are mostly laterally represented (Hast et al. 1974, Gentilucci et al. 1988).

The organization of the ventral part of human inferior frontal lobe comprises in its rostral sector two separate areas (areas 44 and 45) differing for some cytoarchitectonical features, although, according to Campbell (1905), both these areas belong to the same "intermediate (premotor) type of cortex." Area 44 and 45 constitute Broca's region. It is generally agreed that, because of its anatomical location and cytoarchitectonic structure, F5 is the most likely homologue of human area 44 (see Petrides and Pandya 1994). Area F5 is a large area with most of its extent buried inside the lower limb of the arcuate sulcus of which it constitutes the posterior bank. A recent cytoarchitectonical study (Matelli et al. 1996) demonstrated that area F5 consists of several sectors. Mirror neurons are clustered in one of them. This dishomogeneity provides a clue for an initial segmentation of F5 into different areas, suggesting that a similar process could have occurred also in humans. It is possible therefore that human area 45 is the homologue of one of the subdivisions of F5.

Broca's region is by definition related to speech. A recent series of data indicate, however, that the two cytoarchitectonic areas forming it contain also a representation of hand movements. Bonda et al. (1994) showed in a PET study that this region becomes active during the execution of self-ordered hand movement sequences. In another PET study, Parsons et al. (1994) demonstrated a marked increase of Broca's region activation during a task in which subjects were required to imagine to rotate their hands. Furthermore, part of Broca's region is activated when subjects perform mental imagery of hand grasping tasks (Decety et al. 1994, Grafton et al. 1996).

The not exclusive role of Broca's region in speech function is supported also by clinical data on aphasic patients. Many of them show, beside language deficits, difficulties in pantomime recognition (Bell 1994). According to this author, the ability to recognize pantomime is represented in Broca's region as a specific language independent function.

The above listed series of anatomical, experimental, and clinical evidence allows one to conclude that area F5 and at least part of Broca's region can be considered homologue. Both areas are endowed with hand and mouth motor representations. The latter expanded enormously in humans in relation to the high demanding requirements of words emission. The hand-related functions, however did not disappear from Broca's region and, as showed by Bell (1994), retained a role in gestures recognition.

At first glance it might seem counterintuitive, if not paradoxical, to root the origin of language into a system related to gestures recognition, since language means essentially speech production. It would appear therefore more logical to look for a vocal antecedent. Vocal calls are commonly uttered by nonhuman primates. These vocalizations, however, at difference with human speech, are usually emitted in response to emotionally indexed events, and appear therefore related to instinctual behavior. Furthermore, the anatomical structures responsible of the control of vocal calls emission are represented by the cingulate cortex together with diencephalic and brainstem structures (Jurgens 1987, MacLean 1993). All these considerations could lead one to give up an evolutionary explanation of language (see, however, Pinker and Bloom 1990), and accept the nativist, mentalist definition of language as proposed by Chomsky (1986), who asserts that language capacity cannot be derived from lower species of animals. An alternative solution, however, can be found in the "motor theory of speech perception" proposed by Libermann several years ago (Libermann et al. 1967). According to Libermann's theory the "objects" of speech perception are not the sounds but the phonetic gestures of the speaker. These gestures are represented in the brain as invariant motor commands. As stressed by Libermann and Mattingly (1985) the phonetic gestures are the "primitives that the mechanisms of speech production translate into actual articulatory movements, and they are also the primitives that the specialized mechanisms of speech perception recover from the signal." The similarity of this mechanism with mirror neurons is striking: in both cases at the basis of gesture recognition there is an action/perception matching system. The modality is different, acoustic in the case of speech, visual for mirror neurons. Note, however, that language has not to be necessarily and exclusively assigned to the vocal-auditory domain, but can be exhibited also in the brachiomanual visual domain, as in the case of sign language used by deaf people. In fact, deaf signers suffering from left hemisphere lesions show impairments in their visual-gestural language, such as extreme disfluency and almost exclusive use of referential open-class nouns, that are very similar to the impairments that characterize Broca-like aphasics (see Poizner et al. 1984). These data corroborate the notion that the specialization for language of the left hemisphere of humans is independent of language modality.

My proposal is that this specialization resides in gesture recognition. Broca's region likely became a language area within a process of evolutionary continuity between its homologue precursor area, monkey premotor area F5, which well before language appearance was already endowed with the capacity of recognizing gestures. Mirror neurons are the neuronal basis of this capacity.

References

Bell, B. D. 1994. Pantomime recognition impairment in aphasia: an analysis of error types. *Brain and Language* 47:269–278.

Bonda, E., Petrides, M., Frey, S., and Evans, A. C. 1994. Frontal cortex involvement in organized sequences of hand movements: evidence from a positron emission tomography study. *Soc Neurosci Abstracts* 20:152–156.

Brothers, L., Ring, B., and Kling, A. 1990. Response of neurons in the macaque amygdala to complex social stimuli. *Behav. Brain Res.* 41:199–213.

Campbell, A. W. 1905. *Histological studies on the localization of cerebral function*. New York: Cambridge University Press.

Chomsky, N. 1986. Knowledge of Language: its nature, origin and use. *Praeger Special Studies*, New York and Philadelphia.

Decety, J., Perani, D., Jeannerod, M., Bettinardi, V., Tadary, B., Woods, R., Mazziotta, J. C., and Fazio, F. 1994. Mapping motor representations with PET. *Nature* 371:600–602.

Dunbar, R. I. M. 1993. Coevolution of neocortical size, group size, and language in humans. *Behav. Brain Sci.* 16:681–835.

Fadiga L, Fogassi L, Pavesi G., and Rizzolatti G. 1995. Motor facilitation during action observation: a magnetic stimulation study. *J. Neurophysiol.* 73:2608–2611.

Gallese, V., Fadiga, L., Fogassi, L., and Rizzolatti, G. 1996. Action recognition in the premotor cortex. *Brain* 119:593–609.

Gentilucci, M., Fogassi, L., Luppino, G., Matelli, M., Camarda, R., and Rizzolatti, G. 1988. Functional organization of inferior area 6 in the macaque monkey: I. Somatotopy and the control of proximal movements. *Exp Brain Res* 71:475–490.

Grafton, S. T., Arbib, M. A., Fadiga, L., and Rizzolatti, G. 1996. Localization of grasp representations in humans by PET: 2. Observation compared with imagination. *Exp. Brain Res.* 112:103–111.

Gross, C. G., Rocha-Miranda, C. E., and Bender, D. B. 1972. Visual properties of neurons in infero-temporal cortex of the monkey. *J. Neurophysiol.* 35:96–111.

Gross, C. G., Desimone R., Albright, T. D., and Schwartz, E. L. 1985. Inferior temporal cortex and pattern recognition. In: Chagas, C., Gattass, R., and Gross, C. (eds.). *Pattern recognition mechanisms*. Berlin: Springer.

Hast, M. H., Fisher, J. M., Wetzel, A. B., and Thompson, V. E. 1974. Cortical motor representation of the laryngeal muscles in macaca mulatta. *Brain Res.* 73:229–240.

He, S. Q., Dum, R. P., and Strick, P. L. 1993. Topographic Organization of Corticospinal Projections from the Frontal Lobe—Motor Areas on the Lateral Surface of the Hemisphere. *J. Neurosci.* 13:952–980.

Hepp-Reymond, M-C., Husler, E. J., Maier, M. A., and Qi, H.-X. 1994. Force-related neuronal activity in two regions of the primate ventral premotor cortex. *Canad. J. Physiol. Pharmachol.* 72:571–579.

Hyvärinen, J., and Poranen, A. 1974. Function of the parietal associative area 7 as revealed from cellular discharges in alert monkeys. *Brain* 97:673–692.

Jurgens, U. 1987. Primate communication: signalling, vocalization. In: G. Adelman (ed.) Encyclopedia of neuroscience. Boston Birkhauser.

Liberman, A. M., Cooper, F. S., Shankweiler, D. P., and Studdert-Kennedy M. 1967. Perception of the speech code. *Psychol Rev* 74:431–461.

Liberman, A. M., and Mattingly, I. G. 1985. The motor theory of speech perception revised. *Cogn.* 21:1–36.

MacLean, P. D. 1993. Introduction: Perspectives on cyngulate cortex in the limbic system. In B. A. Vogt and M. Gabriel (eds.) *Neurobiology of cingulate cortex and limbic thalamus: a comprehensive handbook*. Boston: Birkhauser.

Matelli, M., and Luppino, G. 1997. Functional anatomy of human motor cortical areas. In: Boller, F., and Grafman J. (eds.) *Handbook of Neuropsychology*, vol. 11. Elsevier Science B. V.

Matelli, M., Luppino, G., and Rizzolatti, G. 1985. Patterns of cytochrome oxidase activity in the frontal agranular cortex of macaque monkey. *Behav Brain Res.* 18:125–137.

Matelli, M., Camarda, M., Glickstein, M., and Rizzolatti, G. 1986. Afferent and efferent projections of the inferior area 6 in the macaque monkey. *J. Comp. Neurol.* 251:281–298.

Matelli, M., Luppino, G., Govoni, P., and Geyer, S. 1996. Anatomical and functional subdivisions of inferior area 6 in macaque monkeys. *Soc. Neurosci. Abs.*: 22.

Milner, A. D., and Goodale, M. A. 1998. *The visual brain in action.* Oxford: Oxford University.

Mountcastle, V. B., Lynch, J. C. G. A., Sakata, H., and Acuna, C. 1975. Posterior parietal association cortex of the monkey: Command functions for operations within extrapersonal space. *J. Neurophysiol,* 38:871–908.

Okano, K., and Tanji, J. 1987. Neuronal activities in the primate motor fields of the agranular frontal cortex preceding visually triggered and self-paced movement. *Exp. Brain Res.* 66:155–166.

Parsons, L. M., Fox, P. T., Hunter Downs, J., Glass, T., Hirsch, T. B., Martin, C. C., Jerabek, P. A., and Lancaster, J. L. 1995. Use of implicit motor imagery for visual shape discrimination as revealed by PET. *Nature* 375:54–58.

Perrett, D. I., Harries, M. H., Bevan, R., Thomas, S., Benson, P. J., Mistlin, A. J., et al. 1989. Frameworks of analysis for the neural representation of animate objects and actions. *J. Exp. Biol.* 146:87–113.

Perrett, D. I., Rolls, E. T., and Caan, W. 1982. Visual neurones responsive to faces in the monkey temporal cortex. *Exp. Brain Res.* 47:329–342.

Perrett, D. I., Mistlin, A. J., Harries, M. H., and Chitty, A. J. 1990. Understanding the visual appearance and consequence of hand actions. In Goodale, M.A., editor. *Vision and action: the control of grasping.* Norwood, N.J.: Ablex, 163–180.

Petrides, M., and Pandya D. N. 1994. Comparative architectonic analysis of the human and the macaque frontal cortex. In: Boller F, Grafman J, editors. *Handbook of Neuropsychology,* Volume IX. Amsterdam: Elsevier.

Pinker, S., and Bloom, P. 1990. Natural language and natural selection. *Behav. Brain Sci.* 13:707–884.

Poizner, U., Kaplan, E., Bellugi, U., and Padden, C. A. 1984. Visual-spatial processing in deaf brain-damaged signers. *Brain Cogn.* 3:281–306.

Rizzolatti, G. 1987. Functional organization of area 6. IN: Motor areas of Cerebral cortex (Ciba Foundation Symposium 132). Chichester, Wiley.

Rizzolatti, G., Scandolara, C., Matelli, M. and Gentilucci, M. 1981. Afferent properties of periarcuate neurons in macaque monkey. II. Visual responses. *Behav Brain Res.* 2:147–163.

Rizzolatti, G., Camarda, R., Fogassi, M., Gentilucci, M., Luppino, G., and Matelli, M. 1988. Functional organization of inferior area 6 in the macaque monkey: II. Area F5 and the control of distal movements. *Exp. Brain Res.* 71:491–507.

Rizzolatti, G., and Gentilucci, M. 1988. Motor and visual-motor functions of the premotor cortex. In: Rakic P. and Singer W. (eds.) *Neurobiology of Neocortex.* Wiley, Chichester, pp. 269–284.

Rizzolatti, G., Fadiga, L., Gallese, V., and Fogassi, L. 1996a. Premotor cortex and the recognition of motor actions. *Cogn. Brain Res.* 3:131–141.

Rizzolatti, G., Fadiga, L., Matelli, M., Bettinardi, V., Paulesu, E., Perani, D., and Fazio, G. 1996b. Localization of grasp representations in humans by PET: 1. Observation versus execution. *Exp. Brain Res.* 111:246–252.

Rizzolatti, G., and Arbib, M. A. 1998. Language within our grasp. *Trends in Neurosci.* 21:188–194.

Sakata, H., Taira, M., Murata, A., and Mine, S. 1995. Neural mechanisms of visual guidance of hand action in the parietal cortex of the monkey. *Cer Cortex* 5:429–438.

Tanaka, K., Saito, H. A., Fukada, Y., and Moriya M. 1991. Coding visual images of objects in the infero-temporal cortex of the macaque monkey. *J. Neurophysiol.* 66:170–189.

Von Bonin, G., and Bailey, P. 1947. *The neocortex of macaca mulatta.* Urbana: University of Illinois Press.

16 Supporting the "Grand Illusion" of Direct Perception: Implicit Learning in Eye-Movement Control

Frank H. Durgin

Part of the "Grand Illusion" of complete and direct perception is the transparency of our eye-movements. We simply don't notice them. The visual information from the retina that supports visual consciousness is sampled discontinuously in the brief fixations that normally occur two or three times per second. Our eyes make abrupt movements called *saccades* nearly every second of our waking lives. These eye "jumps" connect the individual fixations we make, gathering visual information that underlies our actions and our perceptual experience.

Although often crucial to the successful recovery of visual information in which we are consciously interested, our eye movements are, by and large, unconscious actions. They may be said to represent an aspect of the information-gathering control structures postulated by Gibson (1966), though they are not, themselves, part of our awareness. Given the importance of eye-movements for the retrieval of visual information from the environment, the question arises whether the eye-movement control system is capable of implicit learning, or learning without awareness. The present studies were undertaken to investigate this possibility. Can eye-movement patterns show learned sensitivity to environmental regularities of which we are not consciously aware?

In part, the motivation of these studies derived from evidence that visual consciousness often goes beyond the information available to visual cognition. For example, a visual texture can appear to be seen in clear detail—each element clearly represented. Yet studies of texture adaptation (e.g., Durgin and Proffitt 1996) indicate that our perceptual experience is based on processes of "biological image compression." This means that the amount of information actually available in cognition is vastly less than would be required to completely specify the detail that seems to us to be evident in our conscious experience. Similarly, recent interest in short-term perceptual memory has been fueled by the apparent discrepancy between the amount of information that seems to be present in consciousness and our insensitivity to fairly large alterations in the content of our environment from moment to moment (e.g., Grimes 1996, Rensink et al. 1997). In what ways might the sophisticated control of eye-movements help to support the "Grand Illusion" of complete perception?

Part of the motivation for this research came from the literatures on implicit learning (cf. Berry and Dienes 1993, Reber 1993, for reviews). If we are not really "seeing" all that we think we are seeing, might there nonetheless be (unconscious) information available to guide the visual-information-acquisition systems? Might not the whole nature of visual-information acquisition actually involve fairly complicated, yet unconscious, smart routines for guiding the control of eye-movements.

To test this idea, I have developed a paradigm for examining whether eye-movement patterns during a visual search task can be modified in response to hidden contingencies. Because of the phenomenon of change blindness, it is possible to surreptitiously introduce a target into a search display mid-trial, during a saccadic eye movement, so that it appears directly in the line of gaze at the termination of the saccade. From the participant's point of view, the target is simply found on the screen. From the experimenter's point of view, the introduction of the target can be made contingent on particular patterns of eye-movement. In a series of preliminary studies, I found that I could make participants produce larger saccades sooner, if I surreptitiously made target appearance in a visual search task contingent (probabilistically) on large eye movements. That is, in time-limited search trials, success rate at "finding" (eliciting) the target was found to increase over the first 60 trials, and this was related primarily to a decreasing latency for making a large eye-movement during a trial. Eye-movement patterns for controls did not change with time.

The goal of the present investigations was to look at somewhat more complex rules for target elicitation. Specifically, in each of the two experiments to be presented here, an attempt is made to promote either clockwise or counter-clockwise search patterns in a dense display. In Experiment 1, the rules for the clockwise and counterclockwise groups were defined with respect to successive saccade directions. If the change in direction between two saccades made a turn to the right, the clockwise rule was satisfied; if it made a turn to the left, it counted as a counterclockwise. In Experiment 2, the rules for the clockwise and counterclockwise search groups were defined with respect to the screen (i.e., on the right side of the screen a downward saccade would be clockwise, whereas on the left of the screen, an upward saccade would be clockwise). These rules are schematically illustrated in figure 16.1. Intriguingly, implicit learning will be demonstrated in Experiment 1, but not in Experiment 2. Conversely, in Experiment 2 several participants become explicitly aware of a successful search strategy for finding the target, whereas none did in Experiment 1. These findings suggest that implicit learning in eye-movement control systems may be limited to variables associated with the coding of saccades in eye-centered polar coordinates, rather than in world (or display) coordinates, whereas conscious strategies are best developed for world- or display-relative coordinate systems.

Experiment 1

The general form both of the experiments to be presented here is that participants will perform a visual search task in which the "discovery" of a target actually

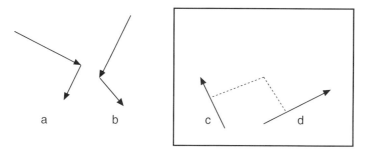

Figure 16.1
Rule definitions for experiments 1 and 2. Panels A and B illustrate "clockwise" and "counterclockwise" saccadic trajectories which could elicit a target in experiment 1. Panels C and D illustrate "clockwise" and "counterclockwise" saccadic trajectories which could elicit a target in experiment 2. Both kinds of rule were intended to foster clockwise or counterclockwise search patterns, but implicit learning was only found with the rules from experiment 1.

depends on first eliciting the target by means of some simple rule concerning the eye-movements of the participants. Preliminary studies had shown improved performance when the rule involved a contingency on saccade velocity (i.e., distance) during search. The present experiment was designed to test whether two different rules could be learned by participants. One rule was intended to promote clockwise search patterns around the screen, the other was intended to promote counterclockwise search patterns.

If implicit learning of these rules occurs and the learning is specific to the rules, then two patterns of results ought to emerge. First, task performance should improve across trials. Second, analysis of saccade patterns ought to demonstrate differential frequencies of clockwise and counterclockwise saccades for the two rule groups.

Methods

Participants.   The participants were 20 Swarthmore undergraduates who were paid for their participation.

Apparatus.   The displays were controlled by a Macintosh PowerPC 7600 and presented on a ViewSonic 17 RGB monitor with a resolution of 1152×870 pixels. Vertical refresh was 75 Hz. The display was viewed from a distance of about 0.5 m without head restraint. An SRR Eyelink® which uses head-mounted 250 Hz infrared video and head movement compensation to sample gaze position at 4 ms intervals monitored eye position. Physical updating of the display could be accomplished within a single video frame (13.3 ms), for a total lag of less than 18 ms. Gaze accuracy was normally well within 0.5 degrees, and the display-center gaze position was recalibrated at the beginning of each trial to avoid systematic drift.

Design. Each participant performed visual search in 150 trials. Participants were randomly assigned to either the clockwise rule condition (N = 9) or the counter-clockwise rule condition (N = 11).

Displays. Search displays were composed of 800 randomly scattered, nonover-lapping line segments (approx. 2×24 min of arc), appearing, with equal frequency, in red, green, blue, yellow and in each of 4 orientations (0, 45, 90 135 deg) against a black background. The target was a red "X" composed of two diagonal lines, (which was not initially present on experimental trials).

Rule for target elicitation. The implicit rules for target elicitation were intended to foster either clockwise or counterclockwise search patterns around the screen by rewarding pairs of saccades that constituted either a right-hand turn or a left-hand turn, respectively. In essence, any large saccade (reaching a velocity of at least 300 deg/sec over an 8 ms period) was treated as the first leg of a turn and immediately subsequent saccades were compared in direction with the first leg. Any turn between 45 and 135 deg was considered clockwise, and turns of 225 to 315 deg were consid-ered counterclockwise. Target elicitation was thereafter guaranteed provided that a candidate target location was available within a deg of final fixation. Since saccadic movements can be detected and their direction well characterized by triplets of suc-cessive gaze samples (4 ms apart) which show large absolute changes in position, satisfaction of the direction-change rule could be computed during the second sac-cade. A target could then be placed near the anticipated landing point of the saccade provided two further conditions were met. Namely, a target could only appear in a location previously occupied by one of the red elements on the screen, and, to avoid detection of the deception, targets could not appear in a location within 2 degrees of any previous fixation position. If no appropriate location was available, target elic-itation was delayed until some further set of saccades satisfied the rule.

The ostensible task. Participants were told that they were in a study of eye-movements during visual search. This served as a cover story for the use of the head-mounted eye tracker. Their task was to find a red "X" on the screen if one was present and to press a button as soon as they found it. They began each trial fixating a spot in the center of the screen and pressing a key which triggered the start of the trial 500 msec later. Trials were always terminated when the response button was pressed or, if no button was pressed, after 3 seconds.

Assessment of awareness. All participants were interviewed at the conclusion of the experiment. Several believed that the target was not always present from the begin-ning, but none believed that target appearance was in any way connected with their search strategy or eye-movements. Only one student mentioned a correlative strategy of examining the corners of the display first (though he did not indicate that he had swept the corners in any particular direction). The results discussed below are unchanged when this student's data are dropped from the analysis.

Analysis of learning.   Because learning curves are often decelerating functions, the analysis of learning was conducted over geometrically increasing numbers of trials. Specifically, the 150 trials were broken into an initial block of ten, subsequent blocks of twenty and forty trials, and a final block of eighty trials. (Analyses by blocks composed of equal number of trials came to equivalent conclusions.) The dependent measure used to assess improvement over time is simply the rate of search success (number of successful searches divided by the number of trials in each block).

Results and Discussion

In order to assess whether participants improved at the task, a repeated measures ANOVA of rate of success at the search task as a function of Trial Block (4 blocks) was conducted with a between-groups factor of Rule Direction (clockwise or counter-clockwise). As anticipated, success rate differed reliably as a function of Trial Block, $F(3, 54) = 8.48$, $p < .001$. More specifically, planned comparisons showed that the mean success rate in the third and fourth blocks (43% and 46%, respectively) reliably exceeded that in the first block (26%), $t(19) = 3.35$, $p < .01$, $t(19) = 4.40$, $p < .01$. The mean success rate in the fourth block also reliably exceeded that in the second block (35%), $t(19) = 2.65$, $p < .05$. There was no reliable difference in success rate between the two different Rule Direction groups, $F(1, 19) < 1$. Overall, as shown in figure 16.2a, there is clear evidence of improved performance at the task in this experiment.

To establish that the learning was specific to the hidden contingencies, a second analysis was conducted to determine whether the two experimental groups differed in their eye-movement patterns. Because trials were terminated upon target discovery, it was necessary to perform the statistical tests of saccade-direction frequency only on the initial portions of trials. A cut-off of 800 msec was chosen, because very few responses were ever generated before this time had elapsed. Only saccades completed prior to this time during each trial were considered. The measure used to assess differential learning of the directional rules was the frequency of clockwise and of counterclockwise saccades per trial. Because the original intent of the experiment was to foster screen-relative search patterns, these directions were defined with respect to the display itself, for purposes of analysis, rather than in the terms used trigger the targets. All saccades with a peak velocity of at least 300 deg/s were checked. If their direction at their midpoint was within 45 degrees of being perpendicular to a line from the center of the display, then they were categorized as either clockwise or counterclockwise.

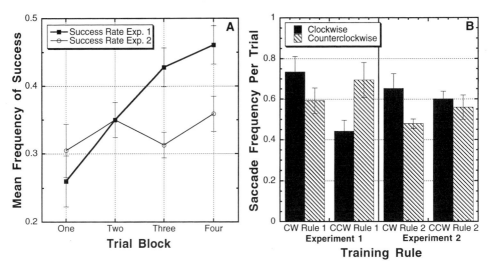

Figure 16.2
Results of experiments 1 and 2. Panel A shows the rate of success as a function of trial block for each experiment. Panel B depicts directional-saccade frequencies during the fourth block of trials for each direction and training condition in the two experiments. Error bars in each graph represent standard errors of the mean.

The frequency of such saccades during the final block of trials was subjected to a repeated measures ANOVA with Saccade Direction as a within-group factor and Rule Direction as a between-group factor. Differential learning would be indicated by an interaction between Rule Direction and Saccade Direction. In fact, as illustrated in figure 16.2b, this interaction was reliable $F(1, 18) = 6.28$, $p < .05$. Overall, the frequency of rule-consistent saccades was 0.715 per trial, whereas the frequency of oppositely directed saccades (i.e., rule irrelevant) was only 0.518 per trial.

In conclusion, the results of this experiment demonstrate clear evidence of learned sensitivity to specific hidden contingencies. Our interviews with participants indicated that none of them imagined that target appearance was in any way caused by their actions. Their eye-movement patterns nonetheless indicate a learned sensitivity to the eye-movement-contingency embedded in the experimental task.

Experiment 2

Saccadic eye-movements are coded in polar coordinates relative to fixation, which was why the rule in the first experiment was expressed in terms of eye-centered saccades. However, it is unclear from Experiment 1 whether a display-relative rule could be learned directly. After all, differential learning was demonstrated when display-based coordinates were used in the *analysis* of data. In the present experiment, the screen-based rule used for analysis in Experiment 1 was used as the target-triggering rule. Apart from the particulars listed below, the methods were the same as in Experiment 1.

Methods

Participants. Twenty-two students were divided evenly between the two training directions.

Design. Each participant performed visual search in 160 trials. The first 120 trials adhered to the training rule. The final 40 trials alternated between the training rule and the untrained rule with the intention that direct within-subject comparisons could be made for the two different trial types.

Rule for target elicitation. Any large saccade (reaching a velocity of at least 300 deg/sec over an 8 ms period) was evaluated for its screen-relative direction. If the saccade was within 45 deg of being perpendicular to a ray to the center of the display when it reached triggering velocity, then it was considered either clockwise or counterclockwise (e.g., an upward saccade on the right side of the screen would be considered counterclockwise). The rules of target placement were otherwise identical to those of the previous experiment.

Assessment of awareness. In addition to questions concerning strategies used, all participants were asked to guess what the underlying rule was after we revealed that a rule had been in operation. They were then told that the rule hinged on either clockwise or counterclockwise eye motions and asked to indicate which direction they had been trained with. Three participants in the clockwise search conditions described strategies of sweeping around the screen prior to being informed of the rule. All three had been in the clockwise rule condition and correctly indicated this. Data from these students will be left out of the main analysis (Two of them were the two most successful at the task overall.) When asked to guess what the rule might have been four more of the participants came up with hypotheses that were correlated with the actual search rule. Three of these four students chose the correct rule direction. Of the remaining 15 participants, only 6 chose the correct direction.

Results and Discussion

Because of the modified design, the division of the first 120 training trials into experimental blocks was modified such that the fourth block contained only 50 trials.

The other three blocks of ten, twenty and forty trials were defined as before. Surprisingly, there was no evidence that students in this experiment improved. The data from these blocks are shown with the data from Experiment 1 in figure 16.2a. In a repeated measures ANOVA with Trial Block as a within-group variable and Rule Direction as a between-group variable, there was no main effect of Trial Block, $F(3, 51) < 1$. Indeed, when search success on the final forty trials was analyzed with Trial Rule (new or old rule) as a within-group variable, no reliable difference in performance was found, $F(1, 17) < 1$, n.s. Moreover, analysis of saccades in the final block of learning trials revealed no evidence of an interaction between Training Direction and Saccade Direction, $F(1, 17) = 1.3$, n.s., though there was a nonreliable trend for all participants to produce more clockwise saccades, $F(1, 17) = 3.46$, $p = .08$.

To confirm that the results of Experiment 2 differed from those of Experiment 1, data from both experiments were analyzed together in a repeated measures ANOVA with Rule Type (Eye-centric or Display-based) and Rule Direction as between-group variables and Trial Block as a within-group variable. As expected, the effect of trial Block differed reliably as a function of Rule Type, $F(3, 108) = 3.41$, $p < .05$. The simplest interpretation of these results is that implicit learning did not occur in Experiment 2, whereas it clearly did in Experiment 1.

On the other hand, seven of the 22 students in this experiment were able to articulate explicit strategies that were correlated with the actual rule, compared with only one out of 20 in Experiment 1, $\chi^2 = 7.68$, $p < .01$. Apparently, the rule was not intrinsically more difficult to learn, though it evidently was not learned by any implicit mechanisms. Indeed, it is a more easily articulated rule, readily available to explicit awareness.

General Discussion

It would appear that, in this novel paradigm, eye-movement control systems can learn a rule which is expressed in terms of eye-centric coordinates more easily than a rule expressed in terms of display-centered coordinates. Conversely, explicit awareness of successful strategies were more likely to occur when the rule was expressed in display-based coordinates. This dissociation is consistent with the idea that the implicit learning demonstrated here is localized in levels of the eye-movement control system that retain locally expressed coordinate structures and are insensitive to scene layout. The formation of explicit rules, on the other hand, probably occurs at level where local coordinates have been displaced by world coordinates.

Previous examples of dissociations between implicit learning and explicit awareness include Berry and Broadbent's (1984) classic sugar production experiment. In their study with a hidden rule, explicit instruction failed to improve task performance, though implicit understanding developed in the uninstructed. In that experiment, the task is presented as a problem to be solved. An important difference between the sugar production task and this one is that participants in the visual search task are unaware that there is even a rule to be learned. From their conscious perspective the ostensible task is transparent in Experiment 1. Although the training rules differed for the two experiments, the same display-relative rule was used to interpret both sets of eye-movement data. It seems therefore all the more surprising that the very same dependent measure of the rule can turn up such different results. If the first rule can be implicitly learned, and the second rule would have been satisfied more frequently by satisfaction of the first rule, why didn't the participants in Experiment 2 simply develop the same implicit strategy as those in Experiment 1? It is possible that intervening rule steps needed to be learned, but it is also possible that the consciously available structure of the task (absence of targets in the middle) somehow interfered with the implicit learning process.

Several participants in Experiment 2 commented that the target never appeared in the middle of the display (a consequence of the display-based rule definition). Perhaps the rotary search strategy they consciously adopted (or which occurred to them even if they did not implement it successfully) was a response to this salient feature of the search environment.

These experiments were intended to study implicit learning in eye-movement control systems that might facilitate the acquisition of visual information. Although the conclusions reached here are tentative, rules based on eye-centered coordinate frames were more susceptible to implicit learning than were display-centered rules. Further research is needed to determine whether this finding is an artifactual result of salient differences between the search tasks, or whether it indeed signals an important limitation on implicit learning in eye-movement control systems.

Acknowledgments

Thanks to Daniel Attig, Sasha Clayton, and David Lewis for assistance with conducting the experiments reported here. This research was supported by the Howard Hughes Medical Institute and a faculty research grant from Swarthmore College.

References

Berry, D. C., and Broadbent, D. E. 1984. On the relationship between task performance and associated verbalizable knowledge. *Quarterly Journal of Experimental Psychology* 36A:209–231.

Berry, D. and Dienes, Z. 1993. *Implicit learning: theoretical and empirical issues.* Hillsdale, N.J.: L. Erlbaum Associates.

Durgin, F. H., and Proffitt, D. R. 1996. Visual learning in the perception of texture: simple and contingent aftereffects of texture density. *Spatial Vision* 9:423–474.

Gibson, J. J. 1966. *The senses considered as perceptual systems.* Boston, Houghton Mifflin.

Grimes, J. 1996. On the failure to detect changes in scenes across saccades. In K. A. Akins (Ed), *Perception* (pp. 89–110). New York: Oxford University Press.

Reber, A. S. 1993. *Implicit learning and tacit knowledge: an essay on the cognitive unconscious.* New York: Oxford University Press.

Rensink, R. A., O'Regan, J. K., and Clark, J. J. 1997. To see or not to see: The need for attention to perceive changes in scenes. *Psychological Science* 8:368–373.

Lianggang Lou

Consciousness and attention are closely related concepts. In this chapter, I will follow the common practice to use the term consciousness to refer to what we can report having been aware of, and the term attention to refer to the selection and maintenance of a portion of information for privileged access, whatever its consequences on consciousness. I will provide a case that seems to illuminate, in an unexpected way, the neural substrate for the distinction and relation between attention and consciousness in vision.

It is well known that if one attends to a stationary point in peripheral vision while maintaining fixation in central vision, the peripheral point will fade from awareness within a few seconds. This effect, known as Troxler fading (Troxler, 1804), has been considered to reflect local adaptations in lower visual pathways (Clarke and Belcher 1962, Millodot 1967). Local adaptation here means that the receptors or neurons responsible for detecting stimulus-background edges by luminance or chromatic contrast cease to respond to steady images. Because in Troxler fading the stimulus is perceptually replaced by whatever in the surrounding area rather than a black patch, it has been likened to the phenomena of blindspot filling-in (Ramachandran 1992). Thus, the conscious percept corresponding to the missing sensory input has been thought to be somehow "fillled in" at higher visual centers by interpolating from the surrounding visual areas. However, it is not certain whether local adaptation is an accurate account of what leads to the missing sensory input in the case of Troxler fading. The following observation suggests that, unlike the blind spots, the voluntary attention required to observe the fading may actually be responsible, at least partly, for the fading.

A circular array of disks, three green and three orange in alternate positions, was presented against a gray background (figure 17.1). Observers (this author and several postgraduate students and colleagues) fixated on the display center and voluntarily attend to three disks of one color (e.g., the green disks) and tried to ignore disks of the other color (e.g., the orange disks). In a few seconds, one or more of the disks faded from awareness. The disks that faded first tended to be those selected for attention. The phenomenal experience was that the background color quite abruptly filled the disk areas. The disappearance of the disks was sometimes quite fleeting and sometimes seemed to last a few seconds.

A similar informal observation was reported by Barbington-Smith (1961), but was never followed up in the thirty-seven years since its publication. A potential problem regarding these observations (henceforth, selective fading of attended stimuli or selective peripheral fading) is how certain one can be that the fading selectively occurs to

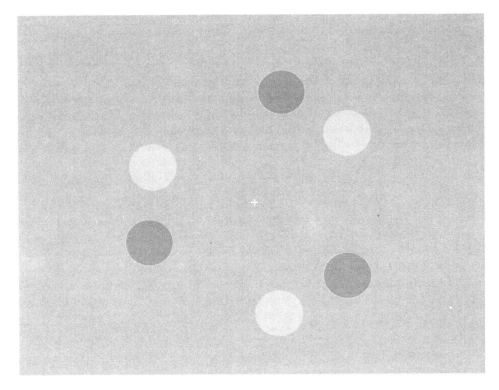

Figure 17.1
The display used in the preliminary observation and the experiment. The display was presented on a 21-inch color monitor with 1024 × 768 pixel resolution and 60Hz maximum refresh rate. For the first two blocks, at 35 cm viewing distance, the disk center and the fixation point subtends 11.3° visual angle (eccentricity). Each disk subtends 4.1° in diameter. Each neighboring pair of disks of the same color subtends 18.9°, and each neighboring pair of disks of different colors subtends 7.7°, center-to-center. The display size in blocks 3–6 were 40%, 20%, 9%, and 7% that in the first two blocks, not necessary in that order. The colors in this figure are close to those seen from the screen. The dark disks were orange and the light ones were green in the experiment.

the attended disks. Suppose lower-level sensory adaptation occurs equally to both the attended and unattended disks; it may be impossible or difficult to consciously perceive the fading of the unattended disks. At least two kinds of evidence may be adduced in support of this possibility. First, recent studies showed that people can fail to detect very salient changes in a visual scene if the change is not relevant to their current goal or intention (Grime 1996). Similarly, subjects could be so occupied with the stimuli selected for attention that they failed to access the changes occurring to the unattended stimuli. Therefore, while they truly perceived the fading of the attended disks, it is unclear whether they perceived, or simply believed in, the constancy of the unattended disks.[1] Second, attention could induce a bias of "prior entry" (Titchener 1908), which leads the sensory adaptation of the attended stimuli to enter the consciousness sooner than that of the unattended stimuli.

To address these concerns, a formal experiment was conducted, in which various parameters of the fading, notably the duration of faded awareness and the proportion of attended disks involved, were measured to see how plausible the alternative explanation of the selective fading can be. On some trials (control trials), a pair of disks, one of which selected for attention and the other ignored, was physically extinguished for a while following a period long enough for attention to be engaged to the selected disks. If attention leads one to be selectively aware of the disappearance of the attended disks, the bias would also be expected in perceiving the fading on other trials, where no disks were physically extinguished from the display. In addition, the extent of the fading was also measured at various eccentricities in order to confirm that, like Troxler fading, it occurs primarily in peripheral vision.

Methods

Eighteen subjects participated in the experiment. They were University of Hong Kong undergraduate or postgraduate students. None of them had previous experience in experiments of visual perception and they were naïve as to the purpose of the study. In a pretest with the above display (figure 17.1), two subjects failed to observe any fading after repeated trying and were subsequently dismissed. Each of the remaining 16 subjects was tested in 6 blocks of trials. The first two blocks consisted of seven trials each, including five test trials and two control trials. The same display (figure 17.1) was presented, rotated randomly from trial to trial. On the control trials, one attended disk and one unattended disk were simultaneously extinguished from the display three to four seconds following the display onset and recovered one second later. Subjects sat 35 cm from the screen and were instructed to fixate the display center, attend to the disks of one color, and ignore the disks of the other color. To facilitate this task, they were told to perceive the to-be-attended disks as forming an equilateral triangle and the to-be-ignored disks as part of the background. Their chin and forehead were supported to minimize fixation shift. Half of them were instructed to attend to the green disks in the first block and the orange disks in the second block, and the other half of them were told to do the reverse. The same displays, but of smaller sizes, hence smaller stimulus eccentricities, were used in blocks three to six, in which attention was directed to the green disks throughout.

Both the perceptual fading and the physical disappearance of the peripheral stimuli were indicated by manual response on a two-key response box. Pressing the left key indicated the onset of stimulus fading or disappearance, and releasing it indicated the recovery of the faded stimulus in awareness. The right key was to be pressed if more disks faded subsequently. The whole display ended one second after the release of the left key or the press of the right key. The maximum viewing time was 40 seconds. After each trial, subjects were prompted to recall the number of faded disks of each color when they pressed the left key.

Results

Table 17.1 presents four different aspects of the fading from each of the 16 subjects: the percentage of attended disks in those that faded first, the latency, the duration, and the number of disks faded simultaneously. Although there were quite a lot of individual differences, it is clear that fading occurred mostly to the attended disks. On average, in about 10 (mean $= 11.35$) seconds of viewing time, some of the six disks

Table 17.1
The means of four dependent measures of fading from the first and second blocks, catch trials excluded. G: Green disks were selected for attention; O: Orange disks were selected for attention.

Subject	% Attended disks		Onset latency (sec.)		Duration (sec.)		Number of disks	
	G	O	G	O	G	O	G	O
1	83.33	43.33	6.12	5.23	2.13	0.72	2.17	2.40
2	100.00	100.00	10.90	8.47	1.30	1.26	1.20	1.40
3	100.00	50.00	9.20	8.71	1.20	1.14	1.60	1.20
4	60.00	90.00	10.00	8.71	1.45	0.89	1.60	1.60
5	100.00	100.00	5.03	9.26	1.03	0.47	1.40	1.20
6	100.00	53.33	8.27	9.90	1.44	1.11	1.40	1.40
7	90.00	50.00	8.38	12.07	1.18	1.47	1.40	1.20
8	100.00	100.00	27.91	17.19	4.31	2.80	1.80	1.60
9	100.00	40.00	14.87	18.58	5.24	2.88	1.80	1.80
10	100.00	50.00	8.99	6.60	1.09	1.04	1.00	1.20
11	80.00	46.67	9.10	6.73	1.90	0.87	2.00	1.80
12	100.00	100.00	20.48	25.71	1.91	1.18	1.00	1.00
13	100.00	0.00	6.90	4.69	2.05	1.09	1.00	1.00
14	100.00	90.00	12.30	12.24	0.98	0.80	1.20	1.40
15	100.00	100.00	12.45	9.45	1.47	1.18	2.20	1.60
16	100.00	75.00	12.18	16.58	1.35	0.81	1.20	1.00
Mean	94.58	68.02	11.44	11.26	1.88	1.23	1.50	1.43

started to fade from awareness. Of the disks that faded, most (mean = 81.3%) were those selected for attention. This was true regardless of attention being directed to the green disks (mean = 94.6%) or to the orange disks (mean = 68.0%). Except for one subject (#13), disks of a particular color faded more frequently when the color was selected for attention than when it was ignored, $t(15) = 7.67$, $p < .001$. The faded disks remained out of awareness for up to a few (mean = 1.55, 95% confidence interval = 0.49) seconds during which the other disks were clearly visible.

On control trials, in contrast, all subjects on all trials perceived the simultaneous physical disappearance of the two disks, one of them selected for attention. The mean duration of the perceived disappearance was 1.12 (95% confidence interval = 0.34) seconds, very close to the actual duration of disk disappearance (one second).

With decreasing eccentricity, the fading occurred less frequently. At the smallest stimulus eccentricity manipulated (0.8°), the fading occurred on less than 30% of the trials, and with longer latency, shorter duration, and fewer number of disks involved. These characteristics suggest the fading to be primarily a phenomenon of peripheral vision.

Discussion

Some obviously implausible explanations can be ruled out in accounting for the selective fading of the attended stimuli. First, while small fixation drifts or short saccades may occur in the present experiment, they are unlikely to account for the effect. The eye movements would either follow a random trajectory or, given the close functional association between attention and eye movements, be biased toward the direction of the attended disks. In both cases, the eye movements would not bring the images of the attended disks to the more peripheral retinal regions, thereby set in their earlier fading.

Second, the disks that faded more frequently were unlikely to have been the less attended. To be sure, attention may be spread or inadvertently directed to the to-be-ignored disks. Indeed, the less than perfect selectivity of the fading (94.6% when the green disks were to be attended and 68.0% when the orange disks were to be attended) may be accounted for, at least partially, by the less-than-perfect selectivity of attention. However, it is extremely implausible that attention was directed primarily to disks other than those specified in the instruction. To suggest the latter would imply either that the brain systematically misinterprets the instruction for the allocation of attention, or that subjects were playing pranks on the experimenter. Both scenarios were implausible.

Therefore, voluntary attention must have facilitated the fading, or inhibited the awareness of the attended stimuli. The problem is how to explain it. Two possibilities were alluded to earlier. First, sensory adaptation occurs evenly at all disk locations of the same eccentricity, but only that at the attended locations is translated into the fading (*the hypothesis of attentional bias*). This hypothesis does not seem tenable. In particular, it does not seem likely that any of the unattended disks would remain visible for 1.5 seconds or longer while its sensory basis has been removed because of adaptation. In addition, because attention was not found to bias the perception of the physical stimulus disappearance, it was unlikely to significantly bias the perception of the fading caused by low-level adaptation either. Therefore, we are left with the second possibility, that attention actually triggers or precipitates the fading of the attended disks (*the hypothesis of inhibitory effect of attention*).

Visual selective attention is known to involve many different cortical areas, notably the V4, IT, posterior parietal and prefrontal areas (Desimone and Duncan 1995). As some of these cortical areas are likely where visual consciousness arises (Crick and Koch 1995), they could underlie both selective attention and its inhibitory consequence on visual consciousness. However, it is equally important to consider the fading as a special case of Troxler fading because of the following defining characteristics: the static stimuli, the low stimulus-background contrast, the specificity to peripheral stimuli and the time (about 10 seconds) that it took for the fading to occur. Thus, what has been known of the neural basis of Troxler fading could also hold true for the selective fading of the attended stimuli. Clarke and Belcher (1962) showed that the saccadic displacement needed for a faded image to recover is too large to suggest a ganglion or preganglion origin of the fading. On the other hand, they failed to find binocular interactions of the luminance threshold for the fading, suggesting a precortical origin of the fading. They concluded, therefore, that Troxler fading most likely arises from the adaptation at LGN, the relay station between the retina and the cortical visual areas. Putting these threads together, the selective fading of the attended disks is likely owing to adaptation at the LGN being triggered, or accelerated, by the activation from cortical areas associated with selective attention.

The above proposal is consistent with the models positing that consciousness relies on the reverberating neural activities in the cortico-thalamic loop (Newmann 1995, LaBerge 1995). To explain the selective fading, it can be assumed that the fading results from a breakdown of the reverberation, and that the breakdown occurs more easily at locations under additional influence from the cortical areas associated with voluntary selective attention.

Implications

The neural mechanism proposed for the selective fading of the attended stimuli allows an evaluation of some common assumptions about the functional relations between visual attention and visual consciousness. The function of attention is commonly assumed to be to select a small set of information from what is potentially available. Indeed, that has been the working definition of attention in this chapter. There has been a lot of debate as to where in the information-processing streams the selection occurs. Early selection theories posit that selection occurs relative early, and leads elementary features of the attended stimuli to undergo further processing and those of the unattended stimuli to be "filtered" (e.g., Broadbent 1958). Late selection proponents (e.g., Deutch and Deutch 1963) argue that selection occurs late in the information processing stream, after much of the semantic processing has been completed. To be compatible with these theories of attention, consciousness has to be conceived as emerging from the further processing after the locus of selection. It is almost certain that neural activities at LGN would not by themselves give rise to visual consciousness; not even those at V1, according to Crick and Koch (1995). Rather, the activities at LGN would provide more or less preprocessed sensory information to be further processed and integrated at the cortical areas, which gives rise to visual consciousness. If, however, attention intensifies and then inhibits the activities at LGN, as has been suggested, then the above explanatory framework has to be modified. It would not be appropriate to assume that visual consciousness is merely due to the additional processing after the locus of selection. For a stimulus to be visually conscious, its retinotopic sensory input (in this case, at the LGN) may need to be amplified by the covert attention directed toward it. Clearly, this proposal is incompatible with the late selection theories. On the other hand, it may be consistent with the early selection theories if the term selection is amended to mean "pick and boost."

As the selective fading of attended stimuli has been found only in peripheral vision and only after seconds of voluntary attention toward the stimuli, it is certainly a special case. Nevertheless, like many visual illusions, it may have revealed a general brain mechanism of visual attention and visual consciousness through its breakdown under special circumstances. Thus, voluntary visual attention may entail a centrifugal influence from extra-striate cortical areas, including the prefrontal areas, to lower visual centers, for example, V1, V2, and LGN. Indeed, evidence from electrophysiological studies of selective attention has suggested sensory modulation by selective attention, but perhaps only at the early extrastriate level (Clark and Hillyard 1996). With more sensitive experimental designs and neuroimaging techniques, direct evidence supporting the notion of selective modulation of cortico-LGN reverberation may be obtainable.

Note

1. This is similar to Dennett's idea about what is involved in the filling-in phenomena that occur at the blindspots (Dennett 1992). Instead of perceptual filling-in (Ramachandran 1992), Dennett believed that the brain simply ignores the blindspot and when forced to report what is in the blindspot relies on conceptual interpolation from what is perceived from the area surrounding the blindspot.

References

Barbington-Smith, B. 1961. An unexpected effect of attention in peripheral vision. *Nature* 189:776.

Broadbent, D. E. 1958. *Perception and Communication*. London: Pergamon Press.

Clark, V. P., and Hillyard, S. A. 1996. Spatial selective attention affects early extrastriate but not striate components of the visual evoked potential. *Journal of Cognitive Neuroscience* 8(5):387–402.

Clarke, F. J. J. 1962. On the localization of Troxler's effect in the visual pathway. *Vision Research* 2:53–68.

Crick, F. and Koch, C. 1995. Are we aware of neural activity in primary visual cortex? *Nature* 375:121–123.

Dennett, D. C. 1991. *Consciousness explained*. Boston: Little, Brown.

Desimone, R., and Duncan, J. 1995. Neural mechanisms of selective visual attention. *Annual Review of Neuroscience* 18:193–222.

Deutch J. A., and Deutch, D. 1963. Attention: Some theoretical considerations. *Psychological Review* 70:80–90.

Grimes, J. 1996. On the failure to detect changes in scenes across saccades. In *Perception*, Edited by A. Kathleen. Oxford: Oxford University Press, 89–110.

LaBerge, D. 1995. *Attentional processing: The brain's art of mindfulness*. Cambridge, Mass.: Harvard University Press.

Millodot, M. 1967. Extra foveal variations of the phenomenon of Troxler. *Psychologie Francaise* 12(3):190–196.

Newman, J. 1995. Review: Thalamic contributions to attention and consciousness. *Consciousness and Cognition* 4(2):172–193.

Ramachandran, V. 1992. Blind spots. *Scientific American* 266(May):44–49.

Titchener, E. B. 1908. *Lecture on the Elememtary Psychology of Feeling and Attention*. New York: Macmillan.

Troxler, D. 1804. Uber das Verschwindern gegebener Gegenstande innerhalb unsers Gesichtskrcises. In *Ophthalmologisches Bibliothek*, Vol. II. Edited by K. Himley and J. A. Schmidt. Jena: Fromann, 51–53.

V EMOTION—INTRODUCTION

Alfred W. Kaszniak

Emotional experience is a ubiquitous component of the stream of consciousness, and emotional "qualia" appear to interact with other contents and processes of consciousness in complex ways. Recent research suggests that important functional aspects of emotion can operate nonconsciously (e.g., Öhman, Flykt, and Lundqvist, in press; Öhman and Soares 1994). Scientific and philosophic accounts of consciousness will require an understanding of the role of emotion. Indeed emotional experience may be a critical factor in key philosophic debates within consciousness studies, such as the plausibility of thought experiments on the functional role of phenomenal conscious states (DeLancey 1996). Specification of neural circuitry critical for the conscious experience of emotion may also provide important clues in the search for neural systems upon which other domains of conscious experience are dependent. The three chapters of this section each provide perspectives on the relationships between brain and emotional experience.

Within the first chapter, Kaszniak and colleagues review theory and empirical observations concerning the interrelationships of emotion and consciousness, and distinguish components of emotional experience and their interrelationships. They then examine evidence supporting dissociability of conscious and nonconscious aspects of emotion, and recently proposed theories concerning the neural systems subserving conscious emotional experience (e.g., Damasio 1994, LeDoux 1996). Particular attention is given to the hypothesis that the ventromedial frontal cortex contains neural systems necessary for "the conscious body state characteristic of an emotion" (Damasio 1994). Kaszniak and colleagues describe their own empirical research motivated by this hypothesis, focusing upon the relationships between self-reports of emotional experience and measures of sympathetic autonomic activation in persons with localized ventromedial frontal lobe damage. Although able to accurately rate visual scenes along a dimension of positive to negative emotional "valence," these individuals show a relative lack of differentiation in subjectively experienced emotional arousal. A corresponding lack of skin conductance response differentiation of these scene categories suggests that both sympathetic autonomic response and the experience of emotional arousal (but not emotional valence) are dependent upon the integrity of ventromedial frontal systems. Kaszniak and colleagues conclude that lesion locations among individual patients within their study, and the recent positron emission tomography evidence of Lane et al. (1997, 1998) suggest a particularly important role for the anterior cingulate gyrus in the conscious experience of emotion.

In the second chapter Doug Watt draws attention to a potentially critical role of emotion in consciousness. Rather than viewing emotion as simply another qualia of consciousness, Watt proposes a more fundamental role of emotion in providing a necessary "valence tagging" fundamental to the gating and feature binding functions of consciousness. He views this role as instantiated by connectivity between sub-cortical affective systems and the hypothesized extended reticular thalamic activating system (ERTAS) subserving a global workspace model of consciousness. Watt makes a case for viewing the three "global state functions" of affect, attention, and executive function as intrinsically interpenetrating in their functional roles and neural archi-tectures. The specifics of neural systems critical for the proposed role of emotion in gating and feature binding are debatable, however Watt's core argument for a "pro-toqualia" role of emotion in the generation of consciousness stands by itself.

Systematic examination of the neural correlates of conscious emotion is limited by constraints in the noninvasive measurement of human brain physiology. Greater precision provided by invasive approaches in animal models would be advantageous. However, in addition to cautions necessary in making inferences from one species to another (see Griffiths 1997), it has been very difficult to infer the presence of emo-tional or other conscious states in organisms that do not provide verbal self-reports. In the final chapter of this section, Panksepp and Burgdorf summarize research which they interpret as providing evidence for a primitive form of "laughter" in rats. The ultrasonic chirping-like vocalizations recorded by Panksepp and Burgdorf are shown to occur as a robust response to "tickling" different parts of rats' bodies, and to vary with previous social experience and gender. Panksepp and Burgdorf argue that the neuroscientific study of this phenomenon may help in understanding the neural basis of positive conscious emotional states, such as joy. Preliminary work by the authors has suggested that circuits within the reticular nuclei of the thalamus and mesen-cephalon are important neural structures in this regard, and that the neurotransmitter glutamate is essential for triggering the response.

The three chapters within this section provide a cross-section of current theoretic formulations and empirical research on emotion and consciousness. Although much remains unknown, the work described makes it clear that the fields of consciousness studies and emotion research have much to contribute to each other.

References

Damasio, A. R. 1994. *Descartes' Error: Emotion, Reason and the Human Brain.* New York: G. P. Putnam's Sons.

DeLancey, C. 1996. Emotion and the function of consciousness. *Journal of Consciousness Studies* 3:492–499.

Griffiths, P. E. 1997. *What Emotions Really Are: The Problem of Psychological Categories.* Chicago: The University of Chicago Press.

Lane, R. D., G. R. Fink, P. M. L. Chau, and R. J. Dolan. 1997. Neural activation during selective attention to subjective emotional responses. *Neuroreport* 8:3969–3972.

Lane, R. D., E. M. Reiman, B. Axelrod, L. S. Yun, A. Holmes, and G. E. Schwartz. 1998. Neural correlates of levels of emotional awareness: evidence of an interaction between emotion and attention in the anterior cingulate cortex. *Journal of Cognitive Neuroscience* 10:525–535.

LeDoux, J. 1996. *The Emotional Brain: The Mysterious Underpinnings of Emotion Life*. New York: Simon and Schuster.

Öhman, A., A. Flykt, and D. Lundqvist. In press. Unconscious emotion: evolutionary perspectives, psychophysiological data and neuropsychological mechanisms. In R. Lane, L. Nadel, G. Ahern, J. Allen, A. Kaszniak, S. Rapcsak, and G. E. Schwartz (eds.), *The Cognitive Neuroscience of Emotion*. New York: Oxford University Press.

Öhman, A., and J. J. F. Soares. 1994. Unconscious anxiety: Phobic responses to masked stimuli. *Journal of Abnormal Psychology* 103:231–240.

Conscious Experience and Autonomic Response to Emotional Stimuli Following Frontal Lobe Damage

Alfred W. Kaszniak, Sheryl L. Reminger, Steven Z. Rapcsak, and Elizabeth L. Glisky

In recent years, there has been an increasing recognition of the importance of emotion research and theory for an understanding of human consciousness. Most all would agree that emotional qualia are a nearly constant aspect of our phenomenal experience. Emotion has been posited to play a necessary role in reasoning processes (Damasio 1994), creativity (Csikszentmihalyi 1990, Nielsen 1998), and any adequate neural network model of mind (Levine 1998, Taylor 1992). Some see emotion and consciousness as interrelated at the most fundamental level, with emotion providing a kind of "global valence tagging" that contributes to the gating and binding functions of consciousness (Watt 1999). Adding to current interest in emotion and consciousness, there has been a growing concern with exploring the neural correlates of conscious versus nonconscious aspects of emotion (LeDoux 1996, Panksepp 1998).

Emotion Components and Consciousness

Although there are disagreements concerning the necessary and sufficient conditions for identifying an emotion (for review, see Griffiths 1997), most analyses typically describe four components: (1) Physiological (CNS and autonomic) arousal, (2) cognitive appraisal, (3) subjective experience, and (4) action tendency (including facial expression). For both the general public and many scientists, emotion is identified with *feeling*, and thus inextricably linked to consciousness. Some theorists (e.g., Clore 1994) assert that conscious experience or feeling is a necessary component of emotion, with cognitive apprasal (of the personal significance of information) seen as preceding other emotional reactions. However, it has become increasingly clear that the conscious experience of emotion is not invariably correlated with other emotion components or a necessary contributor to all emotional behavior. In humans, autonomic physiological and motoric aspects of emotion can occur in response to an emotional stimulus that is not consciously recognized (e.g., in studies employing backward masking of visual emotional stimuli) or outside of attentional focus (Ohman and Soares 1994). Although some cognitive appraisal (in terms of positive or negative valuation in relation to personal goals, need states, or self-preservation) may be a necessary condition for emotional arousal (Lazarus 1991), such appraisals need not necessarily be conscious (Frijda 1993).

Other evidence consistent with the interpretation that important functions of emotion occur nonconsciously comes from nonhuman animal research. As LeDoux's studies of fear (in rodents) have shown, the amygdala appears to be a key structure in both the stimulus evaluation of threatening events and the production of defensive responses (for review, see LeDoux 1996). These defensive responses appear to be evolutionarily selected, involuntary, automatic consequences of the initial rapid evaluation of stimulus significance, and do not require cortical mediation. Thus, LeDoux emphasizes subcortical (e.g., thalamic-amygdala circuitry) emotion systems as involved in fast, evolutionarily selected, and probably nonconscious aspects of emotion. In contrast, he posits cortical inputs (via multiple pathways) as necessary for the conscious experience of emotion. Recent functional brain imaging studies have provided evidence consistent with LeDoux's view that the amygdala can perform its role in the processing of emotional stimuli nonconsciously. Employing functional magnetic resonance imaging (fMRI), Whalen and colleagues (1998) have demonstrated amygdala activation in response to emotional stimuli (facial expressions) even when conscious awareness of the stimuli are prevented by backward masking. It should be noted that in studies such as those of Whalen et al. (1998) or Ohman and Soares (1994), backward masking prevents conscious awareness of the emotionally salient stimulus itself, but does not necessarily prevent the person from being aware of emotional experience in response to the nonconsciously processed stimulus. As discussed below, such conscious experience of emotion, despite unawareness of the eliciting stimulus, might occur via awareness of bodily signals, either through peripheral autonomic feedback or through efferent feed-forward within the brain (Damasio 1994).

Searching for the Neural Correlates of Conscious Emotional Experience

LeDoux (1996) has hypothesized three distinct neural systems to be involved in the conscious experience of emotion: (1) direct cortical inputs from the amygdala; (2) inputs from the amygdala to nonspecific brainstem arousal systems (which then "broadcast" diffusely to the cortex); and (3) feedback to the amygdala and cortical areas from the bodily expressions (e.g., facial muscle movement, autonomically mediated visceral changes) of emotion. One approach to the empirical examination of such hypotheses concerning the neural correlates of conscious emotion examines possible dissociations in persons with neurologic disorders involving theoretically relevant brain systems. For example, one study in our laboratory (Dalby et al. 1995) evaluated the relationship between facial expression and subjective experience of emotion in persons with idiopathic Parkinson's disease (PD). Persons with PD, presumably owing to alterations in necessary dopaminergic inputs to the basal ganglia, often show markedly reduced spontaneous facial expression (termed "masked facies"), despite intact voluntary (pyramidal) control of facial muscle movement. The facial feedback hypothesis (Tomkins 1984) posits that facial expressions provide cutaneous and proprioceptive feedback that is a necessary contributor to emotional experience. This hypothesis would predict that Persons with PD who show masked facies should report proportionately reduced emotional experience in response to salient stimuli. Testing this hypothesis, Dalby and colleagues documented significantly reduced facial expression (as measured by zygomatic and corrugator facial muscle electromyography) in a sample of persons with PD, but unaltered self-reports of experienced emotional valence and arousal. Although these results appear contrary to the predictions of the facial feedback hypothesis, we cannot at present rule out the possibility that persons with PD may alter the subjective scaling of their emotional experience self-reports as their illness progressively reduces spontaneous facial emotional expression.

Another example comes from the study of persons with damage to the ventromedial frontal area, including the anterior cingulate cortex. Damage to the anterior cingulate (e.g., in the case of surgical lesions for treatment of intractable pain) has been associated with alterations in emotional experience, and is thought to play an important role in pain, attention, response selection, and control of autonomic activity (for review, see Devinsky, Morrell, and Vogt 1995). The rostral anterior cingulate has abundant connections with the orbital frontal cortex, the amygdala, and other paralimbic structures (e.g., the insular cortex), all thought to be involved in emotional processes (Price, Carmichael, and Drevets 1996). It has been hypothesized (Lane, in press) that the anterior cingulate cortex may function to provide conscious working memory for "interoceptive emotional information," analogous to the role of nearby dorsolateral prefrontal cortex in cognitive working memory (Goldman-Rakic 1992).

Damasio and colleagues (for review, see Adolphs, Tranel, Bechara, Damasio and Damasio 1996), have shown that patients with ventromedial frontal damage (typically including the anterior cingulate) do not show the normally expected differentiation of skin conductance response (SCR) magnitude to neutral vs emotionally significant visual scenes. SCR is known to reflect eccrine sweat gland changes that are exclusively innervated by cholinergic autonomic neurons (Andreassi 1995). Numerous studies have found increased SCRs to emotionally versus nonemotionally salient stimuli (for review, see Andreassi 1995), and SCRs have been shown to be positively and monotonically correlated with the magnitude of self-rated emotional arousal (Greenwald, Cook, and Lang 1989, Lang, Greenwald, Bradley, and Hamm 1993). Damasio (1994) has hypothesized that frontally damaged patients who do not have an SCR to emotionally salient stimuli will not have the "conscious body state characteristic of an emotion" (p. 209). In support of this hypothesis, Damasio (1994) has provided anecdotal examples of frontally damaged patients who show absent SCRs to strongly negative (e.g., mutilation) pictures and who also volunteered that they did not feel the expected emotion.

Thus, both empirical results and anecdotal clinical reports are consistent with the existence of a close relationship between the conscious experience of emotion, sympathetic autonomic activity (as measured by SCR), and integrity of the ventromedial frontal cortex. However, there remains a need for more systematic study of frontally damaged patients, in which SCR and quantitative self-reports of theoretically distinct aspects of emotional experience are made in response to standardized emotional stimuli. It was in response to this need that we initiated the following experiment.

Participants

Seven adult patients with acquired focal ventromedial frontal lobe damage participated in the experiment. Etiologies of frontal damage in these individuals included head trauma (N = 3), stroke (N = 1), and ruptured anterior communicating artery (ACA) aneurysm (N = 3). Computerized tomographic (CT) and/or magnetic resonance imaging (MRI) lesion localization information was available for each of the patients, and showed all to have ventromedial frontal damage, including the anterior cingulate gyrus (see figure 18.1). An eighth patient with MRI-confirmed damage exclusively within bilateral orbital frontal region was also examined, although data from this individual was analyzed separately from that of the other patients. Patient ages ranged from mid 40s through late 60s, and educational backgrounds ranged from 12 through 18 years of formal education. Ten adults, of comparable age and education ranges to those of the patient group, and without a history of neurological, psychiatric, or major systemic illness, served as healthy controls.

Materials

The International Affective Picture System (IAPS) slides, developed by Peter Lang and colleagues (Lang and Greenwald 1988, Lang, Greenwald, and Bradley 1990, Lang, Öhman, and Vaitl 1988), were employed as the emotionally salient stimuli. These stimuli have been carefully developed to ascertain how pleasant/unpleasant (valence) and calm/excited (arousal) each slide makes an individual feel (i.e., the conscious experience of emotion). A goal of the stimulus set composition was to ease perceptual recognition by increasing the contrast between figure and background. The

R   L

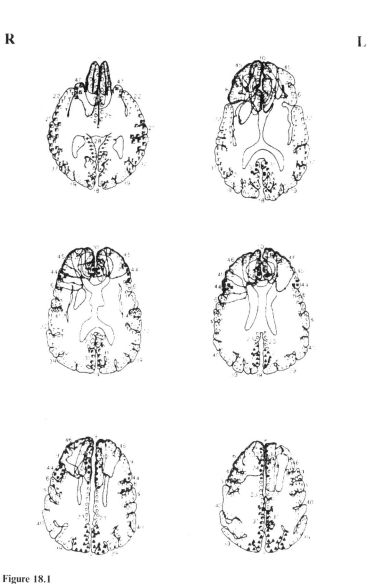

Figure 18.1
Tracings, on standardized brain maps employing Broadman's area locations, of the location and extent of
frontal damage in the patient group.

pictures vary in complexity, color, luminance, content (human, animal, and inanimate photographs are included) and image size. Lang and colleagues have provided extensive normative data on the IAPS slides, with young adult consensus ratings of emotional valence (pleasant-unpleasant) and arousal (calm-aroused) experienced in response to the stimuli. For the present study, valence and arousal ratings obtained from prior validation studies were used to create two valence- and arousal-matched sets of slide images, selected from a 240-slide IAPS set. Normative data provided by Lang and Greenwald (1988) were used to balance the two slide sets with respect to the rating levels of valence and arousal they would likely evoke from study participants. Positive and negative slides were selected from the most valent and arousing slides for both males and females from the IAPS set. Each set consisted of 27 slides (9 pleasant/positive, 9 neutral, and 9 unpleasant/negative), block-randomized in sets of three to distribute the three slide types evenly throughout the presentation. Slides with content of a more distressing nature (e.g., bloody scenes) or of a potentially more shocking nature (e.g., scenes involving full nudity) were not included in the sets. Because the original IAPS set was normed on college students, an attempt was made to also include some slides relevant to older adults (e.g., surgery). Four different block-randomized presentation orders were used for each slide set. Two practice (neutral) slides were included at the beginning of each set.

In evaluation of the IAPS stimulus set, Lang and colleagues had participants report their subjective experience of emotion using the Self-Assessment Manikin (SAM—Lang 1980), designed to minimize the effects that language may have in reporting response to emotionally arousing stimuli. Both the valence and arousal dimensions were ordinally scaled with five cartoonlike figures, and the option was given to make ratings between two figures, providing a scale ranging from 1 to 9 for each dimension. The justification for obtaining separate self-reports on these two dimensions of emotional experience comes from both studies of affective language and psychophysiological experiments. Several studies of the covariation between different emotional adjectives (Mehrabian 1970, Osgood, Suci, and Tannenbaum 1957, Russell 1980) have consistently found that valence and arousal are reliable factorial dimensions that account for most of the variance in affective judgments. Further, self-reported experiences of emotional valence and arousal (using the SAM procedure) have been found to differentially relate to various physiologic measures. Facial muscle EMG, heart rate, and magnitude of the eye-blink startle reflex co-vary with self-reported valence, while SCR, electrocortical activity, and functional brain imaging measures of regional activation co-vary with self-reported arousal (Lang et al. 1993).

Procedure

For all participants, data were collected in two consecutive sessions, in order to limit the length of each experimental session, and hence minimize fatigue and response habituation. The presentation order of the slides and the slide set shown in the first session were counterbalanced across participants. A computerized adaptation of the SAM was used to obtain the subjective ratings of valence and arousal. An electronic box displaying the SAM figures, with 9 buttons positioned underneath the two figure sets, was placed before the seated participant. The box was illuminated during the rating period in which the participant was asked to make happy/unhappy (valence) ratings and excited/calm (arousal) ratings for each slide using the 9-point rating scale. These quantitative responses were automatically stored in computer files for later analysis.

Participants sat in a recliner chair in a small, sound-attenuated, temperature-controlled, dimly lit room during attachment of the electrodes and during experimental stimulus presentation. The experimenter sat out of the participant's peripheral vision during the slide viewing. Slide images were projected directly ahead and slightly above the head of the participant. Slide image size averaged 4 feet × 3 feet, and the images were projected 9 feet from the participant's head.

Slide presentation was controlled by a computerized script that automatically advanced each slide after 6 seconds of exposure. Tape recorded and digitized instructions, under computer control, accompanied the slide showing. Participants were told that they would be viewing pictures differing in emotional content, and that each picture should be attended to for the entire time it is shown. After picture offset, a blank screen was shown during which valence and arousal ratings were made. The digitized instructions requested the participant to rate the slide on both dimensions (valence and arousal) by pushing one of nine buttons placed adjacent to or between the five SAM figures. A variable slide interval of approximately 20–35 seconds occurred between each slide presentation. This allowed time for the participant to self-rate emotion, and also for skin conductance to return to baseline.

A two-minute resting baseline recording was taken before slide presentation to facilitate laboratory adaptation, and two practice slides allowed for adaptation to the procedure. SCRs in response to each slide were recorded with silver-sliver chloride electrodes from the index and middle finger tips of the left hand (12-mm electrode gel contact area), using a 0.050-molar sodium chloride electrolyte in a Unibase cream medium (as recommended by Fowles et al. 1981). A BioPac GSR 100A amplifier (BioPac Systems; Santa Barbara, Calif.), employing a constant voltage technique, sampled absolute (DC) skin conductance at a rate of 120 samples per second and recorded SCRs through BioPac AcqKnowledge software running on a Macintosh Quadra computer (Apple Computer: Cupertino, Calif.). Skin conductance was recorded for 5 seconds before slide onset and for the full 6 seconds of slide viewing. For each stimulus trial, a latency window of 1 to 6 seconds after stimulus onset was used, and the amplitude of the largest SCR (relative to prestimulus baseline) falling within this window was recorded.

Results

Emotional Experience Ratings

Valence and arousal ratings were analyzed with 2×3 (Group $\times$ Slide Type) mixed model analyses of variance (ANOVAs). For valence ratings (see figure 18.2), no group main effect or Group by Slide-Type (positive-neutral-negative) interaction was found. Both patients and controls showed the expected pattern of valence ratings for their emotional experience while viewing the slides (i.e., the negative slides were rated as corresponding to the most negatively valenced emotional experience, the positive slides were rated as correponding to the most positively valenced experience, and the neutral slides were rated as intermediate). For arousal ratings (see figure 18.3), a significant group by slide-type interaction ($F = 3.38$, $p < .05$) was found. Overall, the patient group showed less differentiation between the slide types in their experienced emotional arousal.

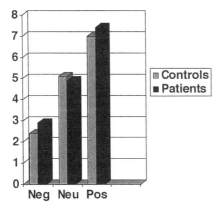

Figure 18.2
Self-ratings of emotional valence experienced while viewing the three different types of slides (Negative, Neutral, and Positive).

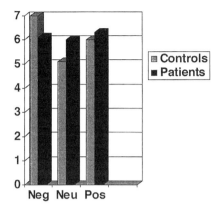

Figure 18.3
Self-ratings of emotional arousal experienced while viewing the three different types of slides (Negative, Neutral, and Positive).

Skin Conductance Responses

SCRs were similarly analyzed with a 2×3 (Group × Slide Type) mixed model ANOVA. A significant ($F = 3.22$, $p < .05$) Group by Slide-Type interaction effect was found, with the patient group showing less SCR differentiation between the slide types than did the control group (see figure 18.4). The control group showed the anticipated result of larger SCR amplitudes to the positive and negative, in comparison to the neutral, slides.

In order to further explore the relationship between SCR and the location of frontal lobe damage, two of the ACA aneurysm rupture patients, with damage in the basal–medial frontal region (including, in both patients, damage to the anterior cingulate gyrus, somewhat more extensive in the right medial frontal lobe for one patient and in the left medial frontal lobe for the other) were compared to the patient with damage limited to the bilateral orbital frontal regions (sparing the anterior cingulate gyrus, and without extension to other medial gray or white matter). The ACA aneurysm rupture patients with anterior cingulate damage showed either absent (for the patient with more extensive left medial frontal damage) or slide-type undifferentiated (for the patient with more extensive right medial frontal damage) SCRs to the emotional stimuli, while the patient with the circumscribed bilateral orbital frontal damage showed a normal pattern of greater SCR amplitude to the positive and negative, in comparison to the neutral, slides.

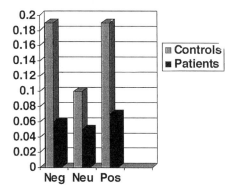

Figure 18.4
SCRs (in micro-mhos) in response to viewing the three different types of slides (Negative, Neutral, and
Positive).

Conclusions and Discussion

In the currently described study, patients with ventromedial frontal lobe damage
show a relative lack of consciously experienced arousal differentiation in response
to neutral versus negative or positive emotionally salient slides. However, patient
valence ratings were similar to those of controls, arguing against the possibility that
group difference in experienced arousal might be explained by any deficit within the
patient group in recognition of the content and general meaning of the slides (all
patients and controls were also able to accurately describe slide content, upon post-
experiment inquiry). These same frontally damaged patients also show a corresponding relative lack of SCR differentiation in response to the different slide types.
This correspondence between the pattern of results for subjective arousal ratings and
SCRs suggests that both sympathetic autonomic response and the experience of
emotional arousal (but not experienced emotional valence) are dependent upon the
integrity of ventromedial frontal structures. These results are consistent with the
clinical examples described by Damasio (1994) of frontally damaged patients who
showed absent SCRs to strongly negative visual scenes and who also volunteered that
they did not *feel* the expected emotion. Thus, the present results support Damasio's
hypothesis that frontally damaged patients who do not have an SCR to emotionally
salient stimuli will not have the "conscious bodily state characteristic of an emotion."

The present comparison of the two ACA aneurysm rupture patients with circumscribed medial frontal (including anterior cingulate gyrus) damage to the patient with
circumscribed bilateral orbito-frontal damage must be interpreted with considerable
caution, given the small number of individuals examined and the possibility that

observed differences could be due to other factors (e.g., differences in duration since damage occurred or premorbid individual differences). However, this comparison does suggest a hypothesis for future systematic testing: It is proposed that among patients with frontal damage, anterior cingulate, but not orbital frontal, damage may result in absent or undifferentiated SCR and subjective arousal in response to neutral versus positive or negative emotional stimuli. The hypothesis of a specific relationship of consciously experienced emotional arousal to anterior cingulate damage is also encouraged by the research of Lane et al. (1998) who examined the neural correlates of varying degrees of "emotional awareness" among normal volunteers, employing positron emission tomography (PET). Differences between these volunteers in emotional awareness were measured with the Levels of Emotional Awareness Scale (LEAS, Lane et al. 1990), which had been shown to correlate with the ability to accurately recognize verbal and nonverbal emotion stimuli (Lane et al. 1996). Higher scores on the LEAS were found to be associated with greater blood flow in a supra-callosal region of the anterior cingulate cortex (Broadman's area 24). In another PET study, Lane, Fink, Chau, and Dolan (1998) found that during attention to subjective emotional experience elicited by visual scenes (as contrasted with attention to the spatial context of the scene), activity was elicited in rostral anterior cingulate cortex (Broadman's area 32) and medial prefrontal cortex. Thus, functional brain imaging studies support a specific relationship between anterior cingulate gyrus activation and the conscious experience of emotion.

In contrast to the hypothesized role of the rostral anterior cingulate gyrus as a working memory (Lane, in press) "convergence area" for bodily aspects of emotion to gain access to conscious representation, the orbital frontal areas may be involved (perhaps both consciously and nonconsciously) in limiting choices, based upon emotional factors (Levine 1998), among courses of action (which themselves may be generated by dorsolateral frontal cortices; see Dehaene and Changeux 1991). This would be consistent with clinical descriptions (e.g., Damasio 1994) of patients with orbital frontal damage who obsessively develop alternative strategies for solving problems but seem unable to decide between them. The orbital frontal cortex, with its connections to the amygdala, also appears to be importantly involved in the inhibition of emotional impulses, given the marked disinhibition that is seen in patients with orbital frontal damage (e.g., Damasio, Grabowski, Frank, Galaburda, and Damasio 1994). In addition, connections between the orbital frontal cortex and the rostral anterior cingulate may allow conscious representations of emotional bodily states (integrated with other conscious representations, such as plans and contextual judgments) to influence impulse control and achieve more adaptive regulation of behavior.

References

Adolphs, R., D. Tranel, A. Bechara, H. Damasio, and A. R. Damasio 1996. Neuropsychological approaches to reasoning and decision-making. In A. R. Damasio et al., eds., *Neurobiology of Decision-Making*. Berlin: Springer-Verlag.

Andreassi, J. L. 1995. *Psychophysiology: Human Behavior and Physiological Response*. Hillsdale, N.J.: Lawrence Erlbaum Associates.

Clore, G. L. 1994. Why emotions are never unconscious. In P. Ekman and R. J. Davidson, eds., *The Nature of Emotion: Fundamental Questions*. New York: Oxford University Press, pp. 285–290.

Csikszentmihalyi, M. 1990. *Flow: The Psychology of Optimal Experience*. New York: Harper Perennial.

Dalby, P. R., A. W. Kaszniak, J. E. Obrzut, G. E. Schwartz, E. G. Montgomery, and L. M. Aleamoni, 1995. Facial EMG and the subjective experience of emotion in idiopathic Parkinson's disease. *Journal of the International Neuropsychological Society* 1:149 (abstract).

Damasio, A. 1994. *Descarte's Error*. New York: Grosset/Putnam.

Damasio, H., T. Grabowski, R. Frank, A. M. Galaburda, and A. R. Damasio 1994. The return of Phineas Gage: clues about the brain from the skull of a famous patient. *Science* 264:1102–1105.

Dehaene, S., and J.-P. Changeux 1991. The Wisconsin Card Sorting Test: Theoretical analysis and modeling in a neuronal network. *Cerebral Cortex* 1:62–89.

Devinsky, O., M. J. Morrell, and B. A. Vogt 1995. Contributions of anterior cingulate cortex to behavior. *Brain* 118:279–306.

Fowles, D. C., M. J. Christie, R. Edelberg, W. W. Grings, D. T. Lykken, and P. H. Venables, 1981. Publication recommendations for electrodermal measurements. *Psychophysiology* 18:232–239.

Frijda, N. H. 1993. The place of appraisal in emotion. *Cognition and Emotion* 7:357–387.

Goldman-Rakic, P. S. 1992. Working memory and the mind. *Scientific American* 267(3):111–117.

Greenwald, M. K., E. W. Cook, and P. J. Lang 1989. Affective judgment and psychophysiological response: Dimensional covariation in the evaluation of pictorial stimuli. *Journal of Psychophysiology* 3:51–64.

Griffiths, P. E. 1997. *What Emotions Really Are: The Problem of Psychological Categories*. Chicago: University of Chicago Press.

Lane, R. D. in press. Neural correlates of conscious emotional experience. In R. Lane, L. Nadel, G. Ahern, J. Allen, A. Kaszniak, S. Rapcsak, and G. E. Schwartz, eds., *The Cognitive Neuroscience of Emotion*. New York: Oxford University Press.

Lane, R. D., D. Quinlan, G. Schwartz, P. Walker, and S. Zeitlin 1990. The levels of emotional awareness scale: A cognitive-developmental measure of emotion. *Journal of Personality Assessment* 55:124–134.

Lane, R. D., G. R. Fink, P. M. L. Chau, and R. J. Dolan 1997. Neural activation during selective attention to subjective emotional responses. *Neuroreport* 8:3969–3972.

Lane, R. D., E. M. Reiman, B. Axelrod, L.-S. Yun, A. Holmes, and G. E. Schwartz 1998. Neural correlates of levels of emotional awareness: evidence of an interaction between emotion and attention in the anterior cingulate cortex. *Journal of Cognitive Neuroscience* 10:525–535.

Lane, R. D., L. Sechrest, R. Riedel, V. Weldon, A. W. Kaszniak, and G. E. Schwartz 1996. Impaired verbal and nonverbal emotion recognition in alexithymia. *Psychosomatic Medicine* 58:203–210.

Lang, P. J., and M. K. Greenwald 1988. *The international affective picture system standardization procedure and initial group results for affective judgements: Technical report 1A*. Gainsville, FL: The Center for Research in Psychophysiology, University of Florida.

Lang, P. J., M. K. Greenwald, and M. M. Bradley 1988. *The international affective picture system standardization procedure and initial group results for affective judgements: Technical report 1B*. Gainsville, FL: The Center for Research in Psychophysiology, University of Florida.

Lang, P. J., M. K. Greenwald, M. M. Bradley, and A. O. Hamm 1993. Looking at pictures: Affective, facial, visceral, and behavioral reactions. *Psychophysiology* 30:261–273.

Lang, P. J., A. Öhman, and D. Vaitl 1988. *The International Affective Picture System [photographic slides]*. Gainsville, FL: The Center for Research in Psychophysiology, University of Florida.

Lazarus, R. S. 1991. *Emotion and Adaptation*. New York: Oxford University Press.

Levine, D. S. 1998. Emotion and consciousness: A shotgun marriage? In S. R. Hameroff, A. W. Kaszniak, and A. C. Scott, eds., *Toward a Science of Consciousness II: The Second Tucson Discussions and Debates*. Cambridge, Mass.: MIT Press, pp. 513–520.

LeDoux, J. 1996. *The Emotional Brain: The Mysterious Underpinnings of Emotional Life*. New York: Simon and Schuster.

Mehrabian, A. 1970. A semantic space for nonverbal behavior. *Journal of Consulting and Clinical Psychology* 35:248–257.

Nielsen, L. 1998. Modeling creativity: Taking the evidence seriously. In S. R. Hameroff, A. W. Kaszniak, and A. C. Scott, eds., *Toward a Science of Consciousness II: The Second Tucson Discussions and Debates*. Cambridge, Mass.: MIT Press, pp. 717–724.

Ohman, A., and J. J. F. Soares 1994. Unconscious anxiety: Phobic responses to masked stimuli. *Journal of Abnormal Psychology* 103:231–240.

Osgood, C. E., G. J. Suci, and P. H. Tannenbaum 1957. *The Measurement of Meaning*. Urbana, Il: University of Illinois Press.

Panksepp, J. 1998. *Affective Neuroscience*. New York: Oxford University Press.

Price, J. L., S. T. Carmichael, and W. C. Drevets 1996. Networks related to the orbital and medial prefrontal cortex: A substrate for emotional behavior? *Progress in Brain Research* 107:523–536.

Russell, J. A. 1980. A circumplex model of affect. *Journal of Personality and Social Psychology* 39:1161–1178.

Taylor, J. G. 1992. Towards a neural network model of the mind. *Neural Network World* 6:797–812.

Tomkins, S. 1984. Affect theory. In K. Scherer and P. Ekman (eds.), *Approaches to Emotion*. Hillsdale, N.J.: Erlbaum, pp. 163–196.

Watt, D. F. 1999. Emotion and consciousness: Implications of affective neuroscience for extended reticular thalamic activating system (ERTAS) theories of consciousness. In S. R. Hameroff, A. W. Kaszniak, and D. J. Chalmers, eds., *Toward a Science of Consciousness III: The Third Tucson Discussions and Debates*. Cambridge, Mass.: MIT Press (this volume).

Whalen, P. J., S. L. Rauch, N. L. Etcoff, S. McInerny, M. B. Lee, and M. A. Jenike 1998. Masked presentations of emotional facial expressions modulate amygdala activity without explicit knowledge. *Journal of Neuroscience* 18:411–418.

19 At the Intersection of Emotion and Consciousness: Affective Neuroscience and Extended Reticular Thalamic Activating System (ERTAS) Theories of Consciousness

Douglas F. Watt

Consciousness and emotion are ancient topics as old as culture, still in their scientific infancy, and both slowly emerging into full respectability after decades of systematic neglect by science. Despite a modest resurgence in interest in the subject, emotion probably remains the most neglected and least understood subject relative to its importance in human life in the whole of neuroscience. This is likely overdetermined. One aspect may be hangover from Lange-James perspectives in which in which the richness of experienced emotion was reduced to a sensory feedback from autonomic and motor efferents, a kind of phenomenologically compelling but ultimately irrelevant "neural mirage" or after image of the "real action" of emotion in autonomic and motor efferentation. Additionally, the explosion of cognitive neuroscience, in concert with the extensive discrediting of much of psychoanalytic thinking, has left emotion in a largely secondary role, despite dramatic lessening of the stranglehold that behaviorism had over thinking in psychology. Cognition is very much in ascendance these days, with some even assuming its foundations are fundamentally independent from affect, a position for which there is little evolutionary or neurological evidence. Finally, the relative disregard for emotion (until recently) in neuroscience may have major contributions from the intrinsic scientific and methodological difficulty of the subject itself:

1. affect is elusively multi-dimensional, a complex composite of disparate elements;

2. there are formidable terminological and nosological issues, as emotion can be defined quite broadly (as emotional meaning, or emotional learning, which is vast and virtually interpenetrant with almost every higher activity in the CNS) or narrowly (the prototype emotional states of fear, rage, sadness, lust, etc.);

3. emotion broadly defined in humans seems to recruit many neocortical, paleocortical, subcortical, diencephalic, midbrain and brainstem systems, eluding localization in any "limbic system" unless that is defined very diffusely;

4. differences between emotion as a conscious event (the activation of a strong feeling), and various unconscious types of emotional processing (i.e., unconscious valence assignments, unconscious aspects of appraisal) have further divided the focus within the emotions research community: should we focus on feelings, or are they just a scientific distraction, while the real action of emotion is largely unconscious.

Although recent work by LeDoux (1996), Panksepp (1998), and Damasio (1994) have moved emotion back onto center stage as a topic in neuroscience, within the burgeoning literature about the neural basis of consciousness, there are still trends strongly paralleling this historical neglect of emotion, probably for the same basic reasons. Cognitive models dominate consciousness theory and research, while affect has been largely relegated to the back of the bus as an interesting "coloration" to the "hard problem" of consciousness (Chalmers 1996), with a few exceptions. Cognition and affect are generally not conceptualized as intimately related, and emotion within consciousness circles is often seen as just an interesting type of "qualia" among many other types of qualia. Not only is affect seen as just another qualia from both sides of the fence (the emotion literature and the consciousness literature), but a disadvantaged poor sister qualia at that, competing with better mapped visual awareness, which several adherents (notably Koch and Crick 1995) offer as a best available neural network model for consciousness itself. Thus, little consideration is given in either "affective neuroscience" (excepting Panksepp (1998)) or in the rapidly expanding body of consciousness theory to any potential role that emotion might have in underpinning or organizing consciousness, or to their potential intrinsic relations, rather that they are two fundamentally orthogonal processes.

Nosological—Terminological Problems—Just What Goes into Emotion Anyway?

To borrow from Chalmers (1996), emotion is no "easy" problem. Just from the standpoint of simple definition, it is illusively, stubbornly, multi-dimensional, as emotion in humans seems to bind together autonomic, endocrine, facial motor and global motor readiness activations, a poorly understood pain/pleasure valence, social signaling aspects, and higher cortical encodings (the high level other/self and social context encodings emphasized by many appraisal theorists) into a composite structure. From this perspective, emotion binds together virtually every type of information that the brain can encode. This composite (supramodal) nature of affect has been a central factor in the morass of controversy and confusion in the various literatures on emotion: with so many disparate features bound together, the study of emotion has often resembled the three blind men inspecting different portions of the elephant. Although this complexity of features is frustrating (particularly for those looking for simple answers), this integration argues for a neglected point: that emotion might be somehow related to or a part of the glue that holds the whole system together. This line of analysis suggests that possibly intrinsic connections between consciousness and emotion may have been generally poorly appreciated. There are parallel blind spots within the emotions research literature, in that in both the harder neuroscience investigations (and in softer cognitive science approaches as well) most emotion research has been largely focused on the top of the processing hierarchy (and analogously the cognitive literature has focused largely on appraisal). There has been much less appreciation of the whole, scientifically formidable and intimidating, neural integration of primitive and higher systems, on the fundamental integration of higher cognition with basic social-biological value which I would argue is the core scientific challenge for mapping emotion in humans, although Lane (1998), Damasio (1998) and others are recently arguing for such hierarchical-distributed approaches. While no definition of affect is going to satisfy all perspectives, there is some consensus that affect at least in humans (where its architecture is frustratingly complex) involves (at least most of the time) a composite of the following elements:

1. a precipitating event, stressor or trigger that can be *external* (social event, threat, or affective expression or behavior of another in social context) or *internal* (a thought, memory, fantasy or other affect) or have related internal and external triggers); precipitants for affect run the gamut of possible stimuli.

2. an assessment ("appraisal") of the precipitating event's meaning, or some degree of cognitive processing that can come either just before the experience of the affect (a vital component of the precipitating process), just after the activation of the affect (a post hoc appraisal), or exist at both positions. This appraisal can be fleeting or detailed, deeply realistic and empathic, or profoundly distorted, or have complex admixtures of both realistic appraisal and distortion); processing of some events may have minimal "cognitive components" (e.g., predatory threats, primary loss experiences), and much of the meaning attribution can also be quite unconscious.

3. subjective experiences along an intrinsic pain/pleasure axis (the crucial and poorly understood "valance" dimension of affect, underlining that emotion is fundamentally a carrier of organismic value). Valence is associated with various perceptions, ideas, sensations, actions, or representations of the precipitating event/trigger/stressor (Ohman (1998) notes that valence can also be assigned unconsciously or "subliminally").

4. motor, especially facial-motor changes, and differential motor "readiness" activations. These reflect the crucial adaptive "priming" of the executive systems by affect typically showing some version of approach vs. avoidance, such as defensive, withdrawn, submissive, aggressive, seductive, affectionate/playful behavior; may show marked behavioral inhibition (freezing, blunting of expression) in the context of fear states, with considerable variability in terms of motor activity. In common English, these reflect our "personal intention," toward the situations/persons/events associated with affect.

5. complex autonomic—physiological changes (the crucial "visceral" aspect of emotion), with the most commonly studied being various cardiopulmonary parameters,

skin conductance, and various muscle tonic issues, but this aspect also could include endocrine and immune system changes.

The Functional Evidence—Intrinsic Interpenetration of Three Global State Functions (GSF)

In general, theories of consciousness have almost completely neglected distinctions between global state functions and channel functions (i.e., perception or any other modular thalamocortical processing channel) of the type proposed by Mesulam (1985), to their consistent detriment. It is as though all psychological functions somehow stand on democratically equal footing in the congress of consciousness, an intuitively appealing but questionable assumption. The distinction between global state functions and channel functions appears to be particularly relevant and informative regarding the conceptual difficulties that have been encountered by leading investigators attempting to construct a general theory of consciousness solely from a theory of vision/visual awareness, as vision is a channel function. No adequate theory of consciousness can be constructed solely from an understanding of a channel function such as vision without mapping global state aspects such as visual working memory, the executive aspects of vision, etc. Recent work by Crick and Koch (1995) stops short of using any version of global workspace theory explicitly, but they do state quite clearly that "the function of visual awareness is to produce the best current interpretation of the visual scene, in the light of past experience, and to make it available, for a sufficient time, to the parts of the brain that contemplate, plan and execute voluntary motor outputs (of one sort or another)." This is an acknowledgement that neuroscientifically valid notions of "visual awareness" cannot be constructed without reference to global state variables, in this case an explicit reference to executive functions supported in prefrontal systems.

In terms of formal neuropsychological categories, the three global state functions (affect, attentional functions, and executive functions (volition)) must be linchpins in any viable theory of consciousness, along with pain and self-representation (which I will not deal with here for space reasons). These GSF (global state functions) are deeply interpenetrating, functionally, and in terms of their neural substrates. The maps we have currently for the neural architecture of these three global state functions are both heavily overlapping and highly distributed:

1. Affective functions (emotion broadly defined) are "localized" to a very diffusely distributed "limbic system" that almost seems to include just about every area of the brain excepting idiotypic cortex—"extended" notions about the limbic system include

a host of prefrontal, paralimbic, telencephalic basal forebrain and subcortical gray matter systems (including the ventral basal ganglia, septal regions, and amygdala) many diencephalic regions, particularly anterior thalamus and hypothalamus, midbrain areas, and the monoaminergic portions of the brainstem core.

2. Attentional functions have been largely "localized" to RAS-MRF-thalamic loops, several other thalamic regions, prefrontal regions/associated basal ganglia, and paralimbic, parietal, and heteromodal right hemisphere systems.

3. Executive functions have largely been "localized" to three parallel prefrontal-striatal-thalamic loops centered in dorsolateral, orbital and medial prefrontal regions.

These three mappings reference nothing that one could consider discretely separated regions or networks, and interestingly, all three are thought to be more crucially dependent upon right hemisphere systems (Mesulam 1985). Lesions studies redundantly support this putative overlap in neural substrates: CNS lesions affecting attentional functions and executive functions (in prefrontal, basal ganglia, paralimbic, limbic, thalamic or brain stem regions) typically produce affective and personality changes and via versa. This suggests that affective, attentional and executive functions should be conceptualized as different aspects of poorly understood global integration architectures, different slices of the consciousness pie. The deep functional interpenetration of GSF (affect, attentional functions, executive functions, along with pain and self-representation) speak to different dimensions of an integrative multi-component neural envelope (supporting consciousness) that we don't have well mapped yet:

a) the most critical aspect of attention relates to its executive aspects (what a person decides to focus upon, or what "grabs" attention), as these frames establish the content of working memory and are much more behaviorally relevant than its simpler "buffer" aspects (Baddeley 1986);

b) goals (invariably wish/fear based), implicit or explicit, conscious or unconscious, inform the frames for working memory (WM); these goals (implicit or explicit, conscious or unconscious) show *embedded value* and the affective significance of virtually all WM frames—what is emotionally important and relevant has a major if not virtually determinant impact on defining foci of attention (the frames for working memory);

c) affective activations critically influence and modulate executive functions, having their strongest impact on learning new paradigms for behavior—affects are the great internal reinforcers, a point neglected by most classically behaviorist points of view to their great (and eventually fatal) impoverishment, as they had to ideologically ignore internal processes about affect to prevent "inner life" from being smuggled in through the back door (these affective processes were relegated to what Skinner called the "black box" of the brain);

d) executive function is geared globally toward the maximizing of pleasurable affect and the minimizing of painful affect (however adaptively or poorly this is conceived and executed, and despite enormous variations across individuals for what is rewarding vs. aversive);

e) diseases that impair affective experience invariably affect motivation, underlining the specious nature of any distinctions between motivation (conceptualized as a core aspect of executive function by most) and emotion.

The Architectural Evidence—the Neural Correlates of Emotion

It is axiomatic these days to think of emotion and memory of as "limbic system functions," but there are serious problems with this concept which I will only briefly touch on here. Current schemes emphasize a division of the limbic system into a paleocortical evolutionary trend (amygdaloid-centered) and archicortical evolutionary trend (hippocampal-centered). Underlining the limitations of any unitary concept of the "limbic system," short-term memory in the hippocampal-archicortical trend is seen currently as more allied with cognitive functions and cognitive mapping. These two evolutionary trends support "episodic memory" (a transmodal serial linkage of cortical sensory-motor encodings with spatiotemporal coordinates to enable short-term memory) and "emotional memory" (the linkage of cortical and thalamic sensory-motor encodings with "valenced" activations of autonomic and other systems (best known for fear). The borders of the "limbic system" are vague and have been extended decade by decade like the erosion of a vast neural shoreline. Various "extended" notions about the limbic system include a host of cortical paralimbic, basal ganglia, thalamic and hypothalamic, basal forebrain, and other subcortical systems, including even monoaminergic portions of the RAS brainstem core (Derryberry and Tucker 1992). In mammals, neural correlates for even the prototype states (from Panksepp 1998)—fear, rage, lust, separation distress, bonding/nurturance, play/joy—are spread out through many systems in the basal forebrain, diencephalon, and midbrain. There even fewer borders to the "limbic system" if one fails to make clear distinctions between primitive or primary emotion (the prototype states) and "emotional meaning," "secondary emotions," and "emotional learning." These are very broad corticolimbic functions, affected by sum total of long-term changes in many systems mediated by synaptic plasticity mechanisms following the activation of primary

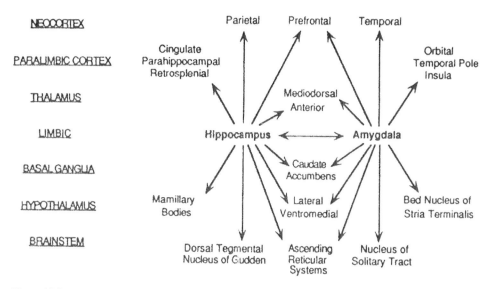

Figure 19.1
"Limbic system" is highly distributed ("fully distributed"?) Highly parallel and globally distributed nature of limbic connectivities running from the brainstem (including portions of ERTAS) to the highest neo-cortical centers. Omitted from this schema are critical limbic inputs into non-specific thalamic systems—(NRT/ILN) from basal ganglia, prefrontal systems, accumbens, and paralimbic cortices, and crucial regions in the midbrain (from Tucker and Derryberry 1992).

affects. This further "spread" of the "limbic system" if one is looking at emotional learning/meaning suggests that the brain is not nonspecifically dedicated to the processing of "information," but to the processing of events in terms of an inter-penetrating hierarchy of biological, social and personal-subjective values, to the deepening interpenetration of "value operators" at many levels of the brain.

A difficult problem has been understanding the biphasic nature of affect (the "plus or minus" nature of all affective valence). This primary feature of affect has been appreciated for as long as there has been human culture: that we have loves and hates, likes and dislikes, attractions and aversions. We are thoroughly ambivalent creatures in our relationships to significant others and we struggle with our ambiva-lence from birth to death. Perhaps the most famous instantiation of this ancient principle was Freud's dual instinct theory, and appreciation for the depth of human ambivalence is perhaps the beginning of emotional wisdom. Yet as fundamental as this is, its neural architecture is not at all clear (although interactions of more dorsal and ventral systems in PAG may be a partial substrate—see next section). There is certainly major evidence for the role of the amygdala in establishing valence (fear conditioning to be more precise) for certain classes of stimuli and for its involvement in negative affect, owing to much elegant work by LeDoux (summarized in LeDoux 1996). This structure acts as a high level correlator associating complex stimuli from thalamus and various cortical regions with autonomic, endocrine and behavioral activations via its outflows from the central nucleus to various targets in hypothalamus, brain stem, and PAG midbrain. One theoretical conundrum in all this, generally not acknowledged, is that a high level correlator structure such as the amygdala cannot by itself supply neural definitions for primitive biological or social value or "valence," only associate those primitive value or "valenced" activations with various encodings from the dorsal portions of neuroaxis such as cortex and thalamus.

The Architectural Evidence (Part II) "Unpacking" Valence and Value into Affective Prototypes

The work of Jaak Panksepp (1998, 1995) is contributory in "unpacking" valence into its fundamental modularity (different kinds of primitive + and −) in terms of core prototypes of social-biological relationship to other species and conspecifics, with these likely fundamental to all mammalian brains. This work has been neglected in most reviews of the neural correlates of emotion. Panksepp (1998) summarizes a group of core networks in the midbrain-diencephalon that support prototype affects or emotional "primitives." Each distributed circuit appears to modulate a prototype "grade A" primary emotion: attachment/bonding/nurturance, sadness/separation distress, rage, fear, play/joy, and a seeking/expectancy system that supplies nonspecific motivational arousal and probably much of the primitive preconscious substrate for the fundamental experience of *hope*. Each circuit is heavily (but not exclusively) neuropeptide mediated, and projects to periaquaductal gray (PAG). (See table 19.1.)

The Architectural Evidence (Part III)—Connectivities between the "Limbic System" and ERTAS Systems

There are many sites for intersection between the basic architecture of value/emotion with the ERTAS networks proposed by several reviewers as the mostly likely neural network architecture for consciousness (Baars and Newman 1993, Newman 1997, Baars, Newman, and Taylor 1998, Taylor 1998). These critical sites for important interactions are seen at each level of the ERTAS, starting with the reticular core and progressing all the way up to the prefrontal systems:

Table 19.1
Distributed midbrain-diencephalic-basal forebrain chemoarchitectures for emotional primitives (prototype emotions) (Extracted from Panksepp 1998)

Affective behavior	Distributed neural networks and major structures	Neuro-modulators
Nonspecific motivational arousal—seeking and exploratory behavior	Ventral Tegmental Area (VTA) to more dorsolateral hypothalamic to periaqueductal gray (PAG), with diffuse mesolimbic and mesocortical "extensions." Nucleus accumbens as crucial basal ganglia processor for emotional "habit" systems.	DA (+), glutamate (+), many neuropeptides including opiods, neurotensin, CCK
Rage/anger—("Affective Attack")	medial amygdala to bed nucleus of stria terminalis (BNST) to anterior and ventromedial and perifornical hypothalamic to more dorsal PAG	Substance P (+) (? ACh, glutamate (+) as nonspecific modulators?)
Fear	central & lateral amygdala to medial and anterior hypothalamic to more dorsal PAG to nucleus reticularis pontine caudalis	Glutamate, neuropeptides (DBI, CRF, CCK, alpha MSH, NPY)
Sexuality/lust	BNST and corticomedial amygdala to preoptic and ventromedial hypothalamus to lateral and more ventral PAG	Steroids (+), vasopressin and oxytocin
Nurturance/maternal care	Anterior cingulate to bed nucleus of stria terminalis (BNST) to preoptic hypothalamic to ventral PAG	Oxytocin (+), prolactin (+), dopamine, opiods
Separation distress/social bonding	Anterior cingulate/anterior thalamus to BNST/ventral septum to midline & dorsomedial thalamus to dorsal preoptic hypothalamic to more dorsal PAG (close to circuits for physical pain)	Opiods (−/+) oxytocin (−/+), prolactin (−/+) CRF (+) for separation distress, ACh (−)
Play/joy/social affection	Parafascicular/centromedian thalamus, dorsomedial thalamus, posterior thalamus, ? all projecting to ventral PAG (septum inhibitory re: play)	Opiods (+ in small–mod. amounts, − in larger amounts), ACh (+)

Keys [(−) inhibits prototype, (+) activates prototype] [PAG = periaqueductal gray, CCK = choleocystokinin, CRF = corticotrophin releasing factor, ACTH = adrenocorticotropic hormone, DBI = diazepam binding inhibitor, ACh = acetylcholine, DA = dopamine, MSH = melanocyte stimulating hormone, NPY = neuropeptide Y] This table deliberately omits biogenic amines, which are nonspecific.

1. There are important afferents from PAG to both MRF and ILN/midline thalamic systems. PAG shows four basic columnar systems projecting (quite differentially) to key nonspecific thalamic systems (the ILN, and other midline systems) as well as feeding back onto hypothalamus and the monoamine "spritzers" (Cameron 1995, Bandler 1991);

2. the nucleus reticularis thalami (nRt) shows dominant limbic, paralimbic, and heteromodal control of nRt gating, with modulation of nRt "gatelets" by nucleus accumbens, paralimbic cortices, BG, and DM thalamus-prefrontal regions; there is NA gating of HC and prefrontal afferents to nRt (Newman and Grace 1998). Taylor (1998) emphasizes that limbic system inputs dominates anterior portions of nRt without reciprocal inhibitory controls;

3. reciprocal connections of ILN to reticular core, midbrain PAG, limbic, BG, and many cortical systems (Newman 1997); There are extensive prefrontal projections to ILN, as part of the top down control of ERTAS, including from paralimbic pre-frontal systems (cingulate and orbital frontal) (Newman and Baars 1993).

Taken together, these argue that "nonspecific" nRt/ILN regions have rich, even dominant limbic, paralimbic, and heteromodal connectivities, which provide a neural basis for: 1) emotionally relevant stimuli to influence attentional content; 2) for different aspects of emotion to possibly enter consciousness; and 3) for limbic inputs to facilitate binding in widely distributed networks (binding and synchronous activation of widely distributed networks being one of the leading mechanisms thought to possibly underpin the integration of features in qualia (Llinas et al. 1994, Engel et al. 1997). These dense limbic and paralimbic connectivities of the nonspecific thalamic systems suggest that affect must be more than simple "coloration" and must make important contributions to gating and binding. Although gating and binding are still not well understood, gating appears better mapped, and dependent on the higher paralimbic, prefrontal-striatal, and limbic inputs into nRt. Binding is less clearly understood, and may have several different neurodynamic dimensions, but PAG projections to ILN and other midline thalamic systems may support aspects of binding, while projections to MRF may support arousal.

PAG's foundational role in affect, and some, albeit poorly understood, crucial role in consciousness, in the context of its many connectivities to reticular tissues in thalamus and brainstem (see Cameron et al. 1995a/b), has yet to be fully appreciated. A key issue here is its receiving projections from all of the affective prototype systems in the basal forebrain and diencephalon, which raises the question (not addressed at all in the PAG literature curiously) of whether it is computing both competition and agonism between these prototype states. If PAG is a clearinghouse for projections from the various distributed affective systems in the diencephalon and limbic basal forebrain, it may function as a primitive ventral nRt—"computing" some version of an ongoing competition between the relative activation states of the prototypes. The various positive and negative (defensive/appetitive) affective systems project quite differentially to four adjacent dorsomedial, lateral, ventral (more positive) vs. dorsal (more negative) columnar systems in PAG. Although it has been understood for years that there is radial organization in these columnar systems, their function has not been mapped, and the radial organization may be a substrate that allows the columns to interact (see Bandler and Depaulis 1991). In any case, the results of PAG "computations" are highly distributed both dorsally and ventrally in the brain, tuning the response of various reticular (including MRF) and monoamine systems, and projecting upward to several key nonspecific thalamic systems that appear to critically underpin gating and binding (Newman and Baars 1993, Llinas et al. 1994, Newman 1997), and feeding back to hypothalamus. Regarding the reticular connectivities, the four columnar systems in PAG project with overlapping as well as differential efferents to the ILN (intralaminar nuclei), MRF (midbrain reticular formation) and several other midline thalamic systems. PAG may even be essential for the arousal or maintenance of a conscious state, or at least for virtually all behavioral intentionality, as PAG lesions seem to have very serious effects on the ability of the organism to maintain a conscious state. Unfortunately, the lesion work on rats has included lesions of superior colliculus in the ablations of PAG, so a clean and complete PAG lesion in rats has not yet been assessed to my knowledge, but full PAG lesions in primates seem to badly impair consciousness, resulting in a dim, profoundly abulic, twilight state. (See Watt, (1998b), and the associated commentaries in the ASSC Electronic Seminar on Emotion and Consciousness at http://server.phil.vt.edu/assc/esem.html for more discussion of the complexities of PAG functional correlates.) Overall, I would argue that PAG is playing some kind of poorly understood role in integration of the most primitive (and essential) features of affect that make emotion intrinsically "valenced" (the essential "plus or minus" nature of affect) but without the essential higher cognitive correlates. By higher cognitive correlates, I mean the crucial adaptive ability of the brain to know when to activate these responses, which depends on appraisals, correlations, and personal meanings that could only be formed in the more dorsal regions of the brain over the lifetime of the organism's affective learning (mediated by various synaptic plasticity mechanisms). This is the crucial distinction made earlier between substrates for primitive affective states of the organism vs. substrates for affective meanings. PAG may be a complex convergence zone that underpins the organization of affective behavior at the most primitive and basic level in the brain, with PAG being quite dependent on various higher systems to adaptively and appropriately trigger the integrated somatic-emotional responses that PAG organizes. PAG then may distribute results of those affective "computations" to core reticular (and monoamine) systems at both the brainstem and thalamic levels that critically underpin conscious states. What these connectivities mean, and PAG's importance for all of the basic global state functions is far from fully appreciated (although its having an important role in pain modulation has been understood for years).

Consciousness Theory and Emotion

Emotion (in the form of these midbrain-diencephalic primitives) defines biologically compelling prototypes for self-world relations based in "primes" for relations to other species and conspecifics, such as the confrontation with a predator (the fear system), the attachment to and/or loss of a mate, child or parent (the bonding and separation distress systems), the confrontation with an aggressor/rival (the rage system), or playful affection with a conspecific (the joyous engagement supported in the play system). These prototype affective states, by initiating various global resonances, may prime the "virtual reality" generation that many (see Revonsuo 1995, 1998) see underpinning consciousness, as consciousness reflects a real time, ongoing "virtual self-world model." Given the assumption (Metzinger 1998) that consciousness depends on coherent self-world models, this set of primitives generates primary "wetware instantiated" models for basic self-world relations that could be (further) cognitively developed. One is led to wonder here if these primes or prototypes operate as resonance points within the global ERTAS architecture for consciousness, whether these primes are essential foundations for primitive qualia. At this point we do not know if self-world models can exist if completely stripped of neural connection to these affective primes or basal neural prototypes for self-world relations, but the richest contents of consciousness suggest that the influence of these primes is deceptively pervasive. It is not some truly isolated "redness of red" that catches our eye, but rather the aesthetic (affective) redness of the rose that reminds us of things and people we love. It is not some isolated motor proprioception that we experience richly, it is the last agonizing and impossible stretch to the ball that scores the winning goal, or fails to.

There are confusing references in the literature to "affective consciousness" which I would argue is a misnomer. A better term might be a "protoconsciousness" in mammals and human infants that has a primary affective base, but one still tied to the crucial integration of value, action, and sense information. In other words, the

segmenting of consciousness into an "affective consciousness," a "cognitive consciousness," an "active consciousness," a more "passive" or "sensory consciousness"
makes no heuristic sense, as it fractionates the very process that pulls these components together, and that derives (I believe) from their living, dynamic interactions.
Consciousness has to reflect global integration, as both agency and value are deeply
embedded in what might initially appear to be passive sensory qualia. Some have
argued persuasively (Panksepp 1998, Cotterill 1995), as agency is central to selfhood,
that the most basal foundations for consciousness must rest on motor maps (which
may have more stability than sensory maps). However, the connectivities between a
primitive value map in PAG, a primitive sensory map largely in superior colliculus,
and primitive motor maps in deep tectal and tegmental areas may form the most
basal neural representation for self (Panksepp 1998). It would be hard to know that
one existed if one could not correlate on-going sensory changes with activated action
schematas, and both of these with value schematas that generate and predict inherent
internal rewards and "punishments." These correlations may enable the most basic
and primitive feeling that we exist, that what we do matters, and has effects, good
and bad. Without primitive value correlates (largely contributed from PAG?) interacting with the primitive sensory and motor mappings, sensory-motor correlations
might not mean much by themselves. This poorly appreciated midbrain integration of
sense, value and action may form foundations for a primitive yet superordinate "self-
model" that Metzinger sees as an essential foundation for consciousness (Metzinger
1998), underpinning the normal "ownership" of qualia, a basic property of consciousness as yet unexplained.

References

Baars, B. J. 1993. "How does a serial, integrated and very limited stream of consciousness emerge from a
nervous system that is mostly unconscious, distributed, and of enormous capacity?" In CIBA Symposium
on *Experimental and Theoretical Studies of Consciousness*, ed. G. Bock and J. Marsh. London: John Wiley
and Sons, pp. 282–290.

Baars, B. J., and Newman, J. 1994. A neurobiological interpretation of the Global Workspace theory of
consciousness. In A. Revonsuo and M. Kamppinen (eds.), *Consciousness in Philosophy and Cognitive
Neuroscience*. Hillsdale, N.J.: Erlbaum.

Baars, B. J. 1996. *In the Theater of Consciousness: The Workspace of the Mind*. New York: Oxford University Press.

Baars, B. J., Newman, J., and Taylor, J. G. 1998. Neuronal mechanisms of consciousness: A relational
global workspace framework. In S. Hameroff et al. (eds.) *Towards a Science of Consciousness II: The Second Tucson Discussions and Debates*. Cambridge, Mass.: MIT Press.

Baddeley, A. 1986. *Working Memory*. Oxford: Oxford Univ Press.

Bandler, J. and Depaulis, A. (eds.) 1991. *The Midbrain Periaqueductal Gray*. Plenum Press: (NATO Asi
Series. Series A, Life Science, vol. 213).

Cameron A. A., Khan I. A., Westlund K. N., Cliffer K. D., and Willis W. D. 1995a. The efferent projections of the periaqueductal gray in the rat: a Phaseolus vulgaris-leucoagglutinin study. I. Ascending projections. *J Comp Neurology* 351:568–584.

Cameron A. A., Khan I. A., Westlund K. N., and Willis W. D. 1995b. The efferent projections of the periaqueductal gray in the rat: a Phaseolus vulgaris-leucoagglutinin study. II. Descending projections. *J Comp Neurology* 351:585–601.

Chalmers, D. 1996. Facing up to the problem of consciousness, *Journal of Consciousness Studies* 2:200–219.

Cornwall, J., Cooper, J. D., and Phillipson, O. T. 1990. Projections to the reticular thalamic nucleus in the rat. *Experimental Brain Research* 80:157–171.

Cotterill, R. 1995. On the unity of conscious experience. *Journal of Consciousness Studies* 2:290–312.

Crick, F., and Koch, C. 1995. Are we aware of neural activity in primary visual cortex? *Nature* 375:121–123.

Damasio, A. 1994. *Descartes' Error: Emotion, Reason, and the Human Brain*. New York: Avon Press.

Damasio, A. 1998. Emotion in the perspective of an integrated nervous system. *Brain Research Review* 26:83–86.

Davidson, R. J. 1992. Anterior cortical asymmetry and the nature of emotion. *Brain and Cognition* 20:125–151.

Derryberry, D., and Tucker, D. M. 1992. Neural mechanisms of emotion. *Journal of Consulting and Clinical Psychology* 60:329–338.

Engel, Andreas K., Fries, P., Roelfsema, P., R., König, P., and Singer, W. 1997. Temporal Binding, Binocular Rivalry, and Consciousness. *Association for the Scientific Study of Consciousness*. On Line Seminar, http://server.phil.vt.edu/assc/esem.html

Kaszniak, A. W. 1998. Conscious experience and autonomic response to emotional stimuli following frontal lobe damage. http://www.zynet.co.uk/imprint/Tucson/2.htm

Lane, R. D. 1998. Subregions within the anterior cingulate cortex may differentially participate in phenomenal and reflective consciousness awareness of emotion. http://www.zynet.co.uk/imprint/Tucson/2.htm

LeDoux, J. 1996. *The Emotional Brain. The Mysterious Underpinnings Of Emotional Life*. New York: Simon and Schuster.

Llinas, Ribary, Joliot and Wang 1994. Content and context in temporal thalamocortical binding. In G. Buzsaki et al. (eds.) *Temporal Coding in the Brain*. Berlin: Springer Verlag.

Lozsadi, D. A. 1994. Organization of cortical afferents to the rostral limbic sector of the rat reticular thalamic nucleus. *J. Comparative Neurology* 341:520–533.

Mesulam, M. 1985. Patterns in behavioral neuroanatomy: association areas, limbic system, and hemispheric specialization. In Mesulam, M. (Ed): *Principles of Behavioral Neurology*. Philadelphia: FA Davis.

Metzinger, T. 1998. "Being No One" Plenary Address, *ASSC Conference on Neural Correlates of Consciousness*, June 21, 1998. Bremen, Germany.

Newman, J. 1997. Putting the puzzle together: Towards a general theory of the neural correlates of consciousness. *Journal of Consciousness Studies* 4(1/2):47–66; 101–121.

Newman, J. and Baars, B. J. 1993. A neural attentional model for access to consciousness: A Global Workspace perspective. *Concepts in Neuroscience* 4:255–290.

Newman, J. and Grace, A. 1998. Newly elucidated circuitry subserving the selective gating of fronto-hippocampal systems contributing to the stream of consciousness: A model for the modulation of attention by affective states and episodic representations. http://www.zynet.co.uk/imprint/Tucson/neuroscience.

Ohman, A. 1998. Distinguishing Unconscious from Conscious Emotional Processes: Methodological Considerations and Theoretic Implications.

Panksepp, J. 1995. Affective Neuroscience: A paradigm to study the animate circuits for human emotions. *In Emotions: An Interdisciplinary Approach*, pp. 29–60. Hillsdale, N.J.: Erlbaum.

Panksepp, J. 1998. *Affective Neuroscience*. Oxford: Oxford University Press.

Revonsuo, A. 1995. Consciousness, dreams, and virtual realities. *Philosophical Psychology* 8:35–58.

Revonsuo, A. 1998. How to take consciousness seriously in cognitive neuroscience.

Schore, A. 1994. *Affect Regulation and the Origins of the Self*. The Neurobiology of *Affective Development*. Hillsdale, N.J.: Erlbaum.

Taylor, J. G. 1999. *The Emergent Mind*. Cambridge, Mass.: MIT Press.

Watt, D. F. 1998a. Emotion, Cognitive Neuroscience and Consciousness Studies: Is Emotion Really One of Easy Problems? On Line Web Seminar at The University of Arizona. http://www.consciousness.arizona.edu/emotion.html

Watt, D. F. 1998b. The Implications of Affective Neuroscience for Extended Reticular Thalamic Activating System Theories of Consciousness. Online Electronic Seminar for the Association for the Scientific Study of Consciousness. http://server.phil.vt.edu/assc/esem.html

20 Laughing Rats? Playful Tickling Arouses High-Frequency Ultrasonic Chirping in Young Rodents

Jaak Panksepp and Jeffrey Burgdorf

Prologue: On the Discovery of "Laughter" in Rats

Laughter is a simple and robust indicator of joyful social affect. All too commonly it is considered to be a unique emotional capacity of humans and perhaps a few other higher primates. If more primitive mammals also exhibit such emotional responses, it would suggest that joyful affect emerged much earlier within mammalian brain evolution than is generally believed. In this chapter we summarize the discovery of a primitive form of "laughter" in rats, and we provide convergent evidence and argumentation that a study of this response may help us decipher the neural basis of joy and positive emotional consciousness within the mammalian brain.

The stylistic approach used in this article is somewhat unique—namely a traditional scientific report sandwiched between a short "prologue" and "epilogue." We do this to share the full text of the manuscript of our initial discovery—a contribution that was rejected by the journal *Nature* in September of 1997, leaving us concerned, once more, over the scientific openness of our present era. One reviewer did enthusiastically support our efforts (accepting this contribution with no major changes as a "scientifically sound" set of studies), while another rejected it outright on the basis of minor methodological concerns. At the conclusion of a harsh review, he asserted that "This is an interesting idea accompanied by some rather bad experiments. So even though the authors' conclusions may be right, it doesn't get a lot of help from the data. I am not sure that even better controlled experiments would be more convincing to readers." Even after we pointed out that most of our "flaws" were largely misinterpretations, the editor refused to reconsider his decision. Now, after a year of additional work and the world-wide broadcasting of our findings in the popular press following the Tucson III meeting (e.g., see *New Scientist*, May 2, 1998 (p. 14) and *People* magazine, June 15, 1998 (p. 105), as well as cameo appearances in "Believe It or Not" and "News of the Weird," we continue to believe that our interpretation of this robust tickling-induced vocal phenomenon in young rats is on the right track. Accordingly, we now share our initial results for the first time and we wish to do it in essentially the form that the work was originally submitted for peer review.

Our Original Findings as Submitted to *Nature*

Abstract: In humans, laughter and giggling are objective indicators of joyful positive affect, and they occur most abundantly during playful social interactions. An understanding of such positive emotions has been hampered by the lack of simple measures of joyful social engagement in "lower" animals. Since the simplest way to induce laughter in children is tickling, we sought evidence for a comparable phenomenon in young rats by studying their ultrasonic "chirping" during vigorous bodily stimulation. Such vocalizations are common during juvenile play (Knutson, Burgdorf, and Panksepp 1998), and they can also be evoked by rapid manual stimulation (i.e., tickling). Stimulation of anterior body areas, which are especially important for arousing playfulness (Siviy and Panksepp 1987) yielded more chirping than stimulation of posterior zones, and full body stimulation with the animals in a supine position yielded the most. Analyses of these vocalizations suggest relationships to primate laughter: Tickling is a positive incentive state, as indexed by classical conditioning induced sensitization and instrumental approach tests; it is also correlated to natural playfulness and is inhibited by fearful arousal. These data suggest that a primal form of "laughter" evolved early in mammalian brain evolution, and provide a new way to study the neural sources of positive social-emotional processes (i.e., joyful affect) in other mammals.

Although laughter is a prominent behavior of the human species, reflecting our ability to experience joy and humor, only fragments of data suggest that other species have similar brain functions. Certain vocal patterns of chimpanzees (Jürgens 1986, Berntson, Boysen, Bauer, and Torrello 1989) and some lower primates (Preuschoft 1992), appear to reflect the existence of homologous processes, but credible evidence for other species is marginal (Douglas 1971, Masson and McCarthy 1996). However, considering the clinical evidence that the primal neural mechanisms for human laughter exist in ancient regions of the brain, including thalamus, hypothalamus and midbrain (Arroyo et al. 1993, Black 1982, Poeck 1969), the existence of such processes in common laboratory species seems feasible, at least in principle. We now report evidence congruent with the presence of analogous, perhaps homologous, responses in domesticated rats.

Adult rats commonly exhibit two distinct types of ultrasonic vocalizations (USVs): Long distress-USVs in the low frequency range (peaking at around 22 KHz) reflect negative emotional arousal related to fear, social defeat and the postcopulatory refractory period (Haney and Miczek 1993, Sales and Pye 1974). On the other hand, short chirping-type USVs in the high frequency range (peaking at approximately 50 KHz) appear to index more positive forms of arousal that occur at high rates during desired social interactions (Knutson, Burgdorf, and Panksepp 1998, Sales and Pye 1974).

Human and chimpanzee laughter tends to emerge most readily in playful contexts (Rothbart 1973, Sroufe and Waters 1976, Van Hooff 1972), and the rough-and-tumble play of young rodents is accompanied by an abundance of short, high frequency USVs (Knutson, Burgdorf, and Panksepp 1998). Although such high frequency USVs have typically been studied in the context of adult sexual and aggressive encounters (Adler and Anisko 1979, Barfield and Geyer 1975, Tornatzky and Miczek 1995), they have also been noted during routine handling (Sales and Pye 1974). In the following experiments, we determined whether the type of chirping seen during play has any resemblances to human laughter which may suggest a degree of evolutionary kinship between the two phenomena.

The easiest way to induce primal laughter and joy in young children is through tickling. This response conditions rapidly (Newman, O'Grady, Ryan, and Hemmes 1993). After a few tickles, one can provoke social engagement and peals of laughter by provocative cues such as wiggling a finger (Rothbart 1973). We have now found that chirping at around 50 KHz is increased markedly in young rats by manual tickling and converging evidence suggests the response has more than a passing resemblance to human laughter.

First we determined whether tickling different parts of the body lead to different levels of chirping, and whether the response varies as a function of previous social experience and gender. Thirty-one Long-Evans hooded rat pups (13 males, 18 females) were weaned and individually housed at 24 days of age. Half the animals were assigned to pairs and allowed two 0.5 hr play sessions daily (alternately, in each other's home cages), while the remaining animals (n = 15) were handled an equal number of times but always left solitary in their own cages. At 41 and 55 days of age all animals were left undisturbed for 48 hrs and then observed during a 2 minute standard dyadic play encounter, during which the frequencies of two objective play activities of each animal, namely pins and dorsal contacts, as well as the number of 50 KHz chirps were monitored (Panksepp, Siviy, and Normansell 1984). Counting of chirps in all experiments was always done by a listener who was blind to experimental conditions. All testing, except as indicated, was carried out under dim (25 lux) illumination.

The next day, all animals were given standardized tickling tests. Animals were transported quietly in their home cages and placed for observation in a quiet observation enclosure. High frequency USVs were monitored with a Mini-3 Bat Detector (Ultra Sound Advice, London), tuned to detect the high USVs. High USVs were recorded during six successive 20 second test periods: 1) an initial no-stimulation baseline, 2) vigorous tickling-type manual stimulation of either the anterior or posterior, dorsal body surfaces, 3) a second baseline, 4) vigorous manual stimulation of the dorsal body surface that had not yet been stimulated (i.e., the sequence of anterior and posterior target areas being counterbalanced), 5) a final baseline, followed by 6) vigorous whole-body playful tickling (focusing on the ribs and ventral surface), with animals being repeatedly pinned 4–6 times, throughout the 15 sec. interval. For all animals, the tickling was done with the right hand and consisted of rapid finger

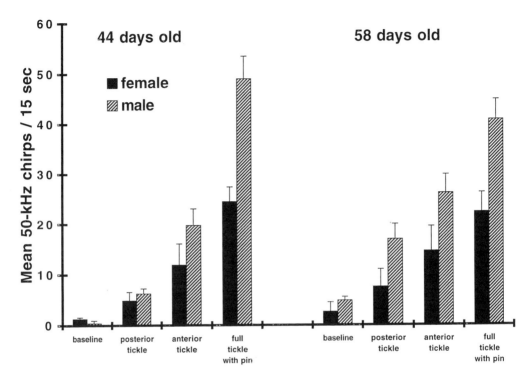

Figure 20.1
Mean (±SEM) levels of 50 Khz chirping in 44- and 58-day-old rats a function of type of body stimulation and gender.

movements across their respective body parts. Even though the stimulation was brisk and assertive, care was taken not to frighten the animal. Chirping typically started immediately at the onset of tickling.

As summarized in figure 20.1, tickling differentially invigorated chirping during all conditions, and the effects were similar at both ages ($F(1, 56) = .52$). Full stimulation was more effective than anterior stimulation, which was more effective than posterior stimulation, which was more effective than no stimulation [overall $F(2, 56) = 86.8$, $p < .0001$ for the three types of tickling, with all successive p's $< .001$]. This effect was larger in males than females [$F(1, 56) = 19.1$, ps $< .0001$], but only marginally more effective in the socially isolated animals than in the play experienced ones [$F(1, 28) = 4.39$, $p < .05$, on day 44, but not significant on day 58; data not shown].

The levels of dorsal contacts during the above play sessions on day 44 were correlated with levels of tickling-induced USVs on day 45 during posterior stimulation

(r = .47, p < .01), anterior stimulation (r = .50, p < .01), and during the full simulation (r = .50, p < .01), suggesting that playfulness predicts responsivity to tickling
prior to puberty. The respective correlations to number of pins were .45 (p < .01), .38
and .20. There were no significant correlations to the recorded behaviors of the play
partners. All correlations at the older test age were negligible, potentially because of
the slight decline and increasing variability/seriousness in playfulness that occur after
puberty (Panksepp 1981). The test-retest correlation between succeeding tickling tests
separated by the two-week interval was r = .41 (p < .05) for anterior, r = .45
(p < .02) posterior, and r = .57 (p < .01) for full body stimulation. Correlations in
other studies using successive daily test days are typically above .75 for this measure.

An additional age comparison contrasted responses of six 17-day-old males and six
7–9-month-old males during five successive daily tests employing full-body tickling.
The young animals exhibited much more chirping than the old ones during the tickle
periods [48.3 (±6.9) vs 15.1 (±3.7) chirps/15 sec, with $F(1, 10) = 17.87$, p < .002] as
well as during the intervening no-tickle periods [22.6 (±2.6) vs 0.7 (±0.4) with
$F(1, 10) = 70.93$, p < .001].

To evaluate the conditionability of the chirping response, another group of 11 male
rats was weaned at 21 days of age and housed individually or 10 days prior to the
start of testing. After two brief sessions to acclimate them to human handling and
following five minutes of habituation to the test arena (a 48 × 38 × 30 cm high open-
topped chamber, with corn-cob bedding on the floor), half the animals underwent
systematic classical-conditioning, consisting of four tests as follows: 1) a 15 sec. baseline recording period, 2) a 15 sec. conditional stimulus (CS) period, 3) a 15 sec.
unconditioned stimulus (UCS) period consisting of full-body tickling with repeated
pinning (i.e., identical to the final condition of the previous experiment), 4) followed
by a 15 sec. post-tickling period. For the six experimental animals, the conditioning
procedure was conducted for five successive trials during three test sessions separated
by at least 8 hrs. The CS was the experimenter's hand, which had a distinctive odor
because of brief immersion in dry coffee grounds. The hand was used dynamically to
follow each test animal around the observation chamber, with gentle touching of the
face and the sides of the animal. A bout of vigorous tickling commenced 15 secs.
thereafter. For the remaining control animals, the experimenter wore a leather glove
dipped into the coffee grounds, but during the ensuing 15 secs, the glove was left
immobile in the corner of the test chamber.

Significant conditioning was evident during the very first training session (figure
20.2). The level of vocalization increased systematically during both the CS and UCS
periods, but only for the experimental animals, as indicated by a significant group by
trial interactions during both CS and UCS periods [F's(4, 9) > 7.0, p's < .001]. This

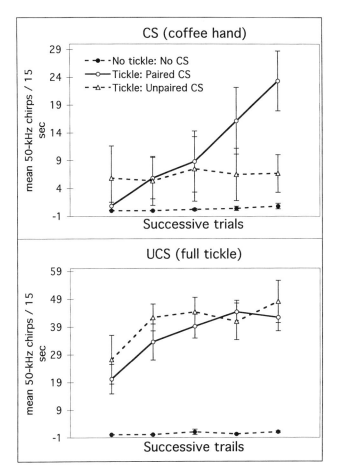

Figure 20.2
Mean (±SEM) levels of 50 Khz chirping during the first day of conditioning as a function of 5 successive training trials during conditioned stimulus (Top: CS—coffee hand) and the unconditioned stimulus
(Bottom: UCS—full tickle) trials. The animals receiving paired CS-UCS trials exhibited clear aquistion of
a conditioned response, while those receiving the unpaired CS-UCS conditons only exhibited sensitization.
Both groups exhibited much more chirping than the untickled controls. The CS presented alone also does
not provoke chirping.

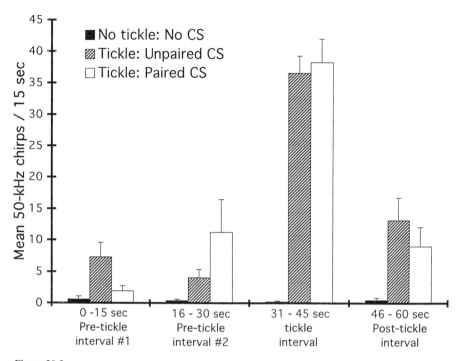

Figure 20.3
Mean ($\pm$SEM) levels of 50 Khz chirping during the four phases of conditioning averaged across the second and third conditioning sessions. First session for these animals is in figure 20.2.

pattern was sustained during the subsequent two sessions (figure 20.3): Although there was no differential chirping during the 15 secs. prior to the CS, elevations were evident during the CS period [$t(9) = 3.4$, $p < .01$], even more marked elevations during the tickling period [$t(9) = 9.2$, $p < .0001$], and a modest differential excitement remained during the 15 sec. poststimulation period [$t(9) = 2.49$, $p < .05$]. To further evaluate the nature of the conditioning, an additional sensitization control group ($n = 6$) was added which received the CS unpaired with the UCS (namely with a 15 sec. interval between CS and UCS), and as is evident in figures 20.2 and 20.3, this group of animals did not show a clear acquisition curve, even though it did exhibit a reliable elevation of chirping over the no-CS group, indicating that part of the elevation of chirping to the CS is due to sensitization rather than associative conditioning.

To determine whether animals would seek tickling, twenty-one 17-day-old group-housed animals were individually placed in one corner of the 48 × 38 × 30 cm high

open-topped test chamber, with the experimenter's hand placed palm up in the diag-
onally opposite corner. When an animal approached to within 2 inches, it was given
15 secs. of tickling. Five sequential trials were conducted with 10-minute inter-trial
intervals (during which animals left individually in holding cages). Animals showed
significantly faster running times during this training session [$F(4, 20) = 4.68$,
$p < .002$], with the mean latencies being 19.2 (± 3.5) secs, for the first trial and 6.9
(± 1.1) secs, for the fifth trial.

To determine how negative emotional arousal would affect tickling-induced
chirping, ten 37-day-old tickle-habituated animals were tested successively using four,
15 sec, test periods (baseline, full body tickle, baseline, tickle), contrasting three pairs
of successive counterbalanced conditions: 1) hunger (18 hrs food deprivation) vs
satiety, 2) dim (25 lux) vs bright (1000 lux) ambient illumination, and 3) exposure to
predatory odors (30 mg of cat fur mixed into the bedding of the test cage) compared
to unadulterated bedding. As summarized in figure 20.4, tickling elevated chirping

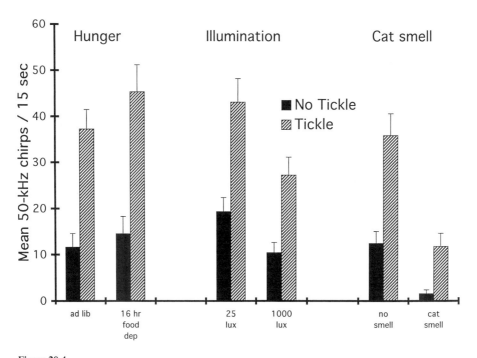

Figure 20.4
Mean ($\pm$ SEM) levels of 50 Khz chirping during three successive counterbalanced experiments evaluating
three types of negative emotional/motivational arousal: mild hunger, bright illumination, and the presence
of cat smell.

under all conditions compared to the nontickle periods. Mild hunger marginally increased chirping [$F(1, 18) = 3.80$, p < .07]. Bright light significantly reduced chirping [$F(1, 18) = 60.82$, p < .0001], with the effect being slightly larger for tickle than no-tickle periods as indexed by an interaction of the two test variables [$F(1, 18) = 4.80$, p < .05]. Exposure to cat-smell had an even larger suppressive effect on chirping [$F(1, 18) = 71.56$, p < .0001], but under this condition a significant interaction indicated that behavioral suppression was greater during the no-tickle period [$F(1, 18) = 10.28$, p < .005]. We would note that chirping during such no-tickle tests is largely a contextually conditioned response. Without prior tickling, chirping typically remain close to zero levels (see figure 20.2).

In additional control studies (data not shown), we determined that gentle touch did not provoke the vigrous chirping evident in figures 20.1–20.4, nor were static forms of somatosensory stimulation effective. Negative touch, such as holding animals by the scruff of the neck or by their tails strongly inhibited chirping. We have also monitored 22 KHz USVs, and they are rare during tickling. Finally, we determined whether this type of manual play would substitute for the satisfactions derived from dyadic play, as measured by the satiety that normally occurs during a half-hour play period (Panksepp, Siviy, and Normansell 1984). Manual tickling-play for 15 mins significantly reduced the ensuing amounts of social play exhibited by pairs of young rats. On the other hand, sustained artificial somatosensory stimulation (animals' bodies restrained snuggly in a hollowed foam pillow connected to a vibrator), had no such effect.

These studies support the possibility that the chirping induced in young rats by manual tickling may be homologous, or at least functionally akin, to human laughter. This conclusion is warranted because of the many similarities between the two phenomena. First, in humans, certain parts of the body are more ticklish than others (Ruggieri and Milizia 1983), and in rats chirping was intensified more by anterior rather than posterior body stimulation, which corresponds to the differential play reductions following anesthetization of dorsal body areas (Siviy and Panksepp 1987). In addition, just as the human tickling response conditions rapidly, so does tickle-induced chirping in rats. Laughter typically occurs during natural play episodes in human children (Rothbart 1973, Humphreys and Smith 1984), and in the present work, as in previous work (Knutson, Burgdorf, and Panksepp 1998), the level of tickling-induced chirping was strongly related to playful tendencies. Tickling was also a positive incentive as measured by a variety of approach and conditioning tests. Although we have yet to evaluate the hedonic qualities of the tickle-induced chirps in animals listening to such vocalizations, we note that comparable high frequency sex-related USVs in adult hamsters have been found to be attractive to conspecifics and to facilitate their sexual responsivity (Floody and Pfaff 1977).

That none of our animals seemed to interpret the tickling stimulation as aggression is indicated by the fact that, during the more than 1000 distinct tickling episodes that we have so far conducted, no young animal has become outwardly defensive. No rat has threatened or sought to aggressively bite the bare hand of the experimenter. However, there have been abundant, nonharmful, play bites. The animals that chirp the most, play the most, and they also exhibit the highest levels of play biting. To all appearances, young animals are aroused by and enjoy this type of bodily stimulation. They readily approach the hand that does the tickling, and they exhibit lots of squirming during the tickling. Many begin to react to the hand as if it were a play partner, exhibiting playful darts and pouncing interactions which appear to fulfill their biological need to play. However, some animals over two months of age have seriously challenged our attempts to tickle them.

It is also unlikely that the tickling provokes much anxiety, even though it can surely provoke some avoidance. In some children tickling can become so intense as to induce transitory avoidance, and excessive tickling has been used effectively as punishment in behavioral modification programs (Greene and Hoats 1971). Some subjectively evident approach-avoidance conflict was evident in a minority of the present animals, especially the ones that chirped least during the tickling. On the rare occassion that an animal has exhibited some apparent anxiety, they have invariably stopped chirping. Likewise, anxiogenic stimuli such as bright light and cat odor unambiguously diminish the response. Clearly, young rats do not regard the smell of a predator as anything to chirp about. The fact that this same aversive stimulus can activate 22 KHz distress calls in adults (Blanchard et al. 1990), further highlights the potential functional and neuroanatomical distinction between high and low USVs in rodents (Brudzynski and Barnabi 1996, Fu and Brudzynski 1994). The present work lends support to the idea that high and low USVs may index distinct affective states in rats.

In sum, the chirping emitted by tickled rats is a robust phenomenon. More than 95% of the young animal we have studied so far have unambiguously exhibited the response, but there are a few animals which chirp rarely during the stimulation. Thus, as in humans (Provine 1996), tickling responsivity appears to be traitlike, suggesting the genetic underpinnings of this reponse may be analyzed in animals. The overall responsivity of animals tends to remain stable throughout early development and is strongly related to playfulness. The slightly elevated levels of chirping in males may correspond to the oft reported elevations of rough-and-tumble playfulness in males, but it may also correspond to the elevated levels of fearfulness commonly seen in females. The onset of puberty does not appear to diminish the reponse, as indicated by the similar responsivities of 44- and 58-day-old animals, although much older animals did exhibit diminished ticklishness.

Since vigorous chirpers were more playful, perhaps one function of chirping is to signal readiness for friendly social interactions. Presumably these vocalizations come to be used in various ways as animals mature, including sexual and aggressive contexts. In the same way, childhood laughter may gradually come to serve several distinct functions in adults, ranging from good-humored social eagerness and communion to displays of dominance, triumph and even scorn. Whether chirping in rats transmits specific information between animals or simply promotes mood states that facilitate certain interactions remains unknown (Nyby and Whitney 1978). We favor the second option, and believe that the study of rodent chirping could be used to index the ongoing socio-emotional states of test animals in a variety of experimental situations.

Although Darwin noted in his *The Expression of the Emotions in Man and Animals:* "Laughter seems primarily to be the expression of mere joy or happiness" (p. 196), we would note that the motor expressions of laughter and the affective experience of mirth may be elaborated in distinct areas of the brain (Arroyo et al. 1993). Many neurological disorders are accompanied by reflexive laughter that is typically distressing to the patient (Black 1982, Poeck 1969). Accordingly, we would suggest that the rapid learning that occurs in this system (i.e., the conditioned chirping response), may be a better indicator for the neural sources of mirth than the unconditional chirping response. We suspect that brain circuits of human laughter and the neural underpinning of rodent chirping do interconnect with brain areas that mediate positive social feelings, but the locations of those areas remain unknown. In sum, although we would be surprised if rats have a sense of humor, they certainly do appear to have a sense of fun.

Rodent chirping may have evolutionary connections to comparable human emotional response systems. Alternatively, it may simply be a social-engagment signal that is unique to rodents. Skepticism about the existence of rodent laughter is to be expected as long as we know so little about the organization of social-emotional systems in the brains of animals, but at present we are optimistic that the intensive neurological analysis of the playful chirping of young rats may help clarify the fundamental brain sources of human laughter and joy. We suspect that both of these responses go back in brain evolution to a time when the readiness for friendly social engagment was communicated by simple acoustic signals. In any event, this work highlights the possibility of systematically analyzing friendly cross-species social interactions in the animal research laboratory.

If a homology exists between joyous human laughter and rodent high frequency chirping, additional work on the topic may yield information of some clinical value. For instance, depressed individuals laugh and play less than normal; the elucidation of neurochemistries that promote chirping and playfulness in rodents may help guide development of new types of antidepressants. Also, the effect of positive emotions on many other bodily processes, such as autonomic reactivity and the vigor of immune responses, can now be studied systematically. If the chirping response has some evolutionary continuity with our human urge to laugh, it could further our understanding human emotions through the study of other animals (Panksepp 1998a).

Epilogue: Relations of this Work to Understanding Affective Consciousness

The objective phenomenon we have discovered is robust. Although the interpretation of the findings is certainly open to other explanations, we have not yet encountered an empirically defensible alternative to the one advanced here. We have shared the above findings with hundreds of colleagues at several scientific meetings, and no one has yet generated an alternative hypothesis that we had not already considered and experimentally disconfirmed. Indeed, all the additional tests we have conducted since completing the work outlined above continue to indicate that rats relish the experiences that evoke high-frequency 50 KHz chirping. To our knowledge, intentional human tickling generates these vocalizations at higher rates than any other social situation.

If there are evolutionary relations between human laughter and this form of rodent "laughter," we may finally have a credible strategy for systematically clarifing the nature of positive emotional consciousness within the human brain. We are now seeking to specify the brain areas and neurochemistries that mediate this positive affective response, and our preliminary work indicates that circuits situated in the reticular nuclei of the thalamus and mesencephalon are important. Also, glutamate is essential for triggering the response, since the NMDA receptor antagonist MK-801 can eliminate tickle-induced chirping.

We currently remain open to the possibility that many other mammals beside humans experience joyful affect during their playful social engagements. The vocal component of this state may have diminished through negative selection in the young of many other species, especially if it served to alert predators in the evolutionary history. Since ultrasonic calls do not travel far, such evolutionary weeding may not have transpired in burrowing species such as rats. The scenario we prefer is that the fundamental process of joy emerged early in brain evolution, even though the external signs of this central state may have diversified considerable among species. Of course, if the response only reflects convergent evolutionary processes in different species, insight into human joy is less likely to emerge from such work. However, if there is an evolutionary relationship between the joyous chirping of rats and the joyous laughter of young children, a study of the rodent brain may provide a compelling way for us to try to understand the nature of a joyful form of affective consciousness within the human brain.

Our provisional conclusion is: Rats do laugh, and they certainly enjoy the frolicing that induces them to do so. We suspect that the nature of their positive internal affective experiences are not all that different from our own, even though the cognitive accompaniments (e.g., a sense of humor) are bound to differ markedly. We remain saddened that many of our colleagues in the prevailing scientific establishment are not more open to entertaining such possibilities. We believe that raw emotional experiences and a primitive sense of self, probably created by deep subcortical structures that all mammals share, may constitute the neural ground upon which the more figurative aspects of human consciousness were built (Panksepp 1998b).

References

Adler, N., and Anisko, J. 1979. The behavior of communicating: An analysis of the 22 KHz call of rats *Rattus norvegicus. American Zoologist* 19:498–508.

Arroyo, S., et al. 1993. Mirth, Laughter and gelastic seizures. *Brain* 166:757–880.

Barfield, R. J., and Geyer, L. A. 1975. The ultrasonic post-ejaculatory vocalization and the post-ejaculatory refractory period of the male rat. *Journal of Comparative and Physiological Psychology* 88:723–834.

Berntson, G. G., Boysen, S. T., Bauer, H. R., and Torrello, M. S. 1989. Conspecific screams and laughter: cardiac and behavioral reactions of infant chimpanzees. *Developmental Psychobiology* 22:771–887.

Black, D. W. 1982. Pathological Laughter a review of the literature. *Journal of Nervous and Mental Disease* 170:67–81.

Blanchard, R. J., et al. 1990. The characterization and modelling of antipredator defensive behavior. *Neuroscience and Biobehavioral Reviews* 14:463–472.

Brudzynski, S. M., and Barnabi, F. 1996. Contribution of the ascending cholinergic pathways in the production of ultrasonic vocalization in the rat. *Behavioral Brain Research* 80:145–152.

Douglas, M. 1971. Do dogs laugh? A cross-cultural approach to body symbolism. *Journal of Psychosomatic Research* 15:387–390.

Floody, O. R., and Pfaff, D. W. 1977. Communication among hamsters by high-frequency acoustic signals: III. Responses evoked by natural and synthetic ultrasounds. *Journal of Comparative and Physiological Psychology* 91:820–829.

Fu, X. W., and Brudzynski, S. M. 1994. High-frequency ultrasonic vocalization induced by intracerebral glutamate. *Pharmacology, Biochemistry and Behavior.* 49:835–841.

Greene, R. J., and Hoats, D. L. 1971. Aversive tickling: a simple conditioning technique. *Behavior Therapy* 2:389–393.

Haney, M., and Miczek, K. A. 1993. Ultrasounds during agonistic interactions between female rats *Rattus norvegicus. Journal of Comparative Psychology* 107:373–379.

Humphreys, A. P., and Smith, P. K. 1984. in *Play in Animals and Humans.* ed. Smith, P. K. 241–270 Blackwell, London.

Jürgens, U. 1986. The squirrel monkey as an experimental model in the study of cerebral organization of emotional vocal utterances. *European Archives of Psychiatry and Neurological Science* 236:40–43.

Knutson, B., Burgdorf, J., and Panksepp, J. 1998. The prospect of play elicits high-frequency ultrasonic vocalizations in young rats. *Journal of Comparative Psychology* 112:65–83.

Masson, J. M., and McCarthy, S. M. 1996. *When Elephants Weep: The Emotional Lives of Animals.* Delacorte Press, New York.

Newman, B., O'Grady, M. A., Ryan, C. S., and Hemmes, N. S. 1993. Pavlovian conditioning of the tickle response of human subjects: temporal and delay conditioning. *Perceptual and Motor Skills* 77:779–885.

Nyby, J., and Whitney, G. 1978. Ultrasonic communication of adult mynomorph rodents. *Neuroscience and Biobehavioral Reviews* 2:1–14.

Panksepp, J. 1981. The ontogeny of play in rats. *Developmental Psychobiology* 14:327–332.

Panksepp, J. 1998a. *Affective Neuroscience: The Foundations of Human and Animal Emotions.* New York: Oxford University Press.

Panksepp, J. 1998b. The periconscious substrates of consciousness: Affective states and the evolutionary origins of the self. *Journal of Consciousness Studies* 5:566–582.

Panksepp, J., Siviy, S., and Normansell, L. 1984. The psychobiology of play: theoretical and methodological perspectives. *Neuroscience and Biobehavioral Reviews* 8:465–492.

Poeck, K. 1969. In *Handbook of Clinical Neurology*, vol 3. ed. Vinken, P. J. and Bruyn, G. W. Amsterdam: North Holland Publishing Co., 343–367.

Preuschoft, S. 1992. "Laughter" and "smile" in barbary macaques *macaca sylvanus. Ethology* 91:220–236.

Provine, R. R. 1996. Laughter. *American Scientist.* 84:38–45.

Rothbart, M. K. 1973. Laughter in young children. *Psych. Bull.* 80:247–256.

Ruggieri, V., and Milizia, M. 1983. Tickle perception as micro-experience of pleasure: its phenomenology on different areas of the body and relation cerebral dominance. *Perceptual and Motor Skills* 56:903–914.

Sales, G., and Pye, D. 1974. *Ultrasonic Communication by Animals.* New York: Wiley.

Siviy, S. M., and Panksepp, J. 1987. Sensory modulation of juvenile play in rats. *Developmental Psychobiology* 20:39–55.

Sroufe, L. A. and Waters, E. 1976. The ontogenesis of smiling and laughter: A perspective on the organization of development in infancy. *Psych. Rev.* 83:173–189.

Tornatzky, W., and Miczek, K. A. 1995. Alcohol, anxiolytics, and social stress in rats. *Psychopharmacology* 121:135–144.

van Hooff, J. A. R. A. M. 1972. In *Non-verbal Communication*, ed. Hinde, R. A. Cambridge: Cambridge University Press, 129–179.

VI EVOLUTION AND FUNCTION OF CONSCIOUSNESS— INTRODUCTION

Stuart R. Hameroff

How did consciousness evolve? Either consciousness is present in all living systems, or it emerged at some point in the evolution of life on earth. If consciousness emerged through evolution by natural selection, then either it was selected for as an adaptive feature, or it emerged as the byproduct of other adaptive features. The dominant view is that consciousness is itself an adaptive feature, playing a crucial functional role.

But this raises some serious questions. What is the function of consciousness? What features of consciousness enhance survival beyond the abilities of increasingly intelligent but nonconscious behavior? How does consciousness exert influence on our biology? When in the course of evolution did consciousness first appear on the scene, and why? Some have argued that any function that consciousness might perform could in principle be performed without consciousness. If this were so, it would be unclear why consciousness should ever evolve. So the search for the function of consciousness is crucial to understanding the evolution of the mind.

The five chapters in this section discuss various aspects of the relationship between consciousness, evolution, and function.

Nicholas Humphrey sees consciousness as having developed from more primitive sensations which lacked subjective qualities. These arose from early organism attempts to integrate sensory inputs into an internal representation of the outside world. Eventually, through natural selection, the signals began to turn in on themselves. These generated internal feedback, formed multiple representations and ultimately "privatized" sensations. Humphrey suggests that within self-sustaining inward loops, the subjective qualities of consciousness played a crucial role in the perception of time.

Richard Gregory builds on this suggestion of Humphrey, stressing that qualia are useful to "flag" the present moment. Gregory points out that increasingly complex organisms developed a need to identify representations of the present, as opposed to past memory and future anticipation. How does the mind know when is now? By adorning representations of the present with conscious qualia, Gregory suggests. Gregory connects the "now" with modern philosophy, cognitive science and physics—a connection worthy of intense pursuit.

But what are qualia? Can they be described within science? Did they evolve and are they describable by physico-chemical systems? Graham Cairns-Smith argues that, yes, qualia belong in our science and their mystery will be solved. He notes that qualia must play a function to evolve, which implies that they must have a physical bases. He suggests that qualia are generated by biomolecular systems ("qualogens") whose diversified phylogeny matches that of the qualia themselves. He suggests that their underlying nature may be quantum-mechanical: feelings and sensations are associated with vast numbers of microscopic processes bound in some type of macroscopic quantum state.

Leaving aside for the moment the original onset of primitive qualia and consciousness, archaeologist Steven Mithen examines the fossil record to try and pin down the onset of the type of complex, higher order consciousness with which we are familiar. This type of consciousness, Mithen observes, must surely have grown from interactions among thought, language, behavior and material culture. He traces the course of human evolution in the 6 million years since humans and apes diverged. Mithen focuses on the construction of handaxes by several types of early humans which first appeared in the fossil record 1.4 million years ago. He argues that their construction required not only sensory-motor control and an understanding of fracture dynamics, but also a desire for symmetry, an ability to plan ahead, and internal (unspoken) language. Toolmaking flowed into art and agriculture some 50,000 years ago, representing, Mithen concludes, the "budding and flowering" of human consciousness.

Like Mithen, neuroscientist William H. Calvin is concerned with higher levels of consciousness, seeing them as the top rungs in a hierarchical series of a dozen-or-so levels. Percolating upward through this hierarchy, Calvin explains, are the substrates for ideas, actions and sensations which emerge into consciousness by winning a competition with other possible ideas, actions, or sensations. Consciousness is the result of a Darwinian process—not only over the course of evolution—but in a moment-by-moment competition for a place in the sunshine of awareness. In Calvin's view evolution is the fundamental process, applicable over various time scales and in systems of all sorts.

21 The Privatization of Sensation

Nicholas Humphrey

D. H. Lawrence, the novelist, once remarked that if anyone presumes to ask *why* the midday sky is blue rather than red, we should not even attempt to give a scientific answer but should simply reply: "Because it *is*." And if anyone were to go still further, and to ask why his own conscious sensation when he looks at the midday sky is characterized by blue qualia rather than red qualia, I've no doubt that Lawrence, if he were still around—along with several contemporary philosophers of mind—would be just as adamant that the last place we should look for enlightenment is science.

But this is not my view. The poet William Empson wrote: "Critics are of two sorts: those who merely relieve themselves against the flower of beauty, and those, less continent, who afterward scratch it up. I myself, I must confess, aspire to the second of these classes; unexplained beauty arouses an irritation in me" (Empson 1930). And equally, I'd say, unexplained *subjective experience* arouses an irritation in *me*. It is the irritation of someone who is an unabashed Darwinian: one who holds that the theory of evolution by natural selection has given us the licence to ask "why" questions about almost every aspect of the design of living nature, and, what's more, to expect that these "whys" will nearly always translate into scientifically accredited "wherefores."

Our default assumption, I believe, can and should be that living things are designed the way they are because this kind of design is—or has been in the past—biologically advantageous. And this will be so across the whole of nature, even when we come to ask deep questions about the way the human mind works, and even when what's at issue are the central facts of consciousness.

Why is it like *this* to have red light fall on our eyes? Why like *this* to have a salt taste in our mouths? Why like *this* to hear a trumpet sounding in our ears? . . . I think these questions, as much as any, deserve our best attempt to provide Darwinian answers: answers, that is, in terms of the biological function that is being—or has been—served.

There are two levels at which the questions can be put. First we should ask about the biological function of our having *sensations at all*. And, next, once we have an answer to this first question, we can proceed to the trickier question about the function of our sensations being of *the special qualitative character they are*.

No doubt the first will strike most people as the easy question, and only the second as the hard one. But I admit that even this first question may not be as easy as it seems. And, although I want to spend most of this chapter discussing sensory quality, I realize I ought to begin at the beginning by asking: What do we gain, of biological importance, from having sensations at all?

To see why this seemingly easy question requires serious consideration and why the answer is not in fact self-evident, we have to take on board the elementary distinction between sensation and perception.

The remarkable fact that human beings—and presumably many other animals also—make use of their bodily senses in two quite different ways, was first brought to philosophical attention two hundred years ago by Thomas Reid. "The external senses," Reid wrote, "have a double province—to make us feel, and to make us perceive. They furnish us with a variety of sensations, some pleasant, others painful, and others indifferent; at the same time they give us a conception and an invincible belief of the existence of external objects.... Sensation, taken by itself, implies neither the conception nor belief of any external object. It supposes a sentient being, and a certain manner in which that being is affected; but it supposes no more. Perception implies a conviction and belief of something external—something different both from the mind that perceives, and the act of perception. Things so different in their nature ought to be distinguished" (Reid 1785, 2: chapters 17 and 16).

For example, Reid said, we smell a rose, and two separate and parallel things happen: we both feel the sweet smell at our own nostrils and we perceive the external presence of a rose. Again, we hear a hooter blowing from the valley below: we both feel the booming sound at our own ears and we perceive the external presence of a ship down in the Firth. In general we can and usually do use the evidence of sensory stimulation *both* to provide "a subject-centred affect-laden representation of what's happening to me," *and* to provide "an objective, affectively neutral representation of what's happening out there" (Humphrey 1992).

Yet, while Reid insisted so firmly on this difference, he never, it seems, thought it necessary to ask the question that so clearly follows on: *Why* do the senses have a double province? Do human beings really need both perception and sensation? If, as might well be argued—especially in the case of vision and hearing—what interests us in terms of our survival is not at all our personal relation to the stimulation at our body surface but only what this stimulation denotes about the outside world, why ever should we bother to represent "what is happening to me" as well as "what is happening out there"? Why should we not leave sensation out of it entirely and make do with perception on its own? Would not such insensate perception serve our biological needs perfectly well?

It is only in the last few years that psychologists have begun to face up to the genuine challenge of this question "why sensations?" And there is certainly no agreement yet on what the right Darwinian answer is. However there are now at least several possible answers in the offing. And I (Humphrey 1992), Anthony Marcel (1988), and Richard Gregory (1996) have all, in different ways, endorsed what is probably the strongest of these: namely, that sensations are required, in Gregory's felicitous wording, "to flag the present."

The idea here is that the main role of sensations is, in effect, to help keep perception honest. Both sensation and perception take sensory stimulation as their starting point: yet, while sensation then proceeds to represent the stimulation more or less as given, perception takes off in a much more complex and risky way. Perception has to combine the evidence of stimulation with contextual information, memory, and rules so as to construct a hypothetical model of the external world as it exists independently of the observer. Yet the danger is that, if this kind of construction is allowed simply to run free, without being continually tied into present-tense reality, the perceiver may become lost in a world of hypotheticals and counterfactuals.

What the perceiver needs is the capacity to run some kind of on-line reality check, testing his perceptual model for its currency and relevance and in particular keeping tabs on where he himself now stands. And this, so the argument goes, is precisely where low level, unprocessed, sensation does in fact prove its value. As I summarized it earlier: "Sensation lends a here-ness and a now-ness and a me-ness to the experience of the world, of which pure perception in the absence of sensation is bereft" (Humphrey 1992, p. 73).

I think we should be reasonably happy with this answer. The need to flag the present provides at least one compelling reason why natural selection should have chosen sensate human beings over insensate ones.

But we should be under no illusion about how far this answer takes us with the larger project. For it must be obvious that even if it can explain why sensations exist at all, it goes no way to explaining why sensations exist in the particular qualitative form they do.

The difficulty is this. Suppose sensations have indeed evolved to flag the present. Then surely it hardly matters precisely *how* they flag the present. Nothing would seem to dictate that, for example, the sensation by which each of us represents the presence of red light at our eye must have the particular red quality it actually does have. Surely this function could have been performed equally well by a sensation of green quality or some other quality completely.

Indeed would not the same be true of any other functional role we attribute to sensations. For the fact is—isn't it?—that sensory quality is something private and ineffable, maybe of deep significance to each of us subjectively but of no consequence whatever to our standing in the outside world.

Certainly, there is a long philosophical tradition that makes exactly this claim. John Locke originated it with his thought experiment about the "inverted spectrum" (Locke 1690, 2: chapter 32). Imagine, said Locke, that "if by the different structure of our organs, it were so ordered, that the same object should produce in several men's minds different ideas at the same time; for example, if the idea, that a violet produces in one man's mind by his eyes, were the same that a marigold produced in another man's, and *vice versa*." Then, Locke surmised, there's no reason to think this difference in inner structure and the resulting difference in the inner experience of the quality of color would make any difference to outer behavior. In fact, he claimed, the difference in inner experience "could never be known: because one man's mind could not pass into another man's body."

Ludwig Wittgenstein would later remark: "The assumption would thus be possible—though unverifiable—that one section of mankind has one sensation of red and another section another" (Wittgenstein 1958, I:272). Indeed this unsettling possibility became one of the chief reasons why Wittgenstein himself decided to call a halt to any further talk about privately sensed qualities. And it is the reason, too, why other philosophers such as Daniel Dennett have been tempted to go even further, and to argue that sensory qualia have no objective reality whatever (Dennett 1988, although compare his more nuanced position of 1991).

Now, we need not go all the way with Wittgenstein or Dennett to realize that if even part of this argument about the privacy of qualia goes through, we may as well give up on our ambition to have a Darwinian explanation of them. For it must be obvious that nothing can possibly have evolved by natural selection unless it does in fact have some sort of major public effect—indeed unless it has a measurably positive influence on survival and reproduction. If, as common-sense let alone philosophy suggests, sensory quality really is for all practical purposes private, selection simply could never have got a purchase on it.

It appears that we cannot have it both ways: *Either* as Darwinists we continue, against the odds, to try to explain sensory quality as a product of selection, *or* we grudgingly accept the idea that sensations are just as private as they seem to be.

So, what is to be done? Which of these two strongly motivated positions must we give up?

I believe the answer is that actually we need not give up either. We can in fact hold *both* to the idea that sensory quality is private, *and* to the idea that it has been shaped by selection, provided we recognize that these two things *have not been true at the same time*: that, in the course of evolution, the privacy came only *after* the selection had occurred.

Here, in short, is the case that I would make. It may be true that the activity of sensing is today largely hidden from public view, and that the particular quality of sensations is not essential to the function they perform. It may be true, for example, that my sensation of red is directly known only to me, and that its particular redness is irrelevant to how it does its job. Yet, *it was not always so.* In the evolutionary past the activity of sensing was a much more open one, and its every aspect mattered to survival. In the past my ancestors evolved to feel red this way because feeling it this way gave them a real biological advantage.

Now, in case this sounds like a highly peculiar way of looking at history, I should stress that it would be not be so unusual for evolution to have worked like this. Again and again in other areas of biology it turns out that, as the function of an organ or behavior has shifted over evolutionary time, obsolete aspects of the original design have in fact carried on down more or less unchanged.

For a simple example, consider the composition of our own blood. When our fish-ancestors were evolving 400 million years ago in the Devonian seas, it was essential that the salt composition of their blood should closely resemble the external sea-water, so that they would not lose water by osmosis across their gills. Once our ancestors moved on to the land, however, and started breathing air, this particular feature of blood was no longer of critical importance. Nevertheless, since other aspects of vertebrate physiology had developed to fit in with it and any change would have been at least temporarily disadvantageous, well was left alone. The result is that human blood is still today more or less interchangeable with sea water.

This tendency toward what can be called "stylistic inertia" is evident at every level of evolution, not only in nature but in culture too. Clear examples occur in the development of language, manners, dress, and architectural design (as has been beautifully documented by Philip Steadman 1979). But I would say that as nice a case as any is provided by the history of clocks and how their hands move.

Modern clocks have of course evolved from sundials. And in the Northern hemisphere, where clocks began, the shadow of the sundial's vane moves round the dial in the "sunwise" direction which we now call "clockwise." Once sundials came to be replaced by clockwork mechanisms with moving hands, however, the reason for representing time by sunwise motion immediately vanished, Nevertheless, since by this stage people's habits of time-telling were already thoroughly ingrained, the result has been that nearly every clock on earth still does use sunwise motion.

But suppose now, for the sake of argument, we were to be faced with a modern clock, and, as inveterate Darwinians, we were to want to know *why* its hands move the way they do. As with sensations, there would be two levels at which the question could be posed.

If we were to ask about *why the clock has hands at all*, the answer would be relatively easy. Obviously the clock needs to have hands of some kind so as to have some way of representing the passage of time—just as we need to have sensations of some kind so as to have some way of representing stimulation at the body surface.

But if we ask about *why the hands move clockwise as they do*, the answer would have to go much deeper. For clearly the job of representing time could in fact nowadays be served equally well by rotationally inverted movement—just as the job of representing sensory stimulation could nowadays be served equally well by quality-inverted sensations. In fact, as we've seen, this second question for the clock can *only* be answered by reference to ancestral history—just as I would argue for sensations.

When an analogy fits the case as well as this, I would say it cries out to be taken further. For it strongly suggests there is some profounder basis for the resemblance than has at first appeared. And in this case I think that, surprisingly, we really have struck gold. For it seems we may be arriving with this clock analogy at the crucial idea we need to unlock the mystery of what sensations are and how they have evolved.

A clock tells time by *acting* in a certain way, namely by moving its hands. And this action has a certain style inherited from the past, a clockwise style, clockwisely.

The remarkable truth is, I believe, that a person also has sensations by *acting* in a certain way. And, yes, each sensory action also has its own inherited style—for example, a red style, redly.

I have no space here to explain the full reasoning behind this theory. But I can at least attempt to sketch in the main themes.

As Reid long ago recognized, sensations are not what people mostly think they are. Our language misleads us. We talk of "feeling" or "having" sensations—as if somehow sensations were the *objects* of our sensing, sense *data*, out there waiting for us to grasp them or observe them with our mind's eye. But analysis shows that this is a mistake. Sensations are no more the objects of sensing than, say, volitions are the objects of willing or intentions the objects of intending.

"The form of the expression, *I feel pain*," Reid wrote, "might seem to imply that the feeling is something distinct from the pain felt; yet in reality, there is no distinction. As *thinking a thought* is an expression which could signify no more than *thinking*, so *feeling a pain* signifies no more than *being pained*. What we have said of pain is applicable to every other mere sensation" (Reid 1764, p. 112).

But I believe Reid got only part way to the truth here. For my own view (developed in detail in Humphrey 1992) is that the right expression is not so much "being pained" as "paining." That's to say, sensing is not a passive state at all, but rather a form of active engagement with the stimulus occurring at the body surface. When, for example, I feel pain in my toe, or taste salt on my tongue, or equally when I have red sensation at my eye, I am in effect reaching out to the site of stimulation with a kind of evaluative response—a response appropriate to the stimulus and the body part affected. Indeed what I experience as my sensation of "what is happening to me" is based not on the incoming information as such but rather on the signals I myself am issuing to make the response happen.

This is how I feel about what's happening right now at my toe—I'm feeling painily about it.

This is how I feel about what's happening right now at this part of the field of my eye—I'm feeling redly about it.

Now, it is true that, today, these sensory responses are largely internal, covert, and private. But, or so at least I want to argue, it was not always so. Rather, these responses began their evolutionary life as full-fledged bodily behaviors that were unambiguously in the public domain—and, what is more, as behaviors with a real adaptive role.

If I try, as I shall do now, to sketch the evolutionary story in cartoon form, it is because I want the general logic to come through rather than to attempt an accurate history. And I must trust you will be prepared to join me at this level.

So, let us return in imagination to the earliest of times and picture a primitive amoebalike animal floating in the ancient seas.

This animal has a defining edge to it, a structural boundary—and this boundary is crucial, serving both to hold the animal's own substance in and the rest of the world out, and as the vital frontier across which essential exchanges of matter and energy and information can take place.

Now light falls on the animal, objects bump into it, pressure waves press against it, chemicals stick to it, and so on. No doubt some of these surface events are going to be a good thing for the animal, others bad. And in order for the animal to survive it must have evolved the ability to sort out the good from the bad and to respond differently to them—reacting to this stimulus with an ow! to that with an ouch! to this with a whowee!

Thus, when, say, salt arrives at its skin it detects it and makes a characteristic wriggle of activity—it wriggles saltily. When red light falls on it, it makes a different kind of wriggle—it wriggles redly. Presumably these are adaptive responses, selected because they are appropriate to the animal's particular needs. Wriggling saltily has been selected as the best response to salt, while wriggling sugarly, for example, would be the best response to sugar. Wriggling redly has been selected as the best response to red light, while wriggling bluely would be the best response to blue light.

Still, as yet, these responses are nothing other than responses, and there is no reason to suppose that the animal is in any way mentally aware of what is happening. Lets imagine however that, as this animal's life becomes more complex, the time comes when it will be advantageous for it to have some kind of inner knowledge of what is affecting it: a mental representation of the sensory stimulation at the surface of its body and how it feels about it. Indeed one of the reasons it may need this kind of representation may be precisely the one we discussed earlier, namely to be able to flag the present.

Now, one way of developing this capacity for representing sensory stimulation might be to start over again with a completely fresh analysis of the incoming information from the sense organs. But, as it happens, this would be to miss a trick. For, the fact is that all the requisite details about the stimulation—where the stimulus is occurring, what kind of stimulus it is, and how it should be dealt with—are already encoded in the command signals the animal is issuing when it makes the appropriate sensory response.

Hence, all the animal needs to do to sense "what's happening to me" is to pick up on these already-occurring command signals. To sense the presence of salt at a certain location on its skin, it need only monitor its own signals for wriggling saltily at that location, or equally to sense the presence of red light it need only monitor its signals for wriggling redly.

Thus the result is that sensations do indeed evolve at first as corollaries of the animal's *public* bodily activity. And since, in these early days, the form of this activity is still being maintained by natural selection, it follows that the form of the animal's mental representation—its sensory "experience" or protoexperience, if you like—is also going to be determined *in all its aspects* by selection.

Yet, the story is of course by no means over. For, as this animal continues to develop and to change its lifestyle, the nature of the selection pressures is bound to alter. In particular, as the animal becomes more independent of its immediate environment, the making of sensory responses directly to the stimulus becomes of less and less relevance to its biological survival. In fact there comes a time when wriggling saltily or redly at the point of stimulation no longer has any adaptive value at all.

Then, why doesn't the animal simply give up on this kind of local responding altogether? The reason is that, even though it may no longer have any use for the sensory responses as such, it has by this time become heavily dependent on the secondary representational functions that these responses have acquired. And since the way it has been getting these representations in the past has been by monitoring its own command signals for sensory responses, it clearly cannot afford to stop issuing these command signals entirely.

So, the situation now is this. In order to be able to represent "what's happening to me," the animal must in fact continue to issue commands such as *would* produce an appropriate response at the right place on the body *if* they were to carry through into bodily behavior. But, given that the behavior is no longer wanted, it may be better if these commands remain *virtual* or *as-if* commands—in other words, commands

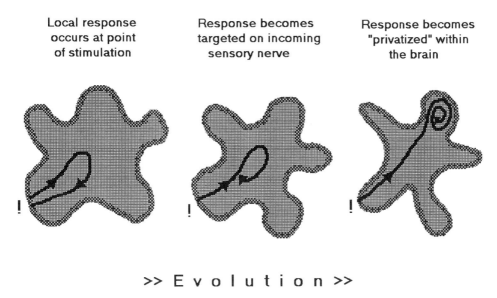

**Local response
occurs at point
of stimulation**

**Response becomes
targeted on incoming
sensory nerve**

**Response becomes
"privatized" within
the brain**

>> E v o l u t i o n >>

Figure 21.1
"Black box" of visual processing. Bottom-up signals from the eyes are "read" or interpreted with specific
Top-down knowledge of objects and with general Side-ways rules—to generate perceptions of the external
world—as hypotheses of origins of sensations.

which, while retaining their original intentional properties, do not in fact have any
real effects.

And the upshot is—or so I argue—that, over evolutionary time, there is a slow but
remarkable change. What happens is that the whole sensory activity gets "privatized": the command signals for sensory responses get short-circuited before they
reach the body surface, so that instead of reaching all the way out to the site of
stimulation they now reach only to points closer and closer in on the incoming sensory nerve, until eventually the whole process becomes closed off from the outside
world in an internal loop within the brain.

Now once *this* happens the role of natural selection must of course sharply diminish. The sensory responses have lost all their original biological importance and have
in fact disappeared from view. Therefore selection is no longer involved in determining the form of these responses and *a fortiori* it can no longer be involved in
determining the quality of the representations based on them. The conclusion is that
sensory experience as such has become privatized.

Note well, however, that this privacy has come about only at the very end, *after*
natural selection has done its work to shape the sensory landscape. In fact there is

every reason to suppose that the forms of sensory responses and the corresponding experiences have already been more or less permanently fixed. And although, once selection becomes irrelevant, these forms may be liable to drift somewhat, they are likely always to reflect their evolutionary pedigree.

It is this pedigree that still colors private sensory experience right down to the present day. If, *I* today feel the sensation red *this* way—as *I* know very well that I do—it is because I am descended from distant ancestors who were selected to feel it this same way long ago.

Here we are, then, with the solution that I promised. We *can* have it both ways. We can *both* make good on our ambition, as Darwinists, to explain sensory quality as a product of selection, *and* we can accept the common-sense idea that sensations are as private as they seem to be—provided we do indeed recognize that these two things have not been true at the same time. But the rewards of this Darwinian approach are I believe greater still. For there remains to be told the story of how, after the privatization of sensory responses has taken place and the command signals have begun to loop back on themselves within the brain, there are likely to be dramatic consequences for sensory phenomenology. In particular, how the activity of sensing is destined to become self-sustaining and partly self-creating, so that sensory experiences get lifted into a time dimension of their own—into what I have called the "thick time" of the subjective present (Humphrey 1992, 1995). What is more, how the establishment of this time-loop is the key to the thing we value most about sensations: the fact that not only do they *have* quality but that this quality comes across to us in the very special, self-intimating way, that we call the *what it's like of consciousness.*

This is however another story for another time. I will simply remark here, with Rudyard Kipling, *contra* Lawrence, that "Them that asks no questions isn't told a lie"—and no truths either.

This chapter will also appear in *The Evolution of Cognition* (ed. C. Heye and L. Huber), MIT Press (in press).

References

Dennett, D. C. 1988. Quining Qualia. In *Consciousness in Contemporary Science* (Marcel, A. J., and Bisiach, E., eds.), pp. 42–87. Oxford: Clarendon Press.

Dennett, D. C. 1991. *Consciousness Explained.* New York: Little Brown.

Empson, W. 1930. *Seven Types of Ambiguity.* London: Chatto & Windus.

Gregory, R. L. 1996. What do qualia do? *Perception* 25:377–378.

Humphrey, N. 1992. *A History of the Mind*. London: Chatto & Windus.

Humphrey, N. 1995. The thick moment. In *The Third Culture* (Brockman, J., ed.) pp. 198–208. New York: Simon & Schuster.

Locke, J. 1690/1975. *An Essay Concerning Human Understanding* (Nidditch, P, ed). Oxford: Clarendon Press.

Marcel, A. J. 1988. Phenomenal experience and functionalism. In *Consciousness in Contemporary Science* (Marcel, A. J., and Bisiach, E., eds) pp. 121–158. Oxford: Clarendon Press.

Reid, T. 1764/1813. *An Inquiry into the Human Mind* (Stewart, D., ed.). Charlestown: Samuel Etheridge.

Reid, T. 1785/1813. *Essays on the Intellectual Powers of Man* (Stewart, D., ed.). Charlestown: Samuel Etheridge.

Steadman, P. 1979. *The Evolution of Designs*. Cambridge: Cambridge University Press.

Wittgenstein, L. 1958. *Philosophical Investigations* (Anscombe, GEM, trans). Oxford: Blackwell.

22 Flagging the Present Moment with Qualia

Richard L. Gregory

Human visual perception is highly dependent on knowledge stored from the past, for seeing the present and predicting the immediate future. This introduces a curious problem: How are present sensory signals distinguished from memory and prediction? How is the present moment—vital for survival—recognized?

It is suggested that qualia of consciousness—sensations, such as red and pain—are evoked by real-time afferent signals, to flag the present moment.

Setting the Scene

Long before there was detailed knowledge of brain anatomy or physiology, John Locke famously said (1690, *Human Understanding*, iii para 19): "Consciousness is the perception of what goes on in a man's own mind." This may be so, though it is now believed that a great deal goes on that is not in consciousness.

The still prevailing mystery of how it is that brain structures, and physiological and cognitive processes generate consciousness was well described by T. H. Huxley (1866, *Physiology*, viii, 210):

We class sensations along with emotions, and volitions, and thoughts, under the common head of states of consciousness. But what consciousness is, we know not, and how it is that anything so remarkable as a state of consciousness comes about as the result of irritating nervous tissue, is just as unaccountable as the appearance of the Djin when Aladdin rubbed his lamp, or as any other ultimate fact of nature.

It is occasionally pointed out, surely correctly, that consciousness is mainly associated with the present moment. The nineteenth century philosopher Sir William Hamilton said this in 1842. (Referred to in the Scottish philosopher Thomas Reid's *Works* (1872), note B 810/1): "Consciousness is a knowledge solely of what is now and here present in the mind." And Reid himself said a little later and less pointedly, in *Philosophy of the Intellectual Powers* (1785): "Consciousness is a word used by philosophers, to signify that immediate knowledge which we have of our present thoughts and purposes, and, in general, of the present operations of our minds."

This emphasis on present time and place is made clearly by the English psychologist Nicholas Humphrey, in *A History of Mind* (1993, 97): "To be conscious is essentially to have sensations: that is, to have affect-laden mental representations of something happening here and now to me." Nick Humphrey goes on to suggest that "I feel therefore I am." So "in the absence of bodily sensations 'I' would cease." This emphasis on sensations of the senses—of the eyes, ears, taste, touch, and so on, and stressing the importance of the here and now—does seem the right place to start for considering consciousness.

We should look at the nature of sensory perception. How does perception work? What is the "status" of visual and other perceptions?

The Nature of Perception

Philosophy has generally held that perceptions are directly related to objects of the external world, and so can be trusted. But the more we know of the physiology of the senses and their immensely complicated brain processes, the more it is obvious that perceptions are only indirectly related to external events and objects, and to one's own body. Apart from the complexities of the physiology intervening between objects and perception, there are other strong reasons for accepting an indirect status for all perception, including even the sense of touch, which may seem direct, though it isn't.

Primitive reflex responses (including blinking to a loud sudden noise) are directly triggered by stimuli. But full-fledged perception is not at all directly related to stimuli; far more subtle, object perception is geared to postulating causes of stimuli. As Helmholtz (1866) pointed out, this must involve processes of inference, for seeing objects as causes of sensory signals.

Traditionally perceptions are made of sensations. But with the realization of the importance of physiology, in the nineteenth century, it became clear that the basis of perceptions are neural signals, which are "de-coded"and read by the brain to generate perceptions and sensations. This is utterly different from classical ideas of philosophy.

In general, perceptions of objects and scenes are far richer than the available data from the senses. In other words, perceptual inference goes way beyond the sensed evidence. This allows visual perception to predict behaviorally important non-sensed properties of objects from optical images in the eyes—such as grainy texture seen as solid wood—though these inferences are never without risk of error or illusion. For example, the wood may turn out to be pretense plastic, or even a picture. Risky perceptual inference allows behavior to be appropriate to hidden and to impossible-to-sense features of objects. But this is only possible when there is sufficient available *knowledge*. Intelligent perception is essentially knowledge-based, which also allows perception to be predictive in time—though of course sensory inputs are always in real-time, and never from the past or the future. This enrichment of sensory signals, for prediction to unsensed properties and into the future, depends on specific knowledge of objects and on very general rules. These are learned and some are inherited.

The perceptual knowledge-base is largely built from interactive experience through childhood.

I like to think of perceptions as predictive *hypotheses*, as having essentially the same "status" as the predictive hypotheses of science (Gregory 1970, 1981, 1997). Both hypotheses of science and perceptions depend on inferences from specific knowledge and from general rules, including more-or-less safe assumptions for applying knowledge from the past to the present and to possible future situations. The principal difference between perceptions and hypotheses of science is that only the former, so far as we know, are conscious.

How closely perceptions match physical reality as known to science is a tricky question. But clearly there are vast differences between how things appear and what they are "really" like. Thus for color, as Newton clearly realized, light is not *itself* colored, but *evokes* sensations of colors in suitable eyes and brains—which somehow *create* the sensations (qualia) of colors. In John Locke's terms, Secondary properties such as color are psychologically *projected* into the physical world of Primary characteristics, such as hard and hot and heavy. But Locke's distinction between Primary and Secondary characteristics remains mysterious, and unfortunately just which characteristics belong in each category changes, especially with new explanations and categories in science. There are overlaps; generally we experience *hot* for things that are physically hot, but the overlaps are not complete. Perceptual hypotheses do not altogether match hypotheses of science, so in this sense much of perception is illusory.

Another difference between Perceptual Hypotheses (perceptions) and hypotheses of science is the significance of time—especially of the present moment. The present is crucially important in perception—crucial for survival. But hypotheses of science are typically timeless, the present having no special significance. In general, present time is far more important in biology than in physics. And the subjective present has finite duration (the "specious present") which may be of several milliseconds (estimates vary widely), but in physics, an instant is indefinitely short, having perhaps zero duration.

Physical events are said to occur as direct results of causes in real time. But intelligent perception and behavior are set by all manner of factors stored in memory from the past, and by present intention, and by assessment of future possibilities. The significance of time is indeed quite different for physical events than for intelligent perception and behavior. We carry our pasts with us in a way quite different from inanimate objects. Perception and behavior depend on knowledge-based inferences and "guestimates" of probabilities for the future, rather than directly and instantly from present causes. I suspect that these two features of perception—being based on knowledge, and projecting the prevailing hypothesis of reality into the physical world—are keys to consciousness.

Plan of Perception

Here it might be useful to outline a plan of the perceptual system. This will not be in physiological terms (though it is mediated by physiology) but rather as necessary processes or functions of perception.

For describing processes of visual and other perception in general terms, it is useful to distinguish between: (1) *Top-down* knowledge from the past, (2) *Bottom-up* sensory signals from the present, and also (3) general processing rules, which we may say are introduced *Side-ways* (figure 22.1).

Top-down knowledge is necessary for sophisticated perception and behavior: for filling in gaps of available data; prediction of non-sensed properties, and into time. The risk-taking of perceptual inference shows most clearly when there are familiar features, but also significant differences from the past. Thus a hollow mask looks like a normal convex face—in spite of normally adequate "bottom-up" sensory data that it is hollow (Gregory 1970, 1997). Here, knowledge from the past is pitted against present-time data. Knowledge can win. (This is contrary to classical Empiricism: we now believe that there are no raw sensory data: all data are cooked!)

Major contributions from stored knowledge are consistent with brain anatomy, as they might be mediated with the recently-discovered richness of down-going pathways. Some 80 percent of fibers to the Lateral Geniculate Nucleus (LGN) relay station come *downward* from the cortex, and only about 20 percent from the retinas (Sillito 1995). Although the plan of visual processing of figure 22.1 is not an anatomical diagram, it is consistent with brain anatomy as currently appreciated.

Qualia

The essential questions of consciousness are (1) How is consciousness generated by physical brains? (2) In which brain regions is it generated? (3) What, if anything, does consciousness *do* causally? The first question will not be addressed, and indeed this author has no answer, beyond a rather vague notion of consciousness as an emergent property, probably of dynamic cognitive brain activity. It is the third question that is addressed here: What does consciousness *do*—what use are *qualia*?

If qualia have a use, most probably whatever causes them has developed with evolution. What has clearly developed in the "higher" animals is cognitive processing

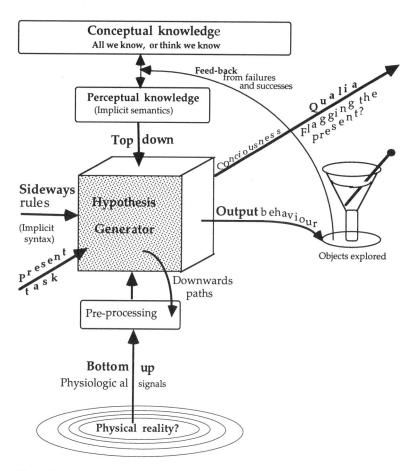

Figure 22.1
"Black box" of visual processing. Bottom-up signals from the eyes are "read" or interpreted with specific Top-down knowledge of objects and with general Side-ways rules—to generate perceptions of the external world—as hypotheses of origins of sensations.

and the intelligent use of *knowledge*. Knowledge is always from the *past*. So as the contribution of knowledge from the past became more important for perception and anticipating the future, surely there must have been a growing problem of *identifying the present* from memory and anticipation. Clearly it is most important for the present to be recognized, and not confused with past or future, or behavior will not be appropriate for current needs. As Top-down knowledge makes such large contributions to sophisticated perception this might too easily happen, though bottom-up signals from the senses do signal some features of the present. When present sensory signals are ignored, we say that someone is "absent-minded." Then memories, or thoughts, swamp present "reality." Though necessary for "deep" thinking, this is dangerous, as we know too well from traffic and other accidents, when the mind wonders.

The working hypothesis is that although the present is *signaled* by the senses, their real-time signals may be ignored if they are not *flagged'* by qualia. In short: reliable present-mind for survival against immediate dangers, depends on flagging the *now* with the vivid qualia of consciousness.

This is the idea. Can we test it?

Some Evidence

A suggestive, very simple experiment, is to look carefully at a distinctive object such as a bright red tie—then shut the eyes and see what happens. As soon as the perception is replaced with memory, the vivid red disappears. (This so for myself, and for everyone I know who has tried it.) So visual qualia do seem to depend on real-time afferent inputs from the eyes.

This extremely simple though surely significant experiment can be reversed: start with the eyes closed, while imagining the red tie. Then open the eyes and compare the real-time perception with the imagined tie. The qualia of vision come with a shock of surprise. For the perception is strikingly vivid compared with the imagination or memory. Whether this is as true for painters is an open question; but artists do seem to look very frequently at what they are painting, as though their memory is a poor substitute for their real-time perception.

Our qualia-hypothesis implies that qualia of vision, and the other senses, are only present with real-time inputs from the senses and so can serve to mark or "flag" the present moment, to prevent dangerous confusions with memory and imagination. But there are some exceptions. These may be evidence against the hypothesis, or they may illuminate what goes on in normal and in abnormal perception—perhaps putting this qualia-hypothesis in its place. We should look at exceptional cases with care, though necessarily briefly.

Some Exceptions

After-images

An after-image from a bright flash of light can give a quale for several seconds following the stimulation. But there are neural signals continuing from the stimulus (owing to breakdown of photo-pigment molecules and so on), so as for normal perception, there is a present afferent input to give qualia from past stimuli.

Dreams

Very differently, qualia unrelated to the senses do seem to be experienced in dreams. It may be suggestive that in sleep the present moment has no special significance, for there is no behavior to be related to what is going on externally. If the flagging-the-present-with-qualia hypothesis is true, we may say that when usual sensory inputs are cut off, or ignored, especially when immediate actions are not needed, the system becomes abnormal. This may occur in isolation situations when sensory stimulation is avoided over many hours; also in hallucinogenic drug-induced states, and in schizophrenia.

Hallucinogenic Drugs

It is often reported that qualia unrelated to the present situation are experienced with hallucinogenic drugs. Evidently the normal active processes of perceptual processing take off from sensory control. It is suggestive that for such drug-states, and schizophrenia, normal brain activity is registered in PET and fNMR brain imaging (Posner and Raichle 1994, Silbersweig et al. 1995). We may suppose that the normally useful system for flagging-reality-with-qualia can go wrong in these conditions, so normal active perceptual processing breaks free of the object world, to lose reality. To some degree this happens whenever there is fantasy; but in these extreme cases, being so absent-minded is behaviorally dangerous.

It is reported that in drug-induced states time may seem to stop. In *Doors of Perception* (1954) Aldous Huxley describes changes of consciousness experienced with mescaline. One ceases to be interested in action, becoming a passive observer ("the will suffers a profound change for the worse"), though ability to "think straight" is little if at all reduced; so he became almost "a Not-self." Most striking: "visual impressions are greatly intensified," while, "interest in space is diminished and interest in time falls almost to zero."

Huxley continually stresses that colors are immeasurably enhanced in vividness, with increased discrimination of hues of super-naturally brilliant colors—ordinary objects appearing self-luminous, with the inner fire of jewels, while time essentially stops, becoming 'an indefinite duration or alternatively a perpetual present'.

In short, under mescaline and other hallucinogens there are enhanced sensations, *super qualia*, and the *present* is emphasized with corresponding little or no flow of time. Thus Huxley writes, again in *Doors of Perception*:

First and foremost is the experience of light. Everything seen by those who visit the mind's antipodes is brilliantly illuminated and seems to shine from within. All colors are intensified to a pitch far removed from anything seen in the normal state, and at the same time the mind's capacity for recognizing fine distinctions of tone and hue is notably heightened.... In this respect there is a marked difference between these visionary experiences and ordinary dreams.

Is there a connection between the super-qualia and reduced sense of time, with the abnormal emphasis on the present moment?

Emotional Memories

Although normally memories lack visual or other qualia, there may be surprisingly vivid qualia of remembered *emotions*, especially when an embarrassing situation is recalled even years later. Why should embarrassment or guilt be special?

It is well known that William James and the Danish physician Carl Lange (James 1890) suggested that emotions have a basis in autonomic changes of the body. The James-Lange theory is that the body responds, for example, to situations of danger, by preparations for sudden action, and these autonomic physiological changes are sensed as emotions of fear, or rage or whatever. For guilt there is a marked autonomic change with visible blushing. Darwin (1872) suggested that blushing is a social signal, warning other's that this individual is not to be trusted. It is perfectly possible to blush at the memory or thought of the guilt-making deed—and to experience qualia of guilt years after the event.

If the James-Lange theory of emotion has truth—that emotions are indeed sensations of bodily changes—then there should be present afferent signals elicited by such memories. So though most memories lack qualia, emotional memories may be qualia-rich without violating our hypothesis.

Individual Exceptions: Luria's "Mr. S"

At least one highly exceptional person, free of drugs or schizophrenia, has been described in detail as frequently confusing memories with present reality. This is the remarkable case of Mr S, described by the Russian neuro-psychologist Alexandr Luria (Luria 1968). At times, in his strange life, S was a professional "memory man."

His vast memory and extremely vivid imagination became confused with real-time reality, to the point of danger.

It may be suggestive that he experienced unusually rich synesthesia. Thus:

Presented with a tone pitched at 100 hertz and having an amplitude of 86 decibels, he saw a wide strip that appears to have a reddish-orange hue in the center; from the center outwards the brightness faded with light gradations so that the edges of the strip appeared pink. (Luria 1968, 25)

... at 500 hertz and 64 decibels, S saw a velvet cord with fibers jutting out on all sides. The cord was tinged with a delicate, pleasant pink-orange hue.... With a tone of 500 hertz and 100 hundred decibels, he saw a streak of lightning splitting the heavens in two.... With 2000 hertz at 113 decibels [extremely loud] S said, "it looks something like fireworks tinged with a pink-red hue. The strip of color feels rough and unpleasant, and it has an ugly taste—rather like that of brine pickle ... you could hurt your hand on this.

Luria adds: "The experiments were repeated during several days and invariably the same stimuli produced identical experiences." Synesthesia accompanied perhaps all of S's perceptions. Luria measured bodily changes—changes of heart rate, or of body temperature—occurring when S imagined running for a bus, or being near a hot stove.

Confusions of memory or imagination with reality could be dangerous—as for crossing a road, are the lights really green?—or merely annoying: "I'd look at a clock and for a long while continue to see the hands fixed just as they were, and not realize time had passed ... that's why I'm often late."

There is much that is suggestive in this remarkable study by Luria, but he confesses to finding Mr. S baffling, as his memory is so different from the normal. Such rare cases must not be ignored.

Qualia in Evolution?

This flagging-the-present hypothesis has implications for consciousness in other animals. We would expect that qualia became more important with increasing use of Top-down knowledge, and as perception and behavior were gradually freed from the tyranny of reflex responses of "primitive" organisms. Primitive creatures should lack qualia, for they would have no trouble behaving to present situations, as they respond almost completely and quite directly to present stimuli.

It "should" be that qualia have developed through evolution, as the difficulty of distinguishing the present from the remembered past increases, with the growing contributions of Top-down knowledge and active cognitive processing. Intelligence cannot be tied to the present. Here there is a balancing act, for what is needed for intelligence is what, in the extreme, pushes the mind to lose reality.

Physiology of Qualia

Visual phenomena of ambiguity—where perceptions flip between alternatives, though the afferent signals are unchanged—show that qualia are attached to prevailing Perceptual Hypotheses, rather than evoked directly from sensory signals. As an example (famously for those of us who study phenomena of perception) the gray region in Mach's flipping corner spontaneously changes brightness—according to whether it is accepted as a shadow or as a feature of the surface—with no change of sensory input (Mach 1886/1959).

This notion, that normally qualia flag the present, does not begin to explain how qualia are produced by brain processes; though much has been discovered recently, especially for vision (Zeki, 1995; Crick 1994). If qualia are associated with the *results* of information processing, as suggested by changes with perceptual ambiguities, doesn't this suggest that qualia result from cognitive processing rather than from the support physiology of the brain? If so, which brain regions are involved should change with changes of cognitive processing, perhaps to be charted dynamically with local changes of blood flow as now recorded by functional brain imaging.

Qualifications

We have, throughout, stressed the vivid qualia of present perception; but is there not run-of-the-mill awareness of (non-emotional) memories and thoughts, quite apart from afferent inputs from the senses or the body? Much of thinking may be accompanied by motions of speech, possibly giving afferent inputs, much as for the James-Lange theory of emotion. This could not plausibly apply to mental imagery, which though feeble compared to real-time qualia, may be said to be in consciousness. They would be beyond this hypothesis. Two alternatives along these general lines present themselves: "cold" thoughts are simply not conscious apart from sensed bodily changes or, it is the special *vividness* of qualia of perception that flag the present. Both are options for future understanding along these lines of speculation.

References

Crick, F. C. 1994. *The Astonishing Hypothesis*. New York: Scribners.

Darwin, C. R. 1872. *Expression of the emotions in man and animals*. London: John Murrey.

Gregory, R. L. 1980. Perceptions as hypotheses. *Phil. Trans. R. Soc. Lond. B* 290:181–197.

Gregory, R. L. 1981. *Mind in Science*. London: Weidenfeld and Nicolson).

Gregory, R. L. 1997. Knowledge in perception and illusion. *Phil. Trans. R. Soc. Lond. B*, 1121–1128.

Helmholtz, H. von 1866. Concerning the Perceptions in General. *Treatise on Physiological Optics.* Volume 3, 3d edition (translated by J. P. C. Southall Opt. Soc. Amer., New York, 1925, Section 26. Reprinted Dover, New York, 1962.

Humphrey, N. 1992. *A History of the Mind.* New York: Simon and Schuster.

Huxley, A. 1954. *The Doors of Perception.* In *The Complete works of Aldous Huxley.* London: Chato and Windus, 1968.

Huxley, A. 1966. *Heaven and Hell.* In *The Complete works of Aldous Huxley* London: Chato and Windus, 1968.

James, W. 1890. *Principles of psychology.* London: Macmillan.

Kosslyn, S. M., Thompson, W. L., Kim, I. J., and Alpert, N. M. 1995. Topographical representations of mental images in primary visual cortex. *Nature* (London) 378:496–498

Luria, A. 1969. *The Mind of a Mnemonist: a little book about a vast memory.* New York: Cape.

Mach, E. 1886/1959. *Analysis of Sensation.* First German edition 1996, republished by Dover, New York, 1959, in English translation from the 5th German edition, revised and supplemented by S. Waterlow.

Posner, M. I., and Raichle, M. E. 1994. *Images of Mind.* New York: Freeman.

Silbersweig, D. A., Stern, E., Frith, C., et al. 1995. A functional neuroanatomy of hallucinations in schizophrenia. *Nature* (London) 378:176–179.

Sillito, A. 1995. Chemical Soup: Where and how drugs may influence visual perception. In *The Artful Eye.* Oxford: Oxford University Press, p. 295.

Zeki, S. 1993. *Vision and the Brain.* Oxford: Blackwell Scientific.

23 If Qualia Evolved ...

A. G. Cairns-Smith

If qualia evolved they must belong to the Physical World. Yet current physics and chemistry, which are supposed to describe this world, has no place for them. On the other hand, if qualia evolved we should expect there to be brain machinery devoted to their production—"qualagens"—and a phylogeny of qualia and qualagens to be discovered.

Consciousness Defined for Present Purposes

There is no agreed scientific use of the word consciousness, so we have to be clear about which of many legitimate meanings we are using. (The *Oxford English Dictionary* gives about a dozen). Our choice will no doubt reflect our particular interests, but if we are trying to understand the nature of consciousness we should not choose a definition that will make the problem too easy. In line with Chalmers's advice to face the "hard problem" (Chalmers 1995), we should choose a definition that makes the problem look as difficult as it really is.

There is a duplicity in terms such as *perception, awareness, thought, intelligence, behavior*. We should say that these all refer to attributes which are indeed often and importantly to do with consciousness. But they are not necessarily to do with consciousness. They need the adjective *conscious* or *unconscious* to make their meanings clear, since there are unconscious forms of each of them. If we concentrate our attention exclusively on the unconscious forms of perception, awareness, etc., we will indeed be able to keep to the language of science—of molecular biology, computing, or whatever. No one will accuse us of being unscientific. But then we will have avoided the question of what consciousness actually is.

For example we may be tempted to say that "consciousness" just means "awareness." That sounds sensible and pragmatic. Indeed it is one of the meanings to be found in the O.E.D. But then we might go on to say that awareness (of a sort) is exhibited by thermostats and burglar alarms, as well as now highly sophisticated computer based recognition systems; adding perhaps that such forms of machine awareness are getting better and better and sooner or later will come to approach human consciousness. Such a line of argument goes wrong at the first step in failing to distinguish between conscious and unconscious awareness.

Or we may be tempted to equate consciousness with *thinking* or even with *intelligence* and use the duplicity of these words to slide away from the real problem. It is reasonable to hope that since thinking, intelligence and consciousness are connected then advances in Artificial Intelligence will help in our understanding of consciousness. And it is part of the traditional strategy of science to go first for those parts of a problem that we have the readiest means to tackle—and seemingly daunting problems sometimes dissolve away if we proceed like this. In support of taking such an attitude to the problem of consciousness one might point, as Dennett does, to the way in which advances in molecular biology have made redundant such earlier ideas as the vital force (Dennett 1991). Indeed vital force was an unreal idea. It was a misunderstanding. But qualia are not like that. Agonizing pain is not a misunderstanding. In discussions of consciousness, feelings and sensations should be on center stage. (Chalmers 1995, Humphrey 1992, Cairns-Smith 1996).

I take the following to be examples of essentially conscious attributes, because they are attributes for which, it seems to me, there are no unconscious equivalent forms:

a feeling

an emotion

a sensation

a mood

These are all qualia, and I define consciousness informally, and for present purposes, in these terms: *a state of consciousness is some kind of arrangement or organization of qualia.*

Perhaps the most significant thing which qualia have in common is precisely that our current hard sciences of physics, chemistry etc., have no place for them. The purpose of this chapter is to show that qualia *should* have such a place—and that there is both bad news and good news here. The bad news is that there is something deeply deficient about current physics and chemistry. The good news is that qualia should be accessible to science.

Our Two Selves

There is a natural dualism in the distinction between the known and the unknown. For example there is a distinction between what as scientists we think we understand in principle about the mind, and what we do not understand at all. Such frontiers are forever changing, the dualism I speak of is strictly provisional, but at the moment it lies neatly between the unconscious and conscious parts of our mind.

We now realize that most of what we do is unconscious (Baars 1988). It is this part of our mind, what we might call our Greater Self, that we can in principle understand in terms of nerve cells and circuitry. To say that our Greater Self is a big unconscious control computer is not so far off. The other part of our mind comes and goes: the Evanescent Self, as we might call it, the conscious mind, the bit that is made of qualia, the bit that switches on every morning.

It often looks as if the brain makes qualia as some kind of add-on activity—because it is conscious only sometimes and to different extents: and because at different moments it may be more or less conscious, and in different ways. An example of this kind of thing is in the acquisition of a skill, where the unconscious systems increasingly predominate. Ask yourself how one rides a bicycle: how for example one can ride a bicycle slowly without falling sideways. There is evidently much manipulation of the handle bars needed, but if you ask most people who can ride bicycles which way they should turn them to stop falling, say, to the left they will probably suggest that you should turn the handle bars to the right. Consciously they seem not to know that this will quickly tip them over. Fortunately their unconscious Greater Self knows the correct answer to the question or anyway it knows what to do.

Functional brain imaging has revealed distinctive alterations in locations and patterns of brain activity during learning tasks (Posner and Raichle 1994), and both Milner (1998) and Goodale (1998) have given us examples of cases where the brain seems to have distinct pathways for conscious and unconscious forms of the same sort of activity. It seems clear now that when a mental activity is qualia laden (highly conscious) or qualia free (unconscious) the brain is operating somewhat differently.

Yet this now-you-have-it-now-you-don't aspect of our consciousness, together with the now well known delays in conscious perceptions and conscious actions, has helped to give an impression that our consciousness does not actually do anything. No doubt consciousness is less intricately involved in our actions that we might like to imagine, but an argument to the contrary—that "feelings are causes"—was put more that a hundred years ago. It is an argument with devastating implications. Not nearly enough attention has been paid to it (Glynn 1993).

The Evolutionary Argument

A Tale of Two Thinkers

The O.E.D. gives, as one of its examples of uses of the term consciousness, a paragraph written by Thomas Huxley in 1866:

We class sensations along with emotions, and volitions, and thoughts, under the common head of *states of consciousness*. But what consciousness is, we know not; and how it is that anything so remarkable as a state of consciousness comes about as a result of irritating nervous tissue, is just as unaccountable as the appearance of the Djin when Aladdin rubbed his lamp, or any other ultimate fact of nature.

It seems a reasonable facing of facts, but then in 1874 he expressed a more positive but, to my mind, more dubious view:

... it follows that our mental conditions are simply the symbols in consciousness of the changes which take place automatically in the organism; and that to take an extreme illustration, the feeling we call volition is not the cause of a voluntary act, but the symbol of that state of the brain which is the immediate cause of that act. We are conscious automata. (Huxley 1874)

William James would have none of it. In addressing the "automaton" issue he gives a robust defence of the efficacy of feelings:

... common-sense, though the intimate nature of causality and of the connection of things in the universe lies beyond her pitifully bounded horizon, has the root and gist of the truth in her hands when she obstinately holds to it that feelings and ideas are causes. (James 1890)

And this was not just oratorical eloquence. By 1878 James had found a wonderful argument for the efficacy of feelings based, paradoxically, on the very idea that Huxley had done so much to promote: Darwin's idea of evolution though natural selection (Glynn 1993, Richards 1987).

In terms of more current language the argument can be put like this. Feelings such as hunger and lust seem so obviously adaptive, "designed" for survival and reproduction, that we can suppose that they evolved. In that case they are effects of genes, effects of DNA molecules, that is, physico-chemical effects. On the other hand feelings such as these have physico-chemical consequences too, in the adaptive activities which they encourage. This cannot be make-believe. In the warnings and encouragements of pain and pleasure it is the feeling that is effective, the feeling itself. If it were only the "neural correlates" of feelings that influenced behavior, not the feelings themselves, then there would be no selective advantage in actually feeling anything. And even if we did have feelings as some kind of accidental side effect there would be no reason to expect them to be appropriate. What would it matter *what* feelings we had if they could have no effects? The appropriateness of qualia, their whole evolution, would be a mystery.

There seems to be no way round it: if they evolved, qualia must have both physico-chemical causes and physico-chemical effects—and thus good enough entrance qualifications to be admitted to The Physical World.

The Bomb in the Basement

This, then, is bomb in the foundations of science: that qualia must belong to the physical world while at the same time physics and chemistry, which supposedly can in principle give us a complete account of this world, have no place for them. We might say that Descartes carelessly left the bomb when he divided the great problem of the Universe into the problem of mind and the problem of matter and gave only matter to science. ("Descartes' error," Damasio [1994] calls it.) It is a bomb that Darwin inadvertently set ticking; and then William James exposed for all to see—but failed to defuse. And it is a bomb that twentieth-century science did its best to bury again. These Tucson meetings have re-exposed the bomb. It is still ticking.

It is not that the hard sciences cannot deal with qualia: that might be of no consequence. Science has no pretensions to explain everything. What is so devastating about the qualia Bomb is that science *ought* to be able to deal with qualia. They are part of the physical world, because they evolved; and they are part of the machinery of our behavior, along with ion pumps, action potentials, reflexes and so on. A hundred years ago there was a similar situation in physics. The way in which the colors of glowing coals changed with temperature clearly *should* have been understandable in physical terms and yet it was to need a revolution in physics for such an understanding to come about. Now it is such things as the sensations of color that are demanding to be let into the Society of Material Things—alongside heredity, and so much else in biology that can now be explained in terms of physics and chemistry and the theory of evolution.

So it is our matter theory that is set to change. Nothing new here, we might say. Think how our ideas of matter have shifted since Greek times. About 420 BC Democritus had a Theory of Everything. There were only Atoms, Motion and Void. The persistence of the Universe depended on the durability of the atoms while the variability of the Universe was to be explained because the atoms could be arranged in different patterns. It was a wonderful idea due to reach a mathematical perfection in the nineteenth-century kinetic theory of gases. But it was not rich enough to explain everything about the material world. Newton was to add forces operating across space and suggested that such would be important in holding the smallest parts of materials together: "Have not the small particles of bodies certain powers, virtues, or forces by which they act at a distance ..." (1730/1979); Faraday and Maxwell were to see fields to be as real as atoms (1844); Planck and then Einstein would upset the whole idea of material substance: quantum energy became the ultimate stuff whose ultimate grain was action. And then, with Heisenberg, atoms had ceased to be *things* at all (1959).

The Fabrics of the World

The fabrics of what we may call ordinary matter are ways of arranging the quantum energy *via* electrons, neutrons and protons to make atoms and molecules; and then higher assemblages of these things: gases, liquids and solids, often with distinctive properties—transmitting or absorbing light, conducting electricity or not, being hard or soft, and so on and on. Then there are more complicated fabrics, such as flames or whirlpools, maintained in flows of matter and energy. And then there is living matter with its layers of complex organization now becoming increasingly well understood in terms of molecular biology, in terms of atoms and molecules and the flow of energy. All these fabrics are more or less "made of atoms."

But there are other fabrics woven differently from the quantum energy, *light* for example. A laser beam is produced by and interacts with molecular matter but a laser beam is not made of atoms and molecules. Light is a different way of arranging the quantum energy.

So here is a tentative minimal conjecture: feelings and sensations are yet another way of arranging the quantum energy. Like light they are produced by and interact with molecular matter—although so far only in brains.

Hunting the Qualagens

We are supposing that the brain *makes* qualia: and also, as part of the unconscious activity of Greater Self, the brain arranges its qualia too, to make the ever changing fabrics of our conscious minds.

To the extent that a state of consciousness is "an organization of qualia," we can claim to be some way along the road to understanding in physical terms what a state of consciousness is: we know quite a lot about the crucial "organization" part of the prescription, about brain pathways and switch-gear for qualia production and control. For example we know quite a lot about what has to happen for pain to be felt, how and why it is wired up the way it is. But how such sensations themselves are made, still eludes us. This may be partly because the mechanisms have not been consistently looked for, in a belief that qualia are irrelevant and/or hopelessly "non physical" concomitants of normal brain activity. But the evolutionary argument shows that qualia are indeed physico-chemical—at least in the sense of having a place in some future physics and chemistry—and if indeed qualia evolved, then there must be machinery that produce these effects in the brain. Let us call such things "qualagens."

The odds are that, like most biological machinery, the qualagens are at root molecular, with protein molecules as key components. I am inclined to agree with those who think that feelings and sensations are large scale effects arising from vast numbers of microscopic processes, and that these are macroquantum effects of some sort (Cairns-Smith 1996, Marshall 1989, Lockwood 1989, Penrose 1994, Jibu and Yasue 1995, Yasue 1998).

Maybe there are special proteins and hence genes out of which the qualagens are made. Alternatively qualagenesis might be a combined effect of activities of not only many, but of many *kinds* of protein molecules that also have other functions; so that one might only be able to say of some brain protein that "when this bit of this molecule wobbles it contributes to making such and such a quale." So perhaps the qualagens are difficult to find because the key proteins are not only widely spread, but have other more obvious functions, as in the Hameroff and Penrose microtubule conjecture (Penrose 1994).

Phylogeny of Qualia

One can roughly sequence qualia according to whether they are more particularly to do with conscious perception, conscious thought, or conscious action.

raw perceptual sensations	*color sensations, smells . . .*
interpretative feelings	*of space, motion, recognition . . .*
intellectual feelings	*feelings of doubt, of certainty . . .*
coercive feelings and sensations	*hunger, fear, pleasures, pains, itches . . .*
volitional feelings and sensations	*curiosity, urges, desires . . .*

And then, outside this scheme there are what we might lump together as background qualia: *moods, attitudes . . .*

Which kinds of feelings and sensations came first? Presumably they would have evolved originally on the back of wholly unconscious nervous systems. To judge from the way new functions usually catch on in evolution, the first step would have been an accidental side effect, a preadaptation with some marginal usefulness. But on the face of it sending neuro-electrochemical signals and making qualia are distinctly different activities, and so it is unlikely that exactly the same equipment would be ideal for each. In that case the first quale having caught on, we would then expect natural selection to have honed increasingly sophisticated devices that became increasingly dedicated to the production of this new class of effect.

We might guess that, to have caught on, the first kinds of qualia must have been both "raw" and "coercive" at the same time, making a direct connection between a simple perception and a simple action. Physical pleasures and pains can be like this. They are nice or nasty in themselves. Smells and tastes are very often like this too, and like pleasure and pain, associated particularly with the brain's more ancient limbic regions.

The in-between qualia of complex perception are presumably more recent—and more neocortical than limbic. Most of our perceptual sensations are not particularly nice or nasty in themselves: patches of color or texture, forms, motions, etc., need interpretation and only begin to push us into action at a high level of recognition—of an apple or a tiger. We often look before we leap.

More remote still would be where we have to think too, perhaps for days, in preparation for action. Then my scheme begins to look a bit too simple, because perhaps part of what keeps us thinking consciously is a coercive emotion, a desire to think it out: "a passion for reason" Demasio calls it (1994). Then we would have to say that coercive qualia are part of conscious thought too—conscious drives, not to immediate action in this case, but to more thinking.

Presumably the qualia of conscious thought are among the most recent. But perhaps we can still see connections in the words we use. Our language often makes connections between abstract thought and bodily sensations. We *feel* that an idea is wrong; we feel *uneasy* about it: we *weigh up* alternatives as if judging them by muscle feel: we *like the sound* of an idea, or find it *distasteful*.... Again and again we use qualia-words. So perhaps the qualia of contemplation did indeed evolve from more immediate and primitive forms, through successive modifications of qualagenic genes and proteins in Nature's usual branching style. If that is the case there is a tree to be found: a phylogeny of qualia and qualagens.

References

Baars, B. J. 1988. *A Cognitive Theory of Consciousness*. Cambridge: Cambridge University Press.

Cairns-Smith, A. G. 1996. *Evolving the Mind: on the nature of matter and the origin of consciousness*. Cambridge: Cambridge University Press.

Chalmers, D. J. 1995. The puzzle of conscious experience. *Scientific American* 273, December 1996.

The Conscious Mind: in search of a fundamental theory New York: Oxford University Press.

Damasio, A. R. 1994. *Descartes' Error: emotion, reason and the human brain*. New York: Avon.

Dennett, D. C. 1991. *Consciousness Explained*. Harmondsworth: Penguin, p. 25.

Faraday, M. 1844. *Matter*. London: Library of the Institution of Electrical Engineers.

Glynn, I. M. 1993. The evolution of consciousness: William James's unresolved problem. *Biological Reviews of the Cambridge Philosophical Society* 68:599–616.

Goodale, M. 1998. Unconscious visual processing for action: evidence from normal observers. Abstract no. 140, Consciousness Research Abstracts: Toward a science of consciousness: "Tucson III," p. 81.

Heisenberg, W. 1959. *Physics and Philosophy: the revolution in modern science*. London: Allen & Unwin, chapter 10.

Humphrey, N. 1992. *A History of the Mind*. New York: Simon and Schuster.

Huxley, T. 1874. On the hypothesis that animals are automata and its history. *Fortnightly Review* 22:555–589.

James, W. 1890/1983. *The Principles of Psychology*. New York: Holt 1890. Reprinted Cambridge Massachusetts: Harvard University Press 1983., p. 140.

Jibu, M., and Yasue, K. 1995. *Quantum Brain Dynamics and Consciousness: an introduction.*

Lockwood, M. 1989. *Mind, Brain and the Quantum: the compound "I."* Oxford: Blackwell, chapter 14.

Marshall, I. N. 1989. Consciousness and Bose-Einstein condensates. *New Ideas in Psychology* 7:73–83.

Milner, D. 1998. Unconscious visual processing for action: neuropsychological evidence. Abstract no. 135, Consciousness Research Abstracts: Toward a science of consciousness: "Tucson III," p. 80.

Newton, I. 1730/1979. *Opticks.* (4th edition) Quest. 31. London 1730. Reprinted New York 1979: Dover, pp. 375–406.

Penrose, R. 1994. *Shadows of the Mind: a search for the missing science of consciousness.* Oxford: Oxford University Press, ch 7.

Posner, M. I., and Raichle, M. E. 1994. *Images of Mind.* New York: W. H. Freeman, pp. 125–129.

Richards, R. J. 1987. *Darwin and the emergence of evolutionary theories of mind and behavior.* Chicago: University of Chicago Press.

Yasue, K. 1998. Physics approaches to consciousness. Abstract no. 289, Consciousness Research Abstracts: Towards as science of consciousness: "Tucson III," p. 131.

24 Handaxes and Ice Age Carvings: Hard Evidence for the Evolution of Consciousness

Steven Mithen

As an archaeologist my interest is not with consciousness as raw sensation, but with high level, access or reflective consciousness—consciousness in terms of thoughts about our own thoughts and about our feelings; consciousness in terms of knowing about one's own mind. This is quite different from consciousness in terms of being and feeling that I guess is the root the matter: those roots are buried much too deep in our evolutionary past for an archaeologist to find; they may go back way before the first hominid like creature appeared on the earth perhaps as Stuart Hameroff (1998) suggests to the Cambrian explosion itself. As an archaeologist concerned with just the last 6 million years of evolution I have what might be the trivial problem to address, no more than the twigs, the buds and then the final flowering of consciousness.

To address this, the first task is to rid our own minds of the idea that the evolution of consciousness is something that can be considered in isolation from that of thought, language, behavior and material culture. These were inextricably linked to each other during cognitive evolution, although the role they played changed as they themselves evolved. This is, of course, quite familiar and obvious. Consider language and thought, for instance. There is a long intellectual history stretching back to Plato's *Theateteus* of considering the relationship between these (Preston 1997); more recently in the work of psychologists such as Vygortsky (1962 [1934]), philosophers such as Dennett (1991) and Clark (1996), linguists such Lock (1993) and Bickerton (1996), and neuroscientists such as Calvin (1997), the notion of language as a tool for thought as much as a tool for communication has gained much support. I am in absolute agreement with this and think that there has been too much stress on language as a tool for communication in the recent work on the evolution of language (e.g., Dunbar 1996). As such, the evolution of reflexive consciousness appears most likely to be entwinned with that of modern language.

The content of the archaeological record suggests that material culture may play a similar role to that of language in terms of structuring, perhaps forming, our thoughts and consciousness. The artefacts from the prehistoric and modern worlds were/are not just tools for hunting animals or using the internet; nor for just decorating bodies or our homes. Material artefacts are as much tools for thought as is language: tools for exploring, expanding, and manipulating our own minds and by that process ridding ourselves of the shackles imposed on our thinking by our evolutionary past. In this regard the evolution of material culture is inextricably linked with the evolution of consciousness. At least, that is the argument I would to pursue in this short chapter.

The Course of Human Evolution

Before developing this argument it is useful to briefly review the course of human evolution, one possible phylogenetic tree of which is represented in figure 24.1. From that basis I will then pick out what appear to be two key moments for the budding and perhaps flowering of our consciousness during the last six million years. This brief review is drawn from Mithen (1996). Jones et al. (1992) and Stringer and McKie (1996) are also excellent sources for further information about the course of human evolution.

Homo sapiens sapiens is closely related to the great apes, having shared a common ancestor with the chimpanzee between 5 and 6 million years ago. It is, of course, usual practice, to assume that cognitively this common ancestor was much like the chimpanzee today. That may be true; or it may be a grave mistake as the chimpanzee mind has also undergone 6 million years of evolution since the common ancestor. But the most reasonable assumption is that the mind of the common ancestor was similar to that of the chimpanzee today, and consequently is likely to lack a fully modern form of reflexive consciousness. As such, this evolved at sometime during the last 6 million years and as the majority of behavior during that period is documented by the archaeological record inferences should be possible as to when, where and within which species this occurred.

Between 4.5 and 1 million years ago, there are several australopithecine species known to us, and probably several more that remain undiscovered. The most famous is Lucy, *A. afarensis*, with her joint arboreal and terrestrial adaptation. The emergence of large brained hominids after 2 million years ago, who were manufacturing Oldowan stone tools and eating greater quantities of meat seems likely to be tied up with significant cognitive developments. The most important of these species is *H. ergaster*, best represented by the fossil skeleton known as the Nariokotome boy which displays various preadaptations for linguistic abilities (Aiello 1996). *H. ergaster* appears to have been the species that diversified and dispersed throughout the Old world soon after 2 million years ago. In Asia distinct species such as *H. erectus* and archaic *H. sapiens* evolved, while in Europe we find *H. heidelbergensis* and then the Neanderthals. All of these species were evidently capable of making complex stone artefacts, such as handaxes, and after 250,000 years ago, levallois flakes and points. They lived in a variety of challenging environments, were able to hunt big game and to live in large, socially complex groups. After 250,000 years ago, several hominid species had brains as large as ours today. But their behavior lacks any sign of art or symbolic behavior beyond pieces such as the engraved Bilzingsleben bones with a few parallel incisions, the purpose of which are quite unknown, and the so-called

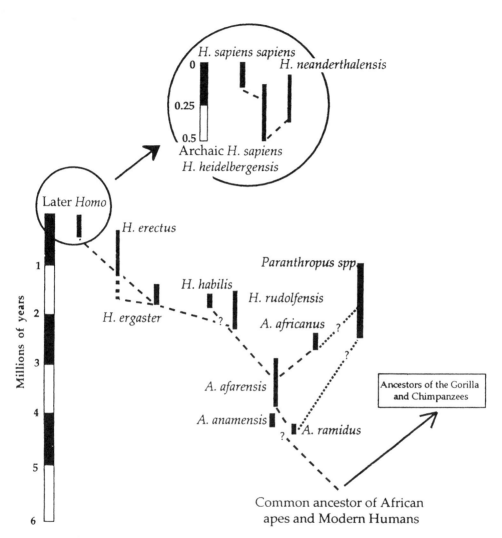

Figure 24.1
Human phylogenetic tree. This is just one of several different trees that can be constructed with the same information depending upon interpretations of how many species exist in the fossil record and their evolutionary relationships.

Berekhat Ram figurine just a few centimetres high but apparently intentionally incised by stone artefacts. This is claimed to be a female figurine (Marshack 1997) and, as such, the earliest piece of representational art.

If we follow the Out of Africa origins for modern humans (Stringer and McKie 1996), then we see *H. sapiens sapiens* first appearing in Africa sometime before 100,000 years ago with the earliest traces being found at Omo Kibish and Klasies River Mouth, and soon after at the caves of Qafzeh and Skhul in the Levant. Modern humans then dispersed throughout the Old and New Worlds replacing all other types of humans so that by 28,000 *Homo sapiens sapiens* was the only surviving member of our genus on the planet. After 50,000 years ago we have unambiguous traces of art and symbols, notably the cave paintings from France first found 30,000 years ago; prior to this we have a few ambiguous traces for art, ritual and symbolic behavior by anatomically modern humans, such ochre crayons from Klasies (Knight et al. 1995).

It is at some time during this evolutionary history that modern forms of consciousness evolve: whether catastrophically or gradually is unknown, whether restricted to just our species or common to all Early Humans remains unclear.

An Evolving Cognitive Package

The argument I want to make—and as a point if principle I am sure that it is quite uncontentious—is that to resolve these issues we need to integrate our study of consciousness with that of thought, language, behavior and material culture. These seem to form a cognitive package. To suggest how we should proceed I will concentrate on two types of hard evidence: handaxes and the first representational art. These show two different relationships arising at different periods of human evolution between the contents of our cognitive package.

Handaxes, Private Speech, and Consciousness

Handaxes, were made by several types of Early Humans and first appear in the archaeological record 1.4 million years ago. They remain a pervasive feature of the archaeological record for more than a million years, and indeed were still made by some of the last Neanderthals in Europe just 50,000 years ago. Handaxes are enigmas (Wynn 1995): many of them show an imposed symmetrical form; they are often found in vast number at single sites; there appears no chronological patterning in their shape or degree of technical skill through time; their form and the investment of time in their manufacture appears quite redundant for the tasks they were used for

(Isaac 1977, Row 1981, Villa 1983, Wynn and Tierson 1990). They are indeed quite unlike any types of modern artefacts. Together with Marek Kohn, I think that many of these peculiar attributes can be explained by considering the artefacts as products of sexual selection and by invoking Zahavi's handicap principle. In essence making handaxes functioned as an indicator of high intelligence and good health (Kohn and Mithen 1999).

With regard to consciousness handaxes provide us with a dilemma, indeed a paradox. On the one hand there can be no question that these artefacts are very challenging to make. This has been demonstrated by many replicative studies and we now have detailed understanding of the knapping procedures used by early humans (e.g., Pelegrin 1993). Often nonarchaeologists speculate that handaxes are equivalent to the complex artefacts made by other animals, such as a beaver's dam, a honeycomb or a spiders web: all complex artefacts with degrees of symmetry but which require neither intelligence nor conscious thought to produce. Well such comparisons are ill founded. A reductive technology is necessary to make a handaxe. One must begin with a nodule of stone and employ a range of different hammers and methods of fracture to achieve the final product. There is a great deal of unpredictability involved: unexpected contingencies arise, plans need to be continually modified. One simply cannot iterate a fixed action routine to produce a handaxe as a spider or a beaver might use for their artefacts. Making a handaxe is a completely different mental ball game. It is one that requires a degree of consciousness, one needs thoughts about thoughts.

The paradox is that the remarkable technological stasis that endured during the Middle Pleistocene (Mithen 1996) suggests that the technical intelligence these hominids possessed was quite unknown to them; that it was something excluded from whatever higher level consciousness that they did possess. So while the form of handaxes tells us that hominids were conscious about their technical knowledge, the distribution of these artefacts in space and time tells us the opposite. Let me suggest how this paradox may be resolved.

To do that we must be a bit more specific and recognised that there are at least four types of knowledge that need to be brought together in the mind for handaxe production (figure 24.2). Each of these four mental components appear to have become part of an evolved psychology long before the first handaxes were manufactured.

First one needs a high degree of sensory motor control. Nodules, pre-forms, and near finished artefacts must be struck at precisely the right angle with precisely the right degree of force if the desired flake is to be detached. It seems unlikely that such sensory-motor control would have been selected for making handaxes themselves. A more likely origin is related to encaphalization and bipedalism. As Leslie Aiello (1996) has discussed, with a large brain there can be a relatively high degree of

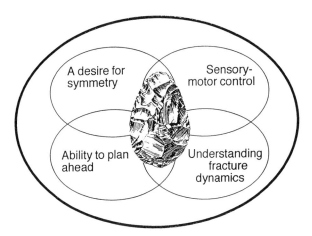

Figure 24.2
The cognitive requirements for handaxe manufacture.

complex sensory-motor control of the body owing to the increased number of nerve tracts and the increased integration between them allowing for the firing of smaller muscle groups. According to Aiello, bipedalism requires a more complex integrated system of balance than quadrupedal locomotion and presupposes a complex and highly fractionated nervous system, which in turn presupposes a larger brain. As substantial encaphalization and bipedalism had arisen prior to the appearance of handaxes in the archaeological record, it is evident that Early Humans were pre-adapted for the sensory motor-control required to make handaxes.

The earlirst hominids prior to the appearance of handaxes also appear to have had a sufficient degree of understanding about fracture dynamics to allow the manufacture of handaxes. This is evident from both the production of Oldowan tools, and from tool use by chimpanzees. As has been made clear by the experimental work of Toth (1985) and Pelegrin (1993), Oldowan tools makers were not simply bashing rocks together (or at least not always). Many choppers and flakes provide distinct traces that Oldowan knappers 2.5 million years ago were able to identify appropriate natural platforms for striking and were selecting hammerstones of appropriate weight and striking at appropriate angles and force. It is also evident from studies of nut cracking by chimpanzees (Boesch and Boesch 1983), that with sufficient experience the direction and power of striking by these animals can be adjusted to crack nuts without destroying the kernel.

A third feature of handaxe manufacture is planning: flake removals happen in a sequential fashion to allow one to move from a nodule to a roughout to a finished artefacts. Each removal both detaches a flake and paves the way for removal of future flakes, perhaps those of a different type. To make a handaxe one must plan; but one must also be flexible, able to modify the plan and react to contingencies, such as unexpected flaws in the material and miss-hits.

Again we can see evidence of planning in the minds of Oldowan tool makers, and in chimpanzees today. With regard to the early hominids there is clear evidence of the transport of artefacts and parts of carcasses around the landscape; these may not have been for great distances but planning with flexibility is clearly required (Potts 1988). We can also see this to some degree in chimpanzee tool use: artefacts such as termite sticks are trimmed to appropriate lengths, sequential uses of tools have been observed, and hammers carried to nut cracking sites in anticipation of use (McGrew 1992). So as with fine-sensory motor control, the ability for planning ahead is likely to have been selected for reasons unrelated to handaxe manufacture and to have already been part of an evolved psychology prior to the first production of handaxes.

The fourth significant feature of handaxe manufacture is the imposition of symmetry. In many handaxes, especially the early protobifaces, this may be no more than an unintentional by-product of the bifacial knapping technique. But in others, the removal of fine trimming flakes is a clear indicator that symmetry was deliberately imposed (Wynn 1995). Now an attraction toward symmetry is also likely to have been part of an evolved psychology, stretching way back in evolutionary time. Many animal species appear to use symmetry as a clue to the genetic health of potential mates (e.g., Møller 1990, Manning and Chamberlain 1993, Manning and Hartley 1991). Also, an evolved ability to perceive and pay attention to symmetry may have been crucial in social interaction and predator escape, as it may allow one to recognise that one is being directly stared at (Dennett 1991). Hominid handaxe makers may have been keying into this attraction to symmetry when producing tools to attract the attention of the other hominids, especially those of the opposite sex. But what is important with regard to consciousness, is that this attraction to symmetry is likely to have evolved for reasons quite unrelated to handaxe manufacture.

It is apparent, therefore, that the four mental resources for handaxe manufacture evolved independently, and were present in the minds of hominids long before the first handaxes were produced. How were these resources combined to produce what I would call the technical intelligence (Mithen 1996) of the Early Human mind? And how does this relate to language and consciousness.

The argument I would like to make is that private speech played a critical role, and here I want to draw directly on Dennett's (1991) arguments for auto-stimulation, or speaking to oneself. He has described this as functioning to "blaze a new trail through one's internal components." Such private speech seems to me as the only means by which that trail between planning, fracture dynamics, motor control and symmetry could have been forged in the early human mind. His figure from *Consciousness Explained*, which can be modified quite easily to relate to handaxe production to suggest how several modules were bundled together to create a cognitive domain within the early human mind (figure 24.3). Here, therefore, we return to the relationship between language and thought. There are many studies and ideas that could be invoked to develop this argument. The most relevant for the evolution of thought and consciousness at 2 million years ago seem to be those by Andrew Lock (1980), arguing that for the child, language makes explicit what is already implicit in his abilities, and by Laura Berk (1994) that a child's private speech is a crucial cognitive tool for problem solving.

So my argument is that when our ancestors made handaxes there were private mutterings accompanying the crack of stone against stone. Those private mutterings were instrumental in pulling the knowledge required for handaxe manufacture into an emergent consciousness. But what type of consciousness? I think probably one that was fleeting: one that existed during the act of manufacture and that did not then endure. One quite unlike the consciousness about one's emotions, feelings, and desires that were associated with the social world and that probably part of a completely separate cognitive domain, that of social intelligence, in the early human mind (Mithen 1996).

Using private speech in handaxe manufacture is but one instance, I would argue, of how early humans began to manipulate, explore and expand there own minds by clever tricks. This clever trick probably evolved hand in hand with another: talking to each other. Both private and public language act as tools for thought and play a fundamental role in the evolution of consciousness: in the opening up of our minds to ourselves. But during the course of the latter stages of human evolution, another tool was found that may have had even greater consequences for the evolution of consciousness: material culture itself.

Material Culture and the Disembodiement of Mind

In my previous work, and notably in my 1996 book *The Prehistory of the Mind*, I have written how the great cultural explosion that happened after 50,000 years ago was a product of co-evolving language and consciousness resulting in minds that I described as cognitively fluid. My argument was that the minds of other Early Humans, such as the Neanderthals were structured by a series of relatively isolated cognitive domains, which I termed different intelligences (figure 24.4). As I have just

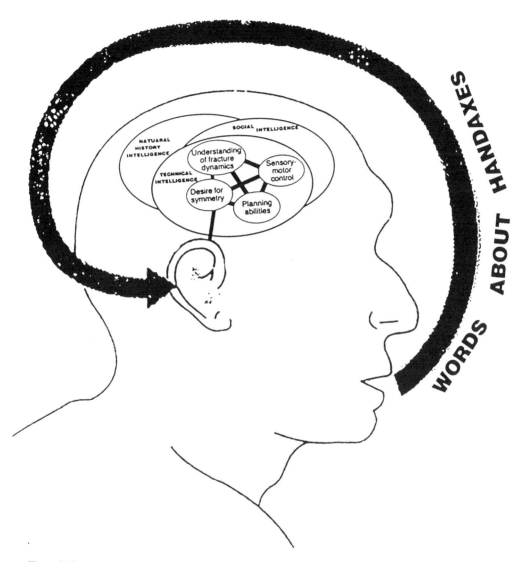

Figure 24.3
A possible role for private speech in handaxe manufacture by early humans (based on an original illustration from Dennett 1991).

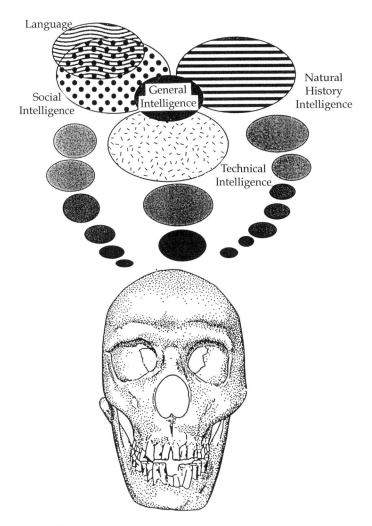

Figure 24.4
Domain-specific intelligences of the Early Human Mind (Mithen 1996).

remarked, I suspect there were different degrees of consciousness about the thoughts and knowledge within each domain: a degree of clear sightedness within that of social intelligence, a murky fog of consciousness within technical intelligence.

Now the modern human mind overcame the barriers between domains so that different types of knowledge and ways of thinking became integrated (figure 24.5). Public language was instrumental. As I discuss in Mithen (1996) the capacity for this is likely to have co-evolved with social intelligence and once public language was used for talking about the nonsocial world, such as about making artefacts and hunting animals, the barriers between those the worlds of society, nature and arte-facts collapsed.

But I now see that this argument was wrong; or rather not as right as it could have been. For I now see that the material culture itself was not just a product of a massive cognitive change, but also a cause of it. An evolved psychology cannot be so easily escaped as I had imagined and the clever trick that humans learnt was to disembody their minds into the material world around them: a linguistic utterance might be considered as a disembodied thought. But such utterances last just for a few seconds. Material culture endures.

To illustrate my argument consider the first, unambiguous representational art, that from the last ice age about 30,000 years ago. Specifically, consider the carving of what most likely is a mythical being from the last ice age, a half human/half lion figure carved from mammoth ivory found at Hohlenstein Stadel, Germany (figure 24.6). An evolved mind is unlikely to have a natural home for this being, as such entities do not exist in the natural world: so whereas evolved minds could think about humans by deploying content rich mental modules moulded by natural selection, and about other lions by using other content rich modules from the natural history cog-nitive domain, how could one think about entities that were part human and part animal? Such entities had no home in the mind. Indeed how can one come up with the idea in the first place.

As I have previously argued a cognitively fluid mind can come up with such enti-ties (figure 24.7), as I show here, but where then to store that entity? The only option is to extend the mind into the material world. Dispense with a reliance on brain stuff and get into rocks and painting, ivory and carving. So artefacts such as this figure, and indeed the cave paintings of the last ice age, functioned as anchors for ideas that have no natural home within the mind; for ideas that take us beyond those that natural selection could enable us to possess. So a better representation of how thoughts about supernatural beings are maintained and manipulated is that of figure 24.8. Without the material culture to disembody such thoughts, they would simply

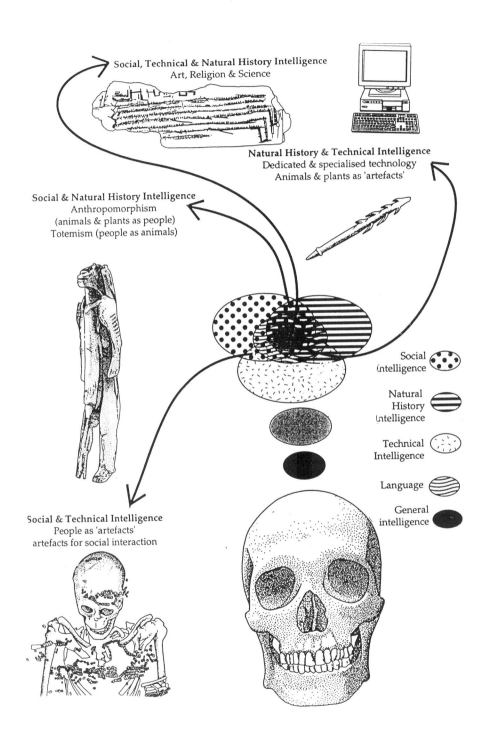

Figure 24.6
The lion/man figurine from Hohenstein-Stadel (Mithen 1996).

dissipate, there could be no fidelity in transmission to another individual or when the idea is recreated within one's own mind (Mithen 1997).

More generally the remarkable developments of material culture after 50,000 years ago should not be seen simply as the manifestation of a new level of consciousness. They are as much a cause as a product. They allowed people to explore, expand, manipulate and simply play with their own knowledge in ways that other humans, even those with private and public language, were unable to do. By doing this, humans loosened, perhaps cut, those shackles on our minds imposed by our evolutionary past. Shackles that always bound the minds of other humans types, such as the Neanderthals.

Summary

The evolution of consciousness is a story entwined with that of thought, language, material culture and behavior. Those big brained ancestors and relatives of ours are

Figure 24.5
Cognitive-fluidity and the cultural explosion (Mithen 1996).

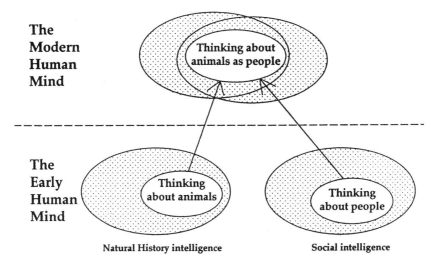

Figure 24.7
Anthropomorphic thinking created by the integration of natural history and social intelligences of the early human mind (Mithen 1996).

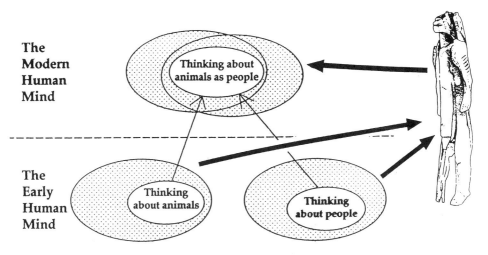

Figure 24.8
Material representation serving to anchor the cognitive representation of supernatural being.

likely to have had the same mental resources as we have today. With private and public speech they began to explore their own minds, creating a fleeting consciousness in some domains, a fully fledged consciousness in social intelligence. But unlike *Homo sapiens sapiens* they lacked the additional tools of material culture that could further discover just what those mental resources were and what they could be used for. We see the first hesitant use of additional tools with the first *H. sapiens sapiens* 100,000 years ago; we see such tool use intensifying after 50,000 years ago with the first art and then continuing with the start of agriculture. Throughout this time new types of material culture helped to pull new types of ideas out of the human mind and into consciousness. Of course this process of exploring our minds continues today: it is seriously unfinished business.

References

Aiello, L. 1996. Hominine preadaptations for language and cognition. In P. Mellars and K. Gibson (eds.) *Modelling the Early Human Mind*, pp. 89–99. Cambridge: McDonald Institute for Archaeological Research.

Berk, L. 1994. Why children talk to themselves. *Scientific American* 271, no. 5:78–83.

Bickerton, D. 1996. *Human Behavior and Language*. London: UCL Press.

Boesch, C., and Boesch, H. 1983. Optimization of nut cracking with natural hammers by wild chimpanzees. *Behavior* 83:265–86.

Calvin, W. 1997. *How Brains Think: Evolving Intelligence, Then and Now*. London: Weidenfeld and Nicholson.

Clark, A. 1996. *Being There: Putting Brain, Body and World Together Again*. Cambridge, Mass.: MIT Press.

Dennett, D. C. 1991. *Consciousness Explained*. London: Penguin.

Dunbar, R. 1996. *Gossip, Grooming and the Evolution of Language*. London: Faber and Faber.

Hameroff, S. 1998. Did consciousness cause the Cambrian evolutionary explosion? In S. R. Hameroff, A. W. Kaszniak and A. C. Scott (eds.) *Toward a Science of Consciousness II: The Second Tucson Discussions and Debates*, pp. 421–437. Cambridge Mass.: MIT Press.

Isaac, G. 1977. *Olorgesailie*. Chicago: Chicago University Press.

Jones, S., Martin, R., and Pilbeam, D. (eds.) 1992. *The Cambridge Encyclopedia of Human Evolution*. Cambridge: Cambridge University Press.

Kohn, M., and Mithen, S. 1999. Handaxes as products of sexual selection. *Antiquity* (in press).

Knight, C., Powers, C., and Watts, I. 1995. The human symbolic revolution: A Darwinian account. *Cambridge Archaeological Journal* 5:75–114.

Lock, A. 1980. *The Guided Reinvention of Language*. London: Academic Press.

Lock A. 1993. Human language development and object manipulation: Their relation in ontogeny and its possible relevance for phylogenetic questions. In K. R. Gibson and T. Ingold (eds.) *Tools, Language and Cognition in Human Evolution*, pp. 279–298. Cambridge: Cambridge University Press.

Manning, J. T., and Hartley, M. A. 1991. Symmetry and ornamentation are correlated in the peacock's train. *Animal Behavior* 42:1020–1021.

Manning, J. T., and Chamberlain, A. T. 1993. Fluctuating asymmetry, sexual selection and canine teeth in primates. *Proceedings of the Royal Society of London*, Series B, 251:83–87.

Marshack, A. 1997. The Berekhat Ram figurine: A late Acheulian carving from the Middle East. *Antiquity* 71:327–37.

McGrew, W. 1992. *Chimpanzee material culture*. Cambridge: Cambridge University Press.

Mithen, S. 1996. *The Prehistory of the Mind*. London: Thames and Hudson.

Mithen, S. 1997. Cognitive Archaeology, Evolutionary psychology and cultural transmission with particular reference to religious ideas. In C. M. Barton and G. A. Clark (eds.) Rediscovering Darwin: Evolutionary Theory in Archaeological Explanation, pp. 67–86. *Archaeological Papers of the American Anthropological Association, No. 7.*

Møller, A. P. 1990. Fluctuating asymmetry in male sexual ornaments may reliably reveal male quality. *Animal Behavior* 40:1185–1187.

Pelegrin, J. 1993. A framework for analysing prehistoric stone tool manufacture and a tentative application to some early stone industries. In *The Use of Tools by Human and Non-human Primates*, eds. A. Berthelet and J. Chavallion, pp. 302–14. Oxford: Clarendon Press.

Potts, R. 1988. *Early Hominid Activities at Olduvai Gorge*. New York: Aldine de Gruyter.

Preston, J. 1997. Introduction: Thought as Language. In Preston, J. (ed) *Thought and Language*. pp. 1–14. Cambridge: Cambridge University Press. (Royal Institute of Philosophy Supplement: 42)

Roe, D. 1981. The Lower and Middle Palaeolithic Periods in Britain. London: Routledge and Kegan Paul.

Schick, K., and Toth, N. 1993. *Making Silent Stones Speak: Human Evolution and the Dawn of Technology*. New York: Simon and Schuster.

Stinger, C., and McKie, R. 1996. *African Exodus: The Origins of Modern Humanity*. London: Pimlico.

Toth, N. 1985. The Oldowan reassessed: A close look at early stone artefacts. *Journal of Archaeological Science* 12:101–20.

Villa, P. 1983. *Terra Amata and the Middle Pleistocene Record from Southern France*. Berkeley: University of California Press.

Vygotsky, L. S. 1962 (1934). *Thought and Language*. Cambridge: MIT Press.

Wynn, T. 1995. Handaxe enigmas. *World Archaeology* 27:10–23.

Wynn, T., and Tierson, F. 1990. Regional comparison of the shapes of later Acheulian handaxes. *American Anthropologist* 92:73–84.

25 Ephemeral Levels of Mental Organization: Darwinian Competitions as a Basis for Consciousness

William H. Calvin

While I appreciate the scientific technique of picking away at pieces of a problem, I think that we greatly underestimate consciousness when we attempt to redefine it as merely awareness or selective attention. These are rather low-level capabilities in the neurologist's pantheon of mental abilities.

Consciousness seems closer to the higher intellectual functions such as structured language, planning ahead in novel situations, composing music, logical chains of inference, our fascination with games and rules, and our delight in discovering the hidden patterns in puzzles and humor—all things that are seldom found even in our closest cousins, the great apes. A richer definition of consciousness must also encompass the transitions from one mental state to another, those dynamics that William James described in 1880:

Instead of thoughts of concrete things patiently following one another in a beaten track of habitual suggestion, we have the most abrupt cross-cuts and transitions from one idea to another, the most rarefied abstractions and discriminations, the most unheard-of combinations of elements, the subtlest associations of analogy; in a word, we seem suddenly introduced into a seething caldron of ideas, where everything is fizzling and bobbing about in a state of bewildering activity, where partnerships can be joined or loosened in an instant, treadmill routine is unknown, and the unexpected seems the only law.

Just as intelligence has been described as "What you use when you don't know what to do," when no standard response will suffice, so too consciousness is prominently involved when the situation contains ambiguity or demands creative responses, ones that cannot be handled by a decision tree. Many mental activities can be handled by subroutines; consciousness helps to deal with the leftovers (and create new subroutines for next time).

But there is some method to all of this floundering around. The first key concept is that of levels of organization, and the second is that of darwinian approaches to creating and stabilizing new levels.

Layers of middlemen are familiar from everyday economics, and our consciousness might well depend on how many there are. As Derek Bickerton (1990) noted:

[T]he more consciousness one has, the more layers of processing divide one from the world.... Progressive distancing from the external world is simply the price that is paid for knowing anything about the world at all. The deeper and broader [our] consciousness of the world becomes, the more complex the layers of processing necessary to obtain that consciousness.

Although it seems to have played little role so far in our modern investigations of consciousness, a hierarchy of levels of organization is a common concept in the sciences and in familiar technologies.

Levels are best defined by certain functional properties, not anatomy. As an example of four levels, *fleece* is organized into *yarn*, which is woven into *cloth*, which can be arranged into *clothing*. Each of these levels of organization is transiently stable, with ratchetlike mechanisms that prevent backsliding: fabrics are woven, to prevent their disorganization into so much yarn; yarn is spun, to keep it from backsliding into fleece.

A proper level is also characterized by "causal decoupling" from adjacent levels; it's a "study unto itself." For example, you can weave without understanding how to spin yarn (or make clothing). Chemistry is a proper level: Mendeleyev discovered the patterns of the table of elements without knowing anything about the underlying patterns of electron shells (or the overlying patterns of the Krebs Cycle).

Mental life can pyramid a number of levels. Some of the major tasks of early childhood involve discovering four levels of organization in the apparent chaos of the surrounding environment. Infants discover *phonemes* and create standard categories for them; six-month-old Japanese infants can still tell the difference between the English /L/ and /R/ sounds but after another six months of regular exposure to the Japanese phoneme that lies in between them in sound space, the baby will treat the occasional English sounds as mere imperfect versions of the Japanese phoneme. With a set of basic speech sounds, babies start discovering patterns amid strings of phonemes, averaging six new *words* every day. Between 18 and 36 months of age, they start to discover patterns of words called phrases and clauses, rules such as add -*s* for plural, add -*ed* for past tense. After *syntax*, then they go on to discover Aristotle's rule about *narratives* having a beginning, middle, and end (and they then demand bedtime stories with a proper ending).

We take great delight in discovering a hidden pattern, whether in a jigsaw puzzle or a subtle work of art; indeed, we often jump to conclusions, finding patterns where none exist. I've often been fooled by the wind blowing around the house, hearing speech and assuming that a radio has been left on in another room. The delight in finding hidden patterns is part of what reinforces doing science (and, for that matter, astrology).

This operates at both subconscious levels (those poorly heard radio voices) and conscious ones ("seeing" the art). As Heinz Pagels pointed out in his posthumous 1988 book, *The Dreams of Reason*, consciousness likely involves operating at a high level:

Such a series of "causal decouplings" may be extraordinarily complex, intricate beyond our current imaginings. Yet finally what we may arrive at is a theory of the mind and consciousness—a mind so decoupled from its material support systems that it seems to be independent of them.... The biological phenomenon of a self-reflexive consciousness is simply the last of a long and complex series of "causal decouplings" from the world of matter.

But how are new levels created? What stabilizes some of them against unraveling? Jacob Bronowski (1973) preached a concept called *stratified stability*: "The stable units that compose one level or stratum are the raw material for random encounters which produce higher configurations, some of which will chance to be stable...." Randomness can, in the right circumstances, be creative.

And the Darwinian process is particularly good at taking random variations and making new stable configurations, ones that would be highly improbable without the Darwinian algorithm. It can combine concepts such as 'horse' and 'rhinoceros' to yield imaginary concepts such as 'unicorn.' Its intermediate stages ought to look something like your nighttime dreams, with their jumble of people, places, and occasions that don't really fit together very well. When we are awake, we are likely only aware of the highest-quality result.

I've mostly studied Darwinian processes for the higher intellectual functions (Calvin and Ojemann 1994, Calvin 1996ab, Calvin and Bickerton 1999); they are indeed capable of providing a Jamesian type of consciousness, with those sudden shifts and improbable associations, simply as a byproduct of copying competitions with playoffs. Here I am going to propose that Darwinian processes invent novelties, bootstrap their quality through a series of generations of improvements on the time scale of thought and action. This can happen at a number of levels of organization, constructing a "house of cards" that, while it may eventually collapse, can attain some heights in the meantime.

Atop a level of codes for objects, one might have a level of relationships (such as simple sentences), and a level of relations among relationships (analogies) atop that. By temporarily stabilizing the intermediate levels, we are sometimes able to tack on an even higher level. A high-level outcome of such a process is what we might want to call consciousness (though the heights vary throughout the day; the relations level may be impossible until after morning coffee). To demonstrate how the cerebral cortex can operate a Darwinian process, and stabilize a new level, I will briefly introduce the essentials of any Darwinian process and then summarize how neocortex can implement one.

Most disciplines within the natural sciences feature only one level of organization; there are, however, at least a dozen levels of organization within the neurosciences. While this makes for a rich subject, it also leads to much confusion and arguing at cross purposes (consider all the conflict over whether learning is a matter of gene expression, ion channel, synaptic, neuron, or circuit-level alterations).

Each neuron has thousands of synapses, producing currents that summate to produce (via a nonlinear input-output transformation) an impulse train. But only rarely does the activity of a single neuron suffice to produce a perception or trigger an action. Mostly, neurons act as members of committees, what Hebb (1949) called a *cell-assembly*; just as in academia, one individual may function in different committees on different occasions. The best-known examples of hard-to-fathom committees, artificial neural networks (ANNs), lack the bi-level functionality of real neural networks, where both synaptic strength and impulse patterning are important; they usually do not incorporate the important wiring principles seen in cerebral cortex, such as the patterned sideways excitation capable of temporarily organizing large areas of cortex into clones (Calvin 1996b).

Real neural networks are also in the business of producing spatiotemporal patterns, the coordinated sequence of activity that it takes to generate the body movements needed for manipulation and speech. Though spatial-only patterns can serve to categorize learned patterns from the input (as "connection strengths" of ANNs show), spatiotemporal patterns are needed to perform most movements or think about something.

Macrocolumns such as the half-mm ocular dominance columns are the best-known intermediate-sized unit of cortical organization, and I earlier predicted (Calvin 1996b) a half-mm hexagonal-shaped module with characteristic spatiotemporal patterns associated with its synaptic strengths. Its defining characteristic is that it can make copies of its spatiotemporal pattern (rather like a little tune, were the cells of the hexagon to be mapped onto a musical scale), cloning it into adjacent patches of cortex. This can temporarily create a hexagonal mosaic of some centimeters square (rather like a plainchant choir, all singing the same melody). Because several mosaics may partially overlap when they encounter one another, composite codes may be created (and harmonylike issues arise), generating arbitrary concepts such as unicorns.

Not only may a hexagon's melody represent an object, but it can code for an action, a relationship, an analogy—even a structured sentence with phrases and clauses. A hexagonal mosaic is expansionistic, rather like a plainchant choir that recruits additional "lay" members in the manner of the expert choir singing the "Hallelujah Chorus" and recruiting the audience. Any level of organization can have a code and exhibit competition for territory.

Though I originally investigated redundant codes because of their importance for precision timing, much needed for accurate throwing (Calvin 1983), another important consequence of cloning and competition for territory is that it can implement a

Darwinian process, our finest example of how quality can be recursively bootstrapped. However, not everything called "Darwinian" has the possibility of recursion.

Simple carving and sorting processes show selective survival at work, for example, beaches that progress from shingle to pebble to sand, all because heavier objects are not carried as far by flowing water. Similarly, one sees selection at work in processes that try a lot, then cull, then try some more, for example, leaves may bud all over the tree, but only the ones on the sunny side survive a drought. Neural connections also have enormous sprouting early in life, then culling during childhood to create the adult patterns, for example, there is a 70 percent drop in the axon count of monkey corpus callosum and a reduction of 30 to 50 percent in the number of synapses per neocortical neuron before maturity. Though we currently lack the techniques to measure it, there is likely a certain amount of weekly turnover: new synapses that are formed "on spec" but culled if they fail to "establish themselves."

Such selection, while very important in wiring up and operating the brain, is not the Darwinian process that so impresses us from the accomplishments of species evolution and the immune response. So far as I can see (Calvin 1996b, 1997), there are six essential ingredients:

1. There's a pattern (genes, memes).

2. The pattern is copied (indeed, what can be semi-reliably copied tends to define the relevant pattern).

3. Variant patterns arise (via copying errors, or recombinations).

4. Populations of some variants compete for a workspace, e.g., bluegrass and crab-grass compete for my back yard.

5. There is a multifaceted environment that makes some variants more common (how often you cut, fertilize, water—this is what Darwin called "natural selection").

6. The more successful variants are the most frequent center for further variants (Darwin's inheritance principle).

Even nonbiological processes may implement the six essentials, for example, storytelling (Calvin 1997) as a basis for history. But if a process lacks any one of the six, it runs out of steam. Neural sprouting and pruning may create a pattern, but it doesn't clone itself to create populations that compete for territory, and so forth. Cloning and competition, if it lacks Darwin's feature of centering the variants of the next generation on the more successful of the current generation, may just wander endlessly. It is unfortunate that Darwin named his theory for just one element of the six, because "natural selection" has misled many people into assuming that variation

(#2) plus selection (#5) buys you the power of evolution—but that recursive boot-strapping of quality that we find so impressive when new levels of organization are discovered, likely requires all six.

There are a number of other things that, while not essential to the Darwinian algorithm in the strict sense, may stabilize it or speed it up, making them particularly important for any Darwinian process involved in thought and action. We often suffer from what the French call *avoir l'esprit de l'escalier*—finally thinking of a witty reply, but only after leaving the party. There are fleeting "windows of opportunity" in more important kinds of behavior, too, whether prey or predator. So we might well expect a brain to find these five additional features of particular importance as well:

7. Stagnation may occur if variants cannot effectively escape a "well" and always backslide—but that can also buy you stabilization.

8. Systematic recombination, e.g., sex doesn't leave variability to chance.

9. Fluctuating climate (more severe selection, more frequent culling—and therefore more frequent opportunities when the climate improves again). Just as in stochastic resonance, noise helps to rapidly discover new niches.

10. Patchy subdivisions (island biogeography promotes inbreeding; also, a higher percentage live out on the habitat's margins where making a living is, well, *marginal*). Fragment-then-reunite sequences serve to "pump" the central percentages of those variants capable of making a living on the margins.

11. Emptied niches to refill (with no competition for a few generations, rare variants get a chance to reproduce—and they may have what it takes to survive the next crunch).

While space does not allow me to summarize the cortical circuitry that makes the hexagonal competitions possible (Calvin 1996ab), it does exhibit all six Darwinian essentials:

1. There's a *pattern* (that spatiotemporal action pattern which fits into a 0.5 mm hexagon).

2. The pattern is *copied* (recurrent excitation with express-trainlike gaps produces mutual connections that entrain and then recruit).

3. *Variant* patterns arise (when hexagons escape conforming neighbors, or when patterns overlap).

4. Populations (hexagonal mosaics) of some variants *compete* for a workspace (there are "dueling choirs" in association cortex).

5. There is a multifaceted *environment* that makes some variants more common (sensory inputs and memorized resonances bias, which pattern succeeds).

6. The more successful variants are the most frequent center for further variants (the bigger a territory, the more edge it has—and thus more opportunities to escape the crystal-like conformity of central regions), giving rise to *inheritance*.

Success and quality are biased by the current sensory inputs and other aspects of the real-time environment, by the synaptic connectivity that has memorized the salient features of prior environments via learning experiences, and by the inborn patterning of cortical connections.

Superficial neocortical circuitry also has all of the four optional catalysts (more later), and it produces in advance the spatiotemporal patterns that are needed for converting thought into action. So copying competitions of neocortex seem to have many appropriate ingredients for portraying the elements of an active mental life— and the dynamics to quickly get from one mental state to a successor.

In this view, the subconscious immediately finds a home. There are many competitions running simultaneously, each with a local winner constituting a subconscious concept or thought (though most are of that low incoherent quality associated with dreams). Each winner can, via corticocortical connections, enter into competitions with more distant local winners. Thus one can have playoff competitions, for temporarily becoming the melody with the biggest choir (and perhaps this is what we'd report as the content of our consciousness if asked, and if we could find means of expressing the concept). Winning doesn't last for very long, habituation being what it is. The content of consciousness shifts unpredictably when a concept choir from a different branch of the playoff tree finally gains the top slot.

There is no "central place" for this kind of consciousness, in agreement with the neurology about what strokes can and cannot eliminate. You'd expect the winner to shift around to a series of places in both left and right brain, in front and rear. But they're all in neocortex in this view, simply because subcortical structures and old-fashioned versions of cortex such as hippocampus aren't known to have the cloning circuitry needed for the copying competitions. So far, that's a feature of the superficial layers of neocortex in many Brodmann areas, and in many mammalian species (rats are the notable exception).

Some of these competitions involve codes (i.e., spatiotemporal firing patterns) that represent words, others relationships at various possible levels. It is tempting to treat consciousness as the current highest level of organization, not simply the one with the most numerous choir. When you first contemplate the toothpaste in the morning, the

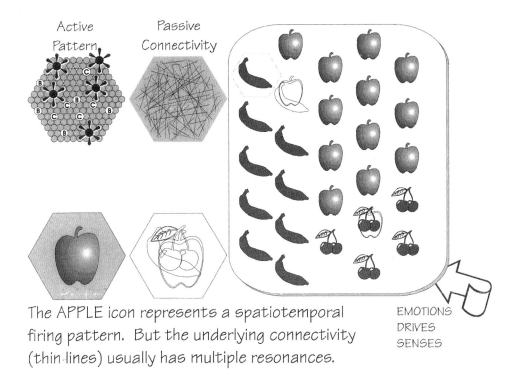

The APPLE icon represents a spatiotemporal firing pattern. But the underlying connectivity (thin lines) usually has multiple resonances.

EMOTIONS
DRIVES
SENSES

Figure 25.1
Any sensory object (say, an apple) activates a number of feature detectors, each of which may form a tri-angular array. Hundreds of different ones are possible; the largest cortical area with one, and only one, member of each triangular array is a hexagon about 0.5 mm across. The spatiotemporal pattern within that hexagon can be considered a cerebral code for apple—perhaps not the most elementary code, but one capable of being copied and superimposed on other codes to form combination codes. Here an apple icon (lower left) is used as a stand-in for the spatiotemporal pattern (upper left). Looking down on the cortex might reveal a territory of apple clones, another of banana or cherry clones, all competing for territory in association cortex. Their success depends not only on sensory inputs and drives, but on specific resonances in the synaptic connectivity of the neural networks; many hexagons will have multiple resonances (lower middle), just as the spinal cord's connectivity simultaneously supports a number of spatiotemporal patterns called the gaits of locomotion. Hexagonal codes can also serve as cortical codes for complex movements.

level of consciousness might not be very high, operating merely at the level of objects or simple actions, barely managing to use the level of relationships. The relations between relationships level (analogies) may require a double espresso. Poets, of course, have to compare metaphors, which requires a series of stage-setting preliminaries to construct and stabilize this ephemeral house of cards. Understanding such staging and scaffolding might someday allow us to spend more time at more abstract levels— or even invent new levels (one can almost imagine meta-poets).

Speed of operation likely involves cerebral versions of the four catalysts seen in more traditional evolutionary media. An animal species, to take a familiar example, has a range; imagine one irregular area, with much mobility and therefore mixing between center and periphery. But this well-mixed population breaks up into a number of fragments as the climate worsens and the population numbers decline. The sub-populations inbreed because there's nothing to eat in between subpopulations to support a journey; effectively, there are now many "islands" where there used to be a single "continent." And a higher percentage of individuals live near the edge of a subpopulation where conditions are marginal for making a living.

If a subpopulation is sufficiently small, it will be atypical simply because of the "luck of the draw" (even if a jury pool is racially balanced, an individual jury drawn from it may be very lopsided). Things that depend on a critical mass of some infrequent characteristic (reciprocal altruism, for example; see Calvin and Bickerton 1999) may finally get a chance, simply because of this random fragmentation of the larger population.

When climate later improves, some of these biased subpopulations may get a major chance to repopulate an abandoned territory, and so increase their percentage in the overall metapopulation. So pervasive fluctuations of any major resource have effects on evolution that go far beyond the caricature of "more severe selection." Furthermore, a series of population bottlenecks with subsequent re-expansion may occur because climate episodes repeat, allowing formerly rare variants to be pumped up until they are the majority type.

We might expect the brain's "weather" (for which EEG rhythms might be an indicator) to do similar things to a neocortical Darwinian process. But with the ease of recombination seen where hexagonal mosaics overlap, the "species tree" is likely to look more like a web; binary trees can be maintained only if hybrids are typically sterile. And, in the cortex, there are all of the interrelationships between levels of organization (that hexagonal code can represent anything from a category to a metaphor) to consider. One level's competition could serve to bias the operation of another. Different levels might sometimes operate on different time scales. For example, a slow Darwinian competition ("agenda") could bias the faster competitions implementing thought and action—perhaps simply by varying the rate and extent of excitability fluctuations (furthermore, randomness is not really a requirement; fluctuations could easily average two little steps left for every big step right).

Backsliding needs to be slowed if new levels of organization are to maintain themselves. Memories are one way; as we know from semiotics and linguistics, symbols can be quite arbitrary and so even inadequate metaphors can be saved, enabling the copying competition to be restarted from some advanced position rather than starting from scratch each time. Ratchets may develop, simply because of the interaction of different time scales.

A neocortical Darwinian regime may also have periods of "monoculture" where a particularly widespread mosaic develops featuring a uniform spatiotemporal firing pattern. In the musical-mapping analogy, this would correspond to a large plainchant choir. If this is maintained for some tens of minutes, it will prevent antecedent patterns from renewing their fading synaptic strengths (recalling something from short-term memory likely serves to restart the clock). Such a monoculture period might serve to allow for fresh starts afterward, with novel spatiotemporal patterns less likely to be captured by the resonances of the antecedent thoughts. Sleep may be one example; meditation with a meaningless mantra, long enough for temporarily enhanced synaptic strengths to fade, might similarly help to "clear the mind."

Though our techniques are improving, no one has yet been able to look down on the cerebral cortex and see what Charles Sherrington predicted sixty years ago in his book, *Man on his Nature*:

The brain is waking and with it the mind is returning. It is as if the Milky Way entered upon some cosmic dance. Swiftly the [cortex] becomes an enchanted loom where millions of flashing shuttles weave a dissolving pattern, always a meaningful pattern though never an abiding one; a shifting harmony of subpatterns.... Dissolving pattern after dissolving pattern will, the long day through, without remission melt into and succeed each other....

Nor have we been able to see those cell-assemblies that Donald Hebb imagined fifty years ago in *The Organization of Behavior*. We only invented the microelectrode techniques, needed to study one cortical neuron at a time, about forty years ago and it is still a feat to study a dozen individual neurons at the same time. The picture that I have painted here predicts much more detail about those subpatterns (my hexagonal spatiotemporal pattern is essentially a candidate for the minimal cell-assembly that has one of everything but no redundancy), yet it too is beyond the bounds of what the microelectrode and imaging technologies can currently deliver.

Fortunately, we have learned a great deal about the evolutionary process in the 160 years since Darwin's discovery. When one sees the patterned cortical circuitry in the neuroanatomy, and combines it with what we currently know of the neuro-physiology of neurons and synapses (and particularly the emergent properties of mutually exciting oscillators), we can at least say that similar dynamics ought to apply in cortical "climates" and "landscapes," that island biogeography ought to operate there just as well as it operates in Hawaii, that repeated bottlenecks could operate in minutes as well as in millennia.

The neocortex has what it takes to run Darwin's recursive bootstrap for quality—and that it helps explain a great deal about how higher intellectual functions could operate. In particular, it gives us a way of thinking about consciousness that is free of dualism and miraculous leaps across a dozen levels of organization from quantum mechanics to consciousness. It is compatible both with the observed cortical local-ization of function and with the apparent lack of a location for consciousness.

Is that all consciousness really is, just the current winner of a widespread copying competition in neocortex, biased by subcortical and sensory influences and the mem-ories of past episodes? It certainly seems to be a good default explanation, the one against which you test your candidates for "something more." While I see no reason to postulate "higher" controlling processes of greater intelligence, I would caution that we understand very little as yet about levels. Or how a Darwinian success can be converted into a "subroutine" that obviates the copying competition after enough experience. But increasingly, consciousness is no longer a mystery (Dennett 1991), something that we simply don't know how to think about—in the same way that the boundary between the living and the nonliving used to be a mystery, or the origin of the universe used to be a mystery. We can now imagine what the brain is doing with those express-train connections of neocortex. For those with enough acquaintance with biology to be able to think in population terms (Mayr 1994), there is now a rich evolutionary carryover that provides a framework for further investigation.

References

Bickerton, D. 1990. *Language and Species*. University of Chicago Press.

Bronowski, J. 1973. *The Ascent of Man*. Little, Brown, pp. 348–349.

Calvin, W. H. 1983. A stone's throw and its launch window: timing precision and its implications for lan-guage and hominid brains. *Journal of Theoretical Biology* 104:121–135.

Calvin, W. H. 1996a. *How Brains Think: Evolving Intelligence, Then and Now*. Basic Books.

Calvin, W. H. 1996b. *The Cerebral Code: Thinking a Thought in the Mosaics of the Mind*. MIT Press, at http://faculty-washington.edu/wcalvin/6k9.

Calvin, W. H. 1997. The Six Essentials? Minimal Requirements for the Darwinian Bootstrapping of Quality. *Journal of Memetics*—Evolutionary Models of Information Transmission, 1, at http://www.fmb.mmu. ac.uk/jom-emit/1997/vol1/calvin_wh.html

Calvin, W. H. 1998. Competing for consciousness. *Journal of Consciousness Studies* 5:389–404.

Calvin, W. H., and Bickerton, D. 1999. *Lingua ex machina: Reconciling Darwin and Chomsky with the Human Brain*. MIT Press, forthcoming.

Calvin, W. H., and Ojemann, G. A. 1994. *Conversations with Neil's Brain: The Neural Nature of Thought and Language*. Addison-Wesley.

Dennett, D. C. 1991. *Consciousness Explained*. Little, Brown.

Hebb, D. O. 1949. *The Organization of Behavior*. McGraw-Hill.

James, W. 1880. Great men, great thoughts, and the environment. *The Atlantic Monthly* 46(276):441–459.

Mayr, E. 1994. Population thinking and neuronal selection: metaphors or concepts? In *Selectionism and the Brain*, ed. Olaf Sporns and Giulio Tonini. Academic Press, pp. 27–34.

Pagels, H. 1988. *The Dreams of Reason* (Simon & Schuster).

Sherrington, C. 1940. Man on his Nature, the Gifford Lectures, Edinburgh, 1937–1938 (Cambridge University Press), p. 178.

VII PHYSICAL REALITY AND CONSCIOUSNESS—INTRODUCTION

Stuart R. Hameroff

What is the reality—space and time—in which we find ourselves? Two types of answers to this question have gone back and forth since ancient Greece. Democritus claimed that empty space was an absolute void, whereas Aristotle suggested some type of background pattern or "plenum." In the nineteenth century Maxwell proposed a "luminiferous ether" to explain the propagation of electromagnetic waves through a vacuum, however the Michelson-Morley experiment seemed to disprove such a concept and the conventional wisdom reverted to an absolute void. Einstein's special relativity with its nonpreferential frames of reference upheld the absolute void context, but Einstein's general relativity with 4-dimensional spacetime curvature swung the pendulum back toward an underlying "plenum," or pattern in basic reality—the spacetime metric. Since then various descriptions of a fundamental quantum sea, vacuum, foam or spin network have been used to describe underlying spacetime geometry. Is this relevant to the understanding of consciousness? Could phenomenological inner space be related to the nature of space everywhere? Historically, panpsychist, pan-experiential and pan-protopsychist views suggest that consciousness, or its raw undifferentiated precursors, are fundamental to the universe (somewhat like mass, spin or charge) accessed by brain processes. If so, qualia may be found at basic levels of reality at which quantum theory holds sway. The chapters in this section address these issues.

Panpsychist, pan-experiential and pan-protopsychist views imply not only that conscious qualia are fundamental, but that somehow the living state—the condition of being alive—is also fundamental. In "What does quantum mechanics imply about the nature of the universe?" physicist Shimon Malin asks the questions: "Is the universe alive?" Conventional physics unavoidably answers "no." Malin explains how the philosophical approach of Alfred North Whitehead gives a qualified "yes." Whitehead (e.g., 1929) perceived the universe as a process of events, at least some of which are imbued with a mental quality ("throbs, or occasions of experience"). Malin draws parallels between Whitehead's view and modern quantum theory, a connection also developed by Abner Shimony (1993). The connection begins a bridge between physics and philosophy of mind, what Chalmers (1996) calls a "psychophysical law."

The psychophysical bridge is fortified in the following chapter, "Quantum monadology." Kunio Yasue begins by reviewing three views of Roger Penrose that have angered conventional scientists and philosophers. The first such view is Penrose's (1989, 1994) arguments regarding the need for noncomputability in conscious thought. Viewing this dispute as irreconcilable, Yasue moves to a second claim of Penrose that macroscopic quantum states exist in the brain. Critics often dismiss this notion out of hand because of the apparent problem of thermal noise causing decoherence. Accordingly technological quantum devices generally involve near-absolute zero temperature to avoid thermal noise and decoherence (though "NMR quantum computing" occurs at room temperature). Yasue (referring to earlier work with Mari Jibu) describes how quantum field theory can enable macroscopic quantum states at physiological temperature. Moreover, he argues, these quantum field effects address both the famous "hard problem" of conscious experience, or qualia, and Penrose's third unpopular claim of a Platonic realm. Yasue makes his psychophysical connection through the ideas of Whitehead's predecessor Gottfried Leibniz who saw the fundamental elements of the world as "monads." Yasue elaborates on the ideas of Nakagomi who put Leibniz's nineteenth-century monads in the context of modern quantum field theory to arrive at "quantum monadology." This synthesis is indicative of a number of approaches linking philosophy with physics at the fundamental level of reality.

In the third chapter in this section "The interface in a mixed quantum/classical model of brain function" Scott Hagan and Masayuki Hirafuji elaborate on quantum field theory in relation to consciousness. They relate differing mental states with differing condensates of the underlying quantum vacuum, and deal further with the thorny issue of how seemingly delicate quantum events can occur in seemingly noisy biological systems. Hagan and Hirafuji describe a necessary 2-way feedback: 1) quantum signals can influence meso-scale neural function, and 2) some level of neural information can translate into quantum encoding. Surveying available biomolecular structures and biophysical mechanisms Hagan and Hirafuji build their psychophysical bridge between ordered dipoles (e.g., in microtubules) and differing condensates of the quantum vacuum.

The chapters in this section reflect the physics of reality meeting the philosophy of mind. Another piece of the puzzle may be information theory, coming to grips with the possibilities of quantum computation. Unlike classical computers in which information is stored as binary bits of either 1 or 0, in quantum computers information can exist in quantum superpositioned "qubits" of both 1 AND 0 that may interact in quantum computation and reduce, or "collapse" to classical, definite states as the output of the computation. As quantum technology arrives as the vanguard of computation, comparisons between the conscious mind and the quantum computer will be inevitable. As quantum computation involves reality itself, the chapters in this section illustrate why such comparisons may have validity.

References

Chalmers, D. J. 1996. *The Conscious Mind—In Search of a Fundamental Theory*. New York: Oxford University Press.

Penrose, R. 1989. *The Emperor's New Mind*. New York: Oxford University Press.

Penrose, R. 1994. *Shadows of the Mind*. New York: Oxford University Press.

Shimony, A. 1993. *Search for a Naturalistic World View*. Vol. 2. *Natural Science and Metaphysics*. Cambridge: Cambridge University Press.

Whitehead, A. N. 1929. *Process and Reality*. New York: Macmillan.

26 What Does Quantum Mechanics Imply about the Nature of the Universe?

Shimon Malin

The Present Paradigm Shift in Historical Perspective

The Copernican revolution destroyed the Medieval paradigm about reality, the paradigm that was so beautifully encapsulated in Dante's *Divine Comedy*. It did not provide Western civilization, however, with an alternative world view. The new paradigm it provided was limited to astronomy. Following Copernicus, for over 100 years Western civilization was devoid of a comprehensive paradigm. The new comprehensive paradigm emerged as a result of advances in physics. It was the Newtonian "clockwork universe."

Our situation at present is similar to the situation that prevailed between Copernicus and Newton in this respect: The theories of relativity and quantum mechanics, especially quantum mechanics, destroyed the prevailing world view (the Newtonian "clockwork universe") without providing us with an alternative comprehensive paradigm. The search for the new paradigm is, in fact, an important aspect of what consciousness studies is about. Will physics come once again to the rescue and provide us with the paradigm we are seeking?

The Field of Inquiry

Let us narrow down the field of inquiry to a more precise question. Although we do not have a comprehensive paradigm, some of its characteristics begin to emerge. These include a movement away from fragmentation and toward holism, away from a mechanical universe and toward an alive one. Let us concentrate, then, on the following question: Does quantum mechanics support the idea that the universe and its constituents, including the so-called "inanimate matter," are alive?

The Principle of Objectivation

The obvious answer to this question is "No. Quantum mechanics does not support the idea that the universe is alive." The reason for this is the following: Quantum mechanics, like the rest of our science, is based on what Erwin Schrödinger called "the Principle of Objectivation." And here it is, in Schrödinger's own words:

By this [i.e., by the principle of objectivation] I mean the thing that is also frequently called the "hypothesis of the real world" around us. I maintain that it amounts to a certain simplification which we adopt in order to master the infinitely intricate problem of nature. Without being aware of it and without being rigorously systematic about it, we exclude the Subject of Cognizance from the domain of nature that we endeavor to understand. We step with our own person back into the part of an onlooker who does not belong to the world, which by this very procedure becomes an objective world.[1]

Since quantum mechanics, like the other branches of physics, obeys the principle of objectivation, it is set up to treat the subjects of its inquiry as lifeless objects. If they are, in fact, alive, their aliveness will not show up under scientific scrutiny, because the alive, or subjective, or experiential aspect was excluded from the inquiry right from the start.

Whitehead's "Process Philosophy"

The negative answer to the question, "Does quantum mechanics support the idea that the universe and its constituents are alive?" is not, however, the whole story. There is a sense in which the answer to this question is positive. To establish this sense we need to make a detour into Alfred North Whitehead's "process philosophy."

Whitehead developed his philosophical system at the same time that Heisenberg, Schrödinger and Co. discovered quantum mechanics. Significantly, Whitehead was unaware of this discovery.

It is, of course, out of the question to present Whitehead's philosophy is a few minutes. If you are interested, read his books (*Science in the Modern World*[2] is an accessible introduction, *Process and Reality*[3] is a much less accessible full statement). Here I wish to present just one of Whitehead's key ideas. According to Whitehead, the fundamental building blocks of the universe, the "atoms of reality," are not enduring objects, but "throbs of experience," which he also calls "actual entities."

Here are some of the characteristics of these "throbs of experience":

1. They are neither purely subjects, nor purely objects; they have both subjective and objective characteristics.

2. They endure only a short time; they flash in and out of existence in spacetime. The apparent existence of enduring objects is due to many collections of actual entities coming one after another in quick succession, like frames in a movie.

3. Each actual entity is a nexus of relationships with all the other actual entities.

4. An actual entity is a process of its own self creation.

5. This self-creation involves accommodating and integrating within itself (comprehending or "prehending" in Whitehead's terminology) all the previous actual entities

as "settled facts" that cannot be changed, and all future actual entities as potentialities. This process of self-creation involves a sequence of phases, which are delineated and analyzed in detail in *Process and Reality*.

An example: Listening to an orchestra playing a symphony involves, at each moment, accommodating the sounds produced by the orchestra. This accommodation depends, in turn, on many collections of past actual entities, such as previous knowledge and training in music, associations with the symphony, etc. Notice that at each instant there is one experience.

6. The end product of the process is one new "throb of experience." The fundamental building blocks of the universe are, then elementary experiences. We do not live in "a universe of objects," but in "a universe of experience."

7. Subjectively, that is, for itself, an actual entity is a throb of experience. The end of the process of self-creation is called "the satisfaction of the actual entity." Its subjective existence is momentary. Objectively, that is, for other, future actual entities, it is a "settled fact": The fact that it did happen cannot be erased. As the Whitehead scholar V. Lowe put it, "The end of... [its] private life—its "perishing"—is the beginning of its public career."[4]

The "Atoms of Reality" according to Quantum Mechanics

According to Heisenberg's mainstream interpretation of quantum mechanics, a quantum system, such as an electron, when isolated, does not exist as an actual "thing." It exists as a "field of potentialities." Potentialities for what? For having certain characteristics, such as certain values of position and/or velocity, if measured. Only a process of measurement, however, brings it into actual (as opposed to potential) existence. When measured, it appears in spacetime as an "elementary quantum event." Its actual existence as an "elementary quantum event" is of short duration. Once the measurement is over, it resorts once again to having only potential existence. According to quantum mechanics, these "elementary quantum events" are the "atoms of reality."

So, Does Quantum Mechanics Support the Idea That the Universe Is Alive?

Do "elementary quantum events" seem similar to Whitehead's "actual entities"? They do indeed. A detailed analysis of these two concepts reveals an amazing correspondence.[5] There is, however, this major difference: Actual entities are "throbs of experience," that is, units of life; elementary quantum events, however, are objective events, devoid of life.

But this is to be expected. As we said before, if there is an alive aspect to entities, there is no way for it to show up in the context of physics, because physics is subject to the principle of objectivation. In view of this fact, it is highly significant that *the "atoms of reality" according to physics come as close as lifeless entities can come to Whitehead's "atoms of reality," which are elements of life.* In this sense the answer to the question, "Does quantum mechanics support the idea that the universe is alive?" is "Yes."

Conclusion

Putting the "yes" and the "no" together, we can formulate the following response to our question: Since quantum mechanics is subject to the principle of objectivation, it treats its subject-matter as inanimate. However, the fact that its "atoms of reality" get as close as objective events can get to Whitehead's "throbs of experience" can be taken as a broad hint that once Western science finds a way to transcend the principle of objectivation, it will discover an alive universe.

Notes

1. Schrödinger, E. 1992. *What Is Life?* with *Mind and Matter* and *Autobiographical Sketches*, Cambridge University Press, p. 118.

2. Whitehead, A. N. 1953. *Science and the Modern World*, The Free Press, New York.

3. Whitehead, A. N. 1978. *Process and Reality*, corrected edition, ed. D. R. Griffin and D. W. Sherburne, The Free Press, New York.

4. Lowe, V. 1951. Introduction to Alfred North Whitehead, in *Classic American Philosophers*, ed. M. H. Fisch, Appelton-Century-Croft, New York, p. 404.

5. Burgers, J. M. (*Reviews of Modern Physics*, 35:145, 1963) was the first to point out that Whitehead's "process philosophy" is uniquely suited to accommodate the ontological and epistemological implications of quantum mechanics. The relationship between Whitehead's philosophy and quantum mechanics was later investigated by A. Shimony (see his paper in *Boston Studies in the Philosophy of Science*, vol. 2, edited by S. Cohen and M. W. Wartofsky, Humanities Press, New York, 1968) H. Stapp (*Foundations of Physics*, 9:1 (1979) and 12:363 (1982) and others, including myself. See my paper in *Foundations of Physics*, 18:1035 (1988) for more references.

27 Quantum Monadology

Kunio Yasue

Penrose's Platonic stance

Roger Penrose has taken unusual and, in some circles, unpopular and disputed positions in relation to the question of consciousness. Within physics the disputes are reminiscent of long-standing arguments regarding the role of the conscious observer taken by John von Neumann and Eugene Wigner, but the current Penrose-generated disagreement seems even more intense.

Reasons for strenuous opposition from computer scientists, philosophers and some mathematicians to Penrose's view seem clear. He claims first of all that our understanding of the characteristic features of natural numbers comes not from computational rules but through contact with a Platonic world. He arrives at this conclusion by complete use of Gödel's theorem to argue for noncomputational effects in human understanding (eliciting strong criticism from many computer scientists investigating artificial intelligence and artificial life). Penrose and some other mathematicians believe that truly beautiful findings come only after a "visit" to the Platonic world of mathematical reality. However it may be that only a select few mathematicians and theoretical physicists are able to have such a highly irregular experience as visiting the Platonic world. A natural consequence of this might be that most mathematicians and physicists cannot understand Penrose's Platonic position (Penrose 1989, 1994). Despite the soundness of his writings, opponents attack him by forcing a conventional materialistic world view of physical reality.

According to Penrose, Gödel's theorem implies that not only mathematical understanding but also human musical, artistic, and aesthetic creativity and appreciation come from contact with the Platonic world of reality. The conventional and common experience of many scientists implies that human creative power emerges from highly sophisticated but certainly materialistic processes taking place in brain tissue. Unable to follow Penrose's experience in mathematical discovery, they disregard his Platonic world view and focus counter arguments against his claim that consciousness is of noncomputational nature as suggested by Gödel's argument. The ghost of the dispute between Turing and Gödel has thus re-emerged.

Of course, Gödel's argument may imply that this dispute cannot be resolved by a sequence of exchanges of seemingly correct discussions. Therefore, it may be hopeless to determine whether consciousness is of noncomputational or computational nature. Therefore I will concentrate my contribution on Penrose's second claim, which irritates not computer scientists, philosophers and mathematicians, but physicists and neurobiologists.

Quantum Coherence

Penrose's second claim is a potential solution to the "binding problem" of how disparate features are bound into unitary mental objects: "Coordination of sole mind can be realized by a certain quantum coherence extended over the whole brain." This potential solution to the binding problem came secondary to Penrose's claim that certain quantum mechanical systems occur inside and among neurons. His original motivation for proposing quantum coherence was to enable noncomputational phenomena such as objective reduction in the brain, thought necessary to interface to the Platonic world. Penrose concluded that objective reduction, or self-collapse of a superposed quantum state by a quantum gravity mechanism could be the only fundamental process in physics of a noncomputational, nondeterministic nature. This led to further suggestions with Stuart Hameroff that objective reduction may be occurring in microtubules inside the brain's neurons.

For Penrose's objective reduction to occur, a critical amount of mass must maintain an entangled superposition (separation from itself) for a critical time. In the brain the necessary entanglement (which could also support quantum computation) must cover a macroscopic volume and would essentially solve the binding problem as well. A superposed state of a quantum system of many degrees of freedom is known to result in a nonlocal interconnection over a long distance, and it was natural that Penrose and his supporters interpreted this quantum nonlocal interconnection (calling it quantum coherence) as the key to reaching brain-wide objective reduction and solve the binding problem. Furthermore, recent interests in quantum information and quantum computing has increased the potential utility of macroscopic quantum state/quantum coherence in future technological devices.

As long as quantum coherence is maintained, that is, as long as the quantum system in question is kept in a superposed quantum state, time development of the quantum state is given in a deterministic but parallel way, thus providing superparallel computing called quantum computing. However, there is a delicate point in the use of such a quantum computer in that the final result of quantum computation cannot be read in a deterministic way but only in an indeterministic way thanks to the quantum reduction. Reduction incorporates either randomness (in the case of environmental decoherence) or noncomputability (according to Penrose, if the reduction is a self-collapse due to his quantum gravity mechanism). Pragmatic scientists have begun to do quantum computation with clever techniques to perform the same quantum computation several times, gathering only the seemingly correct results and putting unexpected results into the trash. By so doing, quantum computing gives an exponentially fast parallel computing architecture with great utility, expected to be the next generation of electronic computers.

Yes, it's a computer. But remember Penrose's first claim: It's a computer because it dumped all the potential noncomputational results realized by the quantum reduction into the trash. Then, where is the potential manifestation of consciousness? Absolutely, it's in the trash. (So if you want to make your billion dollar quantum computer conscious, upset the trash. If not, keep the trash classified. Then, the truth will not be out there.)

Penrose's second claim of brain-wide macroscopic quantum states is very appealing. However use of the concept of quantum coherence—maintenance of the superposed quantum state as a potential solution to the binding problem—is troublesome. Many physicists are uneasy about the stability and maintenance of the superposed quantum state in the highly interactive physical environment of the brain at body temperature. Applying standard quantum statistical mechanics to the microscopic constituents of brain cells, it would seem that superposed quantum states would all disintegrate into mixed quantum states, with no chance for quantum coherence extending over macroscopic regions of brain tissue.

Penrose refers to Fröhlich's theory of coherent quantum vibrations of biomolecules in living cells to provide a possibility of high temperature superconducting phenomena in the brain. At first glance the network of Fröhlich's coherent quantum vibrations may extend the quantum coherence over a considerable number of brain cells or the whole brain, but the chance of realizing such a quantum coherence highly dependent on underlying molecular structures seems extremely small.

Some advocates of a quantum approach claim that so-called Bose-Einstein condensation of some quanta of the material constituents of the brain may take place at body temperature without specifying the constituents and without experimental evidence. This is unacceptable from the point of view of modern physics. The critical temperature T_c is the limiting temperature below which the condensation of the Bose quanta (i.e., boson condensation) can be maintained. The standard calculation gives:

$$T_c \sim m^{-1}$$

The critical temperature is inversely proportional to the mass m of the Bose quantum (i.e., boson) taking part in the boson condensation. Typical superconducting phenomena due to boson condensation of pairs of electrons (i.e., Cooper pairs) in a metal have extremely low critical temperatures. Even for the very small mass of the Cooper pair of electrons, we have a low critical temperature. For other constituent quanta of matter far heavier than the electron, we have even lower critical temperatures, thus eliminating the possibility of body temperature Bose-Einstein condensation in brain tissue.

So referring back to Penrose's "Coordination of sole mind can be realized by a certain quantum coherence extended over the whole brain" we can see two apparent defects: 1) the concept of quantum coherence carried by the superposed quantum state cannot be maintained in brain matter, 2) the concept of quantum coherence carried by the so-called Bose-Einstein condensation of constituent quanta in brain tissue cannot be realized at body temperature. Can there be large scale quantum coherence in the brain?

Quantum Field Theory

For brain-wide quantum states we must progress from quantum mechanics, and go one step further into modern quantum field theory (QFT)—the most fundamental theory of physics at both the microscopic scale and the macroscopic scale. QFT was systematized by a Japanese physicist Umezawa who lived lifelong in Italy, the United States and Canada. Umezawa sowed the seeds of quantum field theoretical methods in Europe and North America after Yukawa received his Nobel prize for the first use of quantum field theory (originally discovered by Heisenberg and Pauli) to predict the existence of a new elementary particle called today a *meson*. Beginning in the 1960s Umezawa developed the theoretical framework of quantum field theory to describe fundamental processes in macroscopic living matter with Italian colleagues. Thus today there are many brilliant Italian physicists in this field of research including Giuseppe Vitiello and Emilio Del Giudice.

In the 1970s Umezawa developed a standard field theoretical model of memory mechanism in the brain with the help of another Japanese physicist Takahashi, famous for the Ward-Takahashi identity, which is the central fundamental equation of modern quantum field theory (Takahashi and Umezawa 1978, 1979). In the 1990s this Umezawa-Takahashi model has been formalized by Mari Jibu and her colleagues (Jibu et al. 1994, Jibu and Yasue 1995, Jibu, Pribram, and Yasue 1996) into a concrete theory related to consciousness called quantum brain dynamics. Italian colleagues of Umezawa also developed a general quantum field theoretical framework to describe fundamental processes of biological cells called quantum biodynamics (Del Giudice et al. 1983, Del Giudice, Preparata, and Vitiello 1988).

Quantum field theory (QFT) applied to the brain (quantum brain dynamics—QBD) may back up Roger Penrose's second claim of a unitary brain-wide quantum state. A sophisticated but concrete version of quantum brain dynamics has been developed by Charles Enz (1997), the last coworker of Wolfgang Pauli and my supervisor in Switzerland.

Quantum Brain Dynamics

Let us sketch the quantum field theoretical (QFT) approach to the brain and consciousness (i.e., quantum brain dynamics—QBD) along lines taken by Umezawa, Takahashi, Vitiello, Del Giudice, Enz, and Jibu. From physicists' eyes, the brain confined within the cranium is a coupled matter-radiation system composed of many atomic constituents and their radiation field, specifically the electromagnetic field. Quantum field theory of electromagnetic field tells us that matter made of atomic constituents can be described as the spatial distribution of quantum electric dipoles in a spatial region, that is, a quantum electric dipole field. Then we see the brain as a quantum electric dipole field coupled with electromagnetic field!

Of course biologists see the brain as a structured mass of brain cells manifesting sophisticated but systematized biomolecular architectures. They see membranes, proteins, cytoskeletons, nuclei, organelles, water, ions, glia, and so on. Here I am saying the brain is a quantum electric dipole field and biologists are wondering: Where are biomolecular structures? Do not worry. They are in the quantum electric dipole field, represented by singularities, topological defects, local symmetries and localizations of the field. Biomolecular architecture provides geometric objects emerging in the quantum electric dipole field. Actual brain tissue can be seen as the quantum electric dipole field equipped with the highly systematized geometric objects manifesting various local symmetries and breaking global symmetries, that is, breaking uniformity of the field.

Umezawa and his colleagues incorporated into modern quantum field theory the capability of dealing with quantum electric dipole fields coupled with electromagnetic fields and manifesting various geometric objects (Wadati, Matsumoto and Umezawa 1978a, 1978b; Umezawa 1993). The physical interaction of the brain's quantum electric dipole field to the environment through neural processes create or change the geometric objects, thus the physical interaction can be understood to be stored as memory (Jibu and Yasue 1995). In other words, memory is stored in the specific biomolecular architectures of membranes, cytoskeletons, and water of the structured mass of brain cells which have a corresponding asymmetric quantum field.

At this point quantum brain dynamics seems not so radical, giving a very standard understanding of memory storing mechanism (expressed in terms of quantum fields).

But what about memory retrieval, and coming to the central question, what about consciousness? I stand on the elegant words of Miguel de Unamuno: "We live in memory and by memory, and our spiritual life is at bottom simply the effort of our memory to persist, to transform itself into hope into our future."

Umezawa and Takahashi provided us with quite an interesting physical process for memory retrieval in terms of general quantum field theoretical concepts (Stuart, Takahashi and Umezawa 1978, 1979): As long as memory is maintained in the form of geometric objects of the quantum electric dipole field, new quanta called Nambu-Goldstone bosons emerge from geometric objects triggered by arbitrarily small incoming energy. Emergence of Nambu-Goldstone bosons is memory retrieval. Then what is consciousness? It should be some kind of physical entity in the brain taking in those Nambu-Goldstone bosons. What could that be?

There is a well known QFT concept called the Higgs mechanism, famous today for its principal role in the standard gauge field theory of elementary particles (Umezawa 1993). It tells us that for a quantum electric dipole field with geometric objects coupled with electromagnetic field (e.g., the case for quantum brain dynamics) Nambu-Goldstone bosons are all taken into the longitudinal mode of the electromagnetic field. In other words, Nambu-Goldstone bosons are transformed into quanta of electromagnetic field: photons. However these are very specialized photons in the sense that they have nonzero mass and do not propagate and remain nearby the geometric objects.

In physics, such a nonpropagating photon of the electromagnetic field is called a tunneling photon or evanescent photon; we may therefore call photons surrounding the geometric objects of biomolecular architecture "biological tunneling photons." A standard calculation shows that the mass of this biological tunneling photon is about 10 electron-volts, which is far smaller than the mass of an electron (Del Giudice et al. 1983).

Extremely smaller than the electron mass?! Remember that the critical temperature for boson condensation is inversely proportional to boson mass. Because of this, the critical temperature for boson condensation of biological tunneling photons of mass about 10 electron-volts turns out to be actually higher than body temperature (Jibu, Pribram and Yasue 1996).

Memory retrieval in terms of Nambu-Goldstone bosons can emerge from the biomolecular architecture of geometric objects of the brain's quantum electric dipole field net. So modern quantum field theory indicates that boson condensation of biological tunneling photons can occur at body temperature. Thanks to Umezawa and Takahashi, as well as Miguel de Unamuno, it seems plausible that the physical correlate of conscious mind might be this boson condensation of tunneling photons manifesting quantum coherence throughout the entire brain.

The "Hard Problem" of Conscious Experience and Frontier Physics

Thus far I have shown that central concepts in modern condensed matter physics within the realm of quantum field theory can account for Penrose's second claim of "binding" via brain-wide quantum coherence which cannot be accounted for by "simple minded" quantum mechanics. So quantum brain dynamics may solve this "easy problem" of consciousness. Our theoretical framework starting from first principles of modern physics allows QFT to reveal the existence of body temperature macroscopic-scale boson condensation of biological tunneling photons manifesting long distance quantum coherence over the whole brain. We regard the quantum dynamics of this boson condensation of biological tunneling photons as a physical substrate of consciousness; memory retrieval in terms of Nambu-Goldstone bosons is shown in terms of the dynamics of biological tunneling photons. Consciousness can be understood as an emergent property of memory.

However it is also true that such an approach cannot solve the "hard problem" of consciousness (Chalmers 1996). As pointed out by David Chalmers and Mari Jibu (1998), the problem of conscious experience is the conceptual limit of the scientific framework based on modern physics. The fundamental concepts and formulations of physics must be extended to solve the hard problem. Penrose's first claim seems to suggest a possible direction. Indeed, he proposed a new space-time framework of fundamental physics called "spin networks" in which not only conventional physical and geometric objects but also protoconscious objects such as qualia can be implemented as underlying mathematical objects. In a sense, he developed a universal mathematical framework simultaneously representing the materialistic world of physical reality and the Platonic world of mathematical reality.

Conceptual extension of fundamental physics is not the normal subject of daily physics in which most physicists are involved, but the subject of "frontier physics." People outside physics research like to hear about frontier physics such as superstrings, blackhole evaporation, Schrödinger's cat, quantum teleportation, quantum time tunnel, however most physicists including myself work toward a common understanding of natural phenomena in terms of daily physics. Thus the QFT/QBD approach taken by Umezawa, Takahashi, Vitiello, Del Giudice, Enz, and Jibu and myself remains concrete but not as sensational as Penrose's approach. The former remain in daily physics, but the latter penetrates into frontier physics. Perhaps Chalmers and Jibu are correct in that the hard problem of conscious experience can be solved only through frontier physics such as Penrose's theory of spin networks.

Referring back to Penrose's first claim regarding the Platonic world view, I now embrace the theory of quantum monadology (Nakagomi 1992) which may solve not only the easy problem but also the hard problem of conscious experience from frontier physics. The Platonic world view may well be implemented in the conceptual structure of quantum monads more naturally than in spin networks.

Theory of Quantum Monadology

Monadology is a famous philosophical framework and attractive world view developed by Gottfried Leibniz in the eighteenth century in which fundamental elements of the world are called "monads." A monad was proposed to occupy the center of human mind, and Leibniz's monadology was aimed at the underlying harmonic order among men, society, nature, and the existence of the God. Whitehead (1929) described dynamic monads with psychological being: "occasions of experience." In its original form monadology was too naive to account for human nature and consciousness. However the formal structure of monadology can be implemented in modern frontier physics to give a very simple but attractive conceptual foundation called "quantum monadology" (Nakagomi 1992). Quantum monadology may be capable of unifying quantum theory and relativity theory, solving the measurement problem in quantum mechanics, deriving and understanding the concept of time, understanding "now," solving the problem of free will, and solving the mind-body problem.

I will briefly describe quantum monadology here; those who want to see the complete picture are invited to read the original paper by Teruaki Nakagomi (1992). For simplicity and brevity I will use minimal mathematical formulation.

In quantum monadology the world is made of a finite number, say M, of quantum algebras called monads. There are no other elements making up the world, and so the world itself can be defined as the totality of M monads; $W = \{A_1, A_2, \ldots, A_M\}$. The world W is not space-time as is generally assumed in the conventional framework of physics; space-time does not exist at the fundamental level, but emerges from mutual relations among monads. This can be seen by regarding each monad A_i as a quantum algebra and the world $W = \{A_1, A_2, \ldots, A_M\}$ as an algebraically structured set of the quantum algebras called a tensor product of M monads. The mathematical structure of each quantum algebra representing each monad will be understood to represent the inner world of each monad. Correspondingly, the mathematical structure of the tensor product of M monads will be understood to represent the world W itself. To make the mathematical representation of the world of monads simpler, we assume each quantum algebra representing each monad to be a C* algebra A identical with each other, that is, $A_i = A$ for all i running from 1 to M. Then, the world can be seen as a C* algebra W identical with the Mth tensor power of the C* algebra A.

It is interesting to notice that the world itself can be represented as the structured totality of the inner worlds of M monads. A positive linear functional defined on a C* algebra is called a state. The value of the state (i.e., positive linear functional) for an element of the C* algebra is called an expectation value. Any state of the C* algebra of the world W is said to be a world state, and any state of the C* algebra of each monad A is said to be an individual state. As the world state is a state of the world W, it can be seen as the tensor power of the individual state. In addition to the individual state, each monad has an image of the world state recognized by itself; it is a world state belonging to each monad.

The world states belonging to any two monads are mutually related in such a way that the world state belonging to the i-th monad can be transformed into that belonging to the j-th monad by a unitary representation of the Lorentz group or the Poincaré group. Identifying the world state belonging to each monad with the world recognized by the monad, the conventional representation of the world as a four dimensional space-time manifold can be derived from the above mutual relation in terms of the Lorentz or Poincaré group. Thus the idealistic concept of the unlimited expansion of space-time geometry in conventional physics is shown to be an imaginary common background for overlapping the world image recognized by every monad.

Each monad has a mutually synchronized clock counting a common clock period, and each monad has a freedom (free will) to choose a new group element g of the Lorentz or Poincaré group G independently with the choice of other monads. If a monad in the world happens to choose a new group element g in G after a single clock period, then the world state belonging to this monad changes in accordance with the unitary transformation representing the chosen group element and the jump transformation representing the quantum reduction of the world state. The world states belonging to other monads also suffer from the change in accordance with the unitary transformation representing the mutual relation between the world state belonging to this monad and the world states belonging to other monads.

For each monad, say the j-th monad, the tendency to make a choice of a new group element g in G after a single clock period is proportional to a universal constant c and the expectation value of the jump transformation with respect to the world state belonging to the j-th monad. Such a change of the world states belonging to all the monads induces the actual time flow, and the freedom to choose the group element is understood as the fundamental element of mind; thus the origin of free will can be identified here. Although I cannot here fully explain Nakagomi's theory of quantum monadology, I want to emphasize that quantum monadology may be the only fundamental framework of frontier physics which can visualize not only the materialistic world of physical reality but also the Platonic world of mathematical and philosophical reality.

Conclusion

To develop a science of consciousness we need 1) an understanding of how a Platonic world could actually exist in frontier physics, as well as 2) a concrete formulation in condensed matter physics of how states may occur in the brain and interact with the Platonic world. To approach the Platonic world, one philosophical avenue involves Leibniz "monads," fundamental pockets of reality. Application of quantum field theory to Leibniz (and Whitehead) suggests quantum monadology in which quantum algebras define spacetime volumes with various properties. Such an approach may form a bridge among philosophical explanations for consciousness, the predictions of Roger Penrose, and the brain.

References

Chalmers, D. J. 1996. *The conscious mind: In search of a fundamental theory.* New York: Oxford University Press.

Del Giudice, E., Preparata, G., Milani, M., and Vitiello, G. 1983. Electromagnetic field and spontaneous symmetry breaking in biological matter. *Nucl. Phys.* B275:185–199.

Del Giudice, E., Preparata, G., and Vitiello, G. 1988. Water as a free electric dipole laser. *Phys. Rev. Lett.* 61:1085–1088.

Enz, C. P. 1997. On Preparata's theory of a super radiant phase transition. *Helvetica Physica Acta* 70:141–153.

Jibu, M. 1998. Consciousness and Quantum Theory. (In Japanese.) *Japanese Psychological Review* 41:215–225.

Jibu, M., Hagan, S., Hameroff, S. R., Pribram, K. H., and Yasue, K. 1994. Quantum optical coherence in cytoskeletal microtubules: Implications for brain function. *BioSystems* 32:195–209.

Jibu, M., Pribram, K. H. and Yasue K. 1996. From conscious experience to memory storage and retrieval: The role of quantum brain dynamics and boson condensation of evanescent photons. *Intern. J. Mod. Phys.* B10:1735–1754.

Jibu, M., and Yasue, K. 1995. Quantum brain dynamics and consciousness—An introduction. Amsterdam: John Benjamins.

Nakagomi, T. 1992. Quantum monadology: A world model to interpret quantum mechanics and relativity. *Open Systems and Inform. Dyn.* 1:355–378.

Penrose, R. 1989. *The Emperor's new mind.* London: Oxford University Press.

Penrose, R. 1994. *Shadows of the mind.* London: Oxford University Press.

Stuart, C. I. J. M., Takahashi, Y., and Umezawa, H. 1978. On the stability and non-local properties of memory. *J. Theor. Biol.* 71:605–618.

Stuart, C. I. J. M., Takahashi, Y., and Umezawa, H. 1979. Mixed-system brain dynamics: Neural memory as a macroscopic ordered state. *Found. Phys.* 9:301–327.

Umezawa, H. 1993. *Advanced field theory: Micro, macro, and thermal physics.* New York: American Institute of Physics.

Wadati, M., Matsumoto, H., and Umezawa, H. 1978. Extended objects created by Goldstone bosons. *Phys. Rev.* D18:520–531.

Wadati, M., Matsumoto, H., and Umezawa, H. 1978. Extended objects in crystals. *Phys. Rev.* B18:4077–4095.

Whitehead, A. N. 1929. Process and reality: An essay in cosmology. Reprinted in 1979 by Free Press.

28 The Interface in a Mixed Quantum/Classical Model of Brain Function

Scott Hagan and Masayuki Hirafuji

Traditional models of brain function, which attempt to provide a dynamical account of the specifically conscious aspects of memory invoke global criteria that cannot be admitted to a causal picture in a classical context. But without such global criteria, features of consciousness like the serial character of conscious recall and the apparent lack of neurophysiological modularity in certain kinds of memory cannot be adequately explained. These features find natural explanation in an account of memory that allows classical mechanisms to be supplemented with one operating on quantum theoretical principles. Such models critically depend on the stability of the quantum mechanism and the nature and efficacy of the interface with classical mechanisms. Such an interface is possible in a theory of macroscopic quantum ordered states in which 1) quantum signals are provided with the means to influence meso-scale neural function and 2) the discriminated information inherent in networks of neurons can be usefully translated into a quantum encoding. Stability in a vacuum encoding can be generically ensured and the conditions for its establishment can be met under the stresses of a biological environment. The vacuum parameter coding memory in the quantum system can be determined in terms of physical parameters, forming the basis of a common language for the quantum and classical systems of memory and allowing information flow from one system to the other.

Why Look Beyond Classical Mechanisms?

Traditional neural network models of brain function have proven to be quite successful in simulating numerous aspects of unconscious cognitive processing so one might ask why we need look any further when it comes to specifically conscious aspects of memory. Indeed if consciousness is understood along emergentist lines, there seem to be any number of proposals to account for its various features. In particular the apparently nonlocal character of memory storage involved in some forms of memory and the predominantly serial manner in which the recall process makes experiential memory available to consciousness have received numerous treatments in a classical framework. Why should these accounts be found wanting?

While the character of connectionist explanation is massively parallel and distributed, the character of conscious recall is roughly serial. Consciousness distinguishes certain memories as *active*, and this distinction passes from one memory to another. Neural networks on the other hand do not, by their very nature, distinguish an active stream of information. The system is disposed to produce particular output given particular input and "memories" are actuated *only* through this dispositional process. It becomes problematic then to explain why conscious recall of "memories" thus conceived should assume features like serial expression, determined within the system, that cannot simply be read out from a consideration of this output.

The emergentist thesis, that neural systems will give rise, at some threshold level of complexity, to ontological features distinct from behavioral dispositions, suffers from the lack of any criterion by which to decide exactly what will become the property of conscious memory, when the mechanism of consciousness should become operable, or why it should be a necessary consequence of the attendant conditions. Some models have attempted to provide answers to these questions by introducing dynamical criteria. Accounts variously identify the contents of consciousness with "vector activations" (Churchland 1995), "concentric epicenters" (Greenfield 1995) or "attractors" (Hardcastle 1994, Port and Van Gelder 1995). Inevitably however such criteria involve *global* discriminations. Typically the global nature of the criteria can be disguised by implementing a description in terms of phase space, a higher dimensional fictitious space that uses the entire collection of local variables as coordinates. This strategy is often convenient in *interpreting* the dynamical behavior of systems, but in a classical context such a device cannot be considered *causally* efficacious. Classical dynamics are determined *locally* at each point in the system. While global characteristics might handily *describe* the dynamics from an external point of view, they play no role in *determining* the intrinsic dynamics. This point will resurface presently in the context of a potentially related problem having to do with the modular character of connectionist explanation.

Some forms of memory have stubbornly resisted explanation by localized storage and recall mechanisms. Much of the success of connectionism in elucidating the workings of the brain has been obtained by modularizing functions and assigning these to localized regions of the brain (see for instance Fodor and Pylyshyn 1988). This methodology was motivated by a recognition of the fact that the discriminatory power of neural networks with respect to input characteristics is read out only in the output since this is the only place where the distributed machinery of the network can be brought to bear. Modularization then allows the intermediate functions of localized areas of the brain to be interpreted as meaningful. While this course has, on most reckonings, successfully accounted for many forms of memory involved in unconscious processing, the kind (or kinds) of memory most directly involved in conscious recall do not appear to be neurophysiologically modular.

The absence of modularization points, in the framework of connectionist thought, to a representation that remains distributed until final output is achieved. Intrinsically—from within the system itself—distributed representation then allows meaningful interpretation only in the final output. Interpretations of distributed processing are, of course, possible but are inevitably made from *outside* the system. They require the acknowledgement of relations, not explicitly represented in the system, that exist between informational elements located at disparate physical locations and therefore constitute an *extrinsic* mode of interpretation. Conscious representation however must require an *intrinsic* mode, since the interpretations of content provided by consciousness are not made from outside the system but rather are provided by the system itself. An explanation of consciousness made in an intrinsic mode would then seem to require the accessibility to and simultaneous availability of the same explicit relationships that facilitate interpretation in the extrinsic mode.

On a classical account, the fulfilment of this requirement is expressly forbidden by the *locality* constraint. Locality[1] constrains the speed of propagation of signals to be less than the speed of light and applies indiscriminately to all classical systems. Its relevance on the scale of brain dynamics stems from the immediate corollary that communication over physical distances, however small, must not occur instantaneously. The determination of relationships existing between informational elements that are physically separated however requires such communication if the relations are to be made explicit, simultaneous with the informational elements themselves. One solution to this apparent impasse is to require that the desired relations be expressed *locally* but such a solution must contend with thermal limits on the possible complexity of a local system, limits far too stringent to allow a realistic description of even very limited conscious processes. Moreover there appears to be no evidence that this is the route pursued in the brain.

What is required then is the means to extend an intrinsic mode of description, in which the elements of the system merely respond in accordance with the principle of locality to the flux of physical conditions in the immediate vicinity, to an extrinsic mode, in which the system itself is capable of providing an interpretation of these activities. Moreover this requirement must apply at every level at which conscious apprehension "binds" information that is not simultaneously available in a local representation. Reinterpreted with this stipulation in mind, the "binding problem" is encountered at a much finer level of psychological structure than is admitted in the traditional reading of the problem. Further, the problem appears not to find an adequate solution in a classical context where the locality constraint is always enforced.

Consider for instance the proposal that temporal synchrony in neural firing offers an explanation of binding in visual processing (Gray and Singer 1989). Since each of the synchronized neurons is firing in response to its own local dynamical situation, oblivious to the fact that other neurons are firing concurrently, temporal synchrony is *recognized* only as a global property, only from outside the system, and therefore must be without causal consequence in the classical context. The encoding becomes local only in the downstream neural dynamics, either through convergence or by the exchange of signals, but at this level there is no longer any reason to anticipate ontological features distinct from connectionist dispositions. Although it originates consequences at the level of neural dynamics, temporal synchrony would seem to be more naturally interpreted as an *effect* of an underlying mechanism that would explain how these neurons are orchestrated to fire simultaneously and it is presumably this mechanism that encodes for psychological binding. But to be efficacious the mechanism must neither encapsulate information that is available only from an outside perspective—that is, the information must inhere in the system itself—nor reduce to local dynamics with only trivial dispositional consequences. On a classical reading however, these would seem to be the only options.

Quantum Memory in a Subcellular Context

Some of these considerations motivated the suggestion that the success of connectionism in explaining many facets of the working of the brain could not be carried over to all aspects of brain function, and in particular that the character of experiential memory would not find adequate explanation within that framework alone. A second and collateral system of memory, operating on quantum theoretical principles, was proposed, originally by Stuart, Takahashi, and Umezawa (1978, 1979) and subsequently elaborated by Jibu and Yasue (Jibu and Yasue 1993; Hagan et al. 1994; Jibu and Yasue 1994, 1995). The necessity of a quantum component to brain function has been suggested, for independent reasons, by several authors (Marshall 1989; Pribram 1991; Penrose 1994; Hameroff 1994; Stapp 1995; Hameroff and Penrose 1996a, 1996b; Hagan 1998). It should be noted that these arguments do not, as some earlier theses did, *use* the mechanism of consciousness to patch up long-standing interpretational difficulties in quantum mechanics, but rather employ physical and mathematical concepts to critique the scope of traditional computationalism to explain consciousness and in particular to suggest that no *purely* classical account can be adequate to the requirements of a realistic theory of conscious processes.

Quantum systems need not be subject to the same locality constraints that always apply in the classical realm and, in particular, macroscopic quantum states allow information about global properties of the system to inhere in the system itself. The proposal of a quantum basis for memory might however introduce potential difficulties in accounting for the long-term stability of memory. And the claim that two separate but interacting systems are, taken together, responsible for determining the nature of memory necessitates a bi-directional flow of information between the systems.

The theory (Jibu et al. 1994; Jibu, Pribram, and Yasue 1996; Jibu and Yasue 1997) situates a quantum component of memory subcellularly in neurons and allows individual memories to be stored in a stable fashion by carrying them into the ground state or vacuum of the system dynamics. This demands that there be a vast multiplicity of different vacuum states to code for different memories. In the quantum mechanics of old this was expressly forbidden by the equivalence theorem, which declared that all vacua were equivalent. Quantum *mechanics* precluded the possibility of describing transitions from one vacuum phase to another phase exhibiting radically different behavior. The advent of quantum *field theory* allowed for the first time a realistic treatment of inhomogeneous media exhibiting domains of differing vacuum phase. To enforce the choice of a particular vacuum throughout a coherence domain, long-range correlations must be established. A well-known theorem, the Nambu-Goldstone theorem (Goldstone 1961; Nambu and Jona-Lasinio 1961), guarantees that in systems exhibiting spontaneously broken symmetries—systems in which the dynamics are invariant under a transformation that is not respected by the vacuum state—gapless modes are spontaneously excited to enforce the choice of vacuum, thereby establishing long-range correlations. These modes, familiar phenomena in condensed matter and high energy physics, arise spontaneously since no energy barrier need be surmounted.

Polariton Basis

In a standard two-state approximation to the energy level structure of the water molecules in the vicinity of cytoskeletal microtubules, two kinds of vacua arise when the system coupling the electromagnetic field and the water dipole field is diagonalized in a polariton[2] basis (Hillery and Mlodinow 1996). One is the standard vacuum and has the same invariance properties as the system dynamics; the other is a set of degenerate vacua of spontaneous symmetry breaking type, labeled by a continuous parameter (see figure 28.1). The gapless excitations that arise in the spontaneously broken phase maintain ordered states that manifest long-range correlations.

The spontaneous symmetry breaking vacua are accessible only in a range of physical parameters relating the energy level difference in the two-state description of water to the number density of participating molecules. The polariton model thus determines the values of the vacuum parameter in terms of classically accessible physical quantities. This relation to physical data is essential to allow discriminated

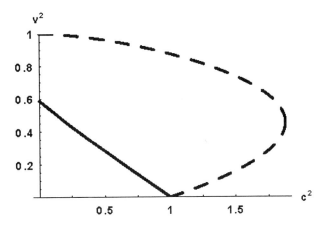

Figure 28.1
Values for the vacuum expectation v^2 over the range of $c^2 = \epsilon_0/4\mu^2 n$ (where ϵ_0 is the energy difference of the levels in a two-state treatment of water molecules, μ is the electric dipole moment of water and n is the number density in the coherent fraction) for which a spontaneous symmetry breaking vacuum is available. The solid and dashed curves correspond to the positive and negative root branches respectively of the relation:

$$c^2 = \sqrt{1-v^2}(\sqrt{1-v^2} + 2v^2(\sqrt{1-v^2} - \sqrt{2-v^2}))$$

information inherent in classical information processing systems to find useful transcription into a quantum encoding and vice versa, essentially providing the basis of a common language for the two systems.

For energy transitions, in the two-state treatment of water molecules, occurring in the far infrared ($\sim 10^{12}$ Hz) one finds a parameter space (see figure 28.2) that easily accommodates a reasonable range of values for the density of the coherent fraction, even leaving considerable room for large-scale biological impurities.

The dispersion relations for the low-lying excitations in the theory are found by linearizing the system with respect to fluctuations about the spontaneously broken vacuum. These dispersion relations determine the energy spectrum in the polariton basis. The relations describe two different modes. One is a gapless mode with a minimum energy of zero. In the Umezawa model for memory, this corresponds to the mode that maintains the stability of memory. The other mode, an effectively massive mode, has a nonzero minimum energy and corresponds to the mode of memory recall. The ensemble of modes of differing vacuum codings that are concurrently active determine the serial stream of conscious recall in a manner consistent with our earlier considerations. Also, because the minimum energy depends on the value of the vacuum parameter coding for a specific memory, some of these modes will require more energy to be excited; that is, some memories will be "harder" to recall.

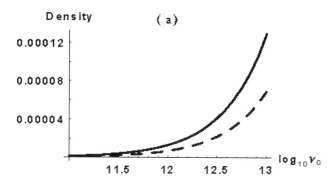

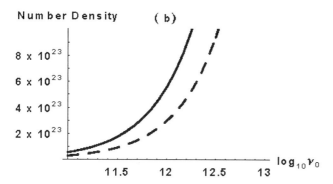

Figure 28.2
(a) Plot of minimum density (in g/cm^3) of the coherent fraction as a function of $log_{10}v_0$ (where v_0 is the frequency of the transition between levels in the two-state treatment of water molecules) required to access spontaneous symmetry breaking vacua. (b) Plot of minimum required number density of participating dipoles (per m^3) against $log_{10}v_0$. The solid and dashed curves in each plot correspond to the positive and negative root branches respectively of the relation between c^2 and v^2.

The dynamics of the interaction between the electromagnetic field and the water dipole field allow for a phenomenon called superradiance to occur in the coherent phase (Jibu et al. 1994; Jibu and Yasue 1997). The phenomenon is related to spontaneous emission in lasers and allows quantum effects to be propagated up to macroscopic levels in systems involving a large number of participating molecular sites. In neurons, such effects might allow the quantum dynamics to exert subtle control over cellular activities, with microtubules acting in the role of a subcellular optical network.

It would seem that information flow in the other direction is *necessitated* by the neural system itself. It is in fact the microtubular network that orchestrates changes to the synaptic "weights" in a connectionist description of neural function. Neurotransmitter vesicles (or their precursors) are conveyed to release along microtubules and other cytoskeletal structures. This suggests that the information needed for the orchestration of these activities at least momentarily inheres in parts of the cytoskeletal network and thereby might be carried into a quantum encoding.

Tuszynski et al. (1995, 1997a, 1997b) have also pointed to the possibility of *classical* information processing in the tubulin ensemble composing the microtubule. The system of tubulin exhibits a spin-glass phase, a description often used to describe information processing in neural networks, and the transition to this phase occurs at biological temperatures. Potentially vast increases in processing power make microtubular involvement an attractive evolutionary option that might later have been adapted to make use of the possibilities offered by the quantum dynamics.

Phase Transitions

In order to take advantage of these properties of the spontaneous symmetry breaking vacuum, a phase transition can be effected by means of a polariton condensation into the ordinary vacuum. It has been demonstrated that such a condensation is an indication that one has moved into an inequivalent Fock space (Umezawa 1993), built on a new vacuum. The new vacuum is moreover a coherent state of the gapless polariton (Vitiello 1995; Hu and Nori 1996).

The means by which it is currently possible to elicit a phase transition to a coherent state can be classified into one of two categories. The first encompasses the well-known method employed, for instance, in attaining superfluid states: Bose-Einstein condensation. Here the parameter that controls the phase transition is generally temperature[3]. Below a critical value, the coherent phase appears.

In the most familiar applications, the critical temperature is often extremely low in comparison to biological temperatures but it is misleading to generalize from these cases. In particular first order calculations depend on particle density and condensate fraction (the fraction of the molecular sites participating in the coherent state) and can easily, without extreme assumptions, assume values greatly in excess of room temperature. Critical temperatures in the theory of magnetism for instance vary considerably, according to the composition of the sample and the nature of the symmetry breaking, ranging from slightly above absolute zero to many times higher than room temperature. Since all temperature dependence is subsumed in the determination of the critical temperature, a discussion of thermal noise would therefore be spurious.

The second category of phase transitions is controlled by an external supply of energy that must be constantly supplied above a threshold value to maintain coherence. This is the kind of phase transition occurring, for instance, in the Fröhlich mechanism (Fröhlich 1968) but is much more familiar as the process governing laser phenomena. Lasers are indicative of the way that coherent states can be maintained by providing a continuous energy supply, a method that has not only been intensively studied from a theoretical point of view but also has been demonstrated experimentally so often as to be commonplace.

In this scheme the external energy provided to the microtubular system might be metabolic energy travelling along the microtubular network. Del Guidice et al. (1985) cite evidence that the water surrounding the cytoskeleton can be brought into an electrically polarized state by very low amplitude, low frequency electric fields when provided with a threshold energy of approximately the same magnitude as is carried by the solitonic waves travelling along the microtubules (Del Guidice et al. 1986). Seen in this context, biological systems become hospitable hosts for coherent states: the continuous provision of energy is ubiquitous in the biological world.

Conclusion

It has been suggested here that classical models of memory cannot alone account for the seriality and nonlocality of conscious aspects of memory. These invariably invoke extrinsic elements—descriptions that do not inhere in the system but are applied from the outside—elements that are expressly forbidden in causal accounts given at the classical level. The establishment of a collateral system of memory based on quantum dynamics allows such elements to be assimilated to an intrinsic description without contravening the locality constraint.

The thrust of this work has been to provide a framework in which to relate the vacuum parameters that act as codes in a quantum field theoretic treatment of memory to physical parameters. This lays the foundation for a system of communication between classical and quantum levels of encoding, and allows the dual system of memory to encapsulate characteristic features of both modes of operation. Microtubules, perhaps in conjunction with the membrane dynamics of the dendritic network, appear to be most strategically placed to effect the transfer of information between the two systems, and in the polariton basis, the physical variable implicated in mediating this transfer is the number density of dipoles in the coherent phase.

Notes

1. The word "locality" refers here to the *physical* concept deriving from the theory of relativity, not the *neurophysiological* concept deriving from an analysis of function in the brain. The coincidence of vocabulary is regrettable but the term is well-established in both fields.

2. Polaritons are the generic quasi-particles that arise in a field-theoretic treatment of the coupling between photon and phonon-like excitations. Here the phonon-like modes are the dipole wave quanta associated with the fact that the molecular field of water is characterized by an electric dipole moment.

3. Pressure and other intensive thermodynamic variables can also play a role to some extent.

References

Churchland, P. M. 1995. *The Engine of Reason, the Seat of the Soul: A Philosophical Journey into the Brain*. Cambridge, Mass.: MIT Press.

Del Guidice, E., Doglia, S., Milani, M., and Vitiello, G. 1985. A quantum field theoretical approach to the collective behavior of biological systems. *Nucl. Phys.* B251:375–400.

Del Guidice, E., Doglia, S., Milani, M., and Vitiello, G. 1986. Electromagnetic field and spontaneous symmetry breaking in biological matter. *Nucl. Phys.* B275:185–199.

Fodor, J. A., and Pylyshyn, Z. 1988. Connectionism and cognitive architecture: a critical analysis. *Cognition* 28:3–81.

Fröhlich, H. 1968. Long-range coherence and energy storage in biological systems. Intern. *J. Quantum Chem.* 2:641–649.

Goldstone, J. 1961. Field theories with "superconductor" solutions. *Nuovo Cimento* 19:154–164.

Gray, C. M., and Singer, W. 1989. Stimulus-specific neuronal oscillations in orientation columns of cat visual cortex. *Proc. Nat. Acad. Sci.* (USA) 86:1698–1702.

Greenfield, S. A. 1995. *Journey to the Centers of the Mind*. New York: W. H. Freeman.

Hagan, S. 1998. Physical and mathematical theory in a scientific approach to consciousness. *Bussei Kenkyu* (Kyoto) 69(6):836–850.

Hagan, S., Jibu, M., and Yasue, K. 1994. Consciousness and anesthesia: an hypothesis involving biophoton emission in the microtubular cytoskeleton of the brain. In Pribram, K. H. (ed.), *Origins: Brain and Self-organization*. Hillsdale, N.J.: Lawrence Erlbaum, pp. 153–171.

Hameroff, S. R. 1994. Quantum coherence in microtubules: A neural basis for emergent consciousness? *J. Consciousness Studies* 1(1):91–118.

Hameroff, S., and Penrose, R. 1996a. Conscious events as orchestrated space-time selections. *J. Consciousness Studies* 3(1):36–53.

Hameroff, S., and Penrose, R. 1996b. Orchestrated reduction of quantum coherence in brain microtubules: a model for consciousness. In Hameroff, S. R., Kaszniak, A. W. and Scott, A. C. (eds.), *Toward a Science of Consciousness—The First Tucson Discussions and Debates*. Cambridge, Mass.: MIT Press, pp. 507–540.

Hardcastle, V. G. 1994. Psychology's binding problem and possible neurobiological solutions. *J. Consciousness Studies* 1(1):66–90.

Hillery, M., and Mlodinow, L. 1996. *Quantized fields in a non-linear dielectric medium: A microscopic approach*. xxx-lanl. gov e-Print archive atom-ph/9608002.

Hu, X., and Nori, F. 1996. Squeezed phonon states: modulating quantum fluctuations of atomic displacements. *Phys. Rev. Lett.* 76(13):2294–2297.

Jibu, M., Hagan, S., Hameroff, S. R., Pribram, K. H., and Yasue, K. 1994. Quantum optical coherence in cytoskeletal microtubules: implications for brain function. *BioSystems* 32:195–209.

Jibu, M., Pribram, K. H., and Yasue, K. 1996. From conscious experience to memory storage and retrieval: the role of quantum brain dynamics and boson condensation of evanescent photons. *Int. J. Mod. Phys. B* 10(13/14):1735–1754.

Jibu, M., and Yasue, K. 1993. Intracellular quantum signal transfer in Umezawa's quantum brain dynamics. *Cybern. Syst. Int J.* 24:1–8.

Jibu, M., and Yasue, K. 1994. Is the brain a biological photonic computer with subneuronal quantum optical networks? In Trappl, R. (ed.): *Cybernetics and Systems Research '94*. Singapore: World Scientific, pp. 763–870.

Jibu, M., and Yasue, K. 1995. *Quantum Brain Dynamics—An Introduction*. Amsterdam: John Benjamin.

Jibu, M., and Yasue, K. 1997. What is mind? Quantum field theory of evanescent photons in brain as quantum theory of consciousness. *Informatica* 21:471–490.

Marshall, I. N. 1989. Consciousness and Bose-Einstein condensates. *New Ideas in Psychol.* 7(1):73–83.

Nambu, Y., and Jona-Lasinio, G. 1961. Dynamical model of elementary particles based on an analogy with superconductivity. *I. Phys. Rev.* 122:345–358.

Penrose, R. 1994. *Shadows of the Mind*. New York: Oxford University Press.

Port, R. F., and Van Gelder, T. (eds.) 1995. *Mind As Motion: Explorations in the Dynamics of Cognition*. Cambridge, Mass.: MIT Press.

Pribram, K. H. 1991. *Brain and Perception*. Hillsdale, N.J.: Lawrence Erlbaum.

Searle, J. 1994. *The Rediscovery of the Mind*. Cambridge, Mass.: MIT Press.

Stapp, H. P. 1995. Why classical mechanics cannot naturally accommodate consciousness but quantum mechanics can. *Psyche* 2(5) http://psyche.cs.monash.edu.au/v2/psyche-2-05-stapp.html.

Stuart, C. I. J. M., Takahashi, Y., and Umezawa, H. 1978. On the stability and non-local properties of memory. *J. Theor. Biol.* 71:605–618.

Stuart, C. I. J. M., Takahashi, Y., and Umezawa, H. 1979. Mixed system brain dynamics: neural memory as a macroscopic ordered state. *Found. Phys.* 9(3/4):301–327.

Tuszynski, J. A., Hameroff, S. R., Sataric, M. V., Trpisová, B., and Nip, M. L. A. 1995. Ferroelectric behavior in microtubule dipole lattices: Implications for information processing, signaling and assembly/disassembly. *J. Theor. Biol.* 174:371–380.

Tuszynski, J. A., Trpisová, B., Sept, D., and Brown, J. A. 1997a. Selected physical issues in the structure and function of microtubules. *Journal of Structural Biology* 118:94–106.

Tuszynski, J. A., Trpisová, B., Sept, D., and Sataric, M. V. 1997b. The enigma of microtubules and their self-organizing behavior in the cytoskeleton. *Biosystems* 42:153–175.

Umezawa, H. 1993. *Advanced Field Theory: Micro, Macro, and Thermal Physics*. New York: American Institute of Physics Press.

Vitiello, G. 1995. Dissipation and memory capacity in the quantum brain model. *Int. J. Mod. Phys. B* 9(8):973–989.

VIII THE TIMING OF CONSCIOUS EXPERIENCE—
INTRODUCTION

Stuart Hameroff

As we walk along a sidewalk, various forms of sensory information from our visual input, sound, swinging arms and contact between our feet and pavement somehow synthesize into a sequence of coherent experiences. Although we take this for granted, exactly how the brain accomplishes this synchronization is not well understood. For example neural conduction time from the sensory neurons of our feet, legs and spinal cord would seem to deliver information about our feet contacting the pavement significantly after visual and auditory experience of the same events. Bergenheim et al. (1996) studied this problem and concluded that the brain somehow compensates by jiggling sensory input to provide a proper frame for timed events. A related problem is how we account for our rapid responses that seem to occur before we are actually conscious of them. In fast-paced activities such as Ping-Pong, and rapid-fire conversation we seem to act almost reflexively, with conscious appreciation lagging slightly behind our seemingly conscious actions (Gray 1996; Penrose 1994). How is this possible?

The whole issue of time in conscious experience is strange, for physics tells us there is no necessary forward flow of time; time just *is* (e.g., as space just *is*). If time were really flowing, then in what medium would it be flowing (e.g., minutes per what?). Nevertheless in conscious experience time does seem to flow, although occasionally at different rates. In certain states subjective (internal) time seems to slow down while the external world speeds up, and vice versa. How does the brain manifest the flow of time?

In 1979 Benjamin Libet and colleagues described a series of experiments performed on patients undergoing neurosurgical procedures under local anesthesia. Thus the subjects' brains were exposed and accessible while they were conscious and communicative. Libet, a neurophysiologist, took advantage of this situation to perform studies that remain widely discussed and enigmatic to this day. Basically Libet and his neurosurgical colleagues stimulated the patients peripherally (e.g., on their finger), and on corresponding regions of sensory cortex and thalamus. They recorded EEG, and most importantly, asked the patients to report precisely when they became consciously aware of the stimuli. As described in the first chapter in this section by Stan Klein, the patients' responses were somewhat surprising. For example when stimulated at the finger, the onset of conscious experience was almost immediate, whereas stimulating the corresponding sensory cortex mapping of the same finger resulted in conscious experience only after a significant delay. To account for these and other results Libet concluded that somehow the brain appreciated sensory input after a significant delay but corrected the timing by referring the conscious signal backward in time! Libet's data and conclusions have been widely debated, with quite different interpretations. Some physicists take the backward time referral seriously, as supportive evidence for a quantum mechanism in consciousness. Others believe classical, nonquantum explanations suffice. The debate continues in the first two chapters in this section.

In "Do Apparent Temporal Anomalies Require Nonclassical Explanation?" Stan Klein reviews Libet's findings as well as the arguments and controversy surrounding them. He comes down on the side of classical explanations. In "A Quantum Physics Model of the Timing of Conscious Experience" Fred Alan Wolf takes the opposing view, explaining how quantum mechanisms can account for backward time referral.

In the final chapter in this section "Conscious and Anomalous Nonconscious Emotional Processes: A Reversal of the Arrow of Time?" Dick J. Bierman and Dean Radin describe a series of experiments that purportedly demonstrate backward referral of emotional experience. Their results have engendered a great deal of controversy because, if true, backward time referral and quantum mechanisms are implicated in day to day, and moment to moment consciousness.

References

Bergenheim, M., Johansson, H., Granlund, B., and Pedersen, J. 1996. Experimental evidence for a synchronization of sensory information to conscious experience. In *Toward a Science of Consciousness: The First Tucson Discussions and Debates* (S. R. Hameroff, A. W. Kaszniak and A. C. Scott, eds.), Cambridge, Mass.: MIT Press, pp. 303–310.

Gray, J. A. 1998. Creeping Up on the Hard Question of Consciousness. In Toward a Science of Consciousness II: The Second Tucson Discussions and Debates (eds. S. R. Hameroff, A. W. Kaszniak and A. C. Scott), Cambridge, Mass.: MIT Press.

Libet, B., Wright, E. W. Jr., Feinstein, B., and Pearl, D. R. 1979. Subjective referral of the timing for a conscious sensory experience. *Brain* 102:193–224.

Penrose, R. 1994. *Shadows of the Mind*. New York: Oxford University Press.

29 Do Apparent Temporal Anomalies Require Nonclassical Explanation?

Stanley A. Klein

1 Libet's Experiment on Backward Referral

Libet (1979) compared the time of subjective awareness produced by cortical or thalamic stimulation while patients were undergoing neurosurgery, to that produced by visual or skin stimulation. He concluded that a backward referral in time (to be clarified) was needed. Penrose (1994, 1997) and Wolf (1998) go far beyond Libet, claiming that Libet's experiments indicate a fundamental time anomaly that requires a quantum mechanical explanation. The present article argues that the jump to quantum mechanisms was premature since simple physiological mechanisms can account for Libet's data.

The critical findings of Libet's experiments on time anomalies can be summarized as:

(i) A cortical or thalamic stimulus requires a duration of more than 250 msec to be felt, whereas a skin stimulus of 20 msec is adequate. The stimulus duration needed to generate a feeling is called the "neuronal adequacy" time (NA). It can differ from the perceived time of the feeling.

(ii) A cortical stimulus whose onset is within 250 msec after the skin stimulus can suppress the skin response if it has an overlapping felt location.

(iii) For a skin stimulus to be felt as synchronous with a nonoverlapping brain stimulus, the skin stimulus must be delayed 250 msec relative to a cortical stimulus or delayed 0 msec relative to a thalamic stimulus. [Section 3 asks whether Libet's raw data is adequate for this claim.]

(iv) Both the skin and the thalamic stimulation, but not the cortical stimulus, generate an evoked cortical potential (E) shortly after stimulus onset.

Instead of NA ≈ 250 msec that appears in item (i), Wolf and Penrose quote a 500 msec delay (however, see footnote 15 of Wolf 1998). The 500 msec value is only found when stimulating the brain with very weak, near threshold, signals. In all the experiments involving backward referral Libet used a much stronger stimulus, with NA ≈ 200–300 msec, see tables 29.2 and 29.3 (Libet 1979). It is strange that Libet himself (1991) says NA = 500 msec when referring to his 1979 data even though his original article is clear that NA ≤ 300 in those experiments.

Items (i), (ii), and (iv) are summarized in panel A of figure 29.1. The XX in connection with the skin stimulation indicates when the skin feeling can be canceled by a cortical stimulus (item (ii)). Item (iii) is summarized in panels B or C by the circled

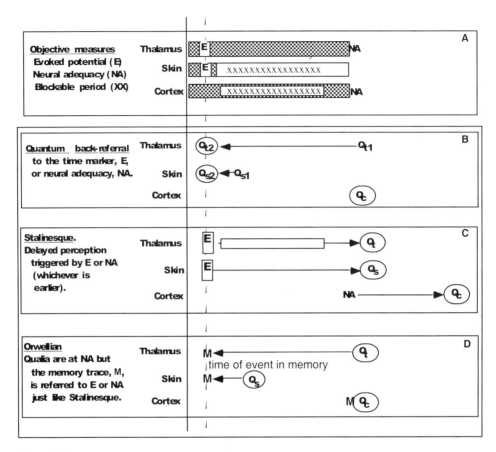

Figure 29.1
Panel A summarizes Libet's data. NA is neuronal adequacy duration indicated by the checkerboard. E is the evoked potential elicited by skin and thalamic, but not cortical stimulation. Q indicates the time of the qualia. Panels B–D are possible explanations of Libet's data. Panel B shows a back-action whereby the qualia occur at the time markers. Panel C shows the case where the qualia occur at a fixed delay from the time marker. Panel D shows all qualia occurring at a fixed time from the time of neuronal adequacy, but the memory marker is placed at the time marker for ecological coherence.

Q's that indicate the timing of the qualia. For this illustration the thalamic, skin and cortical stimuli are assumed to have the same onsets.

Libet argues that his data on cortical stimulation implies a backward referral in time since item (ii) seems to imply that the peripheral stimulus doesn't become conscious for about 250 msec in order that it can be canceled by the cortical masker. Backward referral is then needed to account for the combination of items (ii) and (iii). The backward referral argument is simpler in the thalamic case since there is a decoupling between the duration for neuronal sufficiency and the time of subjective equality of skin vs. the thalamic stimulation. It is unfortunate that Penrose focuses his discussion on the cortical experiments since the "time anomaly" in the thalamic data is simpler and clearer. Libet argues that since the thalamic sensation doesn't reach neuronal adequacy until 250 msec after the pulse train begins (item i) a back referral mechanism is needed with thalamic stimulation to produce the synchrony sensation (item iii) that is perceived.

2   Multiple Explanations of Libet's Data

A number of nonquantum explanations have been proposed for Libet's data. Ian Glynn's (1990) article is short, witty, easily accessible and covers multiple ways of accounting for Libet's cortical stimulation data. The explanation Glynn discusses in most detail is the presence of a time delay following the 250 msec cortical stimulation (item i) before the cortical stimulus is felt (figure 29.1C). That simple suggestion is compatible with all the cortical data. Glynn also rebuts Libet's (Libet vs. Glynn 1991) response to that suggestion. Churchland's (1981) and Honderich's (1984) accounts should also be visited by interested persons. I will focus on the discussion by Dennett (1991) because of his picturesque language that makes the alternative explanations easy to recall.

Dennett points out that our brain has adopted numerous tricks to make sense out of its tumultuous neural activity. He calls some of these tricks Orwellian and some Stalinesque. A Stalinesque account involves hallucinating (misperceiving) whereby the brain generates images not in agreement with the input information (similar to Stalin's staged trials). An Orwellian account involves rewriting history (now called false memories). For example, item (ii) above would be an Orwellian mechanism. Dennett spends the main part of his chapter 6 ("Time and Experience") on Libet's experiments. Further clarification on the application of the Stalinesque vs Orwellian means of dealing with Libet's time anomalies can be found in Libet's (1993) article in the CIBA Foundation Symposium volume. At the end of that article is a discussion by a number of philosophers including Dennett and Searle together with Libet's responses and several counter-responses.

Three explanations of the subjective data are shown diagramatically in panels B, C, and D of figure 29.1. These explanations make use of the notion of a time marker that is either the evoked potential, E, or the point of neuronal adequacy, NA, whichever is earlier (E for thalamus and skin, NA for cortex).

(panel B)   A backward causation explanation, whereby the stimulus is perceived before thalamic neuronal adequacy is reached. The perception is referred back to the time of the evoked potential (E) if an evoked potential is present. Note that since all the time markers and qualia follow stimulus onset there is no violation of physical causality in the data.

(panel C)   A Stalinesque explanation, whereby the time of the sensation is a fixed delay from the time marker. This is also Glynn's (1990) account.

(panel D)   An Orwellian explanation, whereby the qualia for any stimulus are delayed, but the timing of those perceptions is not recorded. What gets into memory is based on the time marker information as in panel B. This explanation actually involves backward referral of memories laid down later, pointing to the time markers, so there is no need for the quantum mechanism suggested by Wolf (1998, 1999) or the causality violating "time symmetric" mechanism suggested by Bierman and Radin (1999).

Dennett does a lucid job of applying the Stalinesque and Orwellian explanations to the Libet data without any need for quantum mechanisms. Dennett goes on to argue that there is no difference between an Orwellian and a Stalinesque account, and concludes that qualia are illusory. I think these claims go too far, and that we will be able to distinguish the two sorts of accounts when the neural correlates of consciousness are discovered. One hopes that discovery will clarify the many issues regarding qualia.

Physicists like Penrose and Wolf tend to find the Stalinesque and Orwellian explanations as ad hoc and distasteful. These explanations lack the elegance of the grand principles underlying many physical phenomena. Psychologists and biologists, on the other hand, are quite familiar with the inelegant contrivances that evolution invents again and again.

Wolf (1998) asks "what purpose could evolution have in allowing such a strange and confused temporal ordering of conscious experiences?" To me the answer seems obvious. The brain has evolved to compensate for delays in timing. It makes ecological sense that the perceived time of touch should be referred back to the actual time of touch to minimize confusions of time ordering. It is known that temporal compensation mechanisms are found throughout the nervous system. Let me give two examples from vision. In the retina there are time delays in the ganglion cell (the output cell of the retina) signals depending on the distance of the ganglion cell from the optic nerve. But by the time the neural activity reaches cortex these delays have been compensated. The second example is from my own research (Baldo and Klein 1995). We used a spatial alignment task to compare the subjective timing of a flashed dot relative to a moving dot (Nijhawan 1994) and found that subjects align the flashed dot to where the moving dot will be about 100 msec later. This predictive mechanism would be a clever evolutionary adaptation for creatures trying to catch flying bugs (among other challenges with moving stimuli). Forward referral has selection advantages when dealing with moving objects, just as backward referral has advantages for designing the motor control system of hand-eye-world coordination. It is not surprising that evolution would come up with the strategy of using time markers to synchronize events across the brain. Time anomalies will occur when an evoked potential time marker is missing, as happens with cortical stimulation. Typically, illusions are a byproduct of sensory mechanisms that were developed by evolution for one purpose being now used in an unusual context (Gregory 1970).

3   A Reanalysis of Libet's Raw Data

I could have stopped my analysis of the Libet data at this point since the classical explanations, given above, seem clear and plausible (once one thinks of them). Rather than quitting here, I want to make a new contribution to the Libet story by questioning the significance of his raw data. I will argue that the slopes of Libet's psychometric functions are sufficiently shallow and the criterion uncertainties are sufficiently large, that the timing shifts between skin and brain stimulation do not need special mechanisms.

In order to clarify Libet's data it is helpful to take a detour and examine a simpler task of comparing the relative location of two arrowheads (upper left of figure 29.2 panels). The lower arrow is always 3.0 mm in length and the length of the upper arrow is randomly varied from trial to trial with the choices being (2.9, 2.95, 3.0, 3.05, 3.1) mm. Suppose each length is shown 50 times and the observer is asked to judge whether the upper arrowhead is to the right or left (longer or shorter) of the reference. Table 29.1 shows a possible dataset. The probability that the upper arrow is judged to be longer is plotted as asterisks in figure 29.2A. This plot of frequency of seeing as a function of stimulus strength is called psychometric function.

Table 29.1
Data for figure 29.2A. The number of occurrences of each outcome.

stimulus offset	−100	−50	0	50	100
upper is shorter	50	49	45	25	5
upper is longer	0	1	5	25	45

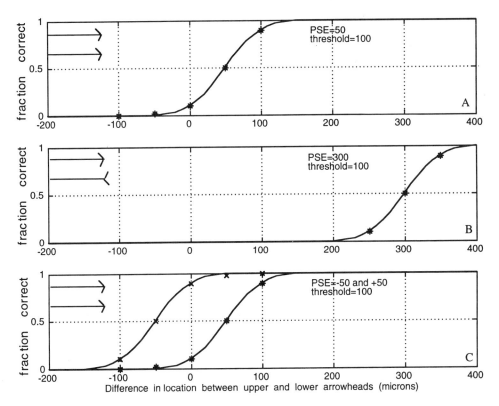

Figure 29.2
Sample psychometric functions are shown to illustrate how they are created and how they are interpreted. Libet's temporal comparison is replaced by the more familiar spatial comparison of two arrowhead locations. Panel A shows a small PSE shift of +50 msec due to a response bias (similar to Libet's shift). Panel B shows a substantial PSE shift due to the Muller-Lyer illusion when the direction of one arrowhead is flipped. Panel C, shows the case with three categories giving two psychometric functions, as in Libet's experiments.

The horizontal axis is the length difference of the upper and lower arrows in microns. The vertical axis is the fraction of times that the observer says the upper arrow is longer. The curve that is fit to the data is a cumulative normal distribution, a form commonly used for fitting psychometric functions (Levi, Klein, and Aitsebaomo 1984). Two numbers can be extracted from the psychometric function: the point of subjective equality (PSE) and the threshold.

Parameter 1, the PSE, is the length difference corresponding to the 50% point. It would be expected that the PSE should be near zero, but often small biases are found in the perceived location of the upper or lower arrow (or perceived time of brain vs. skin stimulation in Libet's case). For example, the lower arrow might seem smaller because of the "moon illusion" caused by perspective cues that make it seem closer, together with a "size constancy" mechanism. Another possible source of the bias is related to what the subject does in cases when the two lengths appear equal. The subject could either: 1) randomly distribute those responses to the two categories (but this introduces noise and gives the psychometric function a shallower slope), or 2) put those responses into one category (this introduces a PSE bias, but the psychometric function remains steep). The latter strategy is the one typically chosen by psychophysicists since the PSE is easily biased, while thresholds (slopes) are more trustworthy.

Parameter 2, the threshold, measures the shallowness (slope) of the psychometric function. In this article, threshold is defined as the abscissa range needed to go from 10% to 90% correct (2.6 times the standard deviation for an underlying normal distribution).

Figure 29.2B is a psychometric function similar to figure 29.2A except that now the test pattern involves comparing an arrow with a regular arrowhead to an arrow with a backward arrowhead. The threshold is the same but now the PSE has increased to 300 microns. In this case the PSE is substantially greater than the threshold and our judgment is called an optical illusion (the Muller-Lyer illusion). When the PSE shift is less than threshold (as in figure 29.2A) the shift is called a response bias rather than an illusion (a point to be remembered for when we look at Libet's data) and one doesn't look for special mechanisms. Only when a true illusion is present as in figure 29.2B does a major industry among perceptual psychologists (or quantum physicists) develop to understand the brain mechanisms that can account for the data.

Figure 29.2C shows two psychometric functions collected using a procedure similar to Libet's where the number of response categories is increased from two to three: a) upper arrow is left of lower, b) upper arrow equal to lower, and c) upper arrow right of lower. A sample dataset using three response categories is given in table 29.2.

Table 29.2
Raw observations for figure 29.2C. Three categories, similar to Libet.

stimulus offset	−100	−50	0	50	100
upper is shorter	45	25	5	1	0
upper is equal	5	24	40	24	5
upper is longer	0	1	5	25	45

Table 29.3
Probabilities for figure 29.2C. The two psychometric functions from table 29.2 data.

stimulus offset	−100	−50	0	50	100
probability that upper is rightward or equal	10%	50%	90%	98%	100%
probability that upper is rightward	0%	2%	10%	50%	90%

The "upper is rightward" category of table 29.2 is the same as in table 29.1, implying that in table 29.1 the "upper is equal" and the "upper is shorter" categories had been combined. The psychometric function for that criterion are given in the bottom row of table 29.3. A second criterion groups the "upper is equal" with the "upper is rightward" as shown in the upper row of table 29.3.

The results of fitting thess data are the three parameters: $PSE_1 = -49.4 \pm 5.0$ microns, $PSE_2 = +49.4 \pm 5.0$ microns, and threshold $= 2.6\sigma = 92 \pm 10$ microns.

I was first inspired to look closely at Libet's raw data by reading Wolf's (1998) article. He reproduced a portion of Libet's table 2a in order to test a hypothesis about a 20 msec delay between thalamic stimulation vs. skin stimulation. Being skeptical about whether the data was good enough to make 20 msec reliable distinctions, I decided to plot and refit Libet's raw data.

Figure 29.3 plots the data from table 2a of Libet (1979). This is just like figure 29.2C except that now the abscissa is the temporal difference rather than spatial difference between two percepts. The vertical axis is the percent of occurrences that a stimulus was perceived to be later than the reference stimulus. The three response categories are: skin first, a tie, and thalamus first (for the skin-thalamus experiment with skin as a reference). The total responses in the three categories were approximately equal (54, 66, 52 trials respectively). The lower curve (diamonds) is the probability that the skin was first. For the upper curve (asterisks) the "equal" votes were combined with the "skin first" results corresponding to a looser criterion for the skin being first. It corresponds to the probability that the thalamus was chosen as *last*. The upper pair of panels are for observer HS; the lower are for GS. The right pair of

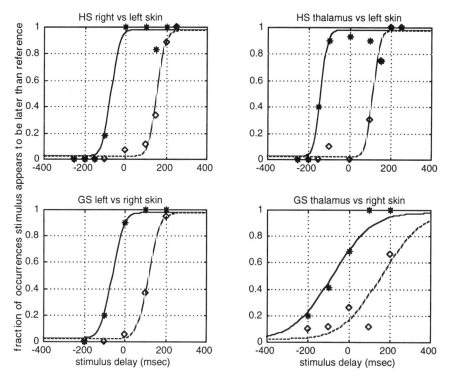

Figure 29.3
Data from figure 2a of Libet (1979). The right hand panels compare the perceived timing of a thalamic stimulus relative to a reference skin stimulus. The left hand panels compare a skin stimulus to the same reference. The upper and lower panels are for two observers. The gap between the two curves shows the fraction of time that the observer felt the two stimuli were simultaneous. This large gap indicates the difficulty of the asynchrony judgment.

panels compares the perceived timing of a thalamic stimulus relative to a non-overlapping skin stimulus; the left compares skin to skin.

The two continuous curves in each panel are the best fits to the data. The fitting function is the standard cumulative normal distribution given by:

$$\text{prob}(z_i) = g + (1 - 2g) \int_{-\infty}^{z} \exp(-(x\text{-}PSE_i)^2/2\sigma^2)\, dx \qquad (1)$$

where σ is the standard deviation (stimulus threshold defined as the stimulus range for 10% to 90% correct is 2.6σ). A guessing parameter, g, has been included (Manny and Klein 1984) to allow for the possibility of making absent-minded errors even when the stimulus delay is large; g was constrained to equal 0.025, a small number.

The chi square goodness of fit is much worse and the thresholds are elevated if $g = 0$. Three free parameters were used to fit the data for each panel: two criteria, PSE_i, (with $i = 1$ or 2) to locate the horizontal position of each curve, and one parameter, s, to determine the slopes (threshold) of the curves. The two curves were assumed to have the same slopes.

In order to help make the connection between figure 29.3 and the raw data in Libet's table 2a we have reorganized the table so that it is similar to our previous tables. Table 29.4 shows the data for the thalamic vs. skin comparison for subject GS. We have switched the sign of the abscissa so that the delay is relative to the skin stimulus reference in all cases. That makes comparing the delays less confusing.

The optimal parameter values were obtained by minimizing chi-square (Levi et al. 1984):

$$\chi^2 = \sum_i \frac{(O_i - E_i)^2}{E_i} \tag{2}$$

where O_i is the raw data from Libet's table 2a and E_i is the expected values based on the fitted curve. The results of the fit are summarized in table 29.5.

The optimal chi-square value is given in the last column of table 29.5. For HS there are nine stimuli, at delays of ± 250, ± 200, ± 150, ± 100, 0 msec. For GS the stimuli

Table 29.4
Table of events (number of observations/total number) for lower right panel of figure 29.3.

thalamic onset time relative to skin onset for GS (msec)	−200	−100	0	100	200
thalamic stimulation perceived last or tied (*)	4/20	7/17	13/19	18/18	18/18
thalamic stimulation perceived last (diamonds)	2/20	2/17	5/19	2/18	12/18

Table 29.5
Parameter estimates and standard errors for the psychometric function fits in figure 29.3.

Subject	PSE_1	PSE_2	10–90 threshold	chi-square
HS, skin-skin	−69 ± 18	153 ± 13	87 ± 26	8.9
HS, skin-thalamus	−139 ± 13	111 ± 13	68 ± 30	16.6
GS, skin-skin	−60 ± 13	115 ± 12	117 ± 25	2.9
GS, skin-thalamus	−78 ± 47	156 ± 56	395 ± 127	17.9

are at ± 200, ± 100, 0 msec. Thus the summation is over $9 \times 3 = 27$ cells for HS and $5 \times 3 = 15$ cells for GS, and the degrees of freedom are $9*(3-1)-3 = 15$ and $5*(3-1)-3 = 7$ respectively, so the chi-square values are reasonable.

The shift in the average criterion between the skin-skin and thalamus vs. skin is -56 and $+12$ msec for HS and GS respectively, (e.g., HS's skin-skin average is $(153-69)/2 = 42$ and the thalamus-skin average is $(111-139)/2 = -14$ giving a 56 msec difference). Libet's average shift from table 2b (his A&C vs B&D) are -12 and -20 msec respectively. The 30 to 40 msec discrepancies between our calculations and Libet's are due to our different methods of fitting the data. Our method (Levi et al. 1984), based on minimizing equation 2, is the standard method for fitting this type of data. In any case, the discrepancy between the two PSE calculations is small when compared to the 10%–90% threshold.

Before further analysis of figure 29.3 and table 29.5, it is useful to present the data from Libet's table 3a comparing touch and visual stimulation with *cortical* stimulation. As with the case of thalamic stimulation the pulse train intensity was sufficiently large so that the train duration needed for conscious awareness was between 200—300 msec. The actual pulse train that was delivered was between 500 and 700 msec.

Figure 29.4 shows the psychometric functions for three observers, JW, CJ, and MT. These are the three observers that Libet considered to be his best examples for illustrating backward referral. The bottom pair of panels is for observer MT who had a slightly different stimulus; a *visual flash* was paired either with a skin stimulus or a cortical stimulus. The results of the chi-square minimization fit are shown in table 29.6.

Standard errors are undefined in several conditions (indicated by ??) because of scanty data. For the skin-skin data of JW and CJ there was only a single point on the psychometric function between 0 and 100% so that the program was unable to estimate the slope error and therefore unable to estimate the threshold error. For the skin-cortex data of CJ there were no trials in which the observer responded that the cortex stimulus was first so the search program was unable to produce a standard error estimate for the right-most criterion. The scanty data also produced abnormally low chisquare values.

Several problems with Libet's data are revealed by examining figures 29.3 and 29.4 and tables 29.5 and 29.6.

1) As seen in figure 29.4 and table 29.6 the PSE shifts in the cortical data are not larger than the thresholds. The entire backward referral enterprise of Penrose and Wolf is based on the belief that there is a trustworthy substantial shift between the time of cortical awareness vs. skin awareness. The shift must be large compared to

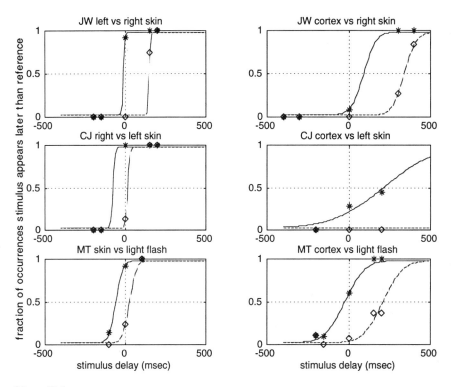

Figure 29.4
Data from figure 3a of Libet (1979). The righthand panels compare the perceived timing of a cortical stimulus relative to a reference skin stimulus (or a visual flash for MT). The lefthand panels compare a skin stimulus to the same reference. Results for three observers are shown. For the cortical stimulation, the large gap between the two criteria curves and the shallow slopes indicate that the shift in PSE is not large enough to warrant special explanations.

Table 29.6
Parameter estimates and standard errors for the psychometric function fits in figure 29.4.

Subject	PSE_1	PSE_2	10–90 threshold	chi-square
JW skin-skin	$-11 \pm ??$	$144 \pm ??$	$19 \pm ??$	1.5
JW skin-cortex	91 ± 60	338 ± 22	154 ± 74	1.2
CJ skin-skin	$-11 \pm ??$	$75 \pm ??$	$23 \pm ??$	1.3
CJ skin-cortex	213 ± 246	$??? \pm ??$	639 ± 452	1.6
MT flash-skin	-58 ± 17	25 ± 17	89 ± 29	0.9
MT flash-cortex	-22 ± 29	208 ± 31	249 ± 78	5.6

threshold for the backward referral to be taken seriously as a real "illusion." For observer CJ the 10%–90% threshold is 639 ± 452. This is much larger than the measured shift of $213 - (-11) = 224$ msec found for the "skin first" criterion (PSE1). For observer MT, the threshold is 249 msec, but the skin to cortex shift is 36 msec for the "skin first" criterion and 183 msec for the "cortex last" criterion (PSE2). Only for JW is the threshold of 154 msec larger than one of the criterion shifts, with PSE $= (91 + 11) = 102$ msec for "skin first" and $(338 - 144) = 194$ msec for "cortex second." Glynn (1990) pointed out these problems in a rough way without having plotted the data or fitted the data with psychometric functions.

2) The average cortex to skin shift is not large when compared to the uncertainty in the shift itself as measured by the separation between the two criterion PSEs. For JW and MT the difference between the two cortical PSEs were $338 - 91 = 247$ msec and $208 + 22 = 230$ msec. These values are large because the observers made very heavy use of the "tie" category where the two stimuli were perceived to be simultaneous. This heavy use of the "tie" category undermines any claim of a substantial shift. For CJ the time difference between the two PSEs was too large to measure (as indicated by the question mark in the PSE2 column). The large number of "tie" responses indicates that the synchrony decision was difficult and not strongly reliable. The PSE shifts could simply be caused by the observer adopting a looser criterion for when he claims the two stimuli are simultaneous.

3) Both of these considerations also apply to figure 29.3 and table 29.5 comparing the thalamic vs. skin stimulation to a skin vs. skin stimulation. The thalamic data are good to examine because they are more robust than the cortical data. For GS the threshold is large and for both observers the separation between PSEs is large, again because of heavy use of the "tie" condition. Thus, the uncertainty in the subjective timings, as evidenced in the raw data, makes it prudent not to develop exotic explanations for the claimed lack of PSE shifts in the thalamic case. The notion that the criterion placement is easily manipulatable was also a theme of my Tucson II article on blindsight (Klein 1998).

4 Summary

1. All of Libet's (1979) data are compatible with normal causality since all responses occur after the stimulus onset.

2. There are at least two reasonable explanations of Libet's time anomaly data: a) there is a fixed delay between the stimulus time marker and conscious awareness of the stimulus; b) the time of occurrence of the qualia that gets placed in memory is the

time of the time marker. In the case of cortical stimulation the evoked potential time marker is missing so the time of neuronal adequacy becomes the marker. Explanation b has evolutionary merit in synchonizing the subjective and objective times of stimulation.

3. By fitting Libet's raw data with standard psychometric functions it is found that PSE timing shifts owing to brain stimulation are relatively small when compared to both the threshold (time between 10% and 90% correct) and the uncertainty in placing the judged time of equality (PSE2-PSE1). The thresholds and criterion uncertainties would have to be much smaller before one should get excited by the PSE shifts.

In summary, Libet's supposed time anomalies provide a weak scaffold on which to build a case that quantum mechanics is needed for brain operation.[1] The duality of quantum mechanics may be needed for philosophical purposes, such as connecting the subjective and objective world views, but not for handling time anomalies.

Acknowledgment

I would like to thank David Chalmers for helpful comments on an earlier version of this manuscript.

Note

1. The causality violating time anomalies of Bierman and Radin (1999) also merit skepticism. These paranormal experiments are missing a key ingredient: the oversight of a skeptic skilled in finding methodological flaws. That missing item may soon be overcome through recent discussions between Bierman and the magician Randi. Randi is offering a large reward for a demonstration of ESP under conditions where care is taken to prevent sensory leakage and improper data handling. Until these controlled experiments are done, it is prudent not to overturn present physics that has otherwise proven so successful.

References

Baldo, M. V. C., and Klein, S. A. 1995. Extrapolation or attention shift? *Nature* 378, 565–566.

Bierman, D. J., and Radin, D. I. 1999. Conscious and anomalous unconscious emotional responses: Evidence for a reversal of the arrow of time. In *Toward a Science of Consciousness III*: The Third Tucson Discussions and Debates. Hameroff, S. R., Kaszniak, A. W. and Chalmers, D. J. (eds.), MIT Press (this volume).

Churchland, P. 1981. The timing of sensations: Reply to Libet. *Philosophy of Science* 48:492–497.

Dennett, D. C. 1991. *Consciousness Explained*. Little Brown, Boston.

Glynn, I. M. 1990. Consciousness and time. *Nature* 348:477–479.

Gregory, R. L. 1970. *The Intelligent Eye*. McGraw-Hill.

Honderich, T. 1984. The time of a conscious sensory experience and mind-brain theories. *J. Theoretical Biology* 220:115–119.

Levi, D. M., Klein, S. A., and Aitsebaomo, P. 1984. Detection and discrimination of motion in central and peripheral vision of normal and amblyopic observers. *Vision Research* 24:789–800.

Klein, S. A. 1993. Will robots see? In *Spatial Vision in Humans and Robots*, Cambridge University Press, 184–199.

Klein, S. A. 1995. Is quantum mechanics relevant to understanding consciousness? A review of *Shadows of the Mind*, by Roger Penrose. Psyche, http://psyche.cs.monash.edu.au/v2/

Klein, S. A. 1998. Double-judgment psychophysics for research on consciousness: Application to blindsight. In *Toward a Science of Consciousness II: The Second Tucson Discussions and Debates*. Hameroff, S. R., Kaszniak, A. W., and Scott, A. C., eds.

Libet, B., Wright, E. Jr., Feinstein, B., and Pearl, D. K. 1979. Subjective referral of the timing for a conscious sensor experience: a functional role for the somatosensory specific projection system in man. *Brain* 194:191–222.

Libet, B. vs. Glynn, I. M. 1991. Conscious vs. neural time. *Nature* 352:27–28.

Libet, B. 1993. The neural time factor in conscious and unconscious events. In *Experimental and Theoretical Studies of Consciousness* (CIBA Foundation Symposium 174), 123–146. Chichester: Wiley.

Manny, R. E., and Klein, S. A. 1984. The development of vernier acuity in infants. *Current Eye Research*, 453–462.

Nijhawan, R. 1994. Motion extrapolation in catching. *Nature* 370:256–257.

Penrose, R. 1994. *Shadows of the Mind: An approach to the Missing Science of Consciousness*. New York: Oxford University Press.

Penrose, R. 1997. *The Large the Small and the Human Mind*. New York: Cambridge University Press.

Wolf, F. A. 1998. The timing of conscious experience: A causality violating, two-valued, transactional interpretation of subjective antedating and spatial-temporal projection. *Journal of Scientific Exploration* 12:511–542. My references to Wolf are based on the long Libet article that is on Wolf's web site (http://www.hia.com/pcr/wolf/libet.html). I have not seen the shorter version that is included in this volume. My rebuttal to Wolf's critique of the present article will appear in my forthcoming article in the *Journal of Consciousness Studies*.

Wolf, F. A. 1999. A quantum physics model of the timing of conscious experience. In *Toward a Science of Consciousness III: The Third Tucson Discussions and Debates*. Hameroff, S. R., Kaszniak, A. W., and Chalmers, D. J. (eds.). Cambridge, Mass.: MIT Press (this volume).

30 A Quantum Physics Model of the Timing of Conscious Experience

Fred Alan Wolf

In his recent book (Penrose 1994) Roger Penrose suggests that "*if*, in some manifestation of consciousness, classical reasoning about the temporal ordering of events leads us to a contradictory conclusion, then this is strong indication that quantum actions are indeed at work!" Here we examine a quantum theory of the relationship between the awareness of timings of events and their corresponding physical correlates and show that indeed not only are quantum actions at work, they are indispensable in explaining the temporal paradoxes inherent in the phenomena.

The problem is that physical events eliciting awareness take place *after* one becomes conscious of them. This has been indicated in experiments performed by Benjamin Libet and his co-workers (Libet et al. 1979) who hypothesize that a specific mechanism within the brain is responsible for the projection of these events both out in space (spatial referral) and back in time (temporal referral). Libet refers to this as the *delay-and-antedating hypothesis/paradox*.

My model (called TTOTIM) provides a plausible resolution of this paradox. It is based the work of Aharonov and his co-workers on two-time observables (TTO) (Aharonov et al. 1985, 1987; Aharonov and Vaidman 1990) and on Cramer's transactional interpretation (TI) (Cramer 1986, 1983).

The Delay and Antedating Paradox

The "delay-and-antedating" paradox/hypothesis refers to the lag in time of measurable cerebral electrical activity associated with a conscious sensory experience following a peripheral sensation. To account for this paradox, Libet suggested subjective antedating of that experience. In a series of studies (Libet et al. 1979, Libet 1996) several subjects' brains showed that neuronal adequacy (critical neural activity) wasn't achieved until a significant delay time D as high as 500 msecs following a stimulus. Yet the subjects stated that they were aware of the sensation within a few msec (10–50 msec) following the stimulation. Put briefly, how can a subject be aware of a sensation, that is, be conscious of it, if the subject's brain has not registered that "awareness"?

Since many plausible arguments have been offered and refuted by Libet et al. and others (Bergenheim et al. 1996) I will not go into them here.

The Two-Time Observable Transactional Interpretation Model (TTOTIM) of Consciousness

According to the TTOTIM, a future event and a present event are involved in a transaction: A real (complex-valued retarded wave) quantum state vector, $|O(1)\rangle$, called the "offer" wave, issues from the present event (1) and travels to the future event (2). The future event is then stimulated to send back through time an "echo" state vector (complex-conjugated advanced wave), $\langle E(2)|$, toward the present event. The probability distribution (probability per unit volume) for a transaction to occur, given by the probability amplitude, $\langle E(2)|O(1)\rangle$, then equals the positive real probability-a correlation between the two events—arising as a probability field around the initial event. This field depends on values acquired at the echo site (2) as well as values obtained from the initiating site (1).

My TTOTIM theory links *mental* and *neural* events. Awareness (mental events) arise as a result of the projection of brain events into space and back in time to the loci of physical events. Thus a conscious experience occurs if and only if at least *two* physical events occur. Hence neuronal adequacy and subjective experience are not one and the same. Neither are peripheral stimulation and subjective experience even though they seem to be. Both stimulation and neuronal adequacy (two events) are needed for conscious experience. The time of that experience is retro-referred close to the time of the elicitation of the sensory signal.

The TTOTIM sheds light on both "subjective referral in time" as well as "subjective referral in space." Libet (Libet et al. 1979) suggests that neuronal adequacy following a peripheral sensation is temporally and spatially projected onto the peripheral site similar to the way visual experience is projected. The achievement of neuronal adequacy following a peripheral stimulus elicits a backward-through-time signal and the somatosensory cortex (*SI*) upon achievement of neuronal adequacy must relay this signal out to the physical location of the stimulus. If the stimulus is applied to the brain itself the theory predicts this projection must occur forward-in-time.

The Quantum Mechanics of the Passive Mind

In the following figures we see how offer and echo state vectors are involved in typical peripheral stimulus response actions. The TTOTIM successfully explains the difference between a phantom sensation elicited by the cortical stimulus and the real sensation elicited by the skin stimulus. The key difference is the impetus for the sensation

Skin with cortical stimulus acting as a blocking signal

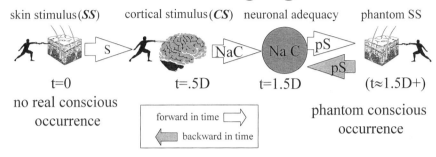

skin stimulus (*SS*)   cortical stimulus (*CS*)   neuronal adequacy   phantom SS

t=0   t=.5D   t=1.5D   (t≈1.5D+)

no real conscious   phantom conscious
occurrence   occurrence

forward in time
backward in time

Figure 30.1
Although a skin stimulus (*SS*) occurs before a cortical stimulus (*CS*) is applied, *SS* does not lead to awareness.

is quite different in that the skin stimulus elicits a time marker signal and the cortical stimulus doesn't.

In figure 30.1 we look at how these two stimuli compare when both are used. We see two signals applied. At *t* = **0**, *SS* causes a quantum wave vector, $|S\rangle$, to travel forward in time. However at *t* = **.5D**, *CS* is applied interrupting and interfering with the state vector. Neuronal adequacy for *SS* is not achieved. Instead a quantum wave vector, $|na\,C\rangle$, travels forward in time. As time continues a train of signal pulses is elicited leading to neuronal adequacy at *t* = **1.5D** (around .75 sec). This in turn elicits a state vector, $|pS\rangle$, that travels forward in time arriving at *t* ≈ **1.5D**+ at the appropriate skin area. Next the time reversed echo state vector, $\langle pS|$, goes back in time to *t* = **D** where it initiates the backward-through-time state vector, $\langle na\,C|$ (not shown), that returns to the onset site of the original cortical stimulus and completes the circuit. There is no awareness of *SS* although a phantom skin sensation produced by the cortical train is felt later if the wave train duration is sufficient. The phantom event for conscious awareness does not occur at a precise time but subjectively accordingly somewhere in the interval Δ*t* between time *t* = **1.5D** and *t* = **1.5D**+ (*t* ≈ **1.5D**+).

One would think from this that the paradox has been resolved. However a question arises when we compare these stimuli with direct stimuli to the thalamus or medial lemniscus just below the thalamus. Signals applied there, unlike cortical stimuli, do elicit time marker signals at *SI*. Thus one would expect according to Libet's hypothesis, a

Comparison of Thalamus roles

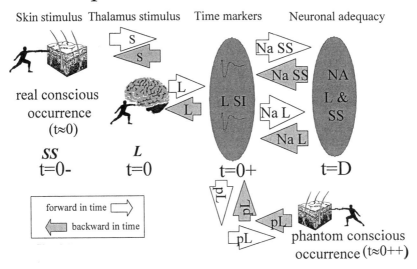

Figure 30.2
The thalamus and skin stimuli are compared.

similar antedating for the awareness of such signals when compared with cortical signals. Although this has been confirmed in a number of studies (Libet et al. 1979) there is a difference in the timings predicted by the TTOTIM.

In figure 30.2 we compare two stimuli (*SS* at $t = 0 - \approx -5$ msec and *L* at $t = 0$) each eliciting a simultaneous time marker signal ($t = 0 + \approx 10$ msec) and achieving simultaneous neuronal adequacy ($t = D$). Yet they are not experienced simultaneously. The thalamus (*L*) phantom skin stimulus is felt slightly later at $t \approx 0++$ (≈ 20 msec) provided the *L* signal train duration is sufficient to achieve adequacy. The real skin stimulus is felt earlier $t \approx 0$.

Both *S* and *L* signals elicit time markers signals at *SI* while *C* signals don't. Libet explains that all signals regardless of where the onset site exists require adequacy—a time delay to become conscious. My theory explains the time order of the awareness of passive stimuli events and predicts that phantom or projected experiences whose origins are brain-based will appear later than their associated time marker events (if they occur) while peripheral stimuli will become conscious earlier than their time markers. It answers the question, "How are we to explain the fact that even though *L* elicits a time marker signal, there is no awareness of this signal unless neuronal adequacy is achieved?" The answer becomes apparent when we realize that spacetime

Cortical-before-skin stimulus cortical-after-skin response

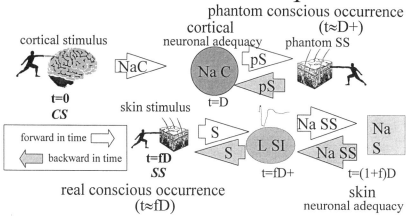

Figure 30.3
An explanation of Libet's hypothesis/paradox temporal reversal relationship between the timings in cortical and skin stimuli.

projection and therefore sensation does not occur unless neuronal adequacy does and then it occurs in reference to the time marker.

In figure 30.3 we see a TTOTIM explanation of Libet's hypothesis/paradox temporal reversal relationship between the timings in cortical and skin stimuli. Here two stimuli are applied with a delay of fD ($0 \leq f \leq 1$), between them. At $t = 0$ a cortical stimulus is applied (CS), which leads to a quantum wave vector, $|Na\,C\rangle$, initiated at the cortical stimulus site SI travelling forward in time leading to neuronal adequacy at $t = D$ and a phantom state vector, $|pS\rangle$, arriving at $t = D+$ at the area of the skin associated with the particular site SI. Next the time reversed echo state vector, $\langle pS|$, goes back to $t = D$ where it initiates the backward-through-time state vector, $\langle Na\,C|$, that returns to the onset site of the original cortical stimulus at $t = 0$ completing the cortical cycle. At $t = fD$ a skin stimulus is applied (SS) leading to a quantum wave vector, $|S\rangle$, travelling forward in time to $t = fD+$ at $L\,SI$ where it initiates a time marker signal. As time contiues the state vector, $|Na\,SS\rangle$, propagates forward in time leading to neuronal adequacy at SI, which occurs after the delay time $(1 + f)D$. Next the time-reversed echo state vector, $\langle Na\,SS|$, goes back in time to $t = fD+$ where it initiates the backward-through-time state vector, $\langle S|$, that returns to the site of the

skin stimulus completing the cycle. Subjectively the phantom awareness of the cortical signal appears to occur in the interval Δt_c between $t = D$ and $t = D+$ ($t \approx D+$)
while the event for conscious awareness of the skin stimulus occurs somewhere in the
earlier interval, Δt_s, between $t = fD$ and $t = fD+$ ($t \approx fD$).

Since the cortical stimulus does not elicit a time marker signal, the corresponding
phantom skin projection occurs well after the skin stimulus projection. It is only
when the fraction $f = 1$, corresponding to the skin stimulus being applied D later are
the stimuli sensed to be simultaneous.

Conclusion

The question, "Is there *really* an 'actual time' at which a conscious experience takes
place?" is answered *negatively* indicating, however, that while a precise timing for
such event does not occur, awareness of peripheral, passive, sensory input must take
place before the cortex has achieved neuronal adequacy while awareness of phantom
or "fill-in" experience produced by cortical stimuli must take place after. Sub-cortical
stimuli, applied to the thalamus or to the medial lemniscus, lie on the borderline
between peripheral and direct cortical stimuli. Stimuli applied here result in the generation of time marker signals that play a role as referents for both temporal and
spatial projection—the specific projection system. Passive, peripheral, sensory inputs
are perceived slightly before a time marker arrives at the somatosensory cortex (SI)
and direct thalamic or lemniscal stimuli (L) are perceived slightly after. We have
come to this conclusion using the TTOTIM, which indicates both initial and final
events are necessary to produce consciousness in the time interval between them.

One of the new and exciting predictions of this theory is the difference between the
timings of phantom (thalamic) and real sensory stimuli. Hence we will sense "real"
things before we project our mental maps of these experiences onto them but will
compare these sensations slightly later. If two time markers are made to simultaneously arise one coming from L and the other from SS, the SS sensation will
become conscious ≈ 10 msec *before* and the L sensation will become conscious about
≈ 10 msec *after*. This appears to be tentatively borne out by experiment (Libet et al.
1979, p. 210). The results are close, to be sure, and it is natural and necessary that
they be close, to be encouraging for a quantum physical theory. Assuming that
images, memories of sensory inputs, and real sensory data involve the thalamus and
the specific projection system within (and consequently elicit time markers), it would
follow that the overlap between what we sense "out there" and what we project "out
there" as experience must occur in close temporal proximity. This may be the reason

for the early evolutionary development of the specific projection (lemniscal) system. Clearly any long delay between sensory inputs and cortical projections (memories or sensory images) that do not elicit time markers could lead to extinction of the species.

Finally I would like to add some thoughts regarding peripheral somatic stimuli, Parkinson's disease, and some prospects for further experimental research regarding the TTOTIM. Libet has already indicated that when the body is subjected to synchronous stimuli, the subject responds without any indication of asynchrony or subjective jitter. If there was no backward-through-time projection from the time when neuronal adequacy was achieved, given that a variety of stimuli would produce a variety of intensities and pulse/train duration, one would expect to experience a lot of jitter owing to the various times when adequacy would be achieved. Since this does not occur it indicates support for the theory.

It is now known that people suffering from Parkinson's disease suffer from what appears to be asynchronous jitter. I suggest that a Parkinsonian subject's thalamus in response to somatic stimuli has lost the ability to provide adequate time marker signals. Consequently synchronous stimuli result in asynchronous behavior or the familiar jitter observed. When electrical stimuli are delivered to the thalamus it is known that the subject's jitter stops or is minimized considerably. I suggest the electrical stimulation provides an artificial supply of time markers. Experiments with Parkinsonian subjects may offer a new source of experimental information regarding the specific projection mechanism and the proposed projection timings indicated by the TTOTIM.

Very little has been done by physicists about subjective experience and for probably very good reasons; no one knows what to do, what to measure, or even if it is ethical to perform such measurements if we knew what we were looking for. Here Libet's remarkable experiments need special mention. At least in them we are provided with a clue concerning subjective time order. Perhaps there is something fundamental in the notion that our equations are not time order unique and (e.g., the theory given here) that we need two or more separate physical events to have a single mental perception. Perhaps this theory that a perceived event requires information flowing from physical end points coming before it and after it, much like a stringed musical instrument requires information coming from its nodal end points to set up standing wave patterns of musical harmony, is a fundamental requirement for both time order uniqueness and subjective experience.

Thus we need to look toward altering our concept of time in some manner, not that this is an easy thing to do. Perhaps we should begin with the idea that a single event in time is really as meaningless as a single event in space or a single velocity.

Meaningful relation arises as a correspondence, a relationship with some reference object.

The resolution of temporal paradoxes particularly as they show themselves in future quantum physical objective experiments and in subjective timing experiments will continue to require a new vision of time and its relation to awareness. Perhaps this chapter will assist us in our search.

Acknowledgment

Supported in part by a grant from The Internet Science Education Project.

References

Aharonov, Y., Albert, D. Z., and D'Amato, S. S. 1985. Multiple-time properties of quantum-mechanical systems. *Physical Review D* 32:1975–1984.

Aharonov, Y., Albert, D., Casher, A., and Vaidman, L. 1987. Surprising Quantum Effects. *Phys. Lett. A*. 124:199–203.

Aharonov, Y. and. Vaidman, L. 1990. Properties of a quantum system during the time interval between two measurements. *Physical Review A* 41:11–20.

Bergenheim, M., Johansson, H., Granlund, B., and Pedersen, J. 1996. Experimental Evidence for a Synchronization of sensory Information to Conscious Experience. In *Toward a Scientific Basis for Consciousness*, ed. Hameroff, S. R., Kaszniak, A. W., and Scott, A. C. The MIT Press, Cambridge, Mass., pp. 303–310.

Cramer, J. G. 1983. Generalized absorber theory and the Einstein-Podolsky-Rosen paradox. *Physical Review D*. 22:362–376.

Cramer, J. G. 1986. Transactional interpretation of quantum mechanics. *Reviews of Modern Physics* 58:647–687.

Libet, B., Wright, E. W., Feinstein, B., and Pearl, D. K. 1979. Subjective Referral of the Timing for a Conscious Sensory Experience. *Brain* 102:193–224.

Penrose, R. 1994. *Shadows of the Mind*. Oxford University Press, New York, p. 387.

31 Conscious and Anomalous Nonconscious Emotional Processes: A Reversal of the Arrow of Time?

Dick J. Bierman and Dean Radin

Two previous experiments have been reported that tried to explore physiological indicators of "precognitive information" in which subjects respond *prior to* presented stimuli. In an elegant experiment in the early seventies, John Hartwell, then at Utrecht University, measured the Contingent Negative Variation (CNV) after a warning signal and before a random selected picture of a face was to be displayed (Hartwell 1978). The CNV is a brain potential that has been associated with anticipatory processes; more precisely the CNV is interpreted as a "readiness for response" preparation. The subjects in Hartwell's studies were asked to respond with one of two buttons depending on the gender of the face on the picture. The warning stimulus was sometimes informative, that is, the subject could infer from the warning stimulus what the gender type of the face on the picture would be. In those trials a mean CNV was observed that clearly differed for the two stimuli categories. In the other case the warning stimulus was uninformative but it was hoped that the CNV still would indicate what type of picture was about to be shown. Such a finding would suggest that in some way or another the subject had nonconscious knowledge of the nearby future.[1]

Nearly 20 years elapsed before the idea of precognitive information reflected in the physiology of subjects was picked up again by the second author of this article (Radin 1996). He used the physiological measures Skin Conductance, Heart Rate and Plethysmography, which reflect behavior of our sympathetic and parasympathetic nervous system. Furthermore, in contrast to Hartwell, he used highly emotional pictures that were presented 5 seconds after the subjects had pressed the button for the next trial. In 3 independent studies Radin found significant differences in physiology, most notably in the skin conductance, preceding the exposure of calm versus extreme pictures. The precognitive response was termed "presponse." Radin discussed a number of possible classical explanations for presponse but concluded that these do not apply.

However one potential "normal" explanation, namely the effect of anticipatory strategies, was not discussed at the time. Subjects who participate in this type of experiment while being aware that once every so often an extreme picture will be displayed may build up (generally incorrect) expectations about the probability that such an extreme picture will be shown in the forthcoming exposure. Indeed, due to the "gambler's fallacy," their expectation may increase after each calm picture and decrease after an extreme. Superficially it appears that this could result in a mean anticipatory presponse that is smaller for calm stimuli than for extreme stimuli.

This possible explanation of the differences in presponse was later modelled through elaborate computer simulations by the first author and by an independent sceptical outsider. It turned out that the effect as described above only emerges when randomization is done without replacement, and therefore it could not explain Radin's original results (see also discussion section).

Thus the experimental results by Radin suggested a true, large and replicable "precognitive" psi effects with a remarkable signal to noise ratio.

The first author of this chapter (DJB) was skeptical of these results and therefore decided to replicate the experiments using the same general procedure and the same picture material but completely different software and hardware and also a different randomization procedure. This would, if the effects could be replicated, make an explanation in terms of technical artefacts or inappropriate randomization less likely.

1   General Procedure

A participant sits in a comfortable chair in a dimly lit room, the index and middle finger of the left hand connected to a skin conductance measurement device. In the instruction the experimenter emphasises that the subject should try to experience each trial as a complete new one. After the instruction and one or more demonstration trials, the experimenter leaves the room and the participant may start the first trial by pressing a key on the keyboard. After 7.5 seconds,[2] a period that we call the *fore period*, a randomly chosen picture, either calm or highly emotional, is displayed for a specific exposure time (for randomization details see appendix 1). Before, during and after exposure the skin conductance is sampled by the computer with a sampling rate of 5 samples per second (see figure 31.1).

Study 1:   This is a rather straightforward replication of the experiments reported by Radin (Radin 1996). However the following modifications were made. Rather than selecting pictures completely randomly from the total pool, pictures are organised in three sets with different ratios between calm and extreme pictures. The set is chosen randomly at the beginning of each experiment such that the ratio is even unknown to the experimenter. Then the pictures in the set are shuffled and presented in the shuffled order. Thus all pictures in the set are presented.

Furthermore, rather than having different exposure times between studies as reported in Radin's original paper, we introduced this variable as a within subject variable. There are always two possible exposure times. Each of them is randomly selected with a probability of 0.5.

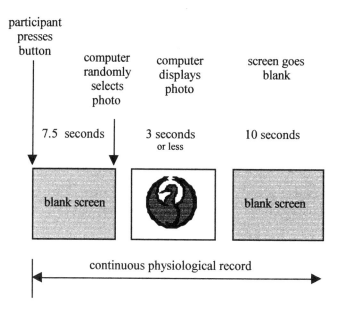

participant
presses
button

computer
randomly
selects
photo

computer
displays
photo

screen goes
blank

7.5 seconds

3 seconds
or less

10 seconds

blank screen

blank screen

continuous physiological record

Figure 31.1
Timing of one stimulus presentation.

Study 2: This is a study with uninformed subjects. They are told that 10 control pictures will be presented in order to establish a baseline in the physiological behavior. According to this cover story the real experiment would begin after establishment of this baseline.

Unknown to these subjects there will be a single extreme picture presented at a random sequence number between 3 and 10. For about half of the subjects this extreme picture is erotic, for the other half the crucial picture is violent.

Study 3: After study 2 the (same) subjects are now completely informed about the fact that occasionally there will be extreme pictures and thus the subject may have similar anticipation strategies as in study 1. Study 3 uses only one ratio (one extreme for every three calms) between extremes and calms, and moreover uses only 48 pictures from the original 120 pictures. These 48 pictures were selected on the basis of their stronger effects in study 1.

1.1   Stimulus Material

The basic stimulus material is identical to the set of pictures that has been used by Radin (1996). It consists of 80 calm pictures and 40 extreme pictures of a violent and erotic nature. This basic set of pictures was slightly updated by the student experimenter in study 1. She adjusted the set for cultural differences, most notably replaced a few erotic pictures that would not be seen as very arousing in Europe with more extreme pictures. A snapshot review of the updated set and other information on this study is available through Internet (http://www.psy.uva.nl/emo_int.1). For the studies 2 and 3 a subset of the 120 pictures of the basic set was used. This selection was based upon a qualitative evaluation of the response effect of each of the pictures in study 1. For the categories, violent and erotic, the most effective pictures were selected while for the calm category a random selection was made. In the category "violent" we included decorative body piercings, including genital piercings. The erotic pictures were of both homosexual and heterosexual nature. We did not make an effort to study the differential effects between these two subcategories.

1.2 Subjects

The subjects in all studies were recruited from the circle of friends or acquaintances of the experimenters. In the first study these were 16 health care professionals who followed a course in Therapeutic Touch. These subjects must be considered as very open minded. In the second and third study most subjects were students at the University of Amsterdam. Seven of the 32 considered themselves as skeptical toward the existence of paranormal phenomena.

1.3 Dependent Variables

The dependent variable in both studies is the behavior of the skin conductance during the 7.5 seconds preceding the stimulus (the fore period). The between-sample correlations and the large number of data points presents us with a problem of how to collapse the skin conductance during the fore period into a single dependent value in order to prevent over-analysis.

We defined the dependent variable P as the mean values of the samples between 4 seconds and 6 seconds after the subjects initiated the trial (which is indicated as the critical interval in figure 31.2) corrected with a baseline value obtained from the samples between 0.6 and 1.6 seconds after the subject started the trial.[3]

1.4 Independent Variables

In the studies the following independent variables are used:

a. Type *of stimulus (StimType)*; For each study this within subject variable has two values: calm and extreme. In the category extreme we discern two sub-categories: violent and erotic. In study 2 the type of stimulus is a between-subject variable.

b. Exposure *Time (Exp. Time)*; For each study this within subject variable has two levels.

c. Subject variables (Ss-X). The gender of the subjects may be an important variable because in normal research on the physiology of emotions gender-typical effects have been reported (Greenwald et al. 1989).

d. *Ratio* between calm and extremes (Study 1 only)

2   Hypothesis and Explorations

Because these three studies were basically done to validate the earlier results obtained by Radin, the major relevant hypothesis concerns the anomalous difference in anticipatory physiology before the exposure of calm and extreme pictures.

Furthermore we decided to explore the potential differences between different classes of emotional pictures and the effect of exposure time.

Finally we planned secondary analyses that could reveal normal sequential effects (study 1 only). This was done because in the studies reported here a "randomization without replacement" was used.

• We will explore the differential effects for calms and extremes matched for sequential position.

• We will explore the effects on the presponse pattern distribution for different extreme: calm ratios.

3   Results of Study 1

3.1   Subjects

In study 1, 16 subjects were tested in the period between October 4 and November 14, 1996. Three were male, and 13 female. Their age ranged from 22 to 57.

3.2   Calm vs. Extreme Effect

Each subject did 40 trials, so the total data set consists of $16 \times 40 = 640$ epochs of GSR. From these 640 there were 428 obtained with a calm stimulus and 212 with an extreme stimulus. These epochs are averaged for each stimulus category and a baseline, which is the mean value of the first sample (at the moment the subject presses the button to initiate the sequence), is subtracted.

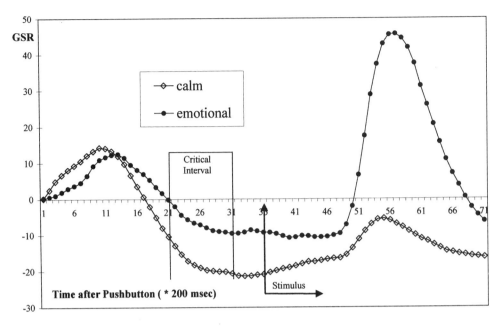

Figure 31.2
The mean GSR[1] as a function of sample number (time) for the two stimulus-categories. Stimulus presentation starts at sample 37. The critical interval where the presponse **P** is measured is also indicated. Note: GSR is used throughout the paper because we measured the phasic response signal and hence slow changing tonic levels are filtered out. The GSR is therefor only given in relative arbitrary units.

In figure 31.2 the average response is given for the calm epochs and for the extreme epochs. No error bars are indicated because error bars presuppose normality of the data-distribution.

The formal test consists of calculating the presponse **P** according to the definition given in the section on dependent variables and performing a Mann Whitney U test on the scores obtained preceding the calm and preceding the extreme stimuli. The resulting z-score is: 2.4 with a corresponding p-value of 0.016.

3.3 Violent vs. Erotic Effect

In figure 31.3 we have plotted the mean presponse pattern for erotic pictures and for violent pictures (NB the mean **calm** presponse is subtracted from both means).

From the figure it appears as if the violent presponse comes early and is the largest. A comparison of the independent variable **P** for the two types of pictures yields a (Mann-Whitney U) z-value of 1.65 (p = 0.09). The results for the violent presponse alone are quite significant (z = 2.94; p = 0.003).

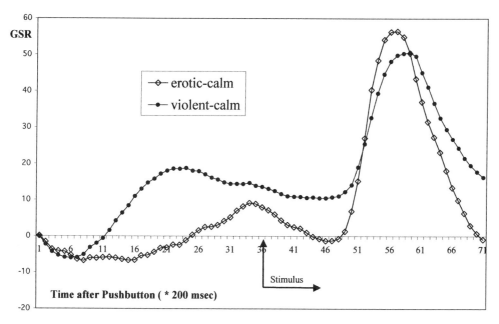

Figure 31.3
mean GSR vs. time for Erotic and Violent stimuli both corrected with the mean GSR for calm stimuli.

3.4 Exposure Time Effect

In figure 31.4 the average difference in presponse between extreme and calm is given for long (3000 msec) and short (400 msec) exposures. Although the differences are in the predicted direction, that is, the presponse effect is larger for short exposures (in contrast to the response effect) the differences when formally tested are near significant. (Mann Whitney U: z-value = 1.72, p = 0.085).

3.5 Secondary Analysis

A number of secondary analysis were done in order to test for sequential explanations. No evidence was found for such an explanation in terms of sequential strategies. (See appendix 2.)

4 Results of Study 2

4.1 Subjects

32 subjects, 16 males and 16 females, were tested in the period from February 17 to March 4, 1997. Their age ranged from 19 to 36.

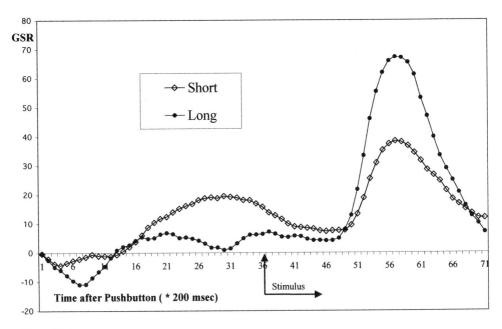

Figure 31.4
The average difference in presponse between extreme and calm trials for two different exposure times.

4.2   Calm vs. Extreme Effect

Each subject had only one extreme exposure, preceded by between 3 or 9 calm exposures. In figure 31.5 the difference between the mean physiological records of 32 extreme exposures and the mean of 184 calm exposures is given. It is clear that the effect is smaller than in study 1.

The formal test yielded a z-score for the difference between Calm and Extreme stimuli of 0.43. It should be noted that the power of study 2 was less than in study 1 (see also discussion).

4.3   Violent vs. Erotic Effect

Figure 31.6 shows the mean physiological record in cases of exposure of an erotic vs. cases with exposure of a violent picture. The over-all pattern is similar to the pattern found in study 1. The maximum value for violent exposures is earlier than for erotic exposures. There seems to be an interesting "symmetry" between presponse and response, especially for the erotic exposures.

The formal test yielded a z-score for the difference between Erotic and Violent pictures of 0.57 (n.s.).

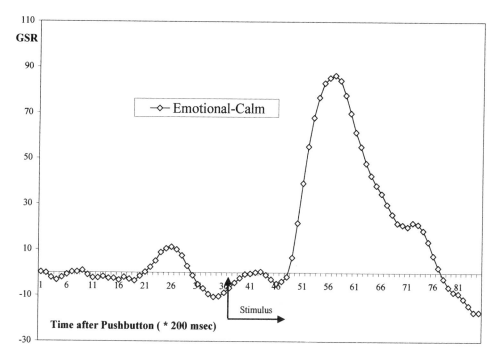

Figure 31.5
The differential effect of Calm vs. Extreme exposures in study 2.

4.4   Exposure Time Effect

Figure 31.7 shows the calm vs. extreme effects split for the two exposure times. In contrast with the findings of study 1 it appears that the shorter exposure time does not have a presponse at all. It should be noted that in study 1 the shortest exposure time is 600 msec while in this study it is 400 msec.

The formal test yielded a z-score for the difference between the two exposure times of 0.67 (n.s.).

5   Results of Study 3

5.1   Subjects

These were identical to study 2.

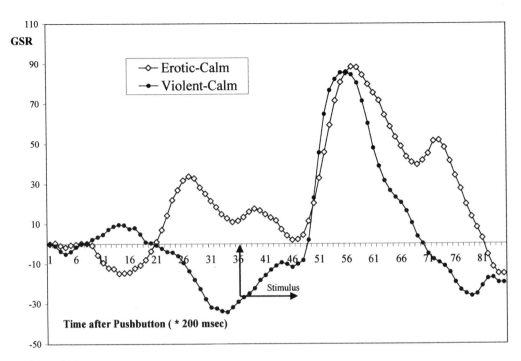

Figure 31.6
Mean GSR for Erotic vs. Violent stimuli, both corrected with the mean GSR for calm stimuli.

5.2 Calm vs. Extreme Effects

Figure 31.8 shows the over-all results of study 3. The presponse is again clearly visible but although the power is even slightly higher than in study 1 the difference in Presponse between Calms and Extreme stimuli doesn't reach statistical significance (z = 0.9; n.s.).

5.3 Erotic vs. Violent Effects

In figure 31.9 we may, with some fantasy, again discern an earlier presponse for violent than for erotic stimuli. The formal test however only deals with the magnitude of the effects during the critical period and hence do not show a significant effect (z = 0.14; n.s.)

5.4 Exposure Time Effects

Figure 31.10 displays the mean GSR for extreme stimuli for short and long exposure times. The Mann Whitney U test yields a z-score of 0.55 (n.s.).

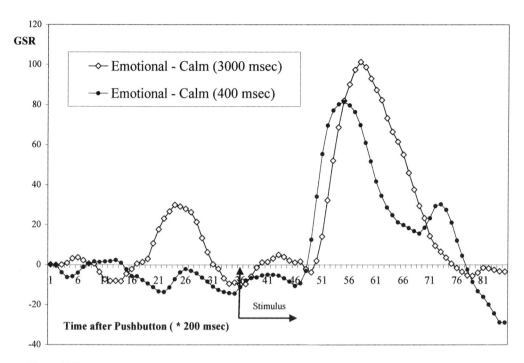

Figure 31.7
Mean GSR for Extreme stimuli for two exposure times. Extreme GSR is corrected with mean GSR for the calm stimuli.

6   Discussion

Table 31.1 reviews the three studies. The effect of a larger presponse for succeeding extreme pictures than for succeeding calm pictures is consistent through the three studies. We have calculated an effectsize measure (the difference in mean ranks for the two conditions that are compared normalised by the over-all mean rank in percent). This allows us to compare the studies quantitatively.

The Extreme vs. Calm effect is consistent throughout the three studies although the effectsize is only one third in studies 2 and 3. This effectsize reduction may be due to the different subject population. The combined result confirms the earlier findings of Radin.

The results of the comparison of violent and erotic stimuli in tabular form are confusing. The direction of the difference is not cosistent across the studies but here, apart from the different subject population, the choice of the dependent variable may

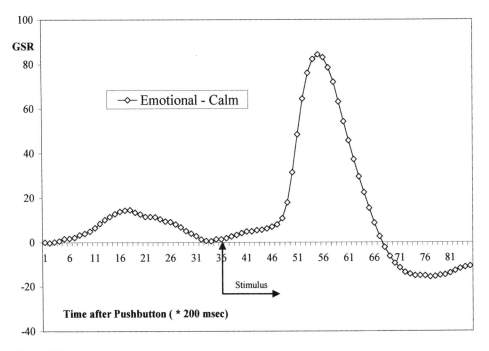

Figure 31.8
Mean GSR for Extreme stimuli corrected with the mean GSR obtained for Calm stimuli.

be questioned. In future research one should use a dependent variable that reflects the specific patterns (i.e., the early and the late phase of the presponse) better.

An interpretation of the exposure times findings is difficult because there were 3 different times used. It appears that an exposure time of 600 msec is better than 3000 msec but an exposure time of 400 msecs is inferior.

It should be noted that for 400 msec exposures the subjects do not always recognize the (emotional) contents of the pictures. So in that condition they may not always consciously experience an emotion.

Radin (1997) has adequately treated a number of potential normal or classical explanations of the effect. The current replication with completely different hard- and software strengthens the conclusion that the results can not be explained by a technical artifact.

The major (and maybe only) source of normal explanations left after Radin's original studies was the hypothesis that subjects developed anticipatory strategies that would result in artifactually different anticipatory physiology preceding calm or

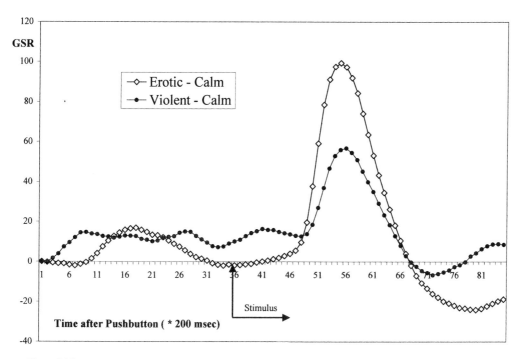

Figure 31.9
Mean GSR for Erotic vs. Violent in study 3.

extreme pictures. As was explained in the introduction this seems at first sight a real possibility. The current results however hardly support this notion because the pre-sponse effect seems not to be dependent on ratio between calm and extremes in a systematic way that should be expected if anticipation strategies based upon the Gambler's Fallacy were employed.

There are three further arguments against an explanation in terms of normal anticipatory strategies. The first one of these is that we find suggestive internal effects that can not easily be explained by this type of strategies. For instance, the difference between erotic and violent stimuli. It would require anticipatory strategies that dis-criminate between the two types of extreme pictures to account for that effect.

The second argument is that an analysis that takes into account the sequential history gives basically identical results. Of course this analysis does not correct for possible strategies that are based upon doublets of extremes and the like.

The final argument is that computer simulations of anticipatory strategies, using ratios and total number of exposures that are also used in the current studies, do not

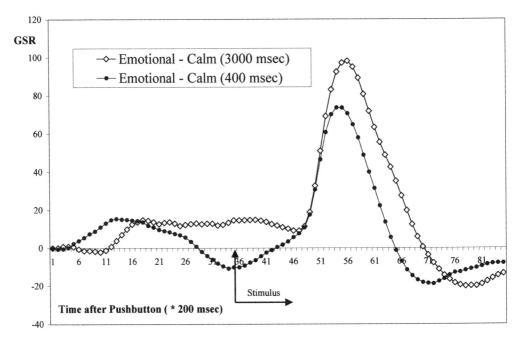

Figure 31.10
Mean GSR for extreme pictures for two exposure times. The data are corrected by the mean GSR for calm pictures with corresponding exposure times.

Table 31.1

study number	study 1	study 2	study 3	combined	p-value
extreme-calm z-score	+2.4	+0.43	+0.9	+2.16	0.016
effectsize extreme-calm	+11.3	+4.7	+4.4	–	–
erotic-violent z-score	−1.65	+0.57	+0.14	−0.54	n.s.
effectsize erotic-violent	−13.5	+12.7	+1.4	–	–
short-long exposure z	+1.72	−0.67	+0.55	+0.92	n.s.
effectsize short-long	+13.7	−13.9	+4.7	–	–

show the expected main calm vs. extreme effects. It turns out that these simulations are extremely sensitive for the type of randomization. If we used a random selection with replacement (open deck) the effects were nil. If we used a random shuffling without replacement then the effects ranged between 0 and 10%. This finding came as a surprise because the reasoning as sketched in the introduction has such a direct appeal.

The following anticipatory strategies were tested:

a) increase anticipation by 1 unit after each calm and resets anticipation to 1 after each extreme.

b) double anticipation after each calm (with a maximum of 500) and reset the anticipation after each extreme to either half or 1.

The simulated effects in the open-deck situation were never larger than 2% while the experimental effects in studies 1 and 2 are generally larger than 10%.

However, these analyses are by no means exhaustive and there may be less plausible models that may result in larger differences. The major point in favour of the psi hypothesis is however that there are no indications in the real data that support any of these sequential strategy models so far.

Is this Effect an Instance of Macroscopic Time Symmetry?

The results indicate a precognitive response—subjects react up to several seconds *before* the stimulus appears. Having ruled out anticipatory strategies, the only remaining explanations suggest some backward time referral. Formally the laws of physics are time-symmetric. Practically this time symmetry is observed in classical mechanics but not in thermodynamics where Boltzmann's second law forces the development of systems toward higher entropy. In a lucid book on time symmetry, Huw Price analyzes this problem and concludes that the standard "explanation" for assymetry based upon probabilistic arguments is incorrect (as Boltzmann himself also realized) (Price 1996). In an analysis of the asymmetry observed in radiation (EM theory) Price suggests that asymmetry here is caused by the spatial arrangements of radiation absorbers and emitters. Absorbers tend to be noncoherent while coherence is often the case for transmitters. According to Price this results in a destructive interference of any "advanced" waves (i.e., from absorber to emitter). Thus we never observe in nature back-action except potentially if we have a coherent absorbing system. Maybe our consciousness is such a system. Price shows also that when allowing for time-symmetry in quantum physics all puzzling paradoxes related to the measurement problem such as nonlocality disappear.

The results suggest that presponse occurs subconsciously but that ("subsequent") conscious experience of the emotional pictures are required. Price's analysis of the problem of lost time-symmetry suggests a continuation of these types of experiments with experienced meditators in altered states. If the meditator succeeds in blocking out the picture of his awareness we may get a complete disappearance of the phenomena. Interestingly this fits with lore about the relationships between meditation and the occurrence of "psi"-phenomena. It is said that on the path toward complete control of one's consciousness at some point psi-phenomena will appear. It is also said that one should not pay attention to these phenomena because that would only frustrate progress in meditation performance.

Within this, admittedly very speculative, framework the expected point of symmetry on the time axis is NOT at stimulus onset but rather at the start of the conscious (emotional) experience which may be around 500 msec later. Therefore the peak of the presponse is not expected around 3.5 seconds before the stimulus onset (where it would be if it was a mirror image of the response with symmetry point at stimulus onset) but rather about 2.5 seconds before stimulus onset, which fits well with the specification of the dependent variable in section 1.3.

Acknowledgments

Dagmar van der Neut was the experimenter in the first study. She was a continuous source of improvements and ideas. Also Rens Wezelman's stimulating discussions and weird insights were and are instrumental in the success of the research program. The Parapsychological Institute offered hospitality for the carrying out of study 1.

Notes

This article is an adapted version of a paper presented by the first author at the Parapsychological Convention (1997, Brighton UK).

1. The results of this experiment were, given the large efforts invested, disappointing. In hindsight it turns out that Hartwell's sensitivity was too low (his design was such that the anomalous differential effect had to be larger than 30% of the normal differential effect in order to be detectable). Also he used stimuli that had only a very low emotional value.

2. Radin originally used a 5 seconds foreperiod.

3. In the original paper, presented at the PA 1997, the first author used a sightly different interval but new theoretical insights suggested to shift the critical interval to one second earlier (see also discussion on time-symmetry). This does not affect the over-all conclusions.

4. GSR is used throughout the chapter because we measured the phasic response signal and hence slow changing tonic levels are filtered out. The GSR is therefore only given in relative arbitrary units.

References

Bechara, A., Damasio, H., Tranel, D., and Damasio, A. R. 1997. Deciding Advantageously before knowing the Advantageous Strategy. *Science* 275:1293–1295.

Bierman, D. J., and Radin, D. I. 1997. Anomalous Anticipatory Response on Randomized Future Conditions. *Perceptual and Motor Skills* 84:689–690.

Hartwell, J. 1978. CNV as an index of precognitive information. *European Journal of Parapsychology* 2:83–103.

Greenwald, M. K., Cook, E. W., and Lang, P. J. 1989. Affective judgment and psychophysiological response: Dimensional covariation in the evaluation of pictorial stimuli. *Journal of Psychophysiology* 3–1:51–64.

Merikle, P. M., Joordens, S., and Stolz, J. A. 1995. Measuring the relative magnitude of unconscious influences. *Consciousness and Cognition* 4:422–439.

Murphy, T. S., and Zajonc, R. B. 1993. Affect, Cognition, and Awareness: Affective priming with Optimal and Suboptimal Stimulus Exposure. *Journal of Personality and Social Psychology* 64(5):723–839.

Price, H. 1996. Time's arrow and Archimedes Point: new directions for the physics of time. Oxford University Press. ISBN: 0–19–510095–6

Radin, D. I. 1997. Unconscious perception of future emotions: An experiment in presentiment. *Journal of Scientific Exploration* 11(2):163–180.

Appendix 1:   Randomization Details

Proper randomization of the presentation order is a critical element in this type of experiments because the basic assumption is that the participant can by no normal means know what the following stimulus may be. Stimulus-arrays were shuffled using a pseudo random generator based upon the standard random function in the CodeWarrior C programming environment (CodeWarrior for Macintosh, version 8.). Sources of the software are available through Internet. It should be remarked that this randomization procedure is done at the start of the presentation of the first trial and therefore an interpretation of the results in terms of clairvoyance rather than precognition is allowed. (http://www.psy.uva.nl/emo_int.1)

Appendix 2:   Secondary Analyses in Study 1

A.1   Ratio Effect

In order to evaluate the effect of different ratios between calm and extreme stimuli, an ANOVA was done using Stimulus category and Ratio as factors and the *P*-score as dependent variable. Given the non-normality of the *P*-score distribution this turns out to be a slightly conservative approach. The results showed that the mean presponse for all stimuli, calms and extremes was heavily influenced by the ratio ($F = 15.36$, df $= 2$, $p < 0.0001$). This is due to the fact that ratio is a between subject variable and subjects do differ greatly with respect to psychophysiological responsiveness. The interaction with stimulus category however was not significant suggesting that the ratio extremes: calms was of no influence on the calm vs. extreme presponse effect.

A.2   Matching for Sequential Position

In the previous analyses the means of the presponses were calculated independent of the sequential position of the specific stimulus. So the average of the calm presponses is composed of presponses of calm trials that were preceded by another calm trial but also of calm trials that were preceded by an extreme trial. This

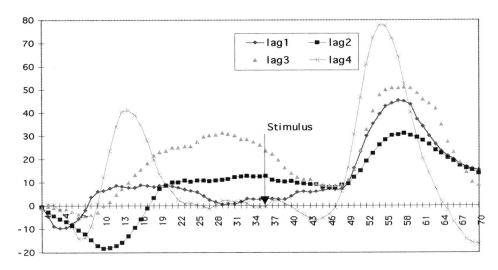

Figure 31.11
Differences between mean presponse on Calm and on Extreme stimuli with matched sequential history.

pooling of trials with different sequential position may result in artefacts as described in the introduction. One solution to this problem is to compare trials only if they have an identical sequential history. The trials in study I were therefore broken down according to their sequential history. We then compared the last Calms and Extremes with the following histories:

lag1:   Extreme-Calm vs. Extreme-Extreme

lag2:   Extreme-Calm-Calm vs. Extreme-Calm-Extreme

lag3:   Extreme-Calm-Calm-Calm vs. Extreme-Calm-Calm-Extreme

lag4:   Extreme-Calm-Calm-Calm-Calm vs. Extreme-Calm-Calm-Calm-Extreme

The results for the different lags are graphically presented in figure 31.11.

It can be seen that, although there are different wave forms for the different timelags, the over-all picture is the presponse for extremes is larger than for calms. Separate Mann-Whitney U tests yield the following z scores:

Lag	z-score	Ncalms	Nextremes
1	0.30	146	77
2	1.74	96	46
3	2.86*	59	34
4	1.15	42	16

All further lags have also a positive z-score. A weighted sum of the 4 different analysis is given in figure 31.12 and shows basically an identical result as figure 31.2.

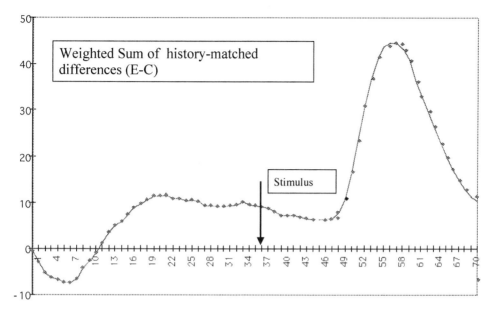

Figure 31.12
Weighted sum of presponse differences between Calms and Extremes over four different sequential histories.

IX PHENOMENOLOGY—INTRODUCTION

Alfred W. Kaszniak

In any attempt to develop a science of consciousness, first-person experience must play a necessary role. Unless introspective data is taken seriously, it is unclear what theories of consciousness or empirical investigations would be seeking to explain. However, there has been much disagreement over the question of how best to obtain first-person data. The formal introspection methods of the early structuralist psychologists (e.g., Tichner) failed, in part because of mistaken assumptions about how perceptual experience is built, and in part because of an inability to replicate across the introspective reports of similarly trained observers. The approaches of European phenomenologists (e.g., Husserl) have not enjoyed wide-spread acceptance within North American philosophy. Meditative and contemplative disciplines employ rigorous training and prolonged practice in introspective methodologies, but are often embedded in religious contexts that do not transport easily across cultures. Within consciousness studies currently, there is an active reexamination of various traditions and systems that have sought to develop reliable methods for obtaining knowledge about first-person experience and its communication across individuals. There is also a growing interest in how these apparently different approaches may overlap or complement each other. The eight chapters within this section examine the variety of methods and assumptions characterizing contemporary approaches to first-person experience and intersubjectivity.

The first chapter of this section is authored by Piet Hut, who provides a comparison of three apparently divergent approaches to answering the question, "What is actual?" These approaches are modern science, Husserlian phenomenology, and Tibetan Buddhist Dzog Chen. As Hut makes clear, however, each of these approaches or world views share an emphasis upon experiment as the ultimate artiber of truth, and all are characterized by theoretical foundations that are in dynamic change. Another commonality Hut finds is that each approach attempts to find "a form of deep truth" that is independent of the culture in which the approach originated. Hut also finds the three world views to be remarkably similar in their respective processes of investigation, despite the markedly different results that are produced. Hut concludes by outlining his agenda for a further comparative study of world views, which he summarizes by the slogan "roots, not fruits." His emphasis, therefore, is on comparing the structure of inquiry rather than resultant cosmologies.

Christian de Quincey, in the second chapter of this section, shifts the focus to intersubjectivity in his discussion of explorations of consciousness from the second-person perspective. In beginning this discussion, de Quincey clarifies differences between psychological and philosophical uses of the term *consciousness*, between two

different meanings of subjectivity ("experienced interiority" versus "private, independent, isolated experience"), and between different meanings of intersubjectivity
(the standard meaning of consensual validation between independent subjects via
exchange of signals, versus the experiential meaning in which mutual engagement of
interdependent subjects conditions or creates their respective experience). The main
thesis of de Quincey's chapter is that of a need to move beyond the limitations of
first- versus third-person arguments to include the second-person perspective. Consciousness, he asserts, involves not only third-person "its" (brains or computer
models) and first-person "I"s (personal experience), but also interpersonal relations
and "I-you" experiences during which something changes in consciousness.

In the third chapter, Arthur Zajonc explores the implications of Goethe's work
for the phenomenological investigation of consciousness. Zajonc makes the case for
experience being an irreducible and essential component of any future science of
consciousness. Goethe, although best know for his literary works, considered his
greatest contribution to be in the sciences, particularly in his criticism of naive scientific realism and his emphasis upon the role of phenomena in the study of color.
Goethe's method of inquiry, Zajonc asserts, offers an approach that holds considerable promise. Summarizing his more extensive reflections (Seamon and Zajonc 1998),
Zajonc argues that Goethe's method opens up new ways of resolving the two forms
of the hard problem of consciousness, by it's commitment to first-person experience
rather than to the establishment of hypotheses as truths about the world. Subject-
object dualism, he asserts, disappears in the recognition that science is actually only
concerned with the subjective world, and the first-person, third-person version will
ultimately find resolution through a basic change in the structure of consciousness
itself.

Within the fourth chapter, Frances Vaughan follows along the themes developed
in the previous three chapters in her discussion of objective, subjective, and intersubjective dimensions of consciousness. Vaughan's main argument is for the importance of epistemological pluralism, with equal attention given to these three different
dimensions. Vaughan finds that within our culture, dominated by a scientific materialism, the subjective and intersubjective modes of knowing have been generally overlooked. Vaughan calls for an integrative approach to consciousness studies in which
there is open and mutually respectful dialogue across the different modes of knowing.
In making this plea, Vaughan draws on the work of Ken Wilber (1997, 1998) who
points out that objective, subjective, and intersubjective modes all similarly employ
the methods of injunction (if you wish to know X you must do Y), apprehension
(direct experience using the methods directed by the injunction), and confirmation
(validation of the direct experience by others who have also followed the injunction).

B. Allan Wallace, author of the fifth chapter, examines the methods of attention training and exploring consciousness in Tibetan Buddhism. Wallace makes it clear that without the subjective evidence provided by introspection, there would be no discipline of consciousness studies. William James (1890/1950) recognized that introspective study requires clarity and sustainability of voluntary attention, but was not convinced that the faculty of attention was trainable. Hindu and Buddhist contemplatives have, however, developed methods for enhancing attentional vividness and stability, and it is these methods, particularly as developed within Tibetan Buddhism, that Wallace describes. He argues that these attention-enhancing methods present a challenge to modern researchers in consciousness studies "to broaden the scope of legitimate methods of scientific inquiry so that the introspective exploration of consciousness may begin to rise to the levels of sophistication of objective means of studying brain correlates of conscious states."

The sixth chapter, authored by Harry Hunt, makes the case for a necessary and reciprocal dialogue between transpersonal and cognitive psychologies of consciousness. As with the other authors of chapters within this section, Hunt sees phenomenology as primary since "... all we ultimately have is our experience, ... all we know about brains and microtubules comes to us refracted through the very medium they are being used to explain." In agreement with Wallace, Hunt sees meditative, transpersonal, and other "altered" states as demonstrating that consciousness can undergo specific transformations and development, and as potentially providing "a kind of microscope" for viewing inner cognitive processes. In this way, cognitive psychology needs the transpersonal. Conversely, Hunt views transpersonal psychology as at risk of remaining mere "magic and only a modern re-recording of lost traditions," without nonreductive neurocognitive accounts of what it is about our minds that allows transpersonal experiences to occur.

The sixth chapter of this section, by Charles Laughlin, summarizes his biogenetic structural theory of consciousness. Resting upon the assumptions that all of science is grounded in experience and that consciousness is a function of higher nervous systems, Laughlin's biogenetic structural theory attempts to integrate research from phenomenology, anthropology, psychology, neuroscience, and physics. Laughlin details the common limitations of other theories within consciousness science, which biogenetic structural theory counters. This theory, including phenomenological, neurobiological, and sociocultural perspectives, attempts to incorporate all of the approaches to scientifically studying consciousness, and places a particular emphasis upon ethnographic and neurophenomenological (drawn from contemplative disciplines linked to current discoveries about brain function) approaches. Biogenetic structuralism holds that all humans share some common experiences of themselves and their world because of "the origins of their cognized environments in species-typical neurognosis." Those similarities between only some human beings are seen as dependent upon "the social conditioning in the development of their individual cognized environments," and unique aspects of persons are viewed as "due to the complexity and uniqueness of each individual's innate temperament and developmental path."

The seventh and final chapter, by Jonathan Shear, focuses upon an experiential clarification of the problem of self. Shear begins by reviewing the attempts at understanding the self made by Descartes, Hume, and Kant, with the resulting paradoxical conclusion being that the "self as single, simple and continuing is at once both absolutely necessary and absolutely unexperiencable and unknowable." The chapter goes on to unpack the logic of the arguments of these three famed philosophers and further demonstrate problems in the notion of self. However, Shear then shifts from discussions of self in Western philosophy to those within Asian civilizations, in which the experience of "pure consciousness" (identified by it's characteristic of being devoid of all phenomenal content) plays a key role. Shear examines the different procedures used in different cultures (e.g., within Zen, Vedantan Transcendental Meditation, and Medieval Catholicism) to produce the common experience of pure consciousness. The chapter provides support for the possibilities that our ordinary sense of self may reflect a subliminal awareness of pure consciousness as a ubiquitous component of experience, and "that after we become clearly aware of it as it is in and by itself in meditation, we can then come also to recognize it as ubiquitous—as self is supposed to be." Shear therefore sees the experience of pure consciousness as capable of resolving some of the major Western concerns about self, and as clarifying commonsense intuition.

References

James, W. 1890/1950. *The Principles of Psychology*. New York: Dover Publications.

Seamon, D., and A Zajonc, A. 1998. *Goethe's Way of Science*. Albany: SUNY Press.

Wilber, K. 1997. An integral theory of consciousness. *Journal of Consciousness Studies* 4:71–92.

Wilber, K. 1998. *The Marriage of Sense and Soul: The Integration of Science and Religion*. New York: Random House.

32 Exploring Actuality through Experiment and Experience

Piet Hut

A comparison is presented of three approaches to an understanding of "what is actual": modern science, Husserlian phenomenology, and Tibetan Buddhist Dzog Chen. In each approach, experiment is the central touch stone, while the theoretical "foundations" are dynamically changing. The roles that consciousness plays in each of the three approaches are contrasted, in a comparative analysis that provides a fresh look at the question of the possibility of a scientific study of consciousness.

Objectivity and Subjectivity

The present conference is dedicated to a search for a science of consciousness. Usually, when we try to establish a science of X, we focus on the unknown properties and structure of X, in order to find a way to provide a scientific treatment of them. Tacitly, we take for granted that we already know what science is, and that we only have to search for a way to apply the scientific method in the proper way to X.

In the case of consciousness, this standard approach may fail. So far, science has only studied *objects* of various kinds. To be conscious is to be a *subject*. To treat consciousness as an object, among other objects, may completely miss the point. In this chapter, I present a comparative analysis of three world views, science being one of them, in an attempt to clarify this issue.

One position, the one that most scientists seem to hold, is to consider subjectivity as a late comer. The world of objectivity is the "real" one, the one that grounds everything else. Its existence originated in the Big Bang, and only after many billions of years did complex surface phenomena on planet Earth result in the presence of life and nervous systems and ultimately brains complex enough to pose the question "what is consciousness?" Subjective experience is thus seen as a byproduct of objective processes, an emerging property that is only present at a few isolated islands in a much vaster sea of objective reality.

Another position, more in line with the world view described by contemplative practitioners in various religious traditions, posits that both subject and object are late comers. In an attempt to interpret experience, we tend to polarize experience, regarding it as a form of interaction between a subject pole and an object pole. This polarization, however, does not affect the underlying "pure experience." The latter remains the more basic aspect of actuality, while the whole interpretive play forms a type of overlay. Note that these brief statements are still cast in a pseudo-objective language; a more careful description would need to rephrase and clarify each of these brief comments considerably.

Figure 32.1
Objectivity and Subjectivity in a naive interpretation of one person's experience. S denotes the total realm of experience of that person; O′ that part of S that is devoted to experiencing the objective world; and S′ that part of O′ that seems to correspond to the experience of that person, viewed as an inhabitant of the world O′. In contrast, the "real" objective world, O, does not and cannot enter directly in the world of experience, S.

At first sight, these two positions seem utterly incompatible. However, it may be possible to bring them into contact, by considering a third approach, that in a way interpolates between the two. If we start from a scientific world view, and ask ourselves how it is, exactly, that a subject deals with objects, we can switch from the usual objective third-person description to a more experiential first-person point of view. An example of such an approach is the philosophical school of phenomenology, founded by the German philosopher Husserl.

Inner and Outer Subjectivity

In an attempt to put these three approaches on the same map, I sketch in figure 32.1 a view of the world that starts from the standard scientific picture. This figure does not represent my own view of the world, and it may not represent the every-day way in which most people, scientists and nonscientists alike, look at the world. Rather, it presents a refinement of the way most of us tend to look at the world, and at our role, as subjects, in that world.

The refinement offered in figure 32.1 consists of an analysis of how a person experiences the objective world O, of which he or she is a part. Within the realm of that person's subjective experience S, many experiences are considered purely subjective, such as fantasies, desires, memories, or dreams. Other experiences are seen as corresponding to the objective world O. For example, when the person looks at a chair, a material object in the objective physical world O, he or she will have a conscious experience of the chair, within that part of the realm S that contains experiences corresponding to the objective world.

In figure 32.1, that subset of S, corresponding to O, is indicated by O′, the realm of experiences of the objective world, as opposed to the objective realm O itself. The distinction is important: we can be conscious of a chair, but we cannot put a chair as such inside our consciousness. The experience of a chair resides in O′, while the chair is considered to reside in O. Finally, the consciousness that we study scientifically can then be called S′, to distinguish it from the real thing, S. S′ is the realm of psychology, while S as such is rarely thematized. S is the universe of experience, within which all experiences of a person are contained.

From a purely phenomenological point of view, the objective realm in which we use our scientific tools is O′. It is distinct from the real thing, O, which is the most concrete realm, as the objective material realm that is posited to ground everything else. But at the same time, O is the most abstract of the four, in that it can, by definition, not be experienced, unlike S, O′, and S′. It is literally abstracted from experience.

One may object that we do seem to experience a chair directly. We certainly do not normally experience the experience of a chair, which would be a rather unnatural type of reflection. Therefore, we usually identify the realms O and O′, and, as a consequence, we also identify S and S′. However, even when we feel that we experience a chair, that experience is still an experience (namely, one of a chair), and as such belongs to realm O′. The experience of the experience of a chair would have to be drawn into a yet more remote realm O″, as the objective subset of S′.

Returning to the title of our conference, "toward a scientific study of consciousness," the question arises, which consciousness are we moving toward a study of? If it is S′, the "inner" realm of subjectivity, then we can try to use our normal scientific approach. But if it is S, the "outer" realm of subjectivity, then such an approach may fail, if it would turn out that the identification of O and O′ could be called into question. A comparison of the three world views mentioned above may help to shed some light here. Husserl, for example, made a sharp distinction between a focus on

S', which he called "psychologism," and a focus on S, which he deemed to be the proper realm of philosophy.

Let us start with the most familiar world view, namely the view that science offers.

Science and World Views

Science is a remarkably successful way of analyzing the structure of the physical world. In a mere few hundred years, it has moved on from a description of the motion of billiard balls and planets to a very detailed analysis of physical phenomena on a huge variety of scales: from subatomic distances to the edge of the visible universe, spanning 44 orders of magnitude, from 10^{-16} cm to 10^{28} cm. We believe that we have a more or less complete understanding of the fundamental interactions governing the physical processes throughout this vast range of length scales. The structure of matter on even smaller scales is still a subject of active research, but on all scales larger than the subatomic, in principle our tool set seems to be complete.

Of course, in practice many of the systems we encounter are far too complex to allow a full calculation of the detailed consequences of the underlying interactions, even though each of those are known. The fastest supercomputers do not suffice for a complete modeling of most complex systems, and therefore we are forced to engage in approximate modeling, often an art as much as a science. But each year our computers are getting faster, and we are also getting new and better ideas about how to use them in more clever ways.

To sum up: We have been successful beyond belief. Science offers us a complete understanding of the physical realm, in principle if not yet quite in practice. And doesn't it seem most sensible that so-called nonphysical phenomena are ultimately nothing more than correlates of complex processes in the brain, itself a perfectly physical piece of matter, obeying the perfectly well known laws of physics?

Well, yes, such a conclusion does seem most sensible, for those who have wholly bought into the prevailing interpretation of what science is, and what it can deliver. In that case, "toward a scientific study of consciousness" is in no way different than "toward a scientific study of superconductivity," for example. Consciousness, like everything else, is then simply seen as grounded in physical reality, as one of many physical phenomena.

But what if we don't buy into such a belief? What if we ask questions like "what is science" and "what is science based on"? To address the latter first, scientific understanding is based on an interplay between theory and experiment, with experiment providing the ultimate touch stone of what is real. Of course, designing, carrying out, and interpreting those experiments, as well as developing and testing theories, are all human activities that take place, for each individual, within his or her consciousness. Doing science is a very specific project, with agreed-up rules, at least at any given time and place.

A modern individual can choose from many projects to engage in, dedicating him or herself to arts, business, politics, or other projects, besides science. And when we compare our own culture with that of others, we are confronted with many other possible projects, valid in other cultures. Thus, as soon as we view science as a project, one project out of very many, we may wonder how unique the world view, presented by science, is.

Two questions arise here. First, are there other valid world views, comparable in their validity to that of science? Second, how valid a world view does science offer? Does it really give us a complete world view, or is something fundamentally lacking? To try to answer these questions, I will briefly discuss two other world views, one from within twentieth-century Western philosophy, and one that can be found within Tibetan Buddhism, with roots that are at least a thousand years old, and probably much older.

Three Approaches to "What Is Actual"

What are world views views of? An obvious answer would be "reality," but that word is already slanted to a particular class of world views. The root "re," of the Latin *res*, or thing, suggest that things are at the base of everything. However, many world views are more dynamic, and do not necessarily base themselves upon things or objects as being most fundamental. Therefore, a more general word would be "actuality," rather than "reality." Whether or not "what is actual" can be explained in terms of things will be left open.

The first approach to what is actual, to be considered here, is the view presented by natural science. The main object of study, in terms of the distinctions made in figure 32.1, is the objective realm O', as it is given to us, that is, in experience. This realm is what is studied by physics, chemistry and biology, for example, and includes the realm of S', the object of study of psychology. The realms O and S, as such, are not addressed by science. This is illustrated in figure 32.2.

The second approach that we will consider is that of a school in modern philosophy, called phenomenology. The term phenomenology, although used earlier by Hegel, was taken up again by the German philosopher Edmund Husserl (1859–1938). He used it to indicate a radical approach to the study of actuality, in which we are invited to shift our focus of attention from O' and S', in figure 32.1, to S. To facilitate this move, he designed a specific experimental method, which he called the

3 Experimental Approaches To
An Understanding of "What is Actual":

Natural Science:	O′, S′
Husserlian Phenomenology:	S, O′,S′
Tibetan Dzog Chen:	A, S, O′,S′

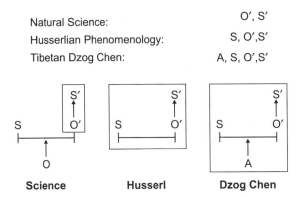

Science   **Husserl**   **Dzog Chen**

Figure 32.2
Three experimental approaches to an understanding of "what is actual." Note that in science, the realms O and S are effectively off-limits.

epoche (from the Greek εποψη for "suspense of judgment"). This shift toward S at the same time enlarges and shrinks the world under consideration, as compared to the world of science. Operationally speaking, it features an enlargement, by adding a third realm S, besides O′ and S′. But given the fact that most scientists automatically posit the realm O as forming an imputed foundation, Husserl's shift constitutes a "reduction," as he also called the *epoche*, by leaving out this fourth realm O. See figure 32.2.[1]

The third approach, that of Tibetan Buddhist Dzog Chen,[2] again invites us to shift our focus of attention. The main topic in Dzog Chen is an investigation of what is actual, while circumventing our habitual tendency to analyze reality in terms of objects and subjects. Prior to the subject-object split, the focus lies on actuality itself, from which the subject and object poles can be seen to arise through a form of polarization. In terms of the classification presented in figure 32.1, the subject pole of this polarization is not S′, which is only a small part of the object pole O′, but the much larger realm S (or, depending on the precise identification, S minus O′). This is graphically indicated in figure 32.2.

At this stage, it is not my intention to consider these three world views in any particular order, or nesting relation. While figure 32.2 could suggest that the view offered by Dzog Chen may contain that of Husserl, which in turn may contain or ground that of science, I prefer to avoid such an interpretation. For one thing, the

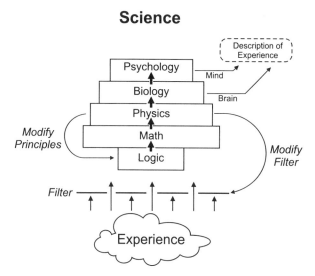

Figure 32.3
The house of science. The internal arrows correspond to a naive view of explanatory power. The two arrows at the side correspond to feedback loops that indicate the hermeneutic character of natural science, as a living and evolving approach to the study of actuality.

roles of S in science and in phenomenology are quite different. For another, the role of O in science and that of A in Dzog Chen are even more incommensurable. For now, I prefer to simply put these three views on the table, so to speak, if nothing else just to show how rich the range of reasonable world views can be. So, rather than trying to relate them immediately, let us first compare their internal structure. Ultimately, for a more detailed analysis, we will have to move beyond the schematic pictures offered in figures 32.1 and 32.2.

Natural Science

Starting with natural science, figure 32.3 illustrates, in the top part, the ordering of disciplines in the "house of science." In this simple picture, physics "rests" on top of mathematics, in the sense that all its laws are couched in the language of mathematics, and all its predictions are derived from those laws using mathematical operations. Chemistry in turn is layered on top of physics, biology on top of chemistry, and so on. Each "higher" discipline uses the entities provided by a "lower" discipline, together with the interactions specified between those entities, as the basis for its own description of what is actual. For example, psychology uses as given the presence and way of operating of sensory organs, described in biology, and biology in turn uses descriptions based on biochemistry, which in turn reduces to interactions between atoms, as specified in physics. For simplicity, only some of the disciplines are sketched explicitly in figure 32.3.

The arrow of explanation thus proceeds from bottom to top from the logical principles that underlie mathematics, all the way to psychology. This is the type of picture that is implicitly presented, in scientific textbooks and popular science books alike. And indeed, when we take a snapshot of the state of science, at any given time, it is quite an accurate picture. However, when we ask the more probing question "what is science?" we have to go beyond that what appears in a single snapshot, and we have to look at how science has developed over the centuries.

The historical picture that emerges from such a longer view is markedly different, and no longer presents the neat picture of a "house of science." It turns out that developments in "higher" floors can necessitate fundamental changes in "lower" floors. For example, the discovery of quantum mechanics, which gave us a more accurate description of the physical world than classical mechanics, forced us to change the underlying principles on which everything else seemed to rest. This change was dramatic: determinism gave way to chance, or spontaneity. Consequently, causality no longer held in the strict way it had been presumed to hold, for hundreds of years. And repeatability, long considered to be the very touch stone of physics, had to be thrown out the window: two radioactive atoms, though fully identical in all their details, yet will decay at different times, in an intrinsically unpredictable way. The picture emerging from a more long-term view of science thus offers a more circular structure of explanation. For example, the chance brought on by the discovery of quantum mechanics is presented by the arrow on the left-hand side of figure 32.3.

When looked at closely, the explanatory structure of science is full of such hermeneutic circles. Another one is indicated on the right-hand side of the same figure, through an arrow that points to the filter separating the experience of the scientist, below, from the product of the work of the scientists, above. At the beginning of modern science, only a few aspects of human experience were admitted as valid topics for scientific investigation. The mass and size of an object, for example, were considered primary qualities, that were allowed to pass through the filter, to be studied by physics. Most other properties, such as its color, or its tactile quality, were designated as secondary properties, less real in a sense, and off limits to scientific investigation. In the course of time, however, the expansion of the framework of physics allowed a gradual widening of the openings in the filter separating science from experience. By now, the color and texture of an object are just as amenable to analysis in physics as are the mass and length of an object.

Note that in figure 32.3 biology and psychology aim at an analysis of human experience, through a study of the brain and of the mind, respectively. However, their area of study, though labeled "experience," is quite different from the experience underlying all of science, and represented by the cloud at the bottom of the figure. This cloud below corresponds with the realm S in figure 32.1, whereas the experience aimed at by biology and psychology corresponds to the much more limited realm S′.

Husserlian Phenomenology

Science starts with a form of *via negativa*, ignoring almost all of what is important in our day-to-day experience. Values, beauty, anything related to social interactions, anything to do with what is considered sacred: all of that does not make it past the filter depicted in figure 32.3. Amazingly, notwithstanding these severe limitations, science has been able to reconstruct a skeleton of the world, as we experience it, in incredibly precise detail. And in the process, it has left in its wake powerful technological tools that have changed the world, for better and worse.

Whether such an approach might ever lead to the construction of a complete world view, is an open question. It may be possible to somehow regain a full understanding of "what is actual," above the filter, of a richness comparable to the more amorphous and ambiguous direct experience below the filter. And then again, it may not be. The only way to find out is to try, and scientific research is doing exactly that, especially in the many branches of cognitive science.

My guess is that anything like a satisfactory understanding of our cognitive processes, in a richness comparable to what we start out from, before applying the scientific filtering operation, is at least a few centuries away. It took us four hundred years to reach our present depth of understanding of the objective side of the world. An understanding of the subject, and of the subject-object interaction, may take at least as much time, and possibly much longer. Therefore, even if we are firm believers in the progress of science toward ultimate completeness, it is not a bad idea to look for alternative approaches. If we want to find a more complete world view within our own life time, we may be better off starting from other angles on actuality.

Phenomenology, the branch of Western philosophy developed by Husserl, offers us such an angle. His key move, in my view, is a replacement of the filter of science by a prism, as indicated in figure 32.4. Phenomenology advocates a thorough description of anything we can discern in our experience of what is actual. In the words of William James, who was a source of inspiration for Husserl, and who used the term

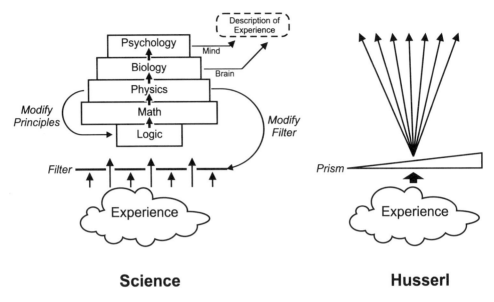

Figure 32.4
Husserlian Phenomenology contrasted with Natural Science.

"radical empiricism" for an approach that was a forerunner of phenomenology: "To be radical, an empiricism must neither admit into its constructions any element that is not directly experienced, nor exclude from them any element that is directly experienced."[3]

At first sight, phenomenology may seem rather flat. While it is very broad, and does not leave out anything, it merely attempts to give a detailed description of what is actually happening. However, such a view is misleading. First of all, an enormous amount of training is required, to learn to become a good phenomenologist. To really see what is going on, we have to learn not to interject our prejudices of what is supposed to go on, and we also have to learn not to overlook the unexpected and so-far unrecognized. Secondly, laying out everything on the table, so to speak, and "staring" at it, letting it organize itself in our consciousness, often leads to unexpected insight. In many areas of science, the key to a new break-through lay in the "seeing" and acknowledging of what had been visible all the time, but had not been noticed before.

Einstein's relativity theories form a beautiful example of what can be won by a patient, honest, and detailed phenomenological analysis. By carefully looking at the behavior of falling elevators and passing trains and light signals, Einstein "saw" some of the fundamental results of both special and general relativity theory, well before he was able to provide detailed and complete mathematical descriptions.

Similarly, Husserl was able to make great progress over and above the insights derived by Descartes, Kant, and Fichte, in "seeing" many of the layers of the processes through which we reconstruct the world in our experience. In fact, much of what is now gradually being discovered about ways to build robots and to let them function as autonomous subjects, was foreshadowed in many of Husserl's detailed analyses of subject-object interactions.

Dzog Chen

In one aspect, natural science and Husserlian phenomenology take an opposite approach to the analysis of experience. The first approach starts with a breakdown into an analysis of a few elementary processes, leaving out almost everything else, followed by an attempt to make a full synthesis, in order to regain what was left out. The second approach starts with the fullness of what presents itself, analyzing everything together.

The former method reminds me of an attempt to copy a complicated piece of machinery. If we somehow acquire a blueprint, with complete instructions to build the machine, we may be able to reconstruct the whole machine, even though in the intermediate descriptive state a lot of unnecessary detail was left out. The reduction from the material machine to a virtual description could be reversed, by adding back what was left out, namely the physical presence of the machine components.

The latter method reminds me of an attempt to read a book that has been dropped in the water. All the pages are wet, and stuck together. The first attempt to read the book will result in a rather unclear story: each time we try to turn a page, we actually turn several pages, and skip over some episodes. The story is still more or less understandable, but many details only make partial sense, or no sense at all. In the course of the phenomenological method of analysis, consisting of "teasing the pages of experience apart," more and more begins to make sense, with many details falling into place naturally.

Notwithstanding the great contrast between both approaches, there is also a significant similarity in that both methods are based upon description. The goal of science is to present a detailed description, as complete and as simple as possible, of what is actual. The goal of phenomenology, too, is to provide such a description, even though the approach is radically different. What would happen if we would try to arrive at a world view not based upon description?

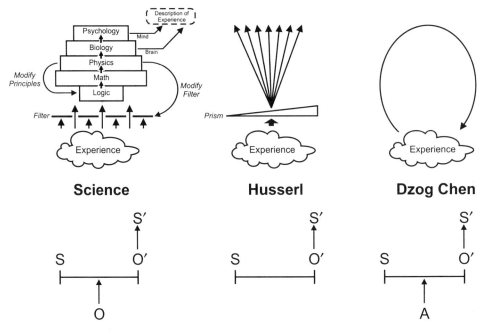

Figure 32.5
Dzog Chen contrasted with Phenomenology and Science.

In our culture, art and religion offer us ways of experiencing the world, or at least part of the world, in ways that are more direct. Similarly, an engagement in sports can lead to forms of experience that are more direct than those based upon description. However, the deep satisfaction that may result from an intimate involvement with any of those approaches, does not easily translate back into a world view. Certainly arts seem to be too much culture bound, but also in the case of religion, not much progress has been made in reaching inter-religious agreement.

It is conceivable that such type of agreement could be obtained, perhaps already during the twenty-first century. Practitioners from diverse religious traditions, such as Buddhism, Christianity, and Islam, could come together, and compare notes. They could try to find a core of common understanding, based on the deepest forms of religious experience they have obtained. Perhaps they could reach a degree of agreement comparable to the way in which physicists from all countries nowadays agree upon Newton's laws or Maxwell's equations.

An example of a world view based directly upon contemplative experience is the form of Tibetan Buddhism called Dzog Chen. My reason to choose this particular approach is related to the very radical nature of inquiry in Dzog Chen. Very briefly, we can divide meditative inquiry into methods based upon renunciation, transformation, and appreciation of actuality "as it is." Most approaches center upon forms of renunciation, with lesser emphasis on transformation, and even less on direct appreciation. Japanese Zen, and the Chinese Chan from which it was derived, are examples of approaches based upon direct appreciation, as is Dzog Chen.

The utterly radical nature of a focus on appreciation, without any attempt to select or transform anything, is what holds the key for an intercultural comparison of these types of world views. One reason to choose Dzog Chen, from among the class of radical approaches, is that there seems to be more of a living tradition preserved, in a direct lineage to ancient times, among Tibetans, both in Tibet itself, as well as among the Tibetan refugee communities.

Conclusion and Outlook

The three world views presented here briefly have the following in common:

• They form three *experimental* approaches to an understanding of what is actual.

Science is based on experiment as the ultimate arbiter of truth. Phenomenology, unlike most other, more speculative branches of Western philosophy, is firmly rooted in experience. And Dzog Chen, in a most radical way, starts and ends with what is immediately given.

• Although originated in a particular culture, each one strives to find a form of deep truth *independent* of that culture;

Science, by and large, has achieved that goal. Whether Husserlian phenomenology and Dzog Chen will be recognized to be particular ways of expressing a similarly universal truth, still has to be seen. My guess is that there is a good chance that this will happen, within another hundred years. I also expect that an appreciation for the one will facilitate an appreciation for the other, given that both are so radical (remember James's description of phenomenology as "radical empiricism"; an excellent characterization of Dzog Chen as well).

• In each world view, the *process* of investigation is remarkably similar, even though the results are markedly different.

An example is the move to step out of the world in order to step into it more fully. In science, a laboratory environment provides a way to shield the investigator from distracting influences, allowing him or her to focus on one particular experimental set-up. In phenomenology, the *epoche* allows the investigator to disengage from the habitual way of viewing the world as given, as objectively existing in a more or less frozen way. And in Dzog Chen, specific forms of meditation and contemplation allow the practitioner to get closer to an immediate appreciation of what is actual, even though the initial exercises may seem to make him or her withdraw from the world.

In this brief summary, I have not been able to give much more than a whiff of what each of the three world views has to offer. I hope that the reader will at least have gotten some feel for the excitement that I have tasted, at discovering these very different ways of exploring actuality. Especially the exhilaration that comes with finding new degrees of freedom in what is actual, is something that I hope has come across, in between the lines.

Freedom, after all, is what a complete world view can offer. We tend to identify ourselves with all the roles we are playing, which can make the play into a burden. In contrast, a complete world view offers us a freedom from identification, an authentic form of freedom, based on a direct contact with what is actual. Without a need to discard any of our roles, seeing them as roles we can play them more lightly, in a less formal and more spontaneous way.

My agenda for a further comparative study of world views can be summarized by the slogan "roots, not fruits." Rather than comparing cosmologies, such a the Big Bang theory and ancient creation myths, I am far more interested in comparing the structure of inquiry in science with that of inquiries in other attempts to arrive at complete world views. Is there a common soil, in which scientific experience, and phenomenological experience, and Dzog Chen experience are all rooted? What can we say about that common soil, and how can that help us to arrive at a deeper understanding of what is actual? These are the questions that I hope to pursue further.

Unfortunately, the current structure of academic research does not naturally leave room for an investigation of world views, as a fundamental discipline. Not only does such an investigation cross many traditional boundaries, what is worse, an emphasis on the living experience underlying each world view is often incompatible with the more indirect and purely descriptive nature of research in most of academia. This situation, one hopes, will soon cure itself, and indeed, the last few years have seen a ground swell of interest into topics such as the scientific studies of consciousness.

In an attempt to speed up this transformation of the academic treatment of direct experience, we have recently founded a nonprofit organization, called the Kira Institute (website: ⟨http://www.kira.org⟩). Our aim is to act as a catalyst, by showing how comparative research of the roots of world views can be undertaken, crossing the traditional academic boundaries, while retaining the standards of academic rigor.

This article was written while I was a visiting professor at Nichibunken, the International Research Center for Japanese Studies in Kyoto. I acknowledge the warm hospitality of Prof. Hayao Kawai, director-general of Nichibunken. I thank Bas van Fraassen for helpful comments on the manuscript.

Notes

1. Husserl's writings, in so far as they are published, are available in: *Husserliana*, Vol. I–XXX (1949–1996), by Edmund Husserl [Kluwer]. A good recent introduction to Husserl's thought is: *An Introduction to Husserlian Phenomenology* (1993), by Rudolf Bernet, Iso Kern, and Eduard Marbach [Northwestern University Press]. For a vivid description of a form of phenomenological *epoche*, refreshingly unsophisticated and down-to-earth, see *On Having No Head* (1961, 1988) by Douglas E. Harding [Arkana].

2. Recently, a large number of books on Dzog Chen have appeared. Here are a few:

The Practice of Dzogchen, by Longchen Rabjam, introduced, translated, and annotated by Tulku Thundup (1989) [Snow Lion Publications];
The Great Perfection (Rzdogs Chen) (1988), by Samten Gyaltsen Karmay;
[Brill]; *Dzogchen, the self-perfected state* (1989), by Namkhai Norbu [Arkana];
Natural Liberation: Padmasambhava's Teachings on the Six Bardos by Padmasambhava, with commentary by Gyatrul Rinpoche (transl. 1998, by Alan Wallace) [Wisdom Publications]. In addition, an interesting world view is presented in the book *Time, Space, and Knowledge* (1977), by Tarthang Tulku, a Tibetan Lama who has presented some of his views in ways that are largely decoupled from his particular background and religion. For the purpose of our present discussion, the vision presented in this book is sufficiently similar to Dzog Chen to play the role of the contemplative world view, indicated in figure 32.5.

3. William James's *Essays in Radical Empiricism* (1912), reprinted in Essays in *Radical Empiricism and A Pluralistic Universe*, by W. James [1967, Peter Smith].

33 Intersubjectivity: Exploring Consciousness from the Second-Person Perspective

Christian de Quincey

The Vitality of Human Engagement

Being intensely engaged in relationship with another person is one of the greatest joys of being human. It is, perhaps, the most vital manifestation of consciousness. Yet it is an aspect of consciousness that, for the most part, has been conspicuously overlooked in philosophy of mind and the emerging field of consciousness studies. This approach to consciousness calls for a shift of perspective—from looking at the world as a collection of objects, or even as a collection of subjects, to a view that sees *relationship* as fundamental.[1]

In this chapter, I argue that in addition to methodologies of first-person subjectivity (exploring consciousness from "within" through meditation and introspection), and third-person objectivity (studying external correlates of consciousness, such as brains and neurons), a holistic science of consciousness would also expand to include second-person intersubjective methodology and epistemology—to account for the inter-reflexivity of consciousness (subjectivity-reflected-in-subjectivity) in "I-thou" relationships.

To clarify what I mean by the second-person perspective, I will begin by discussing the key terms: "consciousness," "subjectivity," and "intersubjectivity." I will then state what I believe to be the central philosophical problem regarding these three concepts, and end by addressing some possible objections.

Clarifying Our Terms

Consciousness

Debates in philosophy and psychology frequently run aground in confusion because participants use the word "consciousness" with different meanings.

The most common misunderstanding arises from a basic confusion between the *psychological* and *philosophical* uses of the term. I find it helpful, therefore, to distinguish between two basic meanings of consciousness:

Psychological consciousness is about the *contents* of consciousness (e.g., thoughts, beliefs, images), and about the mode of access (conscious or unconscious) to these contents. It is also about the *state of awareness*, or *form* of consciousness, characterized by being awake or alert, and is contrasted with the "unconscious," a state of being asleep, and with psychic contents below the threshold of conscious-awake awareness. For example, a person engaged in conceptual cognition is conscious in this sense; a person in a coma, or a worm, are examples of what being unconscious means.

Philosophical consciousness is about the *context* of consciousness; it is about the *mode of being* that makes possible any and all contents and forms of consciousness. Philosophically, consciousness is a *state or quality of being*, the fact of consciousness characterized by having a capacity for sentience, subjectivity, and self-agency. It is contrasted with being "nonconscious," a state of affairs wholly without sentience or subjectivity—that is, brute physicality. For example, a person (awake or asleep), a dog, or a worm exemplify consciousness in this sense; a rock, a cloud, or a computer do not. Looked at this way, it is clear that the philosophical meaning is more fundamental—for without consciousness as a state of being (i.e., an ontological reality) there could be no psychological states or contents. Even the psychological unconscious has something psychic or mental going on. To be unconscious is still to be sentient (worms and sleeping people still feel), whereas to be nonconscious is not (rocks and computers do not feel).

Subjectivity

Subjectivity also has at least two critical meanings:

Subjectivity-1: "*Experienced interiority.*" In the first case, subjectivity means, essentially, a capacity for feeling that is intrinsic, or interior, to the entity under consideration—a what-it-feels-like-from-within. The key notion here is "experienced interiority" as distinct from vacuous (i.e., without experience) external relations. A subject is constituted by internal relations, and these are felt or experienced. Without experience there could be no subjectivity (and vice versa; in fact, the two words are virtually synonymous); and experience is always internal or intrinsic to the subject—that is to say, experience doesn't "happen to" a subject, it is *constitutive* of the subject.

Subjectivity has a point of view. It "takes account of," or feels, its own being. Its being is validated, felt, or known from within itself—hence it is *first-person*—not just from without. It cannot be fully accounted for by external, mechanical relations. A subject lives or endures through time, feeling its own continuity.

Subjectivity-2: "*Private, independent, isolated experience.*" In another, related through restricted, sense, subjectivity means an isolated, independent, self-sufficient locus of experience. Classically, this is the Cartesian ego, wholly private, and independent of all reality external to it. In the first case, subjectivity-1, experienced interiority is not automatically self-contained within its own private domain—it is interior, but not necessarily independent or isolated. The question of whether it is self-contained or interdependent is left open: It is possible for subjectivity-1 to be either interior and shared, or interior and private. In this second, Cartesian, case, the subject is not only interior, it is self-contained and private. Such independent egos, or subjects—Leibniz called them "monads"—can communicate only via mediating signals, whereas subjectivity-1 can communicate by participating in shared presence. With subjectivity-1, interiority or feeling can be "intersubjective" and precede individual subjects; in subjectivity-2, interiority is *always* private, and intersubjectivity, if it occurs, is always secondary.

Intersubjectivity

Again, we should make an important distinction between two basic meanings—standard and experiential—with a further subdistinction of the experiential meaning:

• *Intersubjectivity-1* (standard meaning): "consensual validation between independent subjects via exchange of signals." Standard intersubjectivity relies on exchange of physical signals;

• *Intersubjectivity-2* (weak-experiential meaning): "mutual engagement and participation between independent subjects, which directly *conditions* their respective experience." It is psychological. Weak or psychological intersubjectivity relies on nonphysical presence (e.g., sense of rapport, empathy, love), and affects the contents of pre-existing subjects;

• *Intersubjectivity-3* (strong-experiential meaning): "mutual co-arising and engagement of interdependent subjects, or 'intersubjects' which *creates* their respective experience." It is ontological. Strong or ontological intersubjectivity relies on co-creative nonphysical presence, and brings distinct subjects into being out of a prior matrix of relationships.

The basic difference to note here is between *intersubjective agreement* (1), where my language about the world conforms to yours through exchange of conceptual and linguistic tokens, and *intersubjective participation* (2), or *intersubjective co-creativity* (3), where my experience of myself shows up qualitatively differently when I engage with you as a reciprocating center of experience. The first kind, the standard meaning of intersubjectivity, is used to describe what otherwise goes by the name of "objectivity" in science (Velmans 1993), and is not what I am concerned with in this chapter. I am trying to get at something deeper, something with potentially profound implications for philosophy of mind and consciousness studies in general.

Intersubjectivity-1: This standard meaning derives from Cartesian subjectivity (isolated, independent subjects). Here, individual subjectivity ontologically precedes intersubjectivity. Individual, isolated subjects come first, and then through communication of signals arrive at consensual agreement. Here, the "inter" in intersubjectivity refers to agreement "between" subjects about so-called objective facts—and the subjects don't even have to interact (their agreement could be validated by a third party, as indeed is often the case in science).

Intersubjectivity-2: Here, the sense of individual subjects remains, but now intersubjectivity refers to how the experience or consciousness of participating subjects is influenced and conditioned by their mutual interaction and engagement. The emphasis here is on the shared "experienced interiority" of the subjects as they interact, not on their "objective" agreement about some item of knowledge. Although this is a significant shift of emphasis from the standard meaning of intersubjectivity, nevertheless it is "weak" compared with the "strong" shift we will look at below. It is "weak," not because the participation/engagement involved is weak—indeed it could be intense—but because it refers to changes that happen to the *form* of consciousness of the participating subjects, not to the *fact* of such consciousness. It is "weak" because it still posits subjectivity as ontologically prior to intersubjectivity. Here, the "inter" in intersubjectivity refers to the mutual "structural coupling" of *already existing* experiencing subjects, where the interiorities of the participating subjects are interdependently shaped by their interaction.

Intersubjectivity-3: This is the most radical meaning, and the one that poses the greatest challenge to philosophy of mind. According to this "stronger" meaning, intersubjectivity is truly a process of co-creativity, where *relationship* is ontologically primary. All individuated subjects co-emerge, or co-arise, as a result of a holistic "field" of relationships. The being of any one subject is thoroughly dependent on the being of all other subjects, with which it is in relationship. Here, intersubjectivity precedes subjectivity (in the second, Cartesian, sense, but subjectivity in the first sense, of experienced interiority, is implicit throughout). The *fact*, not just the form, of subjectivity-2 (individual Cartesian subjects) is a consequence of intersubjectivity. Here, the "inter" in intersubjectivity refers to an "interpenetrating" co-creation of loci of subjectivity—a thoroughly holistic and organismic mutuality.

Questions and Implications

Given these distinct meanings of intersubjectivity, we are faced with five questions for philosophy of mind and consciousness studies:

(1) Is the basic distinction between the standard meaning of intersubjectivity as "consensual agreement" and the other two experiential forms identified here legitimate? If we accept the first meaning of subjectivity ("experienced interiority")—and what else could subjectivity mean if we excluded this?—I believe that we need a way to account for phenomenological data, such as experiences of rapport, empathy, and love between interacting subjects, which *prima facie* cannot be wholly explained in terms of exchange of linguistic or other signals. Phenomenologically and logically, therefore, the distinction is valid: Intersubjectivity cannot be restricted to the standard meaning of "consensual validation" of observations via exchange of physical signals.

(2) If the above distinction is valid, do interacting subjects actively shape the form and content of each other's experience? Volumes of data from social psychology, communications theory, psychoanalysis, anthropology, not to mention much commonsense folk psychology—plus the answer to (1) above—hardly leave us any doubt: Interacting people do influence and condition each other's experience and contents of consciousness (how else could communication occur?). If this were the full extent of the expanded meaning of intersubjectivity, the point would be trivial. It is questions (3), (4), and (5) that raise controversial epistemological and ontological issues for philosophy of mind and consciousness studies.

(3) Can one subject have direct access (not mediated by signals) to knowledge of how the other experiences this change? If we can answer yes to this, then the epistemological tradition we have inherited from Kant and the Enlightenment would be radically undermined. The hoary problem of other minds would finally have a solution.

(4) Through knowledge of how "I" show up in "your" experience, can I come to know something about my own consciousness? If the answer to both this and (3) is "yes," the implications for a second-person methodology in consciousness studies would be far-reaching. For one thing, it would indicate, at least, that dialogic interaction could serve as a "mirror" for exploring consciousness; and, more radically, that the consciousness of engaged participants is mutually *constitutive*, not merely reflective. Which leads to

(5) Does intersubjectivity actually create individual subjectivities, is it ontologically primary, or does intersubjectivity presuppose already existing centers of subjectivity? If intersubjectivity is primary, then pretty much the entire edifice of conventional philosophy and science, based on an ontology of substance (both of matter and mind) would be seriously challenged. For how could there be intersubjectivity without there

being always already existing subjects? How could there be relations without pre-existing relata? Commonsense and logic may seem to demand that for there to be relationship there *have* to be things to relate in the first place. Given an ontology of substance (whether of physical energy or of Cartesian minds), the primacy of relata seems compelling. However, we have examples of alternative ontologies from, for instance, Alfred North Whitehead (1979) and Buddhism (Macy 1991), where *process* is ontologically fundamental. These ontologies present coherent accounts where relationships are primary, where relata are *constituted* by their relationships. In such cosmologies, intersubjectivity precedes subjectivity (Cartesian sense). Of course, even in these alternative ontologies, intersubjectivity presupposes subjectivity in the sense of "experienced interiority."

Whereas the *fact* of experienced interiority is a precondition for intersubjectivity, the *forms* of individual subjectivities (how that interiority is shaped and experienced in individual subjects) need not—and in the cases of Whitehead and Buddhism do not—require pre-existent Cartesian subjects. Such transient "forms," co-created as perishable centers of experience in the interplay and flux of intersubjective fact, *are* the individual subjects.

Whether we go all out, and try to make a case for this strong version of intersubjectivity—with its profound philosophical implications—or keep our sights on a closer horizon by focusing on the "weaker" sense of intersubjectivity—with its implications for psychology and studies of the contents of consciousness—we still need to make a break from the conventional dichotomy of studying the mind from either a third-person or first-person perspective. We need to introduce a *second-person perspective* to complement our studies of consciousness in philosophy of mind, cognitive science, psychology, and the neurosciences.

Possible Objections

When there is so much debate these days on whether consciousness should be studied from a first-person or a third-person perspective (see, for example, Hameroff et. al [1996]), a proposal to include yet another perspective is likely to be even more controversial. And, indeed, this is the case. The objections fall into two, related, categories: (1) Whether the notion of intersubjectivity or second-person perspective is logically, epistemologically, or ontologically meaningful; and (2) If the second-person perspective is truly distinctive, in what ways would a methodology of intersubjectivity differ from either first-person subjective or third-person objective methodologies?

Reduction of Intersubjectivity?

One reviewer of an earlier version of this chapter thought it "plausible" that inter-subjectivity could be explained as "a combination of subjectivity and objectivity," and that any description of intersubjectivity must rule out such a reduction. Another objected to the notion that a second-person "you" is a logically and ontologically distinct category between the self and the object. He/she dismisses the second-person as "logically incorrect" and "unnecessary."

As I see it, we have three options: We could take an extreme elminativist position and claim that the notion of a second-person "you" is semantically empty, without any referent. Alternatively, we could say that the second-person referent is ultimately reducible to either of the two other perspectives. I reject the first option for the same kinds of reasons I reject eliminative positions on first-person consciousness. It involves a performative contradiction: In this case, who might the eliminativist be talking to? If there is no "you," no "others," why publish anything at all on this position?

If, then, we reject the hard eliminativist position, is a "softer" reductionist position more viable? On the one hand, we have the first-person subject, and on the other, the third-person object as options for intertheoretic reduction. Now, if the second-person "you" is both "logically incorrect and unnecessary," then it must either fall into the category of first-person subject or third-person object. Which is it? Is another person wholly accounted for from the first-person perspective? This would be tantamount to solipsism, and would deny any experiential reality to the "other"—again leading to performative contradictions. Failing this, is another person (a "you") wholly accounted for as a third-person object or collection of objects? Is there no difference between an entity which might be wholly objective (i.e., without any experiential interiority)—say a rock—and another human being? On experiential and logical grounds, I refuse to accept that "you" (meaning any other person) are nothing but a collection of objective physical things, lacking any sentience and experience with which I could engage in dialogue.

The "you" that the reductionist would like to ignore is any other locus of experi-ence, which both logically and ontologically cannot be accounted for exclusively in terms of either first-person "I"s or third-person "its."

A Third Kind of Knowing?

In connection with this, however, one of the reviewers raised an interesting epis-temological point when he/she doubted that "there is a third kind of knowing."

According to this objection, intersubjectivity would "correspond to introspection and inspection (first- and third-person forms of knowing)." But how can you "introspect" the presence of another person,[2] or "inspect" consciousness in any form (first- or second-person)? The best that third-person inspection can offer is knowledge of correlates (neurological or behavioral) or computer-inspired flow-chart representations of the functions and schemata of mental events.

It is certainly possible that there may be first-person introspection going on simultaneously with second-person engagement—in fact, such introspection is an integral element in the methodology of Bohmian dialogue—where it is called "proprioception" (Bohm 1996). But the point is that both the quality and the content of such introspection is radically different when done in conjunction with another person (or a group of people) similarly engaged, from when done solo. We show up differently to ourselves when we engage intersubjectively. This kind of knowing is pertinent to exploring the "forms and contents" of consciousness (i.e., to a comprehensive *psychology* of consciousness).

I am not sure that a second-perspective alone (using, for example, the methodology of Bohmian dialogue) would be sufficient to enlighten us regarding the *ontological* nature of consciousness. Likewise, I doubt that either the first-person or third-person perspective on its own is sufficient. Part of the point of this chapter is to call for a comprehensive, integral approach that includes first-person introspection, second-person engagement, and third-person rational and empirical analysis.

A "Distorted Mirror"?

This same reviewer raised another valid, and challenging, question: "If the second-person knowing is mirror-like as de Quincey suggests, why should we trust it? I would think it would be more like a fun-house mirror than like a true mirror since human beings are notoriously flexible, fickle, and unstable. Such beings would seem likely to introduce so much distortion into the image that it would be very difficult to glean any information from it."

I can see no way of decisively eliminating all possibility of epistemological error—particularly regarding issues of consciousness. This is as true for first-person investigation of subjectivity, where we must confront the notorious biases and hidden motivations of the unconscious, as it is for intersubjectivity. It is also true, of course, for third-person investigation where the senses can be, likewise, notoriously deceptive. In the case of first-person subjectivity, many spiritual disciplines advocate working with an already-enlightened master to minimize illusion and self-delusion. In the case of third-person investigation, the unreliability of the senses is counteracted by the procedure of peer-review and repeated experiments, leading to what is usually called "objectivity" but which is really "intersubjectivity" in the sense of consensual agreement ("Intersubjectivity-1").

In both cases, the precautions against epistemological distortion involve, interestingly enough, some form of intersubjectivity. In the case of the student-master relationship in spiritual disciplines, that relationship is a quintessential example of second-person engagement. In the case of scientific experiments, scientists take recourse to "standard intersubjectivity" (as defined above). Similarly, I would propose, that the best way to guard against second-person distortion would be to engage with multiple dialogue partners—on the premise that if the reflection of the self in all others is liable to distortion, it is unlikely to be distorted in the same way in every case. A canceling-out effect, and/or repetition of common elements in the reflection from multiple partners, would be the best guarantee of epistemological accuracy.

Conclusion

The thesis motivating this chapter, then, is that we need to move beyond the limitations of first vs. third person argument to include the second-person perspective. Not only are dogmatic subjectivists and objectivists likely to miss essential aspects of consciousness, but, I maintain, so too are those who champion including both first- and third-person perspectives. While we may learn a lot from examination of third-person, objective correlates of consciousness and from first-person investigations of subjectivity, I believe a dual first/third approach still risks leaving out important aspects of consciousness. Consciousness is not to be explained either by an examination of objective third-person "its" (as in brains or computer models) or by an examination of subjective first-person "I"s (as in personal experience), or even by a combination of both. Consciousness also involves *interpersonal relations*, and requires an examination of second-person "I-you" experiences. Something changes in consciousness when two or more people engage each other as communicating subjects—as *intersubjects*. Beyond objectivity and subjectivity, therefore, consciousness studies must also include intersubjectivity.

A longer version of this chapter is available from the author at The Institute of Noetic Sciences, 475 Gate Five Road, # 300, Sausalito, CA 94965. Email: cdeq@noetic.org

Notes

1. This perspective has not been completely ignored in the Western intellectual tradition. For a discussion of scholars who have taken intersubjectivity seriously, see de Quincey (1998).

2. One reviewer challenged my question "how can you *introspect* the presence of another" by pointing out that Husserl, in the fifth of his *Cartesian Meditations*, explicitly lays out a phenomenological method for doing precisely this. But Husserl's phenomenological "introspection" of otherness, in fact, *explicitly* invokes the requirement of intersubjectivity. For Husserl, my first-person apprehension of "otherness" is not constituted by wholly private subjectivity (in the second, Cartesian, sense of independent, isolated ego), but is "other than mine alone" arising in "an *intersubjective* world." In Husserl's own words he expresses, in almost Buberian terms, the mutuality of intersubjective presence:

> I experience others as actually existing and ... not as mere physical things.... I experience them at the same time as *subjects for this world*, as experiencing it (this same world that I experience) and, in so doing, experiencing me too, even as I experience the world and others in it.... In any case then, within myself, within the limits of my transcendentally reduced pure conscious life, I *experience* the world (including others)—and according to its experiential sense, not as (so to speak) my *private* synthetic formation but as other than mine alone *[mir fremde]*, as an *intersubjective* world, actually there for everyone, accessible in respect of its Objects to everyone (Husserl 1995, p. 91; emphases in original).

Like Husserl, we can—and indeed we *must*—access our own personal subjectivity (as experienced interiority) if we are to engage the presence of another subject in the world. In this sense, and only in this sense, do we "introspect" others. The point is, of course, that such "introspection" is conditioned by the Other simultaneously introspecting us. It is a mutual engaged presence, not a lone act of exploration of our own, first-person, private experience. We do not find the Other by introspecting our own "*private* synthetic formation," our own private subjective ego. If the methodology of introspection is to reveal the mutuality of intersubjective consciousness, it *necessarily* implies a second-person methodology of engaged presence—of an "I-thou" relationship. This is not at all the same as mere first-person introspection or contemplation. If there is any intertheoretic reduction to be done between first- and second-person perspectives, it would move in the opposite direction: explaining first-person experience as a derivative of second-person, intersubjective, mutual formations. In a word: Each instance of experienced interiority would be an intersubjective formation—and not strictly "mine" or "yours" in any exclusive first-person sense.

References

Bohm, D. 1996. *On dialogue* (ed. Lee Nichol). London, UK: Routledge.

Buber, M. 1970. *I and thou.* New York: Charles Scribners Sons.

de Quincey, C. 1998. Intersubjectivity: Exploring consciousness from the second-person perspective. Paper presented at Toward a Science of Consciousness-III, Tucson, AZ, April 27–May 2.

Hameroff, S. Kaszniak, A. and Scott, A. 1996. *Toward a science of consciousness: The first Tucson discussions and debates.* Cambridge, Mass.: MIT Press.

Husserl, E. (1995), Cartesian meditations: An introduction to phenomenology (trans. Dorion Cairns). Boston, MA: Kluwer Academic Publishers.

Macy, J. 1991. *Mutual causality in Buddhism and general systems theory: The dharma of natural systems.* Albany: SUNY.

Velmans, M. 1993. A reflexive science of consciousness. In *Experimental and theoretical studies of consciousness.* New York: John Wiley & Sons.

Whitehead, A. N. 1979. *Process and reality: An essay in cosmology* (Corrected edition, eds. D. R. Griffin and D. W. Sherburne). New York: The Free Press. (Original 1929).

Arthur Zajonc

When physics reduces color to a wavelength (or more accurately, to tristimulus values) the loss seems slight. Whether a human visual system is registering red, or an electronic device detects 630 nm radiation, is of little consequence to the science of physics. For that matter the electromagnetic radiation being studied may well be outside the visible region of the spectrum entirely. Thus the qualitative experience of color in humans is purely incidental to the discipline of physics. This situation is emphatically not the case for the science of human consciousness. The phenomena at the center of study are precisely the phenomena of conscious experience. They cannot be replaced or reduced to more material mechanisms without doing violence to the subject itself. One could even go so far as to state that while the neural correlates of conscious experience may be interesting, they are incidental to consciousness studies. Physics aspires to study the physical universe and its laws independent of human experience. Consciousness studies, by definition, must be concerned with conscious experience.

Unlike the emerging science of consciousness, neuroscience can proceed quite satisfactorily without recourse to the idea of consciousness. In this sense neuroscience is like physics. It is the physics and chemistry of particularly complex biological systems. From its standpoint consciousness can justifiably be treated as a "behavior" associated with a tiny part of a much richer range of processes, most of which, like the UV part of the spectrum, do not show up in consciousness at all. If in addition to a science of neurons we are to develop a science of consciousness, then science must investigate conscious experience itself and not reduce it to, or replace it by, unexperienced mechanisms. In such a science the phenomena of consciousness will be systematically studied and carefully analyzed, but, in this instance, no photodetector or even a sophisticated MRI can stand in for the conscious, experiencing subject.

This fact complicates the study of consciousness considerably. For better or worse, the phenomena of subjective, first-person experience are the objects of investigation. This is not to deny or diminish the considerable contributions made by cognitive neuroscience to consciousness studies. Nevertheless, I would like to emphasize the need for a science that concerns itself with the phenomenal field that is subjective human experience itself. We, therefore, require a method of scientific investigation that works intensively with experience. In Goethe's phenomenological method of scientific investigation, especially when developed in the light of recent philosophical and scientific advances, we possess a candidate methodology for a science of consciousness that stays close to phenomena from our first naïve observations to the deepest theoretical insights.

Goethe and the Sciences

While best known for his literary productions, Goethe considered his greatest contribution to be in the sciences, particularly in the study of color.[1] In retrospect it seems clear that Goethe's particular contribution lay not so much in the specifics of his *Theory of Color*[2] but rather in his whole way of doing science.[3] In contrast with the conventional scientific method of his day, Goethe emphasized the role of phenomena at every level of inquiry. In some ways Goethe's criticism of naïve scientific realism anticipated the work of Duhem and van Fraassen, and his stress on lived experience foreshadowed the later philosophical positions of Husserl, Merleau-Ponty, and the phenomenologists generally. Yet Goethe, like J. J. Gibson, distinguished himself not so much as a philosopher but as a practitioner.

As we work toward a science of consciousness, Goethe's method of inquiry offers a distinctive approach that holds much promise. Moreover, implicit within it is a way of re-framing the so-called "hard problem" of consciousness. From this novel vantage point, a way of resolving the hard problem opens out—an important issue to which I will return.

Critical to an appreciation of Goethe's approach to science is a thoughtful understanding of the purpose of scientific investigation altogether. Without such an understanding we might well conclude by holding Goethe accountable to an artificial standard of what science is. In Goethe's time, and to some extent even in our own, the purpose of science was to provide an account of the universe in terms of the dynamics of simple material objects endowed with primary qualities only (extension, position ...). Following Galileo, Descartes and Newton, one reasoned from experiment to the fundamental, if hypothetical, entities that made up the "real" world behind appearances. Goethe was cautious about this as the goal of science.

> The investigator of nature should take heed not to reduce observation to mere notion, to substitute words for this notion, and to use and deal with these words as if they were things.[4]

His objection was not to working hypotheses, but to the establishment of them as truths about the world. Time and again he saw hypotheses become dogmas that dominated thinking for centuries, holding back fresh observation and insight. He would write:

> A false hypothesis is better than none at all. The fact that it is false does not matter so much. However, if it takes root, if it is generally assumed, if it becomes a kind of credo admitting no doubt or scrutiny—this is the real evil, one which has endured through the centuries.[5]

When hypotheses become dogmas they are "the lullabies that the teacher uses to lull his pupil to sleep."[6] Rather we should treat hypotheses in a provisional, workmanlike way. They help us to understand the structure and relationships that exist within and among the phenomena, but they are not themselves the endpoint we seek. Rather,

Hypotheses are like the scaffolding erected in front of a building, to be dismantled when the building is completed. To the worker the scaffolding is indispensable, but he must not confuse it with the building itself.[7]

If the hypothetical model is not the endpoint of scientific understanding, but only a means to another end, then what is the goal of scientific inquiry; what is the building that is hidden behind the dense hedge of scaffolding? In the following quotation we gain a glimpse of that which Goethe saw at the heart of the inquiry.

Yet how difficult it is not to put the sign in the place of the thing; how difficult to keep the being (*das Wesen*) always livingly before one and not to slay it with the word.[8]

Goethe sought always to maintain a living connection to experience, be it a color appearance or a plant. Through lived experiences one could maintain a relationship to *das Wesen*, or the building behind the scaffolding of hypotheses and models. As we will see, it is through the systematic development of this experiential relationship that Goethe sought scientific insight.

At this point one might worry that Goethe is slipping into a vague and mysterious *Naturphilosophie*, or veering onto obscure Heideggerian pathways. While aspects of Goethe's thinking are indeed related to these directions, Goethe developed his own distinct and grounded way of doing science. Thus while Goethe's metaphysics embraced a nonreductionistic conception of nature, he also shunned the speculations of "nature philosophers," so characteristic of his time.[9] Rather he sought a form of empiricism.

Goethe's value to us regarding consciousness studies rests precisely in his reluctance to follow the conventional route of replacing phenomena with mechanical models or "objective" physical process. By insisting on a phenomenological method, Goethe seeks a mode of inquiry that stays with the phenomena of consciousness at every stage. It now remains to explicate briefly this method, and to explore its implications for the "hard problem."

Goethe's "Delicate Empiricism"

Prompted by a question from his friend Schiller, Goethe wrote him a letter describing his method saying, "In my observation of nature and reflection on it, I have attempted to remain true to the following method as much as possible."[10] He then described three stages of his phenomenological method:

1. "empirical phenomena" are the ordinary observations any attentive observer might make,

2. "scientific phenomena" arise through systematic experimentation, including the variation of external conditions,

3. "pure or archetypal phenomena" are the highest form of phenomena, and permit a perceptual encounter with the laws of nature (or consciousness).

At each stage Goethe sought to move deeper into nature, to understand her workings more thoroughly, not by abstracting from phenomena to models but by refining the phenomena themselves.

The process culminates in the encounter with an archetypal phenomenon. When a scientist sees the archetypal phenomenon rightly, he or she sees through it to the pattern or intelligibility of nature. It is the moment of epiphany which every scientist longs for. When Galileo looked at the swinging chandelier in the cathedral of Pisa, in a flash he saw the archetype for isochronous motion of a pendulum. Others in the cathedral were still at the level of empirical phenomena, seeing only a swaying chandelier. But Galileo had been prepared through his long study of mechanics and so had the eyes to see the archetypal phenomenon. This is the moment of discovery, of reaching to the nature of the phenomenon before us. The distinguished philosopher of science N. R. Hanson got it right when he wrote,

Perceiving the pattern in phenomena is central to their being "explicable as a matter of course...." This is what philosophers and natural philosophers were groping for when they spoke of discerning the nature of a phenomenon, its essence: this will always be the trigger of physical inquiry. The struggle for intelligibility (pattern, organization) in natural philosophy has never been portrayed in inductive or H-D [hypothetico-deductive] accounts.[11]

A perceptual encounter with intelligibility is the goal of Goethe's method. He is not concerned to formalize that insight into a mathematical or mechanical model. In his opinion these detract, in fact, from the subjective and personal dimensions of the encounter. Rather Goethe would have the investigator stop here and rest content.

This is perhaps the ultimate goal of our efforts, at least if we have the right sense of our limits.... [It] is the very point where the human mind can come closest to things in their general state, draw them near, and, so to speak, form an amalgam with them.[12]

Yet, of course, it is exactly here that scientists do proceed further, seeking the causes of the observational pattern in terms of underlying mechanisms. This was as true for nineteenth-century physics as it is true today for cognitive neuroscience. For example, explanations for the psychological laws of color perception are sought at the neuronal or cortical level. Goethe was well aware of this tendency, allowing for it when sensible to do so, but also highly critical of it when taken as the only form of explanation.

Goethe's phenomenology is, thus, uncompromising. Theory, for him, is not to be couched in the formal language of mathematics. Rather he understood it in the root sense of the word *theory*, which means in Greek "to behold." Nature only becomes intelligible to the scientist by being rightly beheld. Clearly, naïve empirical observation is insufficient, but one can remain at every stage within the phenomenal and still rise to the theoretical level. The multiplicity of individual phenomena is gathered up into the archetypal phenomenon, which "is to be seen as a fundamental appearance within which the manifold is to be beheld."[13]

The ultimate goal would be "to grasp that everything in the realm of fact is already theory. The blue of the sky shows us the basic law of chromatics. Let us not seek behind the phenomena—they themselves are the theory."[14]

Learning to See

As any science educator knows, students do not instantly "see" the pattern Galileo saw in the swinging pendulum. To move, in Goethe's language, from empirical phenomena through scientific phenomena to archetypal phenomena requires discipline, and most of all, a cognitive maturation of the student. In one sense, the brute facts of nature are forever the same. But as Goethe rightly remarks, every fact is already theory; that is to say, it is already seen in the light of a particular understanding. We bring ourselves to every observation and so see everything in the light of our habits of cognition. Epiphany waits on the remolding of our cognitive capacities: we must learn to see anew. This requires patience and an intimacy with the object of study; active engagement, but also a proper reticence about applying preconceived notions to the novel. This is what Goethe meant by "delicate empiricism."

There is a delicate empiricism that makes itself utterly identical with the object, thereby becoming true theory. But this enhancement of our mental powers belongs to a highly evolved age.[15]

The "enhancement of our mental powers" of which Goethe writes is essential to the education of a scientist, and to his or her continued productivity. Goethe could be describing the marvels of recent research on neuroplasticity when, in a letter to F. H. Jacobi, he writes, "To grasp the phenomena, to fix them to experiments, to arrange the experiences and know the possible modes of representation of them ... demands a molding of man's poor ego, a transformation so great that I never should have believed it possible."[16]

"Molding of the ego" is central to Goethe's understanding of the scientific project. The relationship between the observer and the observed is dynamic and inseparable.[17] For Goethe, every attentive investigation of experience implies the transformation of self. "Every new object, well contemplated, opens up a new organ within us."[18] Scientific discovery presupposes such a transformation of self. Each epiphany waits on the "new organ" required for that specific knowledge. It is this that separates the unseeing novice from the insightful scientist. Information can be found in books and databases, the manipulation of equations is an important technical skill better done by software packages these days than by mathematicians, but the ability to "see" a law of nature is reserved for the human scientist. Here lies the thrill that makes it all worthwhile.

Goethe's approach to science emphasizes this perceptual encounter with the laws of nature and not their abstract or mechanical representation. While important for all forms of scientific inquiry, Goethe's understanding of science is especially useful for the developing science of consciousness where the phenomena of lived experience comprise the very field of study. Increasingly we will need to learn to "see" deeper and more subtle patterns within conscious experience.

The Place of Neuroscience

Unlike Goethe, Paul Churchland and many others have argued for the explanation of consciousness on the basis of neuroscience, likening its role in consciousness studies to that of electromagnetic theory in the study of light phenomena.[19] That neuroscience has much to offer at both the theoretical and practical levels is obvious. Lithium can change the life of a depressed individual profoundly, and brain surgery can provide significant relief to the epileptic. We now largely understand these and other interventions in terms of the neuroscience that underlies consciousness. We can even monitor the neural correlates of specific emotional and intellectual states noninvasively and in real time—all very impressive. And yet we can rightly ask, is this the only or most appropriate form of investigation, and the only modality of explanation applicable to consciousness? At this point it is instructive to look at explanation in physics, especially since Churchland and others often refer to it as the model science.

Explanation of physical phenomena in terms of material mechanisms reached its zenith in the late nineteenth century. The theories of relativity and quantum mechanics both underscored the already growing concern about the fundamental limitations of mechanistic models. Classical physics was too constraining, it simply had no place for the anomalies of the Michelson-Morley ether-drift experiment nor the puzzling spectrum of blackbody radiation.[20] It took many decades until finally the habits of nineteenth-century mechanical thinking could be set aside, and room made for a more sophisticated understanding of scientific theory required by such evidence. Relativity theory says nothing about the particular machinery of nature, but rather works at the level of the fundamental symmetries of space and time. It specifically overturned Fitzgerald's notion of physical length contraction at high speeds, and the mechanical ether theory held on to by all nineteenth-century physicists including Maxwell. In the Copenhagen interpretation of quantum theory, one gives up speaking about a real world of atoms with pre-existing properties and instead sticks with observables, that is, with correlations between specific measurement outcomes.[21]

Understandings at the level of mechanism have tended to come and go. All this is of little consequence to the practicing physicist because he or she has learned to treat mechanistic accounts heuristically, shifting from one account to another as seems useful, even if they are mutually contradictory. In quantum mechanics there is no consistent mechanistic picture. In relativity each observer gives a different and contradictory explanation of "events" depending on his or her state of motion. What remains constant throughout is a deeper pattern recognized within the apparent confusion of outer phenomena. We can represent or account for that pattern in various ways, but at some level Goethe was right we he said, "The constancy of the phenomena is the one important thing; what we think about them is quite irrelevant."[22]

Today's exhilaration within the neuroscientific community is reminiscent of the optimism of late nineteenth-century physics prior to relativity and quantum theory. If we have learned the lessons of physics, we would do well to hold our mechanistic theories of consciousness lightly. Otherwise, for example, we may inappropriately dismiss states of consciousness that cannot be accommodated in our limited models. This is especially tempting in consciousness research because reports of subjective experience are always first-person accounts. From the standpoint of neuroscience, therefore, they are always suspect. Yet if we eliminate experience by replacing it with the output of instruments (as is done in physics), we have changed the field of inquiry entirely. No, the first-person phenomenology of consciousness is essential to consciousness research.

One sensible way of approaching the relationship between phenomenology and neuroscience is that advocated by such individuals as Varela,[23] Thompson and McClamrock.[24] They advocate a "mutual enlightenment" in which both approaches contribute to the joint project of understanding consciousness.[25] But even here, one must be careful not to constrain the introspective data reported by skilled observers because it does not fit existing theory or show up on lab instruments.

Goethe's commitment to first-person experience opens his method, or any method founded on his, to the criticisms leveled at introspectionism.[26] Although much could be said in response, perhaps it is most important to bear in mind that ultimately subjective experience forms the foundation of *every* science including modern physics and neuroscience. The so-called "hard problem" is precisely this troublesome relation between subjective experience and objective reality. By taking its stand on phenomena themselves, Goethe's method opens up new ways of resolving the hard problem of consciousness.

Resolving the "Hard Problem"

The hard problem has at least two distinct forms. The first is the first-person, third-person dichotomy. My subjective perspective on the world is held to be entirely unique, and furthermore I appear to be constrained to my first-person viewpoint. That is, while I can imagine that you have a similar first-person perspective, I can never experience the world as you do. By contrast we can speak of a public, third-person perspective on the world which every conscious entity can assume. It is argued that science concerns itself only with facts that are open to such public scrutiny. Since the subjective experience of individuals is accessible only to first-person investigation, there can be no science of such experience. Rather, it is argued, we should restrict ourselves to the biological correlates of consciousness which *are* open to third-person investigation. Additionally, we can practice a "heterophenomenology" which interprets the first-person accounts of others from a third-person perspective.[27]

A second version of the hard problem is "subject-object" dualism, which is usually taken to be identical with the first-person, third-person dichotomy. I would suggest that we treat these two versions of the hard problem as distinct and that we approach each differently. Subject-object dualism holds that the phenomenal world of lived experience is largely an artifact of human consciousness and so not a fair indication of the "objective" physical world "out there." In the standard scientific analysis, the red of the sunset, for example, is reduced to the differential scattering of high frequency electromagnetic waves from polarizable particles in the atmosphere. The electromagnetic waves make their way to the human visual system where they provoke complex electrochemical reactions. The subjective experience of "red sunset" is explained by an account in terms of supposed, objective realities: electromagnetic waves, molecules, neurons, etc. At this juncture we immediately confront the thorny problem of theoretical entities, hypotheses, and models already touched on. What is the place of these in science?

Bertrand Russell's philosophical development is characteristic of many who have tackled subject-object dualism. Russell initially supposed one could rigorously infer physical entities from sense data. By 1914 he came to realize that Berkeley was right; it is in principle impossible to infer an unexperienced objective reality from sense data.[28] Physics proceeded unaffected by Russell's realization, in large part because physics is not really about objective entities. Rather, physics is about qualities. Physics describes the properties of things (mass, charge, frequency, speed ...) and the lawful relations between these properties. We may measure some with the human sensory apparatus, other properties may be measured by instruments, but one is always working with properties. In quantum theory, for example, we must define a "complete set of commuting *observables*" as the basis for theoretical description. It is simply not possible to make meaningful statements about a reality that is, in principle, beyond description. To borrow a term from Buddhist epistemology, one cannot speak about an "attribute-bearer" that itself has no attributes. According to the above line of reasoning, all science is concerned with "subjective" properties. Rigor and "objectivity" arise not by reference to a hypothetical realm but by care in experimentation and through rigor in theoretical analysis. In this view, therefore, the subject-object form of the hard problem becomes irrelevant to science. If the object of study is beyond experience (whether direct or mediated through an instrument), then it is also not amenable to scientific study. Phenomena are at the heart of science.

The first-person, third-person form of the hard problem remains; namely, phenomena seem to be of two types: private and public. Here too an unwarranted assumption causes the difficulty. Experience is always private. We only have first-person experience. We may compare our individual experiences intersubjectively, but the concept of third-person experience is a philosophical construction. The coin looks round to you and oval to me. We can construct the concept of the coin's shape in itself (Russell's term is "sensibilia"), but no third-person perspective exists from which it can be viewed. Apparently we cannot escape our first-person perspective; it is an artifact of the way consciousness is set up. Implicit in this last statement is, however, a way out of the first-person, third-person dichotomy without falling into solipsism. If consciousness itself can be restructured, then it might (at least in principle) be possible to move beyond dualism or solipsism. From Goethe's perspective the mind indeed is open to development, and every discovery depends on at least a small change in consciousness. Only such change allows one to become "utterly identical with the object," or to "form an amalgam with them." Goethe denies the constraint on consciousness assumed by so many. For him the mind is malleable, even to the point of achieving a nondual form of consciousness. In this, Goethe's view is like that of the contemplative traditions, locating the solution to dualism not in some clever philosophical move, but in a profound transformation of consciousness itself.

The two forms of the hard problem thus find resolution differently. Subject-object dualism disappears by recognizing that science is only concerned with the subjective world. The first-person, third-person version of the hard problem will only find resolution through a fundamental change in the structure of consciousness itself.

Notes

1. J. P. Eckermann, *Conversations with Goethe*, ed. H. Kohn, trans. G. C. O'Brien (New York: Frederick Ungar, 1964), p. 149.

2. J. W. von Goethe, *Theory of Color* in *Scientific Studies*, ed. and trans. D. Miller (New York: Suhrkamp Publishers, 1988).

3. D. Seamon, and A. Zajonc, *Goethe's Way of Science* (Albany: SUNY Press, 1998). See also Zajonc, A. 1993. *Catching the Light* (New York: Oxford University Press), pp. 188–216; and Zajonc, A. 1987. "Facts as Theory," in *Goethe and the Sciences: a Reappraisal*, eds. F. Amrine, F. Zucker, and H. Wheeler (Dordrecht: D. Reidel).

4. J. W. von Goethe, *Theory of Colors*, trans. C. L. Eastlake (Cambridge, Mass.: MIT Press, 1970), p. 283.

5. J. W. von Goethe, *Goethe's Botanical Writings*, ed. and trans. B. Mueller (Honolulu: University of Hawaii Press, 1952), p. 239, and in J. W. von Goethe, *Goethe's Werke, Hamburger Ausgabe*, vol. 13, 5th ed. (Hamburg: Christian Wegner, 1966), p. 51. Henceforth, references to the *Hamburger Ausgabe* are abbreviated *HA* and followed by the volume and page numbers.

6. Goethe, *Maximen und Reflexionen*, no. 557, *HA*, XII:432.

7. Goethe, *Maximen. . .* , no. 554, *HA*, XII:432.

8. Goethe, *HA*, XIII:452.

9. See my "Goethe and the Science of His Time," in *Goethe's Way of Science*, pp. 18–20.

10. Goethe, *HA*, XIII:23, and in Mueller, *Goethe's Botanical . . .* , p. 228.

11. H. R. Hanson, *Patterns of Discovery* (New York: Cambridge University Press, 1958), p. 87.

12. Goethe, *HA*, XIII:24.

13. Goethe, *Briefe, HA*, IV:231 (3 May 1827).

14. Goethe, *Maximen. . .* , no. 488, *HA*, XII:432.

15. Goethe, *Maximen. . .* , no. 509, *HA*, XII:435.

16. J. W. von Goethe, *Briefwechsel zwischen Goethe und F. H. Jacobi*, ed. M. Jacobi (Leipzig: Weidmann, 1846), p. 198.

17. See F. Amrine, "The Metamorphosis of the Scientist," in *Goethe's Way of Science*.

18. Goethe, *HA*, XIII:38.

19. P. Churchland, *The Engine of Reason, The Seat of the Soul* (Cambridge, Mass.: MIT Press, 1995), chapter 8.

20. Zajonc, *Catching the Light*.

21. G. Greenstein and A. Zajonc, *The Quantum Challenge* (Sudbury, Mass.: Jones & Bartlett, 1997).

22. J. W. von Goethe, *Werke*, Weimarer Ausgabe II. 13, p. 444.

23. F. J. Varela, E. Thompson, and E. Rosch, *The Embodied Mind: Cognitive Science and Human Experience* (Cambridge, Mass.: MIT Press, 1991), and F. J. Varela, "Neurophenomenology: a methodological remedy for the hard problem," *Journal of Consciousness Studies, 3* (4), pp. 330–349 (1996).

24. R. McClamrock, *Existential Cognition: Computational Minds in the World* (Chicago: University of Chicago Press, 1995).

25. S. Gallagher, "Mutual Enlightenment: Recent Phenomenology in Cognitive Science," *Journal of Consciousness Studies, 4* (3) pp. 195–214 (1997).

26. See for example H. Hunt, "Cognition and States of Consciousness," *Perceptual and Motor Skills, 60,* pp. 239–82 (1985).

27. D. Dennett, *Consciousness Explained* (Boston Mass.: Little Brown, 1991), pp. 66–67.

28. B. Russell, "The Relation of Sense-Data to Physics," reprinted in *Mysticism and Logic* (1917).

35 Essential Dimensions of Consciousness: Objective, Subjective, and Intersubjective

Frances Vaughan

The process of evolution and growth toward wholeness can be observed to proceed through various stages of differentiation and integration. For example, cells divide and differentiate and are subsequently integrated in a complex organism. At this relatively early stage of consciousness research it therefore seems appropriate to give careful attention to differentiating objective, subjective and intersubjective approaches, with the intention of including all three in a truly integral vision.

Objective approaches study the world of objects—out there. Science provides information about an observable, material universe. Even the brain, as distinguished from mind, can only be studied as an object. Subjective approaches, on the other hand, study the invisible inner world of the psyche which can only be understood through introspection, interpretation and intersubjective dialogue. Intersubjective approaches can also be subdivided into those that are concerned with the exploration of values and meaning, those that are focused on interpersonal relationships, distinguishing between what Martin Buber characterized as I-thou rather than I-it relationships, and those that examine shared cultural values. The more subtle distinctions in the subjective and intersubjective domains may only be apparent to trained observers who have undertaken serious inner work or contemplative disciplines. Intersubjective approaches are particularly relevant to understanding cultural diversity and deepening the dialogue between researchers devoted to objective and subjective approaches.

Common Ground

Before examining these distinctions more closely, we will review some of the factors that objective, subjective and intersubjective approaches to consciousness studies have in common. Each of them is interested in knowledge and the discovery of truth. Every method therefore demands integrity and honesty on the part of the investigator.

All claim to be empirical in the sense of being based on experience, but they do not necessarily agree on the definition of empiricism. Objective approaches that claim to be scientific rely primarily on sensory data, measurement and analysis. Since the social sciences that study subjective phenomenological descriptions of experience tend to be viewed as "soft" sciences in our culture, they also try to be objective in an effort to gain credibility.

All three approaches, objective science, subjective introspection and intersubjective discourse, are subject to injunction, verification, and confirmation by other trained observers. Each approach has its own methods of validation. In other words, we need to remember that each method requires specialized training, and expertise in one domain does not imply expertise in another.

Even within the field of psychology the divisions between behavioral scientists predominantly concerned with the measurement, prediction and control of behavior, and the more introspective proponents of existential and transpersonal psychology concerned with value, meaning and purpose in human life, can be difficult to bridge. Unfortunately people often disparage what they do not fully understand or appreciate.

Objective, subjective and intersubjective approaches to studying consciousness all include rational, emotional, and intuitive modes of knowing. Although intuition and emotion are often perceived as belonging exclusively to the domain of the soft social sciences, objective sciences also rely on the subjective intuition and emotional motivation of investigators.

Any approach can be discussed in objective, descriptive language, but inquiring into the depths of inner experience calls for interpretation and intersubjective dialogue that includes feelings and intuition. Validity in this domain depends, not on objective descriptions, but on the authentic expression of subjective reality. Authenticity, truthfulness, and sincerity are necessary for intersubjective explorations of depth and mutual understanding.

Epistemological Pluralism

In order to make the dialogue between these three approaches to the study of consciousness more meaningful, it seems advantageous to acknowledge an epistemological pluralism in which different modes of knowing, appropriate to these different domains, can be complementary rather than competitive.

We can begin by differentiating three basic modes of knowing: namely sensory, rational and contemplative. These correspond roughly to knowledge of body, mind and spirit. They also correspond to the eye of the flesh, the eye of the mind, and the eye of the soul. Each mode is subject to injunction, verification and confirmation by trained observers. A person trained in only one domain may be quite unaware of the training required in the other domains for adequate evaluation of truth claims.

The problem of scientism arises when scientists believe their discipline is the only valid way of knowing, while being completely ignorant of the stages of development and training required for an adequate understanding of either philosophical discourse or contemplative insight. Communication accross categories can therefore be very challenging. A scientist knows very well that we can easily be fooled by our senses. Likewise, anyone can be fooled by unschooled attempts at introspection.

Even within these broad categories of epistemology people may have difficulty understanding each other. Furthermore, even within one discipline we find people who cannot communicate with each other because their expertise is so specialized. For example, I recently heard two microbiologists commenting on each other's work, each acknowledging that they did not understand what the other was doing. Certainly psychologists sometimes have difficulty understanding each other, and religious practitioners rarely try to understand other faiths. One microbiologist pointed out that while science is literal, art, aesthetics, and spirituality all require interpretation, and this is always vague and messy. He said, "As a scientist I want to know what is definite! But to be true to myself and my internal compass I have tried to develop an I-Thou relationship to my higher Self. This seems unscientific, but it has changed my life."

An integrative approach to consciousness studies calls for dialogue with others whose training and experience may be different from our own, with mutual respect and an open mind. No one of us will be able to cover all the bases. Yet the fact that we may not be trained in all three modes of knowing does not justify dismissing other modes as irrelevant or unimportant. Ken Wilber (1998) points out that the integration of art (subjective phenomenology), morals (intersubjective ethics), and science (objective, concrete occasions) requires that each be recognized in its own right. These three domains cannot be reduced to a single category.

Insofar as the scientific method consists of injunction, apprehension and confirmation, it applies not only to objective, but also to subjective and intersubjective domains. Although transpersonal psychologists have done some mapping of the inner world of consciousness, much work remains to be done in this area. Scholars such as Ken Wilber (1995), Stanislav Grof (1998), and Charles Tart (1983) have attempted to map states and stages of consciousness that transcend the ordinary waking state.

Wilber (1993) points out that it is a mistake to confuse prerational states with transrational states, the former referring to nonrational beliefs and assumptions about reality evident in magical thinking and dogmatic mythological belief systems. Transrational states, on the other hand, refer to those states that transcend and include reason. In prerational states, aesthetics, ethics and science are not yet differentiated. It is the transrational traits and states that need to be investigated further in order to deepen our understanding of the relationship between subjective, objective and intersubjective approaches to studying consciousness.

Many people have observed that humanity is at a crossroads and is undergoing a spiritual crisis. Despite incredible technological advances and a wealth of new information about the brain, we have yet to learn how to cultivate those qualities of

consciousness that are sorely needed, such as wisdom, compassion, and loving kind-
ness. In spite of a wealth of knowledge about physiology, many dimensions of consciousness remain a mystery. We have a tremendous amount of information about
the biological mechanisms underlying consciousness, but very little understanding of
individual conscious experience. Scientific methodologies that are well suited to the
investigation of the mechanistic questions of consciousness are inadequate for investigating qualities of subjective experience. Even the distinctions betweeen the context,
content, and process of consciousness are often overlooked.

In a recent interview following a meeting of the European College of Consciousness Studies, the Swiss pharmacologist Albert Hoffmann commented that people
need a deep spiritual basis for their lives—not dogma or belief, but experience. He
said that many young people are looking for meaningful experiences. The happiness
and satisfaction they seek is spiritual, not material. When there are no sanctioned
paths for this exploration, they sometimes pursue experiences of nonordinary states
of consciousness irresponsibly or inappropriately.

The scientific investigation of altered states of consciousness continues, despite
being hampered by illicit drug use and ensuing legislation. For example, Stan Grof's
work with holotropic breathing has opened a number of people to a deeper awareness of transpersonal realms of the psyche that are usually inaccessible to our ordinary waking state. The popularity of shamanic practices as well as eastern disciplines
of yoga and mediation all attest to the strong and widespread interest in the subjective exploration of nonordinary states of consciousness.

To date a number of different approaches to consciousness studies have been cataloged (Wilber 1997). Among them are the following:

• Cognitive science and neuropsychology.

• Phenomenology and introspection.

• Depth psychology and psychotherapy.

• Developmental psychology.

• Psychosomatic medicine and mind body healing.

• Nonordinary states of consciousness.

• Contemplative disciplines—East and West.

• Subtle energies and quantum theories.

Each of these investigative approaches has made important contributions to the
field. All of them, in addition to others that may be developed, should be included in

an integral view. However, each method offers only a partial perception of the whole. Scholars need to be aware that each perception is partial.

Distinctions

Science tries to describe what is, studying and measuring what can be observed. Religion, on the other hand has traditionally taken the role of telling us what should be, and what values constitute the good life. It offers a creed, a code of ethics, and a community. Science deals with the visible outer world, religion with the invisible inner world. Both worlds need to be included in an integral view of consciousness.

Another distinction that is becoming widely acknowledged is the distinction between spirituality and religion. Perhaps the most succinct way of differentiating them is to say that spirituality refers to subjective experience of the sacred, while religion refers primarily to tradition and organized institutions.

By directing attention to what is, science usually assumes that we inhabit a pregiven world. Claiming to gather objective data from a pregiven world, it does not tell us anything about meaning, intention or values, since these cannot be located in the external world except by inference. These require interpretation and intersubjective dialogue to be discerned. As Huston Smith has said, meaning slips through the instruments of science as the sea slips through the nets of the fisherman.

A postmodern constructivist view argues that our perceptions of the world are constructed and context dependent. This is at least partly true and certainly must be taken into account in studying consciousness. How we perceive the reality that is given, how we experience it and respond to it is largely dependent on our subjective interpretations and cultural mind set. What we believe about reality tends to be reflected and validated by our experience. Consequently experience reinforces beliefs and beliefs shape experience. We are inevitably shaped and affected by our culture, community and interpersonal expectations. We are also the shapers of that environment and culture. In psychotherapy, for example, healing often occurs as a result of new experiential learning in relationship. When the therapeutic relationship provides a safe context in which dysfunctional defenses can be dropped, new ways of seeing oneself and the world can be explored.

Objective Domain

Objective approaches have, up to now, dominated the field of consciousness studies. I will not attempt to examine them here as they are widely acknowledged. I would only like to point out that one can be objective about the inner world and the outer world, the individual and the collective. What objective approaches have in common is that they split the observer from what is observed and describe phenomena in I-it language. Objective approaches therefore describe only observable surface phenomena—the appearance of things. Objectivity does not have depth or meaning. This does not imply that it is not useful or valuable, but only that it is limited. Unfortunately, those who are devoted to objective science are sometimes unaware of its limitations.

Subjective Domain

I first became interested in studying consciousness in an effort to learn about how the mind works and to understand my own experience better. I have devoted most of my attention to the subjective and intersubjective domain, as I have found that it is often overlooked or discounted in a culture that is dominated by scientific materialism. Whereas medicine addresses primarily the physical dimensions of healing, transpersonal psychology attempts to integrate the physical, emotional, mental, and spiritual dimensions of wellbeing, regarding them all as essential to a person's health and wholeness.

In my own work as a psychotherapist, I have had the opportunity to witness the deepening of inner experience in many people's lives, and I have, time and again, observed that, not only are the body and the emotions inextricably interconnected, but that inner work can be profoundly healing. I have sometimes described my work as helping people untie the knots in their psyches. Sometimes I see it as soul work. Physical symptoms are often alleviated, but the interventions are psychological rather than biochemical. We know that physical health, including attention to diet and exercise, can have a positive effect on our emotions. Yet even when we know what we should do in this regard, we do not always do it. The motivation for change is rooted in our emotions—our desires, our hopes and fears, and our beliefs about what is possible.

Intersubjective dialogue in psychotherapy is the means of healing old emotional wounds and developing latent potentials. Inner work may be emotional, cognitive and/or spiritual. Sometimes it is a kind of remedial education that draws out subjective experience in order to reclaim and reintegrate what has been repressed or rejected and facilitate growth toward wholeness.

The idea of multiple intelligences is now widely discussed. Humans seem to develop at different rates along different lines. For example, emotional intelligence may or may not be correlated with IQ as it is usually measured. Physical, emotional, cognitive, and moral development may proceed at different rates and highly developed skills in one area are not necessarily indicative of maturity in other areas.

Howard Gardner (1993) has mapped a number of different types of intelligence and we are all aware of differences between physical, emotional, mental, and spiritual maturity. Dan Goleman's (1995) work on emotional intelligence has brought attention to its importance for psychological health and wellbeing.

Some characteristics of emotional maturity include:

- The capacity to adapt to change.
- The ability to deal constructively with reality and delay gratification.
- Freedom from symptoms produced by tension and anxiety.
- The capacity to find more satisfaction in giving than receiving.
- The capacity to relate to others in a kind, consistent manner.
- The capacity to sublimate and direct hostile energy into constructive outlets.
- The capacity to love.

Lawrence Kohlberg's (1981) work on moral development draws distinctions between preconventional, conventional, and postconventional morality. While preconventional morality is focused only on looking out for number one, conventional morality is determined by what is acceptable to the group, and is governed by the rules and mores of society. Postconventional morality abides by conventional rules when it is appropriate to do so, but is not bound by them. Postconventional morality may be egocentric, sociocentric or world-centric, bearing in mind the wellbeing of the whole, as well as the individual and the social group. However, postconventional morality does not necessarily imply awareness of spiritual development.

The area of spiritual intelligence is an additional domain in which very little research has been done, and yet is clearly needed in these times of spiritual hucksterism and competing religious ideologies. Emotional maturity and moral development may be necessary foundations for developing spiritual intelligence. If we are not to confuse prepersonal fusion with transpersonal integration, we need to map the full spectrum of consciousness across all domains of psychospiritual integration. We have only just begun to explore the implications of this work.

Spiritual development includes and transcends moral development and emotional development. It, too, may be preconventional, conventional, or postconventional, egocentric, sociocentric, or worldcentric. Some popular forms of spirituality use spiritual principles to satisfy ego desires, to get whatever the person desires at a given time. Most religious institutions foster conventional morality. There are also many people who feel they have outgrown traditional institutional forms of religion and yet may be deeply spiritual in their orientation toward life.

Stages of Self

Psychology offers many typologies of personality, and the wisdom traditions identify stages of spiritual development based on changing perceptions of self. The injunction "Know thyself" has multiple levels of depth. For example, a transpersonal map differentiates stages in which the self identifies with the the body, the ego, the soul, or pure awareness (Vaughan 1995). The following outline of stages of self-concept can be easily recognized both within and outside of spiritual traditions:

• Ego: Identified exclusively with ego, the willful self seeks personal, social, and spiritual empowerment. The intentional self may turn attention to developing qualities of consciousness rather than simply focusing on external goals.

• Soul: Identified with soul, the self may identify with being a seeker on a quest. At this stage the person may be inspired by love and devotion to spiritual teachers or mentors. Creativity and love relationships and connections to nature and inner peace become important. A person accepts both joy and sorrow, hardship and good fortune as an opportunity for learning, and is concerned with the wellbeing of others, recognizing that we are all connected. At this level consciousness may transcend time and space.

• Spirit: The self identified with Spirit is at one with all being. All is Spirit or God, as in sahaj samadhi. Spirit is perceived as the ground and the goal of the path, and there is no more preoccupation with self. At this stage spirituality would be world-centric, no longer identified with a specific group, and no longer dividing the world into us and them. This is the domain of nondual mysticism. In the words of Zen master, Dogen:

To study Buddhism is to study the self.

To study the self is to forget the self.

To forget the self is to be enlightened by all things.

   The development of spiritual maturity, intelligence, and freedom depend on the cultivation of love and wisdom. The spiritual path, as a metaphor for the unfolding of consciousness and self-knowledge, demands both inner work and action in the world. Each person begins the quest whenever they begin to ask the deeper questions about life's meaning. Sometimes the quest begins after a close encounter with death, or an experience of illness or depression or disappointment with the fulfillment of unsatisfying ego goals. Stages of faith that deepen awareness of inner realities lead to experience in which one's identity is no longer exclusively defined by the body-ego.

In the subjective domain of consciousness research perhaps every investigator should be required to reflect on his or her own self-concept since that is the lens through which perception and interpretation is filtered. In the absence of self-awareness, self-deception may go undetected. And in the inner world of subjective consciousness, anyone may fall prey to illusions. The way of self-knowledge is fraught with pitfalls as well as possibilities. One anonymous Christian teaching says: "The concept of the self stands like a shield, a silent barricade before the truth...."

Intersubjective Consciousness

Two dimensions of intersubjective consciousness are interpersonal relationships and cross cultural dialogue. Intersubjective approaches to studying consciousness often call for holding different and even opposing views in a larger context that transcends narrow sectarianism. The development of vision logic, the capacity to hold an aperspectival view of relative realities and a network of interrelated ideas is particularly relevant in this domain.

In the domain of interpersonal relationships, intersubjective consciousness is associated with I-Thou relationships rather than I-it relationships, in which another person is treated as an object. Love flows through I-Thou relationships. The depth and truth of another's being is recognized, not learned. A relationship in which one feels seen, heard, and known is a relationship in which mutual respect and a deep connection enables healing to occur. The value of healing relationships is widely recognized in the practice of psychotherapy, but healing relationships are by no means limited to the confines of the consulting room. The power of intersubjective consciousness is pervasive, even if unrecognized.

Dialogues addressing intersubjective consciousness are necessarily culturally conditioned. Nobody grows up unconditioned. Everyone is subject to the social and cultural context in which each individual is embedded. How we address the problem of pure consciousness and whether we take a position for or against the notion of a universal experience depends in part on the depth and extent of mystical consciousness that has been subjectively experienced. Mystics from different traditions recognize each other. I think most would agree that having a mystical experience does not make a person into a mystic. As we take a closer look at the characteristics of mysticism we see that there are different types of mystical experience, although they share certain common characteristics. For example, nature mysticism, deity mysticism, formless mysticism and nondual mysticism may all be transrational and partly ineffable, yet quite distinct. Experience is inevitably reduced when one tries to describe it in words. Language, being linear and temporal, is necessarily reductionistic. An untrained observer can rarely describe the depth and impact of a profound mystical experience.

We see both the inner and the outer world through the filters of our own particular worldview. Images and inner visions—the contents of consciousness—are clearly culturally determined. For example Christians may see Jesus or the Virgin Mary, while Tibetans see Tibetan deities. We all tend to see what we look for, and overlook what we do not believe exists. In the inner world, what is palpably real to one person may appear to be an illusion to another. In the province of the mind what we believe to be true tends to become true in our experience. Intention and belief shape our experiences and we are all prone to self-deception unless we have a community of peers who can test our subjective experiences of nonmaterial realities. On the other hand, the community is not necessarily a safeguard, as we know from observing group delusions in religious cults or in the history of witch hunts.

One of the essential elements in studying intersubjective consciousness is the necessity of holding an aperspectival view that allows for multiple points of view. Every individual exists, not just in one relationship, but in multiple relationships. We all exists in an intricate web of mutually conditioned relationships that affect us as much we affect them. The image of Indra's net, in which every jewel in the net reflects every other jewel is an apt metaphor for this domain. Furthermore, we are affected not only by multiple relationships but also by multiple ideas. The Buddha said, "We are what we think. With our thoughts we make the world." How we think about spirituality, interpersonal relationships, about who and what we are and what is possible for us as human beings affects everything we do. Intersubjective consciousness can constrict, limit and diminish us as human beings as easily as it can heal, uplift, and inspire us. We are usually much more attentive the food we put into our bodies than what we put into our minds. As we learn more about how intersubjective consciousness functions in our lives and how we each contribute to the quality of our collective mindstates, we may begin to understand that downward causation, the role of consciousness in shaping our world, is an untapped resource of astonishing power.

Summary

In conclusion, I want to reiterate the importance of epistemological pluralism, and giving equal attention to subjective, objective, and intersubjective dimensions of consciousness. To date the attention given to physiological correlates of consciousness has far outweighed attention to subjective, internal states. In order to deepen the dialogue between different approaches and support healing the split between the inner life of mind and spirit and our work in the world, it seems necessary to recognize and validate that which has been neglected and overlooked in a culture that has long been dominated by scientific materialism. My hope is that we can listen attentively and be open to learning from our differences as we continue to explore the evolution of consciousness and our part in the process.

References

Gardner, H. 1993. *Multiple intelligences.* New York: Basic Books.

Goleman, D. 1995. *Emotional intelligence.* New York: Bantam Books.

Grof, S. 1998. *The cosmic game.* New York: State University of New York Press.

Kohlber, L. 1981. *Essays on moral development.* San Francisco: Harper.

Tart, C. 1983. *States of consciousness.* El Cerrito, Calif.: Psychological Processes.

Vaughan, F. 1995. *Shadows of the sacred: Seeing through spiritual illusions.* Wheaton, IL: Quest Books.

Wilber, K. 1993. The pre/trans fallacy. In Walsh, R. and Vaughan, F. *Paths beyond ego: The transpersonal vision.* New York: Putnam.

Wilber, K. 1995. *Sex, ecology, spirituality: The spirit of evolution.* Boston: Shambhala.

Wilber, K. 1997. An Integral Theory of Consciousness. *Journal of Consciousness Studies,* 4(1):71–92.

Wilber, K. 1998. *The marriage of sense and soul: The integration of science and religion.* New York: Random House.

B. Alan Wallace

Apart from our first-hand experience, there is no scientific evidence for the existence of consciousness, so if it were not for the subjective evidence provided by introspection, there would be no discipline of consciousness studies, no conference on this topic, and no discussion of "hard" versus "soft" problems of consciousness. Given this fact, it is odd that since the time of William James, while enormous progress has been made in terms of behavioral and neuroscientific studies, no comparable progress has been made in terms of refining the mind itself to make it a more rigorous and reliable instrument for exploring states of consciousness.

Recent progress in developing a psychometer for detecting consciousness may seem to circumvent this issue altogether, but such a conclusion may be misleading. A psychometer designed on the basis of studies of mind/brain relationships may detect the neural correlates for specific conscious states in humans and perhaps other mammals. But the presence of conscious, as opposed to unconscious, mental processes for which such correlates are examined can be identified only on the basis of first-hand accounts and by analogies of such accounts. Thus, such correlates could not be found apart from such introspective knowledge.

Moreover, such a psychometer will unlikely be able to detect the presence or absence of consciousness in reptiles, insects, or micro-organisms or shed any light on speculations about plant or mineral consciousness. In addition, one of the interesting questions to be raised once neural correlates have been identified for a specific conscious process is: does the neural correlate causally produce the phenomenological mental process and therefore precede the latter; or is the mental process a property or function of the corresponding neural process and does it therefore occur simultaneously with it? To answer this question, one would have to know exactly when the conscious process first arises. But for that, one would need an instrument that could detect that process itself, as opposed to its neural correlate. In other words, one would need a genuine psychometer that could detect conscious states, and not simply their neural correlates. And the only real psychometer we have ever had is our own consciousness.

Once again, we are thrown back on subjective experience, and this remains crucial for mind/body studies of all manner of conscious mental states and their corresponding neurophysiological processes. For such research to proceed rigorously, there should be sophisticated methods for subjectively identifying specific conscious states so that one has precise knowledge of the subjective processes that are related to the corresponding brain processes. But once again, no such methods for enhancing the quality or reliability of attention have been devised to complement the increasing sophistication of neuroscientific methodologies.

William James recognized the importance of clear, sustained, voluntary attention for the introspective study of the mind and for the broader context of education and human life in general (James 1890, volume 1, chapter 9). However, when considering the possibility of improving this faculty of attention, he was at a loss and speculated that it was perhaps untrainable (James 1899, volume 1, chapter 11). The problems of scattering and dullness of the attention have long been recognized by many of the contemplative traditions of the world, and nowhere have these attentional defects been more thoroughly addressed than in ancient India and later in Tibet. Hindu and Buddhist contemplatives have long been keenly interested in the nature of consciousness, its origins, and its role in nature; and, unlike modern cognitive scientists, they have devised methods for enhancing attentional stability and vividness so that the mind may become a more precise and reliable instrument for examining a wide array of mental phenomena first-hand.

The following discussion of methods for training the attention in preparation for exploring the nature of consciousness is based on the contemplative literature of Tibetan Buddhism. This tradition was inspired by 1500 years of Indian Buddhist contemplative inquiry, which, in turn, drew from centuries of meditative experience by yogis in ancient India who stepped outside mainstream religious dogmas and devised their own methods for refining human consciousness.

In seeking to use the mind to explore itself, Buddhist contemplatives identified two of the most salient problems as attentional excitation and laxity. When attentional excitation arises, the mind becomes incapable of focusing continuously on its chosen object, whether internal or external. The attention compulsively shifts to other objects, as one forgets the object of one's choice altogether. On the other hand, when the mind settles motionlessly on a given object, it tends to lose its vividness, or clarity, of awareness and thus slips into laxity. Once the mind has fallen into laxity, it may then proceed to the more sluggish state of lethargy, in which a sense of heaviness is dominant; and lethargy in turn may lead to drowsiness and finally sleep.

A mind that oscillates between excitation, in which attentional stability is impaired, and laxity, in which attentional vividness is missing, is of little use for the rigorous examination of mental states. Attentional qualities that Buddhist contemplatives have found to be essential for such inquiry are stability and vividness. To understand these two qualities in terms of Buddhist psychology, one must note that Buddhists commonly assert that the continuum of awareness is composed of successive, finite pulses of cognition; though different schools pose varying hypotheses concerning the exact frequency of these pulses (Vasubandhu 1991, 2:474). Moreover, commonly in a continuum of perception, many moments of awareness consist of nonascertaining, or unconscious, cognition: that is, objects appear to this inattentive awareness, but they are not ascertained (Lati Rinbochay 1981, pp. 92–110).

According to this theory, the degree of attentional stability increases in relation to the proportion of ascertaining moments of cognition of the intended object. That is, as stability increases, fewer and fewer moments of ascertaining consciousness are focused on any other object, which makes for a homogeneity of moments of ascertaining perception. The degree of attentional vividness corresponds to the ratio of moments of ascertaining to nonascertaining cognition: the higher the frequency of ascertaining perception, the greater the vividness. Thus, the achievement of quiescence entails an exceptionally high density of homogenous moments of ascertaining consciousness.

In order to achieve these two attentional qualities and sustain them, two mental faculties must be cultivated: mindfulness and introspection. With the faculty of mindfulness one repeatedly directs the attention on an object with which one is already familiar. The faculty that enables one to recognize both excitation and laxity in the course of one's attentional training is called introspection. While mindfulness focuses on the chosen object, introspection is a kind of meta-cognition that attends to the quality of the attention itself. Thus, the latter is often likened to a sentry who stands guard against the hindrances of excitation and laxity.

In one commonly practiced Tibetan Buddhist technique for developing attentional stability and vividness the attention is focused on a mental image of an object such as a flower or a pebble. With mindfulness one seeks to attend to that image continuously without disengaging from it, but in the early phases of this practice, the duration of such continuous attention is extremely short. Indeed, many novices are astonished and dismayed in the early phases of this training to discover how chaotic their minds actually are! However, by using one's introspective ability to detect the occurrence of excitation, or attentional scattering, the duration of such lapses in focused attention is gradually decreased.

In neither the cultivation of mindfulness or introspection is there a conflation of subject and object, even though these processes are all taking place within one's own mind. With the faculty of mindfulness one focuses on an object such as a mental image, which is itself not a cognition but simply an object of mindful awareness. Thus, the distinction between subject and object persists, as in the case of an observer watching a projected image on a screen. On the other hand, Buddhist psychology defines excitation as an agitated mode of cognition, and laxity as a slack mode of cognition. Moreover, it is said that a single cognition cannot be simultaneously aware of two or more dissimilar objects. When one introspectively detects the occurrence of excitation, this is a type of short-term recollection of a preceding, scattered mode of cognition (Wallace 1998, chapter 3) Introspective awareness of cognitive processes is therefore a kind of "retrospection," in which the distinction between subject and object still holds. Because such introspection actually directs the attention away from the meditative object as it monitors the quality of the attention, if applied too frequently it can actually impair the cultivation of sustained voluntary attention. Thus, one must strike a balance between the continual application of mindfulness of the attentional object and the intermittent application of introspection of the quality of attention.

Tibetan Buddhist contemplatives have mapped out in detail the way the attention develops as a result of such training (Lamrimpa 1995), and they claim that as a result of sustained, continuous training, the attention can be focused for at least four hours, without even the most subtle occurrence of either excitation or laxity. In that state, commonly called "meditative quiescence," the senses are entirely withdrawn as the attention is totally focused into the domain of purely mental experience, so that one no longer even has a sense of having a body. The mind is utterly still, with no thoughts arising, and it is imbued with an exceptional degree of attentional clarity. As William James predicted, if one has been focusing on a mental image, it now appears almost as vividly as if one were seeing it with the eyes (James 1890, 1:425).

At this point this attentional training becomes particularly relevant to the study of consciousness, for now the contemplative is encouraged to disengage from the mental image and leave one's awareness in a still, vivid state free of any appearances (Wallace 1998, p. 206). What remains experientially are the phenomenological characteristics of consciousness itself. Those who have experienced this state describe consciousness as "empty" of substance, as being "clear" or "luminous," in the sense of having the capacity to give rise to all manner of appearances, and as being of the very nature of "knowing." Although all these terms are familiar in common language, it is said that only an experienced contemplative can know their meaning in relation to this immediate experience of consciousness. Others can gain only a metaphorical sense of their import in this context.

Even in this state, in which mindfulness no longer has a mental image on which to focus, the distinction between subject and object remains, for now one retrospectively discerns the nature of preceding moments of consciousness that is disengaged from all appearances. Thus, there is no chance of confusing consciousness itself for some other object appearing to consciousness: consciousness retrospectively folded in upon itself is all that remains. Buddhist contemplatives from various traditions hasten to add, however, that this state can easily be confused with the attainment of nirvana, which it emphatically is not (Wallace 1998, p. 238, 264–266). It simply provides one with direct insight into the phenomenological nature of consciousness, which is knowledge of considerable importance, but not an insight that enables one to accomplish the ultimate aim of Buddhist practice.

If it is possible to experientially ascertain the phenomenological nature of consciousness by drawing the attention inward upon itself, without focusing on other appearances to consciousness, could one not try to do that from the beginning, without focusing on a mental image or any other object? In fact, Buddhist contemplatives have devised another technique that does just that: from the outset, one focuses the attention simply on the mind, immediately cutting off all manner of thoughts and mental imagery (Karma Chagmé 1998, p. 80). As the attention increasingly stabilizes in that state, with a high degree of clarity, one is eventually left with the salient characteristics of consciousness alone.

One could further ask: since consciousness is equally present whether or not thoughts or other appearances are arising to it, could one not focus on the characteristics of consciousness without silencing the mind? In response to this question, Buddhist contemplatives have devised yet another method in which one simply focuses on consciousness in the midst of thoughts and other impressions emerging and passing of their own accord, without intervention (Padmasambhava 1998, pp. 105–114). In all these techniques, it is not a single moment of consciousness apprehending itself, but rather a continuum of moments of consciousness retrospectively ascertaining the nature of preceding moments of consciousness. Especially in the first two methods-of focusing on a mental image and of silencing thoughts-the usefulness of this discipline for observing other mental states is limited, for the techniques themselves inhibit the occurrence of a wide range of mental events. In the final method, however, the contemplative does not intentionally interfere with whatever kinds of mental processes arise. Whether thoughts, emotions, or mental images are rough or mild, long or short in duration, positive or negative, one simply attends to the consciousness of them, without trying either to prolong or cut short those mental events. In this nonintervening state of relaxed yet vigilant awareness, a wide range of mental processes are bound to arise, including long dormant memories and emotions. Thus, this technique can be especially useful in becoming cognizant of mental processes that might otherwise go unnoticed.

As mentioned previously, Buddhist contemplatives were not the first to develop such methods for refining the attention and using it to explore the nature of consciousness. The Buddha himself drew from the experience of Indian contemplatives before him, Buddhist methods were introduced into the Chinese Taoist tradition, and over the course of centuries these methods were practiced and further developed in Tibet, Mongolia, Korea, and much of the rest of Asia. In short, these methods for training the attention have been used for centuries by contemplatives who have embraced a wide variety of religious and philosophical doctrines, including polytheism, monotheism, nontheism, substance dualism, philosophical idealism, and transcendental monism. In the midst of all this diversity of views, it is remarkable that virtually all traditions that have used such techniques claim that they may lead to the development of a wide range of paranormal abilities and forms of extrasensory perception, including the ability to immediately apprehend the presence of another being's consciousness and the contents of that consciousness. In other words, they claim that highly focused, vivid attention can be used as a genuine psychometer not only for apprehending one's own consciousness, but that of other beings, human and nonhuman. Obviously, such claims cannot be taken at face value without being subjected to rigorous, scientific scrutiny, but given the conspicuous absence of such refined techniques for enhancing the attention in the modern West, it would be unscientific to dismiss them merely on the grounds that they are "farfetched." Such techniques present a fascinating challenge to modern researchers in the field of consciousness studies to broaden the scope of legitimate methods of scientific inquiry so that the introspective exploration of consciousness may begin to rise to the levels of sophistication of objective means of studying brain correlates of conscious states.

Buddhist and other Asian contemplative traditions have developed a wide variety of techniques for training the attention, many of them specifically designed for different personality types (Wallace 1998, pp. 143–155; Buddhaghosa 1979, chapters 4 and 5). Such development of sustained, voluntary attention may be of use not only for exploring consciousness and achieving soteriological goals, but it may also be relevant to other fields of human endeavor. William James, for instance, comments, "the faculty of voluntarily bringing back a wandering attention, over and over again, is the very root of judgment, character, and will.... An education which should improve this faculty would be the education par excellence" (James 1890, 1:424). He also observes that geniuses commonly have extraordinary capacities for sustained voluntary attention, but he assumes that it is their genius that makes them attentive, and not their attention making geniuses of them (James 1890, 1:423). This is a plausible assumption, but it would be interesting to test this hypothesis empirically. Finally, it would be well worthwhile to investigate the possible utility of these techniques for helping those who are suffering from various attentional disorders, especially when considering the serious side-effects of the drug therapies that are most commonly in present use today.

Despite centuries of phenomenological studies of different states of consciousness, the Indian and Tibetan Buddhist traditions have produced no compelling view of the brain, a situation that well corroborates John Searle's claim that "the specifically mental aspects of the mind can be specified, studied, and understood without knowing how the brain works" (Searle 1994, p. 44). In the meantime, modern science remains largely in the dark concerning the origins and nature of consciousness. As John Searle comments in a manner reminiscent of William James,

Because mental phenomena are essentially connected with consciousness, and because consciousness is essentially subjective, it follows that the ontology of the mental is essentially a first-person ontology.... The consequence of this ... is that the first-person point of view is primary. (Searle 1994, p. 20)

Despite Searle's reservations about the possibility and utility of introspection, he is certainly correct in his assertion that it is "immensely difficult to study mental phenomena, and the only guide for methodology is the universal one-use any tool or weapon that comes to hand, and stick with any tool or weapon that works" (Searle 1994, p. 23). If the Buddhist and other contemplative traditions have found techniques that work for refining the attention and using it in the exploration of mental phenomena, it behooves us to learn from them and apply their knowledge to the modern world.

An expanded version of this chapter appeared in the *Journal of Consciousness Studies* ... (to be added in proof).

References

Buddhaghosa. 1979. *The Path of Purification*, trans. by Bhikkhu Ñanamoli. Kandy: Buddhist Publication Society.

James, W. 1890/1950. *The Principles of Psychology*. New York: Dover Publications.

James, W. 1899/1958. *Talks to Teachers: On Psychology; and to students on some of Life's Ideals*. New York: W. W. Norton & Co.

Karma C. 1998. *A Spacious Path to Freedom: Practical Instructions on the Union of Mahamudra and Atiyoga*, with commentary by Gyatrul Rinpoche, trans., B. Alan Wallace. Ithaca: Snow Lion.

Lamrimpa, G. 1995. *Calming the Mind: Tibetan Buddhist Teachings on the Cultivation of Meditative Quiescence*. trans. B. Alan Wallace. Ithaca: Snow Lion Publications.

Rinbochay, L. 1980 *Mind in Tibetan Buddhism*. trans. and ed. Elizabeth Napper. New York: Valois/Snow Lion.

Rinbochays, L., Rinbochays, L., Zahler L. and Hopkins, J. 1983. *Meditative States in Tibetan Buddhism: The Concentrations and Formless Absorptions*. London: Wisdom Publications.

Lodrö, G. G. 1992. *Walking Through Walls: A Presentation of Tibetan Meditation*. trans. and ed. Jeffrey Hopkins. Ithaca: Snow Lion Publications.

Namgyal, T. T. 1986. *Mahamudra: The Quintessence of Mind and Meditation*, trans. Lobsang P. Lhalungpa. Boston: Shambhala.

Padmasambhava. 1998. *Natural Liberation: Padmasambhava's Teachings on the Six Bardos*, with commentary by Gyatrul Rinpoche; trans. B. Alan Wallace. Boston: Wisdom.

Searle, J. R. 1994. *The Rediscovery of the Mind*. Cambridge, Mass.: The MIT Press.

Vasubandhu. 1991. *Abhidharmakos'abhāṣyam*. trans. Louis de La Vallée Poussin, English trans. Leo M. Pruden. Berkeley: Asian Humanities Press.

Wallace, B. A. 1998. *The Bridge of Quiescence: Experiencing Tibetan Buddhist Meditation*. Chicago: Open Court.

Wallace, B. A. 1998a. The Buddhist Tradition of *Samatha*: Methods for Refining and Examining Consciousness. *Journal of Consciousness Studies*.

37 Transpersonal and Cognitive Psychologies of Consciousness: A Necessary and Reciprocal Dialogue

Harry T. Hunt

My thesis lies in the title of my talk and its implied dialectic. We begin with a mutual problem shared by both transpersonal and cognitive science approaches to consciousness: their need of each other.

On the one hand, on the cognitive science side, our so called "conscious awareness system" that synthesizes and directs experience is curiously transparent and impalpable—more to be looked through than at, and lacking in the empirical features needed for empirical science. Enter the detailed phenomenologies of altered and transpersonal and meditative states. These show consciousness to be something that can undergo specific transformations and development.

Indeed, transpersonal states may show the very inner cognitive processes of consciousness otherwise invisible within its more ordinary functioning. On this view, transpersonal and altered states would serve as a kind of microscope for the processes behind ordinary consciousness. If so, then consciousness *does* have empirical features after all, and a cognitive science of consciousness will be hobbled without their study. On the other hand, if a cognitive science of consciousness risks having nothing to talk about without its potential for transpersonal development, transpersonal psychology risks remaining mere "magic" and only a modern re-recording of lost traditions, without some account of what it is about our minds, our neurocognition, that allows such experiences to occur. We need a nonreductionistic account here, yet recognizable by modern cognitive science, however thereby opened up and expanded.

Let us explore the first thesis more specifically: cognitive psychology needs the transpersonal. We begin with the strange debate in current cognitive science about qualia. In his book *Consciousness Reconsidered*, Owen Flanagan rejects Daniel Dennett's attempts to deny qualia—the qualitatively sensed dimensions of immediate conscious experience whose supposed privacy places them outside science. But Flanagan also doubts the early suggestion of Charles Sanders Peirce that each day and week has its distinct and unique quale or feel that can be discriminated. This he feels goes too far. So what is the status of these distinct feels and physiognomies, to use Pierce's list—of red, bitter, tedious, and hard?

Dennett intuits correctly that such sensory qualia have nothing to do with functional perception. Since they seem inherently private and indescribable, Dennett argues we can as well imagine them as inverted or eliminated zombie-like without any practical impact on how we live in the world. Certainly, psychologists from William James and Peirce to James Gibson have insisted that perception is not composed of separate sensory dimensions. Instead, sensation is the result of a self-aware analytic abstraction that appears when we ignore the dense tapestry of immediate experience and artificially isolate a single quality for our inspection.

Peirce says that separate qualia—in their irreducible thatness—are not actually present in the immediate moment of consciousness. Rather qualia are only potential or latent within the moment—"maybes" rather than "facts" of ordinary experience. For Gibson, also, "sensations" are not "in" ordinary experience, but they *are* developed out of a more primary perception that is first and foremost always *of* a world and our being in it. In Gibson's terms the first organization of perception is the continually flowing pattern of the ambient array surrounding all moving creatures. So we could say that it is our capacity for the self awareness of our ongoing perception that brings forth specific qualia out of it, either to be manipulated in representational thought or to be felt as such in the direct experiences of the arts. Functional perception comes first and qualia are its "maybe's"—*potential* experiential states *latent* within the more primary envelope of flow.

Now, if qualia are consciously utilized in the arts, we see already that they must be potentially consensual and not private—complexly emergent and not primary or atomic. It is just here that the transpersonal development of consciousness offers a unique contribution to cognitive science. Peirce would be right about his specific quale or felt sense for each hour and day, but they are emergent within a development of self-awareness, and some people are better at bringing them forth as experiences than others. Meditation and mystical experience would then be the major cross cultural settings that foster the development of qualia for their own sake. If qualia are potentials or latencies within our ongoing moments of awareness, these are exactly what meditation prolongs and then develops in their own right.

We can see this in Marghanita Laski's classic descriptions of what she calls the "quasi-physical" qualities of ecstasy. These include expressive and metaphorically rich dimensions of light and darkness, felt bodily expansion, liquidity and flow, and sensed upward surgings and risings. More recently, A. H. Almaas locates separate aspects of mystical or numinous experience such as strength, will, joy, power, and compassion and love—each with its characteristic physiognomy or qualia. For instance, when it is essential strength that predominates in spiritual experience, with its paradoxical sense of vulnerability and openness, there is an expansive aliveness, sense of beauty, bodily heat, and fiery redness. What is striking here, and contrary to philosophical critics of qualia as private and outside science, is just how sharable and consensual the *developed* qualia of transpersonal states can be. Max Weber termed them charismatic in their social impact and Durkheim even thought that such experiences expressed the actual energy binding together the social group.

In short, a cognitive science of consciousness needs the transpersonal because the consciousness it wants a science *of* is not static but undergoes a potential development best reflected in the meditative traditions, and it is that development that may best reveal the inner forms and processes of consciousness itself.

We can go further and see how it is that so called ordinary consciousness already carries within it the seeds of transpersonal development. Peirce defined qualia as the total content of the immediate moment of consciousness—a state that is the whole of our life in that instant—but when we go to ask about it we always arrive too late. Certainly it is not "ordinary" to observe immediate consciousness in its own right. It is more the ocean we swim in, the medium we look through and not at, but our capacity for self awareness allows us to try, and the early history of academic psychology involved just such introspectionism. Contemporary cognitivists love to use William James on the "stream of consciousness," the first phenomenology of immediate awareness, but they usually miss how close James's observations of the flowing moments of awareness are to the states sought in Buddhist meditation. First, he tells us that it is not we who do this streaming but strictly speaking it does or has us—just like more intense mystical experience. It would be more phenomenologically accurate he says, if we avoided saying "I think," and instead said "it thinks" or "thinking going on," in the same way we say "it rains." Second, there is no central self or identity discoverable in immediate consciousness other than the ongoing flow itself. Finally, in his later work he even describes "pure experience" as the sheer "thatness" prior to being taken as any specific "what." Here James approaches the sense of pure presencing or being, the suchness or bare facticity so central to Eastern meditation, Heidegger and Almaas. Along these lines, James even offers this description of coming out of anesthesia: "At the beginning of coming to, one has at a certain moment a vague limitless infinite feeling—a sense of existence in general without the least trace of a distinction between the me and not me." This is the sheer "thatness" prior to any "what," and it may require a self-aware being to become aware of this pure open potentiality of our experience.

We find even more specific examples of meditative-like states in the dry as dust experimental introspectionists like Titchener—so striking precisely because they did not intend it. For instance, in John Nafe's study of affective pleasure in 1924 his laboratory observers eventually experienced the immediate moment of "liking" or "pleasure," in response to the unexpected stimuli being presented, in ways very reminiscent of Laski on ecstasy—that is, as a sense of surging or rising expansion from the abdomen moving into their head and even beyond out into the room, a bit like the beginning of an out-of-body state—all this described with metaphoric and synesthetic references to expansive brightness and luminosity. These ultra-brief, momentary experiences of pleasure, briefly magnified by direct observation, have the same features of the more prolonged ecstasies of advanced meditation. Other studies at this time described the immediate moments produced by such intensified self observation in terms of brief states of timelessness, loss of spatial localization and self identity, synesthesias—or states of inter-modal translation between the patterns of the different senses—and related experiences of subject-object mergence. In its later years Titchener's introspectionist laboratory almost sounds like a mystery school, with its focus on mind moments so reminiscent of Buddhism, its studies showing all recognizable surfaces to be memory illusions, and T-scope studies of the bare experience of light that use the same metaphors as the Tibetan Buddhists.

So we see how the more developed transpersonal states are actually based on an unfolding of the qualia *latent* in the immediate moments of consciousness. Our cognitive sciences of consciousness have missed the fact that the historical core of academic psychology was already transpersonal, and it is only fully understandable from a transpersonal perspective. This material also demonstrates something that the spiritual traditions have always maintained—that the basic features of transpersonal experience *are* actually implicit and potential in the present moment, if we but shift our attention away from what our awareness is "about" or "for" to its more immediate "isness."

So on now to our second thesis: transpersonal psychology needs a cognitive science of consciousness:

First, we must ask why *would* the ongoing moment of consciousness—which it is already nonordinary even to notice in its own right—contain within it the forms whose *development* is the transpersonal, and how do we come to experience this at all? A commonplace of cognitive theory has been that what distinguishes the human mind from that of nonsymbolizing creatures is its capacity for turning around on itself, for taking the role of the other toward our experience, and so transforming and rearranging it—constituting the creativity of the human mind.

If we follow William James on pure experience, then our immediate consciousness is this normally unnoticed thatness—a sense of sheer beingness—prior to its expression as the many "what's" or contents of the different symbolic forms. This moment by moment experiencing—which as self aware beings we have the *potential* to observe—is the context for and contains as latencies all the forms for the more specific functional expressions of consciousness. These are the deep forms or archetypes of experience in Plato's sense. Or in the sense of Almaas, the thatness of immediate awareness flows already in the multiple aspects of strength, will, love, and joy that are a necessary part of our ongoing aliveness. Prolonged into focal consciousness these forms become the different qualities and flavors of spiritual or numinous experience.

We see this same principle in T-scope studies of vision stopped at phases too brief to allow specific visual patterns to be recognized. Instead, what subjects report are the more basic geometric forms underlying ordinary vision—the same forms seen in some altered states and used as such in the arts.

So, if with the cognitivists, human cognition is a turning around on and recombining of the structures of perception, we must ask then about the relation between perception itself and transpersonal states of felt meaning. Is it possible that what stands forth in these states are the basic features of what Gibson calls the ambient array of ordinary perception? For Gibson the kinesthetic or enactive movement of creatures creates a rich pattern of flow that wells forth from the indefinite horizon ahead, expands in the direction in which we are going, and then narrows behind us as we proceed. Like Heidegger's analysis of Dasein, Gibson undercuts the classic dichotomy between subject and object by showing how each specific pattern of flow we make reflects back our unique position and speed. So, each "there" of the moving array casts back its own co-emergent "here" like a shadow—proprioceptively locating our position as specific to just that array.

We find something similar in the more formless levels of mysticism, where in Heidegger's terms a sense of openness that cannot be further specified—he even calls it horizonal—allows or lets us experience a sense of presence or Being as such. Or, for Plotinus, the unspecifiable Absolute gives forth of itself in utter generosity the forms of all existence, whose dynamic flow through time can then be experienced as the highest potential of the human soul. On the more specific level of Almaas on the separate aspects of numinous experience, we can see in Gibson's unfolding perceptual array the basic form of essential strength—as the continuous expansion of horizonal openness, the essential "will" in the directionality and intent of the perceptual flow, the essential power or energy in creaturely movement, the essential joy in the full exercise of these capacities, and the loving and compassionate way in which the presencing of the organism is mirrored by the array surrounding and holding it.

In short, we can see how the fullest development of transpersonal consciousness expresses the fundamental forms of the living, moving sentient creature. It is the basic forms of perception itself that are realized and developed into the metaphors and metaphysics of transpersonal states.

But does that mean that transpersonal states are thereby somehow primitive or regressive? On the contrary, these states also involve an abstract cognitive development. First, there is the witnessing attitude of detached observation that de-embeds consciousness from its usual functions and allows it to develop as such. Second, as I alluded to above, these states seem to involve inter-modal synesthesias that allow different aspects of the numinous to be recognized on a symbolic level. Synesthesias are much broader than the simple color-hearing translations usually described. There are also complex synesthesias in which the tactile-kinesthetic patterning of the body image is cross translated with visual forms and colors, reflected in Almaas's accounts of the cross modal physiognomies of transpersonal states mentioned above. Complex synesthesias also seem to be entailed in the full experience of the chakras, with their multi-modal fusions of muscle groups, colors, geometric designs, and mantras, all with characteristic emotional transformations that sound like a more formal version of Gendlin's focusing.

Here I argue we find a further confirmation of the neurologist Norman Geschwind's theory of the cross modal translation basis of all higher symbolic forms. For Geschwind it is the direct cross translation of the patterns of vision, touch, and hearing across the neo cortex that would allow the multi-modality patterns basic to language and the arts. Transpersonal states would be the experiencing of these complex synesthesias for their own sake and independent of the practicalities of ordinary cognitive functioning. So, for instance, the "white light" experience, with its phenomenology of a sensed all-inclusive totality, felt eternity, and sensed annihilation of the ordinary self, can be understood, in cognitive terms, as the synesthetic translation of the usual body image into glowing light—as both the most basic quality of vision and the perfect metaphor for the openness of time and Being. The full dissolving of the body image into light *should* convey just the sense of dying and disappearing so often described in the mystical literature.

If such states also involve the abstract re-presentation of the primary dimensions of living perception as felt meanings then that would include the sense that we are already somehow familiar with them. Metaphors fully felt in this synesthetic way *become* life-worlds or realms of their own—so there is nothing else the light can be of or about than the light of creation itself, and whether that be truth or illusion can not be decided from the cognitive processes involved.

Such a cognitive account *is* nonreductionistic, in that these abstract synesthetic processes do not create or construct transpersonal states so much as recognize and amplify them on a specifically human level. We *are* present, we *do* exist. The being ness of the universe *is* continually welling forth around us in pure generosity. Consciousness, as our immediate presencing into openness, *is* a fundamental and nonreducible category.

Now I'd like to deal with some implications of a more balanced and reciprocal dialogue between the transpersonal and cognitive perspectives. First, from a transpersonal or spiritual perspective can we really be done so quickly with the spectre of false reductionism? Is not any psychology of the cognitive mediation of higher states of consciousness false if their phenomenology is of an objective, unmediated transcendence? Must not our dialogue break down just here?

Perhaps not. On the one side, we have the metaphysical claims of the spiritual traditions. All the universe is made of consciousness or the singularity before the big bang is somehow consciousness itself. On the other side, for the cognitivist, the experience of light in mysticism appears as a metaphor that *mediates* a felt meaning or felt sense of the source of all existence. How is this line between metaphysics and metaphor to be crossed?

For Almaas and Heidegger what knits them together is the language of being and presence. Within the categories of metaphysics and mystical cosmologies are hidden the primary being experiences that these systems first tried to capture and may yet still evoke if approached more experientially. On the other side, what the felt metaphors within transpersonal states evoke is also this same sheer isness or thatness of Being—which is after all real, and the perfect expression for the root of spiritual experience in our age of the scientifically "factual." What is more of a "fact" than the Being of all that is, welling forth around us?

Yet if the sensory metaphors of light, expansion, and flow that are the vehicles of transpersonal experience are latent within the ambient array of perception does that mean that in these experiences we ultimately just see ourselves, that this approach to the metaphoricity of these states makes them solipsistic? Here we need to recall that the flowing texture of perception in moving creatures is itself nested within the physical universe as science has come to understand it, and that the organization of perception cannot ultimately be inconsistent with the principles of that universe. Certainly we can see the reflection within Gibson's flow patterns of the nonlinear dynamics of water and air, and arguably of other levels of physical reality as well.

A second issue: In the light of our discussion of a nonreducible primacy of experience shared by both transpersonalists and some cognitivists, what of the ongoing debates about the point of emergence of consciousness in nature? There are those who see consciousness—even a simple and immediate one—as only emergent through the evolution of complex enough neural nets. So for Edelman, Crick, and others a neurocognitive perspective is necessarily the most inclusive in any account of what consciousness is and does. Or, there are those who seek to rest a primary or basic consciousness on the field properties of quantum physics.

Where to most plausibly place the emergence of consciousness seems a major key to all subsequent theory and research. If it is placed significantly too high or too low the entire field of consciousness studies will be distorted. I would argue from a primacy of experience perspective—locating the most basic consciousness in immediate perception and its behavioral manifestations—that both the neurocognitive and quantum explanations are ultimately reductionistic and so obscure the most basic features of consciousness itself.

If we assign primary consciousness on a need to know basis then it is probably first visible in all creatures who move enough in relation to their surroundings that some self-location during and after each movement will be necessary for survival. Single cell organisms meet this criterion and show many of the behavioral sensitivities associated with theories of perception—a point first noted by Alfred Binet and Peirce in the late 1800s. In fact the chemical and electrical processes by which single cell organisms move are the same as those in the depolarization of the neuron. Is this too daringly inferential or is it, as the early Darwinians thought, an extension of the same first person based inferring of consciousness that we do with each other? If we are trying to find some midpoint between the spiritual view that the universe itself is conscious and the behaviorist denial of consciousness even in ourselves, then behavioral reflections of Gibson's ambient array of perception seem like the most plausible place to begin. If so, then although the neurocognitive perspective will surely help to explain how consciousness gets gathered and focused in complex organisms, it cannot explain consciousness itself. It cannot solve the "hard problem." Instead, consciousness becomes a defining property of all moving life forms. So from a primacy of experience view, it is not neurocognition that is the all inclusive perspective that explains consciousness, but the phenomenal properties of reality that ultimately may help to explain the neurochemistry and neuroanatomy of neural nets.

What then of the quantum field models so tempting to some transpersonalists interested in the commonalities of physics and mysticism and to physiologists who study quantum events in cells and neurons? If we can speak of an emergence of consciousness at some point in evolution, why not its submergence or latency in the physical order? Some would see such latency in the nonlinear dynamics of the fluid media that first support life and others in the indeterminancies of quantum fields. Certainly there is ample evidence in nature of higher emergent processes utilizing lower supporting ones, but that does not mean that the quantum events posited in cell metabolism somehow *are* already consciousness. For instance, the quantum events posited by Hameroff and Penrose in microtubules may have more to do with the chemical coherence of the cell than with the elementary flow processes common to both movement in single cell organisms and neuronal depolarization. Indeed these quantum events seem as characteristic of stomach cells as neurons. If consciousness is the felt inner side of movement within an ambient array, quantum microtubule events have gone too deep inside to be consciousness. On the present view, mystics and physicists have principles in common because they both develop—in utterly different directions—the same properties of a primary flowing perception.

By way of conclusion, a view of the primacy of phenomenology has consequences for both transpersonalists and cognitive scientists of consciousness. It contextualizes all purported "explanations" for the existence of consciousness and reminds us— with William James—that all we ultimately have is our experience, that all we know about brains and microtubules comes to us refracted through the very medium they are being used to explain. If science itself cannot answer why there is something rather than nothing, maybe it cannot ultimately answer either why there is a consciousness that witnesses that something. Perhaps there are conceptual primitives— like space, time, *and* consciousness—whose *variations* we can trace and even manipulate without being able to explain. Historically psychologists have been far more timid about such speculations than physicists and mathematicians. I personally think it would be more fruitful for the emerging fields of consciousness studies if we leave it open whether what is happening here is a genuine science of consciousness—with a suitable expansion in its methodology to fit its new subject matter—or the spiritualization of science—in which we begin to acknowledge that all our real and emerging knowledge about consciousness does not tell us anything about why it is really there or what it means. To address the questions of meaning, purpose, and existence we must always start, as Kierkegaard says, from the same place as all previous generations, and for such questions we have only our own experience of this life and, one hopes, the integrity and faith to follow where that experience leads—both individually and collectively.

References

Almaas, A. H. 1986. *Essence—the diamond approach to inner realization.* York Beach, Me.

Binet, A. 1888. *The psychic life of micro-organisms A study in experimental psychology.* Philadelphia: Albert Saifer, 1970.

Cattell, R. B. 1930. The subjective character of cognition and the presensational development of perception. *British Journal of Psychology,* monograph no. 14.

Dennett, D. 1991. *Consciousness explained.* Boston: Little, Brown.

Flanagan, O. 1992. *Consciousness reconsidered.* Cambridge, Mass.: MIT Press.

Geschwind, N. 1965. Disconnection syndromes in animals and man. *Brain* 88:237–94:585–644.

Gibson, J. J. 1979. *The ecological approach to visual perception.* Boston: Houghton Mifflin.

Hameroff, S. and Penrose, R. 1996. Conscious events as orchestrated space-time selections. *Journal of Consciousness Studies* 3, 1, 36–53.

Heidegger, M. 1959. *Discourse on thinking.* New York: Harper and Row, 1966.

Hunt, H. 1995. *On the nature of consciousness: cognitive, phenomenological and transpersonal perspectives.* New Haven: Yale University Press.

James, W. 1912. *Essays in radical empiricism and a pluralistic universe.* New York: E. P. Dutton, 1971.

James, W. 1890. *The principles of psychology.* 2 vols. New York: Dover.

Kierkegaard, S. 1843. *Fear and trembling and the sickness unto death.* Garden City, New York: Doubleday, 1954.

Laski, M. 1961. *Ecstasy.* Bloomington: Indiana University Press.

Nafe, J. P. 1924. An experimental study of the affective qualities. *American Journal of Psychology*, 35:507–44.

Peirce, C. S. 1905. The principles of phenomenology. In J. Buchler, ed. *Philosophical writings of Peirce.* New York: Dover, 1955.

Plotinus. *The Enneads.* Trans. Trans. S. MacKenna. Penguin Books, 1991.

38 Biogenetic Structural Theory and the Neurophenomenology of Consciousness

Charles D. Laughlin

For those of you who are willing to accept that consciousness is a function of the nervous system, biogenetic structuralism offers a number of advantages. First, biogenetic structuralism is an interdisciplinary theory, integrating research in anthropology, psychology, neuroscience, physics, and phenomenology. Second, the theory provides a single perspective and language for addressing such issues as the evolution of consciousness, animal consciousness, consciousness in human fetuses and babies, alternative phases of consciousness, the cultural conditioning and transcendence of cultural conditioning of consciousness, and the relations between technology and consciousness. Third, the theory requires grounding in a methodology best described as neurophenomenology—a merger of trained phenomenological skill and an understanding of neuroscience. And fourth, the theory counters some of the more common limitations of other theories currently informing consciousness science—limitations that include the following:

1. *Theories of consciousness are often ethnocentrically naivete.* There may be little or no recognition of the fact that a culture conditions the range of states of consciousness experienced by its members. Theories developed by psychologists, cognitive scientists and neuroscientists very often fail to tap the wealth of cross-cultural data on consciousness to be found in the ethnological literature, and in the personal experiences reported by ethnographers.

2. *Theories are often phenomenologically naivete.* Theories often signal the theorist's limited personal understanding of the essential nature of their own consciousness. As Edmund Husserl (1977) put it, a theorist may be unaware of their conditioned "natural attitude" (or "natural thesis") toward their own states of consciousness. Few theorists in consciousness science are mature contemplatives, or trained phenomenologists, who have learned to examine the structures and properties of their mental acts from a fully empirical standpoint. More on this limitation later.

3. *Theories are often neuroscientifically naivete.* Some theories do not take into account the more than hundred years of developments in the neurosciences. Such theories quite often make claims about consciousness that run counter to how we know the brain has evolved, how it develops during childhood and how it functions. Prior to twenty years ago one could for the most part ignore the neurosciences without contravening the findings of empirical research. But no longer. Modern neuroscience has burgeoned, and consciousness scientists ignore brain research at their peril.

4. *Many theories are limited by mind-body dualism.* Theorists often treat mental and physical phenomena as distinct domains of reality without realizing the ethnocentrism of their dualistic "natural attitude." Consciousness may be defined as an epiphenomenon, as somehow detached from the brain, or as merely mediated by the brain like a radio mediates a program broadcast from another realm of existence. Such theories make it difficult to ground the structures of consciousness in physical reality, or in the processes of the body.

5. *Some theories are hampered by scientistic methodology.* Some theories of consciousness are narrowly grounded upon experimental data, or computer modeling. The methodological strictures of such theories exclude other sources of data such as ethnographic, phenomenological, clinical and naturalistic accounts. Other theories derive from strictly humanistic or "New Age" methodologies that have little reference to scientific experimentation. Again, such theories restrict our point of view in such a way that valuable data and insights are excluded.

Biogenetic Structuralism

What is biogenetic structuralism and how does this formulation avoid these limitations? Biogenetic structuralism is a body of theory that integrates our understanding of consciousness, culture and nervous system in a single perspective. The theory is simultaneously neurobiological, phenomenological and sociocultural, incorporating all the avenues of scientific research relevant to the study of consciousness, with a particular emphasis upon ethnographic and neurophenomenological methodologies.[1] The emphasis upon ethnography works to eliminate the ethnocentrism so common in Western scientific accounts of consciousness. Our understanding of the field is enriched by the full range of experiences and cultural models available to human beings. A neurophenomenological component assures the inclusion of the skills of mature contemplation, and wherever possible, links these phenomenological findings with how we are discovering the brain works.

Consciousness and the Cognized Environment

How does biogenetic structural theory conceive of consciousness? Well, we take the view that our everyday experience arises and passes away between our ears. Our everyday experience is mediated by our brain. Experience is the internally produced play by which the body enacts the world for its own consumption. The body is the producer, the projectionist, and the audience of this ongoing play, which unfolds within the functional space we call *consciousness*. Consciousness is the field of awareness mediated by a dynamic organization of neural structures we call the *conscious network*. What most of us usually mean by "being conscious" is our moment by moment shifting awareness within the field of experience—we are "conscious" of this or that feeling, thing, thought, sensation, etc. Our individual awareness at this moment may or may not include the sound of an air conditioner, the feeling of the pressure of the seat on our behinds, or the sensation of our tongue pressing against our teeth. When we do become aware of such a phenomenon, it means that a new neural model has become entrained to our conscious network.

All properties and qualities of consciousness are mediated by our body's neuro-endocrine systems. These systems function individually and collectively to model reality. The sum total of these models in our individual brain is our *cognized environment* (as the late Roy Rappaport[2] called it). The on-going stream of consciousness is our neurophysiological enactment of our *operational environment*; that is, our local environment, including our physical body. The operational environment is the real world modeled between our ears in our cognized environment. But please be careful here. This is not a mind-body dualism for the very simple reason that the neural systems mediating our cognized environment are part of our operational environment. This is merely a structure-function discrimination, no different than distinguishing between the physiology of the hand and the act of grasping, or the physiology of the GI tract and digestion. There is our real operational body, and our cognized body the latter being a model mediated by cortical networks in our brain[3].

The regulatory function of the organ of experience—the nervous system with its brain—manifests a polarity between the necessity to adapt to the external operational environment on the one hand, and the need to maintain the integrity of the body's own internal organization on the other hand. Our brain thus naturally strives to "autoregulate" its activities in a way that simultaneously answers these twin demands—the result being what Jean Piaget (1971) described as a dynamic state of "equilibration."

Reality Is Transcendental

It seems ridiculous that in science today we should have to mention that there is a real world "out there," that our notions about reality are the constructs of our knowing brain, and that the truth of our notions about reality is determined by their fit with experienced reality. Yet in this era of postmodern relativism, the ontological and epistemological status of reality often gets muddled, and reality as a set of limiting conditions on our knowing requires reiteration (see Krippner and Winkler 1995 for a useful discussion of this issue). In biogenetic structural terms, while the cognized environment is how we know and experience our organism and our world, the system of neurological transformations that produce the cognized environment is part of the operational environment within which we are embedded and to which we must adapt in order to survive. The operational environment, including our own organism, may thus be considered *transcendental* relative to our cognized environment in at least three senses:

1. *The sense of part to whole.*   There is always more to learn about the operational environment, or anything within it, than can ever actually be known. This is true because there is no knowing without the involvement of the "in-forming" process of neural modeling.

2. *The sense of locality.*   Cognized environments reflect the fact that organisms are located in the operational environment. Thus the demands of adaptation privilege local knowledge relative to universal knowledge. Moreover, the cognized environment is organized intentionally, whereas the operational environment is all there all the time, and exists independent of the "searchlight" focus of the knowing brain.

3. *The sense of the invisible.*   Much of reality is invisible to our senses, and thus can only be known by inference. We cannot see electromagnetic waves, only their effects upon our senses. This is especially true of complex causal processes. Causes may be invisible because the effective elements are too separated in space or time to be apprehended, or they may be invisible because they cannot be detected given the limitations of our senses or our technology (see Laughlin 1992a).

The operational environment is mysterious in all these senses. We lose track of the transcendental nature of things when we feel we are in control of events, but when we lose that sense of being in control, a kind of zone of uncertainty reasserts itself. The *zone of uncertainty* is the limit of our knowledge in any domain, and is the "horizon" (to use Edmund Husserl's term) beyond which we may discern the great mystery of existence and the greatest challenge to the cognitive imperative—the biological drive to model and know. Most of reality is invisible to our direct sensory experience and must be imagined and conceptualized in our encounter with the world. By implication, we are each of us a transcendental being that is forever beyond either the grasp of our total self-knowledge, or comprehension of the nature of the world, and our effects upon the world.

The cognized environment is to the operational environment as a map is to a landscape. However, the cognized map is a living, breathing representation produced by transformations in the social life of the living cells that make up our body. At a micro-level of organization, these transformations have their material reality in patterned co-ordinations among neurons whose initial social interactions are largely genetically controlled, whose eventual developmental complexity will be variable, and whose evocation may or may not be environmentally triggered.

Experiencing the Operational Environment

The production of experience by and within our body is a complex process by which cells organize themselves under the simultaneous press of genetic endowment, sensory information about the environment, anticipatory operations in the world, feedback about the efficacy of their own actions in the world, and the lawful demands of autoregulation. The accuracy of immediate sensory experience relative to the operational environment is assured by information derived from past experiences—that is, information stored as developing neurocognitive structures. Developmentally speaking, the person builds an internal experiential world that provides an increasingly more complex informational standpoint from which to act in the world (Maturana and Varela 1980).

Built into this internal experiential world is a focusing function that spotlights aspects of the world for attention, and relegates the rest of the cognized environment to disattention. This spotlighting function is often called *intentionality*, which has been considered the sine qua non in definitions of consciousness since at least the time of Brentano. The intentional function of consciousness is probably the feature that exhibits the greatest evolutionary advance in humans relative to other animals. We know that many of the structures that mediate intentionality are located in the prefrontal cortical lobes, the area of the hominid brain that has exhibited the greatest allometric expansion over the past several million years. It is largely because of the advanced development of the prefrontal intentional structures that we humans are able to develop long-range plans, maintain attention and concentration, and modulate emotional responses (Laughlin, McManus, and d'Aquili 1990:105–108).

Neurognosis

Information from past experiences that becomes enfolded into our stream of consciousness is not limited to that of individual development, but is also enriched from the vast store of species, genus, even mammalian-typical experiences implicit in the initial organization of cells within our nervous system. These nascent structures that we all inherit by virtue of our mammalian, our primate, and our human genome we call *neurognostic*[4] models. The neurognostic models are the seed structures upon which all later development depends. Neurognostic models are the mechanism for what the late Earl Count (1973) liked to call the various levels of our biogram—the mammalian *biogram*, or the way of cognizing and adapting all we mammals share in common, the primate biogram, or the ways all we primates share in common, and the human biogram, the ways all we humans share in common.

Henry A. Murray perhaps said it best when he said "in some ways all humans are alike, in some ways some humans are alike, and in some ways no humans are alike" —or words to that effect. Neurognostic models account for the ways all humans are alike. Neurognostic structures are present in the pre- and perinatal nervous system, and because they are comprised of living cells, they function as soon as they grow and become interconnected (1991). Thus models function as *neurognosis*. That is, neurognostic models mediate genetically patterned, species-typical properties of sensing, perceiving, knowing, intuiting, feeling, etc., as well as of a nascent sense of social self and the intentional organization of consciousness. Neurognosis provides the archetypal framework of experience, which in the very young is very likely the predominant quality of consciousness. Neurognosis patterns our earliest experiences of the world, the archetypal "already there-ness" of our pre- and perinatal lifeworld.

Neurognosis also has a developmental dimension—producing, as Henry Murray said, the ways some humans are alike. Because neurognostic models are living cells, they develop their internal organization both from a plan that is inherent in the genetic makeup of the organism and that guides the maturation of the body, and from the adaptational press of the operational environment. This process begins early in pre- and perinatal life. As soon as neural structures begin to function as models, they begin to develop. Recent research for example has shown that fetal human beings hear and learn about what they hear as early as 20 weeks, well before the development of the cortex. The development of neurognostic models is subject to the tension between conservation of structure and adaptation to the operational environment. Primates are typically social animals, and social cognition is part of the primate biogram. Thus a major orientation of human adaptation is toward the social environment. Enculturation and socialization may be understood as processes of socially guiding the maturation of neurognostic structures. At the expense of appearing too simplistic, certain neurognostic structures are socially selected for development and others are not. Certain domains of experience are socially encouraged to develop while other domains are ignored or discouraged. There exists a great deal of overlap in the experiences of peoples everywhere, primarily because the brains of people all over the planet share the same species-typical neurognosis, which develops along similar lines in roughly the same planetary conditions. Of course the details of development and the entire complement of experiences will vary considerably across cultures and across local environments.

Quantum Relations

Incidentally, some of our recent work has explored neurological-quantum mechanical interactions—a promising avenue of research that may account for some of the universal aspects of traditional cosmologies around the planet. Many cosmologies recognize such phenomena as causation at a distance, co-dreaming, shamanic flying, etc., as well as an essential but hidden wholeness of the energies and forces behind all things. Recent developments in quantum physics[5] and biophysics[6] have layed the foundation for a cosmological understanding of energy relations in the operational environment. Recent explorations have suggested that living cells may interact directly with the sea of quantum energy in the vacuum (see Laughlin 1996a). If it turns out that neural systems may interact with physical reality directly through quantum transformations, it will shed a lot of light on the accuracy and efficacy of very ancient knowledge systems. It may turn out that adepts entering certain states may be able to exercise extraordinary effects owing to enhanced interaction with phenomena via the quantum sea.

Phases of Consciousness

In any event, the patterns of human experience seem to recur and to be distributed across a range of phases of consciousness from those principally oriented toward adaptation to the outer world to those expressing relations internal to the organism. Universal patterns of change in phases of consciousness are neurognostically "wired in," so to speak, to the functioning of the nervous system. The most common universal alternation is between what we call waking and sleeping/dreaming states (see Laughlin, McManus, and Shearer 1993). How such universal alternations develop and how they are interpreted is, of course, influenced by one's culture. In modern Euroamerican cultures, children are typically taught to ignore their dream states and to focus on adaptational interactions with the external world in the waking state. Moreover, ritual practices designed to evoke alternative phases of consciousness are generally discouraged or negatively sanctioned. Thus Euroamerican awareness is primarily concerned with tracking external events while in the waking state. Euroamerican culture thus tends to be *monophasic* in its orientation to experiences of the world.

   This is in sharp contrast to the majority of cultures in which access to multiple phases of consciousness is positively sanctioned and enculturated. We term these *polyphasic* cultures. In these cultures, experiences had in dreams, in visions, under the influence of various psychotropic substances, and under various ritual circumstances are valued and inform the society's system of knowledge. The important thing to remember here is that the brains of people living in all societies, whether they are born into monophasic or polyphasic cultures, are neurognostically prepared to experience a stream of consciousness that flows, as it were, through multiple phases, and not merely in the discrete waking states valued and emphasized by materialist cultures such as our own.

Neurophenomenology

Thus far I have given you some notion of what biogenetic structural theory is about. Summarizing what I have said so far, biogenetic structuralism holds that the world of experience of all people everywhere is mediated by much the same complement of neurognostic models, derived from the human genome and developed throughout childhood in similar ways. Cultural variation in experience occurs because of the variations both in enculturation and in the details of the local operational environment, as well as the remarkable plasticity afforded by neural development. The ways all humans are alike in how they experience themselves and their world is due to the origins of their cognized environments in species-typical neurognosis. The ways some human beings are alike depends largely upon the social conditioning in the development of their individual cognized environments. And of course the ways no human beings are alike is due to the complexity and uniqueness of each individual's innate temperament and developmental path.

Biogenetic structuralism has focussed most intensively on the ways that all humans are alike as a counterbalance to a notable bias in anthropology toward cultural relativism—that is, a professional orientation toward the ways some humans are alike. Because of our concern for the universal properties of consciousness, we have incorporated within our methodological tool kit the advantages of a phenomenological approach. We use the term *phenomenology* in the Husserlian, or Buddhist sense of the study of the essential properties and structures of consciousness by the application of trained introspection. As I said in the beginning, consciousness science is hampered by a great deal of phenomenological naivete. Many of the folks working in consciousness science have not been trained to cultivate phenomenologically productive mind states, nor to systematically explore the structures and operations of their own consciousness. Because of this deficit in methodology, I want to spend the remainder of this chapter exploring this crucially important component of a fully fleshed out consciousness science.

The most direct method for ascertaining the relations between consciousness and the nervous system is by way of combining the methods of phenomenology and neuroscience into a kind of *neurophenomenology*. Neurophenomenology is a powerful method that relies upon a dialogue between descriptions of the essential properties of consciousness as ascertained through trained contemplation on the one hand, and the structures and processes of the brain discovered in neuroscience on the other hand. From the biogenetic structural point of view, phenomenology and neuroscientific research are but two points of view onto the same scope of inquiry. Both viewpoints are required, and neither reduces the other. This is important, for the most common criticism I have heard of a neuroscientific account of consciousness is that it is somehow "reductionistic." A neurophenomenology is reductionistic in neither the popular nor the technical sense. In the popular sense, neither phenomenology nor neuroscience can produce a complete account of consciousness. Therefore neither approach can reduce the other in any imperialistic way. In the more technical sense, neither phenomenological nor neuroscientific theories are sufficiently robust as explanatory frameworks to reduce the theories derived from the other. What combining the respective powers of both windows does do is to broaden the range of empirical observations requiring explanation, thus setting the stage for building a more complete account of consciousness. Again, as William James might well have argued, grounding neuroscience accounts in the phenomenology of experience requires neuroscientists to engage the broadest possible naturalistic scope. For example, phenomenology acts as a corrective to overly narrow conceptions of consciousness inherent in many cognitive science models—models frequently constrained by the limitations of the computer-as-metaphor for the human mind approach. On the other hand, requiring a neuroscience perspective inhibits the tendency toward metaphysical and epiphenomenal accounts of the structures of consciousness that run counter to how we know the brain works. I have already touched on one example of this above. Models of consciousness that deny the consciousness of fetuses and babies, as well as those that deny consciousness in nonhuman animals with brains, reveal both their narrow perspective and their ethnocentric bias, and in addition run counter to pre- and perinatal psychological, neuropsychological, and zoological evidence to the contrary.

Keep in mind that the word "consciousness" is a phenomenological concept. I know about consciousness because I am a conscious being capable of self-reflection. It would seem to be the most natural thing in the world to answer questions about consciousness by examining my own conscious processes. Yet to this day there exists in some scientific circles an outmoded, knee-jerk rejection of introspection as a legitimate source of information about consciousness. The proscription against introspection is as absurd as it is counterproductive to a fully mature consciousness science. The complaint is, of course, that introspection produces soft, inexact, nonobjective, nonpublic, and empirically nonconfirmable statements about the nature of consciousness. Our response is that untrained observation of any scope is marginally useful in science. The greater the training, the more exact and useful are the observations. And in these post-Kuhnian times in the philosophy of science, what objective means has shifted to connote more an intersubjective agreement—which is precisely what trained phenomenologists are able to do. Ken Wilber (1984) put it nicely when he noted that all forms of knowledge about the world are grounded on the injunction: if you want to know this, do this, then when you come to know what you know, you talk to others who have followed the same injunction and see to what extent you agree or disagree. This is what Charles Tart (1975) meant when he noted that all sciences are state-specific. The requisite mind states for whatever exploration must be cultivated, and phenomenology is no different. Mind you, the phenomenological literature is rife with naive philosophical discourses on the nature of consciousness. Phenomenologically speaking, the "as I sit in my study with pen poised and contemplate the qualia making up the tree in my garden" sort of philosophizing is not very productive. One of Edmund Husserl's greatest disappointments was the failure of many of his students to develop the requisite skills in self-reflection without which a deep, penetrating and sustained exploration of one's consciousness is impossible.

The details of training in phenomenology will vary with the school, but almost all approaches depend to some extent upon the practitioner learning to access an extraordinarily deep well of calm from which willful operations may proceed unimpeded by discursive thought, fantasy and the natural inclination of the more excited brain to leap from object to object in its intentionality. In the East the untrained mind is sometimes likened to a monkey holding on for dear life to the tail of a raging elephant, while the trained mind is depicted as the monkey seated on top of and guiding a more placid mount. From the vantage point of deep calm, the contemplative is able to focus the power of intentionality upon whatever property or activity of mind one wishes to examine. In phenomenological terms, the process of focusing upon and exploring attributes of consciousness is called reducing that attribute (not to be confused with the previous use of the term mentioned above—the word "reduce" comes from an ancient root meaning "to return to the beginning"). Some operations of mind are easier to reduce than others, some require more skill than others. And the reduction of some properties does not become relevant until others are realized.

Reductions in Biogenetic Structural Research

Over the last 20 years or so, the biogenetic structuralist group have reduced and offered neuropsychological explanations for a variety of properties and structures of consciousness, and have linked these with the structure of the human biogram. These properties include: (1) the granular texture of all sensory stimuli—what we have called the phenomenology of the "dot" (Laughlin 1992a; Laughlin, McManus, and d'Aquili 1990:108–112), (2) internal time consciousness and temporal awareness (Laughlin 1992a), (3) states of consciousness in meditation (Laughlin 1994b; Laughlin, McManus, and Webber 1984; Laughlin, McManus, and d'Aquili 1990), (4) the causal efficacy of warps over subsequent phases of consciousness (Laughlin, McManus and d'Aquili 1990:140–145), (5) dreaming (Laughlin, McManus, and Shearer 1983, McManus, Laughlin, and Shearer 1993), (6) the archetypes (Laughlin 1996a), (7) the efficacy of portals and skrying devices in transforming consciousness (McDonald, Cove, Laughlin and McManus 1989), (8) intentionality (Laughlin 1992b, Laughlin, McManus, and d'Aquili 1990:103–108), (9) the innate fuzziness of natural categories, especially those used to describe transpersonal experiences (Laughlin 1993a), (10) the nature of psychic energy (Laughlin 1994b), (11) the experience of certainty of knowledge (Laughlin 1994c), (12) intuition (Laughlin 1997a), (13) the body image (Laughlin 1997b), and (14) the effort after meaning and the effort after truth as distinct intentional states (Laughlin 1992a).

Because biogenetic structuralism incorporates an ethnological frame, we have also reduced and built neuroanthropological accounts of a number of sociocultural phenomena, including: (1) the relation between love and ritual gift giving (Laughlin 1985), (2) how ritual and ritual drivers are used by societies to orchestrate the experience of their members (d'Aquili 1983; d'Aquili and Laughlin 1975; d'Aquili, Laughlin, and McManus 1979; Laughlin 1989b, 1990a, 1993b; Laughlin, McManus, and Shearer 1983; Laughlin, McManus, and Webber 1984; Laughlin, McManus, Rubinstein, and Shearer 1986; MacDonald, Cove, Laughlin, and McManus 1989), (3) how symbols penetrate and evoke states of consciousness (Laughlin 1989b; Laughlin, McManus, and d'Aquili 1990:189–195), (4) how technology transforms consciousness (Laughlin 1997c; d'Aquili and Newberg 1996), (5) why gender attributions are used almost universally for aspects of consciousness (Laughlin 1990b), (6) how games sometimes reveal the hidden dimensions of cosmology (Laughlin 1990a, 1993b), (7) How to do transpersonal ethnography and how transpersonal experiences effect the consciousness of ethnographers (Laughlin 1989a, 1994a, 1994b, 1996b), (8) the role of transpersonal experiences in traditional cosmologies (Laughlin, McManus, and d'Aquili 1990:212–237), (9) the relation between abstraction and spirit in traditional and modern art (Laughlin 1997d, 1998), and (10) the use of masks in religious drama (Young-Laughlin and Laughlin 1988).

As we have been able to demonstrate in these various studies, there are numerous advantages of incorporating the reductive power of a mature phenomenology into consciousness science. The simple fact is that very little training in phenomenology is required before one encounters many of the universal properties of consciousness via one's own direct experience, rather than through theories, ideologies, and other cultural views. As Husserl taught, training in phenomenology is a straightforward means to free the mind from conditioned points of view about consciousness and the acts of consciousness. In effect, one learns to correct one's cultural and disciplinary biases in the crucible of ones own expanding self-awareness before unintentionally revealing the biases before the world.

And the curious thing is that the more skilled one becomes at performing reductions, and the more mature one's insight becomes into the essential properties of consciousness, the easier it becomes to map one's phenomenology onto current neuroscience, and even biophysics. As the "natural attitude" of one's conditioned view of consciousness falls away, the view one develops from the direct experience of consciousness looks very much as one would expect from a study of neuropsychology. When one realizes, for example, that one's entire sensory field is made up of waves of particles, or as we say "dots," it is far easier both to understand how neural structures mediate sensation, and to see where the particle-wave ambiguity comes from in quantum physics. Or to give another, perhaps more historically interesting example, when one has reduced the real "now point" in the stream of one's own consciousness, it is far easier to understand what William James meant by "pure experience."

Conclusion

In this brief chapter I have given you a glimpse of the kind of theorizing we have done in biogenetic structuralism over the years. I have indicated some of the limitations the theory is designed to avoid, and have suggested some of the advantages of this view over alternative theories of consciousness. What I have spent more time emphasizing is the crucial importance of incorporating a neurophenomenology into the tool kit of consciousness science. Incorporating such a methodology does not, of course, require adherence to biogenetic structural theory. In principle, any body of theory about consciousness may be tested using neurophenomenology. But it is true that biogenetic structural theory requires a neurophenomenology by logical extension of its fundamental tenets, for biogenetic structuralism is grounded in a "radical empiricism" (to use William James's term; see Laughlin and McManus 1995) that insists that all of science be grounded in experience, and that no experience is beyond the purview of scientific scrutiny. In the future I hope to see more of the properties of consciousness reduced and explained by the application of phenomenological methods (Laughlin 1996b). Whether you buy into a biogenetic structural perspective, or some other formulation that integrates experience and the brain, the incorporation of a full-blown neurophenomenology will certainly aid in bringing a mature consciousness science to fruition.

Acknowledgments

I wish to thank the many people who have made this study possible. I especially want to thank John McManus and Eugene G. d'Aquili who joined me in formulating biogenetic structuralism. Thanks also go to Harold E. Puthoff of the Institute of Advanced Research in Austin, Texas, who has taught me a great deal about the quantum universe. And many thanks to all my fellow members of the International Consciousness Research Laboratories (ICRL) group who have taught me so much and who have supported my efforts over the last few years. This chapter is dedicated to the memory of my friend and colleague, Roy "Skip" Rappaport.

Notes

1. The best single entre into biogenetic structural theory is the book *Brain, Symbol and Experience* (Laughlin, McManus, and d'Aquili 1990).

2. We are indebted to Roy Rappaport (1968) for the concepts of cognized and operational environments. It is clear from Rappaport's (1979:97–144; 1984:337–352) later writings that the meanings we have constructed for these terms are even closer to his thinking than we initially thought. We originally interpreted him as simply equating cognized environment with the native world view and the operational environment with the world as viewed by science. And of course, we consider scientific theories of the world to also be cognized environments. In fact, Rappaport's (personal communication, May 1993) thinking does not differ substantially from our view. For our own development of these crucial concepts, see Laughlin and Brady (1978:6); d'Aquili, Laughlin, and McManus (1979:12ff); Rubenstein, Laughlin, and McManus (1984:21ff); and Laughlin, McManus, and d'Aquili (1990:82–90).

3. See Laughlin (1997b) on the neuropsychology of the body image.

4. The concept of neurognosis is discussed in Laughlin and d'Aquili (1974: chapter 5), Laughlin, McManus, and d'Aquili (1990: chapter 2), d'Aquili, Laughlin and McManus (1979:8ff) and Laughlin (1996a and b)

5. I am especially thinking here of the work by Harold Puthoff (1990) and others on the properties of the random fluctuations of vacuum energies in the so-called Zero Point Energy sea.

6. Here I am thinking of the work of Fritz Popp and his colleagues (Popp, Li, and Gu 1992) on biophoton emission from cells.

References

Count, E. W. 1973. *Being and Becoming Human*. New York: Van Nostrand Reinhold.

D'Aquili, E. G. 1982. Senses of Reality in Science and Religion: A Neuroepistemological Perspective. *Zygon* 17(4):361–384.

D'Aquili, E. G. 1983. The Myth-Ritual Complex: A Biogenetic Structural Analysis. *Zygon* 18(3):247–269.

D'Aquili, E. G., and Laughlin, C. D. 1975. The Biopsychological Determinants of Religious Ritual Behavior. *Zygon* 10(1):32–58.

D'Aquili, E. G., Laughlin, C. D., and McManus, J. 1979. *The Spectrum of Ritual*. New York: Columbia University Press.

D'Aquili, E. G., and Newberg, A. B. 1996. Consciousness and the Machine. *Zygon* 31(2):235–252.

Husserl, E. 1977. *Cartesian Meditations: An Introduction to Phenomenology*. The Hague: Martinus Nijhoff.

Krippner, S., and Winkler, M. 1995. Postmodernity and Consciousness Studies. *Journal of Mind and Behavior* 16(3):255–280.

Laughlin, C. D. 1985. On the Spirit of the Gift. *Anthropologica* 27(1–2):137–159.

Laughlin, C. D. 1989a. Transpersonal Anthropology: Some Methodological Issues. *Western Canadian Anthropologist* 5:29–60.

Laughlin, C. D. 1989b. Ritual and the Symbolic Function: A Summary of Biogenetic Structural Theory. *Journal of Ritual Studies* 4(1):15–39.

Laughlin, C. D. 1990a. At Play in the Fields of the Lord: The Role of Metanoia in the Development of Consciousness. *Play and Culture* 3(3):173–192.

Laughlin, C. D. 1990b. Womb = Woman = World: Gender and Transcendence in Tibetan Tantric Buddhism. *Pre- and Perinatal Psychology Journal* 5(2):147–165.

Laughlin, C. D. 1991. Pre- and Perinatal Brain Development and Enculturation: A Biogenetic Structural Approach. *Human Nature* 2(3):171–213.

Laughlin, C. D. 1992a. Scientific Explanation and the Life-World: A Biogenetic Structural Theory of Meaning and Causation. *IONS Report* CP–2. Sausalito, Calif.: Institute of Noetic Sciences.

Laughlin, C. D. (1992b) Time, Intentionality, and a Neurophenomenology of the Dot. *Anthropology of Consciousness* 3(3–4):14–27.

Laughlin, C. D. 1993a. Fuzziness and Phenomenology in Ethnological Research: Insights from Fuzzy Set Theory. *Journal of Anthropological Research* 49(1):17–37.

Laughlin, C. D. 1993b. Revealing the Hidden: The Epiphanic Dimension of Games and Sport. *Journal of Ritual Studies* 7(1):85–104.

Laughlin, C. D. 1994a. Transpersonal Anthropology, Then and Now. *Transpersonal Review* 1(1):7–10.

Laughlin, C. D. 1994b. Psychic Energy and Transpersonal Experience: A Biogenetic Structural Account of the Tibetan Dumo Practice. in *Being Changed by Cross-Cultural Encounters*, ed. by David E. Young and J.-G. Goulet. Peterborough, Ontario: Broadview Press.

Laughlin, C. D. 1994c. Apodicticity: The Problem of Absolute Certainty in Transpersonal Anthropology. *Anthropology and Humanism* 19(2):1–15.

Laughlin, C. D. 1996a. Archetypes, Neurognosis and the Quantum Sea. *Journal of Scientific Exploration* 10(3):375–400.

Laughlin, C. D. 1996b. Phenomenological Anthropology. in *Encyclopedia of Cultural Anthropology*, Vol. 3. ed. by David Levinson and Melvin Ember. New York: Henry Holt, pp. 924–926.

Laughlin, C. D. 1997a. The Nature of Intuition: A Neuropsychological Approach. in *Intuition: The Inside Story*. ed. By R. E. Davis-Floyd and P. Sven Arvidson. New York: Routledge, pp. 19–37.

Laughlin, C. D. 1997b. Body, Brain, and Behavior: The Neuroanthropology of the Body Image. *Anthropology of Consciousness* 8(2–3):49–68.

Laughlin, C. D. 1997c. The evolution of Cyborg Consciousness. *Anthropology of Consciousness* 8(4):144–159.

Laughlin, C. D. 1997d. Abstraction and Spirit: A Neurocognitive Account of Religious Symbolism in Traditional and Modern Art. Paper presented at the annual meeting of the American Anthropological Association, Washington, D.C., November.

Laughlin, C. D. 1998. Art and Spirit: Brain, the Navajo Concept of Hozho, and Kandinsky's "Inner Necessity." Paper presented at the annual meeting of the Central States Anthropological Society, Kansas City, April.

Laughlin, C. D., and Brady, I. A. 1978. *Extinction and Survival in Human Populations*. New York: Columbia University Press.

Laughlin, C. D., and. d'Aquili, E. G. 1974. *Biogenetic Structuralism*. New York: Columbia University Press.

Laughlin, C. D., and McManus, J. 1995. The Relevance of the Radical Empiricism of William James to the Anthropology of Consciousness. *Anthropology of Consciousness* 6(3):34–46.

Laughlin, C. D., McManus, J., and d'Aquili, E. G. 1990. *Brain, Symbol and Experience: Toward a Neurophenomenology of Consciousness*. New York: Columbia University Press.

Laughlin, C. D., McManus, J., and Shearer, J. 1983. Dreams, Trance and Visions: What a Transpersonal Anthropology Might Look Like. *Phoenix: The Journal of Transpersonal Anthropology* 7(1/2):141–159.

Laughlin, C. D., McManus, J., and Shearer, J. 1993. The Function of Dreaming in the Cycles of Cognition. in *The Function of Dreaming* (ed. by A. Moffitt et al.). Albany: SUNY Press.

Laughlin, C. D., McManus, J., and Webber, M. 1984. Neurognosis, Individuation, and Tibetan Arising Yoga Practice. *Phoenix: The Journal of Transpersonal Anthropology* 8 (1/2):91–106.

Laughlin, C. D., McManus, J. Rubinstein, R. A., and Shearer, J. 1986. The Ritual Control of Experience. in *Studies in Symbolic Interaction* (Part A; Ed. Norman K. Denzin). Greenwich, Conn.: JAI Press.

Laughlin, C. D., and Richardson, S. 1986. The Future of Human Consciousness. *Futures*, June issue, pp. 401–419.

MacDonald, G. F., Cove, J., Laughlin, C. D., and McManus, J. 1989. Mirrors, Portals and Multiple Realities. *Zygon* 23(4):39–64.

Maturana, H., and Varela, F. 1980. *Autopoiesis and Cognition*. Boston: Reidel.

McManus, J., Laughlin, C. D., and Shearer, J. 1993. The Function of Dreaming in the Cycles of Cognition. In *The Function of Dreaming*. ed. by A. Moffitt et al. Albany: SUNY Press.

Piaget, J. 1971. *Biology and Knowledge*. Chicago: University of Chicago Press.

Popp, F. A., Li, K. H., and Gu, Q. 1992. *Recent Advances in Biophoton Research and Its Applications*. Singapore: World Scientific.

Puthoff, H. E. 1990. Everything for Nothing. *New Scientist*, July 28 issue, pp. 52–55.

Rappaport, R. A. 1968. *Pigs for the Ancestors*. New Haven: Yale University Press.

Rappaport, R. A. 1979. *Ecology, Meaning, and Religion*. Richmond, Calif: North Atlantic Books.

Rappaport, R. A. 1984. *Pigs for the Ancestors* (second edition). New Haven, Conn.: Yale University Press.

Rubinstein, R. A., Laughlin, C. D., and McManus, J. 1984. *Science As Cognitive Process*. Philadelphia: University of Pennsylvania Press.

Tart, C. 1975. *States of Consciousness*. New York: Dutton.

Webber, M., Stephens, C. D., and Laughlin, C. D. 1983. Masks: A Reexamination, or "Masks? You Mean They Affect the Brain?" In *The Power of Symbols*. ed. by N. Ross Crumrine and Margery Halpin. Vancouver, B.C.: University of British Columbia Press, pp. 204–218.

Wilber, K. 1984. *A Sociable God: Toward a New Understanding of Religion*. Boulder: Shambhala.

Young-Laughlin, J., and Laughlin, C. D. 1988. How Masks Work, or Masks Work How? *Journal of Ritual Studies* 2(1):59–86.

39 Experiential Clarification of the Problem of Self

Jonathan Shear

I

The topic of self-knowledge has been central to Western philosophy since its inception in ancient Greece. In the modern era the three great philosophers, Descartes, Hume and Kant accordingly held that self-knowledge should be expected to provide the "Archimedes' point" for all knowledge, the "capitol or center" of all human understanding, and the "supreme principle for all employment of the understanding," respectively. Despite its continuing importance, the topic has proven problematic, as Descartes, Hume, and Kant's own analyses clearly illustrate. Descartes held with common sense that we have clear intuitive knowledge of self as single, simple, and continuing. Hume, responding to Descartes, looked within and argued that he could find nothing at all corresponding to the notion, and that it was thus empty of all significance. In return, Kant argued, paradoxically, that both Descartes and Hume were correct: Descartes in that we have to have such a self, and Hume in that there is no possibility whatsoever of experiencing it, or indeed of knowing it as anything but an abstract, vacuous cipher. Since subsequent philosophical discussions of the self have largely been reaction to these analyses and conclusions, it will be worth reviewing them briefly here.

Descartes sought an indubitable ground for all knowledge, and concluded that he located it in awareness of his own self-existence. Cogito ergo sum, or, in modern English, "I am conscious, therefore I exist."[1] For, Descartes argued, one cannot coherently doubt one's own conscious existence, since the very act of doubting implies it. Or, put linguistically, one can never truly say "I do not exist." But if one necessarily exists, what is it that exists? Descartes concluded that the self that we know indubitably exists is a consciousness, the selfsame consciousness, single, simple and continuing throughout one's awareness. This view of course resonates deeply with our common sense. And we should note that it is not only our modern Western, "common sense" that this view accords with, but also that of very different cultures, as, for example, the arguments of Augustine in ancient Rome and Shankara in medieval India clearly show.[2]

Hume's critique of Descartes, however, proved devastating to Descartes's position. For when he looked within he reported that he could not find anything in his experience corresponding to Descartes's single, simple, continuing self:

when I enter most intimately into what I call myself, I always stumble on some particular perception or other, of heat or cold, light or shade, love or hatred, pain or pleasure. I never can catch myself at any time without a perception, and never can observe anything but the perception.   (Hume, p. 252)

These results, of course, have accorded with those of almost every commentator since. Thus, while self is supposed to be "something simple and continu'd," and "that to which our several impressions are suppos'd to have a reference," it is introspectively clear that we have "not the least idea" of what such a thing could be. In short, our ordinary notion of self must be some kind of commonsensical "fiction."

What, then, on Hume's account is the self? Hume offered the first of what later came to be called "logical construction theories" (LCT's), which attempt to account for our concept of self entirely in terms of a "collection" or "bundle" of experiences connected by some "logical" relationship. This approach became the dominant one among English-speaking philosophers in our century. In Hume's original theory the relationships were contiguity and resemblances of our perceptions; later theorists often used complex sorts of memory relationships.

There are, however, real problems with this approach. Indeed, Hume himself rejected it in the famous "Appendix" to his Treatise where his critique and "collection" theory first appeared. The critical passages of this Appendix are very compact, and their argument is not transparent. But the basic idea is clear: the fact, as Hume argues, that each of our perceptions is "a distinct existence," separable (in principle, if not in fact) from all the others, implies that no perception can contain any content implying any real connection with the others. This, however, in turn implies that there is no possibility of properly deriving from the actual content of our perceptions any principle capable of unifying them into a "whole mind" or self. We will return to this line of argument in the next section. First let us now see how Kant's critique strengthened major aspects of both Hume's skeptical difficulty and Descartes's positive claim.

Kant argued, with Hume, that no overall principle of unity can be derived from the content of any of our experiences. Nevertheless, he also argued that such an overall unity, which he called "the transcendental unity of apperception" must be presupposed as "the supreme principle of all employment of the understanding." All of our experience, inner and outer, Kant argued, is extended in time, and all outer experience extended in space as well. Thus, for example, if an experience, whether inner or outer, had no temporal extension, it would be too short to be perceived, and if an outer experience had no spatial extension, it would be too small to be seen. Consequently, Kant argued, every experience, whether inner or outer, must have separate parts. Thus a visual experience, for example, must have a left and a right, and a top and a bottom, etc.

But for any experience to exist as a single experience, all of its parts must be given to a single experiencer. If you look at your hand and see it, you will necessarily see a left and a right aspect. These will be parts of your experience. If, for example, one person saw only the left aspect (say, the little finger) and another only the right (say, the thumb), then these would be different experiences (above and beyond being had by different people) than your original one. And even for each of these different experiences, a single person would have to see both the left and the right aspects, too, or that experience would not have existed either. Similarly, Kant argues, if each of a number of people (heard or) thought only a single word of an extended sentence, no one would experience of the entire sentence or thought. In ways such as these, Kant argued that self as single, simple, and abiding is the absolutely necessary precondition for the existence of any experience or thought whatsoever.

So far, then, Kant would support Descartes. But he also argued, strengthening Hume, that there is absolutely no possibility of having any experience, or even any definite concept, of this necessarily inferred unitary self. Kant's arguments here are complex, and not always clear. But his conclusions are. And one of his major conclusions about the self is that it cannot have any experiential quality if its own at all. That is, it has to be a "pure, original unchanging consciousness," a "bare consciousness" with "no distinguishing features" of its own. We will return to this conclusion in the next section. The next step of Kant's argument is easy to follow, however. For if all of our experience is of qualities extended in time and/or space (as argued above) and the self is necessarily qualityless with no distinguishing feature of its own, there is no possibility either of experiencing it, or even generating any graspable concept of it. Therefore the self, however necessary it might be, is knowable only as a blank abstraction, "a something = X," as he puts it, completely ungraspable, as well as unexperienceable, in itself.

Thus the paradox: self as single, simple and continuing is at once both absolutely necessary and absolutely unexperienceable and unknowable. In other words, Descartes and Hume are both importantly correct—and this amounts to a paradox that, as Kant put it, "mocks and torments" even the wisest of men. In short, the concept of self is at once both (i) absolutely necessary and (ii) entirely vacuous and ungraspable.

II

These arguments are all well-known to students of philosophy. But since they underlie so much of our contemporary discussion of self, it will be worthwhile to unpack their logic a little more. Hume's rejection of the existence of any internal perception adequate to our ordinary notion of self is of course well-known and well-accepted. But his rejection of his own—and all other—LCT's is neither so well understood, nor so influential. It is not, however, hard to see how, as Hume suggested, all LCT's must be inadequate to capture our ordinary notion of self. Suppose, for example, the self to be some collection of perceptions defined by an empirical relation R. That is, suppose that there is some such R capable of defining one's self. Then R must be able to distinguish between (i) perceptions that it includes in the collection identified as one's self and (ii) those that it excludes. Next consider any one, say P, of the possible perceptions outside the collection R specifies as (supposedly) constituting one's self. Since P is a possible perception, one can (without contradiction) imagine having it. That is, it is logically possible, if not possible in empirical fact, that one could find oneself having just this particular perception. But then one would be having a perception outside the bundle specified by R and supposedly constituting one's self, contrary to the definition of R. The conclusion, of course is that no such relation R could serve to define our ordinary, commonsense notion of self.

Since the above argument is a bit abstract, let me give a concrete example. Suppose, in accord with Hume's original proposal, that every member of the collection of perceptions (supposedly) constituting one's self has to be related to the others by the relation R, "recognized spatial contiguity," that is, that all of one's perceptions must be connected by the recognized spatial contiguity of their content. This would make it impossible for one to become unconscious and wake up in an environment having no recognizable spatial relationship to the environment where one went to sleep. For one would then be having perceptions P outside the collection, defined by the contiguity-relation R, supposedly constituting the self. Yet we can easily imagine people having such spatial discontinuities in their experiences without having to be different selves. Indeed, people obviously sometimes do have such spatial discontinuities in their experience, as, for example, happens when people become unconscious and wake up in environments perceptually noncontiguous to those where they went to sleep. And surely no-one would want to say they had to become different individuals for having done so. Alternatively, consider a relation R' defined in terms of "perceived contiguity to one's (physical) body." This relation would imply that it couldn't be the case that one's body could be destroyed, and one find oneself in heaven, or reincarnated, or simply disembodied in some realm or other. Now it may be the case that one will in fact cease to exist if one's body is destroyed. But it is surely not impossible to imagine otherwise. Indeed, most of the people of the world indeed believe otherwise (i.e., that they will somehow survive bodily death). Thus it is clear that this R', too, is incapable of capturing our ordinary notion of self as something that can (at least logically, if not factually) undergo such a sequence of experiences.

Such examples can be multiplied without end. They illustrate that there is an important sense in which we conceive of ourselves purely as experiencers, capable in our conception, if not in objective fact, of being independent of any particular context and/or set of experiences. And this implies, as the above argument in terms of P's and R's showed in abstract general form, that our selves, as ordinarily conceived, cannot be captured by any set of experiences. In short, Hume's skeptical despair ever coming to an adequate account of self by virtue of any LCT whatsoever appears very well taken.

Let us now turn to Kant's conclusion that the self must be a "qualityless pure consciousness," a "bare consciousness" with "no distinguishing quality of its own." Kant's arguments are embedded in the details of his epistemological and psychological theories, and are, as noted, often difficult to follow. But the gist of his reasoning is easy to understand. Roughly put, he argues that the self has to be an aspect of (or at least connected to) all of one's possible experiences. Otherwise these experiences would not be one's own, and one would not be able to say of them "I have them," "I recognize them," "They are mine," etc. So far, this seems sensible enough. But, strikingly, in itself it seems to imply that the self must be qualityless. For suppose the self did have some distinguishing empirical quality Q. Then Q would have to be an ubiquitous quality, since self has to be an aspect of (or connected to) every part of every one of one's experiences,[3] and as the distinguishing characteristic of self, Q would have to be there, too. That is, it would be impossible for one to have any experience where Q was absent, and Q could never be identified as an empirical quality or distinguishing characteristic in the first place. Thus, by analogy, suppose the self to be the glass of one's glasses. If the glass had any color, say green, this color would color all experiences equally, and this would imply that the color would not be knowable as an empirical quality or distinguishable characteristic at all.

In short, Hume and Kant's analyses appear to lead to the striking conclusion that self cannot be experienced, or even defined, in terms of any empirical quality, or even any empirically significant set of empirical qualities, at all.

III

Indeed, it is easy to see from the perspective of common sense, that is, quite aside from formal philosophical analyses, how problematic the notion of self really is. Each of us naturally feels we are a person, a single continuing something. As James put it, each of us feels that we are an "Arch-ego, at the center of our own experiences, which, as Locke put it "owns and imputes its experiences to itself," one and the same throughout one's life. At least this is what common sense would hold, unless we become confused by reading too much philosophy. But what is this sameness? It seems to be extremelhy difficult to identify. Consider, for example, the body. One's body changes throughout one's life. One can remember events that one experienced as a small child, and one remembers them as one's own, despite the fact that one's body was very different. One's personality changes, too, yet one remembers events from the time one was a young child or a teenager as one's own, even if one had a very different personality then. These observations clearly suggest that there must be an aspect of one's ordinary concept of self that one takes to be different from either one's body or one's personality, all matters of abstract philosophical analysis aside.

This is even easier to see if we turn our consideration from waking consciousness to that of dreams. One common type of dream involves experiencing oneself as having a different body than the one one has in reality. This dream-experienced "body" can even be a nonhuman type of body, such as that of an animal. Yet when one wakes and remembers the dream, one is sure that it was one's own dream, that one had the dream one is remembering. This makes it clear, again, that there is an important aspect of our commonsense notion of self that is independent of identification with one's body (various philosophical arguments for the necessity of body-grounded self-identification notwithstanding). Of course, the point here is not that one is, or even could in fact be, independent of one's body; it is just that people sometimes do experience themselves (as well as naturally conceive themselves) as being independent of it. This independence is made even clearer by the common sort of dream where one appears to be a disembodied spectator, watching the dream action from some vantage-point or other, like a video-camera.

The case of personality is similar. People often do things in dreams that they "wouldn't dream of" doing (in the waking state). In other words, we often do things in dreams that lie entirely outside our consciously conceived personality. Even more, it is also a common experience to observe the dream-action in a completely impersonal, emotionally neutral way when one finds oneself a disembodied dream-spectator. Nevertheless, even if there is neither body nor personality there (in the dream), one is sure that one was there, oneself, watching the action. But what was watching? It seems ungraspable.

These experiences, of course, are not universal. But they are very common. Each time, for example, I poll groups of philosophically innocent students, easily one-fourth or more say they have had the above experiences. At the very least these experiences show something of how discoordinated a basic aspect of our deeply held, naive commonsensical notions of self are from anything graspable in terms of body, personality or, indeed, any identifiable empirical qualities at all.

Such simple reflections on common sense in short make it clear that the puzzles about self generated by Descartes, Hume, and Kant's philosophical analyses are not off the mark. For a deep aspect of self as we ordinarily conceive it does seem to be both continuing ubiquitously throughout our experience and completely ungraspable in terms of empirical qualities whatsoever. It is thus not hard to see why Hume ended his analysis with skeptical despair, and Kant with mocking and tormenting paradox.

IV

The above analyses reflect the problematic sorts of discussions of self in Western philosophy over the past few centuries. Interestingly, if we turn from Western analyses to those of Asian civilizations, however, we find their philosophical discussions in general, and discussions of self in particular, often embedded in what amounts to an expanded experiential context that includes experiences generally not even referred to, much less emphasized, in Western discussions of self. These experiences have been taken seriously enough by a variety Eastern traditions that they have developed a variety of meditation procedures designed specifically to produce them. One of the experiences, often called the "pure consciousness" experience, will prove to be highly relevant to our own discussion. Different traditions use different terminology to refer to the experience, and they interpret it from different metaphysical perspectives. But its identifying characteristic, namely, that it is devoid of all empirical content whatsoever, is found in common in tradition after tradition. This identifying characteristic, to be sure, is at first likely to appear a bit odd to us, if not simply unintelligible. It will therefore be useful to take a brief look at standard accounts of the experience, taking them at face value, and suspending for the moment all questions about their reliability and intelligibility.

We should first note that nothing much can be said about the experience itself. For its identifying characteristic is that it is devoid of all empirical content. That is, as texts from many traditions emphasize, the experience has absolutely no discernible sensations, perceptions, images, thoughts, etc., in it. Indeed, by all reports, it does not even have a spatiotemporal manifold for such phenomenological objects to be located in. What than is the experience like? It is not *like* anything. What is it remembered as? Not *as* anything. Nevertheless it is remembered. One remembers having the experience, but there is nothing "to" it. No content, shape, structure, or anything else. Thus, not surprisingly, it is often referred to as "pure consciousness" (since there had to be consciousness for there to be a rememberable experience), "pure being" (since nothing positive can be said about it except that it was), and "pure void" (since it is utterly devoid of content).

More, of course, can be said about the procedures developed in different cultures and traditions to produce the experience. Many such procedures exist, with those of

Zen and TM being the most widely known throughout the world. Some of these procedures are easy and widely applicable, others are very difficult and masterable only by a few people after years of dedicated work. The methods range, for example, from Zen's koan practices (concentration on intellectually unsolvable connundra to "freeze" the mind) and "doubt sensation" (to loosen one's attachment to everything) to TM's use of mantras (mental repetition of specific sounds to let one relax utterly, while remaining awake). Although less widely known, Western practices, such as Medieval Catholicism's focusing on "unknowing" (to cause all ordinary mental processes to stop), exist as well. The proponents of such procedures appear to be unanimous in their claims that the procedures actually have to be practiced to really be understood. Nevertheless something of their overall logic is easy to comprehend. For they are all designed allow one's attention to withdraw from all ordinary contents of awareness, including finally even the procedure itself, the idea being that once all phenomenological objects (including the components of the procedure itself) are gone from one's awareness—while one nevertheless stays awake—what remains can only be awareness or consciousness itself.

Thus, particularities of methods aside, what remains, according to a wide spectrum of traditional accounts, is what can be called pure qualityless conscious itself. Consider, for example, the following accounts from several different traditions. First, from Chinese Ch'an (Zen):

When the mind is reduced to impotency, it is compared in the Ch'an [Chinese Zen] texts to that of a withered log, an unconscious skull, a wooden horse, a stone girl and an incense burner in a deserted temple.... The mind, thus stripped of all its activities [thought, feeling, experiencing, etc.], will be reduced to impotency and will vanish sooner or later.... This death of the mind leads to the resurrection of the self nature. (Luk, pp. 20–21)

Japanese Zen:

The time comes when no reflection appears at all. One comes to notice nothing, feel nothing, hear nothing, see nothing ... But it is not vacant emptiness. Rather it is the purest condition of our existence. (Katsuki Sekida, in Austin, p. 473)

The ancient Indian Mandukya Upanishad:

Turia [the "fourth" state of consciousness, after deep sleep, dreaming, and ordinary waking] is not that which cognizes the internal (objects), not that which cognizes the external (objects), not what cognizes both of them, not a mass of cognition, not cognitive, not non-cognitive. (It is) unseen, incapable of being spoken of, ungraspable, without any distinctive marks, unthinkable, unnamable.... The fourth [state, turia] is that which has no elements, which cannot be spoken of ... non-dual.... He who knows it thus enters the self with his self. (Radhakrishnan, pp. 698 and 701)

And modern Vedantan TM:

When the subject is left without an object of experience, having transcended the subtlest state of the object, he steps out of the process of experiencing and arrives as the state of Being ... beyond all seeing, hearing, touching smelling and tasting—beyond all thinking and beyond all feeling. This state of ... unmanifested, absolute, pure consciousness. . . ." (Maharishi, p. 52)

From the above examples we can immediately see two things, first that texts from different traditions, in different cultures with different metaphysics, take great pains to emphasize that the experiences they are describing are to be understood as absolutely devoid of phenomenal content. Secondly, they also associate the experience with what they take to be the true, underlying nature of self. Similar descriptions, and similar claims of relation to the self, are also found (although, to be sure, less frequently) in Western texts as well, as in the following example from a Medieval version of Christianity's Pseudo-Dionysious:

Through ... passing beyond yourself and every other thing (and thereby cleansing yourself from all worldly, physical, and natural love, and from everything that can be known by the normal processes of mind). . . . Enter into this darkness with love ... this supreme and dazzling darkness ... [and experience] the self in its naked, unmade, unbegun state. (Pseudo-Dionysius, pp. 209–213)

Such texts and claims raise many questions of course. These include hermeneutical questions about the appropriateness of taking descriptions from different cultures as being of the same (type of) experience, and methodological questions about how seriously to take subjective reports of unusual experiences in the first place. We will return to these questions later. For now, however, let us turn to the question of the significance of the experience for our examination of the nature of self.

V

As we have seen, identification of the experience in question with a fundamental underlying stratum of self is quite common. However our concern here is not so much with how ancient traditions have interpreted the significance of the experience vis a vis the self, but only with how *we* should interpret it.[4] Nevertheless, the basic intuition underlying the common identification of the experience of pure qualityless awareness with the self is not difficult to understand. For, as noted above, from the perspective of common sense it seems apparent that if one takes everything away while remaining conscious, what remains has to be one's self.

It is also easy to see that the analyses of Descartes, Hume, and Kant outlined above serve to identify the experience in question as experience of self. For it is obvious (i) that this experience, and only this experience, can fulfill Kant's otherwise paradoxical "pure consciousness," "bare consciousness" "devoid of all distinguishing marks. It is also (ii) the only experience that could give experiential significance to the notion of the commonsensical simple consciousness, underlying but distinct from all our changing perceptions, proposed by Descartes and Locke but rejected despairingly (as unexperienced) by Hume. And (iii) it is the only experience that could give experiential significance to the notion of self as independent of all collections of experiences, as implied by our analysis of common sense. In short, this and only this experience can allow us to resolve the relevant tensions within and between Descartes, Hume, and Kant, not to mention the tensions between these philosophical analyses and common sense, in an experientially significant way.

Thus, in sum, we can see both (1) how the expansion of the domain of experience provided by Eastern meditation techniques helps us resolve major Western philosophical problems about the self, and (2) how the same Western philosophical analyses in turn help identify the experience as being of self.[5] This analysis also (3) allows us to "save" common sense, at least to the extent indicated above. But common sense would naturally also ask: If this qualityless pure consciousness is the self, and it is ubiquitous, why is it so obscure? The answer, I think, is straightforward: it is ordinarily obscure precisely because it is (a) qualityless and (b) ubiquitous. It is a psychological commonplace that that which is constant in experience becomes "filtered out," with attention going to what is changing (compare information theory's definition of information as "news of a difference"). Thus if pure consciousness is constant, it is easy to see why it is not attended to until attention is drawn to it—much, for example, as one is unlikely to notice the background temperature of a comfortable room. For since infancy our attention, in the name of functional efficiency, has been drawn to the ever-changing qualities of our environment in order to learn to deal with them properly. Moreover, because pure consciousness has no distinguishing characteristics at all, the only way to actually draw attention to it is to allow all the other objects of attention to be withdrawn from our awareness while we remain awake. (By analogy, one may be unlikely to notice anything but the images projected on the screen while a movie is playing, but one can easily be led to become aware of the flat imageless screen itself if the moving images are brought to a halt with the light still on.)

On this account, then, it should not be surprising that after one's attention has been drawn frequently to pure consciousness in meditation (with all other objects of awareness absent), it should become possible to recognize it at will afterward, even when the other ordinary components of experience have returned to one's awareness (much, perhaps, as one may notice the flatness of the screen even after the movie has started up again), as meditation traditions often report.

In short, these experiential reports suggest (1) that pure consciousness may well be an ubiquitous component of our experience, (2) that our ordinary (and ordinarily paradoxical) sense of self reflects a subliminal awareness of this ubiquitous pure consciousness, and (3) that after we become clearly aware of it as it is in and by itself in meditation, we can then come also to recognize it as ubiquitous—as self is supposed to be.

VI

The above analyses have proceded by taking the widespread, cross-cultural accounts of pure consciousness experiences at face value, and assumed the appropriateness of talking about a single identifiable pure consciousness experience. But serious questions about this approach can be raised here, and the most important critiques and questions at least be mentioned, namely, the (i) hermeneutical—questioning whether there can be one experience, the same across different cultures, (ii) phenomenological—asking if the experience can really be qualityless, and (iii) methodological—asking how can we determine if these odd experiential reports have any objective significance at all? These critiques all involve complicated issues. Nevertheless a few brief remarks may be useful.

(i) The hermeneutical critique is based on the following line of reasoning: All experience, as a matter of empirical fact, is shaped and constructed out of culture-dependent components (symbols, images, expectations, etc.). This obviously implies that it is impossible to have the same experience across different cultures. This critique had been influential for a decade or more. Yet it is quite easy to respond to: The defining characteristic of the pure consciousness experience is the complete absence of all empirical content. Thus any experience properly identified as a pure consciousness experience is outside the range of all the components (symbols, images, expectations, etc.) hermeneutical thinkers are concerned with. Furthermore, it is easy to see that the pure consciousness experience is logically unique. For if two experiences are phenomenologically different, at least one of them must have some content and cannot be an instance of a pure consciousness experience. In short, any two experiences that fit the defining characteristic of pure consciousness experiences have to be the same, whatever the surrounding cultural context might be.[6]

(ii) The phenomenological critique has more substance. For it is not implausible to suspect that putative examples of pure consciousness experiences might have some content, though too abstract to be noticed and identified by the ordinary observer. That is, there might be some content in the experience that would be apparent to one who had undergone sufficient phenomenological training to uncover typically unnoticed subtleties of one's experience. Here one can readily allow this logical possibility. Nevertheless, there would still be a family of closely related experiences well-defined here, and the members of this family would, at least to a first approximation, still serve (with slight modification) to fulfill the arguments about self outlined above.[7]

(iii) The methodological question is, I think, the most important one, namely, how to tell if reports of pure consciousness experiences are anything more than mere reports. Here some kind of objective corroboration is needed. But how could this be possible for such contentless subjective experiences? The response is in terms of actual research on meditation subjects. Quite a bit has been done here, much of it on subjects practicing the TM technique (presumably, according to the research literature, because of the ease of the practice, consistency of results, and ready availability of experienced subjects). Here we have the ordinary methodological constraints on subjects' reports, typical of those in psychological research in general. More to the point, a variety of physiological correlates of the experiential reports has been observed, including unusual EEG coherence, marked reduction of metabolic activity, and, most strikingly, periods of complete cessation of respiration (measured, for example, by essentially flat pneumotachygraphic tracings) highly correlated ($p < 10^{10}$) in experimental settings with reports of the experience (Farrow and Hebert 1982). Furthermore, this same correlate (cessation of respiration) of the experience is reported and emphasized in meditation texts from ancient and contemporary China and India, in the contexts of Zen, Yoga, and Tibetan Buddhism.

Thus, when the same unusual experiential accounts, found in very different belief-contexts, are correlated with the same unusual (often unconscious) physiological parameters, it would strain credulity to think that these correlations occur just by chance. The reasonable inference is that the experiential accounts reflect the natural subjective response to the unusual correlated physiological state, rather than to the radically different, often opposing cultural, belief, and expectation-contexts in which the reports happen to be embedded. In short, the reasonable conclusion is that the reports do indeed reflect an objective phenomenon, namely, the culture-independent psychophysical state in question. Finally, we can also note that this common psychophysiological conjunction across very different cultures and belief-contexts reinforces the lack of relevance of the hermeneutical culture-embeddness objection, and the phenomenological objection as well.[8]

VII

It is important to note here, however, some things that the above account does not do. In the first place, the account is purely phenomenological (a matter of experience and its relation to our concepts), and not at all ontological. Indeed, this is part of its strength. No particular ontological position is presumed, and the analysis is compatible with substance and nonsubstance theories of self and nondualisms (whether idealist, materialist, or neutral-monist) and dualisms indifferently. For it is derived from examination of our experience and ordinary concepts, quite apart from any determination of these ontological questions. And however these questions may be resolved, our experiences, our commonsense concepts, and their relations remain what and as they are. But while the above account of self has no ontological significance, it does appear to enable us both to clarify the significance of our commonsense intuitions and to resolve long-standing conceptual problems about the self in a way compatible with common sense.

All of this, one hopes, is enough to show something of the potential value for our traditional philosophical discussions of self and mind of taking into account the pure consciousness experience, widely discussed in Eastern, but not Western, philosophical traditions. For if the phenomenological analyses above are even roughly correct, it appears that this experience is capable of resolving some major Western issues about self, clarifies our commonsense intuition, and is properly identified by philosophical analysis as being experience of self itself.

An expanded version of this chapter appeared in the *Journal of Consciousness Studies* 5, no. 5/6 (1998): 673–686.

Notes

1. Traditionally, Descartes's *cogito* used to be translated as "I think." Yet Descartes, in both the Latin and French editions, makes it clear that what he intends is what we would now call "being conscious" rather than merely "thinking," including, for example, willing, sensing, and imagining, as well as such things as asserting, understanding, and doubting. Compare, for example, Anscombe and Geach's now widely used translation of the Meditations in their *Descartes: Philosophical Writings* (Indianapolis: Bobbs-Merrill, 1971).

2. Thus the fashionable view, often expressed by philosophers from Ryle onward, that we modern Westerners find Descartes's view "commonsensical" only because of the influence of his views today, is clearly incorrect. For a discussion of the cross-cultural commonality of core components of our notions of self, see Shear 1996.

3. Indeed, as Kant put it, all of one's experiences are in one's self. Thus self has to be there wherever any part of any one of one's experiences exists.

4. This identification, to be sure, is not universal, and there are Buddhist traditions that, while clearly identifying the experience in question, also hold, in opposition to the Zen, that there is no true "self" to be discovered in the first place.

5. Thus this analysis also supports, with uniquely Western lines of reasoning, the identification of the experience with the self, common to many but not all Eastern traditions. That is, it gives independent grounds for siding with Yoga, Vedanta, and Zen, for example, which emphasize the identification of the experience and the fundamental nature of the self, versus Therevada Buddhism, for example, which emphasizes the (apparently opposing) doctrine of "nonself."

6. For extended discussions of the hermeneutical critique, see Shear 1990 and Forman 1990.

7. For further discussion of these phenomenological questions see Shear 1999.

8. For further discussion of these methodological questions see Shear 1999.

References

Austin, J. H. 1998. *Zen and the Brain*. Cambridge: MIT Press, 1998.

Farrow, J. T. and Hebert, R. 1982. Breath suspension during the transcendental meditation technique. *Psychosomatic Medicine* 44, no. 2:133–153.

Forman, R. 1990. *The Problem of Pure Consciousness*. Oxford: Oxford University Press, 1990.

Hume, D. 1740, 1978. *A Treatise of Human Nature*. Oxford: Oxford University Press.

Luk, C., ed. and trans. 1961. *Ch'an and Zen Teaching*. Vol. 2. London: Rider and Co.

Maharishi, M. Y. 1967. *Bhagavad Gita: A New Translation and Commentary*. Washington, DC: Age of Enlightenment Press, 1984.

Pseudo-Dionysius. 1978. *Pseudo-Dionysius' Mystical Theology*, from the Medieval English version by the anonymous author of *The Cloud of Unknowing*. In *The Cloud of Unknowing and Other Works*, translated by Clifton Wolters. Penguin Books.

Radhakrisnhan, S. 1981. translator, *The Principal Upanisads* (London: G. Allen & Unwin).

Shear, J. 1990. Mystical Experience, Hermeneutics, and Rationality. *International Philosophical Quarterly* 30, no. 4 (December 1990): 391–401.

Shear, J. 1996. On a Culture-Independent Core Component of Self. In *East-West Encounters in Philosophy and Religion*, ed. Ninian Smart and B. Srinivasa Murthy (Long Beach: Long Beach Publications, 1996).

Shear, J. and Jeuning, R. 1999. Pure Consciousness: Scientific Exploration of Meditation Techniques. *J. of Consciousness Studies* 6, no. 2–3 (1999): 189–209.

Index